ECONOMICS
for DEVELOPMENT

PRENTICE-HALL INTERNATIONAL, INC., *London*

PRENTICE-HALL OF AUSTRALIA, PTY., LTD., *Sydney*

PRENTICE-HALL OF CANADA, LTD., *Toronto*

PRENTICE-HALL FRANCE, S.A.R.L., *Paris*

PRENTICE-HALL OF INDIA (PRIVATE) LTD., *New Delhi*

PRENTICE-HALL OF JAPAN, INC., *Tokyo*

PRENTICE-HALL DE MEXICO, S.A., *Mexico City*

ECONOMICS

for DEVELOPMENT

STEPHEN ENKE

Professor of Economics
Duke University
              and
Assistant to the President
Institute for Defense Analyses

PRENTICE-HALL, INC.
Englewood Cliffs, N.J.

Dedicated
To All
the Peasant Cultivators
of Asia, Africa, and the Americas,
Who Remain
the Forgotten Men and Women
of Economic Development

Preface

The Cold War is not going very well for the western world. Soviet or Chinese influence is infiltrating into many of the undeveloped countries, in Asia, Africa, and Latin America. The next twenty-five years may indicate which system of government and economics is going to prevail outside the North Atlantic basin.

There are many reasons for the continual gains of communism. For one thing the Soviets, during several decades, have come near to perfecting their techniques of subversion. They know what issues to exploit both with the masses and with intellectuals. They are masterful in their ability to use perfectly patriotic and well intentioned people for their purposes. And, where not yet in power, they can make extravagant promises of material well being later.

In such an ideological struggle one would think that the countries of North America and Western Europe would have nearly all the advantages. Their own extraordinary prosperity, contrasted with the Soviet Union and Communist China, should be a convincing proof of the superiority of their political and economic systems. Their cultures, techniques, and institutions, if they could only become established in today's poor and backward countries, would provide economic development with personal freedom.

The peoples of the undeveloped countries sense that adopting communism means sacrificing their cultures and losing many freedoms. But perhaps a majority is prepared to suffer these losses in exchange for the rapid economic advance that they now believe can come only through international communism. They know that their countries are barely developing now. Because they do not have state socialism now, many believe that they have already tried the best that private capitalism can offer and have found it wanting.

What they do not realize is that in the main they have never really experienced American-style government and economics. True, there has been a certain amount of direct investment in these countries, operated by American, French, British, or Dutch companies: but these activities have not had much cultural impact on a majority of the population. Given a measure of political maturity, and a willingness to change traditional attitudes that are uneconomic, these peoples could have development *and* freedom.

But it is hard to persuade the officials and natives of these undeveloped countries that the opportunity to have development and freedom really exists. This is partly because our own government officials often do not understand that political liberty and economic liberty are indivisible. Many of our representatives do not realize how it is that market-directed and free economies allocate resources efficiently in the main. They have accepted unwittingly the communist contention that there is no natural order in economic affairs and that there will be chaos and waste without a government plan. Why should foreign governments believe in the "western" way of life if we ourselves do not really understand the remarkable social organization into which we were born?

The western world has lost its missionary zeal. It is no longer intellectually fashionable to assert the superiority of "European" (including American) institutions and attitudes. Instead, too many people have come to believe that the development of backward countries can be accomplished merely by spending money, and that almost anything can be accomplished if only enough "capital" is transferred in loans or grants.

This superficial emphasis on financial foreign assistance can be extremely dangerous, for it is far from being a sufficient condition of economic development. Countries with backward and uneconomic cultures lack the capacity to usefully absorb large increments of capital. What they often need far more urgently are extensive technical assistance and guaranteed markets for their products in North America and Western Europe.

It is also unfortunate that when foreign aid is given by one government to another, bureaucratic emphasis tends to be on economic plans and controls. Many a country has been unable to "collect" in Washington until it had assembled a rather detailed economic development plan. If a serious attempt is later made to adhere to these plans, despite all sorts of unpredictable events occurring, there are certain to be shortages and gluts that "invite" government taxes, subsidies, and regulations.

*   *   *   *   *

It was with this background of concern that the present book on economic development of backward countries was written. Starting in 1958, and except for a year as a visiting professor at Yale University, the author traveled during four years through dozens of undeveloped countries. He tried to understand some of the reasons for the west's losses in the cold war, and particularly to learn where our development policies have gone awry.

The general conclusion was that the U.S. Government, and some other Western countries also, are trying to *buy* support and popularity abroad with *money*. The basic causes of slow material progress in these countries, which are deeply rooted in tradition or are the consequence of strongly vested interests, are frequently not mentioned for fear of giving diplomatic offense. But granting financial assistance in this way often defers reforms that otherwise would have to be made by the country itself.

A more specific conclusion was that many officials who make economic policy, although they may have a great deal of factual and necessary knowledge, are largely unaware of economic principles essential to their work. Instead they have acquired a smattering of superficial ideas and a meaningless jargon that through repetition have become accepted without question. Economics is not a simple subject. True relations are often the opposite of what at first they appear to be. There must be more *economics* in economic development if there is to be more *development*.

The purpose of this book is, accordingly, to emphasize the economics of development and to stress principles rather than description. An intelligent reader who has had a really sound introductory course in economic theory, and thoroughly understood its content, should have no trouble in completing this book during a semester course. The material presented here has been included in courses given at Yale University, Cape Town University, and Duke University, and has presumably benefited from this practical test.

*　　*　　*　　*　　*

A word is in order regarding the bibliography. There are references relating to each Chapter, extra references relating to each Part, and, in addition an extensive general reference list. No citation appears in more than one place though. The reason for this arrangement is that it seemed desirable to relate each citation as specifically as possible to the appropriate section of the book—although this is often not easy to do. Finally, given the immense flood of literature concerning economic development now being published, many excellent writings have had with regret to be omitted.

Acknowledgments

It is always difficult to acknowledge by name those who have assisted one's own intellectual development and understanding. For one thing, it is hard to know where to draw the line; for another, the views presented in this work are the author's, and cannot coincide entirely with those of anyone else. But mention should be made of Professors Basil Yamey and Mark Perlman, both of whom read the manuscript and made many useful comments. Appreciation is also extended to all those officials in foreign countries who, despite other demands on their time, provided the author with information. Thanks to Mrs. Mary Ellen Earp, the manuscript has been typed quickly and efficiently, despite many imperfections in the original copy.

Also, the author is grateful for ability to draw upon earlier writings that have appeared in economics journals, including the *American Economic Review, Canadian Journal of Economics and Political Science, Economic Development and Cultural Change,* the *Journal of Political Economy, Kyklos, Oxford Economic Papers, Population Review, Quarterly Journal of Economics, Review of Economics and Statistics, South African Economic Journal,* and the *Southern Economics Journal.*

Finally, and more formally, he wishes to acknowledge permission from numerous publishers to quote excerpts from the works of others, and specifically:

Anglo-American Corporation; American Economic Association; American Farm Economics Association; Center for International Economic Growth; University of Chicago Press; Economic Society of South Africa; United Nations Food and Agriculture Organization; Glyn, Mills and Company; Harcourt, Brace, and World, Inc.; Harper & Row; Harvard University Press; Institute for Population Research; Richard D. Irwin, Inc.; Kyklos-Verlag; London School of Economics; Macmillan and Company, Ltd.; Massachusetts Institute of Technology Center for International Studies; National Bureau of Economic Research; New School for Social Research; Oxford University Press; Princeton University Press; Routledge and Kegan Paul Ltd.; Royal Economic Society; Southern Economic Association; University of Toronto Press; World Health Organization; Yale University Press.

Contents

xiii

IV. LABOR AND DEVELOPMENT

VI. PROSPECTS FOR DEVELOPMENT

ECONOMICS
for DEVELOPMENT

I

Environment for
development

THE economic development of backward countries is very much in the fore today. But what is the nature of these less developed countries? What is the environment to be developed?

People who have always resided in advanced nations, however great their interest and motivation, will always be handicapped in their understanding of what is needed. It is almost impossible for a person who has not lived and worked in a number of underdeveloped countries, and preferably on more than one continent, to appreciate fully the enormous gap that separates people living in the backward countries of the tropics from those in the advanced nations of the temperate zones. Without this appreciation, it is all too easy to suggest policies and promote programs that are unrealistic and wasteful, and which in the end will result in widespread frustration and political instability.

Unfortunately, few students of aggregate economic growth in undeveloped countries can arrange to live and work abroad in these countries, although opportunities are increasing slowly through the Peace Corps and other institutions. Part I, although a poor substitute for personal experience, is included for the majority of people who must stay at home. It attempts to explain how the inhabitants of the underdeveloped countries tend to think and feel, how they earn and survive, and the important ways in which their economic situations differ.

1

The politics
of development

One of the most striking features of the world we live in is the marked range in per capita incomes of different countries. At one extreme are countries such as India and Egypt with annual average incomes of under $100; at the other is the United States with a per capita yearly income over 30 times as great. And in most cases the gap in average income between the richest and poorest countries is increasing. Such extreme contrasts, even allowing for the impossibility of exactly estimating income differences, must have political consequences. The concurrence of such wealth and poverty among nations is a challenge to governments and their economic advisers. It has also been made part of the Cold War between East and West.

RISING ECONOMIC ASPIRATIONS

Poverty is as old and widespread as mankind. A majority of the human race has always suffered intermittent hunger. What is new is that people in all countries are demanding an improvement in their economic lot. It is this "revolution in expectations" that is creating such a ferment in the underdeveloped world. And these new attitudes are a political force that cannot be ignored.

Why should so many people now refuse to accept poverty after so many centuries of resignation?

There are several answers. One is an "international demonstration effect." Another is Soviet propaganda that the "colonial" peoples are victims of exploitation—past and present. Still another is the world-wide tendency to look to government for economic progress. Moreover, there is a tendency toward urbanization throughout the world, and town life gives a new role to the ordinary man.

The demonstration effect

It is very human to want the better things that someone richer than oneself can be seen enjoying. In suburban America, this is called "keeping up with the Joneses," and many a housewife has plagued her husband with accounts of the new refrigerator in a neighbor's kitchen. To some extent this phenomenon occurs internationally, among those people in poorer lands who have an idea of how people live in advanced countries. Some economists have termed this the "demonstration effect," although it might in this connection be better termed the "emulation urge."

Before World War II only a very few people in underdeveloped territories had much contact with the living standards of the Western world. Of the few who did, many were extremely wealthy in their own right and well able to indulge their liking for conspicuous consumption abroad in Europe.

All this has begun to change. Throughout the world there are movie theatres in even modest towns. Except in those underdeveloped countries that have a local movie industry—e.g., India—most of the movies shown are American or European. And in these movies almost everyone seems to have fine clothes, eat well, and live in luxurious surroundings. In addition, but again only in the towns, there are magazines with photos displaying the vastly higher consumption levels of the Western world. During and following World War II, American and European armed forces were stationed in many parts of Asia, and the realization of how lavishly even foreign soldiers live came as a shock to many natives.

Finally, the development of air travel has enormously increased the number of American and European tourists annually streaming through the major cities and tourist attractions of Latin America, Africa, and Asia. Their possessions, spending habits, and behavior have all been noted. And a small but growing stream of officials and merchants has traveled from the more backward countries to Europe. The rapidity and economy of air transport vastly increase contacts in official and business circles between advanced and backward countries.

In these and other ways, but mostly in the urban areas of underdeveloped countries, there has grown a strong desire to emulate Western ways. Among the young this may reveal itself in T shirts, blue jeans, and rock 'n roll. The young white collar worker, in his business suit, admires his new fountain pen and wrist watch. The businessman admires his new office air conditioner—whether it works or not. One and all, this new class of educated city people wants more of what it knows Westerners have.

This is of enormous significance for economic development because these emerging urbanites are a powerful class. They constitute an elite group having considerable influence both officially and intellectually. It

is primarily due to them that many backward countries are now on the
move.

Alleged "colonial" exploitation

It is also significant for Western relations with the underdeveloped
world that the very real disparity that exists between their consumption
levels is often attributed to colonial exploitation. This allegation is not
only made by Soviet propagandists, but also by many others whose
hearts can sway their heads. Moreover this recurrent theme refers not
only to imperial colonialism as practiced by some European powers until recently, but also to "economic" colonialism as supposedly practiced
today by American corporations with international markets.

The Soviet charge, put bluntly, is that the Western world is rich
because the underdeveloped world is poor. Western Europe and North
America have supposedly taken the tin, nitrates, copper, oil, rubber,
copra, tea, coffee, sugar, jute, and cotton, produced by the backward
countries at prices that were "unfairly" low. In return, the underdeveloped world has had to buy the West's manufactured producer and
consumer goods at prices that allegedly were and are unfairly high.

It is very natural to ascribe one's poverty, not to one's own short-
comings, but to the malevolence of others. Economic backwardness is
often attributed by Western writers to an unfavorable native culture, an
untrained labor force, and an unwillingness to make social changes. It
is one thing for backward peoples to recognize the truth of such charges
privately, but quite another to admit it publicly. The Soviet allegation
that these current inadequacies are the result of a "colonial" system that
prevents local development, imposed now by concerted Anglo-American
economic pressure rather than through political hegemony, is often
welcomed by local politicians in poor countries.

Of considerable help to governments of backward countries in negotiating loans, is the Soviet claim that past and present instances of colonial exploitation result in a Western "debt" to the underdeveloped
countries. The United States and Western Europe are said to "owe"
large-scale foreign aid as a sort of financial compensation and moral
restitution for past spoliation. Such propaganda has the effect of excusing
ingratitude by poorer countries now receiving economic aid.

Later we shall examine these claims that the advanced countries have
been exploiting the backward ones through international trade. We
shall argue that in material, but not in human terms, the colonialism
of the past constituted the only kind of development that was practical
prior to 1914. But these are technical arguments that require economic
understanding. The politically important fact is not only that the
emerging people of many underdeveloped countries want to live as

people do in advanced countries. In addition, because of allegations regarding colonial exploitation, they have often been led to believe that they have a *right* to a less disparate standard of living. They feel the developed industrial countries must make reparation in some way.

According to the Soviet view, this colonial exploitation is not coming to an end merely because former colonial territories are now politically independent. Even the countries of Latin America, although legally independent for a century, are still held to be economic colonies of the United States and Western Europe. Somehow limited to exporting primary products, and importing manufactures in exchange, their terms of trade are said to be inevitably and increasingly disadvantageous to them. That they do not industrialize themselves, always assuming that this would be beneficial, is attributed to the unwillingness of Western capitalists and governments to provide the necessary technical knowledge and funds. So the end of political domination allegedly does not mean the end of economic "colonialism."

Emotionally—as distinct from logically—these are powerful arguments indeed. They are directed at college students in particular and the educated urban classes of the poorer countries in general. These people would not be human if they did not resent the great disparity, of which they are now aware, between consumption levels in their countries and those in the Western nations.

Expectations regarding government

In the backward countries, and more so perhaps than in the advanced ones, there is an increasing tendency to suppose that economic development can be assured by government action. This is especially true in former colonial territories, where much of the current poverty is bitterly ascribed to recent foreign rule. However, even in Latin America there is a deeply rooted belief that a sovereign people can alleviate grinding poverty through their own government if only the will is sufficiently strong and interference from outside is sufficiently weak.

It is hard to realize how comparatively late in the world's history have governments come to be held responsible for continued economic progress. This is one of the consequences of universal suffrage in most countries. However, it is also in part a result of advances in the science of economics, modest though this progress has been.

Until a half century ago, people looked exclusively to their own efforts for improvement in their economic situation. The role of government was for the most part limited to protecting people and their property, enforcing contracts, and providing a monetary system. In addition, many of the more advanced countries stimulated invention and provided for vocational training through patent and apprenticeship laws, respectively.

Public education and health, although of great economic consequence, were largely provided for other social reasons. No government considered that its major responsibilities included preventing unemployment and guaranteeing higher per capita incomes.

The great depression of the early 1930's, at least in the more advanced and industrialized nations, changed this permanently. Governments have ever since been judged at election time according to the economic state of the nation. It is generally felt that governments have the means—if not always the ability and will—to forestall mass unemployment. Absence of economic advance is blamed on the party in office. Annual percentage increases in gross national product (GNP) have become a campaign issue in countries other than the United States.

These attitudes have spread to more backward countries. Nowadays political ideas travel around the world almost as fast as the daily news. Moreover, this view of government responsibility for economic progress is now seeping down from intellectuals to workers and from city dwellers to rural peasants.

In those countries that have recently gained independence and are still eliminating colonial ways with vigor, economic expectations are likely to be especially high. Before independence, poverty was often attributed to colonial status and imperial greed, so that the public at large came to equate political freedom with increased consumption. Now they still await these anticipated economic fruits. In some cases these expectations may be met, and in many others they will not, but in all instances the new government will be held accountable for the people's economic progress.

This extreme dependence on government to make and implement economic development plans can be partly attributed in many poor countries to the absence of a substantial middle class. In Western Europe it was the bourgeoisie—the merchants of the towns—who innovated and saved. Much of the economic growth of these countries was due to their entrepreneurial vigor and accumulating capital. But most underdeveloped countries do not possess such a middle class. Instead, between the poor peasants and the privileged rich, there often is a gap. Hence governments may have to assume more responsibility for economic plans and operations than would be desirable in countries having a broad middle class of private managers and proprietors.

RIVAL DEVELOPMENT OBJECTIVES

Most people are in favor of economic development, but few agree—except in the most general terms—as to what it should entail. It is one thing to want more goods, to expect them to be provided through government planning, and to demand technical and financial assistance from more advanced countries. It is quite another to specify the kinds of outputs and incomes that are to be increased. In fact the objectives of development most often advocated are incompatible because they compete for resources so that successful attainment of one goal must often mean comparative failure in reaching another. If one objective is desired sooner, some other must wait until later. No rational planning can take place until these incompatibilities are understood.

Increasing real incomes

Superficially, one might think that no one would be against increasing per capita incomes, for after all this is tantamount to increasing national output. However, in every country the distribution of incomes is very uneven, with a few rich at one extreme and many poor at the other. With such a skewed income distribution, median income is far less than the mean income, and many humanitarians might urge that the first consideration should be to improve the lot of the very poor. This might require the development of plans which place more emphasis on assistance to peasant farmers and cottage industry. As a result, some potential increase in aggregate national income might have to be sacrificed, involving a partial "trade-off" of one objective for another.

For example, in order to increase the average annual income of the poorest one-fifth of the country's families by $10, it may be possible to increase all other family incomes by an average of only $4 instead of $8. Accordingly, per family income for the country as a whole might increase by $5.20 instead of $6.40. A potential increase of $1.20 in per capita income has then been sacrificed for a larger increase in the incomes of the poorest fraction of population.

The geographic distribution of benefits also must be considered. A specific development project may primarily benefit the people in one region. Its construction and later operation will provide local employment. Its main raw material needs may be supplied from some quite small area of the country. This uneven geographic incidence is often quite incidental to some other decision—e.g., that there should be more rope output, in which case the sisal growing areas benefit—but sometimes a deliberate effort is made by government to favor certain regions which may be exceptionally poor, or pivotal in supporting the administration, or in a border area where some other country is seeking to gain influence. To increase incomes in a particular province, the rest of the country may have to sacrifice a larger potential income increase.

It is also not unknown for government to favor one kind of productive agent over another. If landowners are politically unpopular and powerless, a forced fragmentation of their holdings may be undertaken. This may reduce agricultural output, but increase the real incomes of former tenant cultivators. If a prime objective is the creation of new jobs for unemployed urban labor, all sorts of intensive labor projects may be undertaken in the towns, with a resultant diversion of investment from possibly more productive rural enterprises. The earnings of industrial labor may increase, but by less than the loss of gross national product.

Increasing particular outputs

Government-financed projects may have only an incidental effect on real incomes. The actual objective may be to increase the supply of certain commodities that for some reason are considered especially vital to the country. Of course all goods are scarce, but it may be thought by the authorities that certain goods are overly scarce, in the sense of being far too high priced. By undertaking increased production, the government not only provides employment and income but also benefits users of the good in question because they can now obtain it more readily or at a lower price.

Accordingly, in poor countries where food is a major item, there have often been demands for governments to increase grain output. Plans to build fertilizer plants and construct irrigation systems have been supported by the urban population in the hope of obtaining more and cheaper food. However, because rural cultivators have a high income elasticity of demand for food, often only a fraction of the extra food output has reached urban consumers.

However, governments of most underdeveloped countries are more interested in expanding industrial than agricultural output, despite the meager diets of their peoples. Industrialization, for many officials, has become synonymous with development. And it is hard to untangle the emotions and thinking that prompt this attitude

First, there is the emulation urge, and the belief that industrialization is a cause rather than a result of successful economic development. The advanced countries now emphasize industry and so the backward ones wish to stress it too. It is not generally recognized that the industrial revolution came to Europe together with an agricultural revolution.

Second, manufactured goods comprise a large fraction of the total value of imports, and most underdeveloped countries wish to become less dependent on external trade. There are many reasons for this attitude, as we shall see later. And, as already explained, most policy makers in these countries believe that somehow the local economy receives less than it should when it sells primary products and buys manufactures. Through industrialization they hope to produce import substitutes and perhaps, through new industrial exports, to "exploit" more backward countries in turn.

Third, industrialization has a cultural impact in many diverse ways.

The very experience of working with machinery in a large plant cannot help but change even an unskilled employee. As a part of a larger organization, in which each person must often do certain things at specified times, a new understanding of precision and timing may be implanted in people whose former motto was *mañana*. Industrialization may cause factory workers to understand rudimentary physical processes and encourage them to seek more formal education. And industrialization means urbanization, which involves not only overcrowding and dearer food, but also readier access to new ideas. For those who live in towns, there are newspapers, magazines, books, and movies. Also, there are strangers from other regions of the country, with different customs to observe and ideas to discuss.

It must be admitted too that many governments favor industrial projects for their display value. Oil refineries and steel mills fall within this category. So too do large river dams, major bridges, modern airports, four-lane highways, and enormous government buildings. A few spectacular projects, if sufficiently well publicized internally, may do more for morale than a widespread but small increase in material well-being and "progress."

Government's timing of increased consumption

A fundamental issue in every country attempting a rapid increase in national output is the degree to which it should invest in future capacity or present output. This decision has to be made whatever the level of resource employment. But it is of course less obvious and agonizing if formerly idle factors of production can now be put to work. Here again is a trade-off—this time between present and future consumption—and one that is usually reflected in prevailing interest rates.

Government leaders in underdeveloped countries usually incline to a higher rate of investment—especially in government-operated projects— than the economy itself can use. There is ample evidence to indicate that few such governments can borrow domestically—after obtaining abroad all the capital they can—the money needed to finance their favored projects. Specifically, at anything like "normal" interest rates, these funds are not forthcoming. And if such funds are borrowed at very high interest rates, few of the government's industrial projects would appear profitable.

But governments do have the right to levy taxes and regulate the supply of money. Unfortunately, quite apart from political objections to heavy taxes, there are many other reasons why governments of backward countries have difficulty in levying and collecting taxes that will yield the revenues they feel are needed. It is therefore not surprising that they often resort to hidden methods of expropriation and to the financing of deficits with newly created money. The resultant price increases reduce consumption and thereby free resources for use by the government. In this way a government can impose its notion of the relative need for present versus future consumption. Immediate utilities are traded for a postponed output of consumer goods.

Politicians, in expounding their development plans, do not customarily dwell on the existence of all these cruel and inevitable alternatives. Perhaps this is because the government's ability to create money and increase taxes prevents resource constraints for the economy from being sufficiently obvious. But for any country—given the level of foreign assistance—constraints do exist. Usefully employed resources are limited. Opportunity costs are very real; so far as these are measurable by economists. it is well that they be ascertained. Decisions can then be made by politicians aware of what is being sacrificed to attain some favored goal.

How should decisions among economic alternatives be made? In a country where government intervention is slight, these decisions are made by the economy itself. The numerous consumers, investors, lenders, workers, and owners of other productive factors, competing in their respective markets, determine the prices of goods and services. Resources are simultaneously allocated among alternative uses. The output mix is thereby determined. So also are factor and personal incomes. Invariably, some of these results will be disliked and criticized, and if there is enough resentment the government will act to set these market decisions aside. It can either intervene indirectly (as by altering property rights so that former landowners have less income) or directly (as by setting maximum interest rates, minimum wage rates, or rationing foods).

Such intervention usually cannot be justified on economic grounds alone. Hence it must be political. This is because any intervention affects individual real incomes by altering the prices of goods. Normally some people will be benefited, and others injured, by government alteration of the economy's own decisions. Only in very rare cases will *everyone* be better or not worse off. Except in these cases, the policy maker will have to decide whether to make *A* better off and *B* worse off, or vice versa. There are really no obvious ways in which such interpersonal comparisons can be made. A subjective political decision—based on "judgment," or "prejudice," as one prefers—must be rendered.

Hence economic development involves political decisions. They are inseparable. And no choice among development objectives can be wholly scientific and objective.

WESTERN MOTIVES FOR GRANTING AID

The more advanced Western countries assisting economic development in poorer lands are also faced with alternative goals and policy doubts. What are their motives? What are they trying to accomplish?

Many people in the United States support government aid to backward countries—whether it takes the form of technical assistance, "soft" loans, or outright grants—on the grounds of humanity. There is the feeling that at slight real cost to them a great deal of good can be done for others. Of course any form of charity can weaken efforts at self-help and often causes furtive resentment. But the humanitarian spirit that prompts such help is certainly laudable.

There are, however, interests that support foreign financial aid on quite selfish grounds. When the United States makes loans or grants to underdeveloped countries in dollars, nearly all these dollars are eventually used to buy United States exports, although not always by the initial beneficiary. Within limits, one can predict that these funds will be spent for certain kinds of products, such as earth-moving equipment, heavy electrical machinery, and steel products. It is therefore not surprising that certain industries within the United States are not exactly opposed to foreign aid. Moreover, if the United States government makes a practice of "selling" very large quantities of food and fibers to governments abroad, certain sections of United States agriculture are likely to support this aspect of foreign aid. Of course, that certain domestic interests benefit from government aid to underdeveloped countries in no way subtracts from the moral credit due the taxpayer, who may quite unselfishly favor limited aid to poor countries.

It is evident, moreover, that the Western world would make fewer development loans and grants to backward countries were it not for the supposed exigencies of the Cold War. Such assistance is widely held to be one of several useful weapons that can be employed against the spread of Communism. Why should the United States spend fifty-odd billion dollars a year on land, naval, and air forces—one purpose of which is to prevent certain territories coming under the control of less friendly governments—if this same danger can be avoided by economic assistance costing far less?

One might think that to ask the question is to provide the answer. However, the best allocation of expenditures between military systems and economic assistance is far from clear. For one thing, it is not obvious exactly what economic aid is supposed to "buy."

One school of thought is that the United States can help to maintain friendly and democratic governments in office by extending economic aid to their countries. If people are living better, there may be less likelihood that the existing government will be replaced either by ballots or bullets. Moreover, if the present government *is* replaced by another, there is a greater probability that the new government will be equally friendly if United States assistance has tended to benefit many people and has been widely publicized.

According to this view, it is important to ensure that our economic assistance penetrates to the public at large and is made known. As assurance, we attach various conditions to granting aid and have stationed local inspectors of our own. Moreover, we may choose not to assist in projects that the recipient government wants, but offer to finance others instead, because we feel that they will be of more general benefit. But such inspection and selection are not likely to make the recipient government as appreciative as it might otherwise be.

Another and more cynical school maintains that the United States should support any government that will support us, as for instance by giving us military bases or voting with us in international organizations. This means that on occasion we may be supporting personal dictatorships or socialist governments. It also means that we may have to finance projects that are of more propaganda value to the existing government—or perhaps to the private financial interest of government leaders—than to the people. Finally, should there be a revolution, the incoming government is likely to view the United States as an ally of its political enemies; our influence, at least temporarily, will then be less than nothing.

A corollary of both these views is that we concentrate our assistance on those countries which for some reason we wish to influence. The reason may be military, as in the case of countries on the Asian perimeter of the Soviet bloc. Or, through influencing some particular government, we can perhaps affect events in surrounding countries that normally look to it for diplomatic or cultural guidance. But such concentration means a comparative neglect of other undeveloped countries, which may then promote links with the Soviet bloc in order to give themselves a nuisance value and so qualify for greater economic aid from the West.

A third school eschews all such *Realpolitik,* denies the desirability of trying to influence foreign governments however suavely, and instead maintains that the best safeguard against more countries "going" Communist is a steady if slow advance in their personal consumption levels. A sometimes associated objective is the strengthening of private enterprise and capitalistic institutions, through the growth of a middle class, in which case assistance may be conditional upon the recipient government's treatment of private enterprise. But governments sympathetic to international Communism or simply in favor of state socialism on economic grounds do not come into power only in the poorest countries. Cuba provides an outstanding example. Also, by the time an imminent *coup* becomes sufficiently apparent, it is far too late for such long-run measures. And the alternative policy, that of granting assistance without strings to all underdeveloped countries, means of course that its scale and effectiveness in any particular country are decreased.

These difficulties are not presented as an argument against the extension of increased foreign assistance by the advanced Western nations to poorer and more backward nations. But a consideration of these various political perplexities suggests that it is not realistic to suppose that any specific *quid pro quo* can be demonstrated or expected. Assistance must be rendered in the belief that generosity and sympathy may be rewarded in some now unpredictable way. And, where this is patently improbable, assistance should be refused.

POSSIBILITIES OF FRUSTRATION

Enough has been said already to indicate that the people of backward countries demand an escape from crushing poverty, expect their governments to alleviate their miseries, and believe that the advanced countries have a moral obligation to assist them. Although for mixed motives, the countries of North America and Western Europe (and, independently, the Soviet Union) are prepared to provide capital funds and technical assistance within limits. One might accordingly think that it is just a matter of a decade or so before all these underdeveloped countries "take off" into sustained economic growth.

Such heady optimism may lead to bitter frustration: the roots of poverty lie deep in cultural and economic circumstances. These causes cannot be removed overnight by angrily changing a government or belatedly realizing that a few other countries are comparatively rich.

It is one thing to recognize that a country is poor and backward. It is quite another to agree on the causes of its poverty and to remove them. Some of these causes—such as poor soil, a harsh climate, a lack of mineral resources—can be offset but never altered by man. And an "uneconomic"[1] culture, in which there are few individual incentives to earn extra income and people have too many children, is subject to human change only over a generation or so.

A poor and backward country is hence truly "underdeveloped" only if there are reasons for supposing that it has unused but valuable natural resources or an uneconomic but alterable culture. What natural resources are in fact valuable depends upon available techniques for exploiting them. And cultural adaptability varies considerably from country to country: Japan and India exemplify this in Asia, and Holland and Spain in Europe. However, if a poor and backward country lacks both valuable natural resources and a potentially materialistic culture, its economic prospects are bleak indeed. The high hopes of today will not be realized tomorrow.

It follows that large capital transfers from rich to poor countries are an insufficient and perhaps unnecessary condition of material advance. Of course this assertion flies in the face of much that is written about

[1] In this work, "uneconomic" means a failure to maximize material opportunities.

economic development, whether by governments that hope to receive additional funds or by bureaucracies that are maintained to supervise such transfers. But the truth is that recipient countries cannot use large capital increments without also training management and workers in new techniques and often inducing new consumer tastes.

Economic development can in many cases be accelerated by technical assistance and capital advances from the more advanced countries. But the main source of economic progress must be the peoples of these lands. They must open their minds and accept change. Family ties must be loosened and traditions discarded. They must work in new ways and perhaps harder. Except for the very poorest, these peoples must save and invest more—through some form of compulsion if necessary. Some spiritual values must give way to more material ones. Hence all sorts of psychological traumas are part of the price of material progress. But the inhabitants of a backward country must be prepared to pay this price if they really want economic development.

It is here that government can play a role. Government leaders, in these days of mass communication media, can do much to make new ideas and ways respected and favored. The State cannot create wealth of itself, but it can sometimes engender a national sense of dedicated effort, so that millions of individuals in their daily lives are more willing to work, save, and change. This is perhaps the major way in which a common will to prosper may help to end the worst poverty.

2

Common characteristics
of poor countries

The poorest countries of the world share a number of features that distinguish them from the more advanced ones. Many of these distinctive characteristics are really specific aspects of general poverty. However, some may be causes of economic backwardness, and so of greater analytic interest. In many cases too—such as low savings per capita—the result of poverty in one generation is one cause of poverty in the next. Of course there are also many important economic differences among the poorer countries (see Chapter 3), but this chapter will examine only those social and economic characteristics that are common to all.

WHAT IS AN UNDERDEVELOPED COUNTRY?

An impressionistic word picture of an underdeveloped country has been skillfully painted by a general manager of the United Nations Special Fund (for economic development):

Everyone knows an underdeveloped country when he sees one. It is a country characterized by poverty, with beggars in the cities, and villagers eking out a bare subsistence in the rural areas. It is a country lacking in factories of its own, usually with inadequate supplies of power and light. It usually has insufficient roads and railroads, insufficient government services, poor communications. It has few hospitals, and few institutions of higher learning. Most of its people cannot read or write. In spite of the generally prevailing poverty of the people, it may have isolated islands of wealth, with a few persons living in luxury. Its banking system is poor; small loans have to be obtained through money lenders who are often little better than extortionists. Another striking characteristic of an underdeveloped country is that its exports to other countries usually consist almost entirely of raw materials, ores or fruits or some staple product with possibly a small admixture of luxury handicrafts. Often the extraction or cultivation of these raw material exports is in the hands of foreign companies.[1]

[1] Paul G. Hoffman, "One Hundred Countries—One and One Quarter Billion People," (Washington, D.C.: Committee for International Economic Growth, 1960), p. 14.

In practice the United Nations considers any country underdeveloped if it has a low per capita level of income. Altogether about two billion people—or three-quarters of the human race—live in almost 100 countries where the income per head is below $300. These countries were once simply called "poor" or "backward." But these terms seemed too accurate for diplomatic use in the mid-twentieth century. Hence, for a brief period, they were called "undeveloped." In time this adjective in turn gave way to the more euphemistic "underdeveloped." Still later the most commonly adopted term came to be "less developed." The latter adjectives also have more optimistic implications and so are usually preferred by international development agencies.

A stricter use of language might distinguish between "undeveloped" and "developed" and between "overdeveloped" and "underdeveloped." There are several *un*developed regions of the world, such as the Antarctic and parts of the Sahara, where man has had little impact and has no settled habitation. In contrast, a developed region is one which contains population, and hence economic activity. In this sense all countries are developed, but they may contain large undeveloped regions, such as the central arid areas of Australia. An *under*developed region might be considered one in which population and economic activity per capita are likely to increase; examples are British Columbia, Southern Rhodesia, and Queensland. *Over*developed countries can then be viewed as overpopulated, given their present productive methods, so that income per head hardly increases even though population itself may do so.

Some of the poorest countries are overdeveloped in this sense. Located where man in his early history was best able to cultivate food, and where the earliest civilizations flourished millennia ago, these countries in time became overpopulated. Their ways of life also became rigid. Examples of such countries are Egypt, China, and—to some extent—India.

These various distinctions are too academic though. In accordance with now accepted nomenclature, "underdeveloped," "poor," and "backward" will be used synonymously.

VARIOUS ASPECTS OF GENERAL POVERTY

Poverty has many different aspects, and all are found in varying degree in all underdeveloped countries. Poverty, in human terms, means little to eat or wear. Its more abstract consequences are a propensity to consume rather than to save income, and hence low ratios of capital to labor (see Part III, which elaborates on the problems of accumulating and investing real capital).

The most obvious meaning of poverty is of course low income per capita. Table 2-1 gives some published statistics in this connection. However, for various reasons (see pp. 41–44) these estimates must not be taken

Table 2-1

INCOME PER CAPITA OF THE UNDERDEVELOPED WORLD: 1959

	Asia and Micronesia		Sub-Sahara Africa		Near East and North Africa		Latin America and Caribbean		Totals		
	Population (millions)	Territories	Population (millions)	Territories	Population (millions)	Territories	Population (millions)	Territories	Population (millions)	Percentage of Population	Territories
Under $100	657	16	146	23	22	4	7	3	832	71	46
$100–199	33	4	17	1	69	5	94	9	213	18	19
$200–299	12	7	1	1	10	2	50	6	93	7	16
$300–699	—	—	—	—	4	3	45	6	49	4	9
	702	27	164	25	105	14	196	24	1,177	100	90

Principal Source: United Nations, *Demographic Year Book*, 1961.
N.B. Includes Communist China.

at their face value; not only are they usually based on very dubious and sparse data, but their conversion into dollars at official exchange rates is questionable. It is clear that at United States prices no population could survive on a per capita real annual income of $100.

It is really more informative to consider typical *consumption* in the poorer countries. Food, clothing, and housing are the most important items. Table 2-2 gives data on average calorie intake, but the situation in some respects is worse than that indicated. The diets of backward peoples include a great deal of cereals and other starches. Even though they do not refine these foods to the extent that most Western peoples do—and so preserve more of the vitamin content—their diets tend to be very deficient in animal protein. There is a lack of "building" foods such as meat, fish, dairy products, and eggs.

There are very few statistics on housing in the underdeveloped world, in part perhaps because, except in towns, a house comprises little else than a shelter. And two-thirds or more of the population is rural. "Housing" for them consists of dried mud walls with some strengthening timbers or plaited palm fronds with stick supports. A Central African can build his rondavel hut in a few days with a little help. Rural housing in backward countries has nothing to do with plumbing. The village women carry their water from a nearby stream, well, or tank. There are no sewers ("night-soil" is used as fertilizer) and heavy rains mean mud and stagnant puddles. The nearest electricity is as far as the nearest town.

Poor health is to be expected. Many human ailments follow prolonged malnutrition. Contaminated water results in a variety of intestinal infections. All sorts of parasites flourish in the tropics, from bilharzia in African rivers to liver flukes in the Amazonian jungles, while the ubiquitous mosquito spreads malaria. Tuberculosis saps the vigor of many throughout the less developed world. In poor countries there is almost no personal medical care available for most of the population. Superstition and self-help must take the place of medical knowledge and hospital nursing. It is not surprising that in some countries (see Table 2-3) the infant mortality rate is around 250 per 1,000—in some regions 500 per 1000—and that life expectancy at birth is only about 30 years.

A simple but striking illustration of the poverty of backward countries is that almost nothing is ever thrown away. There are none of the street litter and junk yards of America. Old oil drums continue to do service as ovens and water containers—and even as musical instruments in the West Indies—and there is a use for every old nail or piece of wire. Axes may be made from sharpened spring leaves of old cars. And when some piece of equipment breaks down it is not replaced with a new part, as in advanced countries, but is actually repaired. Mechanics in backward countries often have more ingenuity and manual skill than those in more advanced countries.

Table 2-2
INTAKE AND AVAILABILITY OF FOOD: 1959

	Calories per capita per day	Protein of animal origin (%)	Kilograms available per capita annually				People per animal		
			(meat)	(eggs)	(fish)	(milk)	cows	pigs	sheep
Latin America									
Argentina	3040	52	100	7	2	126	.4	4.6	.3
Brazil	2500	20	29	5	—	58	.7	1.2	2.6
Ecuador	2230	18	15	5	4	93	.2	3.0	2.1
Guatemala	—	—	—	—	—	—	2.4	6.9	3.5
Mexico	2330	20	24	7	2	94	1.6	3.7	6.0
Peru	—	—	—	—	—	—	2.0	2.0	.4
Venezuela	2300	27	25	4	8	141	.7	2.0	—
Asia									
Burma	—	—	—	—	—	—	.6	4.8	50.7
India	2080	6	2	0	1	50	2.8	88.8	11.2
Japan	2210	18	6	4	23	20	30.0	42.0	108.0
Fed. of Malaya	—	—	—	—	—	—	—	—	—
Pakistan	1930	—	4	0	2	47	3.9	—	14.0
Thailand	—	—	—	—	—	—	5.0	6.3	—
Africa & Near East									
Egypt	2650	13	14	1	6	43	19	1534	21
Ghana	—	—	—	—	—	—	18	—	15
Guinea	—	—	—	—	—	—	—	—	—
Iran	—	—	—	—	—	—	37.1	—	1
Iraq	—	—	—	—	—	—	—	—	.7
Lybia	2180	10	10	2	1	58	—	—	.9
Tanganyika	—	—	—	—	—	—	1.1	—	3.0
R. S. Africa	2580	30	—	—	—	—	1.3	—	.4
Advanced									
United States	3130	66	94	20	5	307	1.9	3.2	5.4
Canada	3150	64	82	16	6	274	1.6	2.3	13.9
W. Germany	2890	46	54	13	7	220	4.2	3.5	45.8

Source: Food & Agricultural Organization, *The State of Food and Agriculture*, 1961.

Table 2-3
DEMOGRAPHIC DATA: 1959

	Population (millions)	Crude annual birth rate (per thousand)	Crude annual death rate (per thousand)	Infant mortality rate	Life expectancy of males (aged 1 yr.)	Crude annual increase (%)	Fertility (women 10–49 years per yr.) (%)	Urban population (%)
Latin America								
Argentina	16	23	8	—	62	1.5	7	62
Brazil	52	—	—	170	39	—	—	36
Ecuador	3	46	—	106	57	—	—	35
Guatemala	3	50	17	90	48	3.3	17	25
Mexico	35	47	12	76	44	3.5	15	44
Peru	6	40	11	85	51	2.9	—	
Venezuela	5	47	9	59	—	3.8	—	
Asia								
Burma	29	38	18	134	—	2.0	—	10
India	438	26	12	100	39	1.4	—	17
Japan	93	18	7	33	67	1.1	5	56
Fed. of Malaya	6	42	10	66	—	3.2	17	43
Pakistan	94	—	—	—	—	—	—	10
Thailand	26	37	—	—	52	—	—	12
Africa & Near East								
Egypt	26	40	17	141	42	2.3	—	36
Ghana	7	52	21	90	—	3.1	—	—
Guinea	3	62	—	—	41	—	22	—
Iran	19	43	—	39	—	—	—	30
Iraq	6	12	—	—	—	—	—	37
Lybia	1	—	—	—	—	—	—	—
Tanganyika	9	—	—	—	—	—	23	4
R. S. Africa	16	48	16	107	48	3.2	—	43
Advanced								
United States	179	24	9	26	68	1.5	9	64
Canada	16	28	8	28	69	2.0	10	67
W. Germany	51	18	11	34	68	.7	6	71

Source: United Nations, *Demographic Year Book,* 1960.

UNPRODUCTIVE AGRICULTURE THE DOMINANT OCCUPATION

A majority of the people of backward nations live, not in towns, but in the bush, jungle, veld, or whatever the local name for "countryside" may be. The main occupation of rural inhabitants—apart from a little cottage industry and minor processing of agricultural raw materials—is cultivating the land. Statistically, peasant cultivators and their families really *are* the underdeveloped world, for they are a majority of the population. But they are the forgotten people of economic development. Government, in almost all poor countries, is really more concerned with the urban population. Unemployed workers in cities who may riot for food are politically far more dangerous than hungry peasants in remote areas.

Agriculture is the dominant occupation in poor countries. Table 2-4 indicates that there are four times as many people occupied in agriculture in some backward countries as there are in advanced countries.[2] This very considerable concentration in agriculture is both a symptom and an explanation of national poverty. Its significance has often been overlooked or misunderstood.

Throughout the world, as a family's real income rises, it consumes absolutely more food but spends relatively less on it. A wealthy family may devote only 10 per cent of its income to food—even though it eats more expensive foods of animal origin. The other 90 per cent may go for travel, entertainment, durable consumer goods, and so forth. But such families are so few that, although always conspicuous, they should be ignored. Average families in the poorest countries may spend almost half their energies and income on food. Apart from a little expenditure of effort and money on shelter and clothing, the struggle for food is the story of their lives.

The extent to which a country as a whole devotes its energies to obtain food also indicates its degree of poverty. Hence the percentage contribution of agriculture to total GNP is usually significant. There are two reservations however. Agricultural output includes various producer goods—cotton, wool, and hemp, for instance—and these values should be excluded if known. On the other hand, some overpopulated countries import food, and the percentage productive effort of the nation devoted to eating is then greater than the share of agriculture in the national product. This is true, among the less advanced nations, of Malaya. Among the more advanced countries this is notably so in the case of Japan and Great Britain.

[2] In estimating occupations in backward countries, "agriculture" is often a residual category: that is to say, men of working age living in rural areas are often considered to be engaged in cultivation if they are not evidently occupied otherwise.

Table 2-4
LABOR FORCE AND RESOURCES: 1959

	Population (millions)	Population density (per sq. kilometer)	Percentage of land arable*	Population to arable land (per sq. kilometer)	Percentage of males economically active	Percentage of females economically active	Percentage of population active in agriculture
Latin America							
Argentina	16	7	—	—	63	17	—
Brazil	52	8	2	400	56	10	35
Ecuador	3	15	4	375	56	20	80
Guatemala	3	34	3	1112	60	9	90
Mexico	35	17	5	340	57	9	66
Peru	6	8	1	800	55	28	52
Venezuela	5	7	1	700	55	12	50
Asia							
Burma	29	30	13	225	54	19	70
India	438	123	39	307	54	24	73
Japan	93	251	16	1564	58	41	—
Fed. of Malaya	6	51	16	318	51	17	82
Pakistan	94	92	22	416	—	—	85
Thailand	26	43	10	430	52	50	90
Africa & Near East							
Egypt	26	25	2	750	54	6	75
Ghana	7	21	—	—	—	—	—
Guinea	3	11	—	—	71	16	—
Iran	19	12	15	802	57	6	85
Iraq	6	16	8	200	55	4	—
Lybia	1	1	—	—	58	8	—
Tanganyika	9	10	—	—	53	7	—
R. S. Africa	16	12	5	240	—	—	—
Advanced							
United States	179	19	24	72	56	26	19
Canada	16	2	3	67	53	18	24
W. Germany	51	213	—	—	65	34	25

* Rand-McNally, *Commercial Atlas*, 1962.   *Principal Source:* United Nations, *Demographic Yearbook*, 1960.

No country would be poor if it were able to feed itself adequately—either directly or by external trade—through the efforts of a small fraction of its labor force. Poor countries are poor, partly because they have nothing to export in exchange for food imports, but mostly because it takes too many people too much time to feed the population. In other words low output per worker in food production is to blame, and this is very approximately suggested by the last column in Table 2-4. However it must be realized that the figures for agricultural labor force in backward countries include relatively more part-time labor of women and children.

What is surprising is that agricultural output per unit of cultivated area is also usually lower in backward countries. In rather densely populated areas, such as the Philippines, Burma, and Indonesia, one would expect that intensive use of land might reduce output per cultivator. But one might also expect that output per hectare of cultivated land would be rather high. However rice output per hectare is higher in advanced countries such as Australia, Japan, and Italy than in backward and densely populated countries.

There are many explanations, among them a paucity of capital per hectare or per cultivator, imperfect occupational specialization, lack of knowledge, and fragmented land holdings. (Some of these causes are examined in Chapter 8.) Until agricultural output per worker is increased, most of these countries cannot divert many resources into other occupations. Food comes first. Only after a country has satisfied its essential food requirements—unless it has something to export—can it start producing anything but the most necessary manufactures.

A common fallacy is to believe that countries are poor because they have relatively few people occupied in industry. However, with the exception of advanced countries that are able to export manufactured goods despite fierce competition from other nations, backward countries have relatively few people in industry because they have a low agricultural output per cultivator. Under such circumstances, large-scale industrialization without exports would invite mass starvation, especially in the overpopulated countries. It is easy to confuse cause and effect.

DUALISM

Nearly all underdeveloped countries exhibit marked dualism in their economies. In and near the towns, there is an industrial market-money economy; in the rural areas, a subsistence agricultural economy. In addition, in some backward countries there may be foreign-directed enclaves (which makes for triplism). These last are highly capitalistic, and are usually found in petroleum, mining, and "plantation" (or "estate") agriculture.

The market economy

Centered in the towns is a market-money economy. The towns themselves, often seaports, are in direct contact with the rest of the world by ship or air, and by radio and telephone. Foreign trade, moving to and from the hinterland, passes through these *entrepôts*. Such industry as exists is mostly located on their outskirts. Here are to be found government offices, schools, movie theaters. Here too is an emerging middle class of merchants, officials, teachers, doctors, lawyers, and white collar workers.

The urban population uses money for almost everything. Its members, if employed, have particular activities. The occupation may be quite lowly—such as portering or sweeping—but it is specialized. Accordingly, most of what these people consume must be bought with money earnings, for little can be self-produced.

Wage rates for regular urban jobs are usually rather high by rural standards. Sometimes this is due to minimum wage laws that apply only to urban occupations. Sometimes, in the case of foreign-owned firms, wages are higher than they need to be because overseas wage rates constitute a subconscious standard for management. But there are two other reasons, probably far more important.

First, urban living costs are high. The towns are growing, their populations are increasing, and urban occupations and jobs are becoming relatively more numerous. Shelter is therefore perennially scarce and expensive and extra housing is always being planned and built. Associated projects, such as public utilities, sewers, and streets, must also be constructed with public or private capital. In one way or another, taxes and the current cost of all this extra social overhead investment, needed only in the towns, must be paid by their inhabitants. Food costs, especially if internal transportation is expensive, are also likely to be high. Urban wages for regular jobs must hence be sufficient to offset these considerably higher urban living costs.

Second, the sort of people who can hold permanent jobs in the towns are often above average in education, intelligence, reliability, diligence, and industry. Because these people tend to be somewhat superior, compared to their compatriots, they tend to get superior wages. In a very real sense they are often a quality group.

Of course this may not be realized by bush natives and country peasants who hear possibly exaggerated rumors of easy earnings in some distant town. In any event there is always the lure of the bright lights, both figurative and literal, in countries where rural electrification is unknown. And in bad times, as after a crop failure, hunger and desperation may cause the less resigned to try for a last chance in the city. These varied reasons explain the large floating population that is to be seen in the towns, hanging around during the daytime and often sleeping on the streets at night. Odd jobs may keep them for a while, but most of these people, unless they find work or can doss-down indefinitely with some relative in town, eventually drift back to their village. But some remain. And it is this steady net immigration, together with the many floaters, that causes the urban overcrowding so typical of most underdeveloped countries.

The urban population is necessarily dependent on imports, largely from the surrounding countryside, of food and fuel. Also, urban industry may require rurally produced materials for processing. These purchases introduce money into neighboring areas. Peasant families may sell increasing amounts of their surplus food to the town. They may even begin to cultivate cash crops—such as rice or tobacco—not for consumption, but for sale. Because internal transportation is usually expensive—grain prices may double every hundred miles in some cases—this penetration by the market economy of the subsistence economy tends to be limited.

The subsistence economy

The other aspect of dualism is the subsistence economy, starting some distance from the towns and stretching back into the hinterland, desert, or outer islands, as the case may be. The point at which the subsistence economy starts is hard to define. There are few if any rural communities left in the world today that do not have some interchange with the outside economy. But in most backward countries over half the output of rural families is still consumed within the same village. In many cases less than a fifth of a village's production is considered surplus and sold or exchanged outside the community.

In normal years, a village with a subsistence economy is not only self-sufficient in regard to food but also provides its own fuel for cooking and perhaps for heating, too. Cottage weavers may make cloth if the necessary fibers are locally grown. Village artisans make or repair baskets, earthenware, leather goods, footwear, carts and wheels, and fishing nets. A local smith will shape metal into nails, hooks, blades, and simple tools. In these and many other ways a large village, or a cluster of small villages, can look after most of the needs of the inhabitants.

Within these rural communities, especially in the more backward countries, much of the trading may be in kind rather than in money. Tenant cultivators usually pay their rent to the landlord in produce. Peasants who are in debt to a moneylender often repay in grain.

The moneylender, most commonly found in the large villages of South and East Asia, usually performs several economic functions. Because he accepts payment in cereals, he is a grain merchant as well. Selling some of this grain to the nearest town for money, he may buy goods that are not made in the village, and there sell them for money or trade them for more produce. In this way the capitalist merchant reduces the village's need to acquire and use money in its daily transactions, and he links the subsistence economy with the market economy.

Middlemen—and especially moneylenders—are unpopular the world over. Certainly they do not perform these important services gratuitously, and the traders of South and East Asia are notorious for their rapacity. However, much as these men may be disliked in the villages, their economic role should be understood. Their activities serve to bring food to the towns. In fact, the higher the interest charges, the more surplus grain the peasant cultivators must relinquish. Moreover, and something that economists should appreciate, within the entire rural community these money-lending and grain-trading merchants do most of the monetary saving that is usually considered so necessary for development. Asian Communists usually make this sort of merchant, together with the landlord, the object of organized hatred and envy. These emotions can sometimes be translated into rural violence. The Communists privately recognize the merchant, a vigorous practitioner of private enterprise, not only as a class enemy but as an enemy of the system.

But villagers must have money for some purposes. One of the most important of these is to pay poll or land taxes. Or a peasant may want to buy some metal hand tool from a resident or itinerant trader who will take only money. To obtain such money the peasant must sell something— whether it be rice, copra, or a goat—usually to a middleman who later sells it in town.

Another source of money for the village is relatives who have migrated, usually temporarily but sometimes permanently, to a town. Relatives who go away and find work remit funds to their families, especially during the first year or so. This is considered a filial obligation and is also reasonable since the absent son or nephew often leaves his wife and children in the patriarchal home. Sometimes, as in Africa, he is away several years; but he intends to return one day, and meanwhile, to preserve his place in village society he sends not only funds but also advice regarding family or tribal affairs.

This limited and temporary exodus of young males, to try their luck in the world outside, is a common feature of many underdeveloped countries. Its economic importance is that the rural areas, insofar as they receive these money remittances, can consume more of their own produce. In other words the villages send labor, as a partial substitute for produce, to the towns.

The villages are a residual habitation for those who have little to do, either because of their sex or age, or simply because they cannot find gainful employment in town. Compared with urban living, there are almost no money costs, and fewer apparent real costs connected with living in a small village as part of a large family. Accordingly, even in rather underpopulated and poor countries, there tends to be a certain amount of underemployment in the rural areas (except at certain times, such as harvest season).

In many respects villages are more remote from the towns than the towns are from the Western world. This remoteness of the villages is physical and psychological. Transportation, in regions without hard surface roads, is mostly by foot. During the rainy period all movement of goods by vehicle must cease. News and ideas are spread by word of mouth. In primitive areas, where illiteracy is prevalent and there are no radios, there can be little communication with the outside world. Rumor is rife. Because only a few national political leaders are known by name in the villages and there is little understanding of public issues, voter apathy is not surprising. Life continues without much change from year to year, and even from generation to generation, so that anything novel is suspect. Most major events, such as droughts, locusts, and earthquakes, are of natural origin. Children are born and people die, but the village endures.

The "foreign" enclaves

In many underdeveloped countries there are small enclaves where foreign corporations are engaged in large-scale and highly capitalistic undertakings. Some of the more obvious examples involve petroleum extraction in the Middle East, Venezuela, and now Lybia; mining for copper in Central Africa, tin in Bolivia, and gold in South Africa; and plantation cultivation of tree rubber in Malaya, tea in Ceylon, and cane sugar in Cuba (before the rise of Castro). According to Communists and their sympathizers, these enterprises constitute economic colonialism.

Actually, these foreign-owned and foreign-managed concerns produce almost entirely for export, and so their main impact on the domestic market economy is usually through their local payrolls. (Many of the economic effects of this direct investment are considered in detail in Chapter 26.) These disbursements are respent by recruited native employees, partly as remittances to their villages, but to a considerable extent on imported consumer goods of a kind that are not made in the home country. Housing, utilities, and sometimes rations are often supplied by the company.

These "foreign" oil and mining enclaves also have a considerable cultural impact. The company township will tend to be laid out and governed according to Western patterns. The native labor, although usually confined to semiskilled and unskilled categories, has contact with Western supervisors. This experience of living and working in an alien cultural environment causes ethnic bitterness. But a little vocational training is inevitably acquired. And a few local workers will become "straw bosses" or fill clerical positions. Thus they will gain an idea of organization, responsibility, and efficiency. These virtues are scarce and valuable in many poor countries.

Also noteworthy is that these foreign-operated communities, alien "pockets" in a backward land, are in many ways in closer contact with the Western world than with the surrounding country from which labor is recruited. For one thing, because the output is exported, there is return transport available for imported consumer goods such as canned foods, flashlights, knives, bottled soft drinks, shoes, store clothes, bicycles, and all the other lures to work a while for the Yankee dollar. There will also be foreign movies. The bush native hired for manual work and assigned company housing enters a different world.

This is also true, but in a more limited way, in the case of large-scale agriculture financed and managed by foreigners. These plantations—or "estates," to use the British term—are very different from the small-scale cultivations of native land holders. Plantations often involve a very large total investment. For example, in the case of tree rubber, there is a long waiting period from the clearing of the jungle to the first tapping of the trees. In addition, all plantation agriculture uses mechanical equipment and extensive terracing, irrigation, or drainage projects, all of which make the operation extremely capitalistic. Moreover, the local labor force is supervised to a degree that is unknown in native agriculture, and in this way expensive mistakes that reduce yields can be avoided. Although plantation agriculture often is found within a few miles of competitive native holdings, and in the same sort of soil and climate with the same kind of labor, the differences between them regarding technique, supervision, capital, and—above all—output, make them entirely different kinds of enterprise.

Many underdeveloped countries really have triple economies: the subsistence economy of the rural areas, the native market economy in and near the towns, and the foreign enclaves. The last two obtain labor from the subsistence economy and have direct contacts with the more advanced world outside. One aim of development, especially if most of the population now lives in the subsistence economy, is to have the market economy and the foreign enclaves encroach increasingly upon it. Only by penetrating the subsistence economy and introducing cultural and economic changes within it can the development program of a government really benefit all the people of a country.

A TROPICAL CLIMATE

A remarkable fact is that the poorest countries are nearly all in or near the tropics. In contrast, all the more advanced countries are north of

35° N. Latitude or south of 20° S. Latitude. These include Canada, the United States, Western Europe, the Soviet Union, and Japan in the north, as well as Australia, New Zealand, the Union of South Africa, Argentina, and Uruguay in the south. In between, and straddling the tropics, are the really poor and backward countries of the underdeveloped world.

This association of poverty with latitude cannot be a coincidence. What then is the explanation? Many theories have been offered and debated. Some of the more common ones are (1) lower human effort, (2) prevalence of disease, (3) unfavorable agricultural conditions.

Lower human effort

A once popular but now rather discredited theory—given great publicity a generation or so ago—was that only in the temperate zones did people have the necessary energy to work hard and produce, to acquire knowledge, and to advance their society economically and culturally. The climate in the tropics was said to sap the energy of the inhabitants, so that physical tasks are postponed and mental effort is avoided. The only exceptions were supposed to be where high altitudes—such as around Mexico City—offset the debilitating effects of low latitudes.

In rebuttal, it has been stressed that even white people live healthily and work actively in many tropical areas. Examples are the Panama Canal Zone, Northern Queensland, and—until recently—the Congo basin. But usually these white people are supervisors or do mechanized rather than manual work. Some of the southern states in the United States, such as Mississippi, are just as hot and humid in summer as parts of the tropics, and yet people there work effectively, though perhaps at a somewhat slower pace than they do further north. There are no physical reasons why people cannot be as active in tropical as in temperate zones. Perhaps the real question is whether, after several generations, there are subtle attitude changes that are prejudicial to regular hard work.

A more sophisticated view is that a tropical environment does not challenge man to give his best. Life is too easy. Coconuts, bananas, pawpaws, taro root, sweet potatoes, and many other vegetable foods can be grown abundantly, and are sometimes in sufficient wild profusion to sustain life without work in underpopulated areas. The absence of cold means that shelter and clothing can be minimal and fuel is needed only for cooking. Where and when epidemics and war have limited population, a few hours' work every day or so can provide enough simple food, and this may be the extent of economic activity. In the Marquesas, for instance, a family can eat without working for food; such cultivation and fishing as is done is mostly for the sake of a more varied diet.

It is outside the tropics, where winter cold or seasonal water shortages force people to prepare against these difficulties, that man has become more competent and energetic in economic matters. Progress seems to have been greatest where the environment is neither too favorable nor too unfavorable. Food must not be too readily available; but climate, terrain, and resources must not be so unfavorable that all energies are lost in a struggle to survive. But what is a favorable or unfavorable environment also depends on population pressure and technical knowledge. In parts of the tropics—and the Caribbean islands are a good example—public health measures have so reduced the natural check on population growth that an otherwise auspicious environment has become a rural slum.

Prevalence of disease

The tropics have always been notoriously unhealthy and associated in the minds of white people with malaria, typhoid, yellow fever, and cholera, even though some of these diseases have been previously known in temperate climates also. The Panama Canal could not be completed until the area had been made free of yellow fever. However, until introduced by the first Westerners, tuberculosis, smallpox, and venereal diseases seem to have been unknown in many tropical areas. All in all, the tropics remain one area of the world in which many of man's oldest diseases continue to cause a serious economic loss.

Although all these afflictions are today found in the tropics, public health measures have enormously reduced their frequency. Even malaria, through mosquito control, is being eliminated in many tropical areas as it has been eradicated in the subtropics.

The situation as regards parasites is far less heartening though. Bilharzia, which lodge in the kidneys (causing "black water fever"), debilitate many natives of tropical Africa. Filiriasis, which cause elephantiasis, are the curse of Polynesia. Various kinds of parasitic worms, such as the liver fluke, attack certain internal organs. Intestinal amoeba are often malignant and a cause of dysentery. These are but a few of many familiar examples.

These parasites and infections, together with the malnutrition prevalent in overpopulated areas, reduce energy and shorten life. These difficulties do seem to be presently more serious and prospectively less tractable in the tropics than in more temperate lands. (See also Chapter 22.)

Unfavorable agricultural conditions

The luxuriant vegetation of the tropics misleads many into believing that they should be a cultivator's paradise. The opposite is the case however. It is true that in a natural state there is rank tropical growth—

including some things that are edible—but increasing population requires systematic and intense cultivation of a few selected plants and eradication of all other competing vegetable life in the immediate area. Clearing out unwanted roots, vines, and shrubs is a never-ending chore.

Tropical soils are often found to be poor and fragile once the land has been cleared and cultivated for a few seasons. The sun beats down on the now unprotected earth and heavy rains wash away the topsoil. Once the surface deposit of humus left from the cleared bush or forest has been lost, the soil is apt to become sandy.

Fertilizers are not always the answer. Animal manure may not be abundant because the necessary animals are too few in number. The main exception is of course India, which suffers from deforestation and where the many bulls and cows eat so poorly that their droppings are used for fuel instead. Human excreta—"night soil"—is the most common fertilizer in populated Asia. But its supply is of course limited. Commercial fertilizers, often unavailable or too expensive, may not be compatible with the acidity of the soil. Moreover, especially if the soil is sandy, these costly fertilizers may be washed away by the first rains.

Sun and humidity also favor unwanted weeds and pests. Although mechanical weeding is sometimes physically possible between rows of maize, tobacco, and other crops, it must be done manually among plants in a given row. And in any event, mechanical equipment is financially out of the question, except for large plantations.

Nearly all crops are subject to attack by insects and fungi. Because spraying with insecticides can be time-consuming and costly, it is seldom attempted by peasant cultivators. Frequently they may not even know what parasite is destroying their crop, or the proper insecticide may not be available when needed.

In some countries there are also religious scruples against eating meat. But animal husbandry in general is pathetically primitive in most tropical countries. There is little attempt at selective breeding and unsuitable male stock is seldom castrated. The manner in which desirable but possibly recessive characteristics can be transmitted to progeny is not generally understood. Without fencing or corrals to segregate male from female, breeding is unsupervised, and eugenics an impossibility.

The familiar barnyard animals of Western Europe do not thrive in the tropics. The local vegetation does not include the grasses needed by cows, sheep, and horses, although it will usually sustain goats and donkeys. Domestic animals are debilitated by many of the same parasites —such as flukes and ticks—that weaken human beings. Cattle are likely to become infested unless frequently dipped, and in tsetse fly areas they cannot survive without repeated inoculations. Such practices require more capital and technical knowledge than a native family possesses. Chickens do thrive, but they are allowed to run loose, so their eggs are seldom found while still fresh. Finally, in seriously overpopulated regions, it is more economic to use land to feed people directly by raising food crops rather than domestic animals.

Tropical agriculture does not currently produce many kinds of food. However its future is not hopeless. Scientific and experimental work, comparable to that which developed better crops and animals in the Western world during recent centuries, has not yet been devoted to their tropical counterparts. The kind of effort that developed hybrid corns and rustless wheat needs to be devoted to native cereals and tubers. Selective cross breeding of tropical cattle may also result in great improvements. So far the effort has not been commensurate with the need.

HIGH BIRTH RATES AND TOO FEW ADULTS

An outstanding demographic feature of all poor countries is the high crude birth rate, which in most of them approximates 40 per thousand of population a year. Some are higher—such as Mexico, with 47—and some are lower—such as Argentina, with 23. However, as Table 2-3 shows, there is a marked difference in crude birth rates between advanced and backward countries.

Many reasons for this contrast have been advanced. An immediate explanation is that in most tropical countries nearly all girls marry young. And for this reason India has raised the minimum legal age of marriage for men and women. But a question still remains: Why is it that a majority of girls in the poorest countries are married before they are 18 years old whereas a majority of Irish women are certainly not? Possibly, it is because girls attain puberty sooner in the tropics, partly because there is more of an urgency to reproduce in countries where life expectancy is short, and frequently because children (and sons particularly) are viewed as a sort of old age insurance. Another probable explanation is that young women have few economic alternatives except marriage in poor and backward countries.

These same reasons, reinforced by all sorts of cultural attitudes that stress the importance of children, explain the high fertility rates of Table 2-3. For a woman of 25 there are few worse social stigmas than to be barren. And, especially in countries where "marriage" is seldom legalized, only a few urban, emancipated, and "westernized" women ever seem to be without children.

An important consequence of high birth rates is that an unusually large proportion of the total population is too young for serious work. In the long run, the age distribution of a population is primarily dependent on the birth rate and not on the death rate. Thus countries such as Venezuela (whose crude birth rate is almost 50 per thousand) have almost 40 per cent of their population under 15 years of age. In contrast, Great

Britain (whose birth rate is about 20 per thousand) has about 25 per cent of the population under 15 years. A high proportion of children in the population constitutes a serious economic burden because children consume and do not produce.

Backward countries also have a smaller fraction of their population available as an effective labor force because of shorter life expectancies. Death rates, although differing considerably among poor countries, are higher at every year of age than in advanced countries. Thus, to take extreme examples, life expectancy at birth is roughly 40 years in Egypt and 70 years in the United States.

Demographically, underdeveloped countries suffer not only from high birth rates that increase the proportion of children, but also from short life expectancies that reduce the working years of persons who survive their fifteenth year. The economic outcome is that there are relatively more children to support and fewer adults to provide for them. Thus all backward countries, even those which are not overpopulated, carry the burden of a very uneconomic age distribution.

AN UNECONOMIC CULTURE

Last, but far from least, poor countries have what might be termed an uneconomic culture. Primarily this means that traditional attitudes discourage the full utilization of human resources. More specifically, it means that men are less likely to strive for extra money and extra consumption. Compared with the so-called advanced countries, this is a major difference. Thus the vociferous demands of backward countries for higher consumption levels sometimes conflict with their natural desire to maintain their traditional cultures. But no nation can have a drastically more productive economy and preserve its old ways of life.

Some philosophical and religious handicaps

In most backward countries, and especially in the rural areas, there is a widespread acceptance of poverty as the only condition most people have ever known. There is little realization of the extent to which man can make nature serve him. The general feeling is that nothing can be done. There is just so much good, happiness, or wealth in the world. Why struggle against fate? This attitude is not prevalent in the urban areas, where luxurious living can often be seen and envied and where there is a greater awareness of what technology plus capital can do.

Moreover, particularly in South and East Asia, more thought and effort may be devoted to ensuring one's position in the next world than in this one. Unnecessary consumption may be considered vulgar or sinful. The Hindu and Buddhist religions, for instance, consider asceticism a virtue.

The impecunious are not thought contemptible, and begging—which has religious origins—is not considered immoral. All this is in marked contrast with the common American suspicion that poverty is somehow a personal fault attributable to lack of industry and thrift.

Among primitive people a great deal of superstition exists. Even in Latin America, where most people are at least nominal Catholics, peasants still solicit the favors of pre-Christian deities and watch for auspicious "signs." Many people in backward countries believe that the success or failure of an enterprise results from the intervention of some special god who had best be propitiated. Any important event, such as planting a field, roofing a house, or starting a journey, may be undertaken only after an offering to the proper god has been made. Time spent looking for omens and placating local godlings has an opportunity cost. And continued belief in the supernatural mitigates against acquiring technical knowledge and becoming self-dependent.

Sources of status

Anthropologists have shown that in all cultures a great deal of human effort goes to the acquisition of social status. In the United States, the surest way to enhance one's status is to engage in the conspicuous consumption that is made possible by a high income, and usually one cannot earn a higher income without being more productive. In other countries, while established wealth is always respected, earned income often is not.

In all countries, except perhaps the United States, Canada, and Australia, unearned income from inherited wealth is socially the most desirable. Income from one's own efforts—although earned in a respectable profession—can be quite another thing. Even wealth is not enough to open all doors. The form in which it is held may be important; for instance, the ownership of land usually is considered preferable to the ownership of shops. A person's social position also tends to be related inversely to the degree that he personally supervises his wealth. A landowner or magnate who can employ an agent or manager is thought superior to one who personally supervises his own affairs. In such a culture it is an unusual man of wealth who seeks actively to improve the farming of his tenants or the operations of his factories. He is more likely to win admiration by developing his skill as a sportsman or perhaps as a scholar.

The native culture may determine the uses to which income is put. In Asia a rich man may be esteemed because he has built a temple. In Central Africa a prosperous chief may be envied for the extra wives he brings into his kraal. Only in a few countries is the rich man lauded for investing income in new and productive enterprise.

For the vast majority of people who must earn their income, status derives from occupation: manual work is universally despised; government positions usually have more prestige than other clerical jobs. Among the professions, lawyers are more esteemed than engineers, while veterinarians and agronomists are suspected of having peasant origins. Depending upon the country, military officers, scholars, or priests have the highest status, never the merchant who devotes his energies to making money. All this is very different in the United States, where men seek status and emotional satisfaction in business, and success is measured in dollars.

In some countries, status (or lack of it) is not earned, but is inherited. India, despite constitutional provisions to the contrary, still has its "untouchable" class. In not a few backward countries, despite official avowals, too dark a complexion is a social handicap that can hardly be overcome by economic success.

Immobility among occupations

In many poor countries, certain occupations are in practice reserved to members of some particular caste, religion, race, tribe, or sex. In African mines, certain tasks tend to be in the monopoly of specific tribes. No high-caste Hindu would work as a janitor, because sweepers have always been Untouchables. In some areas of Latin America, various cloth-making jobs are done only by women. All this results in considerable inflexibility and wasted labor.

The family's role

In the West, and in North America especially, a young man—married or not—is expected to earn his own income. Except in agriculture, and unless his family is wealthy, he must fend for himself. In backward countries economic satisfaction is not sought by adults as individuals but through the family.

Nor is the family the same. In advanced countries a young man establishes his own household when he marries, or as soon afterwards as possible, and sometimes while still a bachelor. In backward countries the family household normally includes three generations. A man, on marrying, brings his wife to live in his parents' household. There, although they will have private sleeping quarters, they will live with his unmarried sisters and his brothers. If his brothers are married, their wives and children will be part of the same extended family household. New family groupings may be formed when a man becomes a grandfather or when the old grandfather dies. But in regions where there is limited housing and no extra land, the families of all the male descendants live in close proximity and even eat together.

The resources of the entire family are largely shared. The family as a whole cultivates its land. If some of the menfolk go off to the towns, look-ing for work, they frequently leave their wives and families with their parents, and the men send money home for their support. These remit-tances will usually go not to the man's wife but to his parents, who sell produce from the land, pay the taxes, and manage the finances of the three-generation family.

The economic disadvantages of this family structure probably outweigh its advantages. Certainly the family constitutes a form of insurance against illness and old age; it can pool resources and often provides a trading network between town and countryside. However, it tends to encourage high birth rates (see Chapter 18). Moreover, because personal earnings—whether in money or kind—are shared, there are fewer in-dividual incentives to work harder. A sub-family which decided not to pool surplus earnings, but to save and invest them for itself, would be considered immoral. And a married son can hardly decide on his own to cultivate the family's land in some new and supposedly better way. Hence saving and innovating must be left to the family as a whole. Certainly the extended family blunts individual economic initiative, and thus is a serious matter.

Grip of custom

The force of custom in the rural areas of backward countries is almost inconceivable to Westerners who have not personally experienced it. Everything is done in a customary way which is handed down from gen-eration to generation and which must not be questioned. Experimentation is scorned as due to ignorance of the "proper" way; it is resented and feared. A family that seeks to introduce a new crop may be blamed by the villagers for a supposed increase in pests and weeds. The drilling of a bore hole may be the alleged cause of a water shortage in a neighbor's holding. Rural people are always extremely loath to alter their diet. A nutritional crop may not be sown or planted because it is not a traditional food.

In a stationary economy a great deal can be said in favor of custom. It constitutes the accumulated experience of society. A person who conforms to custom may often be following the best course—but he will not know why. Past deviations from tradition that failed have long since been for-gotten. It is enough for him to know that the old way is the safe way.

However, no one today is living in a stationary world. New ways of doing things, and new equipment to aid in their innovation, are con-stantly being devised. But experiments in production are sometimes dismal failures. For a family producing barely enough to survive, there is a real danger in change. So young agricultural experts sent out by the gov-ernment may be viewed with suspicion and hostility. Yet there can be no

progress without change, no permanent change without initial experimentation, and no experimentation without breaking away from custom.

Uses of money

From what has been written it follows that there are few incentives
for an individual to earn money in a backward economy. For one thing,
he will have to share it with his entire family, so that the money he earns
is less rewarding to him personally unless his affection for them all
(brothers, sisters-in-law, nephews, and nieces) is equal to his love for his
own wife and children. Second, money will buy fewer material things
than in advanced countries. Third, extra production does not necessarily
bring a higher social status.

There are various reasons why money earnings above a certain level
have sharply reduced utility in a backward country. In rural areas many
consumer items are not available. They may even be unknown. Also, many
modern consumer goods can only be used with other goods that are not
available. Bicycles are of little use unless there are paths to ride them on.
Electrical equipment is useless without electric power. Books have limited
utility unless their owner can read. Consumer goods are becoming increasingly complementary with advancing technology. But the other jointly
demanded goods, services, or abilities are often lacking in backward areas.

The economic significance of this is that people in poor countries are
more likely to produce—after some minimum cash has been earned for
taxes and the like—for direct consumption or direct investment. Extra
food output may be eaten or stored by the peasant family rather than be
sold for money. Or savings may alternatively result in direct, on-the-spot
investment. Surpluses, whether ultimately used for consumption or investment, are not inevitably "monetized."

All this is so much in contrast with advanced economies. There people
become more economically active—whether as workers, investors, or
entrepreneurs—because they want more money. Economic incentives are
extremely strong and personal. More money will buy them status and an
endless variety of goods, services, and gadgets. Advertising, children, the
envied possessions of others, all combine to urge the individual to greater
feats of production.

Superficially, it may seem paradoxical that money should count for
more in the richest countries of all, while in poor economies it can buy
fewer of the things that people want. However this really is not so
strange. A country where money has a limited importance is one in which
many resources—especially human resources—are not fully employed. It is
also one in which the market economy—and the specialization in production that attends it—has not yet replaced the subsistence economy.

The ability of money to buy the tangible and intangible things that people want is one indication of whether a country's culture is economic. Although economic cultures may not really promote more human happiness, there is little question but that they are far more productive of goods. And one can say that a country which does not make full productive use of its human resources, because it has an uneconomic culture, is truly underdeveloped.

SUMMARY

It is clear then that all backward countries have important similarities. These include:

1. Low per capita income, with attendant malnutrition, poor health, low literacy, and primitive shelter;
2. Inefficient agriculture occupying a large fraction of the labor force;
3. A dualistic—or even triplistic—economy, including a large subsistence sector;
4. A tropical, or near tropical, climate and location;
5. High birth rates, resulting in too few adults available for work;
6. An uneconomic culture, in which individual incentives to earn money are unduly limited.

Of course these attributes are found in varying degree, but they are common characteristics of all backward countries.

It is also obvious that the typical features of poverty can be elaborated upon in detail. For instance, poor and backward economies are not going to have developed banking systems, high literacy rates, or female emancipation. Poverty has a thousand faces.

3

Economic differences
among poor countries

The time has come to consider, in addition to the many common characteristics of backward countries, some of their economic differences. Although they are all poor—compared with, say, the United States—they are far from being equally poor. The extent to which they save from income differs, the extent being sometimes but not always associated with per capita income. Some economies, such as that of Mauritius, are highly "monetized"; others, such as that of Ethiopia, are not. There is a marked difference in various countries' possession of known and usable natural resources. Some have proven reserves of oil, coal, or mineral ore, potential hydro power, or just good agricultural land, but no really poor country has more than a few of these assets and some—so far as is yet known—have none. In many cases neither capital nor resources are particularly scarce in terms of one another, although both are often far too scarce in terms of labor. In most of the Asian countries there is too much population, given present techniques of production, for a high per capita income to be possible; but in parts of Africa, underpopulation is still a problem, although it probably will not be by 2000 A.D. Some countries participate far more than others in the world economy, exporting a fifth or more of their domestic product, and these tend to have higher per capita incomes; it is the stagnant economies that have the least international trade.

Because many of these differences tend to be associated, it is possible after a fashion to categorize underdeveloped countries into several broad classes (see pp. 60–62).

NATIONAL DIFFERENCES IN ECONOMIC WELFARE

There are enough published statistics to prove that some underdeveloped countries are much poorer than others. However, national income data for many of these countries are unreliable and subject to misinterpretation. Accordingly it is often useful to supplement these income estimates with more accurate and specific economic series—such as production and net imports of cloth, number of bicycles, pounds of mail—although particular series need to be interpreted with care.

National income per capita estimates

A preliminary indication of differences in per capita income among countries has already been given in Table 2-1, which shows that over 800 million people live in almost 50 territories where the annual income per capita is under $100.

It would be interesting to classify these countries in various ways to see what association there is between per capita income and such things as climate, extent and duration of permanent settlement by people of European descent, and lapse of time since political independence. Another possible classification would be according to population per hectare of arable land. Of course any causal link between income and any one attribute cannot readily be isolated because of the simultaneous influence of many other characteristics.

One striking tendency—as revealed by Table 2-1—is that the countries and people of Southeast Asia are somewhat poorer than in the Middle East and Africa. And, in contrast to these three broad areas, Latin America is prosperous. Over 90 per cent of the population of Southeast Asia live in countries where the annual per capita income is estimated to be under $100. In contrast, over 90 per cent of the inhabitants of Latin America live in countries where income per capita is thought to be over $100. If China is included this contrast is even more striking. To what extent this notable difference is attributable to differences in population density, religious beliefs, or social culture is hard to say.

Problems of measuring differences in income

It goes almost without saying that estimated per capita income statistics are always unreliable and sometimes misleading.

They are unreliable because the basic data are always incomplete, non-homogeneous, and inevitably subject to error. Statistical definitions vary among nations; within a single country (India, for example), different units for measuring the output of grain and other produce may be used. Even if governments had the resources to improve their economic statistics, peasants, artisans, and petty traders have no idea of bookkeeping, and keep few records other than of debts owed them.

Most national income estimates published by poor countries are inherently misleading, especially when compared with those of advanced nations. The annual per capita income of India is set at about $75; this means that because of the "skewed" income distribution, over half the population actually has less. Even so, this amounts to roughly 20 cents per head per day, or about $1 a day for a typical married couple, say with one aged dependent and two children under fifteen years old. It seems impossible for such a family of five to survive on so small an income. They certainly could not in North America. What is the explanation of such apparent differences in welfare?

First, obvious perhaps but worth mentioning, differences in happiness and welfare are not commensurate with differences in the money value of goods and services consumed. A man in the United States who has $100,000 a year after taxes is not really ten times better fed, clothed, or housed than one with $10,000. Sumptuary pleasures require leisure, and no rich man has time to enjoy all his pastimes to the full. So, simply because of the declining marginal utility of money, a Canadian, say, with $10,000 a year should not be considered 100 times better off than an Indian with $100 a year.

Second, most of the people of underdeveloped countries are able to avoid many expenses that are physically or socially unavoidable in advanced countries. In backward countries, unlike richer ones, a majority of the population lives in rural areas where huts can be constructed without reference to building codes and people can answer nature's frequent calls by going behind a bush. In cities, however, because many people are forced to sleep and work literally on top of one another, buildings must be better constructed and utilities and sewage must be provided. A vast majority of the world's poor people live in or near the tropics, where cold does not compel insulated shelter, heating fuel, or warm clothing. In fact young children, except in towns, can run around naked.

Third, national income comparisons are necessarily biased by the necessity of converting national outputs, measured in pesos, bahts, riels, and so forth, into some single currency such as United States dollars. Official rates of exchange tend very roughly to equate the prices of goods that are traded internationally. But many goods, especially local services, are never traded internationally. Many of these "untraded" goods tend to be comparatively lower priced in backward than in advanced countries. Moreover, the essentials of life, which bulk so large in the budgets of people living in poor countries, always tend to be rather lower priced than they are in advanced countries. Durable consumer goods (*e.g.,* washing machines) are fantastically expensive in poor countries. But the necessities of life, while expensive in terms of the work required to produce them, are usually cheaper in dollar terms at going exchange rates. So an estimated per capita annual income, converted into the currency of an advanced country, has actually more local purchasing power in the backward nation than might be supposed.

Fourth, the conventions of national income accounting include as received (or "utility") income many items that could better be treated as a cost of producing or guarding such income, and these bulk large in advanced nations. All current government expenditures are normally classed as "income," but almost 10 per cent of the national "income" of the United States consists of national defense expenditures. In a complex culture people must be literate, if only to understand tax bills and traffic signs; a rudimentary education is one cost of operating a society. Also, while the economies of North America and Western Europe are physically most productive, to be so their populations must live in a certain way. Many aspects of this life are expensive and reflected in GNP but provide little or no satisfaction. For example, a businessman who lives in a suburb must use money and resources for daily commuting and city clothing; but it is doubtful whether, on a hot summer's day, the crowded commuter train or his suit and tie really give him pleasure. However, because resources are being used, all this is accounted a contribution to national income, consumption, and utility. The apparent national income of advanced societies includes items that are really costs of producing real utility income rather than utility income itself.

Finally and most important, national income accounting in backward countries is likely to omit, by necessity or design, a great deal of accruing real income. A subsistence economy occupies the lives of many or most rural people in poor countries. A great deal of what they produce is at worst ignored and at best understated.

Most governments of underdeveloped countries guess the value of output by the subsistence economy of those things that are customarily marketed in whole or in part. Thus most food grains, and other produce such as cotton, are marketable goods. Government may estimate their output by village or district. It will then apply a price to obtain a value estimate. It will also try to include that fraction of the output that is not marketed but consumed on the spot. But subsistence farmers are mixed producers. Typically they produce a dib of this and a dab of that during the year—things that are not sold but locally consumed, such as chickens for the pot, fuel for cooking, articles of clothing, and perishable fruits and vegetables. These outputs will not all be included in national product estimates.

National income accounts also exclude economic services performed within the family—e.g., constructing a hut or cabin—but include them if done commercially outside the home. "Income" is not statistically increased by washing clothes in a nearby stream, but it is augmented when an American housewife sends things to the laundry. To make a meal a peasant woman may start with grain, which has to be ground into flour and then baked, but these services are not considered income because they are not performed by a miller or baker. One way for backward countries to increase their national incomes, according to income accounting conventions at least, is to do less work at home and buy ready-made dresses and TV dinners! Hence national income disparities are exaggerated, because consumers in poor countries usually buy rudimentary goods to be worked into usable form, while in wealthier nations they buy final goods ready for use.

Specific indications of economic welfare

If per capita estimates for countries are suspect, additional impressions of comparative national welfare can sometimes be had from physical rather than value statistics. For example, in Table 2-2, calorie intakes were cited for different countries. And, in Table 2-3, estimates by country of life expectancies at birth were given. Not only do these two series vary to a marked extent, but together they provide one of the best comparisons available, in real terms, of differences in economic welfare among the poorer countries.

Other physical series are far more specific and hence can be treacherous when used for comparisons. For example, one of the best measures of native "emergence" in sub-Sahara Africa is the ratio of bicycles to population: but some of the more advanced countries of Latin America are graduating from the bicycle stage, and so by this test might seem poorer than they are. The point is that many goods are "superior" goods at low incomes only to become "inferior" goods at higher incomes; examples are potatoes, oil lamps, and motor scooters. Comparisons involving such items are only valid among countries of roughly the same culture and per capita income.

Some statistical series, while they have welfare implications, are also measures of the degree of urbanization. Examples are the percentage of homes having electricity and inside water closets. The number of telephones per thousand population is correlated with both better living and city living.

In poor countries, sample surveys of families to see what they own in the way of durable consumer goods may give a good idea of their economic condition. Do they have a stove for cooking? Do they sleep on the ground or in some sort of bed? Do the men have another set of better clothes for special occasions? In underdeveloped countries, it is often easier to take stock of physical wealth used by consumers than it is to estimate current output, and the resultant data may be more reliable.

A count of publicly owned assets is also often instructive. How many miles of paved highway and rail track are there per 100 square miles? How many hospital beds are there per thousand of population?

The partial check list (Table 3-1) shows the sort of physical data that may be indicative of economic activity and welfare. Because these items are very specific, and at different income levels and in different regions are substitutes for possibly unlisted items, temporal and national

Table 3-1
INDICATIONS OF ECONOMIC WELFARE: PHYSICAL STOCKS OWNED AND CONSUMED*

Annual Use**

Food intake (in calories)
Cloth (in yards)
Electric power production (in kilowatt hours)
Petroleum products (in metric terms)
Newsprint and printed matter (by weight)
Mail (number of pieces handled)
Soap (by weight)

Stocks of Durable Goods†

Private

Radios, battery and other
Cooking stoves with ovens
Bicycles, pedal and power
Metal cooking utensils, pots and pans
Dresses, saris, and the like
Square yards of ground within homes covered by flooring, mats, rugs, and the like
Pieces of furniture
Oil lamps and electric bulbs in use

Publicly owned assets

Paved highway or rail track (in miles)
Telephone and telegraph line (in miles)
Hospital beds
Seating capacity of all buses and all railroad carriages
School rooms

Economy's human resources

Licensed doctors, dentists, and veterinarians
Teachers
Literate adults
Males of working age

* Quantity (per 1000 population) unless stated otherwise.
** Consumption must usually be estimated from domestic production plus net imports.
† Private stocks can only be estimated from sample surveys of families.

comparisons can be treacherous. This problem may sometimes be mitigated by combining two or more known substitutes in a single series. For example, rail and road transport of passengers are substitutes, so it is best to aggregate the seating capacity of road buses and rail coaches. Use of a single item can suggest much sometimes: for example, the number of pounds of soap used annually per thousand population. Of course, some of the items on the list—as, for example, petroleum products—are used by producers as well as consumers, but economic activity by producers indirectly results in consumer welfare, so this does not matter very much.

Bearing in mind that physical economic data are always specific, and so can never tell the whole story alone, Table 3-2 is included.

NATIONAL DIFFERENCES IN SAVING AND CAPITAL WEALTH

Before the twentieth century, economists were not so much interested in national income as they were in national "wealth," for it was generally held that accumulation of goods would increase economic welfare *ipso facto*. Accordingly great stress was laid on thrift as evidenced by the amount of annual increase in accumulated goods of all kinds. Today, with national income estimates more available and reliable, it is possible for some countries to relate income and wealth to savings.

Differences in savings

Table 3-3 includes a comparison of annual savings, relative to output, of a number of countries. As might be expected, the richer countries save a higher percentage of their national income than do the poorer ones, recent estimates, for example, being 24% for Canada and 13% for Ecuador. Here is yet another of the vicious circles so commonly encountered in economic development.

One must not exaggerate the meaning of these differences though. Because capital depreciation is hard to estimate, many governments publish statistics of gross national product and gross savings. And the gross savings rates of advanced countries are higher, with few exceptions. But it is precisely these countries that have a large accumulation of capital relative to output. Such capital depreciates. The advanced nations must have a high gross saving if they are not to suffer net disinvestment.

The following is a hypothetical example. All the values are in billions of dollars. It is supposed that already accumulated capital, of which there is three times as much per dollar of income in the advanced country as in the backward one, has an average service life of twenty years in both cases.

	Advanced Country	Backward Country
(a) Net national product	100	10
(b) Capital accumulated already	300	10
(c) Depreciation of capital	15	.5
(d) Gross savings	20	1
(e) Net savings	5	.5
(f) Gross domestic product	120	11
Gross savings rate (d/f)	.17	.09
Net savings rate (e/a)	.05	.05
Net increase in capital (e/b)	.017	.050

As can be seen, the net saving rate is the same for both countries, namely 5 per cent. But the gross saving rates for the advanced and backward countries are 17 and 9 per cent, respectively.

It is customary to compare the savings—either gross or net—of different countries to their respective *incomes*. But such comparisons are not necessarily the most relevant. For certain purposes, national net savings can be better related to already accumulated *capital;* thus in the above example, the percentage net increase in capital is only 1.7 per cent for the advanced country but 5.0 per cent for the backward one. Some economists have suggested that percentage increases in national income are some ratio of percentage net increase in capital stock (see Chapter 9). If this were the same for both countries, in the present imaginary example, the 4 per cent gross savings rate of the backward economy will contribute a threefold greater per cent national income increase than will the 17 per cent gross savings rate of the advanced economy. A small absolute amount of saving in a country having little accumulated wealth may be more significant than is generally realized.

In practice, because accumulated wealth estimates are highly subjective in all countries, savings are seldom related to existing total capital stocks. But it is feasible to relate gross savings to labor force to see how much "more" capital workers will have on an average to help them. As might be expected, domestic gross investment per worker is very low for the Southeast Asian countries, and rather higher for those of Latin America.

Some difficulties in estimating investment

For many reasons it is extremely difficult to estimate a nation's savings and investment. Some of these hazards are the usual ones of error, omission, and double counting. But there are very serious conceptual problems also.

In underdeveloped countries a great deal of direct investment by peasant cultivators and small business proprietors is never recorded. If one drains a swamp area, or terraces part of a hillside, such improve-

Table 3-2

	Life expectancy (males aged 1 yr.)*	Persons per passenger car**	Newsprint per capita (annual, in kilos)	Percentage of dwellings with piped water inside
Latin America				
Argentina	62	47	8.5	—
Brazil	39	213	3.2	16
Ecuador	57	422	1.6	—
Guatemala	48	701	.9	—
Mexico	44	148	2.4	17
Peru	51	331	1.3	—
Venezuela	—	82	4.5	30
Asia				
Burma	—	1977	.4	—
India	39	2513	.2	—
Japan	67	3392	6.2	81
Fed. of Malaya	—	253	.4	—
Pakistan	—	4446	.1	—
Thailand	52	2996	.7	—
Africa & Near East				
Egypt	42	335	1.2	—
Ghana	—	—	.5	—
Guinea	41	—	—	—
Iran	—	1969	—	—
Iraq	—	640	.3	—
Lybia	—	—	—	—
Tanganyika	—	—	—	—
R. S. Africa	48	29	5.0	—
Advanced				
United States	68	4	33.7	82
Canada	69	8	15.5	87
W. Germany	68	—	7.9	—

° United Nations, *Demographic Yearbook.*
°° Rand McNally, *Commercial Atlas,* 1962.
† World Health Organization, *Annual Epidemiological and Vital Statistics,* 1958.
Principal Source: United Nations, *Statistical Yearbook,* 1960.

Table 3-2

(cont.)

Percentage of dwellings with electricity	Steel consumption per capita (annual, in kilos)	Inhabitants per physician†	Persons per hospital or medical center bed†	Persons per secondary school teacher	Percentage population literate (15 years and over)
60	97	760	160	849	86
25	37	2500	280	975	49
—	—	2900	—	1026	56
39	—	6300	360	1273	29
—	37	1700	810	2419	57
—	9	2400	480	746	43
41	105	1700	330	1508	53
—	—	2900	1600	—	57
—	9	5000	2000	1176	17
82	163	940	120	320	—
—	33	7300	—	—	47
—	3	15,000	—	1774	19
—	10	6900	1100	1941	64
—	9	—	510	954	23
—	—	25,000	1800	1281	—
—	—	—	—	—	—
—	21	4500	1000	—	15
—	38	5500	750	1499	31
—	—	7800	320	2074	21
—	—	19,000	600	15,309	—
—	134	190	200	100	29
92	491	790	120	365	97
97	355	930	90	544	96
88	444	730	100	266	96

Table 3-3

ORIGINS AND DISPOSITION OF GROSS NATIONAL PRODUCT FOR SELECTED COUNTRIES: 1959

	From agriculture, fishing, and forestry (%)	From mining and manufacturing (%)	To gross capital formation (%)	From net inflow of long-term capital and grants (%)
Latin America				
Argentina	23	21	18	0.5
Brazil	26	25	15	1.3
Ecuador	37	18	13	1.3
Guatemala	—	—	6	2.7
Mexico	—	—	17	1.9
Peru	24	29	23	—
Venezuela	6	43	18	—
Asia				
Burma	43	14	19	0.9
India	50	17	—	0.2
Japan	17	29	35	—
Fed. of Malaya	—	—	12	—
Pakistan	55	12	—	—
Thailand	40	15	17	—
Africa & Near East				
Egypt	33	13	—	0
Ghana	—	—	13	0
Guinea	—	—	—	—
Iran	—	—	—	—
Iraq	—	—	—	1.0
Lybia	—	—	—	—
Tanganyika	59	11	15	—
R. S. Africa	12	38	22	.8
Advanced				
United States	4	31	17	—
Canada	7	30	24	—
West Germany	7	46	23	—

Source: United Nations, *Statistical Yearbook*, 1960.

ments will seldom if ever be included in official statistics. Agricultural investment is hence always understated. Analogously, a petty artisan may himself enlarge his workshop and make some of his own equipment, but these improvements have not been "monetized" and so will never be recognized as investment.

Even "monetized" investment, in backward countries, may be understated. This is because these countries have usually adopted certain national accounting conventions evolved for advanced countries. Goods that are used as consumer goods in the Western world may be capital goods in poor countries; examples are bicycles adapted into pedalcabs, and hand sewing machines acquired by individuals for making clothes commercially. In backward countries such goods are really producer goods and should be included as investment.

On the other hand, if investment were defined to include expenditures that increase human productivity, the advanced countries would on paper annually accumulate a great deal more capital than is usually supposed. The countries of North America and Western Europe devote considerable resources to education. Much of this education increases the productivity of people who are or will be economically occupied, so this "production" really represents a form of gross investment—although it is not usually so classified.

Even when there is agreement on what assets should be considered producer goods, there is still the question of whether to estimate their value by cost of acquisition or by value in use.

Consider a bore hole that has been dug to raise water for irrigating some cultivated fields. Theoretically, the production cost will be no more than the present discounted value of the additional crop output attributable net to the bore hole. Because an expenditure has been incurred, and its cost is more or less known, it tends to be taken as a measure of the investment's value. But time may prove that the landlord was far too optimistic or pessimistic, for agricultural yields are hard to predict, and prices for farm produce no less so. Moreover, it is the net increase in output that must be estimated, which means deducting the cost of raising the water and reaping any larger crop. Finally, because present values can only be computed on the basis of assumed discount ratios and because future interest rates are also highly conjectural, all estimates of the capital use value of real investments are rough estimates at best.

Concept of capital

Capital itself is often confused with capital funds and capital values. (For systematic definitions of such overlapping concepts as capital, investment, and saving, see Chapter 11.) But here capital, in the sense of real accumulated capital, refers to produced means of production. That capital goods are *produced* means of production distinguishes them from natural resources—such as land—also used in production. That they are *means of production* distinguishes them from consumer goods, which are also produced.

Capital goods can be classified as *working* or *fixed*. Working capital is normally altered, destroyed, or resold within a short period of time in the course of business. Examples are raw materials, fuel and power, and component parts to be assembled. Fixed capital can be subdivided into stationary capital (such as factory buildings and railway sidings) and movable equipment (such as machinery and tractors). Some modern writers, unlike the classical economists, seem to forget that working capital is just as necessary as fixed capital. This may be because, as an economy emerges from a more primitive state, working capital becomes less important compared with fixed capital. But all accumulated resources, if they add to the flow of goods and services over time, constitute real capital.

Net investment in a closed economy is usually an estimate of the increase in stock of capital, during some time period, valued at cost of acquisition. The investment itself is a *flow*. And depreciation during the same time period must be deducted to obtain a net investment estimate. But depreciation is so hard to value, for more than one season, that few statisticians in underdeveloped countries do more than "guestimate" net investment. Hence the data of Table 3-3 need to be taken with a grain of salt.

NATIONAL DIFFERENCES IN NATURAL RESOURCES

Natural resources, together with labor, are the original and basic means of production. Although natural resources constitute part of the wealth of a country, together with produced means of production, they are not capital. But natural resources are often a substitute for capital, as when navigable rivers lessen the need for railroads, or better soils reduce the need for irrigation. The existence of natural resources may also make the accumulation of capital easier. For these and other reasons the possession of abundant and usable natural resources is of great importance to a country. On the other hand, the existence of poor resources has stimulated some nations to great economic advances (*e.g.*, Japan and Holland).

What is included in natural resources? To the early economists, natural resources meant land, and they stressed the "original and indestructible powers of the soil" used in agriculture. A natural resource is any material thing of economic value which man did not bring into existence: mineral and oil reserves, fisheries, virgin forests, and the objects of all "extractive" industries. Climate, topography, and geographic location relative to world markets should also be included.

The first part of the definition—"any material thing of economic value"—means that a natural resource must command a price. Application of this pragmatic test eliminates many supposed natural resources. There is nothing more futile than the practice, common among some development engineers, of listing all sorts of mineral deposits and water power sites as national assets although they have zero value. Quite a few economists have made themselves unpopular by showing that such "assets" are really useless. Physical existence and economic value are not the same thing at all.

There are many mineral deposits in the world, some long known, which are not now worked and may never be. Nor are these ores necessarily of low grade. They are not extracted because it would not be profitable to do so. And this may be either because the deposits are too inaccessible or because labor or other necessary factors of production are lacking.

A mineral deposit, or any other natural resource, will have no current commercial use unless all sorts of prices are right. These include, in addition to the market price of the product, costs of transporting the extracted goods to market, labor wages in regard to their effectiveness, cost of acquiring and moving to site the equipment and materials needed in the enterprise, and interest on capital funds. It does not matter how low some of these prices are. If the combination of prices does not promise a profit, the deposit will not normally be developed now.[1]

In many underdeveloped countries, the main obstacle to the use of virgin natural resources is transportation cost, especially if all sorts of equipment has initially to be moved into some inaccessible place and the output subsequently transported to a market. Often an extracting company would have to construct its own railroad, flume, conveyor belt, or highway. Local labor may be not only unskilled, but entirely primitive—apt, unless closely supervised, to ruin expensive equipment. Under such circumstances, true labor costs cannot be low enough to offset high transportation costs, and it is not to be wondered at that some rich and known mineral reserves have been left untouched for posterity.

Many estimates of potential water power are economic dreams. There are numerous rivers in the world that *could* be dammed to generate power. But no one should do so. Thus it is estimated that over three-quarters of the world's potential hydro-electric power is in Africa, with its major rivers descending from a rain-soaked inland plateau; however, only a small per cent of the world's actual hydro power is generated in the "dark" continent. The explanation of this disparity is that electric power, because of high transmission costs, must normally be used within 500 miles of its place of generation. And most of Africa's potential power, even if subsidized to be sold at a zero price, could probably not attract enough users because of other cost disadvantages. There are only a few industries—such as aluminum-making from bauxite—for which power costs are more than a small fraction of total production costs.

What constitutes an economic resource depends in large measure upon rival supply sources and the current state of the arts. Thus the wild rubber trees of the Amazon basin were a natural resource until stolen

[1] Even so, unworked mines may have a capital value, in the sense that potential profits from future contemplated operations have a positive discounted present value.

seedlings were taken to Malaya to begin a still more profitable industry. A resource that cannot be worked profitably now may be exploitable in another decade or so—not because a market has come into existence or cooperating factors have become available—but because of new techniques not yet discovered. The silver deposits of Great Bear Lake and Flim Flon, in northern Canada, really became commercial propositions with the advent of aircraft able to provide economic transportation. The Zambesi would never have been dammed at Kariba for use in the "copper belt" of Northern Rhodesia before low-loss transmission of electric power at high voltages had been developed. New methods of oil drilling and transportation have helped to make petroleum extraction profitable at Magdalena, Colombia. The uranium deposits of the Belgian Congo had little value before the development of atomic weapons; and the later development of thermonuclear bombs has again impaired their value. Changes in the state of arts are constantly altering the *economic* resources of nations, although there may be little change in their *physical* reserves.

The passage of time also brings new discoveries of resources. Only a few years ago, Lybia's important oil reserves were unknown, and there may be other happy surprises for other underdeveloped countries that are not now oil producers. Central Africa may prove to have unsuspected mineral treasures.

Such discoveries are partly a function of deliberate search, and prospecting and exploration in turn depend upon commodity prices, which again reflect scarcity and usefulness. In the case of petroleum, and certain minerals such as bauxite and copper, giant international companies can be counted upon to locate and prove enough new reserves to satisfy probable demands as they materialize for the next few decades. And where they prospect and explore is not unaffected by government policy.

But many other underground resources are prospected by small companies and individuals. Their search may be more superficial. Some countries now think they are lacking in natural resources of various kinds only because there has been inadequate search.

Thus the apparent generosity with which different nations have been endowed with economic resources varies from generation to generation. Over time, this is the result of at least three kinds of change. First, changes in the nature and size of the market, the supply of cooperating factors, and ease of transportation, as reflected in the prices of outputs, inputs, and freight. Second, changes in techniques of extraction, recovering, concentration, and even use. Third, changes in known reserves, which to some extent depend upon the energy and skill of search. A country's original natural endowment cannot alter. But an inventory of its economic resources can and does change.

One can never be sure whether the extraction and proving of mineral reserves is a cause or effect of economic development. Certain regions really "got their start" following the discovery of gold, diamonds, or oil. Many of these countries are now far from backward. And yet there is always the lingering suspicion that, except in the case of the richest deposits, the development of latent resources depends upon the culture itself. The mineral wealth of Africa, like that of North America, remained unexploited until the arrival of Europeans. There is a fatalistic phrase that "gold is where you find it." Perhaps, to some extent, "minerals are where you seek them."

This is an analogy in the case of agricultural goods that depend on a country's soil, climate, and topography. For example, a number of regions *can* grow tea competitively; but *where* tea is grown depends on the development spirit. Ceylon would never have become one of the main tea producers of the world had it not been for private enterprise by people of another culture. The same is true of the establishment of rubber estates in Indonesia before political independence.

It is to be hoped that the exploitation of natural resources is partly a *result* of economic development and not entirely its cause. If so, the current resource poverty of some poorer countries is more apparent than real. For a few countries, there may be some promise of cumulative economic progress, with advances in income and wealth leading in turn to the discovery and development of resources now unknown.

NATIONAL DIFFERENCES IN LABOR AVAILABILITY

The availability of labor differs sharply among the underdeveloped countries. Of course the abundance or scarcity of labor is a relative concept, and any international comparison should be made relative to the supply of natural resources and accumulated capital. The labor force of a country—*i.e.,* the number of people who are and would like to be economically active—obviously depends more on population size than anything else. But this is not the whole story, for the ratio of labor force to total population is not the same from country to country, but depends also on birth rates and other influences.

Population size and growth rates

In the preceding chapter it was indicated that all poor countries have high birth rates. But it does not follow from this that they all have a similarly high rate of population growth, for there is a considerable difference in death rates among them. Also, it does not follow that they are all "overpopulated," in some economic sense that will have to await definition. In many of them the death rate has been almost as high as the birth rate until the present century, and has included many deaths from causes other than poverty, such as tribal wars and occasional epidemics.

In nearly all countries there is some natural annual increase in population. However, primarily because of differences in death rates rather than birth rates, the population growth rates among underdeveloped countries range from about 3 to 1 per cent a year. Thus the estimated annual birth and death rates per thousand population are, respectively, 42 and 10 for Malaya and 23 and 8 for Argentina.

A country with a rapid rate of population increase is not necessarily one that has a great deal of available labor relative to land and capital. The United States has a very low labor to capital ratio, and yet has an annual population growth rate approaching 2 per cent—not so very much less than that of India. Most of Africa and South America have labor to land ratios considerably below that of Western Europe, but the birth rate is far above the death rate.

The sources of these discrepancies are to be found in the timing of past changes in the death rate. In Central Africa, until almost the present century, hunting accidents, tribal wars, and medical ignorance made for high death rates that kept population in check. Within half a century, colonial law enforcement and public health probably halved the death rate, but the population was so small previously that it is still only about 10 per square mile today. In India, as a contrast, the death rate has probably been 10 points below the birth rate for centuries. Thus the incidence of modern public health and organized famine relief in India came upon an already densely populated subcontinent. It is this that has caused current Indian population densities of approximately 300 per square mile.

The case can be put in rough magnitudes. Most backward countries have birth rates of around 40 per thousand a year. It is one thing for the death rate to drop to 20, if until recently it has been 40, for the previously stable population may still be too small for any immediate catastrophe. It is quite a different situation if the death rate has been 30 for a century or so and drops to 20, because then there may be a rather large population already. This seems to be approximately what has happened in the Caribbean and most of Southeast Asia.

Table 2-4 (p. 23) gives estimated population density per square kilometer of area for some selected countries. A more meaningful comparison, but not often available, is population per hectare of what is now considered to be arable land. In some cases, for example Egypt, there is a great difference between total land area and usable land area.

Labor force to population ratios

There are limited job opportunities—especially for women—in poor and backward countries. But in addition, because young adult women are more preoccupied with bearing and rearing children in high birth rate countries, they are also less available for other jobs or self-employment. These are two reasons why, in addition to cultural limitations on women's activities outside the home, one does not normally see women waiting on tables or behind store counters in underdeveloped countries.

In countries with high birth and death rates, the percentage of total male population at age groups above 25 is distinctly lower. But a larger fraction of the male population, at any given age class, is usually reported to be in the labor force than would be normal in advanced countries. Adolescent boys between 12 and 18, who in North America would be in school, are already at work in poorer countries. And few men in backward countries, if they do survive to 60 years or more, ever think of themselves as retired. So the influence of high death rates at each age is partly and superficially offset by a general poverty that precludes education and retirement. Of course much of the work that the very old and young can do in a rural community—such as taking goats to water or watching cattle treading out the grain—is a rather easy and occasional sort of "work."

Hence the labor force estimates of Table 2-4, and their relation to total poulation, may be somewhat exaggerated for backward countries. Even so, compared with advanced nations, the labor force is comparatively small. And, partly because nourishment and education are lacking, the labor force's output is even smaller relative to the total population of consumers. This is probably true despite the longer hours often worked by employees in underdeveloped countries. (See Chapter 19.)

Different occupations of labor force

The emphatic role of agriculture in poor countries has been mentioned in Chapter 2. Typically, a high proportion of the labor force is occupied in agriculture, just as agriculture contributes a high proportion of the national income. But the nonagricultural labor force tends to be occupied differently from country to country. Unfortunately, "industry" is a broad term that can include anything from crude oil production to food processing. The backward countries, as is well known, stress production of primary products. These include, along with agricultural foods and fibers, the output of mine and forest. (See Table 3-3.)

It is also commonly believed that to increase the relative importance of service industries is a "good" policy objective. Undoubtedly, a comparison of rich and poor countries indicates that there is a covariation between relative economic well-being and relative size and number of service industries. But it would be a mistake to think that the services performed by such businesses in advanced countries are not available in backward ones. Families in Thailand, for example, get their clothes laundered, eat cooked meals, and have their hair cut, even though they may not patronize laundries, restaurants, and barber shops: all these services are normally available within the home, sometimes being performed by servants. If there is any inherent superiority in the way that advanced economies provide these services, which is through a business that hires employees who might otherwise be domestic servants, it is probably due to the usual efficiencies of specialization.

Nevertheless, inasmuch as advanced economies are so organized that services are performed commercially, the relative extent of employment in service industries is a reasonable index of development. However, like all indicators, commercial service industries are primarily a symptom and not a cause. Hence government regulations designed to increase employment in service businesses will not of themselves increase economic welfare.

VARYING PARTICIPATION IN FOREIGN TRADE

Through historical accident, and because of an apparently unequal distribution of specific mineral and other natural resources, underdeveloped countries do not participate to the same degree in foreign trade. This is indicated in Table 3-4, where exports and imports are given as a relative of gross domestic product (GDP), by country. A few high income nations have very high ratios.

It is sometimes held that backward countries are poor because they have been made to participate unduly in foreign trade. But Table 3-4 would seem to give the lie to this assertion. The ratio of exports to GDP is estimated to be about equally low for India as for the United States, but the first is poor and the second is rich. On the other hand, this same ratio is almost as high for Thailand as for New Zealand, two countries again having very different per capita incomes. These ratios tend to be overstated in backward countries because foreign shipments are recorded and a great deal of subsistence income is not.

It cannot be said that those underdeveloped countries that do export a high fraction of their national product do so *because* they are poor. The reason is frequently that mineral or oil reserves have been discovered, or that the climate is well adapted to some agricultural product, and alien brains and capital have organized to take advantage of these opportunities. Nor is it fair to say that these countries are poor *because* they are export-oriented. Does anyone seriously contend that per capita incomes would be higher in Iraq if it had no petroleum, in the Congo if it had no copper, or in Brazil if it had no coffee?

The confusion seems to be as follows. Underdeveloped countries are poorer countries by definition. If an underdeveloped country specializes heavily in making one commodity, it will have to be for a foreign mar-

Table 3-4

	Currency	Unit	Gross domestic product	Gross capital formation	Exports	Imports	Relation of exports to GDP (%)
Latin America							
Brazil	cruzeiros	millions	1837	228	135	120	7
Ecuador	sucres	billions	12.9	1.6	2.5	2.1	19
Guatemala	quetzales	millions	659	84	122	148	19
Mexico	pesos	billions	122	18	18.2	18.6	15
Peru*	soles	billions	37.7	8.6	8.3	10.0	22
Venezuela	bolivares	billions	24.9	6.7	7.2	6.7	29
Asia							
Burma	kyats	billions	5.5	1.0	1.1	1.2	20
India	rupees	billions	125	—	7.1	11.2	6
Ceylon	roupies	billions	6.0	.8	2.1	2.2	35
Fed. of Malaya**	malais	billions	5.3	.6	2.3	1.8	42
Thailand**	baht	millions	41.4	6.4	8.9	9.5	21
Africa & Near East							
Ghana	ghaneenes	millions	512	64	140	122	27
Rhodesia & Nyasaland	pounds	millions	498	131	227	211	45
Tanganyika	pounds	millions	188	29.1	50	43	27
R. S. Africa	pounds	billions	2.4	.5	.75	.58	31
Advanced							
New Zealand	pounds	billions	1.25	.25	.33	.29	26

* 1958
** 1957

Source: United Nations, Yearbook of National Account Statistics, 1960, Table C.

ket, because there is of course a quite inadequate domestic demand. And if foreign capital and enterprise had not originally come on the scene and developed these specialized export lines, most of these countries would now have exports earning little if any domestically retained income. Actually, the governments of many primary producing countries obtain a large share of their revenues from these exports, good examples being Bolivia (tin) and Ghana (cocoa).[2]

Of course no one would deny that there are serious uncertainties attached to the export of primary products having fluctuating prices. And the chances of large gains or losses in any one year for the economy are greater if it is a "one product" country such as Venezuela (oil). But it is probably better to mitigate these difficulties (perhaps in one of the ways suggested in Chapter 25) than to produce little or nothing that

[2] The Ghana cocoa industry was developed largely by small holders and not by large foreign owned plantations.

other countries want to buy. The really stagnant countries are those with hardly any foreign trade.

If a country does not export, it cannot import—except on credit or charity—for the payments made and received must always balance. Hence, exports tend to match imports in value over long periods, during which loans and gifts become relatively unimportant. A country that has a small domestic market can only make a limited range of products economically. If it is to enjoy other products in consumption at all, it must import them. Accordingly, to the extent that export earnings are retained by residents of the producing country, they provide them with more imports and a better life.

This author and many others feel that the progress of underdeveloped countries must come largely through some sort of participation in world trade. In the past this has been most obvious in the case of the recently settled lands—such as Canada and Australia—where there was no strong and uneconomic native culture to oppose development. Where such an uneconomic culture does exist, as in Southeast Asia, more progress seems to have been achieved in countries that do trade more per capita. The contrasting well-being of Ceylon and India is suggestive. And foreign trade can often instigate the cultural changes required for economic development. (See also Part V.)

ATTEMPTED CLASSIFICATION OF UNDERDEVELOPED COUNTRIES

The underdeveloped world encompasses too much variety and too little similarity for easy description and analysis. There are not many policy recommendations that will apply to all backward countries irrespective of their differences. And yet, if too much weight is accorded dissimilarities, economic development can have no general principles.

Any classification scheme must accordingly be broad enough so that a number of countries will have sufficient common characteristics to appear similar. Some of these attributes are likely to be reasonably objective (*e.g.,* per capita income), but others will be quite subjective (*e.g.,* whether the culture is "economic" or not). Moreover, for each of these dimensions, not more than two or three ratings may be possible; for example, in the case of population, it may not be possible to do more than assert that a country is or is not overpopulated.

Thus, on the basis of what has already been written, one might attempt to locate a country in a matrix of attributes. Each cell might be defined in terms of the following seven characteristics, taken together:

1. Per capita income (or savings)—low or very low;
2. Population—excessive or satisfactory;
3. Culture—economic or uneconomic;

4. Natural resources—adequate or inadequate;
5. Foreign trade participation—active or stagnant;
6. Market economy—widespread or very limited;
7. Political maturity—developed or undeveloped.

Many additional dimensions are obviously possible, such as the proportion of the labor force engaged in agriculture, the proportion of issued money in bank deposits, or the quality of the civil service.

Even this scheme—assuming that certain concepts such as political maturity could be adequately defined—would be rather too complex. With seven attributes, and two ratings for each, there are 7^2-1 (or 48) possible combinations. With only about 75 underdeveloped countries in the world, there are altogether too many categories. What is really needed is a classification scheme that will permit discussion and analysis of a dozen or so countries at the same time.

If one does not examine individual countries too closely, and is willing to consider only the first three attributes listed above, it will be found that these three characteristics roughly distinguish the countries of Southeast Asia, the Middle East (including adjacent Arab countries), sub-Sahara Africa, and Latin America (including the Caribbean) from one another. Of course every country in each of these continental arrangements is not the same, even in respect to these three characteristics. But, for some purposes, it is often possible and indeed necessary to consider the underdeveloped countries of Southeast Asia as one subset, those of sub-Sahara Africa as another, and so on.

These four continental areas can be approximately ranked from unfavorable to favorable as follows:

Per capita income	Population pressure	Economic culture
Southeast Asia	Southeast Asia	Southeast Asia
sub-Sahara Africa	Middle East	sub-Sahara Africa
Middle East	Latin America	Middle East
Latin America	sub-Sahara Africa	Latin America

Some of the intermediate rankings are uncertain. Nor do all the countries within a particular continental area share uniform characteristics. But in general the degree of poverty and general backwardness is greatest in Southeast Asia and smallest in Latin America, And, for political and cultural reasons in addition, the problems of Asia, Africa, and Latin America tend to be distinct.

Although Southeast Asia has an uneconomic culture, it possesses some of the oldest civilizations and has produced two of the four great religions of the world. The same is true of the Middle East. While the native culture of sub-Sahara Africa is not only uneconomic, but really primitive, it is not cursed with many of the caste rigidities of some Asian lands. On the other hand, Latin America has looked culturally to Europe since the Spanish and Portuguese invasions, and the more influential classes are essentially Western in their economic attitudes.

These continental areas can also be distinguished on political grounds. Latin America has been politically independent from Europe for a century. Most of Southeast Asia became independent shortly after World War II. For sub-Sahara Africa, 1960 was the great year of political independence—almost a dozen new nations coming into being. It now remains to be seen whether all these new states can have political independence and economic development.

II

Innovations and

development

EXPERIENCE and logic suggest that the most powerful engine of economic development, and hence the most potent source of rising living standards, are innovations. "Innovations" are here not limited in meaning to new products and new methods of making them; they also include new markets and organizations, and even new economic principles as a guide to policy. Accordingly, attention is first given to theories of the "classical" economists, for these once-revolutionary ideas still form the core of development theory today. Second, economic theories of innovation and development are outlined, together with a survey of the process of innovation. Third, the ways in which factor prices influence and are affected by innovations are included because they are so relevant to capital-poor and labor-rich countries. Fourth, the choice between stressing innovations in agriculture or industry is argued. Fifth, possible schemes for promoting agricultural and village development are described. Sixth, various growth models that relate innovations, capital, or labor to increasing output per head are examined. Finally, past and current historical notions regarding "stages" of economic growth are discussed, without much conviction. However, despite this variety, the central theme of this Part is development through innovations. And it is innovations—*i.e.,* useful changes in human economic methods—that can probably contribute more eventually to income per head than additions to capital stocks and labor availability.

4

Development ideas
of early economists

Economic development is not a new subject. Mercantilist pamphleteers were beginning to advocate certain development policies four hundred years ago. And *The Wealth of Nations,* written by Adam Smith almost three centuries ago, is usually considered the first "professional" book ever published on this subject. Within the next eight decades, a series of writers, including Malthus, Ricardo, and Mill, continued to concern themselves with problems of overpopulation and national economic welfare. But by Marshall's time, toward the end of the nineteenth century, economists were already interesting themselves more in theories of price determination and income distribution. And until recently, most novelties in economic science have been more relevant to advanced than backward countries. The intense postwar concern regarding economic development of backward areas has done much to restore professional interest in the views of the first economists. Nor is this so surprising, for in many important respects the eighteenth century Britain of Adam Smith was not too dissimilar from some underdeveloped countries of the twentieth century, being largely agricultural with a considerable subsistence economy, and yet beginning to experience the impact of industry and a new technology. Accordingly, in this chapter, an attempt will be made to summarize those principles of the mercantilist and the so-called classical economists that seem most pertinent to economic progress in today's backward countries.[1]

MERCANTILISM: THE NEW MERCHANT CLASS

It is difficult to understand Adam Smith, or the classical writers that followed him, without some knowledge of Western Europe, and especially England and Scotland, during the seventeenth and eighteenth centuries. Adam Smith became famous for, among other things, his attacks on

[1] Theories of later economists, pertinent to economic development, will be examined as occasion demands later in the book.

what he called "mercantilism." As a result the mercantilists, at least among economists, have ever since had too bad a name.

The new merchant class

By the seventeenth century Western Europe had emerged from feudalism and the Middle Ages. The comity of Europe—long maintained by the Catholic Church—was shattered by the Protestant Reformation. Real power was now held by the strong central governments of the new national states of England (with Scotland), France, Spain, and the Netherlands. People were coming to think in national terms and to believe that a country could increase its wealth and power by adopting proper government policies. This nationalist spirit of the mercantilists and their faith in government intervention are typical of many an underdeveloped country today.

The end of the Middle Ages was also marked by the emergence of a new merchant class that soon became a political force. These merchants were townspeople; they had no inherited titles, and their wealth did not come from ownership of land. They were a self-made class, springing sometimes from the lowest orders, and the ancestors of not a few included runaway serfs. They understood the virtues of thrift and industry and tended to despise profligacy of the gentry. In many ways they were apart from, and had conflicting interests with, the old aristocracy.

These bourgeois are important in the history of economic development because they were the first entrepreneurs of any note. They advanced and risked capital, organized resources, and saw and seized new opportunities. The more prosperous might be goldsmiths and silversmiths, doing a little banking on the side; or they might be successful artisans—coopers, wrights, or tailors—now employing journeymen and apprentices. These merchants were not only traders—buying and selling some commodity—but included manufacturers. Nothing quite like them had been known before.

With increasing prosperity, this new merchant class gained political influence too, and it not unnaturally used it to further its own interests. It wanted liberty, and above all legal protection against arbitrary exercise of power by the Crown, so that it would be safe in its property and persons. It wanted freedom from taxes imposed without its own consent. In England it was the main proponent of parliamentary government. Its special and new philosophy sparked the American Revolution.

Their economic views

These merchants were not exactly inarticulate. Many of them turned pamphleteer. They all agreed upon the desirability of (1) enhanced national power; (2) intervention in economic affairs by the central authority; (3) unification of the country through scrapping internal trade restrictions; (4) a favorable balance of trade, and (5) a large population. But as regards specific means to attain their goals, except for gaining a favorable balance of trade, they were often far from being unanimous. They were not economists, although they naturally had many decided, if simple, views on economic matters; in fact, until Adam Smith in a later century called them "mercantilists," as a group they even lacked a name.

National power. Mercantilist pamphlets were primarily concerned with increasing the power and wealth of the nation. In many respects these were considered synonymous. And like many others since, but perhaps with more sincerity than most, the mercantilist writers identified their own class interests with those of the nation. This supposed merging of interests often led them to advocate policies that seem almost totalitarian today. Certainly, as compared with the utilitarians of the next few centuries, the mercantilists were not primarily concerned with individual happiness.

Intervention. Nearly all the writers of the period were convinced that the political economy of the nation, if properly directed by the state, could make greater contributions to the wealth and power of the realm. They definitely did not believe in any natural law that would suggest the desirability of *laissez-faire*. They were prepared to give up some freedom in what they bought and sold, and at what prices, if this were in the interests of the nation.

Unification. Many of the new states of Europe, although politically unified, still suffered economic dismemberment as a result of innumerable petty restrictions and tolls left over from the Middle Ages. Some of these had been imposed by local rulers, chartered towns, or merchant guilds. Internal transportation was so harassed by imposts, although less so in Britain than on the Continent, that often merchants and farmers could only trade with profit in the local town. Other regulations limited entry into certain privileged occupations. The new merchant class was largely instrumental in removing many if not most of these local restrictions. Because the mercantilists were not opposed to intervention by the central government, their very great contribution in removing internal barriers has often been overlooked, although this clearing of the restrictive underbrush was a precondition of the industrial revolution.[2]

Favorable trade balance. As regards external trade, patriotism and profits combined to make the merchant class strongly protectionist. Imports of goods were in general held to be undesirable, because they occasioned a loss of gold and specie, although a few writers conceded that raw materials might be imported if needed for domestic manufac-

[2] See Eli F. Heckscher. *Mercantilism,* rev. ed. (New York; The Macmillan Company, 1955), especially Part I.

ture. But the wealthy were criticized for importing luxuries, and advised to drink good English ale instead of Portuguese wine, for example, while Puritans were especially fond of criticizing the fripperies imported by the gentry from Italy and France.

What logical economic reasoning led the mercantilists to favor protection has never been entirely clear. A great many, unlike medieval writers who identified *goods* accumulation with wealth, seem to have considered acquisition of gold and silver to be the goal of economic activity. Many trade associations today are apparently no less muddled. But some of the mercantilist writers—such as Mun—seem to have been far less naive. And there are other possible and more charitable explanations.

Trade in Western Europe—and only Spain and Portugal had gold and silver mines in the Americas—was constrained by a coinage supply that was not keeping pace with increasing productivity and a growing population. There was no central bank that could increase the money supply overnight. Paper bank notes were still a rarity. Hence a favorable external balance of trade appeared to offer the best means of increasing the supply of circulating coinage, facilitating trade, and increasing output.

Still another consideration, in a period when gold and silver were deemed the "sinews of war," was that military power and the Crown's war chest went hand in hand.

A third possible explanation is that the new merchant class, often from personal experience, was obsessed by the need to save and invest. And what benefited a household was by analogy supposed to benefit a nation. Each nation, because of its natural endowment, would tend to produce some things in excess of domestic demand. Foreign markets provided a place to sell this surplus. But during the mercantilist period, nearly all imports into Britain were consumer goods, and most of them luxuries at that. How much better—it was perhaps "reasoned"—to accept payment in gold and use these proceeds to employ idle workers at home in improving bridges and harbors, draining bogs, and building ships. This reasoning rested on certain special assumptions: (1) that the export surplus is a datum and that the resources making it cannot be shifted to another kind of production; (2) that export earnings cannot be advantageously used to finance capital imports but must be taken either in gold or luxury consumer goods; (3) that there are idle domestic resources which can be employed on useful capital projects if the means to finance them exist. Granted these assumptions, this is not an entirely frivolous argument, but unfortunately it is often hard for a present-day economist with his special concepts and language to read between the often ambiguous lines of the mercantilist pamphleteers.

Population. Almost to a man, the mercantilist writers seem to have been in favor of a large and increasing population. A larger population meant more workers, consequently more output, and hence supposedly more national power, it being assumed that a worker typically produces a surplus over and above his own consumption. Some mercantile authors simply saw more consumers for their wares in a larger population. Others appealed rather blindly to supposed experience, as when a dogmatic rector asked rhetorically: "Was a Country thinly inhabited ever rich? Was a populous Country ever poor?"[3] It is an old, if mistaken, idea that national power, economic progress, and population necessarily march in step.

Significance for development

The new merchant class of the sixteenth and seventeenth centuries, whose rather unorganized but vocal views have been labelled "mercantilism," are of historical interest to anyone concerned with economic development today. Because of their views on foreign trade, they have been pilloried by Adam Smith and almost all economists ever since, and on the whole there is little question about the naïveté of some of their economics. But the mercantilist writers included many astute observers and imaginative thinkers. And so it is a great mistake to regard them in a cavalier manner.

It is the philosophy of the new merchant class, from which the mercantilist writers mostly sprang, that is important. They were nationalists and interventionists for the sake of national wealth and power, and this same attitude is very common among officials and politicians in the underdeveloped countries of today. They did much to achieve national economic unity, and many backward countries of the twentieth century still suffer from local economic restraints of one kind and another. They favored all sorts of foreign trade and exchange restrictions, as do many recently independent governments today. In some ways mercantilism is very modern.

But it is in other and less controversial ways that the new merchant class contributed most to economic development. Its political victory over the Crown in England, with the establishment of parliamentary government, was a necessary condition of further progress. The establishment of civil liberty and property rights must have done much to improve economic inducements and increase investment. Above all the new upper middle class—largely comprised of entrepreneurs—demonstrated that industry and thrift are practical virtues. Previously wealth has been considered to be for enjoyment, not for use in production; the Protestant ethic was now coming to the fore. It is a moot point whether

[3] Josiah Tucker, "Reflections on the Expediency of a Law for the Naturalization of Foreign Protestants," London, 1751.

some of today's backward countries can achieve substantial economic development without first achieving some of these same political, social, and cultural advances. They may still be "preconditions" for economic progress in a free society.

"CLASSICAL" PRINCIPLES OF ECONOMIC DEVELOPMENT

The economists of the English classical school, like the mercantilists they attacked, were strong exponents of parliamentary government, law and order, private property rights, and the virtues of industry and thrift. They too would have opposed, had they still existed, the numerous internal restrictions on transport and occupation that the mercantilists had slowly overcome in England and which were swept away by the Revolution in France. But in other respects they were far apart.

For one thing, starting with Adam Smith they all believed in natural law as a philosophy of life, which in economic affairs meant *laissez-faire;* as a natural consequence of being opposed to government interference, they were free traders. From Malthus on, they feared that population pressure on resources might become chronic and keep wages of common labor near a subsistence level. And, beginning with Ricardo and continuing through Mill, they evolved an increasingly deductive body of economic theory that related capital, resources, and population in the development process.

This entire evolution of thought was offered to the world during the short span of seventy-two years separating the publication of Adam Smith's *The Wealth of Nations* in 1776 and J. S. Mill's *Principles of Political Economy* in 1848. During this time, the world around these men was changing rapidly; Adam Smith was developing his views before the onset of the Industrial Revolution, whereas the younger Mill was writing after many of its economic impacts were recognized. Although the classical principles are supposed to apply to a country whether it be primarily agricultural or industrial, rural or urban, this claim has of course often been disputed—notably, during the same period, by Fredrich List in Germany and Alexander Hamilton in America. And the German historical school was later to argue that classical economics might be all very well for Britain but that "Manchesterism" did not necessarily apply to less advanced nations. It is therefore interesting to note that Adam Smith was asserting his free trade principles when Manchester and the Lancestershire cotton textile industry were barely in existence.

What are the classical principles of economic development? Any simple list of relevant ideas must of course be arbitrary, but it would certainly include:

1. Natural law and a government policy of laissez-faire toward private economic affairs;
2. Division of labor, limited only by the extent of the market;
3. Free foreign trade, to export each nation's comparative advantage in production;
4. The use of paper money and the need for institutions to provide it in appropriate quantities;
5. Capital accumulation, financed from surplus value, as a means to increase the output from labor;
6. Diminishing returns, as an explanation of land rents and a potential limit to growth.
7. Threat to progress of population growth when combined with fixed natural resources, unless offset by increased capital and improved technology.

A short explanation of these ideas, followed by a demonstration of how they can be related to make an aggregate dynamic model of development, is in order.

Laissez-faire

Adam Smith was one of the first and most persuasive writers to assert that natural law also extended to economic affairs. In the eighteenth century—prompted by Newtonian physics and other scientific explanations of what had previously been mysterious phenomena—people came to believe that many activities within the universe are not random events but are ordered in obedience to some grand design. Smith felt that this same natural order related prices, the supply of labor, land rents, and, indeed, most economic affairs.

Behind the "invisible hand" of natural law was self-love or selfishness. Smith observed that people produced goods and useful services, not out of altruism, but from self-interest:

. . . every individual necessarily labours to render the annual revenue of society as great as he can. He generally, indeed, neither intends to promote the public interest, nor knows how much he is promoting it. . . . and he is in this, as in many other cases, led by an invisible hand to promote an end which was no part of his intention.[4]

He also recognized that voluntary transactions of all kinds, whether the exchange of goods or the provision of factors of production, normally benefit both parties to the deal. And it is this mutual search for gain that motivates trade and commerce:

[4] Adam Smith, *An Inquiry into the Nature and Causes of the Wealth of Nations* (1776), Cannan ed. (New York: The Modern Library, 1937), p. 423.

Whoever offers to another a bargain of any kind, proposes to do this. Give me that which I want, and you shall have this which you want, is the meaning of every such offer; and it is in this manner that we obtain from one another the far greater part of those good offices which we stand in need of. It is not from the benevolence of the butcher, the brewer, or the baker, that we expect our dinner, but from their regard to their own interest. We address ourselves not to their humanity, but to their self-love, and never talk to them of our own necessities but of their advantage. Nobody but a beggar chooses to depend chiefly upon the benevolence of his fellow-citizens.[5]

Of course this does not mean that the gain is equally shared, for buyers and sellers do not necessarily have equal bargaining power. But where there is government that maintains law and order, and does not support unjust monopolies, selfishness cannot be predatory and is instead harnessed to a social end.

It followed, so far as Adam Smith was concerned, that the self-interest of capitalists, landlords, and workers, together with that of merchants, would do more to provide the realm with opulence than any direction from a presumptuous and ignorant government. As he himself put it concerning public interference in private investment decisions:

. . . The Statesman, who would attempt to direct people in what manner they ought to employ their capitals, would not only load himself with a most unnecessary attention, but assume an authority which could safely be trusted, not only to no single person, but to no council or senate whatever, and which would nowhere be so dangerous as in the hands of a man who had folly and presumption enough to fancy himself fit to exercise it.[6]

Accordingly he believed, as many once did but few do now, that the best government is the one that governs least: his advice to a government that sought to interfere with the natural economic order would have been: "Let be."[7]

Division of labor

The first sentence of *The Wealth of Nations* is:

The greatest improvement in the productive powers of labor, and the greater part of the skill, dexterity, and judgement with which it is directed, or applied, seem to have been the effects of the division of labour.[8]

[5] *Ibid.*, p. 14.
[6] *Ibid.*, p. 423.
[7] Although Adam Smith is often considered the father of *laissez-faire*, he never once used this term of the French Physiocrats, despite their influence on his thought.
[8] *Op. cit.*, p. 3.

And Smith continues to give an example of a pin factory, where ten workers, each performing only a few specialized jobs, could make 48,000 pins a day, or several thousand times more than 10 men could who each worked alone. This great increase in productivity he attributes to three things:

First, to the increase of the dexterity in every particular workman; secondly, to the saving of the time which is commonly lost in passing from one species of work to another; and lastly, to the invention of a great number of machines which facilitate and abridge labor, and enable one man to do the work of many.[9]

There can be little argument regarding the first two reasons offered. But the third cause of increase in productivity is attributable not to labor but to capital. And occasionally nowadays, as when extremely specialized machinery is developed for a high wage country but used in another low wage country, specialized human work may be due to the use of such machinery rather than the other way around.

The mention of machinery is also a reminder that some kinds of equipment can hardly be used with profit below some given volume of sales. This was well recognized by Smith. And one of his most famous *dicta* is that "the division of labor is limited by the extent of the market":

There are some sorts of industry, even of the lowest kind, which can be carried on nowhere but in a great town. A porter, for example, can find employment and subsistence in no other place. . . . It is impossible that there be such a trade as even that of a nailer in the remote and inland parts of the Highlands of Scotland. Such a workman at the rate of a thousand nails a day . . . will make three hundred thousand nails a year. But in such a situation it would be impossible to dispose of . . . one day's work in the year.[10]

The "extent of the market" means the intensity of demand at the point of production. Where transportation is cheap—as for example when a good is easily carried or water freight is available—more can be sold if other things are equal. The intensity of demand will also depend upon the tastes of people in the area, their incomes, and their numbers.

The policy consequences of these ideas are enormously imporant. As we shall see, for some products at least, free international trade is needed to extend the market enough to permit useful specialization. But, perhaps more important, the ability of people to produce far more than they need of one thing, so that they can exchange some of it for part of another's different surplus, is greatly dependent upon the use of money in such transactions. Local monopolies are also less probable if the market is

9 *Ibid.*, p. 7.
10 *Ibid.*, pp. 17–18.

great, and self-interest and social usefulness are more likely to correspond if competition is strong.

Adam Smith considered the division of labor between town and country to be one outstanding example of its benefits, and we can do no better than to close with excerpts from the opening paragraph of Book III, on the progress of opulence:

> The great commerce of every civilized society is that carried on between the inhabitants of the town and those of the country . . . The gains of both are mutual and reciprocal, and the division of labor is in this, as in other cases, advantageous to all the different persons employed . . . The inhabitants of the country purchase of the town a greater quantity of manufactured goods, with the produce of a much smaller quantity of their own labor. . . . The town affords a market for the surplus product of the country, or what is over and above the maintenance of the cultivators, and it is there that the inhabitants of the country exchange it for something else which is in demand among them.[11]

Free foreign trade

Any one who subscribes to a philosophy of *laissez-faire,* and believes in the advantages of productive specialization, will in general be a free trader. And so Smith, Ricardo, and Mill proved to be among its foremost proponents. But while Smith largely contented himself with ridiculing the mercantilists in scathing prose, Ricardo evolved the principle of comparative demand and Mill, through his statement of reciprocal demand, determined the rates at which commodities would exchange in foreign trade. This whole line of theoretical development has been frequently traced elsewhere.[12] So it will be given short shrift here.

Absolute advantage or foreign trade. Adam Smith felt that all trade was beneficial, whether foreign or domestic, for people will only trade if it is to their advantage and they can thereby obtain goods more cheaply. To him this was a self-evident truth. It was accepted as regards domestic trade, so why would it not be true of foreign trade? As he said:

> Among all the absurd speculations that have been propogated concerning the balance of trade, it has never been pretended that either the [rural] country loses by its commerce with the town, or the town by that with the country. . . .[13]

And he had little love of tradesmen's ethics:

> The Portuguese, it is said, are better customers for our manufacturers than the French, and their imports should therefore be encouraged in preference to

[11] *Ibid.*
[12] *E.g.,* S. Enke and V. Saler, *International Economics,* 3rd ed. (Englewood Cliffs, N.J.: Prentice-Hall, Inc., 1957), Appendix B.
[13] *Ibid.,* p. 357.

them. As they give us the custom, it is pretended, we should give them ours. The sneaking arts of underlying tradesmen are thus erected into political maxims . . . .[14]

His main concern was that the source of goods be determined according to cheapness, or by what has sometimes been termed "absolute advantage":

. . . By means of glasses, hotbeds, and hotwalls, very good grapes can be raised in Scotland, and very good wine too can be made of them at about thirty times the expense for which at least equally good can be brought from foreign countries. Would it be a reasonable law to prohibit the importation of all foreign wines, merely to encourage the making of claret and burgundy in Scotland?[15]

Ricardo's principle of comparative advantage. David Ricardo, successful city financier, member of Parliament, and one of the first abstract analytical economists, stated the advantages of foreign trade in comparative form. Like other classical economists, he assumed that commodities exchanged within a country in relation to the labor cost of producing them. Thus, if England required 100 men for a year to produce x yards of cloth and 120 men for the same period to produce y barrels of wine, the cost to England of domestically producing this amount of wine is $1.2x$ yards of cloth. But the labor theory of value was supposed not to determine the prices at which goods exchanged in foreign trade. Accordingly, even if it took Portugal only 90 man-years to produce x yards of cloth and only 80 to produce y barrels, it does not follow that Portugal with lower costs for both outputs cannot trade wine advantageously for English cloth.

For, as Ricardo says:

Though she [Portugal] could make the cloth with the labor of 90 men, she would import it from a country where it required the labor of 100 men to produce it, because it would be advantageous to her rather to employ her capital in the production of wine for which she would obtain more cloth from England than she could produce by diverting a portion of her capital from the cultivation of vines to the manufacture of cloth.[16]

The point is that the English, with their internal labor costs, will be prepared externally to pay up to 12/10 yards of cloth to buy y barrels of wine. Analogously, the Portuguese will sell y barrels of wine at any price above $8/9x$ yards of cloth, so mutually advantageous exchange between

14 *Ibid.*, p. 460.
15 *Ibid.*, p. 425.
16 D. Ricardo, *Principles of Political Economy and Taxation* (1817), edited by Piero Staffa with M. H. Dobb (Cambridge, England: Cambridge University Press, 1951), p. 135.

the two countries is almost inevitable. The significant conclusion is that backward countries having low outputs per worker can still benefit from trading with advanced countries *if* the productivity differences between the two countries are not the same in every line of enterprise. And, of course, normally they never are.

Mill's equation of international demand. John Stuart Mill, in his *Principles of Political Economy* (1848), explained how the barter terms of trade are established. Ricardo, in the above example, indicated that there would be an exchange of wine and cloth between Portugal and England. But he did not state what the commodity exchange rate would be, except that it would have to be somewhere between the rates that left one or the other country indifferent to trade. To answer this question, Mill had to introduce demand considerations and price, and a concept he termed *the equation of international demand* (or, as it is sometimes called, *the principle of reciprocal demand*).

The essential idea is that in equilibrium the value of all the English export must equal that of all of the foreign country's export, the value being measured in one or other of the two commodities. Continuing with Ricardo's example—which Mill did not use—we can assume that yards of cloth are priced in barrels of wine. There will be some one wine price of cloth that will make the number of wine barrels the Portuguese are then willing to sell equal to the same price multiplied by the number of yards of cloth the English are then willing to sell.

This idea, although hard to put into words, has often been illustrated with simplicity in a diagram. Mill himself tried to sum it up when he wrote:

> The values at which a country exchanges its produce with foreign countries depend . . . on the amount and extensibility of their demand for its commodities, compared with its demand for theirs. . . . The more the foreign demand for its commodities exceeds its demand for foreign commodities, . . . the more favorable to it will be the terms of interchange: that is, the more it will obtain of foreign commodities in return for a given quantity of its own.[17]

In other words a country has less bargaining power, and must pay higher prices, if it tends to want other nation's goods more than that nation wants the first country's exports. As usual, trade benefits both nations, but not equally. In the modern world, a common complaint among backward countries that specialize in primary products exports is that the gains from trade go mostly to the advanced countries, although this is not necessarily so. (We shall return to this allegation in Chapter 25.)

[17] John Stuart Mill, *Principles of Political Economy* (1848), rev. ed. (London: Longmans, Green and Co., 1920), p. 603.

Money and credit

The seventy-odd years between Smith and Mill greatly changed the kinds of money and credit in use and the monetary needs of the times. For Smith the problem was that there was not enough money—or money substitutes—in circulation. For Ricardo and Mill, with the paper money issues of the Napoleonic period in mind, it was inflation that had to be controlled if money was to serve its functions.

Adam Smith was a strong proponent of bank notes, assuming safeguards against excessive and unsecured issue, as a means of supplementing the gold and silver coinage in circulation. For one thing, in a country of growing population and productivity, an almost fixed stock of specie money must at constant prices limit demand and hence the division of labor. For another, if coinage could be supplemented by paper notes of domestic banks, one of the more respectable arguments of the mercantilists for a favorable balance of trade could be turned against them. An increase in the domestic money supply could then be independent of an import balance; and in fact, needing less coinage at home, England could afford to lose bullion in exchange for imports of real capital. Or, in Smith's own words:

The substitution of paper in the room of gold and silver money replaces a very expensive instrument of commerce with one much less costly, and sometimes equally convenient.[18]

J. S. Mill, while agreeing with this point, was also concerned with the individual injustices and public disasters following inflation. Or, as he stated it:

The substitution of paper for metallic currency is a national gain; any further increase of paper beyond this is but a form of robbery.[19]

Hence it was his position that paper money—whether issued by a national bank or private banks—should never be more than a substitute for coinage. If it became an addition, prices would rise, and the issuers of the paper money would obtain an unconscionable gain. Even when this gain accrues to a government, so that it has in effect taxed all those whose incomes are defined in relatively fixed money terms, Mill considered this incidence arbitrary and unjust. Moreover, and the depreciation of the French *assignats* was well-remembered, he had little faith in the restraint of government if once permitted to issue paper money that was not convertible into metal. And so we find him asserting:

[18] *Op. cit.,* p. 276.
[19] *Op. cit.,* p. 551.

The temptation to overissue, in certain financial emergencies, is so strong, that nothing is admissible that can tend, in however slight a degree, to weaken the barriers that so restrain it.[20]

These varied views all have application to backward economies of to-day. As their subsistence economies are slowly penetrated by the market economy, there will be an increased need for means of payment, and it is monstrous to suppose that this must comprise a metal coinage obtained through a "favorable" trade balance. The potential blessings of paper money and central bank credit as a means of increasing the division of labor are very great. But there have been too many instances of the curse of overissue for Mill's warning to be academic. The need for an adequate supply of money and credit and the dangers that inconvertibility will be abused by weak governments are perhaps even greater today than a century ago.

Capital accumulation from surplus value

Like many modern economists, those of the classical school considered capital accumulation to be the *primum mobile* of economic development and the main requirement of steady progress to be continued saving and investment. They were all capitalists in spirit. Living in a time of many new inventions, all could see (especially by the nineteenth century) the ability of machinery to increase output. So the problem of development, as they saw it, was largely the ability of a country to accumulate "capitals." The more people saved from their income, and the more investment, the more wealth. But "people" in this case were not workers, who as we shall see were considered incapable of any significant savings, but capitalists (including landowners). And the greater "wealth" that resulted from more investment was not higher per capita incomes for the working classes, but more possessions, both productive and for pleasure, of the upper classes.

Kinds of capital. The productivity of capital was taken to be a self-evident fact. However, the classical economists distinguished among various kinds of capital, and especially between fixed capital and circulating capital. Fixed capital is exemplified by factory buildings and machinery, agricultural drainage or irrigation systems, and the like. Circulating capital takes two main forms: first, the working capital of an enterprise, such as raw materials, semiprocessed goods, and seed for planting; second, resources in effect advanced by employers, or consumed by independent proprietors, while waiting for the final output of sumptuary goods. This last is the notorious "wages fund."

These early economists were all very conscious of the time interval

20 *Ibid.,* p. 546.

between the start of production and its final result in some consumable form.

As Mill says:

When the labourer maintains himself by funds of his own, as when a peasant-farmer or proprietor lives on the produce of his own land, or an artisan works on his own account, they are still supported by capital, that is funds provided in advance. The peasant does not subsist this year on the produce of this year's harvest, but on that of the last. The artisan is not living on the proceeds of the work he has in hand, but on those of work previously executed and disposed of. Each is supported by a small capital of his own, which he periodically replaces from the produce of his labour. The large capitalist is, in like manner, maintained from funds provided in advance.[21]

If a people engage in "roundabout" methods of production, making machinery and intermediate goods in order to consume more eventually, the economy must previously have accumulated goods that directly or indirectly can be used in the meantime for subsistence.

This may all seem very obvious. But in the development plans of backward countries it is not uncommon to find that the need for circulating capital—of both types—has been overlooked. The emphasis is too often all on fixed capital, with depreciation ignored, and gross fixed investment identified with net additions to capacity.

Source of capital. The source of capital was always held to be saving; that is, denial of personal consumption now. And almost all saving was from income obtained from the investing of capital or the renting of land; for practical purposes, capitalists and landlords were considered to be the only people able and willing to save. The laboring classes, as a general rule, were held to be incapable of saving; this was partly from lack of restraint, but primarily because their usual wages were supposed to be barely adequate to enable them to reproduce themselves. (This is explained further in the next subsection.)

An essential part of the classical theory—and the cornerstone of later Marxian economics—was the theory of surplus value.[22]

Under normal conditions of production, the value of a worker's output is greater than the wages that are paid to him. This is because part of the output is attributable to the capital—intermediate goods and fixed facilities—he has had to help him. And where the occupation involves growing or extracting something, part of the output is also attributable

21 *Ibid.*, p. 58.
22 However, as between Malthus and Ricardo, there were major differences. Malthus stressed that the level of profits depended primarily upon the quantity of capital relative to that of labor. Ricardo held that the values of goods were proportionate to the labor directly or indirectly embodied in them, and that profits were this value minus wages paid, so that lower wages meant correspondingly greater profits.

to "land," because a given set of workers would produce less if they worked with fewer or poorer natural resources.

This surplus value, the excess of the value of output over the real wages paid to make it, is the source of income to capitalists and landlords. And, because their incomes are usually considerable, they can normally save. The higher their incomes, the larger their savings, and the more rapid is economic development.

However, this development is for the greater indulgence of those who own the means of production, and for no one else. Laborers, in the long run, are neither harmed nor helped by this kind of development, except that the country can then continuously maintain more of them. The per capita incomes of workers—except in the short run—will remain about the same. Although this is a pessimistic view of the development process, and so has often been decried, several economists have independently advanced very similar theories of development during the past few decades. (See Chapter 18.)

Theory of wages

The belief that only capitalists and landlords can provide private savings depends upon the classical theory of wage determination. The commonest and soundest view was that, while wages depend upon demand and supply in the short run, in the long run they depend primarily upon supply. And the cost of supply, in the case of labor, is the cost of perpetuating a labor force. If wages should temporarily rise, the most likely result is that fewer children will die prematurely and that couples will marry sooner, so that within half a generation or so there will be an oversupply of labor to depress wages. For opposite reasons, still another half generation later, falling wages will render the labor force too small. Thus wages will oscillate around a level corresponding roughly to the cost of "reproducing" a working-class family.

Written views of the classical economists regarding the natural level of wages are actually far less rigid or pessimistic than many of the popular caricatures of classical wage theory. Among the economists themselves, it was generally held that wages were determined by supply and demand in the short run. Supply was held to be the number of available workers, and demand to be the capital advanced by employers for production.

J. S. Mill summed it up when he said:

Wages depend, then, on the proportion between the number of the labouring population and the capital or other funds devoted to the purchase of labour. . . . It is not the absolute amount of accumulation or of production that is of importance to the labouring class; it is not the amount even of the funds destined for distribution among the labourers: it is the proportion between those funds and the numbers among whom they are shared.[23]

However, this is still far from a complete statement. The size of the so-called wages fund, and how this is determined, were always a matter of uncertainty and later of dispute. The root idea was that, as work precedes output in agriculture and indeed in all lines of production, the employer must advance subsistence in money or kind to his laborers during the wait for output. Thus an upper short run limit to total wages paid by all employers was supposedly the stock of capital available for this purpose. But this is not a very exact concept, and the amount involved may be discretionary; in fact, if wages were for some reason "high," employers might find their way to advancing more funds for wages.

The lower long run limit to wages was commonly held to be the cost at which the laboring class could reproduce itself, although in the short run wages might be considerably higher. All the economists pointed out that in an expanding economy—North America usually being the example —the relative stock of capital and workers might be much in the laborers' favor. In fact, for this reason, wages in a stationary but wealthy country might be lower than in a growing but poorer one.[24]

Also, despite a common misconception, it was not held that wages in the long run would necessarily tend to fall to a minimum of subsistence. The more educated view was that, although this might happen in very poor countries where the people were brutish and despotically governed, in more fortunate countries the lower orders would gradually become accustomed to more than bare necessities. Having tasted of a better life, they would be less improvident in having families during bad times. Thus Malthus asserts:

The rate at which the resources of a country increase is . . . liable . . . to great variation; and the habits of a people . . . can scarcely ever be considered as permanent. . . . When the resources of a country are rapidly increasing and the labourer commands a large portion of necessaries, it is to be expected that if he has the opportunity of exchanging his superfluous food for conveniences and comforts, he will acquire a taste for these conveniences, and his habits will be formed accordingly.[25]

This slow progress could be abetted by civil liberties and public education; thus, concerning the possibility that an independent people will be more likely to practice moral restraint and have small families, Malthus wrote:

23 *Ibid.*, p. 350.
24 Smith, *op. cit.*, pp. 70, 71: J. S. Mill, *op. cit.*, pp. 350, 351.
25 T. R. Malthus, *Principles of Political Economy* (London, 1820), p. 248.

Of all the causes which tend to generate prudential habits among the lower classes of society, the most essential is civil liberty. No people can be much accustomed to form plans for the future, who do not feel assured that their industrious exertions, while fair and honorable, will be allowed to have free scope; and that the property which they either possess, or may acquire, will be secured to them by a known code of just law impartially administered.[26]

Mill wrote similarly, regarding the effect of education on the birth rate:

An education directed to diffuse good sense among the people with such knowledge as would qualify them to judge of the tendencies of their actions, would be certain, even without any direct inculcation, to raise up a public opinion by which intemperance and improvidence of every kind would be held discreditable, and the improvidence which overstocks the labour market would be severely condemned, as an offense against the common weal.[27]

Thus the classical writers did foresee the possibility of improving the economic lot of the common people, and through government action at that, great importance being placed on civil liberties and public education.

Even in Adam Smith's time, although a majority of workers were no more than unskilled laborers, some were acquiring skills and knowledge that set them apart. And, as he stated:

A man educated at the expense of much labour and time to any of those employments which require extraordinary dexterity and skill, may be compared to expensive machines. The work which he learns to perform, it must be expected, over and above the usual wages of common labour, will replace to him the whole expence of his education, with at least the ordinary profits of an equally valuable capital. It must do this too in a reasonable time, regard being had to the very uncertain duration of human life. . . .[28]

In other words, even in the eighteenth century a certain amount of vertical mobility was recognized to exist. Otherwise the classical economists saw contemporary English society much as it was, with landlords and capitalists on the one hand, and on the other laborers owning no means of production save their own bodies.

Diminishing returns to increasing population

If the classical economists saw saving and investment as the main cause of development, they saw a growing population and limited natural re-

26 *Ibid.*, p. 251.
27 *Op. cit.*, p. 381.
28 *Op. cit.*, p. 101.

sources as ultimate checks, operating through the principle of diminishing returns.

In each and every line of enterprise, there are usually one or more employed agents of production that are in comparatively fixed supply. Therefore, in order to obtain more output, other productive agents must be combined in ever greater quantities with them. A point of diminishing returns will be reached when a given percentage increase in the quantity of variable productive agents gives a smaller percentage increase in output. The most familiar example is agriculture, where a country may have a comparatively fixed acreage of arable land: a continual doubling of labor, fertilizer, and so forth, used in combination with this land, will eventually result in a less than double output.

This principle of diminishing (average) returns to a continuously increasing labor force, because of inherent limits on natural resources, was also part of the classical theory of land rent. As population increases and greater efforts are made to produce food from a given land area, there will be a change in the so-called *extensive* and *intensive* margins. Ever poorer quality land, which earns no rent, will be brought into use at the extensive margins, thereby increasing the premium or rent that can then be obtained by the owner of more productive land already cultivated. This "better," or intramarginal, land also comes to be used more *intensively;* that is, more units of other productive agents are now combined with it. Hence "land," the comparatively fixed and increasingly scarce element in the combination, comes to earn a larger income.

Although rents rise during certain stages of development, they are far from being a true cause of wealth, and, in countries where natural resources are abundant, rents may be almost nil. As Ricardo put it:

The rise of rent is always the effect of the increasing wealth of the country, and of the difficulty of providing food for its augmented population. It is a symptom, but it is never a cause of wealth; for wealth often increases most rapidly while rent is either stationary, or even falling. Rent increases most rapidly as the disposable land decreases in its productive powers. Wealth increases most rapidly in those countries where the disposable land is most fertile, where importation is least restricted, and where through agricultural improvements, production can be multiplied without any increase in the proportional quantity of labor, and where consequently the progress of rent is slow.[29]

In the classical scheme of things, high rents are associated with increasing population, and may be coincident with accumulations of capital. But in later stages of development they may retard economic progress, as we shall see.

[29] *Op. cit.,* p. 77.

Threat of population

The eighteenth century was in many ways a period of great optimism among those who today might be considered "New Frontier liberals." This easy faith in the coming perfectibility of man and his condition irked the Reverend T. R. Malthus so much that he wrote an "Essay on Population,"[30] and subsequently an economics textbook. It was mostly as a result of his views that Thomas Carlyle was later to call economics "the dismal science."

Malthus had two simple and very undeniable postulates: "First, that food is necessary to the existence of man. Secondly, that the passion between the sexes is necessary, and will remain nearly in its present state."[31] From these premises he reasoned that "the power of population is indefinitely greater than the power in the earth to produce subsistence for men."[32]

Yet the human population of a country does seem somehow to be kept in check. It does not keep doubling every quarter of a century or so. Malthus lists various "positive" checks that operate through the death rate, such as wars and pestilence and—above all—malnutrition and poverty. He noted that child mortality rises when wages fall due to overpopulation. He also noted, especially in what today might be called "emerging" cultural groups, a "preventive" check. Many people, in order to climb the social ladder, will postpone marriage so as not to be unduly burdened by the expense of many children. Deferment of marriage—sometimes termed "moral restraint"—was the only manner of reducing the birth rate that Malthus considered practical and acceptable. He was opposed to all methods of preventing conception as a result of sexual intercourse. And he was not at all sanguine regarding the possibility of reducing the frequency of intercourse within marriage.

In later life Malthus was to accord more importance to the preventive check. There was evidence to be seen in Britain of improving conditions among the lower classes. Regarding this phenomenon, he commented in his subsequent *Principles:*

This great increase of command over the necessaries of life did not . . . produce a proportionate increase of population. It found the people of this country living under an excellent government and enjoying all the advantages of civil and political liberty in an usual degree. The lower classes of people had been in the habit of being respected, both by the laws and the higher orders of their fellow citizens, and had learned in consequence to respect themselves. And the result was that, instead of an increase in population exclusively, a considerable

[30] T. R. Malthus, *First Essay on Population* (1798) reprinted by The Macmillan Company (London, 1926).
[31] *Ibid.,* p. 11.
[32] *Ibid.,* p. 13.

portion of their increased real wages was expended in a marked improvement of the quality of the food consumed, and a decided elevation in the standard of their comforts and conveniences.[33]

Unfortunately it is the earlier dogmatic and more hopeless views of Malthus' first essay that are usually remembered.

Today, in the third quarter of the twentieth century, there is again a lot of easy optimism regarding development in countries that have uneconomic cultures and serious overpopulation. In such circumstances the forebodings of Malthus and other classical writers cannot be ignored by either economists or politicians. These gloomy prospects need constant restatement "from a conviction that they are really in the picture. . . . and not from a jaundiced eye, or an inherent spleen of disposition."[34]

DEVELOPMENT "DYNAMICS" OF CLASSICAL ECONOMICS

Classical economic theory—always recognizing differences of viewpoint between Malthus and Ricardo and among other writers—contains the elements of a highly aggregate and dynamic model of economic development. The entire model itself is not explicit, nicely and tidily described in one place, but the main components are all there. And in general terms the recurrent theme is that pressure of population on limited natural resources, despite increases in capital stock during the interim, will finally prevent further economic improvement.[35]

Aggregate dynamic model

The main elements of this dynamic system—allowing a little license for synthesis—are illustrated in Fig. 4-1. The horizontal axis represents population, or labor force, it being assumed that these tend to vary in the same proportions. (If one wishes to assume a steady annual percentage increase in population, this axis could be given a logarithmic scale, and designated "time" instead.) The vertical axis represents the money value of total national output and of various factor's aggregate shares in it.

First, the real wage of common laborers stays near the subsistence wage (w), so that aggregate payments as wages (W) are a constant multiple of L, the labor force (i.e., W equals $L \cdot w$): the W curve, a straight line from the origin in the diagram, shows total real wage payments as a function of population (also a constant multiple of L).

33 Op. cit., p. 253–254.
34 Malthus, First Essay on Population, op. cit., p. iv.
35 Chapter 18 includes a neo-classical reformulation of some of these same ideas (see pp. 342–345).

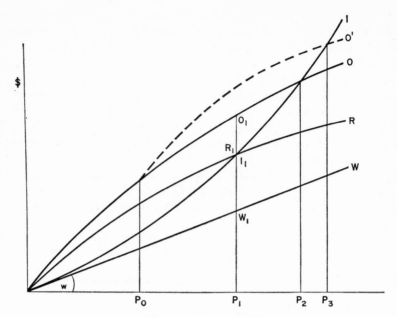

Fig. 4-1. Classical Growth Model.

Second, there is a national output curve (O), which rises as labor (and presumably capital) increases. For a while, if capital accumulation is rapid enough, the absolute output increment may suffice to raise income per head (despite no new inventions), but this case is not illustrated in the diagram. In the end, because of population pressure on limited natural resources, these absolute increments will become smaller and the O curve will rise less rapidly and curve increasingly toward the right. The vertical difference between the O curve and the W line is Marx's surplus value. And surplus value, whether paid to capitalists or landlords, is the main source of savings.

Third, as diminishing returns worsen, rents per acre of the fixed land resource will increase. The total real income of landlords from rents will increase. And this is shown by the vertical difference between the O and R curves.

Fourth, there is some minimum total amount of income that capitalists must receive as profits and interest if they are to maintain—and not start to consume—the stock of capital already accumulated and used in production. The simplest notion is that they will only keep and add to the capital stock if some minimum yield is received from current aggregate investment. Hence the total "minimum necessary interest" earnings can be estimated from existing real accumulations and appear in the diagram as the vertical difference between curves I and W, where I (referenced ordinately to W) is necessary aggregate interest on current total investment. (Incidentally, landlords and capitalists are not two mutually exclusive groups. Many landlords will also be capitalists. Both may consume less than their incomes, which are derived from surplus value, and so invest.)

Fifth, given the state of arts, any increase in national income from year to year is attributable to increased labor and capital. However, because of diminishing returns, capital to labor ratios must increase if total surplus value is not to diminish. The rise in the O curve, relative to the W curve, depends very considerably upon the ability and willingness of factory owners and landlords to invest.

All the makings of eventual stagnation are now in the model. The working population cannot grow unless total wage payments increase proportionately. As population increases, rents must increase more than proportionately. The fraction of total output that remains as a reward to capitalists—*i.e.*, that does not go to workers or landlords—must decline with population growth. However, if absolute surplus value is not to decline as population increases, total capital accumulation must be increasing proportionately more than population growth.

But it cannot do so. In the end, capital accumulation will come to a stop, because the minimum necessary payments to capitalists, even to maintain capital investments, cannot be covered. If there is no more net capital accumulation, output can only increase if there are more workers; but if total absolute income to landlords and capitalists is to be maintained, aggregate real wages cannot increase enough to support extra working-class families.

Diagrammatically, because it is where the R and I curves cross, there is a crisis at P_1. Surplus value (O_1W_1) is just enough to pay rents (O_1R_1) *plus* the minimum necessary interest (W_1I_1). This last magnitude is based on the total capital stock that, together with P_1, was able to produce O_1. Net investment ceases. And, without more accumulations of capital, there is not enough extra subsistence to support more workers.

Of course, although the classical economists would not readily have admitted it, private land ownership is a social institution and not an economic necessity. The productivity of land does not depend upon whether it is privately owned. If all landlords suddenly died, or all rents ceased to be paid, the land and its uses would continue to exist.

Accordingly, at the price of a social revolution however, an economy could eliminate private land ownership and so continue to P_2. At this point the O and I curves intersect. And, unless some way is contrived to occasion net investment at a lower yield, capital accumulation and population growth cease.

All this ignores inventions, however. If the nation in question is now at P_0, and there are significant improvements in technology, the economy has a new lease on life as it were. The output curve will be raised (dotted O' curve), partly because of the advanced state of art, but also because with more surplus value there will be more annual net investment and a greater total capital stock. Hence there would really be a new and higher minimum necessary interest curve (not shown). Final stagnation, assuming no landlords, will be approximately where O' and I intersect with a P_3 population.

It should be stressed again that this graphic presentation appears nowhere in classical economic literature. It is merely a rational and more or less consistent summary of not always unanimous views. The often prolix prose style of the early nineteenth century did not always lend itself to succinct theorems.

Critique of system

Many criticisms may be made of this far too simple and abstract scheme of development.

The classical economists were thinking in terms of the Europe they knew, and especially of Britain, and they often seemed to assume that the only possible division of society was a rigid one between capitalists (including entrepreneurs), landlords, and workers. They accepted the institution of private property, and especially ownership of land, as something inviolable. Public enterprise being unknown on any scale, it did not occur to them that part of surplus value might be taken by the State, and so be added to society's stock of capital.

Land rents, although useful as a means of determining how land is to be used, are not needed to make it physically available. Natural resources, unlike capital and labor, already exist to be used. So rents are in a sense artificial, a result of property rights, and are usually justified because it would be highly inequitable to prevent their payment to persons who have chosen to buy land, rather than other earning assets, with their savings or wealth.

It is also obvious that the whole concept of surplus value depends upon a rather rigid theory of long run wage determination. Experience has shown that a middle class can emerge from the lowest orders and that its per capita income can vary greatly. Much of an advanced society's savings come from those who own no property but instead earn their incomes.

One of the greatest omissions in the classical schema is the part played by technology and science in economic development. Extra output was mostly attributed to extra capital—which "fructified" labor—and increased division of labor. Invention and innovation to the classical economists seem to have been a discrete rather than a continuous affair. There are reasons for this blind spot. The great inventions of the Industrial Revolution had not been made when Adam Smith was writing: even in Mill's time, these are mentioned as though they were unusual events. The very term "industrial revolution," which was not commonly used until the latter part of the nineteenth century, implies an unusual rather than a normal series of events. Consequently, although all economists have always set some hopes on improvements in the "state of arts," until the twentieth century this seemed a very trivial weight to set against high birth rates as a threat to economic welfare.

In defense of the classical economists, who were all men of great intellectual attainment, they should never be judged according to more familiar popularizations of their views. The political history of Europe during their times describes how the emerging capitalist classes overcame the privileged positions of the landowning nobility. Repeal of the Corn Laws, which accorded protection to agriculture, became one of the most famous battles of this war. The new industrialists found that almost everything the classical economists wrote could be simplified to serve as arguments in this domestic struggle. *Laissez-faire,* free trade, wages "naturally" limited to something like a minimum of subsistence, all this was very much to their taste. Nor were capitalists averse to an economic doctrine that cast landlords as the enemy and themselves as the ally of economic progress. Hence the views of men like Ricardo were given the greatest possible publicity. Even young ladies were instructed by popular writers in political economy. For every person who has ever read Smith, Malthus, or Mill in the original, there must be a hundred who have only read *about* their views, which is a very different matter.

Applicability to today

In the underdeveloped countries of today, among the officials who evolve their development plans, classical economics are customarily not thought to be of much use. Certainly, as regards analytic techniques, economics has come a long way in the last hundred years. For example, the classical writer had no theory of demand and supposed that commodity prices are based on the labor cost of producing them; they had no principle of marginal productivity to explain distribution of output among factors; and they tended to think in terms of wealth stocks rather than income flows. But, in broader terms, the classical doctrines are both highly relevant and perhaps irrelevant to economic development in backward countries.

The economic similarities between today's undeveloped countries and the Europe of 1750 to 1850 are fairly considerable and have been remarked upon. Then as now there were limited capital stocks and high birth rates. Much of the economy was of a subsistence nature. There was limited specialization in production. Industrialization was beginning. The common people earned little more than a bare livelihood.

However, there are many economic, political, and social differences.

In Britain, at least, there was already an important stock of techniques and ideas. An agricultural surplus was developing. A substantial middle class of entrepreneurs and traders already existed. There was law and order. Despotic rule had been replaced by parliamentary government. Economic progress was seen as the result of private enterprise. The entire population spoke the same language and subscribed for the most part to the same cultural values. Almost none of these circumstances exist in many backward countries of today. Accordingly, although certain principles—such as those of diminishing returns and the division of labor—are universal, it is uncertain whether the policies of the classical economists can prove effective in the absence of something like the political and social conditions that prevailed in Europe in the eighteenth and nineteenth centuries.

5

Development through
science and technology

One of the paradoxes of economic history and thought is that early nineteenth century writers feared eventual stagnation when all around them were ever more examples of the amazing ability of science and technology to multiply output. In fact, the material record of the Western world during the past century is essentially one of how novel and vastly improved ways of satisfying man's wants were discovered and adopted. Even so, with a few exceptions, professional economists have paid little systematic attention to this process of *innovation*—the embodiment in commercial practice of some new idea or invention. One of these exceptions was Joseph A. Schumpeter, who sought to show that the source of private profits is successful innovation, and that this in turn is the essence of economic development.

Since then, there has been an increasing awareness that improvements in practiced arts involve various distinct stages, namely disinterested scientific discovery, useful invention, and finally a profitable innovation. Economic progress in the advanced nations has included all three stages. But in the world's backward countries the principal need is for innovation, for they can often draw upon the world's backlog of knowledge and invention. Selected innovations alone, without another new invention anywhere on earth, could raise their incomes enormously.

But this still leaves important questions. How are the backward countries to select and make desirable innovations? Will innovation be made by government? Or, if undertaken by private enterprise, how can innovations be expedited through incentives, education, and knowledge?

TECHNOLOGY A FACTOR OF PRODUCTION

Events in the Western world during the past one hundred years suggest that something that might be termed "technology" may well be a fourth factor in addition to labor, "land" (natural resources), and capital. During this period there was at least a threefold increase in the popula-

tions of the advanced nations. Their per capita incomes also increased
severalfold. "Classical" economics—as shown in the last chapter—included
this possibility in principle. It was always recognized that what was
termed the O curve in the last chapter might keep shifting and inclin-
ing upward because of improvements in the arts. But this was not expected to be enough to prevent population pressure from eventually
bringing economic progress to a halt. Something unexpected and important has obviously happened in the interim. And that something was
an unprecedented rate of scientific and technical advance.

Physically, natural resources are as limited as they always were. But
they have come to have new uses, exploration for resources has become
more effective, and distant mineral, soil, and climatic assets have become
economically useful through better transport. These changes are attributable to technology.

Economists used to fear that population would outstrip available food.
However, very large and previously unused areas of the world have since
been put into food production, largely through a revolution in transport.
New steamships came to link Europe and the newly settled countries of
America and Australasia. This had the effect of encouraging immigration to them. Sure and rapid transportation by ship made it economical
to import all sorts of foods and fibers from these countries. The penetration of their hinterlands by rail also increased the land area that could
be used for cultivation and grazing. Refrigerator ships made it possible
to bring chilled and frozen meats over long distances. All these innovations had the effect of extending overseas the land area used for feeding
Europe. The economic result was to raise the effective land to population
ratio by placing the new world's territories at the service of the old world's
population.

Agricultural techniques also made enormous strides during this period.
Although many books have been written on the subject, city-dwelling
economists tend to neglect these advances, and a few examples will have
to suffice here. Research revealed the principles of nitrogen fixation and
the proper use of fertilizers. Biologists developed new strains of seed,
such as Northern wheat and hybrid corn. Selective breeding of livestock
increased yields of meat, milk, and eggs. The Industrial Revolution also
aided that in agriculture. The farm implement industry enormously increased rural labor productivity. The internal combustion engine obvi-
ated the cost of maintaining horses for power. Ocean freight brought
Chilean nitrates within economic reach, and later chemistry enabled artificial fertilizers to be produced. Even such a simple innovation as barbed
wire markedly cut the cost of supervising livestock and facilitated selective breeding. For these and other reasons, the growth of population in
the Western world did not prevent a rising level of individual food consumption.

Power for use in production has always been a limiting factor in economics. The eighteenth century knew only the power of wind and water and the strength of beasts and humans, but it was on the eve of the steam engine. Oil began to replace coal as a source of heat for generating steam late in the nineteenth century. During the present century the internal combustion engines not only replaced steam engines in many uses but also came to power new products, such as motor cars, farm tractors, and airplanes. Today economic and peaceful uses of atomic power may be only a decade away.

Exploration for minerals, and particularly for petroleum, has become far more effective during the past quarter-century. New oil and ore reserves are constantly being proven so that the world's known reserves tend to increase despite constant depletion. Large oil reserves may yet be found in sub-Sahara Africa.

Water has long constrained development in some areas. But many of these areas have ready access to salt water. Economical methods of desalination will almost certainly be available soon.

Until twenty-five years ago, man had to use the wood, stone, and fibers that nature provided. Nylon, a synthetic fiber, became available for public use in 1939. Since then an entire family of synthetic materials has come into being. Plastic products of all sorts are now made, including sailing yachts that can be made in molds.

New products, as well as new materials and processes, have become commonplace. The twentieth century has welcomed airplanes, telephones, radios, antibiotics, computers, and electrical domestic appliances. The electronics industry, including commercial television, has come into being during the lives of present college students.

No one questions the ability of Man increasingly to control his environment and produce more efficiently. Scientific discovery and economic innovation seem to be proceeding at an accelerating pace that sometimes wearies the mind although easing the body. To many people, in both advanced and backward countries, the innovation of these wonders seems to be the essence of development. Many economists are of the same opinion.

Various studies of advanced countries suggest that increases in national output are primarily attributable, not to increases in capital and labor, but to increases in something called "productivity." Thus, National Bureau of Economic Research estimates for the United States, during the eight decades from 1869–78 to 1944–53, indicate that (1) net national product in constant prices increased about twelvefold; (2) population and labor force approximately tripled, and (3) capital—as usually defined—increased nearly ten times.[1] *Per capita*, net national output quadrupled,

[1] M. Abromovitz, *Resource and Output Trends in the United States Since 1870*, Occasional Paper 52, National Bureau of Economic Research, New York, 1956, pp. 6–12.

the capital input tripled, and the labor input remained about the same.

Superficially, it might be inferred from these estimates that most of the output increase was due to capital increase, but this is neither probable nor logical. Capital, relative to labor, actually made a comparatively unimportant contribution to extra output during most of this period. At least this is so if the relative contribution of capital and labor to output is indicated by their relative earnings. And, if the changing contribution of capital to output per head can be assumed to be proportionate to changes in capital per head, nearly all the per capita output increase during this period must be attributed to "the complex of little understood forces" that comprise "productivity."

Abromovitz' own explanation is as follows:

Suppose we combine our indexes of labor input *per capita* and of capital supply *per capita* with weights proportionate to the . . . incomes going to labor and property, respectively. If we may equate productivity with earnings, we obtain a combined index of resources which has a particular meaning. It tells us how net national product *per capita* would have grown had the productivity of resources remained constant at base levels while only the supplies of resources per head increased. Such an index, based on the 'twenties, rises only some 14 per cent between the 'seventies and the last decade. To account for the quadrupling of net national product *per capita,* the productivity of a representative unit of all resources must have increased some 250 per cent. This seems to imply that almost the entire increase in net product *per capita* is associated with the rise in productivity.[2]

This striking conclusion, as Abromovitz points out, is subject to various reservations. One is the weighting of labor and capital inputs according to their relative incomes in a particular decade. Another is the concept of "capital," namely: the net increase of land, structures, durable equipment, commodity stocks, and foreign claims. If the capital concept were broadened to include expenditures for health, education, and training, more of the output increase would be held attributable to "capital," and hence less to "productivity." In a market economy, producing far above the minimum of subsistence, more types of expenditure, including some for recreation even, may incidentally increase output.

The basic finding, even including expenditures for health, education, and training in "capital," is of extraordinary importance nevertheless. It is that an unspecified amalgam termed "productivity" is many times more

---

See also related studies by John W. Kendrick, *Productivity Trends: Capital and Labor,* Occasional Paper 53, 1956; and Solomon Fabricant, *Basic Facts on Productivity Change,* Occasional Paper 63, 1959. These studies make use of pioneer research by W. I. King and Simon Kuznets.

2 *Op. cit.,* pp. 10, 11.

important than extra "capital" in explaining increases in per capita output. A great deal of this increased "productivity" must comprise innovations—*i.e.*, new and improved ways of doing things—that have resulted from scientific discovery, technical inventions, and entrepreneurial experiment. If so, something called "technology" may in some senses be considered a fourth factor of production, along with labor, capital, and land.

PROGRESS THROUGH INNOVATION AND PROFIT

One of the first economists since Adam Smith to make economic development his principal concern was Joseph A. Schumpeter. The classical school, since Ricardo, had become increasingly involved in questions of value and distribution. Meanwhile the economies of Western Europe and North America (such was the force of new techniques in industry and agriculture) had been experiencing an explosive growth. Contemporary economists were, of course, quite aware of the increasing importance of the new technology. But the first economist to incorporate innovations within economic theory, and to make them the main explanation of growth and profits, was the young Schumpeter of 1911.[3]

Although he had the private capitalist economies of the advanced countries primarily in mind, Schumpeter's views on innovations are relevant to still backward economies. Certainly no underdeveloped country of today will achieve real economic progress without widespread innovations. But to what extent these will be made by private or public enterprise is another matter.

Equilibrium without innovation

The impact of innovations on an economy can best be understood by considering the equilibrium that would result if there were no innovations. If there are no new products, no new ways of doing things, no new markets, no new raw materials, and no new organizations for production, the economy will come into a sort of equilibrium. This equilibrium is typified by what Schumpeter termed the *kreislauf*—the "circular flow."

The circular flow has many characteristics. For every producing unit, costs equal receipts, so that prices everywhere equal average costs. Actual or potential profits do not exist without innovations. There is no involuntary unemployment of resources. Households neither save nor dissave and cannot change their expenditures to advantage. Farmers cultivate their land in the same way from decade to decade.

The economy can grow physically without developing economically. A

[3] Joseph A. Schumpeter, *The Theory of Economic Development* (Cambridge, Mass.: Harvard University Press, 1934); the subtitle of Schumpeter's classic is "An Inquiry into Profits, Capital, Credit, Interest, and the Business Cycle."

slow increase in population, unless accompanied by some *qualitative* change in the economy, exemplifies growth but does not constitute development. Changes in the circular flow attributable to external causes—such as favorable weather for a large crop—may occasion short run adjustments and a temporary increase in welfare. But economic development stems from within the system, and depends on innovations attempted despite present prices and costs.

Unless for some strange reason the disutility of working or saving is lessened, no person can improve his lot in this equilibrium state without innovation. Because of competition, no producer can raise prices or find equivalent factors at a lower price than his rivals. Landlords can find no producer who will pay a higher rent.

Business uncertainties are presumably all of a kind that can be insured against. The necessary premiums against fire and flood, and other acts of God, can then be considered a normal cost. Because prices and costs are predictable, there are no uninsurable risks that capitalistic purchasers cannot escape, and so society does not have to pay them profits as a reward.[4]

If an economy were to continue year after year without any innovations, it should eventually reach some sort of capital saturation point at which extra net capital adds nothing to output, especially if population is constant. Whether such a stage can be reached when community time preferences are positive is debatable; and whether there is any warrant for assuming high enough incomes to obviate time preferences is extremely doubtful. In any event, because of the supposed certainty of the circular flow, Schumpeter postulated zero interest rates in the absence of innovations, and he envisaged a stationary state as the final fate of such an economy.[5]

The impact of innovations

Innovations prevent the attainment of such stability. Schumpeter asserts that new credits are introduced into the system so that innovating entrepreneurs can break into the circular flow and divert resources to new employments. And because investment in innovations is very risky, such funds must earn interest.

[4] The idea of profits as a reward for bearing uninsurable risks is not explicit in Schumpeter. Its genesis is to be found in Professor Frank H. Knight's theory of risk, uncertainty, and profit. But as Schumpeter assumed no profit in the circular flow, he was implicitly anticipating Knight.
[5] Several writers have debated the compatibility of zero interest rates and constant capital stocks, including Professor Lionel Robbins ("On a Certain Ambiguity in the Conception of Stationary Equilibrium," *Economic Journal*, June, 1930) and Professor Paul A. Samuelson ("Dynamics, Statics, and the Stationary State," *Review of Economic Statistics*, February, 1943). This assumption of Schumpeter's is more essential to his theory of the business cycle than to his economic development theories.

It is now necessary to distinguish between ordinary producers who do the same old things and entrepreneurs who innovate. The latter think they see new ways of satisfying human wants with scarce resources. Events may prove them wrong, in which case there will be a loss of capital, suffered by those who advanced it. Or the innovation may be successful, in which case those who invested will be secure, and receive interest besides.

Schumpeter conceives the functions of the entrepreneur and the capitalist to be quite distinct in an innovating economy, although in practice they may be performed by the same person. If the innovation is a success —as indicated by a profit above interest and other costs—this accrues to the entrepreneur. But if the innovation is unsuccessful, so that a loss ensues, this actually, if not legally, will fall on the capitalist. Hence the profits of successful entrepreneurs are not a reward for taking risk.

Profits may reward the work and discouragement often incidental to innovation. Or perhaps the sort of people who innovate are motivated by desires other than for money. The profits of innovation are then not a necessary incentive but may be an incidental consequence. Logically, profits are then unearned income, and the economy may not have to reward those who are compelled by temperament to innovate. Schumpeter ascribes three motives to entrepreneurs: the desire to found a private commercial "kingdom" and family dynasty to rule it, the will to conquer and prove one's superiority, and the joy of creating and contriving. The last two motives can be satisfied outside a free enterprise economy. An acquisitive profit-motivated society is best adapted to providing the first incentive however.

What is innovation? Schumpeter conceived of five kinds. First, producing a new good, or one of different quality. Second, producing a good in a new way, which has not yet been tried by anyone. Third, entering a new market, which a particular industry has never previously penetrated. Fourth, taking raw or partly processed materials from an existing source not formerly used by an industry. Fifth, organizing production in a new form, such as creating or breaking a monopoly.

Thus the concept of innovation is a broad one, including changes that improve output-to-input ratios, increase effective demand, reduce input prices, and realize latent economies of scale. Innovation may take the form of supermarkets or industry licensing-pools as well as the introduction of cellophane and automation. It excludes, however, the act of invention itself. To conceive of a safety razor is one thing; but to find funds to develop and produce it as a commercial good and put it on sale is quite another. Invention can remain in the mind; innovation involves action. Inventions that are never innovated have no effect on the circular flow.

Innovations may be undertaken by large existing producers. However, especially in earlier stages of free enterprise development, a majority of innovations may be introduced by new firms established for this very purpose. At any moment there are many new firms attempting through some innovation to shoulder their way into the economy. That a majority may soon fail does not lessen the importance of the others' survival.

A firm that has made a profitable innovation will soon have imitators. But the entrepreneurs that follow are not as original and the capitalists who finance them take less risk. Eventually, the "innovation" is no longer a novelty, and it becomes absorbed into the circular flow.

In a developing economy, innovations in one area may induce other innovations in different but related areas, partly because prices and costs are altered and new supplies and demands result. A successful department store may make it profitable to have an adjoining parking lot. The innovation of an entirely new and major industry, such as automobile-making, may in turn stimulate investment in gas stations, motels, and drive-in movies. These irregular bursts of activity which follow a really major innovation may contribute in advanced countries to economic fluctuations.

Critique

In certain respects the Schumpeterian system, as a theory of economic development rather than one of business cycles, may be too rigid. It is not clear that, even if only indirectly, the cost of innovations must be matched by additions to credit. It is not evident why interest rates must be zero in the circular flow. But it may not be logically necessary to insist that an innovating entrepreneur takes no capital risk and that a capitalist earns no interest unless financing an innovation. And one suspects that in the real world all capitalists and entrepreneurs take some risk at all times, although more so when they are joined in an act of innovation.

One proven innovation may certainly induce additional but related innovations. But the same changes in prices and costs that induce these novelties may also constrain or eliminate some existing operations that are now rendered "obsolete." New firms, with their novel combinations, may lessen profits and capital values for older firms. Some of their recent capital investments might not have been made had certain innovations been foreseen by them. An important social question, which is left begging, is whether private or public enterprise is most likely to innovate at a rate that is higher in some sense.

Schumpeter describes innovation as practiced during the nineteenth century in the advanced countries. Thus the applicability of his description to a backward country with a large public sector is not immediately evident. And some of the distributional aspects of his theory are certainly less relevant when the entrepreneur is a government. A great deal of significance for backward countries remains however. Among the most important of these ideas for development are probably the emphasis on innovation as distinct from invention, the use of profits as a measure and expeditor of improved resource allocation, and qualitative changes as the essence of true economic development.

The distinction between innovation and invention is an encouraging one for backward countries. In many instances, necessary inventions have already been made in advanced countries, and it remains for the backward country to make the indicated innovations. This means that public and private entrepreneurs of underdeveloped countries must somehow select a few innovations from a long list of possible improvements. And those entrepreneurs who wish to innovate must somehow come into command of the necessary resources. These are not minor tasks. But at least the first step of invention has been already accomplished by others.

Profits are still a good first approximation of how usefully economic resources are being employed. In the absence of monopoly, and for goods and services that can be sold, it is reasonable to suppose that resources that yield a profit in a new employment have been reallocated to advantage. Profits are some incentive to innovate. Also, if the making of profits is not a completely fortuitous affair, and people who have made profits in the past are rather more likely to make profits in the future, it is fortunate that these are the very people most likely to command resources for subsequent innovations.[6]

Schumpeter addressed himself in the early twentieth century to one of the main questions of economics. His great spirit was concerned with explaining a nation's increasing income and wealth. He was not so interested in the more niggardly question of how a given national income is distributed; accordingly he underlined the theoretical importance of innovations as the essence of economic development and the main source of increased welfare. He showed that a country that did not develop qualitatively through innovation, but merely grew quantitatively through extra labor and capital accumulation, would in reality remain underdeveloped. Advanced countries, as indicated by historical and empirical studies, confirm these theoretical views.

The moral for all those who seek to improve the economic lot of now backward countries is both obvious and important. Investment without innovation is not good enough. Capital loans without technical assistance are largely a waste.

[6] The ideas contained in the last sentence, perhaps because they would have been considered platitudes at the turn of the century, are implicit rather than explicit in Schumpeter's early writings. It is also worth noting that, despite such views, Schumpeter liked on occasion to assert that he was a Marxist But Marxists did not usually agree!

CONDITIONS THAT FAVOR INVENTION
AND INNOVATION

It is remarkable that, of all the countries in the world, Great Britain, the United States, and Germany, followed by the Soviet Union, Sweden, and France, have contributed nearly all the important economic inventions of the past two hundred years. And it is also remarkable that, insofar as the more backward countries have adopted these inventions, innovation has more often than not been effected by aliens. There must be some broad cultural reasons for this amazing disparity between advanced and backward countries.

The technological process: invention to innovation

Some remarks concerning the process of innovation are in order before considering possible cultural explanations. Some innovations—but by no means all—have their roots in one or more scientific discoveries. The discovery may be made in a laboratory by a university scientist who is quite uninterested in any possible commercial consequence. His discovery may concern the behavior of high-frequency radio waves, the collision of atomic particles, or the chemical reactions of previously unobserved micro-organisms. Major discoveries of this kind are, with few exceptions, made only in the advanced countries.

Inventions are more practical ideas. The biographies of most inventors reveal that they were obsessed by the desirability of finding a better way to fulfill some particular need. With this requirement almost constantly in mind, they often stumbled, almost accidentally, upon a solution. In other cases, and increasingly nowadays, inventors have worked deliberately in search of the "invention." In so working, they have tried, more or less systematically, to apply certain scientific discoveries to human needs.

Case studies of inventions during the past fifty years suggest that more often than not these have been individual rather than team contributions. Such lone inventors, although often prompted by hopes of financial gains, usually have other motives also. In this connection, a recent study of inventions observes:

It may be true that in these days the search for new ideas and techniques is pursued with more system, greater energy, and, although this is more doubtful, greater economy. Yet chance still remains an important factor in invention and the intuition, will and obstinacy of individuals spurred on by the desire for knowledge, renown, or personal gain the great driving force in technical progress. . . . In many fields of knowledge, discovery is still a matter of scouting about on the surface of things where imagination and acute observation, supported only by simple technical aids, are likely to bring rich rewards.[7]

[7] J. Jewkes, D. Sawers, and R. Stillerman, *The Sources of Invention* (London: The Macmillan Company, 1958), pp. 223, 224.

The same study remarks that all new inventions do not have their roots in new scientific advances: there are myriads of technical possibilities inherent in the existing stock of scientific knowledge but only a few people seem to have the gift to see and exploit them.

The exploitation of an invention normally involves hand production of prototypes, pilot plants, or "breadboard" models. The "proving" costs that are thus incurred may amount to several millions of dollars in extreme cases, and in all cases will require the cooperation of some individual or corporate capitalist. Traditionally, inventors have joined hands with a capitalist by borrowing funds or selling patent rights. Nowadays, the inventor may be salaried and simply sign his rights over to his employer.

The next stage of development is engineering for production. The prototype may have been put together by skilled workmen using simple tools. The entire product may now have to be redesigned for large scale production. Specialized equipment, which can be tended by relatively unskilled workers, will be needed. Materials have to be put to new uses. Launching a product into mass production involves technical novelties that really constitute subsidiary inventions.

Introduction of a new idea to the market is the final step in the innovation process. In fact, many innovations do not depend directly on new scientific inventions, but constitute the marketing of a novelty. Drive-in movies are an example: talking movies, mobile loudspeakers, and automobiles already existed when the first entrepreneur conceived of this new, cheaper, and in some ways more enjoyable way of seeing motion pictures.

Circumstances favoring invention

The conditions that favor patentable inventions are not necessarily the same as those that favor innovations. They are in some respects more rigorous. For several decades to come, most new inventions are likely to be made by persons who, by virtue of education and training, are of European (or North American) culture.

Inventions germinate in the soil of intellectual freedom. The culture must encourage scepticism toward existing practice, a pragmatic rather than a doctrinaire approach to problems, and expression of independent views. Novelties must not be suspect because they are new. Ideas must be valued for themselves and not for their conformity with dogma. It may or may not be a coincidence that most of the inventions associated with the Industrial Revolution were made in predominantly Protestant countries.

A majority of inventions are an attempt to match existing technical knowledge with human needs. The inventor who makes the match must know something of both. It follows that inventions are most likely to occur where there is ready access to such knowledge—through professional journals and meetings, for example—and where human needs are both varied and changing. The advanced countries have many advantages in both respects. It is not that they possess a greater store of knowledge—for backward countries can subscribe to most periodicals—but that they have so many more people with the professional training necessary to understand what mankind has learned. This particular division of labor, permitted by the size of the economy, is a necessary condition of further technological advance.

The very increase of existing products induces additional ones. Electricity within the home makes electric vacuum cleaners possible. Suburban life, based on the automobile, occasions supermarkets. Television sets beget TV dinners. So many goods are in joint demand with others that, even at constant incomes per head, there is a tendency for the variety of goods to increase exponentially.

Government policy can do much to help or hinder invention. Nearly all governments, through the grant of patents, attempt at least to stimulate invention through the hope of profit. In countries with high income taxes a further encouragement for profitable firms is deductability of research and development costs from taxable income. And it should go without saying, such are the costs of bringing out a new product, that any owner of a successfully innovated invention should be secure against arbitrary exactions by government officials who wish to share in his profits.

Encouraging innovation in backward countries

At present there are many circumstances that actively discourage innovation in backward countries. The pervasive and inhibiting influences of an uneconomic culture, in which money incentives are dulled, have already been touched upon in Chapter 2. Innovators encounter and cause social antagonism. Poor people cannot afford to satisfy more than their most obvious and immediate needs. Inventions that have already been developed abroad, and that would be suitable to a backward country, may simply remain unknown. The time and capital required to adapt equipment and labor may be lacking. Government, at the instigation of rival interests threatened by some innovation, may intervene to render it unprofitable or illegal.

A major handicap of many underdeveloped countries is that they have lacked an entrepreneurial middle class. It is these people—in some respects equivalent to the bourgeoisie of Europe one and two centuries ago—who almost alone have the personal and financial abilities needed for successful innovation. As Bauer and Yamey state:

The ability of individuals to perceive new opportunities for profit and the ability and willingness to exploit them are indeed crucial in economic development. The activities of . . . entrepreneurs who introduce new crops or techniques of production or open new trading routes and areas of cultivation, and of those who appreciate the potentialities of new ideas and novel methods and adopt and adapt them for local use, raise the level of the economy. The economy is especially fortunate when the qualities of the entrepreneur are possessed by individuals who are also resourceful, thrifty, and industrious.[8]

Unfortunately, although races born of different cultural traditions presumably possess the same distribution of intelligence among individuals, there do currently seem to be differences in their possession of entrepreneurial attributes.

It has often been remarked that innovations are often made in backward countries by alien races. The record of Europeans throughout the rest of the world is familiar. Not so well-known are the activities of Chinese traders in Malaya, Indonesia, and French Oceana, of Indian traders in East Africa and Fiji, and of Levantine traders on both African coasts. In the present century, these immigrants have done for the Malays, Bantu, and Polynesians what the Jews did for Europeans in the late Middle Ages.

It is hard to say why foreign traders so often are needed to leaven a country's development. Not all Indians in India are shrewd and resourceful contrivers. Among possible explanations are that only the enterprising migrate, a new environment has a stimulating effect, and that there are fewer social pressures upon alien immigrants to conform to their own traditional customs.

Of course aliens are not usually popular, especially when they are too successful. Their incomes, although due to ingenuity and energy, will be considered a sort of robbery. Their eventual wealth, although sorely needed by a capital-poor economy, may be circumscribed. Discomfited native traders will agitate against them. Thus, even as European princes would from time to time expel the Jews, so have Panama and Indonesia forced many of their foreign traders to leave. This may also happen in some of the new African states. In such cases the envy and greed of the native population cause them to rid themselves of the very persons who possess the complementary aptitudes that they require.

A regrettable truth is that human nature often stands in the way of developing poor countries. Arthur Lewis writes that:

Many underdeveloped countries, awakening in the middle of the twentieth century to a strong desire for economic development, are embarrassed by what it seems to require in terms of inequality of income, whether as between the "middle classes" and the farmers, as between foreigners and natives, or as between profits and other incomes. For the climate of our day is hostile to income

[8] P. T. Bauer and B. S. Yamey, *The Economics of Under-Developed Countries* (Chicago: University of Chicago Press, 1957), p. 102.

differentials in general, to foreign differentials in particular, and to handsome profits in the extreme. These, however, are part of the cost of development.[9]

It takes a long time for people to understand that, in economic affairs, equity is often impossible without inequality. It is some simple and arithmetic notion of equality that is frequently inequitable.

The prospect for innovation in backward countries is not one of unrelieved gloom however. Certain native races seem almost to be born with an entrepreneurial sense, and are constantly seeking new ways to "turn a penny" in business. Writing about the rural Guatemalans, Sol Tas has observed:

I know of boys eight and ten years of age who have set themselves up in business, buying and selling independently of their parents. Boys of 12 or 14 are apt to be pretty sophisticated traders. I doubt if I know even one man in the region who is not interested in new ways of making money, who does not have, typically, an iron or two in the fire, and who does not make his living partly as a business enterpriser. His wife is often the brains behind the business, too, and women also independently engage in business enterprises of one kind or another. It is therefore easy to go from descriptions of Panajachel [a Guatemalan village] to the writings of classical economists. . . .[10]

However, as already noted, these attributes do not seem to be possessed to date by Bantu, Malays, and Polynesians.

Backward economies may also not be so reluctant to make useful innovations as outsiders may superficially assume. Certain complementary factors that may be taken for granted by imported technical experts may in reality be lacking. A new seed may have a high yield but cannot be ground in primitive mills. Quite simple equipment cannot be maintained by local smiths who only know how to heat and hammer metal. Although tractors might replace bullocks, they use gasoline or oil that is costly and perhaps unavailable, and in regions where there is no other fuel the excrement of cattle may be needed for cooking. Village economies, especially when they barely provide a means of living, are often too integrated to permit of many innovations that seem desirable to an outsider.

Westerners are sometimes too prone to identify innovation with the introduction of revolutionary new equipment such as cotton pickers, electronic computers, or cargo aircraft. A great deal of innovation is rather unobtrusive. A byproduct that used to be thrown away may now be processed and marketed. Some needed material may now be bought rather than inefficiently produced within the family. Spoilage may be

[9] A. W. Lewis, *The Theory of Economic Growth* (Homewood, Ill.: Richard D. Irwin, 1955), p. 182.
[10] S. Tax, *Penny Capitalism—A Guatemalan Indian Economy* (Washington, D.C.: 1953), p. 18.

reduced through improved storage. A new crop may be tried. Or, by new methods, a special attempt may be made to get two harvests instead of one each year. Independent private innovations of this kind involve small changes and limited outlays, but what each lacks in magnitude they together can make up in numbers.

The governments of backward countries can do a number of things to encourage private innovations. Some are fairly short-run, such as the provision of small productive loans, agricultural extension services, and technical advice to small-scale business. There are always selected tax remissions or explicit subsidies by which entry into new activities can be stimulated. Various public utilities, including transportation and communication services, can be undertaken by government: some of these may so reduce certain business costs as to instigate private investment and innovation. Good airport facilities may help to put certain cities internationally "on the map" and so lead to an increased flow of travellers and information. Better newspapers and technical periodicals can be subsidized through zero postal rates on their distribution. Radio, despite the fact that multiple languages are used in many underdeveloped countries, can transmit useful information to rural people through village loudspeakers. In the longer run, all sorts of investments in education are possible, ranging from vocational training to university scholarships abroad.

There are some people, though, who would prefer that government itself perform many of the innovations that have hitherto been left to private enterprise. It is often argued that if there is only a very limited entrepreneurial class, government can save time by establishing and operating various new industries. Whether a man who in private life would be no better than a clerk can be converted into a qualified and imaginative manager by placing him on the public payroll is not entirely certain. Nor is it evident that government alone is able to hire foreign technicians and managers. On the other hand, government commercial operations do have certain advantages, one of them being a comparative immunity from obstruction by other government agencies. Their credit is often, but not always, better than that of a private concern.

We shall turn to these matters again. There is, of course, a great deal of controversy and uncertainty regarding the extent to which government should either encourage private entrepreneurship or engage in industry, commerce, and perhaps agriculture, on its own account. But there is no disagreement or doubt that innovation, one way or another, does have a most important part to play in the development process. Most economists would also probably agree with Schumpeter that:

The slow and continuous increase in time of the national supply of productive means and savings is obviously an important factor in explaining the course of economic history through the centuries, but it is completely overshadowed by the fact that development consists primarily in employing existing resources in a different way, in doing new things with them, irrespective of whether those resources increase or not.[11]

In other words, during the immediate future, an increased tempo of innovation is the principal condition of economic progress. And every society, if it wishes to develop rapidly and economically, must leave a role for Schumpeter's heroic innovator to play.

[11] *Op. cit.*, p. 69.

6

Economics
of innovation

The economics of innovation are not simple and so are frequently misunderstood. Some optimistic officials, planning large loans to under-developed countries for new industries, forget that innovation requires new kinds of capital and labor. Capital must, then, comprise different sorts of equipment and structures, while labor must acquire new skills and attitudes. The economists' distinction between "labor-saving" and "capital-saving" innovations, and the consequences of this difference for the economy, often seems the opposite of common sense to the man in the street. There is no unanimity as to whether labor-saving inventions are made because wages are rising relative to interest rates or whether wages tend to rise because most inventions just happen to make labor more productive compared to capital. Although most people would hold that underdeveloped countries, because they are comparatively short on capital and long on labor, should favor capital-saving innovations, not a few economists have cited special instances where the opposite may be true. Finally, because new innovations often waste resources only recently invested in previous processes, there has been some debate as to whether private enterprise can and will innovate at a proper pace in an under-developed country. These issues need to be understood.

NEW KINDS OF PRODUCTIVE AGENTS

Innovations are often prevented in backward countries because they use kinds of capital and labor that are not readily available. There may be enough capital and labor in general but a lack of, say, metal-working lathes and machinists in particular. The important distinction here—an old one now fallen rather into disuse—is between general factors and specific agents of production. Thus labor is a productive factor, but veterinarians and pharmacists are productive agents. Similarly, capital is a factor, but wire fencing and long-handled hoes are agents. This distinc-tion is relevant to economic development because all innovations require the employment of new or additional productive agents that the actual innovator initially lacks.

A few examples of necessary agents may help. A peasant who used to grow corn and now wants to raise a wheat crop instead will have to acquire a mower or a scythe. "Modernization" of a railroad by replacing its old steam locomotives will require not only diesel electric engines but also diesel fuel. The establishment of any new industry in a country involves a wide variety of fixed and working capital; thus a leather shoe industry may occasion new demands for both shoe machinery and hides. In the case of industry, rather more than in agriculture, innovation is often too narrowly identified in the public mind with the introduction of some kind of novel machine.

Of course the domestic economy does not necessarily have to produce these new or additional kinds of capital goods. They can be imported, assuming there are exports or loans to finance them. Development planners, however, although conscious of new fixed capital costs, have sometimes forgotten the continuing need for imported materials as working capital.

Innovations usually create a joint demand for both new capital and new labor agents of production. This is also often overlooked by the enthusiastic. But the introduction of farm tractors means that people must be trained to maintain and repair them. The installation of dockside cranes is useless unless men are trained to operate them. Large-scale manufacturing concerns cannot operate unless there are accountants who know how to establish and supervise a set of books that goes beyond merely recording monies received and disbursed. In really backward countries, although most people may be skilled in their own traditional ways, very few are trained in any of the extremely diverse skills that characterize modern commerce, industry, and even agriculture.

Unfortunately it is often much simpler and quicker to provide new capital goods than it is to obtain new labor skills, for where money is of little concern the former can be imported. But in a free society, except at salaries that would be so high as to create all sorts of frictions at home and abroad, one cannot ship the necessary specialist along with every dozen crates of exported equipment. Some of the most notorious development "boondoggles" in recent history have involved the shipment of expensive and intricate equipment to overseas regions where there were almost no people trained to maintain or operate it. Experience has shown that innovation must often wait, not upon specific capital goods, but upon local labor skills.

The apparently obvious alternative of training some of the native population is at best a long run solution. Some "skills" which require only an ability to understand, calculate, and reason may have to begin with an elementary education in reading and arithmetic. This may take a decade.

Still less is the inculcation of certain human qualities and attitudes a short run affair. Honesty, reliability, and self-discipline, all necessary in many employments, cannot be taught in a six-week course. But workers that do not possess these virtues may have a negative value. Expensive equipment can soon be ruined by native labor that forgets to follow a lubrication schedule. Containers that are not properly sterilized or cleaned may spread infection or bring a firm into disrepute. Prize livestock, imported for breeding, may become mysteriously "sick" and die; the herder's family may appreciate them more as immediate food than as progenitors of a new blood line. Thus, in not a few countries, "trained" native labor must initially be closely supervised by foreigners.

The capacity of a country to absorb capital is intimately related to the same lack of specific capital and labor agents that so often prevents more rapid innovation. In a closed economy, where there is no way of importing produced means of production, there might be adequate domestic savings but no new type machinery to buy. In an open economy, and especially one that can finance imports by borrowing from abroad, lack of specific labor agents will be the constraint. Most backward economies find themselves in an intermediate situation; that is, they could import more capital goods if they would increase their exports, but even so they are restrained from innovation by the inferior quality of the domestic labor force.

LABOR SAVING OR CAPITAL SAVING?

Poor countries lack financial capital. It is hence important that their innovations make better use of the scarcest factor. But when is an innovation capital-saving or labor-saving?

Most innovations—in addition to permitting larger outputs or reduced inputs—occasion a change in the relative productivity of the employed factors. After making an innovation, an individual producer may find that at the same wage and interest rates as before he now uses more capital and less labor. In this case, paradoxical though it may seem, the innovation is said to be capital-saving because the marginal productivity of capital as used by him has increased relative to the marginal productivity of labor. However, if this same innovation were made by numerous producers throughout the same industry, other things being equal, it would have the effect of raising interest rates relative to wage rates; the producers in other industries, faced by higher interest rates, would begin to "save" capital by substituting labor for it. In this case the innovators use more capital, but the rest of the economy tries to use less. The conventional terminology is based on the wider viewpoint of the economy.

This can all be better explained by a diagram. Figure 6-1, constructed for a single producer, represents capital (K, measured along the vertical axis) and labor (L, measured along the horizontal axis) employed by him. The units of measurement are money and labor hours, respectively. It is simplest to assume that the enterprise has a single kind of output. The "producer indifference curve" Z then shows all the other combinations of capital and labor that would provide the same output as the producer is making with K_1 and L_1 (capital and labor, respectively). The line iw shows all the other combinations of capital and labor that occasion the same total factor costs as the producer is in fact incurring. Given the scale of inputs, and the relative cost of capital and labor, A marks the most profitable proportions in which to employ these productive factors. The iso-output curve Z is the highest of all such curves that intersect or touch the iso-value input line, iw.

If Z represents a constant physical output, the "cost" of capital must include depreciation of the real capital stock as well as interest expense. If interest rates rise relative to wage rates, the equal factor cost line will become flatter. Lower wage rates will have the same effect.

Suppose now there is an innovation. There will be a new map of iso-output curves having a somewhat different slope and shape. Perhaps the producer wishes to make the same combined money outlay for capital and labor as before, in which case we shall assume that the broken Z' curve

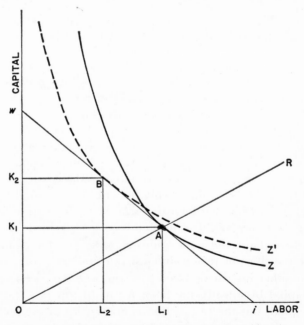

Fig. 6-1. A Capital Saving Innovation (single producer).

is the highest attainable iso-outlay curve of the new family, being tangent to iw at B. A comparison of Z' with Z shows that, after making the innovation and producing a larger output with the same value of inputs, the producer is using less labor (L_2) and more capital (K_2).

If one compares the intersection of Z' and OR with that of Z and OR, it will be seen that Z' is flatter there than Z. Economically, this means that had capital and labor been employed in the same proportions as before, the innovation would have rendered a unit of capital more productive relative to labor than before. Of course the innovation may have made both factors increasingly productive, but capital more so. A unit of capital is now the productive equivalent of more labor than hitherto. Hence this single firm substitutes capital for labor, because its relative prices have not yet changed, and specifically it should employ the quantities of capital and labor indicated by K_2 and L_2.

Innovators have imitators if successful. In time all the producers in the same industry may likewise substitute some capital for a little labor. Other things equal, and unless this industry is an insignificant part of the national economy, there will be a tendency for the price of capital to rise relative to that of labor.

This is schematized by Fig. 6-2, drawn for an entire economy, it

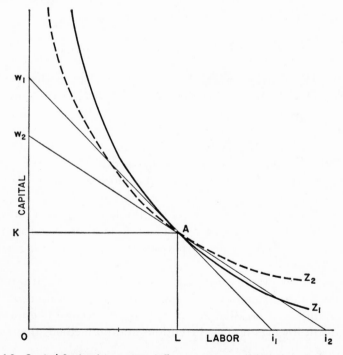

Fig. 6-2. Capital Saving Innovations (effect on wages and interest in the economy).

being assumed that the country has a constant employment of K (capital) and L (labor). The output curves Z_1 and Z_2 are now some index of national output. And Z_2, partly reflecting the altered factor productivities in the industry of innovation, is flatter than Z_1 at A. Assuming the owners of capital and labor services accept the market's dictates, and given constant quantities of capital and labor seeking employment, there must be a new monetary exchange value of capital and labor. The fact that i_2w_2 must be flatter than i_1w_1, if these lines are drawn tangent to Z_1 and Z_2, respectively, at A, shows that interest rates will rise relative to wage rates.[1]

Supposedly all the producers in the economy will tend to adjust to these new factor prices, seeking to use a little less capital with a little more labor. This will very slightly offset the first change in factor prices. But the outcome is that existing producers in all except the innovating industries will try to "save" capital by replacing part of it with labor.

To sum up, a spontaneous innovation that raises the marginal productivity of capital relative to labor at previous factor proportions initially causes producers in the affected industry to use more capital. But as this raises interest rates relative to wage rates, producers in all other industries try to "save" a little capital by replacing it with labor. Therefore, if there is a constant amount of capital and labor to be hired, the innovating industries have taken capital from other industries and given them labor in exchange.

PRICE-DETERMINED INNOVATIONS

The preceding section traced the factor price changes that can be expected to follow an innovation that is "exogenous" in the sense that it came into being independently of factor prices. But many innovations are induced by factor price changes. They are the result of entrepreneurs seeking to introduce entirely new methods that increase the productivity of those factors that are becoming more expensive.

During the past fifty-odd years, in the more advanced countries at least, the value of invested capital (in constant dollars) has increased about three to four times more than has the labor supply. Consequently labor has become more expensive relative to capital in these nations. And the reactions of firms has in turn contributed to the rising wages of labor.

There is an important conceptual distinction between adjustments of a firm along an existing output isoquant and the innovation of entirely new techniques that occasion an entirely new isoquant. The former sort of adjustment involves no new inventions and no methods that were not

---

[1] Depreciation of capital stocks is assumed unchanged.

formerly known. But adoption of an isoquant from an entirely new family of hitherto unrecognized isoquants constitutes a change in the state of arts. It is one thing for a firm to alter its operations in a way that may be new to it but not to others in the same industry. It is another to introduce methods that have never been used before in the country.

This sort of innovation is often undertaken in response to a persistent tendency for one factor to become relatively more expensive. Once such a trend is recognized, industrial inventors will concentrate their attention on making better use of the appreciating factor. And firms may introduce methods that may not be much more economical now, but promise to be so when labor, for instance, becomes still more expensive later.

Even if inventions by scientists are "neutral" as between labor and capital, the innovations of producers may be induced, for they tend to exploit only those inventions that offer a way of escaping the higher priced factor. It is as though producers are diners in a restaurant where the chef invents new dishes. If meat is becoming more expensive, the diners select from the menu those new recipes that make a little meat seem to go further. Producers similarly favor innovations that promise to make labor more useful when wages are rising.

This spiral effect—labor being rendered more productive because it is becoming scarce relative to capital—is of course very advantageous to labor in advanced countries. But in many backward countries, where it is capital that is becoming relatively scarcer, the spiral tends to be downward for labor. The common people, who live from their work, may benefit only very indirectly from capital-saving innovations. In poor countries where labor is not the scarce factor, a majority of innovations are perhaps induced by comparatively high capital costs, and the marginal product of labor falls relatively as a result.

SHOULD CAPITAL-POOR ECONOMIES FAVOR CAPITAL-SAVING INNOVATIONS?

A common characteristic of underdeveloped countries is a low ratio of capital to labor. Evidence of this is high interest rates (sometimes double comparable rates in advanced countries) and low wages for common labor (perhaps fifty cents a day). Capital scarcity is also revealed by the lives of the people. Women fetch water from a well, goods are carried inland by human porters, and messages are sent by runners. The importance of even simple capital equipment can be seen from the frantic efforts made to get broken-down trucks and bicycles going again. In everyday occupations the addition of simple capital goods, such as saws, drills, and pumps can enormously increase output. Under these conditions, economic theory assumes that the most desirable innovations are capital-saving ones.

Practice and theory often diverge, however. In many underdeveloped countries the most favored innovations are extremely capital-intensive. There are many human reasons. Such projects are more spectacular and evoke more political support. They are the ones that government can most easily administer. The establishment of modern industries, which are always highly capitalistic, is identified with development. But governments often "develop" even small and existing industries by innovations that require a great deal of extra capital but not much more labor. In this way "show case" companies that have been selected for modernization can demonstrate large gains in output per man. But how economic are such isolated and capital-intensive innovations?

Some of the reasons why most economists are doubtful of these publicized innovations can be explained by Fig. 6-3. Here, Z_1 shows the various combinations of capital and labor that, using old methods, produced 100 units of output at A; and, at the prevailing wage to interest rates of $i_1 w_1$, K_1 capital and L_1 workers are employed. If the decision is made by government to introduce new methods and equipment, so that the 100 output isoquant becomes Z_2, management should suboptimize by using K_2 capital and L_2 labor at B. It is at once evident that output per hour has increased, for the output is still 100 units and L_2 is much less

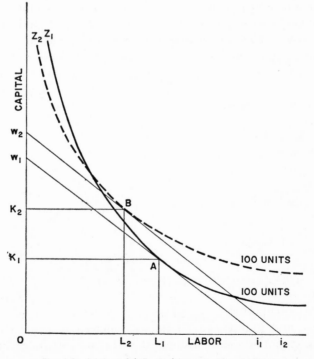

Fig. 6-3. A Wasteful Capital Intensive Innovation.

than L_1. But before everyone congratulates himself unduly, it should be stressed that output per unit of capital has decreased.

The difficulty here and always is that economic efficiency can never be assessed by comparing ratios of output to one of several scarce inputs. A real evaluation must ascertain whether the value of the inputs which produce the constant output has decreased. In the present case, if the interest and wage rates prevailing in the economy have any meaning, inputs of greater value are used after the innovation. The extent of the loss can be represented by i_2i_2. This is a measure of the superiority of other uses of capital and labor that have had to be foregone.

A possible rejoinder is that i_2w_2—parallel to i_1w_1—does not reflect the "true" alternative use values of capital and labor. Perhaps the opportunity costs of labor are really much higher and those of capital much lower. For example, if the factor cost line were steeper than i_2w_2, the capital-intensive innovation could be "economical."

All rules have their exceptions. An imaginative economist, armed with a few special assumptions, can always make a case for capital intensity in capital-poor countries. Five different arguments come to mind.

First, the labor skills needed in new factories may hardly exist in the country, and only people of rather unusual native intelligence may warrant training. Or, with partially trained labor, its true cost may not be wages but damaged equipment and spoiled output. In this case a factor cost line that supposedly relates ordinary wages and interest rates may not be very relevant. The true cost of finding adequate labor and training may be such that it is not really capital but labor that is the scarcer factor.

Second, if a new plant has to be located in an uninhabited area (mining installations, for example, are often in remote regions), the full cost of labor includes the amortized expense of the townships and utilities that must be constructed for the workers and their families. A factor cost line such as i_2w_2, which considers only the wage cost of labor, is irrelevant. (This argument does not apply, of course, to new industrial facilities established in old population centers.)

Third, it is often impracticable to have imported equipment redesigned and specially made for use in low-wage countries. Most underdeveloped countries import the special capital goods they need for oil refineries, shoe factories, canning plants, and the like, from the advanced countries. This imported equipment was originally designed to be economical in plants where labor is highly paid. It is then asserted that the backward country has no discretion: if it wants a particular industry and output, it must take the only producer indifference curve available (*e.g.*, Z_2 in Fig. 6-2). However, while the central processes of many new industries may have to be performed by equipment already designed for use in advanced economies, there are always many ancillary functions that can be made more or less labor-intensive. Materials handling is a case in point.

In a lumber mill, the main log carriage-way and saws may comprise a highly mechanized unit, but the maneuvering of logs and the moving to storage of finished lumber can be done largely by hand. Finally, backward countries need not always import and install the very latest equipment; sometimes a wiser possibility is to purchase second-hand capital, not fully depreciated physically but no longer competitive in high-wage countries. Unfortunately, although military equipment provides a precedent, the sale and purchase of used capital goods are often beneath the dignity of new sovereign governments.

Fourth, it is sometimes held that backward countries need entirely new product industries rather than modernization of existing ones because a greater variety of consumer goods to buy increases incentives to produce and earn. And factories that make ballpoint pens, cameras, electric fans, and so forth, tend to be capitalistic. This argument implicitly assumes, however, that the country in question should produce capital intensive consumer goods rather than import them in exchange for more labor intensive exports. The case collapses if this assumption is invalid. Normally, a capital-poor country should specialize in labor-intensive production and make use of the world economy.

Fifth and finally, a modified version of an idea first advanced by Hirschman,[2] gives theoretical support to the contention that backward countries should always use somewhat more capitalistic processes than advanced ones if the ratio of wages to interest is the same in both countries. Hirschman's argument rests on the assumption that although capital goods in a given industry are the same in both advanced and backward countries, available labor is less reliable and disciplined in the underdeveloped ones. This inferiority is especially evident in operations where the workers are not forced to maintain a certain pace by the machinery they are tending. They are likely then to be lackadaisical, take long breaks, or even wander off. But continuous process plants and assembly line factories—such as canneries and packing plants—compel attendance and application. Although these latter facilities are usually more capitalistic, the extra capital increasingly offsets inferior labor by preventing slackness. And so extra capital may be economical.

This theorem is given in Fig. 6-4. All the producer indifference curves represent the same quantity of output. That for the backward country (Z_b) always lies to the right of Z_a because its labor is inferior. If the same wage and interest ratios prevail in both countries—i_1w_1 and i_2w_2 are parallel in the figure—it is evident that the backward economy should use relatively more capital and less labor in this line of production. At any given K/L ratio, the marginal product of capital is relatively greater in the backward country, because of the inferiority of its labor.

Hirschman's argument can be given a more general applicability. His

[2] A. O. Hirschman, *The Strategy of Economic Development* (New Haven: Yale University Press, 1959), Chapter 4.

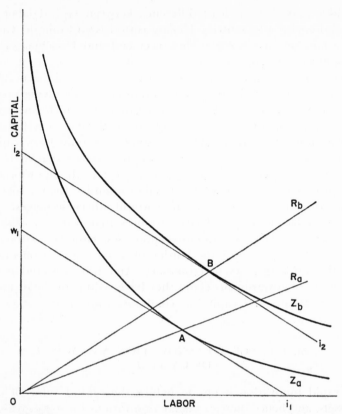

Fig. 6-4. Capital Intensity as an Offset to Inefficient Labor (comparison of single firms producing the same output in an advanced country and a backward country).

diagram has two isoquants almost converging at the most capitalistic processes. Thus he supposed that labor performance in advanced and backward countries is almost identical when a lot of capital is used. This requires an assumption that extra capital investment means capital goods of a specific kind that will pace workers and compel effort.

A more general and equally valid argument can be made by merely assuming that labor in backward countries is inferior to some constant degree. For example, irrespective of the amount of capital combined with them, perhaps one worker in a developed country is the equivalent of two workers in an underdeveloped country. Then, as in fact it has been drawn in Fig. 6-4, the abscissa values of Z_b are always twice as great as those of Z_a for a given ordinate magnitude. The conclusion still holds that the backward country should innovate somewhat more capitalistic processes if its wage-to-interest ratio is similar to those in advanced countries. There is no need to make a special assumption that a higher capital-to-labor ratio reduces the comparative inferiority of labor in backward countries. It could be argued that it is when workers have almost no capital aids that there is least difference between typical labor in advanced and backward countries. Hoeing cotton is an example. Curves Z_a and Z_b would then converge at the lower end and Hirschman's conclusions would be reversed.

The practical significance of this fifth exception to the general rule— *i.e.*, that capital-poor countries should innovate capital-saving processes— should not be exaggerated. Wages are customarily much lower relative to interest rates in underdeveloped countries. Because they are not the same, one cannot state that backward countries should favor capital intensive operations as a rule. The conclusion is rather that, if backward country labor is inferior to some constant degree, the appropriate production process will be somewhat less labor-intensive than a comparison of factor prices in an advanced country would otherwise suggest.

There may be other special circumstances that justify a capital-poor country's innovating capital-intensive processes. However, although few axioms are universally valid, the burden of proof is always on those who gainsay the working rules of economics. And it is a sound principle, especially where governments claim they have redundant labor and must receive loans, that scarce capital be combined with many workers rather than with a few.

RESISTANCE TO INNOVATION AND WASTE
OF CAPITAL

Very rapid innovation is apt to reduce the capital value of existing firms' assets, and hence they may delay innovations for selfish reasons. Although such delay may also be desirable for the economy, because it reduces capital wastage, this is not readily apparent. It is sometimes argued instead that if innovation is left to private enterprise, its pace will be too slow. A common implication is that government, being less sensitive about existing capital values, will innovate more rapidly. Although the "proper" rate of innovation is an extremely complex problem and cannot be treated adequately here, the main elements can be explained. There are some theoretical reasons for supposing it is economic for backward countries to innovate more slowly than advanced countries because of capital scarcity.

Innovation timing by existing firms

There is no special reason why, unless they are in rival supply, a firm making one product should not innovate another. In advanced countries large firms are continually spreading into new industries. If there is a social problem, it is most likely to arise when new and more economical methods are not introduced because management refuses to scrap existing capital that is not yet worked out.

The usual and simple rule is that a firm should not scrap existing equipment and replace it with more efficient capital unless the total unit cost with the new process is less than the variable unit costs with the old. For example, suppose a company produces 1000 units of output a year, has annual variable (prime) costs of $200,000, and total fixed costs attributable to existing equipment of $100,000. (The price of the product does not matter so long as it exceeds $200 a unit.) If new and more efficient capital becomes available, and the physical service life of existing capital has not expired, any contemplated modernization will not be profitable unless the total unit cost with the new method is under $200 and so less than the unit variable cost with existing equipment. At least this is the "static" rule for a private concern.

Observance of this axiom is also in the public's interest. This is a little difficult to understand as the best explanation is a "dynamic" one that involves discounting future receipt and payments to obtain present values. It is also necessary to make some assumptions regarding physical durability of fixed capital. We shall suppose that all a firm's fixed capital must be replaced for physical reasons every twenty-five years and that our specimen firm is currently in its twentieth year. Hence it can use its present equipment for another five years.

If it innovates now, there is a gain and a loss, but the loss is greater. The gain comes from the fact that, with output always 1000 units a year, it will obtain a reduction in variable costs of say $50,000 a year for the next five years that otherwise it would not enjoy: the present discounted value of this gain, at 10 per cent a year compounded, is about $180,000. The loss arises from having to re-equip the plant now and so invest over $700,000 of resources today rather than in five years' time.[3] With discounting at 10 per cent a year compound, such a sum, in five years' time, has a present value of roughly $420,000. Hence, in present value terms, postponing the investment gains about $280,000 (*i.e.*, a present value of $420,000 is $280,000 less than a capital expenditure today of $700,000). Deferring the improvement in operating efficiency loses about $180,000. Thus wastage of fixed capital, from innovating now as against five years from now, is greater than the recovery of working capital by a present value of about $100,000 (*i.e.*, $180,000 − $280,000).[4]

[3] A rough estimate of over $700,000 is obtained by assuming that the $100,000 of annual fixed costs attributable to fixed capital comprises depreciation at 4 per cent a year (25-year service life) and a "necessary" 10 per cent rate of return on the investment. Hence, the "return" portion of the fixed annual costs is a little over $70,000 or 10/14 of $100,000, so at 10 per cent the value of the principal is a little over $700,000.
[4] Logically, one should also consider successive generations of capital and the present value of bringing "forward" in time all their associated fixed and variable costs. Replacement theory is extremely complex. An excellent book, although written from the private rather than public interest, is G. Terborg's *Dynamic Equipment Policy* (New York: McGraw-Hill Book Company, 1949).

The public's concern in this matter has, of course, nothing to do with the private financial fortunes of the owners of the business. That the owners might throw away existing equipment costing over $700,000 five years prematurely, and so lose part of their original investment, no longer concerns the economy. Investments once made are historical costs that logically should not affect decisions of the moment. The public's interest in not having an existing firm innovate now lies in its desire to defer the investment of resources in new fixed capital until such investment is economical.

Innovation timing by new firms

New firms are no respecters of the capital values of existing companies. They are eager to start in business with the most economical capital and methods possible. In so doing they may increase the total supply of a product and thereby cause a price reduction indirectly, or they may deliberately undercut the prices of rival brands. In either event, older firms will obtain reduced receipts; and, as their variable unit costs are presumably constant, they will suffer a decrease in surplus income.

Assuming the same magnitudes of the preceding example, imagine a new firm that uses the new methods already mentioned, so that its unit variable costs are $150 and its unit fixed costs are $100. Perhaps it sets a price of $250. This is met by previous companies that used to charge $300. These older firms still have unit variable costs of $200—unlike the new companies—and so on an output of 1000 units a year only $50,000 rather than $100,000 of surplus income remains for their fixed capital assets. (This remaining income—equal to total receipt minus total variable costs—is sometimes termed *quasi-rent* because in certain ways it constitutes an implicit rent of existing real capital.) If the prospective income of the fixed capital goods is halved, their capital values will also be halved, and so it is that new firms through innovation are constantly threatening the worth of already established rival companies.

Why should society shed tears over such losses? One rather intangible reason is that if there is a widespread expectation of rapid technological change, firms may be inhibited from investing in new processes because an even more efficient one may become available a little later. The decision whether or not to innovate now becomes analogous to a motoring family looking for a good motel to spend the night: this one on the right looks pretty good, but there may be a better one a few miles ahead, but then again delay may mean no vacancies remaining. And, inasmuch as innovations by new firms increase the risks of all other investors, the cost of hiring capital funds is likely to rise.

A more concrete public objection to rapid innovation by new and rival firms rests upon the same reasoning as before. After all, if one thinks of the economy as one large firm, the same principles apply as in the preceding example. If it is uneconomic for a single firm to innovate in order to save working capital having a present value of about $180,000 and thereby waste $280,000 of fixed capital, it is also uneconomic for the country as a whole.

Where the management of an economy is in the hands of numerous and independent private firms, the profit interests of the new firms are in conflict both with those of older firms and perhaps those of the economy in general. It is profit calculations of existing firms—if properly made— that seem to be most in accord with public interest. At least this would be so if there were any assurance that existing firms would be equally vigilant in their search for better methods were there no danger of competition from new firms. Thus new firms may increase capital wastage by innovating—if existing firms would make the same innovations but at the proper time—but they do ensure that new and better processes are introduced.

Time preferences and innovation rates

There are, of course, many reasons why innovation seems to occur at a slower pace in backward countries. Lack of education and knowledge, small markets and ineffective demand, plus disorderly government are some of the explanations frequently advanced. Are there any other inherent economic characteristics of backward countries that otherwise cause them to innovate even more slowly?

Backward countries have been more or less identified in this work with countries that have low incomes per capita. Poor families have a high time preference. Parents with hungry children are apt to place far less value on food a year from now than on food today. Events even a few months away may be discounted heavily. High time preferences are all pervasive in a poor country. They give rise to high interest rates. Hence resources will be invested in additional or better productive processes— and so be lost to producing more goods for current consumption—only if such investments are likely to be highly productive. High interest rates in poor countries indicate not a plenitude of productive investment possibilities but a paucity of loanable funds.

There is at least one way in which high time preferences, reflected in high discount rates, deter innovations by existing firms. If annual discount rates were zero instead of, say, 10 per cent (and reverting to the preceding example), the present value of a $700,000 equipment replacement in five years is $700,000 today. Capital wastage—$700,000 minus $700,000—is zero. A firm (if we assume it has access to capital at no interest) might as well innovate the process today and be done with it. At some positive discount rate below 10 per cent, the present value of postponing the fixed investment is just about equal to the recalculated present value of the potential saving in working capital, at which discount rate the firm and the economy would be more or less indifferent to the question of whether or not to innovate. And, as we have seen, at 10 per cent discount there should not be innovation now.

Granted that innovation in backward countries may tend to be deferred because of high discount rates, is this good or bad from the economy's viewpoint? One could very well argue that in regions where capital is scarce, and interest rates are high, it is more often best to defer innovations that require the premature scrapping of fixed capital that still has many years of service life. If a country has to live from hand to mouth because of its poverty, a slow rate of innovation in existing industries may not be too slow a pace.

High interest rates may in one way encourage innovation by inducing producers to install less durable equipment. Suppose an entrepreneur is about to have a ferry built, with which he will take passengers, livestock, and freight across an inlet, charging toll for the service. Should he invest $50,000 in a scow and engine having a thirty-year life, or should he pay another $15,000 for better materials and construction, so that the ferry will probably last an *additional* twenty years. The present value of tolls to be expected from the thirty-first through the fiftieth year will not justify an extra $15,000 construction cost unless the compound discount rate is very low. Backward countries, where interest rates are high, can make fixed capital goods more durable than they often do. But if resources for investment are very scarce, it is economic to make equipment and structures of a shorter service life than in more advanced and prosperous countries.

If fixed capital has a shorter life, existing producers have more frequent opportunities to innovate. If their capital goods have to be replaced every fifteen years, instead of every thirty on an average, they have twice as many occasions to innovate a new type of equipment or to build a better designed plant. Thus, for *existing* firms, high discount rates make it more likely that new processes will be innovated when and not before old capital expires. Necessary replacement comes sooner and there is a greater penalty attached to junking before wear-out. Scrapping half-used equipment may "pay" in advanced countries where interest rates are low. But it would be a great mistake to suppose that a similar innovation and replacement tempo is appropriate to backward countries.

Much innovation in underdeveloped countries is in entirely new industries. These new industries, making new goods, usually have a very limited impact on the capital values of established companies. In these cases, there is no advantage to prolonging the employment of old equipment because there is none to use.

Even so, high interest rates tend to discourage innovation—but for a different and more general reason. The special inhibiting capital cost in this case is not the cost of new capital goods but the cost of trying to train labor to perform new jobs. These costs include not only the actual costs of training before production begins, but also the subsequent waste of materials and damage to equipment that inadequately skilled workers will always cause. The establishment of a conventional plant where there is already a supply of trained labor does not have these unusual costs. But all innovations, whether they be new products or new processes, do have these extra costs to some degree. They constitute capital costs because they have mostly to be incurred in advance or at the start of production. And so, if interest rates are high, there will be less willingness to provide labor with new skills.

Innovation is costly, involving several kinds of special expenses. If the innovation is a new way of making an old product, and it is necessary to junk still serviceable equipment, this is an extra sort of cost that is less likely to be warranted in high discount rate economies. In all cases, whether or not a new product is involved, there will be extra labor costs. Both these types of cost are peculiar to innovation and so constitute additional costs. Moreover, as they have to be met in advance, they are capital charges. Incurring these costs is less likely to be truly economic where discount rates are high. And in poor countries, where time preferences are extreme, this is likely to be the case. Accordingly, there are *a priori* reasons for expecting innovation to be less rapid in poor countries, but this may constitute the most economic use of a very limited capital surplus and is not necessarily to be deplored.

7

Expansion of agriculture
or industry?

Granted the importance of innovations and the need to apply new kinds of labor and capital to increase output, there is always the question of what to expand. As more resources become available and can be used in better ways, should they be employed mostly to advance industry or agriculture? Or should individual projects be selected and rejected according to some investment criteria, with the comparative emphasis on agriculture and industry being an incidental result of these more numerous and specific decisions? Should an attempt be made to produce a little more of everything, according to the country's market demand patterns, or should output of a few products be stressed so that the country participates increasingly in world trade? Some knotty problems remain even though extra resources and useful innovations are available.

Only the comparative expansion of agriculture and industry will be considered in this chapter. Narrower allocation questions, and the matter of investment criteria, are considered in Part III. The "industry or agriculture" issue is a heated and crucial one. The controversy concerns not only the broad composition of national product but also the division of population into rural and urban. A way of life is also at stake.

In many countries—rightly or wrongly—industrialization has become identified with economic development. It is pointed out that industrial countries (*e.g.*, the United States) are rich and that poor countries (*e.g.*, Burma) are agricultural. It is usually not mentioned that there are some countries (*e.g.*, New Zealand and Denmark) that are both agricultural and wealthy. Hence, and all too often, industrialization is seen as a cause rather than a result of true economic progress. As a symptom of success, the industrialization that accompanies rising consumption levels is certainly to be welcomed, but an industrialization that is premature and forced by government can be economically wasteful and politically dangerous.

Urbanization is often sought as an end in itself. Living in cities, rather than in innumerable rural villages, people are exposed to more new ideas and are less hidebound by custom. Women become emancipated, are often available for employment, and perhaps have fewer babies. Children can be educated more effectively and given better medical care. Partly for these reasons the twentieth century has been characterized by urbanization even more than by industrialization.

A major consideration regarding the growth of industry, and one too often overlooked, is that innovation requires a great deal of human persuasion. People must be induced to abandon customary procedures, to risk failure and ridicule, all on the advice of some outside expert. In agriculture, where millions of peasants must be convinced that unfamiliar ways are better, there are simply not enough officials and experts to "sell" them new methods. It is easier in industry: new kinds of equipment can be imported, some foreign technicians can be temporarily hired, and the total number of workers that must be trained is comparatively small. Moreover, if these workers are new to industry, they will not have set ideas on how to do everything. Therefore, quite apart from the physical discomforts of rural travel and the social stigma attached to agriculture, it is not surprising that most officials lean to programs that stress industrial rather than agricultural expansion and innovation. The resource in shortest supply, in most backward but developing countries, is officials who can argue ordinary people into forsaking tradition and risking new ways.

THE SUPERFICIAL VIEW

Some of the economic arguments in favor of forced industrialization are less convincing. Of course they vary somewhat from country to country, but the following is a reasonably fair caricature of one commonly held and widely publicized view.

It is alleged that the marginal product of labor in rural employments is extremely low—if not zero. The basis of this impression is not clear. Sometimes Asian examples are cited. In these cases observers feel that a change in the number of village workers would not alter village agricultural output. (From this it has been somewhat illogically inferred that the marginal product of an hour's rural labor is practically zero.)

A considerable fraction of rural labor is therefore supposed to be available to industry as a "free" good. After all, if it has no opportunity costs in agriculture, why not use it in industry? It seems to be assumed that a 48-hour industrial work week, as distinct from rural underemployment, will not involve additional disutilities that must be compensated with pay and goods by a free society.

The only costs of industry, with labor supposedly being freely available to it, are those of capital. Accordingly the best industrial projects are held to be those that have the highest output value, net of material purchases, per unit of employed fixed capital. Hence rival projects, competing for limited capital funds, should allegedly be ranked inversely according to their incremental capital-output ratios (ICOR). In practice, those industrial projects that are labor-intensive will naturally tend to have the lowest ICOR's and so appear preferable.

Of course, if an unkind aside may be permitted, many small scale agricultural operations would also have very low ICOR's. Whether or not real and money capital are the scarce resource, they should be allocated to maximize the total value of all output increases, which means that the value of the marginal product of extra capital in all employments should be as nearly equal as possible. There are no economic grounds for being so prejudiced against agriculture that only industrial projects are considered.[1]

This popular "analysis," although once supported by a few economists, has all the characteristics of an engineer's approach to development problems. This is seen, for example, in the failure to realize that labor is not a free good if the extra disutility of industrial employment must be compensated. But it is most strikingly manifested in the easy assumption that almost any kind of industrial output will have a higher market value per unit of capital than will extra agricultural output.

Who will be willing and able to buy the output resulting from forced industrial expansion? Industrial workers cannot buy it all. Their total pay will be less than total costs of industrial production. And some, if not most of their wages must buy food. There is a limit to the total demand of an agricultural sector for the output of domestic industry. Of course there is always an export demand—but often only at a price below domestic unit costs of production—so this is not a sure solution.

It does not necessarily follow that because a marginal worker in agriculture now has a zero output, a country should industrialize. The product of an hour's rural labor may yet be positive and can perhaps be increased by capital and innovations. And the composition of the economy's output must have some relationship to domestic and international demands.

Any economy, whether its resources are allocated by private or public decisions, presumably wants to produce those goods that will most satisfy its people's wants. This satisfaction is partly indirect—as when a country exports some of its production and imports some of its consumption—for no nation is an entirely closed economy. And in a free enterprise

---

[1] This is so even if the distribution of labor between industry and agriculture is arbitrary, subotimum, and unalterable. The marginal value product of labor may then be higher in industry than in argiculture. But, given the principle of variable proportions, this may mean that an optimum allocation of capital will result in a greater investment in agricultural enterprises.

economy the wants that count most are those of people who can afford to assert them in the market. Hence the composition of a country's domestic product is determined both by supply considerations—including the country's own comparative endowment of factors and location—and by demand conditions. And the character of demand, so far as domestic consumers are concerned, depends very largely upon their individual levels of consumption.

INDUCED INDUSTRIALIZATION THROUGH INCREASED PRODUCTIVITY

The world over, consumers spend proportionately more on food and less on other things the lower their real incomes. Thus Egyptians spend relatively more on food than Canadians do, although in actual fact they eat far less. Hence, unless a poor country has a comparative disadvantage in agricultural output and imports food, rather a large fraction of its labor force will initially be in rural occupations.

Some major determinants

As an economy advances, and family incomes rise, there will usually be an internal transfer from agricultural to nonagricultural employment. Labor, and other productive factors, will migrate to industry. These changes may be slow due to psychological inhibitions, paucity of profitable opportunities for industry, and the associated costs of urbanization. And they will be extremely slow for national economies that are expanding but hardly advancing, with gross domestic product increasing only slightly faster than population, and per capita incomes remaining almost stationary. The important thing is that the rate of transfer out of agriculture—whether fast or slow—be compatible with the rise in individual consumption levels.

Some of the ways in which the character and level of consumption are related can be understood by considering the following questions. If the productivity of labor should increase in agriculture, compared to that in industry, will this increase or decrease the fraction of total labor force that is employed in agriculture? Will workers be attracted into agriculture by increased earnings there? Or will the larger output so reduce agricultural prices that the real wages of industrial workers will increase proportionately more? Can anything be said *a priori?*

The answer is complex. Suppose an economy is divisible into two sectors, one rural-agricultural and the other urban-industrial, each sector producing one output that both consume. Whether earnings per head of rural population increase more or less than those of the urban population will depend upon both sectors' comparative income and price elasticities of demand for each product. However, it can be demonstrated that, given usual conditions, increased agricultural productivity must improve the economic condition of the urban sector more than that of the rural sector, in a closed economy with a free price system. Hence one can expect a migration of workers and families out of agriculture and into industry.

Zero price elasticity case

It is no easy matter to determine algebraically the outcome of interacting price and income elasticities of demand in two sectors for two goods. Consider first a case of zero price elasticity of demand for industrial and agricultural output. Then the consumption mix of each sector depends on income alone. And, to simplify matters still further, assume that the average propensity to consume agricultural output (grain) relative to industrial output (cloth) is a physical constant (θ, theta). In physical terms θ must of course be consistent with the production mix of this closed economy. Under what conditions will such a two-sector economy be in equilibrium?

There are two equilibrium conditions. First, the output mix is determined by θ. The output of grain will be $P_r \cdot \phi_a$, where P_r is the rural population and ϕ_a is the output of grain per head of rural population. Similarly, the output of cloth will be $P_u \cdot \phi_i$, where P_u is the urban population and ϕ_i is the cloth output per capita of urban population. Hence:

$$(1) \qquad \theta = \frac{P_u \cdot \phi_i}{P_r \cdot \phi_a}$$

Second, if there is to be no net migration between the two sectors, the value of output per capita must be the same in each sector. If cloth is employed as a *numeraire* instead of money, the value output per head of urban population is ϕ_i. And the value output per capita of rural population, where p_a is the price of agricultural grain measured in cloth, is $\phi_a \cdot P_a$. Hence:

$$(2) \qquad \phi_i = \phi_a \cdot p_a$$

With these two conditions of equilibrium, the effects of changes in productivity and taste can be assessed. The basic parameters are θ, ϕ_a, and ϕ_i. These in turn determine the ratio of P_u to P_r and the price of grain (p_a).[2] For example:

$$(3) \quad \frac{P_u}{P_r} = \frac{\phi_a}{\phi_i} \theta$$

[2] To substitute numbers, if ϕ_a is 1.5 bushels of grain, ϕ_i is 3.0 yards of cloth, and θ is 1 yard to 2 bushels, the ratio of P_u to P_r will be 1:4. And the price of a bushel of grain will be 2 yards of cloth.

And

$$(4) \quad p_a \; = \; \frac{\phi_i}{\phi_a}$$

It follows from (3) that an increase in the ratio $P_u : P_r$ (*i.e.*, "urbaniza-tion") requires either an increasing demand for cloth (relative to that for grain) or an increasing productivity of agricultural labor (relative to that in industry); assuming θ is constant, it is changes in comparative labor productivity that will be decisive, and the sector that becomes com-paratively less productive gains population.

An arithmetic example may help. If the ratio of $P_u : P_r$ is 1:4, and it is hoped to make it 2:3, what must be the change in comparative sector productivity if θ remains constant? The ratio 2:3 is 2.67 times larger than the ratio 1:4. Hence, in order to transfer one-fifth of the total population from rural agriculture to urban industry, agricultural pro-ductivity must increase by 2.67 times as compared with that of industry. And the transfer will be associated with a 2.67 increase in the price of cloth measured in grain units.

The mechanism of migration is really as follows. One sector—say the agricultural—becomes more productive. Initially the output of grain in-creases proportionately. But tastes have not altered, and so, at unchanged prices, people do not want more grain unless they can also consume more cloth. The price of grain must fall relative to cloth. Consequently, the urban population has more real purchasing power although its out-put of cloth is the same as before. In the present simplified model, where the influence of taste (θ) is dominant, the price of grain must initially fall enough for real per capita incomes in industry temporarily to rise relative to those in agriculture. Otherwise there will be no migration to the towns. The rural population, even though it is producing more grain physically, has less command over economic goods. All this is contrary to the usual official view in underdeveloped countries which maintains that the way to industrialize is to equip new factories with the latest machinery and ignore agriculture, but in economic affairs it is not uncommon for policy makers to grasp the wrong end of the stick.

Complex elasticity case

It is, of course, more realistic to assume a negative price elasticity of demand for each output. Also it is more sensible to suppose that, as real incomes rise but prices remain unchanged, each group's demand for agricultural goods will increase less than proportionately. Finally, in the region of equilibrium, it is valid to suppose that peasant households typically consume rather more of their own given output if its price rises. In other words, when agricultural goods come to be higher priced in terms of industrial goods, rural households have a more pronounced income than substitution effect. This is because agricultural output is their sole source of real and money income. But it is only one of many sources of consumer satisfaction.

A comparative increase in agricultural productivity—say 20 per cent per worker—will then cause a proportionately greater decrease in the price of agricultural output. The urban-industrial sector will then find that its income, measured in agricultural goods, has increased more than 20 per cent. The point is not merely that agricultural prices will fall if rural households try to sell rather than consume their extra output. This is obvious. The noteworthy result is that the decline in agricultural prices will be proportionately more than the increase in agricultural output. Hence real earnings will become comparatively greater in industry, and there may be a migration of labor out of agriculture.

The validity of these assertions can be demonstrated algebraically or geometrically (see Appendix). But it does not take much intuition to see that if one sector increases its productivity and output, the price of its produce will fall more drastically if the public at large wishes to consume very little more of it at higher incomes regardless of price. A low income elasticity of demand and an even lower price elasticity mean that an increase in sector productivity must expel resources for it. As consumption levels rise, the willingness of the market to absorb increased agricultural output is diminished, and small percentage increases in productivity will occasion larger percentage reductions in rural population. But in poor countries, where extra food intake is still a major consideration, quite large advances in agricultural productivity may be necessary to shift resources into urban industry.

The conclusions are not vitiated because rural households produce primarily for their own consumption and sell only a fraction of their output. They are not altered because rural households may consume most of any output increase (so long as their output elasticity of consumption is not greater than 1). Nor are they invalidated because each rural worker, as a member of a large peasant family, may consume an amount that is more akin to his average than his marginal product.

FORCED GROWTH THROUGH GOVERNMENT INTERVENTION

It is not every government that is content to have industrialization wait upon comparative increases in agricultural productivity. An attempt may be made to force industrial production at the expense of agricultural output. Industrialization is then neither a natural consequence of economic development nor a reliable index of increasing personal well-being.

Closed economy case

Consider Fig. 7-1 and suppose that government is anxious to expand industrial output from I_1 to I_2. The economy is now at R. However, as indicated by the social indifference curve S_1, those consumers that can assert their wants apparently do not wish I_2 industrial output unless they can also have A_2 agricultural output (see Point B). The economy wants economic development to proceed along a production and consumption path, at present prices for sector outputs, indicated by RZ. But this will not happen if government wants increased industrial output before innovations and capital have shifted the transformation curve upward and to the right to T'. There is clearly an impending conflict between the consuming public, which prefers industrialization to wait upon productivity, and an impatient government.

A resolute government can obtain I_2 industrial production without waiting for increased output per worker in either sector if it is prepared to force consuming households on to the lower social indifference curve marked S_0. It must also subsidize production of industrial goods and tax

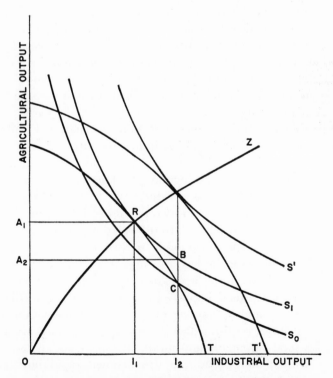

Fig. 7-1. Forced Industrialization Before Increased Productivity.

consumption of agricultural goods, so that their marginal rates of substitution in output and use can be sufficiently dissimilar. Then C will
constitute a market equilibrium.

Alternatively, the government can take over all distribution, becoming a monopsonistic buyer of all consumer goods from producers and a
monopolistic seller of them to households. By adjusting prices, it can
then achieve a production and a consumption of C. This is, of course,
very easy to do in a socialist state, where the government organizes production and there is no private sector.

In all these cases the government must make extensive use of its police
power. Even when a supposedly democratic government depends on
differential subsidies and taxes, the government must seek to prevent
home consumption of agricultural output, which means considerable
intervention in the lives of "subsistence" producers. Some freedom is
always lost when government officials come to think they know better
than the market what is needed and are sufficiently opinionated to impose their views on the economy.

Open economy case

All countries, even the poorest and most backward, engage in some
merchandise trade with other nations. And most of them now receive
loans or grants, transferred as net imports, which temporarily permit
consumption and use to exceed domestic production in value. One
method of accelerating industrialization without decreasing consumption of agricultural goods is for international assistance to be extended
through food shipments.

Figure 7-2 shows a country which, thanks to international trade, is able
to consume more agricultural and less industrial output than it produces.
The line Pp, indicative of relative world prices for say grain and cloth,
links consumption (C) with production (P). There are no capital movements, and imports equal exports in value.

Government may want again to increase industrial output from I_1 to
I_2. However, given an unchanged transformation curve, the maximum
consumption line through world trade is then Bp' rather than Pp. As
consumer satisfactions must be less, this may involve political difficulties.
These can be resolved, however, if loans or grants are obtainable that
will permit unrequited food imports amounting to AB (*i.e.*, the vertical
distance between Pp and Bp'). Some advanced Western governments with
agricultural surpluses resulting from "support" programs, are prepared
to make such food shipments and await later payment in local currencies (as the United States does). In this manner, rapid but "painless"
industrialization is possible.

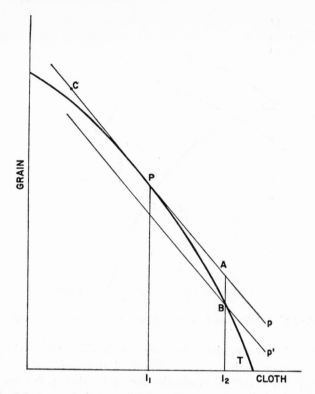

Fig. 7-2. Losses from Forced Industrialization of an Open Economy.

Food constraints on forced industrialization

In really poor countries, lack of food is a very serious limitation on industrialization, and food imports can be a most effective way to relax this constraint. A government may be quite prepared to alter prices so that the economy is induced to produce what its households do not want most to consume. But no government that rules by consent of the governed can force a decision to industrialize if there is insufficient food for the inhabitants.

Some of the forces at work are depicted in Fig. 7-3. The domestic transformation curve is again T. However, two new curves have been introduced, both as functions of industrial output; one (A_f) shows the maximum available food, the other (R_f) shows the minimum food requirement for the economy.

The derivation of A_f is as follows: maximum food availability is the sum of domestic food production and food imports. At a given domestic production mix, such as F, it would be possible to exchange nonfood output for food imports at a rate determined by world prices. The line GF has a slope representative of such external exchange rate between

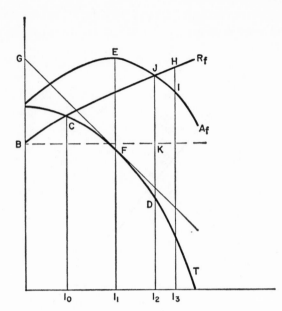

Fig. 7-3. Food Availability and Requirements with Varying Degrees of Industrialization.

grain and cloth. Hence, given domestic production and world prices, the maximum food availability at I_1 degree of industrialization is G. This provides a point E on A_f. Similarly, for each other point on the transformation curve (*e.g., D*), there is a corresponding point on A_f (*e.g., J*). (The highest point on A_f must be immediately above F, as the international price line is tangent at F to the transformation curve.)

The minimum food requirement curve is probably below the transformation curve at zero industrialization. Backward countries, unlike some advanced countries perhaps, can usually feed themselves if enough resources are devoted to agriculture. But (and this is a marked characteristic of backward countries with partially subsistence agriculture) increased industrialization probably increases the minimum food requirements for the population to survive.

The explanation is that more industrialization means more people moving from a rural to an urban habitat. The people who leave their village also leave their former share in its subsistence output. The rest of the family, who remain behind, consume most of this "abandoned" share. The amount of agricultural output that the peasant family sells to the city does not increase enough to feed the migrants. And yet this extra urban population must have food or it will go back to the countryside. The urban inhabitants may eat only enough to stay alive, substituting other satisfactions for some food, so they are not to blame. The trouble is that the rural population will eat more per head as a result of the exodus from agriculture. This is why the R_f curve, which indicates minimum food requirements as a function of industrialization, is positively inclined.

An example may help to explain. Imagine a village of 100 people producing 1250, consuming 1000, and exporting 250 units of food a year. Now 20 people leave, but output is the same. The remaining 80 relatives subsequently have 12.5 units of food per head instead of 10.0, even though food "exports" to the town remain the same. They choose to increase their consumption by 2.0 units a head and increase their sales of food by 0.5 units a head. Hence they increase their total sales to the city from 250 units to 290, or by 40 units. However, the village has contributed 20 people to the city, accustomed to eating around 200 units a year altogether. The demand for food has increased by 200 − 40 units. But although the minimum requirement has thus increased by 160 units, total food availability is at best constant and rural output could decline.

It is now possible to see how lack of agricultural output can limit industrialization, because government is not prepared to risk famines. For example, if the economy does not trade externally, the intersection of R_f and T at C marks I_0 as the greatest possible industrial output. And, in the case of an open trading economy, the intersection of R_f and A_f at J indicates I_2 as the maximum industrialization compatible with survival. The latter is an absolute limit, for at I_2, although there is considerable industrial production, only agricultural goods are presumably consumed. (But more food is consumed than would be possible if the economy refused to trade and concentrated on agricultural production alone.)

Incidentally, if agricultural produce (or "food") is scarce, the transformation curve has an ambiguous meaning beyond the critical degree of industrialization where starvation begins. It may be conceptually interesting to know that if more labor would and could remain employed in industry, there would be such and such increase in its output. But this has little significance if much of this labor would be expiring for lack of food. This is the situation to the right of I_2. However, if world prices for agricultural goods decline relative to those for industrial output, more of the transformation curve would become relevant. So it does have some significance. But only to the extent, as it were, that adequate food "brings it alive."

A temporary palliative is for foreign governments and investors to give or lend sufficient funds to import extra food. Thus unrequited food imports of HI quantity would permit I_3 industrialization with survival. Otherwise it is clear that this output mix would never be the market choice of the country's population.

Were it not for the positive inclination of R_f—attributable to the sharing of food within the extended families of the subsistence rural sector—the people of this economy might choose I_2 industrialization. (If food requirements did not increase with migration from village to town, the minimum food requirement function would be a horizontal straight line extending from B, and the economy would produce an output mix indicated by F.) But I_2 industrialization means less domestic urban non-food consumption.

The long run remedy is undoubtedly to encourage all social changes that will reduce the positive slope of the minimum food requirements curve. Anything is beneficial that tends to restrict the consumption of each rural worker, plus that of his wife and children, to his own marginal product. The three-generation extended family, with consumption determined by communal sharing, guarantees economic backwardness. Unfortunately, in democratic societies, the only permissible ways to prevent the remaining rural population from consuming the share of the absent relatives are likely to be both indirect and slow in taking effect. But the only alternative is to substitute police action for market forces.

Associated urbanization costs

In many backward countries, producers, consumers, and workers—at least as regards their observed economic behavior—seem to favor a less rapid pace of industrialization than official utterances often demand. These people may one and all identify themselves proudly with the nation's more spectacular new industrial plants. But as workers they often prefer to stay in their village. And as consumers they often do not spend enough of their income on industrial output to finance that sector of the economy. Some of the circumstances that inhibit a faster expansion of industry have already been described. But there are other obstacles to industrialization, some recognized and some ignored, and one of these is the associated costs of urbanization.

The labor force that is employed in industry, together with all the other local trades that provide these workers with goods and services, is an urban population. In a developing economy, in which there is a steady migration from rural to urban living, there must also be a steady investment in housing, streets, utilities, sewers, schools, and other improvements that in agricultural areas are conspicuous by their absence. All this investment for associated urban facilities is just as much part of the capital cost of industrialization as are actual plant facilities.

Although estimates are difficult to obtain, and vary greatly from country to country, it may be that the urban capital costs occasioned by an extra worker and his family are sometimes a substantial fraction of the factory investments that are combined with that worker. Of course this is particularly evident in the case of company townships that have to be constructed when a mineral or petroleum deposit, located in a previously uninhabited region, is to be extracted for the first time. Associated urban costs are just as real, although far less obvious, where an existing town has to expand in order to shelter and serve those workers and their families who are attracted to its expanding industries.

A transformation curve between "agriculture" and "industry" for a developing economy can have two different meanings under these circumstances. A worker who is marginal to both sectors may produce an extra bushel of grain for every extra 2.5 hours of work in "agriculture" during the year. And in "industry" he may on an average add a yard of cloth to his employer's textile output every half-hour that he works. Superficially, the "transformation" is 5 yards to 1 bushel, if one compares only the change in output occasioned by moving a worker from a job in one sector to another.

But supposing that, for every extra two men in, say, "industry" one extra man must be employed in the same town in providing the extra housing, utilities, and so forth, that are a peculiar cost of urban living. This "shadow" man is part of the real cost of expanding industry. He must be included in the economy's transformation function too.

It is also evident that someone must pay for this "shadow" man who is a measure of the extra urban costs associated with industrialization. If employers meet these costs, as they do where there are company townships, they will pay lower wages. But if workers must pay these costs, through higher housing rents and special municipal taxes perhaps, their net wages are really less than they seem.

If associated urban costs are included in the analysis, as they should be when one examines an industrializing economy, apparent disparities between real and money costs of labor in agriculture and industry may prove illusory. For example, suppose hired rural labor is paid 50 cents an hour and hired industrial labor 75 cents an hour, and the physical products of marginal workers are 0.2 bushels and 1.0 yards an hour, respectively. If private employers are trying to maximize profits, the prices of the two commodities should be $2.50 for a bushel of wheat and 75 cents for a yard of cloth, and this involves a market exchange rate of 1 bushel to $3\frac{1}{3}$ yards of cloth. But a comparison of the marginal products gives a transformation ratio of 1 bushel to 5 yards. Some people would seize upon such a situation as justification for protection against textile imports.[3]

However, if one extra worker is needed to provide urban amenities for every two additional workers hired directly into industry, there will

---

[3] E.g., Professor E. Hagen, "An Economic Justification of Protection," *Quarterly Journal of Economics*, November, 1958. However, see this author's "Food Constraints on Industrial Development," *Southern Economic Journal*, April, 1961. In this latter essay it is argued that protection, even when there are no associated urban costs, is a third-best policy.

be no disparity between money and real costs in the two sectors. The
real alternatives for the economy, unless the "shadow" worker is ignored,
are either three men making together 0.6 bushels an hour or three men
together making only 2.0 yards an hour. This is because only two men
are actually making cloth. The third man is providing social overhead
capital. This is equivalent to an exchange of 1 bushel for $3\frac{1}{3}$ yards and
is confirmed by a comparison of the market prices of grain and cloth.
And if the difference in wages between 75 and 50 cents an hour does
not evoke a stampede of labor into industry, one can only assume that
almost 25 cents an hour of the "high" industrial wage do not buy
satisfactions but are needed to pay for food and housing that are more
costly but no better.

The moral is that a comparison of marginal products in private agricultural and industrial *employments* does not indicate the marginal substitution rate of the *economy* in production. Nor does a difference in
wage rates between industry and agriculture demonstrate a market
aberration that needs to be rectified by government intervention. If the
special and associated urbanization costs usually incurred by rapid industrialization are ignored, bad policy recommendations are likely to
result.

IS UNDEREMPLOYED RURAL LABOR FREE?

A striking feature of many poor and backward countries, although
less so in Latin America, is apparent underemployment in agriculture.
During most of the year, a great deal of the rural population may not
work many hours a day. Several Occidental economists, observing this
underemployment and the scarcity (in Asia) of usable land, have assumed
that the marginal product of labor must approach zero. Why else would
these people, hungry at times, not work harder to feed themselves? And
if labor in agriculture has an almost zero marginal product, is it not a
"free" service without opportunity and disutility costs if used in another
sector of the economy?[4]

A few economists have reached more penetrating conclusions, however.[5] In their opinion, extra rural work hours—but not necessarily extra
rural workers—are usually still far from being unproductive. The difficulty lies in social customs that prevent an individual worker in agri-

[4] This is often advanced as a justification for using capital-to-output ratios to compare
the "desirability" of alternative investment projects. After all, if labor is free, capital
is the only important scarce factor to contribute value added in industry. Unfortunately for this view, labor in industry is not a normally free good for reasons given
below.
[5] See T. W. Schultz, "Latin-American Economic Policy Lessons," *American Economic
Review, Papers and Proceedings*, May, 1956, where he denies that rural labor has an
almost zero marginal product.

culture from receiving exactly his actual or potential marginal output.

Custom is often the determining factor where agricultural tasks are decided by the family or village as a whole. Certain lands are ploughed, certain paddies replanted, certain areas cleared each year. The magnitude of these annual projects having been determined long ago, when the village had a smaller and more stable population, it now takes fewer hours per worker to complete these tasks during the year. A one-fifth change in the village labor force will then result approximately in an inverse one-fifth change in hours worked by each person. So although the marginal product of an hour of work may be considerable (relative to the average product of an hour), the marginal product of a worker may be very low indeed (relative to the average product of a worker). Migrant workers, then, have a low opportunity cost in agriculture, not because their "labor" is unproductive, but because custom rather than individual self-interest determines what work is to be done.

Where land is communally used, and output is communally shared, the incentive for each person to work is considerably dulled, whether the community is a small village or a large extended family. Within such a community, much as a man may be fond of his nephews, nieces, sisters-in-law, and neighbors, he knows that more work on his part will have little effect on the food intake of his own children. Suppose there are twenty family members of working age in an extended family. Someone who then applies one extra hour of total family labor to the acreage will increase his immediate family's consumption by only about one-twentieth of the extra output he occasions. With such reduced incentives he may be prepared to work an extra hour only if the other nineteen potential workers do also.

This is one reason why it is often left to custom, rather than to frequent and difficult negotiations, to decide how much labor is to be provided and how output is to be shared. In this way no one works notably more or receives less than others of the same age and sex. The unfortunate outcome is often too few hours of agricultural work and a diversion of effort into petty trading and casual portering at nearby towns. More of this "outside" income is kept by the individual. Such a misallocation of effort from the economy's viewpoint is largely attributable to communal sharing of work and output in agriculture.

There is yet another reason why a change in rural labor force may be reflected more in hours worked per individual than in total labor application and agricultural output. When people are very poor, and far from satiation, the utility of the "last" unit of consumption is about the same as the "next" unit would have were it available. Also, where malnutrition makes work more arduous and land scarcity makes for low marginal product of labor, there are hedonistic temptations for each man to work only a few hours a day despite his real poverty. The "next" hour of work that is not performed may not yield enough output utility to offset its labor disutility. And in the extreme case of a constant marginal disutility of work hours and a constant utility from consumption of output, a halving of the work force should double the hours applied by each remaining worker.

All this throws considerable light on whether labor transferred from rural agriculture to urban industry is somehow "free." Either there is a loss of agricultural output and hence an opportunity cost (where other rural workers do not change their hours of work), or there is a disutility cost (assuming remaining labor works enough more to maintain aggregate output). The probable outcome combines some opportunity costs and some disutility costs. A more complete analysis should distinguish the incidence of a marginal transfer on the migrant himself, the rural sector he leaves, and the industrial sector he enters.

As for the migrant, it is generally true that he will not transfer except for higher net earnings, if only because eight hours a day of factory work and discipline may involve more disutility than four hours a day of family farm work. The economy must compensate him for this extra disutility. So he must expect to be better off by transferring.

The rural sector, if hours per person remain unchanged, loses the migrant's marginal output (not now produced) but gains his average output (his former consumption). As the latter exceeds the former, the rural sector—and specifically his family—are better off. This is also true if it adjusts hours to produce the same total output.

The urban sector, exclusive of the migrant himself, is worse off. The value of his contribution to output as a marginal worker is presumably given to him for his own satisfaction. This must be at least enough for him to command through the market the equivalent agricultural output that was formerly his subsistence share. The increased food consumption of the rural sector is hence the decreased consumption of the urban sector minus the migrant. And the economy as a whole is not demonstrably better or worse off. A numerical representation may help. Suppose the migrant, when previously in the rural sector, was working four hours a day and had an average product of 0.2 bushels an hour; a bushel being worth $2.50, his daily real subsistence income was $2.00 a day. If he migrates, output declines say 0.4 bushels a day, against which must be set his former share of 0.8 bushels, so the rural sector is better off, without additional work, by 0.4 bushels a day. His marginal contribution during the day is 8 yards of cloth worth altogether $6. Of this, $2.00 goes for associated urban improvements of a kind that give him no obvious pleasure, as explained in the preceding section. The remaining net wage of $4, which is $2 over his agricultural subsistence share, is necessary to compensate for four extra hours of work. And his budget includes a $2 a day outlay for agricultural output. The rest of the urban sector, unless it is able to exploit the migrant, gains nothing from his industrial employment. But it has lost 0.4 bushels a day, for the migrant is still eating his 0.8 bushels a day, and his transfer has cut output by 0.4 bushels. In value terms the rural sector's gain—which is the migrant's previous average minus marginal product in agriculture—is the urban sector's loss.

The sad truth is that any significant increase in well-being under existing social arrangements must come, not from transferring labor, but from making it more productive in its current employments. When this has been done, and if it occurs at a differential rate in various sectors, some reallocation of resources is desirable. But the case for labor transfers must then rest on changing productivity differentials and not on the notion that some fraction of the rural labor force is a free service to the economy.

SOME POLICY CONCLUSIONS

No government that wishes above all to increase national domestic product will tolerate a large rural labor force that works only a few hours a day during most of the year. It then has two broad alternatives: it may either draft rural labor and commandeer its output, or introduce marginal product rewards into the subsistence economy.

In countries where government is by consent, economic development is supposedly for the advantage of man, and not man for economic development. The government must then try by every acceptable means to introduce profit calculations into subsistence agriculture. Specifically, it must seek to reduce communal sharing except within subfamilies, and to bring individual rewards into correspondence with marginal productivity.

As peasant families are brought into closer contact with the towns through improved transportation and communication, their agriculture tends to become commercialized. More of the output is marketed, decisions are more often made according to profit calculations, and members of one family may be hired by another. A revolution occurs when most workers' real income is an earned wage and not a share enjoyed by right of consanguinity.

This constitutes a fundamental change, because agriculturists as employers will pay a daily wage that is no greater than the marginal product. Hence employers will pay only the old consumption per head to a reduced number of workers for more hours of work a day than each customarily performed before. In this way a great deal of superfluous labor will be expelled from agriculture.

The situation is somewhat different where there is also rural underemployment in the sense that the utility from the "last" hour worked is still greater than its disutility. This may occur where there is communal agriculture and certain customary tasks and practices are no longer compatible with current labor-to-land ratios. The object of government is then to induce the village, tribe, or family, through technical advice and credit extension, to try different crops and adopt new practices. Unfortunately, if ownership and use of land are communal, such innovations require community consent and cannot be undertaken independently by one or two subfamilies. Moreover, when peasants have only part of last year's crop between them and starvation, they are reluctant to risk experiments.[6]

These voluntary ways of releasing labor and output from the rural sector all take time. The market economy can only commercialize a small fraction of subsistence agriculture each year. Customs are not suddenly discarded but slowly worn away.

Some political leaders—as Lenin clearly stated in his *State and Revolution*—will not let their countrymen wait for progress to evolve without compulsion. In all Communist countries it has been traditional to employ force. Rural labor is either compelled to work longer hours in agriculture or forcibly transferred to work on other projects. Peasant families cannot choose how much of their output they wish to consume but are set quotas they must deliver. Most of the economic problems that have been considered in this chapter are, then, not resolved but made to "disappear" superficially. But the human cost of forced labor and commandeered output is high. Economic production may increase, but human liberty is lost. Only the poorest people would ever willingly and knowingly pay such a price.

6 In this case of underemployment, it is also desirable to substitute marginal product rewards for average product shares.

8

Agricultural innovations and community development

The rural village is still the center of life for over a billion inhabitants of the undeveloped world. These small villages, often comprising a hundred-odd people and a few extended families, are important units of the rural economy. If these people are to improve their lot, it will be through interacting schemes of agricultural and community development. But more than their own welfare is at stake. As we have seen, unless food supplies can be increased, industrialization will find itself checked. A rather stark program for agriculture is essential to any over-all plan of forced economic development. Whether this can be accomplished in a free society is not at all certain.

ROLE OF AGRICULTURE IN DEVELOPMENT

Agriculture and peasants are the twin rocks upon which all Communist and most "neutral" governments have almost foundered in their voyage toward industrialization and development. This is not because the Communist states have ignored and neglected agriculture; on the contrary, attempts to mechanize the cultivation of certain crops have been an outstanding feature of Soviet agricultural programs, and the Chinese have deliberately revolutionized the village communities for economic and political reasons.

Thus the attitude of non-Communist governments to agricultural innovation and community development is in sharp contrast. Their educated white collar officials tend to know little of village life and seem to care less. As the Food and Agricultural Organization has stated:

The comparatively junior position which agriculture occupies . . . tends to be reflected in the low priority given within (member) governments to agricultural matters. Even when very large sums are being allocated to economic development schemes, the emphasis may be largely on the industrial side, and although the idea of achieving balanced development may be present in the minds of the planners, agriculture may in the end have insufficient funds for this to be achieved.[1]

The low status of agriculture in most undeveloped countries is also indicated by the disinterest of ambitious young officials. How to use manure and skin animals, for example, are not subjects likely to help them professionally. Some of these men are only a generation or so removed from village life themselves, and they wish to make good their escape by securing a government post in some provincial or national capital. It has been aptly remarked that "agriculture is regarded as an unprofitable and undesirable career, with little prestige value, small chance of promotion, and few of the other rewards that go to attract young men into public service."[2]

One of the important contributions that the Ford Foundation has made to Indian development is the example of interest and participation set by its senior mission officials in agriculture. That important and successful Americans and Britons should bother about the dirty and ordinary details of farming and village life is a constant source of surprise to minor bureaucrats, who are far too proud of their clean hands, white collars, and limited education. (The importance attributed to agriculture and conservation by imperial governments is also one of the offsetting and positive characteristics of recent colonialism.)

The widespread neglect of agriculture in poor and backward countries, however understandable it may be psychologically, makes no economic sense at all. Directly or indirectly, agriculture contributes about half the gross national product of many of these countries when subsistence output is adequately valued and included. And economic planners, even if their only goal is industrialization, should realize two logical and associated requirements for agriculture and village life.

First, as developed rather fully in the preceding chapter and in Appendix A, industrialization and urbanization require a greater total food availability. Most of this increment must usually come from domestic output. For centuries economists have agreed that more wage goods are a prerequisite of industrial expansion and urban growth.

Second, although the pace of industrialization may be established in part by capital accumulation rates, the industrial sector must receive its labor force from the original subsistence subeconomy. If agriculture becomes too productive, there will be a tendency for rural communities to withhold their labor from the rest of the economy. Only as the terms of trade shift against agriculture will labor tend to be released. This natural process of reallocation may be too slow for planners. In order to hasten

---

[1] United Nations Food and Agricultural Organization, *Millions Still Go Hungry* (Rome, 1957), p. 6.
[2] *Ibid.*

the migration from country to town, they may wish to extract all incre-ments of agricultural output from village communities, making these extra supplies available exclusively to city inhabitants.

Putting it bluntly, if planners wish to force the pace of industrializa-tion and urbanization, they must arrange that (1) villages produce more food, (2) villagers have less to eat per capita, and (3) extra food is made available to urban families at what amounts to subsidized prices.

The Communist method has usually been to establish collective farms, conscript rural labor into them, and require these collectives to surrender or "sell" large output quotas to government for urban sale and distribu-tion. Even if the Communists had no ideological need to terminate own-ership of the land—private ownership of the means of production being counter to socialism—the exigencies of industrialization would have re-quired some kind of food exactions by government. Unfortunately for the Soviets, their methods have not encouraged peasants to grow food for others' consumption, and it may be that economic growth would have been more rapid had the State placed less heavy a hand on agriculture.

Supposedly, democratic governments determined to force industrializa-tion may have to use less obvious methods of extortion and coercion. They may be able to use the price system, if it is supplemented by taxes and subsidies, and if they will take the lead in sponsoring experimental innovations. Because they are not opposed to private ownership of the means of production, democratic nations may be able to make private land ownership an important incentive to medium-scale farmers. In this respect the non-Soviet countries have an important advantage—if they can learn how to use it. But so far, land "reform" has tended to fragment land use and reduce output, as explained in a following section.

City dwellers and most economists do not seem to realize the extent to which modern science is continuously revolutionizing agriculture in the advanced countries. In Great Britain, the agricultural revolution was as drastic as the Industrial Revolution, and the latter would have been im-possible without the former. And it is still continuing. The ability of a little over 10 per cent of the United States labor force to produce agri-cultural goods for the entire American people, and to create surpluses for export besides, would never have been possible without new and better seeds, fertilizers, breeding, equipment, and widespread application of scientific methods. Can a similar revolution be expected among the primi-tive agriculturalists of today?

It is instructive to realize how these innovations have come to be made. In Great Britain, but far more so in the United States, the government has supported experimental stations to evolve and prove new strains of seed and livestock. Agricultural colleges have long been a landmark of nearly all the states. Many farmers have subscribed to technical farm periodicals, sent for pamphlets, listened to extension agents' lectures, and generally sought to improve their operations. In all this they have enjoyed many advantages. They are nearly all literate, and many have attended agricultural colleges or extension courses.

A substantial minority of farmers are well-to-do, have large holdings, and constitute good loan risks. Hence economies of scale—except in parts of the Old South in the United States—accrue to their farms and ranches. Moreover, where the operator owns his own land, apart from government regulations he is an independent decision-maker when it comes to land use, selection of crop, methods of cultivation, and so on. He does not have to make his operation conform with the practices of all his neighbors. Farming is not a community affair.

The situation is very different in most parts of the undeveloped world. Land is often owned and used by the subtribe, village, or extended family, and no important innovation in agriculture is possible without the agreement of the group. There is sometimes no way in which the community as a whole can borrow for equipment or improvements. Moreover, each family may cultivate its own paddy, or strip, or terrace. Where land is scarce, these individual plots may be small indeed. With small holdings, no single family can afford or justify the use of mechanical aids which are often commonplace in the Western world. Communal grazing makes it difficult or impossible to improve livestock by selective breeding. Peasant cultivators often know little more about agriculture than has been handed down as traditional wisdom from father to son. Few of them are really literate, most are superstitious, and there is a general resistance to outside ideas. When one realizes that a single crop failure can mean starvation, and that the advice of government officials has not always proved to be successful, one can understand the conservatism of villagers.

The first question therefore is whether today's villagers and primitive agriculturalists can significantly improve their operations within the present rural context. Or must small holdings be combined? Do current landlord-tenant relations have to be revised or abolished? Can agriculture be advanced without drastic alteration in the structure and organization of tens of millions of villages? Can anything be done within the existing rural framework?

POSSIBILITIES OF INNOVATION WITHOUT REORGANIZATION

At the outset, it is important to realize that many private innovations regarding domestic animals and crops *have* taken place, although sometimes this has taken a century or so of trial and error. Thus "Indian" corn (or maize), from which "mealies" are made throughout Africa, was introduced from the New World. Although sweet potatoes are indigenous to Peru, they are also grown throughout the tropics and subtropics.

Manioc is another case in point. Cocoa was introduced into Ghana by small cultivators rather recently. Turkish tobacco originated in the Near East, but is now grown in parts of Asia, Latin America, and Africa as a cash crop by peasants with limited capital. Wheat and barley are today grown throughout the world, but they originated in Asia Minor. Long staple cotton has been transplanted from the Nile Valley to coastal Georgia and elsewhere. Chickens and goats are now commonplace in Latin America, but they were introduced by the Spanish and Portuguese. Brahmin bulls from India are being crossbred in the United States, Australia, and Africa. Eucalyptus or "gum trees," grown in many countries for posts, shade, and fuel, come from Australasia. The Israeli citrus fruit industry is not truly indigenous. The palm tree, useful for copra and much else besides, was imported into Oceania. Coffee and cane sugar are now grown around the world. Caribbean breadfruit was introduced from Tahiti. And the tree rubber industry of Malaya was founded upon seedlings smuggled from the Amazon Valley. Similar innovations are still continuing as private farmers and government agricultural stations experiment to discover what crops and animals can be made suitable for regions that have never known them before. A striking aspect of development is that one increasingly finds the same domesticated flora and fauna in all parts of the world where climate is similar.

Seemingly ignorant villagers have always made rather more innovations than is always realized. This is especially so where agricultural change requires little capital and is possible without wrenching the social structure. Dr. McKim Marriott's description of innovations in a small Ganges valley community could have been written of many other undeveloped villages:

I was very impressed by evidence of American influence—influences much older than those of Point IV. Farmers were cultivating potatoes, maize, tomatoes, and a strain of improved cotton, all of them imported from America. I was surprised, too, to find many crops in the village which I knew were not native to the Ganges valley. Carrots, originally from Asia, were being eaten in huge quantities by men and beasts instead of the native turnip. Mustard oilseed plants were crowding wheat and barley in the grain fields; villagers told me that there had been none two generations ago. Sugar cane of an improved variety was being cultivated in my village as a valuable small cash crop, while it had become the only crop in other villages beside the canal a few miles away.[3]

But although some change is always occurring, the juxtaposition of new and old methods of village agriculture is often surprising, especially in Asia and Africa. The village flour mill may be powered by a gasoline engine, but the grain may be threshed by the hooves of circling oxen.

[3] McKim Marriott, "Technological Change in Overdeveloped Rural Areas," *Economic Development and Cultural Change,* December, 1952.

Homemade seed-drills may be used instead of hand sowing, but reaping may be done with a short-armed hand sickle. The raising of water for irrigation, using traditional methods, may require several men, a span of oxen, and a week's work to water a single acre of land under cultivation.

The task of technical assistance to agriculture is therefore not to introduce change where there has been none. It is to ascertain what further innovations are practicable and worthwhile, given the numerous constraints imposed by the villagers' poverty, their other economic and social needs, and sometimes their overpopulation relative to land. The following examples give some idea of what can be done within the present context of village life.

1. It sometimes happens that, although a crop may have been grown in some area for thousands of years, scientific plant breeding for seed production can increase yields, reduce losses to local diseases, and provide a food of higher nutritional value. Thus, during the 1950's, improved strains of wheat and barley were developed for use in the Near East. Some twenty-five nurseries were established within the region, plus another ten outside, growing identical collections of wheat and barley varieties. Tests were made according to a uniform plan for resistance to bunt and rust. When improvements can be made by outside technicians in seed strains of crops that have been planted in the same area for millennia, one realizes how great are the potential gains from introducing novel grains, vegetables, and fruits, and adapting them to local environments.

2. Many cash crops have to be processed close to where they are grown because of the inevitable waste of material and loss of weight. Examples are sugar cane crushing and sisal pulping. Many other plants—such as *cabuya*—require decorticating. Small holders who grow such crops for cash are usually faced with the choice of tediously transporting their bulky crops to the nearest mill, or inefficiently removing some of the wastes themselves. And yet, assuming that improved roads and transportation are often uneconomic, a little ingenuity, capital, and enterprise can often evolve an economical and movable machine for processing these crops. Compared to a large permanent mill, such devices must be very inefficient by physical standards, but portable decorticators have proved themselves in Costa Rica for *cabuya,* and experiments have been made elsewhere in pulping sisal and crushing sugar cane. Too often the problem now is not that the peasant can't grow a crop, bad though the soil and climate may be, but that he cannot make adequate use of what he has raised.

3. Fish are potentially an important source of animal protein, and an important fraction of the undeveloped world's villages are on a coastline. These people are accustomed to fishing, often using methods "perfected" thousands of years ago, but a night's work for a boatload of men may

result in a very small catch. Often fishery experts, by suggesting the use of different lines and hooks, or different kinds of nets and methods of casting, can significantly increase the landed catch. Even the installation of a small motor in each fishing boat, so that further banks can be reached or a deeper drag can be made, may pay for itself within a season. Techniques of commercial fishing have been changing rapidly during the past fifty years in the Western world, but few governments of backward countries have taken steps to communicate these improvements to their own fishing villages, let alone make the necessary gear available for rent or sale or loan.

4. Leather from animal hides is an important material for making shoes, harness, belts, and the like. But the value and quality of leather is affected by the method of skinning, curing, and tanning. In countries where cattle are not slaughtered (for religious reasons), leather must be obtained from "fallen" animals, which must be found before vultures and hyenas spoil the hide. In India, the flayers or *chamars* are of low caste and little education. However, several experimental projects under technical assistance programs have resulted in increasing the number of skins recovered and improving the quality of tanned leather. Improvements in curing and tanning are probably also possible in other backward areas of the world. Moreover, as hides and leather can always be sold, there is an immediate cash incentive to making these changes.

5. Selective breeding and slaughter of domestic animals would increase food and protein availability in almost every undeveloped country. The situation in India, where 200 million starving cattle are competing for food and land with 400 million starving people, is altogether too familiar; were it not illegal to kill bovine animals, slaughtering three-quarters of the cattle population would probably double meat production permanently, significantly increase the availability of food grains to humans, and cereal shipments by the United States to India under P.L. 480 might be unnecessary. But quite apart from India, in many other countries male domestic animals are neither segregated nor sterilized, so that reproduction is indiscriminate. If livestock improvements in Europe and North America give any indication, meat production in many backward countries could be more than doubled through selective breeding and slaughter. Unfortunately, livestock ownership is often for status rather than food, and in parts of Africa cattle can be used to pay the bride price irrespective of their health or quality. A first and essential change is for backward peoples to consider livestock from an economic rather than a religious or social viewpoint.

6. Many areas of the world possess a comparative advantage in fruit and vegetable production, and could have a considerable domestic and export industry besides, if there were only adequate canning and preserv-

ing facilities. Foods that spoil very rapidly, such as fish and milk, would often be produced in greater quantity if the practical market were not limited to the immediate village. But in hot countries, where transportation to the nearest town may be slow or uncertain, spoilage is too great a risk and cost. Government might make a major contribution in some localities by organizing low-investment and small-scale canneries that can be supervised by a single, skilled foreman. Probably the development of such plants is technically feasible and economically worthwhile. But small canneries are not a very dramatic form of industrialization unfortunately.

7. Increased use of fertilizers is often advocated by agricultural experts from advanced countries. But the use of manure is well understood in countries where there is population pressure, and Asiatic peasants have been known to walk a mile or more in order to defecate on their own land. In seriously overpopulated areas, few trees or bushes remain for fuel, and so animal dung must be burned for cooking. Dung that might be used for crops is also needed to plaster walls and harden floors of huts. If artificial fertilizers are not employed, it is often because of their cost, or their unsuitability to local soils, or the fear that when the rains come these relatively concentrated fertilizers will be washed away in the flood.

It must never be forgotten that in many poor countries, and especially those of ancient culture and excess population, the problem is in a sense one of overdevelopment. In the fertile areas that have water, every scrap of land is exploited, and even the roots of grass are used for nourishment. Marriott[4] mentions that improved wheat seed, advocated by government, was found most unsatisfactory by several Indian villages. Admittedly, with good weather the crop was doubled, but the grain from the new crop was so big and tough that the village women could hardly grind it in the old stone flour mills. Dough made from the new flour was difficult to knead and hard to bake into the usual consistency. The peasants didn't like the taste of the bread anyway. The cattle refused to eat the straw from the new strain of wheat. And the old straw was better for thatching roofs. All in all, the experiment was not a success, and what seemed like a promising innovation failed because it was incompatible with traditional village life.

In a closely integrated village economy, no useful innovation is likely to be a casual matter. What appears as a simple improvement to a Westerner may have quite unexpected consequences. If this is true of the minor changes considered so far, none of which alter even land tenure and use for instance, the revolutionary nature of modern and specialized capitalist agriculture can perhaps be appreciated. Everything is so interacting that any "minor" change has wide repercussions.

4 *Ibid.*, p. 428.

LAND REFORMS AND AGRICULTURAL EFFICIENCY

A powerful countercurrent, running across the economic need for larger agricultural holdings, more trained supervision, and the use of equipment, is the almost universal political demand for what has loosely been called "land reform." There is land hunger everywhere. And "popular" governments, if beholden more to the masses than to any landlord class, have in many cases sought to satisfy this demand through ownership limitations and partial expropriation.

Some degrees of land reform

Land reform can take many patterns, varying in degree of intervention by government, and is hardly a recent phenomenon. The French Revolution led to the end of feudal land tenure in Western Europe. Widespread agrarian reforms occurred in Eastern Europe following World War I. The occupation authorities in Japan after World War II tried to enforce maximum size holdings. Hope of land reform was an important stimulus to the Mexican revolution. And in Latin America and the Near East today, much of the potential revolutionary discontent among tenant cultivators is strengthened by the prospect of land seizure, these expectations often being sedulously spread by pro-Communists.

"Land reform" often means something less violent than revolution however. There are at least three degrees of government intervention that can be distinguished. The milder versions are usually to be found in countries with more established government and less uneven distribution of land ownership.

First, almost all governments during the past half-century or so have come to "codify" in statutes the old common law arrangements between landlords and tenants. These customary principles are often of long evolution, going back centuries in parts of Asia, while in Latin America many land tenure arrangements follow the pre-independence customs of Spain. The purpose of these laws has usually been to give the tenant at least the nominal protection of the courts against his more powerful landlord.

Thus the landlord by tradition may have had the right to evict a tenant for not fully working his holding, resulting perhaps from the death of a son and the failure of the tenant to hire a substitute; making such a provision statute law means practically that the landlord cannot simply give notice of eviction, but must convince a judge that the tenant is underworking the holding—and meanwhile the tenant is protected. Or the custom may be that a tenant is entitled on quitting to have the value of approved improvements he has made during the past five years; if this provision is legislated, the courts can be called upon to assess what is owed to the tenant, and this possibility may prevent landlords from capriciously evicting tenants who do improve their holding. Existing tenants often are granted "pre-emptive" rights by statute, the purchase price being a prescribed multiple of the lease rental; provisions of this nature prevail in various of the Indian states, Uruguay, Japan, and other countries. By enacting land use and tenure statutes, governments have almost universally tried to improve the bargaining power of tenants versus landlords. Practically, though, this reform is too often limited by the inability of lowly and poor cultivators to afford the cost of advocates and litigation.

Second, governments have often tried to transfer income and wealth from landlords to tenants, typically by means of rent restrictions, limitations of maximum land ownership, and forced sales to small-scale cultivators. It may be required that to be enforceable rents must be approved by a local government agent. Landlords who own more than some maximum land area may be required to sell the excess on demand in parcels of prescribed size and at low prices established by public authority; to facilitate transfer of ownership, government may advance part of the purchase price to land purchasers as a low interest and long maturity loan, any subsequent price inflation giving the new "owners" a windfall. In other cases, large landowners have been given a certain number of years to disinvest themselves of all holdings above some maximum area, with the threat that land not so disposed will be confiscated by the State; the effect of course is that land prices are forced down to very low levels if the announced State policy is taken seriously, and if owners cannot divide their land among relatives. One form or other of these methods has been used to a limited extent by Pakistan, Egypt, and Mexico, and other countries besides.

Third, "revolutionary" governments in China, Cuba, and other countries have expropriated land from large owners, and divided their acreage into either individual peasant holdings or collective community farms. There will undoubtedly be other instances of such confiscation during the next decade in the Near East and in Latin America. A vital issue though is whether the new owners are to be individual families—in which case land ownership may eventually fragment or consolidate depending upon inheritance laws, population growth, and the advent of specialized farming—or whether "collectives" will be forced upon the peasants.

Politically, one of the most powerful propaganda weapons of the West against the Communist world is the desire of peasants everywhere to own land, not collectively as members of some government farm station providing food for the cities at low prices, but as private owner entrepreneurs. This is something the Communists cannot offer. But free countries must make sure that where land reform means extended peasant ownership, economic efficiency is not needlessly sacrificed.

Some land reforms and their economic impact

Many of those who advocate land reform most stridently do so on supposedly humanitarian grounds. They observe poor cultivators in undeveloped countries, and these peasants are tenants, so it is concluded they would be better off if not tenants but owners. Or it is supposed that, because absentee landlordism and agricultural poverty are now associated, the end of the former would terminate the latter. The truth seems to be though that land reform, if supplemented by many other essential changes and improvements, is a necessary but *insufficient* condition of increased agricultural efficiency. Moreover, without these other reforms, drastic alterations in land ownership and tenure may actually reduce agricultural output per worker. Land reform and agricultural efficiency are not inexorably associated with one another. Hence, in a sense, it is dishonest to urge land reform as a means of increasing farm output unless plans are also advanced for ensuring larger holdings, investment of capital, specialization of output, innovation of crops and methods, and more aggressive entrepreneurship.

Land rental limitations. In most rural areas of backward countries, rents are contracted in kind rather than money, and the landlord's claim is usually defined as some percentage of the output. Sometimes the divided output is net of replacement seed and stock necessary for next year's operations and some very minimal subsistence allotment for the cultivator. The landlord's share may be some traditional fraction, more or less unchanged for decades or more, but in the absence of legal restrictions this fraction is likely to increase as families and population increase in number.

The great merit of a sharing arrangement is that the tenant does not then bear all the risk of fluctuating output. Agriculture is notorious for dangers of loss from drought, flood, hail, disease, and pests, so that a poor tenant may seem perhaps to be the last person who should be called upon to assume all these hazards alone. This would be the case were he to pay a rent defined not as a share but as a fixed physical quantity.

The disadvantage of share rentals is that the tenant's incentive to produce is somewhat blunted. Extra output from capital improvements made by the tenant will accrue to the landlord in proportion to the rental share. Extra output from extra work enriches the landlord more, and fills the tenant's stomach less, than it would under some absolute rental arrangement.

All in all, if output rather than the tenant's income security is the test, land rental reform might usefully include the substitution of fixed rather than share rentals. By defining them in kind rather than money the tenant is at least accorded some protection against having to provide more output to his landlord in years of low product prices. Moreover, low city prices for food grains may be caused by good crops in other areas, which local cultivators did not enjoy in their region.

Most reformers are more interested however in seeing the average real level of tenant's rents reduced substantially by government *fiat*. The immediate outcome is without a doubt pleasant for the cultivator. He will eat better and can work less. Whether he will save more and invest these savings in agricultural improvements are another matter. Aggregate national capital accumulation will be less if the saving propensities of poor tenants are less than those of rich landlords. Another consideration is that, if land rents are kept artificially low by government, there will be more would-be tenants than available holdings. Potential tenants who cannot find tenancies will have to migrate to the cities or work as hired hands for those fortunate enough to be tenants when rent controls were introduced. The "shortage" of land holdings thus created will tend to freeze existing tenant-land relations. Where agriculture is undertaken for market rather than for subsistence, rental ceilings will prevent superior farmers from extending their cultivated acreage. Land rent controls can prove to be a very mixed blessing after their full effects have had time to prove themselves.

Encouraging farm improvements. One common argument for land reform is that a tenant will be less inclined to make capital improvements to a holding that he does not own. Indeed, if he can find another farm later, he may deliberately overcrop and overstock and so exhaust the soil and grazing. As the Food and Agricultural Organization has stated:

The purpose of tenancy legislation is to establish equitable tenure relations which provide for continuous farming operations, sustained production, a reasonable standard of living for the cultivator, and his protection against undeserved eviction. Assured of the benefits derived from his additional efforts and from his permanent and semi-permanent investments the tenant will be encouraged to make all the improvements he possibly can and to develop the agricultural resources. Insecurity, on the other hand, and in particular, lack of adequate compensation for unexhausted improvements and disturbance of occupancy, will not only discourage initiative but may permanently damage the land by inviting soil-exhausting practices.[5]

The essential problem in any owner-tenant agricultural relation is to ensure that one or the other has an incentive to improve the holding and that neither has a motive for exhausting it. Where there is a comparative abundance of land, and tenants can move to other farms, economic policy should probably stress the protection of the landlord against malpractices by tenants. The usual situation is the opposite however. With the exception of certain areas in Latin America and Africa, most of the

[5] United Nations Food and Agricultural Organization, *Principles of Tenancy Legislation* (Rome, 1957), p. 52.

poorer regions of the world are characterized by acute land scarcity, in which case all economic bargaining power lies with the landlord class. But even here it is necessary to distinguish several situations. In some countries there may be many landowners, some of whom may not be much wealthier than their tenants, and in fact the same family over several generations may graduate from tenant farmers to cultivating owners to absentee landlords. However, this sort of mobility is not typical, except in relatively prosperous areas, and it is really more characteristic of agriculture in advanced nations. The usual situation in old and backward nations is that a few wealthy families own most of the usable land, that these absentee landlords live in the capital city or abroad and have no knowledge of agriculture, and that it is left to the tenant to make improvements and initiate changes.

It has often been stressed that tenants do not make significant investments and innovations in countries where land ownership is extremely unequal. But the usual inference that this is because the cultivators are tenants is not necessarily valid. In many of these same countries, as explained in the following subsection, the tenant now is protected against eviction without cause. He and his sons and grandsons are reasonably assured of farming the same holding, perhaps at a rental share that will not change, so that as a tenant he need not reasonably fear eviction from the land before improvements of his making have been fully depreciated.

However, it is still true that as a share tenant some fraction of extra output will go to the landlord, so that the rate of return to the tenant is less than the real output rate of return. An investment that earns 20 per cent for the economy, may earn only 12 per cent for the tenant, with the remaining 8 per cent going to the landlord. This must diminish tenants' incentives to improve the holding, and, usually being poor, their high time preferences already inhibit investment to some extent.

The ideal situation is where absentee owners, possibly through local farm agents, seek to improve the output from their lands through innovations and investment. Such enlightened self-interest might even cause owners to share in the expense of improvements in the same proportion that they share in output. Often landowners, or at least their agents, do suggest certain improvements and so are innovators in a sense. Best of all, some agents have been trained in agriculture at college, so that as paid employees of the landowners they become introducers of progress. In these ways large and wealthy landlords can often do more to improve agricultural practices than government can.

The pity is that only a few large owners of land seem interested in stimulating such improvements. Their daily social activities do not usually bring them close to their land or to their tenants. Often they do not feel any great need to increase their incomes, for taxes may not be really burdensome, and an ever-growing population increases their rents without effort to them. With thousands of tenants, no single landowner can bother about particular land leases, and his agents are normally promoted for their ability to collect rents and not for their proclivity to suggest capital expenditures. It is normally where an owner has a few tenants whom he knows, and lives in the countryside and gets around his own land, that unequal land ownership is associated with agricultural improvement.

Nevertheless, where tenants are secure in their holdings, one must not exaggerate the evils of having ownership concentrated among a few families who have no contact with their land. Under such circumstances, so far as the tenant is concerned, an absentee and renting landlord is little different from an absentee and taxing government to an owner cultivator. Thus some of the large landowners of Latin America, whose ownership may derive from a royal land grant of centuries ago, still function really as tax collectors for the State. The owners collect rents from tenants and pay taxes on their land to government. The landlord's share of tenants' agricultural output has the same incidence as a proportionate income tax. And if crop sharing inhibits investment by occupiers, the true issue may be whether the rents that become government's taxes and landlords' consumption should not be defined absolutely instead of relatively, even if this does make the tenant cultivator suffer more during bad years.

The failure of peasants to invest may really be caused by factors other than their tenant status. So long as holdings are small, cultivators are limited in the kinds of innovations they can make, and practical objects of investment may require some extra work but few extra funds. It is not just that peasants are poor and so save little. The ability of agriculture to absorb capital improvements may be very limited within the existing social context and economic organization of village life. Schemes of irrigation and drainage require community agreement, and very often cooperation of neighboring villages too, so that there is little that an individual cultivator could do even if the project were not beyond his own strength. A single livestock owner cannot begin selective breeding where there is only communal grazing. And people who are poorly nourished, yet must work fairly long hours to feed their families and pay their rents or taxes, usually lack the physical vigor and spiritual energy to introduce major improvements. Impoverished peasant cultivators, whether tenants or owners of the land they work, cannot be counted upon for outstanding feats of agricultural enterprise. The real problem is how to reorganize village farming so that capital and entrepreneurship can be applied by government, landlords, or the community itself.

Legal protection of tenancy rights.   In many countries the peasant cultivator, although legally a tenant, is protected in his holding and cannot be evicted without cause. Tenancy rights often accrue to heirs. Sometimes the owner can remove a tenant only in order to place his own son on the land. National laws often facilitate land purchase by the tenant, giving him the right to purchase at some preferential price, or perhaps allowing him to apply some of his rent to the purchase price. The object of such provisions is to help the peasant tenant climb the agricultural "ladder" to independent ownership. It is rather generally held that steady occupancy and eventual ownership should be within reach of thrifty and industrious cultivators and that these prospects are a strong incentive for him to increase his efforts.

Such legal provisions make most sense where agriculturalists can produce and earn enough above their immediate consumption needs to save the reduced purchase cost of the land they are cultivating. Where holdings are of reasonable size, where there is specialized production for commercial sale, and where perhaps farmer cooperatives and tenant associations enhance the peasants' influence and bargaining power, a substantial transfer of ownership may occur over several decades. Moreover, the tenants' savings that purchase the land may in turn be invested by the former owner in industry, so that this variety of land reform may channel rural savings into urban capital.

Unfortunately, there are many areas of the world where poor soil, unfavorable climate, fragmented holdings, lack of capital, and excessive population all combine to limit agricultural output and hence tenants' real incomes. In such situations tenants have no surplus to purchase land at anything like its real value. The very pressure of population that causes land to be cultivated intensively so that its rents increase, and which therefore elevates the capitalized value of its future income, prevents most tenants from saving enough to become landowners. The only price they can afford to pay is something a little greater than zero. And for government to compel sales at such a price would be confiscation.

Nor are there necessarily any economic gains to be had from dividing the land among small peasant cultivators. The erstwhile tenant will certainly have no rent to pay, and so will live better, and for many reformers this is a sufficient end in itself. But output from the land may be no higher. The new owner may work less hard if all the output belongs to him and there are no easy ways to market the surplus he does not wish to consume. He will not invest in farm improvements if the holding is so small that he cannot employ most kinds of equipment profitably. This was well stated by one expert on Near East land use and tenure when she wrote:

. . . social change alone will not help, if there is no change in the methods of production: if the entire landlord class were abolished, while the methods of farming remained the same, bad years would still bring starvation to the cultivator and force him to borrow from one source, if not another.[6]

Where there is a large rural population relative to usable and available land, holdings tend to be small whether cultivated by tenants or peasant owners. The State can hardly make it easy for some favored peasants to acquire substantial land holdings if this means that the rest of the rural adult population must become a hired laborer class. When government seeks to satisfy land hunger, the results may be fragmented holdings, zero investment, and technological stagnation.

What is needed?

The basic economic inadequacies of land reform are well summarized in the following quotation:

In most land reform countries labor is cheap while land is the scarce factor of production. . . . In the economic development of these areas emphasis must be placed upon means of increasing both individual productivity and the productivity of land. One of the best means for attaining this end in agriculture calls for providing each farm operator with a unit of economic size and with the capital and training he needs to operate it. Unfortunately, this approach is often disregarded for the simple reason that there are far more people claiming land than there is land to go around. Too often land reform leaves the peasants with units of less than economic size or with units that permit subsistence but little margin for improvement. These units provide a poor base for the effective use of credit and for economic development in agriculture.[7]

The simple truth is that, unless supplemented by many other economic improvements, land reform of itself may accomplish little more than changes in the legal title to land. Otherwise, land reform does not normally result in increased output, and production may actually decline if the former landlords provided knowledge, supervision, capital, and perhaps marketing assistance. Giving land to peasants is not the answer. And even intelligent land reform tends to be a necessary but insufficient condition of agricultural improvement.

If agriculture is to contribute to economic development, both by producing more food and by supplying some of the labor and capital needed in industry, means must be evolved to introduce aggressive entrepreneurship. This is unlikely to come from the small-scale tenant, who lacks not only capital but also knowledge of what else he might plant and when. In some countries, where landlords are not too isolated from the land,

[6] D. Warriner, *Land and Poverty in the Middle East* (London: Royal Institute of International Affairs, 1948), p. 121.
[7] R. Barlowe, "Land Reform and Economic Development," *Journal of Farm Economics*, May, 1953, p. 185.

incentive taxation may stimulate them to greater efforts. In other cases, government may have to abolish individual land holdings and vest local agricultural resources in the villages, appointing officials to supervise collective farm operations. In all cases, with means of transportation to market improving, agriculture must become more specialized. Extra value output must be sold to industrial workers. So-called "land reform" that does not introduce entrepreneurship to the village will be almost useless so far as economic development is concerned.

MODERNIZING SUBSISTENCE AGRICULTURE

There will have to be drastic changes in village life if subsistence agriculture is to be "modernized." As suggested above, "modernization" includes at least the following: (1) combining land holdings, (2) specializing in output for market, and (3) introducing improved methods. These are now briefly outlined in turn.

Combining land holdings

Units of cultivation are often smaller than units of ownership. In countries where the peasants are poorest and the ratio of rural land to labor is lowest, individual family operations are usually too small to be efficient. Land fragmentation and parcellation, especially in countries where the law gives all immediate relatives equal inheritance rights, sometimes reaches such extremes that different branches of an olive tree may have different owners. A single family, instead of working a compact land parcel, may have strips of land in different fields several miles apart. And as population inexorably increases and more and more land is put under cultivation, the livestock have ever poorer land upon which to graze.

Simple arithmetic demonstrates that individual family operations cannot be enlarged unless other tenants or owners are forced off the land they are cultivating. Conceivably, where there are several families in a village that have more land and capital and ability than others, these families might be encouraged to "purchase" the rights in land of their neighbors. Government might acquire the land in the first place, indemnifying existing tenants and owners, and then lease compact land parcels to these "superior" and large-scale operators. The outcome would be something like the enclosure movement in Britain during the late eighteenth and early nineteenth centuries, except that it would be initiated presumably by government in selected villages, rather than at the request of influential local families. The dangers of such a program are considerable and obvious however. Corrupt government officials, responsible for determining whom to evict and what their land is worth, would have unparalleled opportunities to collect bribes from all parties.

And only a very secure government could take the political risks of creating a large rural proletariat.

An alternative is to make existing villagers part owners, part cultivators, and part laborers, by "collectivizing" the useful land surrounding each village. The village then becomes an economic unit operating a single large farm. Existing owners (and perhaps tenants with inheritable rights) get some first claim on output, larger land owners presumably receiving less than proportionate liens on output. The rest of the village product, after subtractions for taxes and servicing capital borrowings, would be "sold." Some of this residual output would actually be marketed in town. But much of it would be paid as wages in accordance with the skills of laborers and the number of days worked.

The administrative problems and difficulties of "collectivization" are considerable of course. A supervisor would have to know the work contributions of each adult villager. Unless a strong *esprit* develops, villagers will be tempted to steal from the community's paddies and stocks, and to loose livestock they might still own upon communal grazing land. A perennial issue, especially if government extracts too much of the village output, would be the right of families to cultivate the land around their huts for themselves. In any event, there will be an unprecedented requirement for bookkeeping and supervision, lack of which will force government to experiment with only a few village "farms" at the outset.

Another burning issue would be treatment of underemployed living in each village. Is everyone to be put to work who asks for employment, in which case the worth of a daily work "ticket" at the end of the crop year may be small, reflecting a low marginal product of labor time. Or, if more labor is offered the village farm supervisor than he "needs," shall he take only what he wants; and, in this case, should he share the work and unemployment among the village's inhabitants by hiring them all a little, or should he fully employ a few workers, leaving it to them to share their earnings among relatives if they will. The answer is probably that labor should be accepted only so long as its marginal value product equals net urban wages, after deductions for special living costs in cities, and that hired hands should be as fully employed as possible so that others will be free to migrate to other jobs including those in industry. However, as the village farm supervisor who makes such decisions will be a government employee, politically these are all very difficult questions to settle.

Combining land holdings into larger units, even though the result is several large family operations rather than a single and integrated village farm, brings obvious benefits. One is that internal economies of scale can be realized through the use of more equipment and improvements, such as bore holes and reservoirs, power driven pumps, cattle dips, seed drillers and grain thrashers, and vehicles for transporting produce to market. Another gain from integrating land holdings is that a larger farm owner and operator can often borrow on easier terms. Still another advantage, explained in the next subsection, is that a larger unit can better afford to specialize in output. And such division of labor, partly because cultivators learn more about raising a particular good, is likely to increase productivity further.

Specializing in output for market

Land parcellation (or fragmentation) is both a cause and effect of mixed subsistence farming. If a family is to produce most of what it consumes, it needs perhaps some paddy for rice, some land for barley or wheat, some other piece of ground for root and fodder crops, another strip for sugar cane, and so on. Around a village, because of differences in soil and topography, certain land will be best suited for one use and other lands for alternative uses. Thus subsistence farming almost requires that each family have strips of several kinds of land. If each village family were to have a single compact land parcel, assuming that the land around every village is not uniform, such families would have to choose between less efficient subsistence farming or small-scale specialization. (Of course unless the size of holding can be increased, the latter may be inefficient also.) Land consolidation tends to encourage production for market because it discourages subsistence agriculture of mixed outputs that are too varied for efficient cultivation.

Specialization obviously incurs peculiar costs. Most of the output must be sold or exchanged for other produce, and selling and exchanging take time, especially if frequent and tedious trips have to be made to a market town some distance away. Unless these diseconomies are more than offset through enhanced productivity, specialization cannot be really advantageous, and it is exactly such problems of transportation that have encouraged the continuation of subsistence farming in many regions. This is undoubtedly one case where "social overhead capital," invested in railroads, highways, ferries, and the like, can contribute to the commercialization of agriculture. Output for market must evidently start in those areas from which towns are accessible.

Scale of operation and specialization for market are closely interacting. Without some minimum quantity of output to sell, taking goods to market is hardly worthwhile, especially where perishables cannot be stored and have to be sold upon ripening. Moreover, where a small-scale farmer has to carry his produce on his own head or on a donkey's back, a larger farm can perhaps afford to share the expenses of operating a truck.

Population pressure inhibits agricultural specialization for commercial sale. Where too many people are dependent for their livelihood upon not enough land, little remains for market after the family has satisfied its immediate needs, and there is really no reason to incur the additional trouble and cost of selling some goods to buy others. It is when families can produce more food than they can consume that the question of exchanging the surplus for nonfarm goods arises. And once it is realized that some of the output should be marketed anyway, the extra transport costs of output specialization are seen to be slight. Hence more productive farmers are more inclined to specialize, which in turn tends to make them more productive.

An important consequence of marketing agricultural output is that money is introduced increasingly into rural life. If the cultivator has cash for his output, he will pay wages and other debts in money, so that more people come to satisfy their demands through purchases. If a man has money to spend, he consumes what he wants, and not what he happens to have grown or raised. And the money that flows into a village from the sale of agricultural output eventually flows back to the town through the purchase of industrial goods. This means that both industrial and agricultural goods must be transported between village and city, and in opposite directions too, so that the cost of movement per item is reduced by eliminating "dead-heading."

Introducing improved methods

The greatest problem of all is to introduce improved agricultural practices into the villages. Part of this difficulty is that what constitutes better methods and crops is not always known with certainty. However, even when a desirable innovation is known to central government experts, it may require considerable investment. And even if no great capital requirement is involved, there is the difficulty of explaining and demonstrating the new method to villagers. Often they must also be persuaded that it is worth the risk of a trial.

Here it should be stressed that alleged "better" methods may actually prove to be worse. Many advanced practices in temperate zones are not necessarily advantageous under other climatic and cultural conditions. One example must suffice for now.

Superficially, the pointed nail plow that is common to so much of the Near East seems grossly inefficient, for it only penetrates a few inches into the ground. A modern molded board plow of Western design, which can invert a seven-inch sod in a continuous row, seems vastly more efficient. However, in hot countries with long dry seasons, deep plowing may cause a loss of moisture from the soil. Shallow groundbreaking with a nail plow may be good enough for the eradication of weeds that took root in the last wet period. Moreover, unless cultivators are willing to adopt contour plowing exclusively, deep plowing could increase soil erosion disastrously in some climates. Another problem is that a modern board plow requires a great deal of power, so that a pair of oxen might not have the strength to draw it, a motor tractor being required for the purpose. Not only do tractors cost money to buy and maintain, but fuel must be bought for them also, and their use is seasonal compared with oxen.

In most backward and tropical countries, a great deal of scientific research and experimental farming are needed to discover innovations that are biologically feasible and economically advantageous. Desirable methods vary considerably from region to region. Oil refineries of similar design using similar crude petroleum will have similar yields wherever located. But the same seed, although planted in the same way, may produce a very different crop in say the Orinoco Valley than in the Ohio Valley. This is so obvious when stated that it appears trite. The less evident corollary of course is that application of the same sort of experimental biology that caused the initial agricultural revolution in Western Europe, and which even in the last twenty-five years has more than doubled output per man for many crops in North America, is desperately needed in most poor and backward countries. Experimental agricultural stations, with trained staffs and adequate budgets, could be worth more than many spectacular industrial projects. New factories and machines are easy to see. But new knowledge of how a people can feed themselves better may be far more important in countries where a majority of the inhabitants are undernourished.

Once better agricultural methods have been proven to the satisfaction of agricultural experts, the problem remains of "selling" the new practices to ordinary peasants, many of whom do not wish to gamble a certain small crop against what they consider to be an uncertain though possibly larger one. At the outset, government may have to give new seed for planting, or it may have to guarantee free distribution of food grains should the experimental crop fail. Combining land holdings, especially where an entire village is consolidated into a single farm under government auspices, makes the introduction of new methods somewhat simpler. The village farm supervisor, probably hired by government anyway, can be instructed to institute certain crops and practices. Undoubtedly he will meet resistance, especially if no other village in the area has made the same experiment successfully, but free seed and fertilizers and guarantees against famine may assist in convincing the doubtful to make a trial.

Innovations always require some advance of funds or work. This is true even when purchases of equipment and materials with money are unimportant. The reason why "savings" are required is that any new method requires advance preparation, and this extra labor must be financed or fed ahead of output. Therefore accumulations of money or produce are needed.

Sometimes these advances may be considerable. For example, a new strain of rubber tree has been developed since World War II which yields several times as much latex as prewar trees did. Most of the rubber plantations in Malaya have been replanted with the new tree strain, but small holders have for the most part not made this change, largely because they lack capital. A new rubber tree does not yield for roughly five years after planting, and establishing new trees requires either clearing extra ground or destroying mature but old-type producing trees, so that initially the cost in capital of this eventually profitable innovation is considerable.

There are enough examples of plantation (or estate) agriculture in underdeveloped and tropical countries to suggest that modernization of agriculture involves not only consolidation of land holdings, and specialization of output for market, but also capitalization. Familiar instances are copra estates in Oceania, banana estates in Central America, cane sugar in the West Indies, coffee plantations in Kenya, and tea plantations in Ceylon. In all instances, scientific knowledge, strict labor supervision, and large capital sums have combined to produce exports, increase total employment, and earn investors a profit. The capital sector of a modern and developing economy should include agriculture as well as industry. And capitalist agriculture is as different from subsistence agriculture as chalk is from cheese.

In simple terms, development of backward economies is not exclusively a question of moving underemployed rural labor into industry and combining it with city-located plant and equipment. Another aspect of development is the moving of foreign and urban capital into agriculture and combining it there with rural labor. One advantage is that many of the associated and special living costs of town life are thereby avoided. Another gain is that increased agricultural output and lower food prices prevent unduly high urban wages and so render industrial exports more competitive abroad. Balanced economic development requires expansion of both a capitalist industrial and agricultural sector.

OVER-ALL COMMUNITY DEVELOPMENT

The development of a village can hardly be considered complete when its agricultural activities have been "modernized" in the sense described above. The health and education of its inhabitants are still important needs. There is little object in having people eat more unless the incidence of gastroenteritis can also be reduced. If many of the village children will eventually work in industry, now is the time to give them the rudiments of an education so that they can manage later in an urban environment. Investment is out of balance when expensive equipment is used to clear and prepare land for planting but the village's water supply must still be carried from some distance away by its women.

Thus complete village development should normally include a safe water system, sanitary means of disposing of human wastes, and at least four to six years of schooling for children. These improvements all require labor, and a certain amount of material, and the supervision of someone who knows a little about civil engineering. Government may be able to provide the engineer during construction, and it may give or loan the village such materials as pipe, but the inhabitants will have to provide most of the labor and make some items—such as bricks—themselves.

Most of this labor will have to be "conscripted" in some fashion or other. The taxpaying capacity of most villages is not adequate to pay wages for community development. Government's police power can, however, be used in other ways to provide necessary labor.

One obvious possibility is for each local authority to impose a poll tax on all its villages, with the understanding that this can be paid in cash, in certain readily marketable food grains, or in labor for local public works. The rates of exchange between these three ways of meeting the tax would of course have to be stipulated. Then a man who had enough training to earn a good wage would pay in cash, and a man with a productive farm holding would pay in produce, while the comparatively underemployed and undertrained would pay with work.

The public projects financed in this way could include a water and sewage system, dams to prevent run-off during floods, a school house with classrooms for different grades, perhaps a local mill and smithy, paved streets in the main village, and a better road to town to facilitate transportation of produce to market. Such projects are well worth their cost to most villages. But they will never be undertaken without organization, some outside financial aid for materials that cannot be made locally, and enforced contributions of labor, produce, or money.

Complete village development in this sense can only be undertaken slowly at first. Even a country with a population of only ten million may have roughly fifty thousand villages. Few governments can simultaneously hire and deploy so many experts to initiate and supervise community projects, innovate agricultural improvements, and complete all the necessary bureaucratic forms. Moreover, until a decade or so of experience has been amassed, there can be no assurance as to what are the most productive improvements and innovations. So lack of personnel and expertise together require and ensure that over-all community development will proceed experimentally and selectively.

This necessity has other virtues however. It means that the first villages scheduled for agricultural innovations and community development can be chosen with an eye to cooperativeness of inhabitants, potential output increment, proximity to market, and so on. Government cannot afford to have its first model villages be anything less than successes, and so it had better select its experimental communities with care. Also, by locating model villages throughout the country, the demonstration effect will be increased. This should facilitate the indoctrination of other communities later.

The popular success that attends these community development programs of government will obviously depend considerably upon the amount of extra real income that villagers are allowed to retain. If the cultivators are tenants of private landlords, the State can tax away much of the owners' economic rent while limiting the maximum rent liability of tenants. In this way the cooperation of the villagers—and also of course the political opposition of the landlords—should be ensured. If the State has consolidated village land holdings into a few large private farms, it can again tax economic rent more heavily, but this will hardly win for government the cooperation of what are now the most influential families in the local community. And if the State has instituted a single collective farm, increased exactions of produce will be bitterly criticized and become generally known elsewhere.

Most governments are anxious to force the pace of industrialization. And the tendency of most Communist governments has been to finance these industrial ambitions partly at the expense of agriculture. The "people's democracies" also afford a striking example of industrial growth that has been financed in part by forced collections and continued poverty for peasants. These examples suggest that taxation of the economic surplus realized by cultivators as a result of land redistribution, rent reductions, or other land reform programs can indirectly provide an important fraction of the resources needed for industry and associated urbanization. How large this fraction should be is largely determined in a free economy by commodity prices and prevailing rates of interest. How large it *can* be is something that only those versed in the art of politics and power can hope to discover.

9

Some growth and development models

Some theories of economic development are sufficiently explicit that they can be illustrated geometrically or expressed algebraically. Such statements must be extremely abstract, because mathematical formulations of economic processes cannot usefully include more than a few variables and their interactions. The art of economic model construction, even more than theorizing in prose, is to select and include only those elements that most affect the outcome.

Many of the most familiar models of economic development rather myopically stress the role of capital saving and investment. A number of them concentrate upon the transfer of resources from subsistence agriculture to commercial industry. Only a few include the enormously important effect of technological advance. Some are implicitly closed economy models. A small minority concern themselves with changes in labor force and population.

Of course just because a nation's income is expressed as an equation it does not follow that it is predictable. Nearly all the parameters and variables will have uncertain magnitudes. So it is important to realize that the main use of mathematical statements of economic growth is not computational but conceptual. Such representations serve to indicate what the analyst considers most important. This is often an important first step toward understanding economic growth processes.

CAPITAL SECTOR EXPANSION BY EQUIPPING
SUBSISTENCE LABOR

One of the more interesting and systematic theories of economic development in backward countries has been advanced by former Professor W. Arthur Lewis.[1]

He sees development as the accumulation of capital that is used

[1] W. A. Lewis, "Economic Development with Unlimited Supplies of Labor," *The Manchester School*, May, 1954; "Unlimited Labor—Further Notes," *The Manchester School*, January, 1958.

initially to equip labor drawn from a subsistence agriculture. His theory envisages an economy divided into a subsistence sector and a capitalistic sector. The capital sector is primarily industrial but can include commercial agriculture.

Economic growth entails the slow penetration and eventual absorption of the subsistence sector by the capitalistic sector. The essence of development, if income per capita is to be increased, is that the labor force be given more capital to use. At first, when there is little capital, it is important to "widen" its use and have people using some equipment. Later, as the capital-to-labor ratio rises, there can be capital "deepening." But these two stages of growth—capital-widening followed by capital-deepening—are basically different. In the first stage, but not in the second, there is an "unlimited" supply of labor available to the capitalistic sector from the subsistence sector.

Stage one—unlimited labor supply

All backward economies have a subsistence sector within which output is shared by each family among its members. The "wage" in this sector is sometimes said to be average product and sometimes viewed as output per head. In either case it is low, for people work with very little investment to assist them and saving is also negligible as a consequence. However, there is an adjoining capitalistic sector where there is enough investment from domestic saving and foreign loans to give each worker a certain minimum investment to help him. Hence the output per worker—but not the net productivity attributable to labor—is much higher in the capital sector than in the subsistence sector. However, because the supply of labor from the rural areas is "unlimited," all this additional output must return to capitalists. Industrial workers cannot demand higher wages if there is always a competitive supply of available labor from the subsistence sector at the same wage rate.

The wage of labor in the capital sector cannot be less than the average product that is available to workers as family members in the subsistence sector. It may be somewhat higher, especially if food and shelter cost more in the capitalistic sector, or if leaving home occasions psychic disutilities. But if there is a difference, it is likely to be fairly constant, and so the supply of labor to the capital sector appears to be almost infinitely elastic during this stage. Of course if the marginal product of a worker in the subsistence sector is less than his average product, an exodus of such workers presumably raises the average consumption share available to those who remain. But perhaps this is a second order effect and can be ignored.

If the capital sector has economic contact with the outside world, the cost of any capital it uses is more or less determined by external interest rates. And the cost of labor to the capitalistic sector is determined as explained. Hence, at the given ratio of wage-to-interest rates, there is likely to be a given capital-to-labor ratio that is most profitable. And this may not vary significantly with the output scale of the capitalistic sector. (Something like a homogeneous production function is implicitly assumed.)

Additional capital will be used during this stage to employ more labor in the capitalistic sector at the same K/L ratio, and not to increase the quantity of capital combined with each worker. This is because it will be unprofitable for private entrepreneurs to vary the ratio of capital to labor—and hence their relative marginal products—in the absence of a change in wage rates or interest rates. Accordingly, there is a constant and minimum capital-to-labor ratio throughout this stage attributable to constant factor price ratios.

The expansion path during the first stage can be depicted by AB in Fig. 9-1 (Lewis does not employ such a diagram in his presentation). Factor price ratios are constant, as are K/L ratios. It might be a little more reasonable to suppose that the average consumption product in the subsistence economy is slowly rising, and hence that K/L ratios in the capitalistic sector should be increasing somewhat also. But the more important point is that during this stage wages are determined for the whole economy by the average product of subsistence labor, and not by marginal labor productivity in the capitalistic sector.

One point needs clarifying: when K_1 capital is available to be com-

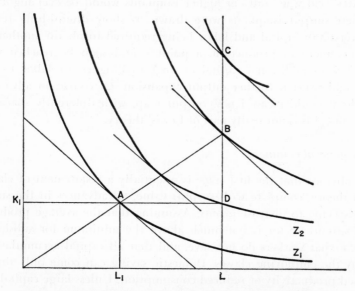

Fig. 9-1. Economic Growth with Unlimited and Limited Labor Supplies.

bined with L labor, why does the economy not move to D on Output Curve Z_2, instead of combining K_1 with L_1 labor at A on Z_1? Three possible reasons come to mind. First, the flat slope of Z_2 at D indicates very low wage rates relative to interest rates, and so if interest rates are set at world levels the wage that entrepreneurs could offer would be less than the average subsistence product and hence unacceptable. Second, it must be remembered that the isoquants refer only to the output of the capitalistic sector, and so total output value at D is only greater than at A if labor's marginal product in the capitalistic sector is greater than that in the subsistence sector. Third, it may be extremely difficult to combine capital with labor in the subsistence sector, so that in practice capital can be invested only with labor that has migrated from the rural hinterland to the modern capitalistic sector.

Stage two—limited labor supply

Eventually, if the economy can obtain more and more capital, it will reach point B. The subsistence economy is then no more. Additional capital will involve not capital-widening but capital-deepening. The supply of labor becomes virtually inelastic. Wages are hereafter based on marginal productivity in the capitalistic sector.

As can be seen from the diagram, successive output isoquants intersect the vertical labor supply ever more steeply. A tangent indicates that at C a unit of extra labor is equivalent in production to a larger increment of capital than at B. So assuming interest rates are still based on world loan rates, real wage rates at higher isoquants would be ever higher too.

If these output isoquants were drawn to show diminishing returns, with ever more capital and labor being required to obtain another constant increment of production, a point would soon be reached where either lack of additional capital or an unwillingness of labor to work more could prevent further output expansion. Of course an advance in technology would mean a new output map, with differently spaced isoquants. But this is not really part of Lewis' theory.

Some general comments

It is obvious that the first stage is essentially a restatement of classical growth theory, complete with surplus value, all advances in the state of the art serving to increase profits. Assuming that the average product in the subsistence sector is not much above the minimum for subsistence, it is clear that workers do not save, and that all capital accumulation is done by the employing classes. Domestic saving can come only through increased productivity or reduced consumption. Unless large capital sums can be borrowed from abroad, and most national investments must usually be saved domestically, anything that reduces profits or raises the cost of "wage" goods (*i.e.*, the products that workers buy) will reduce the rate of real capital accumulation and hence slow down progress from *A* to *B*.

Economic development during the first stage is not of much benefit to anyone but the capitalists. The workers who transfer from the subsistence sector to the capitalist sector are not appreciably better off. Only the people remaining in the subsistence sector may have somewhat more to eat.

The welfare significance of the first stage is that it has to be traversed en route to the second stage. In the second stage, technological advances can benefit workers as well as capitalists. Labor, being in limited supply, has effective bargaining power, even though this is exercised only through competition. Factors are rewarded according to marginal productivity. The developing economy can now be understood better in terms of neoclassical rather than classical theory.

The outstanding merit of the Lewis analysis, with its emphasis on equipping subsistence labor with new capital, is that it is a two-sector model of development and treats both labor and capital. It does not seek to prescribe rigidly either the rate of capital accumulation or its productivity. Size of the labor force and advances in technology are neither excluded nor included explicitly. Its refusal to treat these variables in a rigid and mechanical way is both a weakness and a strength of the approach. The theory loses specificity but gains realism.

GROWTH MODELS THAT STRESS CAPITAL

Very popular among development agencies are those one-sector economic models that consider capital to be the sole source of increased production and ignore changes in the size of the labor force. But such models can stress—by including an incremental capital-to-output ratio—the changing productivity of savings and investment. The most familiar examples of this approach are probably those of Harrod and Domar,[2] originally evolved for analysis of advanced nations, and concerned in Domar's case with maintaining effective demand in a mature economy. They are not very appropriate to backward economies that have rapid increases in labor force and considerable direct investments by householders. However, because of the current popularity of incremental capital-to-output ratios in economic development planning, they cannot be ignored. And they can be modified in ways detailed below that make them more useful in analyzing underdeveloped countries.

[2] R. F. Harrod, "An Essay in Dynamic Theory," *Economic Journal,* March, 1939, and "Domar and Dynamic Economics," *Economic Journal,* September, 1959; and E. Domar, "Expansion and Employment," *American Economic Review,* March, 1947.

Incremental capital-to-output ratios

It is a very simple and attractive idea to suppose that national output increases as some linear function of additions to real capital stock. But it needs to be recognized that this incremental capital-to-output ratio need not be constant over time. And it is of course quite invalid to suppose that annual national output can increase only through annual net investment.

The very concept of an incremental capital-to-output ratio (ICOR) for a single company—let alone an entire economy—is difficult to define for reasons listed below. Suppose that engineering and cost studies indicate that a single investment of $1 million will occasion the following annual increments:

Value of output (constant prices)	$500,000
Materials used in production	250,000
Gross value added	250,000
Depreciation	50,000
Net value added	200,000
Payroll for labor	100,000
Return on investment	100,000

An ordinary entrepreneur would say that his $1 million investment yielded $100,000 a year for a rate of return (ROR) of 0.10.[3] But some economic planners would hail this as an incremental output-to-capital ratio of 0.25 ($250,000, gross value added, divided by $1 million, initial investment). Thus the ICOR, which is a reciprocal, is 4.0. This rather remarkable difference between 0.10 and 0.25 arises because the planner does not deduct payroll, and perhaps does not deduct depreciation from gross value added, whereas the capitalist does.

The planner might argue that various items that are costs to an entrepreneur are not costs to an economy and can be ignored when one is formulating development programs. For instance, he might argue that aggregate employment is constant, so why consider the cost of labor to a single project? The answer is that if payroll is not deducted from the value added by this project, the reduction in the values added by all other enterprises that have lost labor to this project should be deducted from its value added. Or the planner might argue that the labor employed by the new investment was previously out of work; but then the payroll represents the real utility of leisure as against this work, and not to deduct the payroll from value added reflects a callous disregard of

[3] The incremental rate of return is sometimes termed the marginal efficiency of capital.

human sensibilities. Those who labor are not slaves of the state to be worked or not without a change in their remuneration.

Depreciation is a very real cost both to a government project or a private enterprise. And if projects are being ranked because insufficient capital funds require that some be excluded, it is important that differences in depreciation be considered. For example, if one project is a wharf whose pilings will soon become worm eaten, whereas another is a steel toll bridge, it would be folly to ignore differences in depreciation.

In reality the ICOR of a *nation* ($\Delta K/\Delta Y$) may be less than individual plant possibilities suggest. This is because \$1 million invested in one project or firm may cause other facilities to be withdrawn from use earlier than would otherwise be the case. Premature scrapping of equipment elsewhere is a very real cost of investment, but cause and effect are extremely indirect, and so cannot be predicted.

Practically, a nation's ICOR has to be estimated by observing historic macro-economic relations, always recognizing that national income statistics of backward countries are extremely unreliable. Conceptually what is wanted is a value ratio that seeks to express quantity changes at constant prices. The numerator should be the value increase in stocks of all produced means of production, including not only fixed capital, but all forms of voluntarily accumulated working capital besides. The denominator should be the net value added output of the economy during the same period.

For example, the ΔK of the numerator might be the net annual investment aggregated from 1950 through 1959, and the ΔY of the denominator might be the national income of 1960 minus that of 1951. Accordingly, an ICOR for the 1950's might be estimated. In this case the increases in income flow lag behind the increases in capital stocks by a year in an attempt to allow for the fact that new capital goods do not start producing immediately.

Assume that observed $\Delta K/\Delta Y$ is 4.0. The mathematical definition of the ratio is clear, but the resultant quotient has no economic meaning whatsoever. It does not follow that in future \$4 of extra investment will always yield \$1 extra output.

Careless thinking about capital often results in just this sort of nonsense inference. Increases in national income result from increases in the stock of capital, a larger labor force, or improvements in technology. If the entire national income increase is then attributed to a single cause—such as investment—some very unfortunate policy decisions can be made.

Imagine a small backward country which for the past decade has been enjoying an annual national income increase of \$10 million. Annual investment, that is, additions to the aggregate capital stock, has also been \$10 million a year. Superficially the ICOR appears to be unity. But perhaps, of the $10 million annual increase in national income, $4 million is attributable to innovation and $4 million to an expanding labor force and population. Suppose the government wishes to force an annual national income increase through additional government investments.

Specifically, government may desire an annual increase in national income of $20 million, not $10 million as hitherto. If the planners casually assume that the observed ICOR of unity has a causal significance, they will be in trouble. The rate of return on capital is really not 1.0 but 0.2. An extra annual government investment of $10 million will not raise national income by $10 million but by only $2 million a year. The real capital cost of annually increasing national income by $20 million is annual investments of $10 million + $50 million a year. And most economies cannot immediately absorb such a large proportionate increase in annual investment even if made available from abroad.

One can of course imagine circumstances that render these dangers more apparent than real. One ingenious assumption would be that innovations must wait upon new capital goods that embody improvements in the state of arts. But new capital goods include all replacement investment, as well as net investment, and many innovations depend more on people working in different ways than upon substituting new forms of capital for old.

Ignoring innovation and technology, observed aggregate ICOR's have causal significance only in certain special instances. One is when capital and labor are employed in fixed proportions. (This is Lewis' first stage: capital-widening.) If extra capital always puts extra people to work, according to some fixed proportion, estimates of future output can, in the absence of innovation, be based on capital or labor employment alone. But because extra output then involves extra worker disutility, its welfare significance is less certain.

Like most analytic tools, aggregate ICOR's must be used with caution, and only under very special circumstances is their employment justified. Careless employment of them in economic development can lead to exaggerated ideas regarding the efficacy of extra capital to accelerate national economic growth. These hopes must often be frustrated.

Saving rates and capital productivity: Harrod

If additional investment and increased productivity of extra capital are the only sources of increased output, it is evident that the rate at which national output grows will depend exclusively upon the rate at which annual income is saved and the rate at which net investment contributes to output in value terms. For instance, if the savings rate is 0.1 and the ICOR is 4.0, national output increases by 0.1 over 4.0 or 0.025.

Like most fundamental truths, when barely stated, this notion has a rather obvious quality.

This idea was advanced by Sir Roy Harrod as long ago as 1939. He called the proportionate output increase, which results from dividing the current savings rate by the current ICOR, the warranted growth rate.[4] Symbolically expressed as G_w, he defined this as s/C_r, where s is the ratio of annual savings to annual income and C_r is the incremental capital-to-output ratio when all physical accumulations are put to their best productive use.

The warranted growth rate refers to a point in time. There is no supposition that the values of s and C_r are constant parameters from year to year. Hence there can be a steady growth rate, even though s and C_r are varying over time, so long as they change in the same proportion and direction. Nor is there any assumption that the average saving propensity is equal to the marginal saving propensity. In fact there is no mention of the latter.

There is no assurance that $\Delta Y/Y$ in the future will be equal to the past value of s divided by the past value of C_r. In future, at the warranted growth rate of the past, savings might exceed intended investment; then some physical accumulations (*e.g.*, unintended inventory additions) will not be "normally" productive. Or the quota of extra labor and natural resources, as previously combined with each unit of investment, may not be available in future. In this event C_r will have a higher value than formerly.

A complete agnostic might assert that there is neither a stable savings ratio nor a stable ICOR in most economies. The values of these ratios derived from the past have no predictive value then at all. In fact it could be argued that the warranted growth rate is nothing but an identity restated in a way that seems to imply—at least so some have inferred—that s and C_r are parameters. Are these ratios *ex post* observations or *ex ante* guides? Logically they are only the former, but the temptation to use them for extrapolation is very strong, and some analysts will always do so. The warranted growth rate, where A represents accumulations, is identical with $\Delta Y/Y$. This is because s is defined as A/Y and C_r as $A/\Delta Y$; this cancels to $\Delta Y/Y$.

Growth without inflation

Investment, when it is independent of current national income levels, has a dual impact on an economy. On the one hand it adds to productive capacity. On the other it constitutes a monetary injection, which may be multiplied by the tendency of people to respend extra receipts, according

[4] R. F. Harrod, "An Essay in Dynamic Theory," *Economic Journal*, March, 1939.

to conventional Keynesian analysis. In some advanced countries there have been fears in the past that this monetary augmentation of effective demand might not be enough to buy the potential output increase resulting from investment in plant capacity. But in backward countries, during recent years, the problem has not been deflation but inflation. Governments have so expanded bank credits in order to finance ordinary operations and investment projects that rapidly rising prices have hampered economic development in other sectors. Growth without inflation is still beyond the competence of weak governments.

In 1947, a decade later and independently of Sir Roy Harrod, Professor Evsey Domar[5] stated what he considered to be the incremental annual investment requirement for a constant rate of income growth without inflation or deflation. Unlike Harrod, he made two very specific assumptions, and these predetermine everything else. He assumed that "savings" (e.g., hoardings) are equal to $Y \cdot a$, where Y is income and a is the constant average and marginal propensity to save. And he seems to have assumed that the incremental and average output-to-capital ratio—designated by σ—can be treated as a parameter. It is also clear that he made the usual assumptions of that time and supposed that all "saving" is income induced and that all investment is income autonomous. What is required then for $\Delta Y/Y$ to be constant over time? And what determines this rate of income growth?

On "physical" grounds it is evident that if σ is the constant ratio of $\Delta Y/I$, $\Delta I/I$ must be equal to $\Delta Y/Y$ where I is investment.[6] A given percentage change in annual income requires an equal percentage change in annual investment. This essentially assumes that advancing technology and increasing labor force make no contribution to output.

Monetary savings equal $Y \cdot a$, and in equilibrium this will be equivalent to I. And ΔY equals $I \cdot \sigma$. So, substituting $Y \cdot a$ for I, ΔY equals $Y \cdot a \cdot \sigma$, or

$$\frac{\Delta Y}{Y} = a\sigma$$

In those cases where Harrod's s is Domar's a, and where Harrod's C_r is the reciprocal of Domar's σ, it is apparent that Harrod's warranted growth rate is Domar's stable growth rate.[7] Ex post, they are identical, and this explains perhaps why their theories are so often considered to be similar. But Domar assumes that the marginal propensity to save is the same as the average propensity.

[5] E. Domar, "Expansion and Employment," American Economic Review, March, 1947.
[6] I, investment, has previously been designated ΔK; we are here using Domar's symbols.
[7] Harrod's equation is identical with the right side of Domar's. Domar's $\Delta Y/Y$ equals $a\sigma$ or I/Y times $\Delta Y/I$. Harrod's G_w is s/C_r or I/Y times $\Delta Y/I$.

It has already been indicated that $\Delta I/I$ must equal $\Delta Y/Y$ for physical reasons in Domar's scheme. So $\Delta I/I$ equals $a\sigma$ also. If we multiply both sides by I/a:

$$\frac{\Delta I}{a} = I \cdot \sigma$$

which is also equal to ΔY.

Does this exercise in symbolic logic lead to a significant economic revelation? In this case, where the average and marginal propensities to consume are equal, I/a appears to be the Keynesian multiplier. And if investment is autonomous of income, ΔI appears as an incremental monetary injection or *extra* multiplicand. The stable rate of income growth can only be maintained if each year there is a changing but specific ΔI. Each year the increase in investment must be enough to produce both the ever-increasing output and the additional effective demand to buy it at constant prices. The extra output is $I \cdot \sigma$; the extra effective demand is $\Delta I/a$. They must be equal at the equilibrium growth rate.

Domar's essential contribution is that he stressed the inability of an economy—assuming a constant linear ICOR—to sustain an equilibrium growth unless $\Delta I/I = \Delta Y/Y$. An economy with a constant I, year after year, would not be in balance. Initially, it would suffer from inflation, as I/a would exceed $I \cdot \sigma$ in the first year. But after, say, ten years, when demand had still increased by only I/a but output had now increased by 10 times $I \cdot \sigma$, it would suffer from deflation. Equilibrium requires not a constant absolute income increase but a constant relative income growth. This is the real moral of the model.

This approach, however, still makes assumptions regarding the behavior of investors and of consumers that are not very realistic for backward economies. It ignores the contributions of additional labor force and improving technology to national income. But although the analysis is all in terms of a closed economy, it does relate production or supply to the consumer demand. And that is a step in the right direction.

FORCED GROWTH IN BACKWARD ECONOMIES

It may be true in advanced economies of Western culture that investing firms and saving households are two distinct groups whose only contact is indirect, through the capital fund markets. It may also be true that firms usually decide to invest independently of national income levels and that households consume and save solely according to money income. But this is not true of many backward economies. Most such economies produce partly for subsistence. Some of the family output is consumed directly; some is used directly to improve the farm property or family business. Part of the money receipts from the output that is sold may be spent for consumer goods, part for additional stocks of producer goods, and part may be "saved" or hoarded. So there are five ways in which output may be used by households, two entail direct use of output, and three involve the use of money.

In poor countries industry is organized, not into giant corporations, but into small partnerships and proprietorships. These small businesses do not raise capital funds by selling securities, and they have limited access to bank credit. An investment decision of any magnitude therefore cannot be made independently of a consumption decision. In order to invest more, many households must simultaneously decide to consume less.

Macro-income theory, evolved initially to analyze advanced economies, has often assumed that investment is autonomous of income and consumption is induced by it. But in backward countries investment seems to be partly income autonomous and partly income-induced. And the same is true of consumption. It is unfortunate that these complications involve a somewhat more elaborate theory. But the importance of the subject would seem to warrant some extra realism.

First of all we shall suppose that the constant marginal and average propensities to use net output, taken for an entire economy in some average sense, are:

α	(alpha)	to sell output, and hoard the proceeds;
β	(beta)	to sell output, and spend to improve own enterprise;
γ	(gamma)	to sell output, and spend on consumption;
δ	(delta)	to use output directly to improve own enterprise;
ϵ	(epsilon)	to use output directly for consumption.[8]

Second we may suppose that national output will be exhaustively distributed among the following six components:

I_a	autonomous money investment
I_i	induced money investment
C_i	induced money consumption
I'_i	direct induced investment
C'_i	direct induced consumption
C_a	autonomous money consumption

The ΔY for a given year, taking the supply or production side first, is then

$$[Y(\beta + \delta) + I_a]\,\sigma$$

8 The sum of α, β, γ, δ, and ϵ is unity.

Of this extra output, ΔY $(a + \beta + \gamma)$ will be marketed, and $\Delta Y(\delta + \epsilon)$ will be used directly where produced. The extra "missing" monetary demand—due to "saving" or hoarding—is hence $\Delta Y \cdot a$ of the total output increase or $\Delta Y a/(a + \beta + \gamma)$ of the increased *market* output.[9]

If extra demand is to match extra supply, an additional autonomous injection must occur, equal to $\Delta Y \cdot a$. This extra injection will be the sum of autonomous extra investment and autonomous extra consumption. The relevant sum is of course algebraic. And a positive autonomous investment may be partly offset by negative autonomous consumption. In any given period there will be a matched increase in demand and supply if

$$\Delta I_a + \Delta C_a = [Y\ (\beta + \delta) + I_a]\ \sigma a$$

The *rate* of growth, $\Delta Y/Y$, is given by dividing either side of this equation by $Y \cdot a$.

What is required for some *steady* rate of income growth? If σ remains constant, and so do all the marginal propensities listed above, the rate of growth will depend upon the proportionate increase that occurs in the autonomous investment I_a. In turn, given a constant σ, this will require the same proportionate increase in $\Delta(I_a + C_a)$ for demand to match supply.

Suppose Y is \$100 million and a steady 5 per cent annual increase in income is required. Then, assuming σ is 0.2, total investment I must equal \$5 million divided by 0.2, or \$25 million. If the sum of $\beta + \delta$ is 0.15, induced investment will be \$15 million. Hence autonomous investment I_a must equal \$10 million in the first year. The extra "missing" demand, if a is 0.1, is \$0.5 million. If Y is increasing at 5 per cent a year, and σ is constant, I_a must be increasing at 5 per cent a year also. So ΔI_a will be .05 of \$10 million or \$0.5 million. In this case the autonomous change in consumption can be zero, and demand and supply will balance as they grow.

This is a rather special rate of growth. It is the growth rate that occurs when ΔI_a is equal to $\Delta Y \cdot a$. It is the maximum possible rate of growth not requiring some enforced decrease in autonomous consumption to prevent inflation. It is the minimum possible growth rate without some action being needed to prevent deflation. This fiscally "neutral" growth rate might be designated G_n. It is equivalent to $(a + \beta + \delta)\sigma$.[10]

[9] It may be useful at times to distinguish between the market output, Y_m, and the subsistence output, Y_s. Y_m is $Y\ (a + \beta + \gamma)$. And Y_s is $Y\ (\delta + \epsilon)$.

[10] The two consuming propensities together may be taken to equal 0.75, the two investing propensities together may equal 0.15, and the hoarding or saving propensity 0.10.

This is very much like Domar's equation for $\Delta Y/Y$, but it takes into account the influence of induced investment on potential output, which may be important. Because this induced investment is not autonomous of income, it is not a multiplicand to be multiplied by the reciprocal of the saving propensity. (The *basic* equation also recognizes that households may autonomously reduce consumption when they autonomously increase investment.)

Government may not be content with this monetarily "neutral" G_n rate of income increase, assuming autonomous investment brings it about, and may wish instead to force the growth rate. Perhaps a 10 per cent annual rate is the politically approved percentage. Given such income increases, how much consumption must then be slowed by taxes and borrowing if inflation is to be avoided?

Using the same parameter symbols and values as before, and assuming a base Y of \$100 million again, it is apparent that a total investment of \$50 million will be needed in the first year for a ΔY of \$10 million. Induced investment again will only amount to \$15 million of this sum. So autonomous investment of \$35 million is needed. But the "missing" demand—$Y \cdot a$—is only \$10 million. Consumption spending amounting to \$25 million needs to be prevented by government taxes and borrowing. This is the inflationary gap that needs to be closed.

Going into the next period, ΔY is \$10 million, and the extra "missing" demand (ΔD_m) is $\Delta Y \cdot a$ or \$1 million. If a steady income growth of 10 per cent is required, induced and autonomous investment must also be increasing by 10 per cent, which means that ΔI_a in this period will be \$3.5 million. Hence autonomous consumption must be reduced by a further \$2.5 million so that $(\Delta I_a + \Delta C_a)$ will equal \$1.0 million.

It is *basic*, for growth with balanced supply and demand, that

$$(\Delta I_a + C_a) = \Delta Y \cdot a$$

where

$$\Delta Y = \sigma[I_a + Y\,(\beta + \delta)]$$

Symbolically, if G_g is the government required rate of growth and asterisks indicate necessary values, the following equations hold:

(1) $I^* = (G_g \cdot Y)/\sigma$
(2) $I_a{}^* = (G_g \cdot Y)/\sigma - Y\,(\beta + s)$
(3) $D_m = aY$
(4) $C_a{}^* = aY - I_a{}^*$
(5) $\Delta D_m{}^* = a\Delta Y^*$
(6) $\Delta I_a{}^* = G_g \cdot I_a{}^*$
(7) $\Delta C_a{}^* = a\Delta Y^* - G_g \cdot I_a{}^*$

This is really not so formidable as it may appear. It says that given a desired increase in income, a certain autonomous investment is required over and above that normally induced. This autonomous investment may well prove to be greater than "savings." If so, to avoid inflation, other spending must be curtailed. The spending to curtail is that for consumption, so long as investment is "needed" for growth. Such an autonomous reduction in consumption, by government taxes, borrowings, and the like, is the human price that must be paid for a rapidly growing domestic national product.

One merit of the foregoing analysis, as compared with the one preceding it, is that the "neutral," "stable," or "warranted" growth rate is not the only one considered. "Forced" rates can be examined. And their cost in lost consumption can be assessed.[11]

THE CONTRIBUTIONS OF LABOR AND TECHNOLOGY ALSO INCLUDED

The great defect in most development models, and of all those considered in the last section, is that they ignore the possible contributions to output of an expanding labor force. And all the formulations described so far in this chapter ignore the very potent influence of advancing technology on production. Fortunately, it is possible to supplement what has gone before in such a way as to remove these inadequacies.

Labor and capital when productivity is constant

The neglect in Harrod-Domar models of labor's contribution to aggregate output is perhaps explained by their original purpose, which was to understand the growth and occasional overcapacities of advanced economies such as those of Western Europe and North America. In most of these countries population has been growing at about 1 per cent a year. In contrast, gross investment in these same countries has often been around 20 per cent of national income, which means that their total stock of capital has been increasing perhaps 5 per cent a year. In relative magnitudes capital stocks were increasing about five times as rapidly as labor force—assuming the latter to be some more or less constant fraction of population—and so it is not surprising that investment received primary attention.

In some of the more poor and backward countries, population—and

11 To simplify the above presentation, it was assumed that growth occurs at the same rate in the output of things to be sold (Y_m) and of things to be used by those who produce them (Y_s). One might assume that output increments occur only in the money-market sector. This makes for more complicated but also more interesting cases.

hence the labor force—is increasing at around 2 to 3 per cent a year. Net investment may be around 5 per cent of the existing capital stock. And so, although the absolute stock of capital may be increasing at a higher proportional rate than the labor force, the difference is not so marked. Under these circumstances almost any method of including labor's con-tribution is preferable to omitting it. There is really no warrant to ignore it.

One of the simplest production functions that includes labor and capital is one that assumes each has a constant physical product irre-spective of the ratios in which they may be combined. Then an extra man has a given physical product whether he is the 10th, 100th, or 1,000th man to be combined with $100, $1000, or $100,000 worth of capital. Capital and labor are then linear substitutes for one another.

Symbolically, this can be expressed as

$$V = L\theta + K\sigma'$$

where V is value of output, L is the employed labor force, K is the original value of the total stock of capital, θ (theta) is the constant value product of a unit of labor and σ' (sigma prime) is the value product of a unit of capital.[12]

But why the prime on sigma? This brings us to depreciation. And we must digress briefly.

A production function basically relates physical output to various in-puts. The inputs in the present case are producer goods stocks and "stocks" of labor. The output by a production function for a given period is estimated independently of the future longevity of the capital and workers. It makes no difference to the input-output relation that workers die and capital depreciates. Output as estimated by a production function is neither gross nor net of capital depreciation. Output is output.

A stock of capital results in two things happening in a given unit of time: one is output, at a rate σ' per unit of capital; and the other is depreciation at a rate d per capital unit. The depreciation rate has no effect on output or, therefore, upon gross value added, if the capital is always maintained. But it must be taken into account in determining net value added and the net incomes of capitalists and workers.

This can be done by making $\sigma' - d$ equal σ, which last is the net value product of a unit of capital, σ' and d both being measured in dollars per capital unit. Then $K \cdot \sigma$ equals $K \cdot \sigma' - K \cdot d$, and we can write:

$$V - K_d = Y = L\theta + K\sigma$$

[12] ΔK is periodic investment and equal to I in the preceding section.

The σ is then a net coefficient and identical with that of the preceding section (see pp. 175–177).

It is worth noting that σ' is based on technology, as is θ, and both are independent of changes in the stock depreciation rate d. A rise in depreciation rates, if technology is otherwise unchanged, will reduce the net value added occasioned by a fixed K and L. The net aggregate income of workers, $L \cdot \theta$, is unchanged. However, the net income of capitalists, $K \cdot \sigma - K \cdot d$, will decline. Labor's net income is not immediately affected if the factor combination cannot be changed. In macroeconomics this differential incidence of depreciation on factor incomes is important where capitalists rather than workers do most of the saving.

This two-factor production function can be combined with some of the preceding equations to indicate what is required to obtain a given increment in income with balanced demand and supply. Such an equation for ΔY is

$$\frac{\Delta I_a + \Delta C_a}{a} = \Delta L \theta + \Delta K \sigma$$

where ΔK has been substituted for the previous I and ΔI is $\Delta \Delta K$. Only $(a + \beta + \gamma)$ of extra output occasions money income. And the fraction of this that is hoarded is $a/(a + \beta + \gamma)$. However, as $(a + \beta + \gamma)$ cancels, this can be omitted—and has been previously.

Inclusion of labor's contribution to production lessens the inflationary pressures that would exist without an autonomous consumption decrease. Reverting to the previous example, suppose again that base Y is $100 million, that ΔY of $10 million is "required" by government, and that $\Delta L \cdot \theta$ is worth $5 million. Then a new investment of $25 million will suffice to provide the other 5 million of extra income desired by government. The induced investment of $15 million, plus an autonomous investment of $10 million will suffice. And an I_a of $10 million, together with a zero C_a, will provide the "missing" demand of $Y \cdot a$ (or $10 million) from the preceding period.

Models that ignore all contributions to income save that of capital's tend to exaggerate the incidental inflation of any forced rate of income growth.

Labor and capital: constant substitution elasticities

One thing most economists would probably agree upon is that the marginal products of labor and capital do vary when these factors are combined in altered proportions. The 100th man will usually contribute less extra output than a 10th man if both are working with the same total quantity of capital. This principle of diminishing returns, applied to labor when land is fixed in quantity, is of course one of the oldest of economic theories.

How factor marginal products change with altered combinations is much more debatable, obviously varies from industry to industry, and is very hard to measure. Accordingly, it is customary to make some simple and rather special assumption. One such supposition is that, for an economy as a whole, a given proportionate change in the quantity of labor is always the output equivalent of some other constant proportionate change in the quantity of the other factor. Thus a 1 per cent increase in labor with a 2 per cent decrease in capital quantity may leave output unchanged. Or a 10 per cent decrease in labor may be a perfect substitute for a 20 per cent increase in capital. And so on.

In addition, constant returns to scale are usually assumed, so that if both labor and capital are doubled, output will be doubled too. If a production function is homogeneous in this sense, and factors always are paid unit prices in accordance with their relative marginal products, the total output will be "exhausted." The total claims upon output of all the factors, determined by competition, will then exactly equal the gross value added of all that has been produced.

The Cobb-Douglas function has all these characteristics. It can be written:

$$V = \phi \cdot L^l \cdot K^k$$

Here V is annual gross value added again, L is the labor force, K is the producer goods stock (or "capital"), and ϕ is a conversion coefficient that relates worker-capital units to gross income. The sum of the exponents l and k must be unity if all the product is to be claimed. And the values of these exponents indicate the constant fractional shares in gross value added that each factor will obtain. For instance, if l is 0.67 and k is 0.33, then 0.67 of the gross value added will be paid as aggregate labor earnings and 0.33 will be paid as aggregate gross interest. In other words, V_L is $V \cdot l$ and V_K is $V \cdot k$ where V is gross value added and the subscripts indicate the factor recipient of the gross factor incomes.

Real values for the exponents that define each factor's constant share in gross value added can often be estimated from national income data. For instance, suppose GNP is \$100 million, labor's income is \$67 million, and income from capital before depreciation is \$33 million. Then l is V_L/V or 0.67 and k is V_K/V or 0.33.

Aggregate net income, and its distribution to labor and capital, cannot be determined without considering capital stock depreciation. Y, the net income, is $V - K \cdot d$. Y_K, the net income of capitalists, is $V \cdot k - K \cdot d$. And we can perhaps suppose that the net and gross incomes accruing to labor are both equal to $V \cdot l$. The net interest rate is then $(V \cdot k - K \cdot d)/K$ and the wage rate is $V \cdot l/L$.

There is still exhaustion of the product. A doubling of capital with a doubling of labor results in twice as much gross value added, twice as much depreciation, twice as much net interest payments, and twice as much labor earnings. But the expansion path will involve less capital than *net* formulations of the Cobb-Douglas functions usually presume.

A production function of this type, assuming values of, say, 0.67 for l and 0.33 for k and a present GNP of \$100 million, can give some indication of what awaits a national economy over the next five years or so. For example, suppose population and labor force are expected to increase by 15 per cent over the next five years, and that gross capital formation for this entire period is expected to be 50 per cent of current annual GNP. How much greater is GNP likely to be at the end of these five years?

The contribution of the extra labor force is clear. If l is 0.67, and the increase in L is 15 per cent, this will occasion an increase in GNP of 0.67 of 0.15 or 0.10. In other words, extra labor will have provided an increase of \$10 million to the higher GNP of the fifth year.

The contribution of capital is a little more difficult to estimate. The gross capital formation over five years will be 0.5 of \$100 million, or \$50 million. Let us assume that the initial value of K was \$80 million and that during this five-year period there is depreciation of \$26 million. A net capital increase of \$24 million is 0.3 of the initial \$80 million capital stock. And, if k is $1/3$, this will also occasion a 0.1, or \$10 million increase of initial GNP by the fifth year.

This means that GNP will rise 20 per cent from \$100 million to \$120 million in five years, for an average yearly increase of 4 per cent. If population has increased 15 per cent during the same period, there has been an annual increment of no more than 1 per cent in per capita GNP. And yet the magnitudes used in this example are not atypical of poor and backward countries.

Incidentally, the gross ICOR in the above example is \$50 million divided by \$20 million over five years, or 2.5. However, as a little arithmetic will show, an additional \$50 million gross investment would only add about \$10 million. The gross rate of return on capital is about 20 per cent.

Advances in technology

The conversion coefficient ϕ in the Cobb-Douglas function can be increased to allow for the effects of advances in technology. If these improvements in efficiency cannot be linked to either one factor or the other, and statistical methods of estimation are usually far too rough to permit such attribution, it is not uncommon to assume some constant rate of increase in the conversion coefficient. This could increase compound according to some function of gross income from some base date. But it is more usual to compound such an increase in efficiency with the passage of years.

If this relative efficiency increase is designated by a^t, where t is the number of years since the base period, it is as though L and K had each been increased by a^t times. Or, if the production function has been represented graphically by an output isoquant map, it is as though all the isoquants had been renumbered and given new values a^t times greater.

Improvements in efficiency, when incorporated in this way as "shift" effects, are neutral as regards factor rewards. If a is 1.02 a year, the gross incomes of capital and labor (K and L being unchanged) will both increase by 1.02 each year. However, there is no reason for supposing that depreciation will increase by a, and so net incomes of capitalists may increase by a larger proportion.

Conceptually, one might allow for increases in labor efficiency, on account of improved health and training, by having the effective (but not real) magnitude of L increase relatively as some function of time. Given a constant actual L, population being unchanged, one might apply the exponent l to a magnitude $b^t \cdot L$. Similarly, for some reason or other, one might increase the effective (but not real) quantity of K over time and apply the exponent k to a magnitude $c^t \cdot K$. The revised equation would then be

$$V = a^t \phi (b^t L)^l (c^t K)^k$$

There is such a thing as being too sophisticated, however. It is doubtful whether economic statisticians, especially when using sketchy data from backward countries, can estimate the various coefficients included in such a theoretically refined statement. In attributing improvements in productivity, the best that can be done is probably to assume some over-all advance, rather than to attempt measures and extrapolations of each factor's special increases in productivity.

A GENERAL MODEL OF ECONOMIC DEVELOPMENT
IN BACKWARD COUNTRIES

Enough has now been stated, in describing various models of economic growth that have been proposed, to form some idea of what might be included in any minimum model of development that is likely to be useful. Such a model must inevitably be more complex than some of those considered to date. But the general characteristics of such a model can be described in literary rather than numerical terms.

Multisector. An essential aspect of all backward but developing economies is that they are "dualistic." There are at least two distinct sectors, of which one is primitive and largely given over to subsistence, while the other is capitalistic. A major constraint on output in the primitive sector, which produces agricultural goods and primarily food, may be scarcity of land which results in diminishing returns to labor; the major constraint in the capitalistic sectors may be lack of capital. Labor will be allocated among these two sectors so that workers are as well off in one sector as the other. In the subsistence sector there may be no distinction between income from labor and income from rent, the apparent "wage" being sector output divided by sector labor force. (If there is a distinct landlord class in agriculture, other assumptions must be made.) Labor in the capitalistic sectors is rewarded according to its marginal product.

Sector production functions. Each sector has its own production function. The most useful form of such a function may be a modified Cobb-Douglas formulation; that is to say, each factor has a constant supply elasticity of output. In the subsistence sector, the factors could be labor and resources (land); in the capitalistic sector, labor and capital. Each sector's production function should include an improvement in technology coefficient that might be time dependent.

Population. The simplest way to treat population increase is to consider it exogenous, with population increasing by some given percentage every year, labor force being a constant fraction of total population. More intricate formulations might consider the crude death rate to be some function of per capita income. Exogenous variations in the birth rate might be linked to a changing ratio of labor force to total population.

Capital. Accumulation of capital from domestic saving can be considered some function of per capita income. Capital inflows from abroad, whether as private investment or intergovernment aid, had best be considered autonomous. It is probably too much of a complication to relate the demand and supply of investible funds to rates of return.

Consumption. All economies within reason prefer a "balanced" consumption. In a closed economy this means that the capitalistic sector must produce nonagricultural goods if the economy is to advance. The preferred consumption mix of agricultural and industrial (*i.e.,* nonagricultural) goods will be some function of per capita income.

Foreign trade. "Balance" between sectors is far less constrained in the case of an open economy in trade with the outside world. Then each sector's output does not have to conform to preferred consumption mixes at home. The capitalistic sector, depending upon the economy's comparative advantage, can specialize either in industrial goods (importing some agricultural produce in part exchange) or in agricultural output (exchanging some for industrial imports).

Forced growth through government efforts. It is possible that government, at a cost, can increase the annual rate of technological advance in one or both of the sectors. Or, once again at some cost, it can increase capital accumulation. It can be shown that if such government expenses are met from extra taxation, there will be a partially offsetting diminution of private investment.

Such a model is, of course, only one of several possible variants. But it covers the essentials. By having two or more sectors it can recognize "dualism." Its production functions do not make capital the only source of extra output but recognize the contribution of extra labor force from population growth: more important, they permit the effects of improvements in technology to be felt, and over the long run this may be the most important influence of all. The model also accepts the fact that there are preferred consumption mixes that can be satisfied with less constraint through international trade. The model permits exogenous increases in population to affect output, the consumption mix, and levels of saving. The possibilities of government intervention to accelerate output increases are also included. It is hard to see how the model could exclude any one of these elements and still reasonably describe a backward but developing economy.

A final word on macro-economic development models is in order. Almost any national economy, with its various external links, is an extraordinarily complicated affair. No model can ever do more than caricature reality. Making a model more and more complex may only give it a formal realism. The various parameters are not always susceptible of estimate. On the other hand, a really simple growth equation that relates "output" to "capital" and nothing else, is probably worse than useless; it is dangerous in that it may seem to imply policies that are far from optimum. A model's real purpose is to relate major forces conceptually rather than to calculate GNP increases. A useful model is one that, by relating all the important variables, is an aid to thinking. Then a growth model can be a good servant rather than a bad master.[13]

13 Appendix B gives an idea of what is involved in a simple two-sector and two-capital growth model.

10

Historical stages
of economic growth

At the other extreme from mathematical growth models are historical descriptions of economic development in advanced countries. Whereas the former are highly abstract, concentrating upon a few supposedly crucial variables, the latter possess all the rich variety that verbal description alone permits. But they are both alike in being highly subjective, for just as the econometrician must decide which variables to include in his model, so must the economic historian survey the past record of each country over the centuries and judge when some discontinuity warrants the assertion that one stage of development has been completed and another begun. Moreover, inasmuch as historical "stages" of successful economic development can describe growth only in what are now advanced countries, there is a real question regarding their applicability to backward countries. For even their location may render the stages of growth experienced by, say, Great Britain quite irrelevant to what lies in store for, say, Indonesia. Hence it is not always evident how economic histories of advanced countries can suggest wise policy decisions regarding the development of still backward ones.

DESCRIPTION OR THEORY?

There is no *a priori* reason why a historical approach should not contribute to an understanding of the processes of economic development. Conceivably it could provide more insights than an abstract mathematical model. But for economic history to be of positive service it must be much more than a description of what took place as nations happened to advance. The real use of economic history is to induce a theory of why national economies evolve. The contribution of an economic historian having true insight is that he can identify stages and show why each stage necessarily entails the next.

Mere description is not enough. There is no great art in describing the economic path followed by those nations that have "arrived." Expanding output and higher personal income are usually associated with increased savings, greater use of equipment and energy, improving transportation services, a smaller fraction of workers in agriculture, larger urban populations, lengthening life expectancies at birth, growth of secondary and tertiary industries, expanding social services by government, and so on. Inasmuch as all nations that have largely eliminated poverty possess a basically European culture—except Japan—it is not surprising that the economic development of Britain, France, Germany, Sweden, Canada, Australasia, and the United States should exhibit many similarities. But a chronicling of similarities does not constitute a theory of growth. In itself it contributes no understanding as to why France, for instance, developed but Spain did not.

A possible analogy would be a description of how people develop from birth. After a while they start walking, after another dozen years they enter puberty, and so on. All this would be true and not too uninteresting. But typical case histories of what happens as individuals grow older would not explain why these changes occur. Our understanding of the forces of life would be no greater.

A historical theory of economic growth, on the other hand, might take one of several forms. From past events it might be possible to induce an integrated dynamic theory in which each stage gives birth to the next in an understood manner. Or the records of nations that have achieved economic development might suggest that there are certain points at which there is a pause until some particular event stimulates another advance.

An integrated dynamic theory would be something like a real business cycle. Just as certain unleashed forces during an upswing of economic activity may in turn propagate another force, which slows expansion and ultimately leads to an upper turning point, one stage in a nation's secular economic growth may itself create the next stage. Such a theory, whether of a business cycle or economic growth, would be an integrated theory because each stage grows out of the last. And it would be dynamic, as the whole system would be self-propelling. It would provide its own inner logic as well as auto-power, and so continual economic growth would be inexorable, largely proceeding neither despite nor because of government actions.

Another use of growth stage theories induced from economic history would be to suggest points in development at which national economies typically pause until some one of several prescribed events occurs to move them forward again. Identification of these "waiting" points, and of subsequent "moving" events, would be difficult but useful. Perhaps the Old World of Western Europe was ripe for the discovery of the New World at the close of the fifteenth century. Perhaps Great Britain was

waiting for steam power in the early nineteenth. But, if these events had not occurred, might not other events have served as well? And as these occurrences were "once-forever" events, they cannot be repeated now for the benefit of countries still less developed today. Hence the policy uses of historical growth theories are somewhat obscure.

GROWTH STAGES IN PAST THEORIES

The German historical school of economics, which flourished in the nineteenth century and was partly a reaction against the deductive theorizing of the English "classical" economists (see Chapter 4), sought inductively to determine national policies that would promote economic growth. Almost to a man, they were concerned to promote industrialization in Germany against the severe competition of already established British manufactures. From their studies of history they thought they discerned various stages in the development of national economies, although no two writers of the historical school seem to have perceived the same stages. The most important writers of this group include Friedrich List, Bruno Hildebrand, Karl Bucher, Gustav Schmoller, and Werner Sombart.

List

Almost all the leading writers of the historical school addressed themselves to identifying transition points from one stage to another, and to discovering laws of development for national economies. In this respect Friedrich List's work—*Das National System der Politischen Oekonomie* —is not atypical. Accordingly, it is worth noting some of his particular views, some of which were shared by Alexander Hamilton in the United States.

First, except as regards the protection of "infant" industries from imports, List was a believer in *laissez-faire*. He believed that this was the surest guarantee of an optimum allocation of resources. He was an unequivocal free trader when it came to agriculture.

Second, he was preoccupied with economic policy, and the ways in which material human welfare flows from political associations of ever larger scope. It was his view that economic development depends upon the state of government and private organizations. He felt that general and abstract principles of economics that ignored society's cultural environment had a very limited usefulness.

Third, he asserted that growth can occur only in societies in which there is freedom of political organization and freedom of the individual. Thus he writes:

. . . it is in vain that individuals are industrious, saving, intelligent, and inventive; . . . free institutions are still needed for the proper application of these qualities. History teaches, in fact, that individuals draw the greatest part of their productive power from the social conditions and the institutions of society.[1]

In other words, economic advance and human freedom are indivisible, the more of one bringing more of the other.

List's own selection of stages of growth is not demonstrably superior or inferior to those of others before and since. He happened to distinguish five stages: (1) savage, (2) pastoral, (3) agricultural, (4) agricultural and manufacturing, and (5) agricultural, manufacturing, and commercial. The last three stages—and occupational classifications—are common to several economists and statisticians, among them Colin Clark.[2]

Of more interest to modern readers is probably the gist of List's economic "theory" and its policy implications. He believed that only countries in the temperate climatic zones were suitable and destined for industry. The tropical countries were advised to continue their specialization in agricultural exports. For temperate countries, industrialization —with all its attendant gains—rests on three conditions: there must be a fairly dense population to provide a market for increasing returns manufactures; agriculture must be reasonably efficient so that labor can be released to industry and so that the standard of living can be sufficiently high to provide a market for manufactures; and the nation must have varied natural resources, and preferably mineral reserves of some importance. It was also List's view that a society, once industrialized, would undertake agriculture in a more scientific, less traditional way.

For countries that could "qualify," the proper national policy was to establish manufactures as promptly as possible, even if this required protection of infant industries against imports. Manufactures were considered the *sine qua non* of continued and successful economic development for such nations. However, List did not assert that industrialization was an appropriate panacea for all countries seeking material advance, and certainly not for those located in the tropics. They had also to qualify by meeting the three requirements listed above—population density, efficient agriculture, and varied natural resources. Hence List's views do not support indiscriminate industrialization within the backward nations of today, although many officials in these countries have been more than willing to quote his views on infant industry protection out of context.

[1] *National System of Political Economy* (Philadelphia, 1856), pp. 178–179.
[2] Colin Clark, *The Conditions of Economic Progress,* 3rd ed. (London, 1957).

Hildebrand

Bruno Hildebrand[3] was subsequently to take List to task on various points. For instance, he felt that List was generalizing too much from British experience, and in this the critic had the advantage of additional hindsight. But more important here is Hildebrand's view that the only invariant feature of developing societies is, not some characteristic of production or consumption, but the method of distribution that is practiced.

Accordingly, Hildebrand's stages—of which there are three—concern the system of exchange that is prevalent. He distinguished (1) a natural or barter economy, (2) a money economy, and (3) a credit economy. But the general consensus is that he failed to indicate how one stage evolved into the next according to some definite inner logic. Some writers have complained that these stages are descriptive symptoms rather than analytic elements. Moreover, in concentrating on the advantages of money over barter and credit over money, Hildebrand was to some extent anticipated almost a hundred years earlier by Adam Smith.

Bucher

Since List, and excluding such modern "stage" economists as Rostow, one of the most widely read has been Karl Bucher.[4] In many ways Bucher was able to synthesize the ideas of previous writers such as List and Hildebrand. His particular view of historical economic development also contained three stages.

Bucher's first stage is one in which the economy is primarily characterized by numerous independent households, ideally producing for their own consumption, with no formal market institutions for commodities. His second stage is characterized by a town economy, the nation now comprising a number of more or less independent market towns where producers mostly pass goods directly to ultimate users. The third stage of national economy is marked by the dominant role of the middle man: goods are produced wholesale for market with no idea of who the final users may be, and in time small independent producers may become hired or otherwise absorbed by a new type of commercial entrepreneur. These three stages are certainly descriptive of German evolution. But Bucher did not make much use of his stages after describing them. Al-

3 Hildebrand's works were republished in 1922 in Jena under the title *Die National-oekonomie der Gegenwart und Zukunft und Andere Gesammelte Schriften.* Most of them were first published between 1848 and 1864.
4 His first and most important contribution was included in the first edition—*Die Enstehung der Volkswirtschaft* (1893)—of a work that was to pass through several editions and enlargements.

though a deservedly renowned scholar, and an expert on Frankfurt, today he could hardly be considered an economic theorist.

Any assessment of Bucher's stages, as of List's and Hildebrand's, is
rendered difficult by lack of criteria. What constitutes a "good" stage
theory of economic growth? Descriptions and distinctions of the analyst
that conform with the impressions of his readers? The fact that "history
repeats itself," and scholarly government officials can thus aid rather
than hinder in their own country the "natural" evolutions they have
learned about? Or is social evolution essentially a continuous phenomenon so that all attempts to establish segments—whatever the
breadth and depth of the latest perceiver of stages—can never be more
than pretention? No answer is really possible. The only certainty is that
stipulations of economic stages, and assertions that these stages somehow
constitute an economic theory, are an exercise that someone in each generation seemed compelled to undertake.

A MODERN VERSION: WALT ROSTOW'S "STAGES"

One of the most popular and persuasive current writers on historical
stages of economic growth is Professor W. W. Rostow. He has sought to
distinguish five stages: (1) the traditional society, (2) preconditions for
take-off, (3) the take-off, (4) the drive to maturity, and (5) the age of
high mass consumption. Not unnaturally most attention, especially in
still underdeveloped countries, has been concentrated on the so-called
take-off stage.[5]

The traditional society

The history of man records that many peoples have existed and multiplied over centuries with little economic change. When change did occur,
often as an incident of armed invasion that brought a new material
culture with it, it was discontinuous. Thus people "suddenly" discovered
the advantages of settled cultivation, the domesticating of animals, the
smelting of metals, the use of the wheel, the possibility of writing, the
practicability of aqueducts, the principle of carrying over the harvest of
fat years for survival during lean ones, calculations with numbers, the
employment of money to facilitate exchange, and so on.

[5] Three of the most comprehensive statements by Professor W. W. Rostow have ap-
peared in *The Process of Economic Growth* (Oxford, 1953), "The Take-Off Into Self-
Sustained Growth," *Economic Journal*, March, 1956; "The Stages of Economic
Growth," *The Economic History Review*, August, 1959; and *Stages of Economic
Growth: An Anti-Communist Manifesto* (New York: Cambridge University Press, 1960).
Another useful reference is W. W. Rostow and M. F. Milikan, *A Proposal: Key to an
Effective Foreign Policy* (New York: Harper & Row, Publishers, 1957). However there are
considerable differences among these three statements as regards emphasis, and where
in one case there are five stages in another there are three. Accordingly, the following
paraphrase, except where quotations are used, is necessarily selective and free.

But centuries often intervened between each such increment of technology and its consequent exploitation. Each advance in knowledge came rather as an accident and could not be counted upon to generate another improvement in technology, at least within any predictable time. Or as Rostow has said:

> . . . limitations of technology decreed a ceiling beyond which they could not penetrate. They did not lack inventiveness and innovations, some of high productivity. But they did lack a systematic understanding of their physical environment capable of making invention a more or less regular current flow, rather than a stock of *ad hoc* achievements inherited from the past. They lacked, in short, the tools and the outlook toward the physical world of the post-Newtonian era.[6]

Each new advance in the state of the arts probably permitted some increase in population and the possibility of a temporary productive "surplus." Because the community could temporarily more than feed itself, a fraction of the population could become potters, smiths, and weavers, rather than cultivators or fishermen. For a while the temporal and spiritual rulers of each civilization were able to divert resources from subsistence to the construction of temples and the prosecution of wars. But the income of the State and the nobles came from the ownership of land, not from trade or manufacturing, and agriculture was far and away the dominant occupation.

The preconditions for take-off

The preconditions for sustained economic growth were developed slowly in Western Europe, and especially in Great Britain, during the two and a half centuries or so preceding the French Revolution. Among the more important influences were the end of feudalism, the rise of the bourgeoisie in the mercantile cities, the elimination of many internal trade barriers after the establishment of the new national states, the assertion of spiritual independence as expressed in the various Protestant religions, and the decline of superstition in the face of increasing scientific knowledge during the Age of Reason. Many of these "preconditions" were indirectly initiated or encouraged by the discovery of the New World at the very end of the fifteenth century. And upon the continent of Europe—as distinct from the British Isles—they ended three hundred years later with the domination of Napoleon. The new ideas and attitudes followed hard behind his armies as they "liberated" one foreign population after another. The old structure of privilege, together with various constraints through local customs, never really recovered.

Specifically, according to Rostow, the preconditions for sustained

6 W. W. Rostow, "The Stages of Economic Growth."

industrialization have usually included radical changes in three non-industrial sectors. First, an accumulation of social overhead capital in transport, so that the extent of the market could be enlarged and productive specialization increased. Second, a revolution in agriculture, so that a growing urban population that possessed industrial knowledge could be fed. Third, an expansion of imports, including capital, financed perhaps by exporting some natural resource.[7]

Political forces are also important in the case of undeveloped countries. An international demonstration effect may cause people in backward countries to want the products of industry to such an extent that they are prepared to discard old cultural values. Or, in the case of lands that were long under the domination of Europe, the experience of subjugation may harden an indigenous resolution to acquire the special techniques and "magic" of the foreign masters.

In any event, the evolution from traditional society to "take-off" occurs along more or less the following lines:

We start with a reasonably stable and traditional society containing an economy mainly agricultural, using more or less unchanging production methods, saving and investing productively little more than is required to meet depreciation. Usually from outside the society, but sometimes out of its own dynamics comes the idea that economic progress is possible. . . . More often than not the economic motives for seeking economic progress converge with some non-economic motive, such as the desire for increased social power and prestige, national pride, political ambition and so on. Education, for some at least, broadens and changes to suit the needs of modern economic activity. New enterprising men come forward willing to mobilize savings and take risks in pursuit of profit, notably in commerce. The commercial markets for agricultural products, domestic handicrafts and consumption-goods imports widen. Institutions for mobilizing capital appear: or they expand from primitive levels in the scale, surety and time horizon for loans. Basic capital is expanded, notably in transport and communications, often to bring to market raw materials in which other nations have an economic interest. . . . And, here and there, modern manufacturing enterprise appears, usually in substitution for imports.[8]

Of course the precondition stage must be rather different as among (1) the Western European nations that gave birth to modern economic progress (e.g., Great Britain, France, and Germany), (2) the new and empty lands of recent settlement that were born capitalistic (e.g., Australia, Canada, and Argentina), and (3) the densely populated areas of older and nonadaptive civilizations (e.g., India, China, and Mexico.) And it is exactly these differences that make the subject of economic development so difficult. Is it possible for countries such as Indonesia,

7 Ibid.
8 W. W. Rostow, "The Take-Off Into Self-Sustained Growth," pp. 29, 30.

Egypt, and Brazil to take the same steps along the same path as did Sweden, Japan, and the United States?

Take-off

The take-off is supposed to be a relatively short period of time, lasting not more than two or three decades, during which a series of events combine to ensure that per capita income will in future rise regularly almost every year. A people can be confident in their economic future after take-off. Before take-off there is no assurance of a steadily improving level of consumption.

Clearly, take-off is a dramatic if short period in a people's economic history, and trying to isolate and define this period must be an intriguing task. Rostow has proposed the following tentative dates for those countries now actually or almost deemed to be airborne:

Great Britain	1783–1802	Russia	1890–1914
France	1830–1860	Canada	1896–1914
Belgium	1833–1860	Argentina	1935–
United States	1843–1860	Turkey	1937–
Germany	1850–1873	India	1937–
Sweden	1868–1890	China	1952–
Japan	1878–1900		

It is obvious that any such list of dates for take-off must be debatable, and in fact a number have become controversial already.[9]

The requirements of take-off are probably numerous. But it has been suggested that at least three conditions must *all* be satisfied. First, a rise in the rate of productive investment from under 5 per cent to over 10 per cent of net national product. Second, the development of one or more substantial manufacturing sectors with a high rate of growth. Third, "the existence or quick emergence of a political, social, and institutional framework which exploits the impulses to expansion of the modern sector . . . . and gives to growth an on-going character."[10] The first and second criteria at least give some opportunity for quantitative research. But there remains the question as to why these three particular conditions must be satisfied.

Investing over 10 Per Cent of National Income. For economic advance, if a country's population is increasing, annual net output must also increase by more than enough to maintain per capita incomes. In other words, extra national net income must suffice to occasion the extra capital needed to provide the extra population with a rising level of consumption. Or, to give Rostow's argument:

[9] See D. C. North, "A Note on Professor Rostow's 'Take-Off' Into Self-Sustained Economic Growth," *Manchester School*, January, 1958.
[10] W. W. Rostow, "The Take-Off Into Self-Sustained Growth," *op. cit.*, p. 32.

If we take the aggregate marginal capital-output ratio for an economy in its early stages of economic development at 3.5 to 1 and if we assume, as is not abnormal, a population increase of 1 to 1.5% per annum, it is clear that something between 3.5 and 5.25% of NNP must be regularly invested if NNP *per capita* is to be sustained. An increase of 2% per annum in NNP *per capita* requires, under these assumptions, that something between 10.5 and 12.5% of NNP be regularly invested. By definition and assumption then, a transition from relatively stagnant to substantial, regular rises in NNP *per capita,* under typical population conditions, requires that the proportion of national product productivity invested move from somewhere in the vicinity of 5% to something in the vicinity of 10%.[11]

The most noteworthy feature of this statement, asserted as though commonly accepted without question, is the supposition that net national product increments are contributed exclusively by additions to the capital stock. There is an implied denial here that extra labor force or improved technology can or do make any contribution to annual increases in national income. This is evidenced by the uncritical way in which the same incremental capital output ratio is used first to estimate the annual rate of saving needed to sustain per capita incomes, and second to raise them 2 per cent annually, population increasing by the same percentage in both instances (see also pp. 172–174 above).

Alternatively, if it is assumed that extra labor force and improved technology do contribute something to extra national product when per capita incomes are constant, it will take more than 12.5 per cent national saving from income to increase per capita incomes 2 per cent yearly with an annual population increase of 1.5 per cent. For example, suppose that 1.0 per cent of extra income came from extra labor force when per capita incomes were constant, population always increasing by 1.5 per cent annually. And suppose that a 5.25 ratio of saving to income had been associated with the 0.5 per cent annual income increase not ascribed to labor and technology and so attributable to investment. Then, although $\Delta K/\Delta Y$ may be 3.5, $\Delta K/\Delta Y_K$ is 10.5, where ΔY_K is the increment in income occasioned by investment. And the necessary ratio of savings to income to provide a 2 per cent annual increase in per capita income, with a 1.5 per cent annual population increase, is not 12.5 per cent but 26.25 per cent (*i.e.,* 10.5 [2% + 1.5% − 1.0%]) where the 2% is per capita increase, the 1.5% is population increase, and the minus 1.0% is the output increment due to extra labor force.)[12]

The moral for take-off is significant, especially as some important

11 *Ibid.,* pp. 29–30.
12 Simply, assume $\Delta Y > \Delta Y_K$, which means that some of ΔY is attributable to extra labor and improved technology. Then $\Delta K/\Delta Y_K$ does exceed $\Delta K/\Delta Y$. But the only ratio that matters as regards forcing a larger ΔY through ΔK is $\Delta K/\Delta Y_K$. The calculation made by Rostow in the above quotation is valid only if $\Delta Y = \Delta Y_K$.

underdeveloped countries have an annual population increase of around 2 per cent, or a third as much again as is assumed in the example. If backward countries have been obtaining part of their annual income increments from extra population and improved technology, which seems incontrovertible, the relevant incremental capital-to-output ratio is considerably higher than generally assumed. Hence, if forced growth is attempted only through capital, the savings and aid requirements are enormous. Fortunately, extra population is not an unmitigated curse from a per capita income viewpoint, for the marginal product of labor cannot really be zero. And as evidenced by advanced countries, an even greater potential blessing is the possibility of raising national income through technology and innovation.

Rapid Growth of Leading Sectors. In any economy experiencing take-off there will be rapid growth in one or more leading sectors. Historically these have ranged from textiles (Britain and New England), to railroads (the United States, Germany, and France) to modern timber cutting (Sweden). How are these "leading," or primary growth sectors, to be recognized?

Rostow feels that they have four characteristics. First, there must be a rather sudden increase in effective demand for their output, occasioned perhaps by sudden dishoarding, imported capital, or a sharp increase in real incomes. Second, in these sectors there must be a new production function as well as expanded capital. Third, there must be a high rate investment of profits or other savings in these leading industries. Fourth, they must through Leontieff input-output linkages induce output expansion in other sectors (see Chapter 17). Leading sectors tend to have a rapid growth phase, early in their life, and as one set of leading sectors slows it will be overtaken by another, once sustained growth has been achieved.[13]

An interesting question is whether one leading sector can include modern agriculture. Most people infer that it cannot. But on occasion Rostow implies that it might, if capitalistic-market and not subsistence agriculture is involved; and, without this concession, it might be difficult to explain the sustained growth of countries such as New Zealand (lamb and butter) and Denmark (eggs, bacon, and butter.)

Cultural Framework that Exploits Expansion. The third stated requirement for take-off is the existence or emergence of a political, social, and institutional framework which exploits impulses to expansion in the modern sector. They are presumably required so that the economy does not stall and crash on take-off. One important requirement is for mechanisms by which savings from extra income can be mobilized. There must be entrepreneurs ready to come forward and invest in industries said to

[13] W. W. Rostow, "The Take-Off Into Self-Sustained Growth," *op. cit.,* p. 47.

benefit from external economies created by the leading sectors. In short, to quote Rostow again:

. . . the take-off usually witnesses a definitive social, political, and cultural victory of those who would modernize the economy over those who would either cling to the traditional society or seek other goals. . . . By and large, the maintenance of momentum for a generation persuades the society to persist and to concentrate its efforts on extending the tricks of modern technology out beyond the sectors modernized during take-off.[14]

The drive to maturity

Following the take-off period, according to one Rostowian scheme of things, comes the "drive to maturity." Economic growth and higher per capita incomes are now regular and expected. New leading sectors take the place of former ones. Modern technology is now applied to almost all the country's resources. Investment continues to be well over 10 per cent or so of national income. Unexpected shocks to the now resilient economy can be withstood. The over-all concentration on material advance, so characteristic of the early take-off, gives way to a mellowing regard for values not based on consumption. Humanity is no longer trodden underfoot, as sometimes occurs during the initial rush to industrialize.

Rostow has suggested the following symbolic dates for the attainment of technological maturity in the following countries:[15]

Great Britain	1850
United States	1900
Germany	1910
France	1910
Sweden	1930
Japan	1940
Russia	1950
Canada	1950

And they are probably as good a set of dates as any other that people might agree upon. Because the very concept of maturity is so hard to define there is little object in arguing over when a country did or did not become "mature."

The way of living changes for most people during the drive to maturity. The population becomes primarily urban rather than rural. The proportion of semi-skilled and white-collar workers increases. Rugged individualists give way to salaried managers and compromising committee men.

[14] W. W. Rostow, "The Stages of Economic Growth," *op. cit.*
[15] *Ibid.*

The new soft-handed urban proletariat looks increasingly to the State to provide a measure of social and economic security.[16]

The age of high mass consumption

The twentieth century, after World War I, has witnessed one country after another in North America and Western Europe attain the age of high mass consumption. This stage was first reached by the United States in the 1920's. In Great Britain it began in the 1930's but was interrupted by World War II. On the western European continent it was a feature of the 1950's. In all cases the stage of high mass consumption has been characterized by the automobile, the move to suburbia, and the use of innumerable durable consumer goods and gadgets. In these countries, except for families in the lowest third of the income distribution, there are beginning to be signs of substituting leisure for consumption. And the increasing sense of financial security, due partly to government social services and to continued full employment, seems to have induced an increase in the birth rate. For most of the people of these countries, hunger is something that one reads about, and poverty a memory. In short, although man may not have subdued himself, he has conquered his environment.

SOME REAL DANGERS

The notion of take-off, after which a nation experiences an uninterrupted output expansion per capita, is extremely plausible when advanced by a skillful writer. It is also attractive to those who want to be optimistic about the economic future of the poorer undeveloped countries. Hence it is not surprising that Professor Rostow's theory of "stages," and especially the apparent promise of sustained growth in the near future, should have had a *succès fou* among those whose interest in development is unrelated to any professional training in economics. The truth is that people and officials are now exploiting the idea of take-off— and sometimes propagating caricatured versions—in much the same way that capitalists took political advantage a century and a half ago of the *laissez-faire* ideas they attributed to Adam Smith. In fact, as one critic has complained, "probably no theory has been so widely circulated from so slight a base of organized fact and careful analysis."[17] Therefore it becomes almost a duty to comment on the "stages of growth" approach to economic development.

[16] *Ibid.*
[17] Ian Drummond in his review of *The Stages of Economic Growth: A Non-Communist Manifesto* in *Canadian Journal of Economics and Political Science,* February, 1961, pp. 112–113.

Are there stages?

Whether there are definable and ascertainable stages of growth typical of nations that develop economically is something that each person must decide for himself. Some people can look at the stars and discern constellations that resemble a dipper, a belt, a cross, and so on: others, with less imagination, can observe these same stars and see only stars. The history of business cycle theory is similarly replete with instances of people who thought they saw short, medium, and long cycles rather than mere fluctuations in activity.

Among economic historians there seems to be no general acceptance of the stages proposed by Professor Rostow. As one reviewer has written:

Many scholars have found the stages—especially the take-off—inherently plausible. It is easy to believe in an industrial revolution, especially if one's historical knowledge is scanty and out of date. But historians are almost certain to reject the take-off's implication of sudden change. . . . Years of research and controversy will be required to determine whether the idea of take-off is empirically sound, and whether Rostow's own take-off dates are correct. Rostow himself has marshalled some evidence—plausible, but insufficient to prove his case. Unfortunately, he has defined his criteria so vaguely that they will stretch to cover any likely instance. And he seems willing to admit "exceptions" when take-off occurs at a time different from the time his tests would suggest. The stages of growth are not defined with sufficient precision.[18]

And Professor D. C. North has also been skeptical about the take-off dates suggested for the United States.[19] It may be significant that, from publication to publication, the number and the essential characteristics of the various stages are not always the same.

Particular attention naturally focuses on the alleged take-off stage. Or, as Professor A. K. Cairncross has stated:

The stage that has struck the public mind most forcibly is undoubtedly that of the take-off: largely, no doubt, because of the aeronautical metaphor—prolonged in the phrase "into self-sustained growth" suggests at once an effortlessness and a finality congenial to modern thought. The reactions of economists and historians have been less favorable. They have grown accustomed to emphasizing the continuity of historical change, to tracing back to a previous age the forces producing a social explosion, and to explaining away the apparent leaps in economic development. They are inclined therefore to regard Rostow as . . . stressing a discontinuity that is no more than symptomatic of the underlying forces at work. . . .[20]

18 *Ibid.*
19 *Op. cit.*
20 A. K. Cairncross, "Essays in Bibliography and Criticism, XLV: The Stages of Economic Growth," *The Economic History Review*, April, 1961, p. 454.

Hence a fundamental question is whether the "stages"—including that of take-off—are mere description or the basis for some sort of theory.

There even seems to be some doubt as to whether the "stages" constitute description. Professor Simon Kuznets, in a paper presented to the International Economics Association in 1960, ended a long and painstaking assessment by remarking: "Unless I have completely misunderstood Professor Rostow's definition of take-off and its statistical characteristics, I can only conclude that the available evidence lends no support to Professor Rostow's suggestions."[21]

Neo-Rostowian policies

The take-off, as described by Rostow, is ideally suited to those who want to industrialize backward nations with the assistance of loans and grants from foreign governments. A reader can select from Rostow what he likes and reject the less appetizing. Government officials are not above ignoring the lack of preconditions in their own country when applying for grants-in-aid to achieve immediate take-off. It is also easier to understand the specific than the vague. And the most uncompromising features of the stages of growth are two of the three necessary conditions for take-off; namely (1) capital accumulation equivalent to over 10 per cent of income, and (2) one or more leading manufacturing sectors.

Capital accumulation means capital funds. If this purchasing power to make investment is not saved domestically, or is not accumulated through higher taxes and budget surpluses, the East-West struggle may make it available on "soft" terms from abroad. Most governments favor commanding more resources than fewer, prefer to receive gifts than loans, and incline toward increasing taxes in countries other than their own. The take-off doctrine, with its great stress on capital investment, suggests that massive foreign aid can within a decade or so give backward countries that extra acceleration needed to make them airborne. Or, forgetting the aerodynamics, the suggestion is that the giving of a little more money now will make a country able to advance itself faster and faster forever after. This is essentially the same beguiling tale that many an insolvent debtor has for centuries told his creditors when asking for just one more credit advance.

It is therefore extremely unfortunate that, in the one instance when he descended to arithmetic, Professor Rostow suggested that a necessary condition of take-off was capital accumulation about 10.0 to 12.5 per cent of income. For, as has been explained above (see p. 198), the extra capital requirements are likely to be very much greater than he

[21] Simon Kuznets, "Notes on the Take-off." A paper presented at the International Economics Association, Lake Constance, 1960, and shortly to be published by The Macmillan Company, New York.

supposed. This is because despite his numerous verbal allusions to the importance of innovations, his arithmetic assumed that improved technology and increased labor force contribute nothing to national output. Consequently the capital-output ratio observed from the past cannot be applied to the future. This confusion has unfortunately been compounded by many people carelessly inferring that this erroneous minimum capital requirement is a *sufficient* condition of take-off. And this is not at all what Professor Rostow said.

Another misfortune has been the improperly inferred approval of indiscriminate industrialization. Considerable emphasis is placed upon the one or more leading sectors that are such a feature of supposed take-offs. Rostow always refers to them as "industries," and this is generally presumed to exclude agriculture. If this were so there would be no explanation of the take-off of countries such as Denmark and New Zealand, both of which have among the highest national per capita incomes in the world, and base their prosperity on exporting agricultural produce. Moreover, although countries such as Canada are given take-off dates at a time that they predominantly exported raw materials, this particular source of development is minimized in the "stages of growth" schema. All this is extremely palatable to newly independent countries, which view primary product exports as a sort of colonial hold-over. And of course it suits the prejudices of governments, which have identified industrialization with development. What is too often overlooked is that Rostow also stresses the necessity of an agricultural revolution as one of the preconditions for take-off.

The great danger of any "stages of growth" doctrine—and especially the one currently so much in vogue—is that it can be all things to all men. Almost every possible condition favorable to growth has been mentioned without really connecting it to anything else. Thus support can superficially be found for any policy, but in reality for none.

Why should history repeat itself?

A fundamental doubt must be whether the development of advanced nations is any guide to the economic future of still backward countries. Can one expect the development stages of Germany to be repeated by Ghana, those of Canada by Ceylon, or those of Belgium by Brazil? Or are the people of the backward countries so basically different in culture from those of advanced countries that no amount of capital loans and gifts can make much difference over a period as short as a decade or so?

The "stages of growth" approach to development would have more significance if it were possible to regard each country as a member of a culturally homogeneous global population of nations. Then the nations that have advanced could be considered a sort of random sample from all countries. Somehow they had luck and happened to be drawn first by a fickle but provident fate, but the turn of the others will come soon. Then they will be "selected," and experience the same sort of take-off in all essentials as the advanced nations once did.

This would seem to be a completely untenable view however. Nations of an essentially European culture are fundamentally different at the present time from many of those in Asia and Africa. And in between are most of the Latin American peoples. This does not mean that Europeans are different at birth from Asians or Africans in any significant sense. But they are born into a very different culture, so that by the time they are adults they are different people, perhaps superior only in their ability to produce and distribute more and better material goods.

It is for this reason that there is no parallel between Marshall Plan reconstruction of Europe following World War II and economic aid at the present time to the underdeveloped world. The war left much of Europe physically smashed and with depreciated capital. Loans and gifts, used to finance imported materials and machinery, expedited the recovery. But there is an enormous difference between reconstructing a devastated economy that once existed and developing a modern economy where there was never one before. It happens that Europeans still lived in Europe, understood capitalism and an exchange economy, and possessed technical knowledge instead of customary superstitions. The same expenditure of funds in Asia or Africa could never have the same effect during the same time interval.

It is worth noting that many circumstances that favored the advanced countries over a century ago are still not present in many of the backward countries. One was freedom from the sort of population pressure existing in many parts of Asia and Latin America today. Another, except during the Napoleonic period, was a sound currency and rather stable prices. Still another advantage, except for the period of the French Revolution, was a climate of law and opinion favorable to private capital investment and entrepreneurial innovation.

The great issue remains though. Why can some already advanced countries expect ever-rising per capita incomes while others are backward and hardly improving their situation? The usual retort is that poor countries cannot save the capital necessary to make the useful innovations already invented. However, and especially during the colonial era, Western capitalists were eager to invest wherever effective demand for new products might render their supply profitable. But the effective demands of the native markets were inadequate. Hence Western investment was usually direct and oriented to the primary product needs of Western Europe and North America.

There was little effective demand in the undeveloped countries for new products—except government purchases of utility and transportation equipment—because the native peoples were for the most part too poor. Merely feeding themselves absorbed too much of their daily efforts in Asia. In Africa, their leisure time was devoted to beer-drinking, religious ceremonies, and tribal wars. And in most areas superstition, ignorance, and custom prevented any significant improvements in agriculture.

Thus cultural change and technical innovations within rural communities may be the most important of all preconditions. And it is a gigantic task to make over a billion people, in millions of villages spread over almost a hundred territories, go about raising their food and providing their other essential wants in new ways.

There can be no argument about whether it will and must be done eventually. However, for these countries, there is no imminent take-off period of a decade or so. Nor is its immediate advent being postponed only by the refusal of richer countries to provide capital. Thus it is neither in their nor our best long run interests that false hopes be raised. Save in exceptional cases this can result only in frustration and bitterness.

III

Accumulation and
use of capital

Enough has already been said to indicate that the contribution of capital to growth and development, while only one element combined with labor and technology, is a most important one. Accordingly, this section describes the various ways in which capital can be accumulated and used. This includes a study of private saving and investment of domestic resources and the means by which a government can mobilize domestic savings. Various criteria that governments might or do use to determine priorities among development projects are described. Certain suggestions that development is possible only if many projects are undertaken simultaneously are critically examined. The opportunities and dangers of stressing social overhead capital are outlined. Some of the special fiscal problems of governments in underdeveloped countries are described. How rapidly backward economies can really absorb capital is also considered. Although capital is not the whole solution to development problems, it is certainly an important part of the answer, as the following seven chapters are designed to show.

11

Private saving and
domestic investment

In advanced nations of the Western world, most saving and investment are undertaken privately. Households save and invest. Firms save and invest. And over the decades a formidable accumulation of capital has been stocked. Poorer and more backward countries cannot save so much per capita, as their incomes per capita are much lower. And there is considerable uncertainty as to whether private savings under these circumstances can be "adequate." Accordingly, it is often proposed that governments, through fiscal deficits or current account surpluses, should seek to supplement the investment that flows from the private sector. Such policies may sometimes be necessary during early stages of development. There is more unanimity, however, regarding the necessity for considerable private savings if economic development is to be sustained in later years. Savings by households and firms, except in Communist countries, are the main sources of extra investment. It is therefore important to understand the economics of private saving and domestic investment.

SOME CONCEPTS DESCRIBED

Economics has many terms such as *saving, investment, capital,* and *interest,* which have more or less exact meanings when used professionally.

Savings

A national economy is said to save if it produces more than it consumes. The difference can take various forms. Additional structures, extra equipment, and larger inventories of goods are the most obvious examples. Some of these "investments"—such as larger inventories of goods—may be involuntary in the sense that producers would have liked to sell most of them but consumers would not buy. Under most definitions of social economic accounting, aggregate savings must equal the total value of all forms of investment, internally and externally.

Not all an economy's savings need result in domestic accumulations of producer and consumer goods, however. A country may be exporting more than it is importing in value terms. It is then acquiring claims against foreign residents (or canceling their claims against the domestic economy). Such international saving must be summed with local capital accumulation to obtain the nation's saving.

Most backward but developing economies are debtor countries. And in early stages of development they are usually going into debt each year on balance. Then the rather considerable domestic investment that may be occurring is somewhat offset by the increasing international debt that is also being undertaken.

Governments are said to "save" when they receive on current account more than they disburse on current account. The government sees this surplus as extra bank deposits, debt redemption, or capital investments. The great question, however, is: What is meant by "current" account?

Most tax receipts are current account receipts. Funds received from the sale of government obligations are not. Some desperate governments permit taxes to be paid in advance at a substantial discount, and these receipts may be called tax payments, but they are really a form of borrowing against the future.

On the disbursement side, the distinction between the current account and the capital account is often very vague, and open to abuse by governments that categorize their accounts in this manner. The purchase of railroad freight cars may be accounted a capital disbursement although in fact more such cars were retired in some year than were purchased. Maintenance work on highways may be hailed as a capital charge. Whether an expenditure for the purchase or production of durable physical assets is "current" or "capital" often cannot be determined unless a depreciation allowance is established for each different class of property. On the other hand, in countries where government services are improving public health and increasing general literacy, the cost of these increments is properly a capital rather than a current charge.

A firm saves to the extent that its net worth increases. Some of the accounting problems that are thereby raised are familiar. Depreciation allowances may be too low. Bad debts may be carried at face value. Inflation may occasion revaluations that increase the apparent net worth but hardly constitute savings for the economy.

Urban households usually imagine they are saving if their money incomes exceed their consumer spending. Theoretically, if property such as housing, clothing, and furniture is not being maintained, the real saving may be less than the apparent. But such considerations do not have much practical significance in backward countries, where most households own few durable consumer goods.

Rural families, especially those that engage in subsistence cultivation, can usually see their savings. A good year may mean more corn in the cribs, additional livestock grazing around the village, or some new improvement such as a well. (Whether accumulations of any sort of good are necessarily productive will be considered below.)

Investment

Investment, for purposes of economic development, is not merely the voluntary or involuntary accumulation of producer and consumer goods that is the physical counterpart of financial savings. Investment here means accumulations of goods that are ordinarily productive. Inventories that a firm accumulates because it cannot sell them are not themselves productive. Highways are ordinarily productive, but some governments for prestige purposes have built six lane highways—often into the capital city from the airport—when four lanes would be more than adequate. A peasant village may grow more rice than it eats one year, but this accumulation is not productive if it results in the same village working less next year, except insofar as the utility of leisure is given a value.

Some writers deplore investment in land as being unproductive, if not downright wasteful. They complain against speculative "investments" that raise the price of land. Somehow they suffer from the quaint idea that savings "invested" in land are somehow lost or buried in it. But land exists. It is not created from scarce resources at time of sale. And the purchase price is paid not to the land but to the seller. The acid test of whether or not such land purchases result in output depends on what the former owner does with his sale proceeds. If he imports luxury automobiles, the buyer's savings have been spent on the seller's consumption, and there has been no net saving or investment. If the seller of land invests in some industry, and perhaps contributes to the importation of machinery for it, the buyer's savings eventually become an industrial investment although initially spent for land. Actually, in some countries, a considerable amount of investment in industry is financed by large landlords selling portions of their estates to small cultivators who have some savings and a hunger for land. And unless there are legal restrictions on the division of estates into smaller parcels, the availability of land for sale may be a powerful incentive for peasants to save.

It has been pointed out above that the local moneylender and grain merchant is one of the more important capitalists to be found in agricultural areas. His interest rates may often be unconscionable, but he is a source of net saving. Loans that he makes to very poor families, so that they can buy grain, of course simply increase the effective demand for consumer goods. But a portion of the profits that a moneylender wrings from villagers may be invested in agricultural improvements and even in industry. So his activities have a limited economic usefulness. (There may be alternative and less miserable ways of mobilizing rural savings however.)

Capital

Capital goods are the physical object of investment. Net investment results in a larger stock of such capital goods being held. And aggregate capital in the real sense comprises the total stock of produced means of production. (Consumer goods accumulation is excluded.)

This definition distinguishes capital from land and labor because they are not produced (in the normal meaning of the word). It is true that slaves may have been deliberately bred as a form of investment in certain places and times. And reclaimed land may partially be considered capital. But these are exceptions.

Capital goods stocks are sometimes divided into fixed capital (such as factory buildings and installed equipment) and working capital (such as goods in process and fuel). Both are essential to production. A plant that had no stocks of working capital would perforce have a zero output. Inadequate inventories of materials on hand result in delays involving idle labor and machinery. Profit maximizing requires that marginal outlays for both kinds of real capital earn the same level of return.

It is surprising that government planners often seem unaware of the importance of working capital and occasionally neglect to budget for it. There is also a common tendency to believe that only fixed capital is productive. This error may arise because many working capital items—such as energy—disappear during production.

Capital funds are the monies advanced so that production can be undertaken. Fixed real capital obviously incurs considerable costs of construction before it can be used, and long before these expenditures of money or resources have been recouped from the sale of its output. Stocks of real working capital must also be produced before they can be used. Labor that is directly employed in an enterprise must usually be paid before the results of its work can be sold. Even a subsistence farmer, while working toward the coming harvest, can eat only the produce of earlier years, so in effect he advances himself food in the interim. An expansion of output, however organized and whatever the good produced, requires that resources be advanced pending the useful outcome of the activity. These goods and services are usually purchased by industry with capital funds that may or may not be borrowed. In primitive agriculture the advance is in real goods and is largely self-provided. But in either case all such advances have a monetary value and their aggregate can be considered the (imputed) financial capital investment.

Capital values are the present discounted values of goods having future income or utility streams. A piece of land that can be rented at $1000 gross a year indefinitely has a capital value of $1000/.05 if the discount rate is always 5 per cent. Both land and consumer goods, in addition to real capital goods, have finite capital values if they are useful and durable, and if interest rates are above zero. The capital values of real productive assets depend in addition upon the duration and timing of the receipts and disbursements they occasion in the future. It is possible for a "valuable" asset, such as unexploited mineral rights, to incur costs only in the immediate future so long as sufficiently large net receipts are estimated for later. Capital values are always very conjectural because they depend on current estimates of future events and uncertain interest rates.

Rate of interest

The rate of interest is the price that borrowers must pay for capital funds. Hence it is in theory the rate of return that marginally acquired capital goods should earn. It is reasonable to suppose that managers will always pay a bonus to have money receipts now rather than later. Pure interest rates reflect these preferences. And the relative importance of future and present events to an economy is expressed by the spectrum of interest rates that in some sense can be represented by a single percentage.

Conceptually, the pure rate is determined in the market for loanable funds, where lenders negotiate with borrowers. One can imagine a supply schedule and a demand schedule with their intersection determining the funds loaned and the interest price. Producers comprise most of the demanders, and the premium they are prepared to pay depends upon the estimated productivity of their investment opportunities. Households comprise most of the suppliers—although some people always borrow to consume more now—and their willingness to lend will vary inversely with the strength of their time preferences. The desire for liquidity, although probably of far less quantitative importance, activates some borrowers and some lenders.

It is evident that strong time preferences will result in high interest rates if other things are equal. But in many backward countries financially profitable investment opportunities are limited, in part by reason of the same poverty that makes for reluctant lenders, so that the modest supply of loanable funds is matched by a very modest demand for them. Also, real capital investments are often in competition with extra labor that can be hired at low effective costs, and which accordingly proves a very competitive substitute for extra real capital. For these and other reasons, pure interest rates are not over twice as high, on an average, in backward countries than in advanced nations.

Interest rates have an all-pervasive influence in a free market economy. They partially determine the extent to which current production is for investment rather than consumption. They affect the durability of structures and equipment. They provide a criterion for accepting or rejecting many proposed development projects. They help to indicate whether savings should be invested, rather than held in liquid form, and also whether such investments should be at home or abroad. Only an arrogant or ignorant government would disregard without cause a free society's time priorities as reflected by market interest rates.

INCENTIVES TO SAVE

Saving by households in underdeveloped regions is often undertaken for different reasons than one might expect from a knowledge of wealthier and more industrial areas. Certain incentives to save may exist that count for little in advanced countries. And saving to invest may be inhibited in backward countries because certain institutions for channeling savings into profitable investments are lacking.

Saving against disasters

Primitive economies do not have a complex of insurance schemes to protect families against losses from bad harvests, floods, illness, and all the other calamities that afflict mankind. It is for each large family itself to save against such disasters or to repay debts incurred upon past calamities. (Paying off debts constitutes saving.) In any large country most of the saving of temporarily prosperous families is offset by the dissavings of families in trouble. Hence the net savings of households, especially among the poorer classes, is likely to be very small despite the existence of considerable gross saving in any year.

People who save against a rainy day must find some object for their saving. But peasants the world over are suspicious of banks and afraid of losing their savings. So they seldom deposit in a savings account even where such banking facilities are available. They are distrustful of paper money because governments have a reputation for multiplying their obligations and so depreciating them. There is also a great deal of political unrest in many backward countries, and hence families like to store their wealth in forms that can be closely guarded, easily hidden, and readily carried elsewhere.

This explains the considerable demand in many Asiatic countries for precious stones and gold bullion. Coins are not esteemed except in those rare cases where their inherent metallic worth is at least equal to their nominal value. Whether "investment" in jewels and bullion is wasteful depends on how the sellers use the funds received from the purchasers. In some cases the sale of precious stones and monetary metals by the wealthy has channeled the savings of families in modest circumstances into large industrial projects. On the other hand, the urgent demand for "safe" ways to store wealth has led to some economies buying gold and jewels from abroad. Such imports are usually illegal. But distrust of government is so great they continue to occur. The economic result is that the buying country exports useful goods and resources that have required scarce resources for their production in exchange for objects that would have no special usefulness if only domestic governments would provide a stable currency and maintain law and order.

Family saving for direct investment

A great deal of private saving in backward countries, and especially where a subsistence economy predominates, is undertaken by families for direct investment in their own agricultural or commercial enterprises. Statistical estimates of the magnitude of such investments in backward countries cannot be very reliable and in fact are seldom attempted. So it is not surprising that there is uncertainty and controversy regarding the importance of direct family investment.

In agriculture, some Occidental economists tend to think that direct investment of this kind is very small, and perhaps they are influenced in this belief by the failure of governments in poor countries to estimate it. But the lack of official reports is not conclusive. And, on the other hand, agricultural experts who travel in rural areas of these countries are often impressed by evidence of agricultural improvements. This is especially so where peasants own the land themselves. Most families that cultivate the soil, wherever they live, are emotionally and economically identified with their own property. Farming is to them a way of life. They know little and perhaps care less about investment opportunities hundreds of miles away and managed by some stranger. Hence, if landowning cultivators have a surplus in a good year, the only practical alternative (apart from storing wealth or eating more) is to improve their holding. The physical surplus that constitutes saving can then be used in two ways. Some of it may be sold for better draught animals, plows, pumps, or whatever else may be traditionally used as real capital. In exceptional cases, where the cultivator has a "modern" orientation, he may experiment by purchasing new and improved seeds, fertilizers, and so on. Or the surplus may be "used" in the sense that, because some labor can now be diverted from producing for current family consumption, work on new clearings, terraces, wells, dipping tanks, fencing, and so on, can be undertaken. However, and this needs stressing, a cultivator who is a tenant and not an owner will have few incentives to improve the property unless he is protected in his occupancy for a long enough period to share in the benefits.

Families that do not work the soil, but gain their livelihood from some sort of petty trade, are not usually inhibited in making direct improvements by tenancy arrangements. Hence families that make pots, footwear, clothing, baskets, handtools, harness, and the like, are inclined to invest any surplus in improving their enterprise. This may take the form of buying some better equipment (such as a newer sewing machine), adding more shelves and lockers, or putting on a new roof to keep things dry during the wet season.

All direct improvements add to capacity. More can now be produced with the same hours of applied work. And this raises an important distinction between direct investment in agriculture and trade. In poor countries almost any increase in food and agricultural output can be used by the very family that raises it. But when a smith increases his capacity to make tools by purchasing an additional forge, for example, he must find extra customers. A peasant family can eat its own output, but a smith's family does not want to use all the tools it can make. Direct investment in making a specialized output will occur only if there is an adequate effective market demand.

In all backward countries there are a few extremely wealthy families engaged in major enterprises such as textiles, hotels, bus lines, warehousing, processing raw materials, and so on. These firms are usually not limited companies with many unrelated shareholders. They are businesses owned and operated by and for some powerful family. Many of these concerns are profitable and their surpluses are an important adjunct to national savings.

Ordinarily these profits would be invested again by the owning family in some private sector enterprise. But governments too are eager to "invest," and they are frequently tempted to impose taxes in order to divert some of these private surpluses into government operations. In this way it is thought that the private sector can be made to finance part of the public sector.

Private capitalists in many countries are well aware of such government attitudes. They hence prefer investments where a quick profit can be taken and assets can be sold before government introduces special imposts that make it an unwelcome partner, sharing the profit but not the risk. This is one explanation of the preference of many capitalist families in backward countries for "speculative" investments.[1] The great attraction of such an investment, if it succeeds, is that the capitalist is in

[1] Although the word *speculation* has a bad connotation with the public, most economists recognize that speculators normally perform a useful function in taking risks that ordinary businessmen can thereby shift through "hedging" transactions. A lot of apartment building in underdeveloped countries has also been stigmatized as "speculative" because the construction is financed by interests that sell on completion to other longer term investors. But this is really a kind of specialization in investment.

and out of his commodity or property speculation in a very short time. He can usually take his profit before a curious and possibly corrupt tax collector can also introduce himself to a good thing.

A family that gives hostages to fortune by purchasing a business with fixed assets of considerable value and durability must be able to withstand tax encroachments over long periods of time if it is to profit from its investment. If it owns a successful hotel, the property may be reassessed. If it owns a business that has to comply with numerous and vaguely defined safety and sanitary regulations, it may be at the mercy of dishonest government inspectors. If it owns a plant that must import raw materials under license, it is obviously vulnerable to a shakedown. In backward countries that have only a single government party, any successful business must make political contributions to the party. If a revolutionary movement exists that one day may come into power, no owner of a business with fixed and durable assets of value knows how he will end financially.

Under these circumstances, unless they are in the rare position of controlling the government, wealthy families are loath to make any long term investments. Speculators are not exposed to the same risks, because each operation is so short term. Writers who complain about the prevalence of speculative investment—and the absence of supposedly "productive" and longer term commitments—should really be lamenting the lack of good and stable government.

Private savings for indirect investment

Saving and investment are far more personal transactions in backward than advanced countries. North Americans and Western Europeans think nothing of buying securities issued by limited liability corporations. And yet the managers, and all the other shareholders who "own" the same company, usually are personally unknown to the investor.

In backward countries, to a considerable extent still, there is a great reluctance to invest outside family concerns and also a prejudice against hiring anyone not a relative for a responsible position. These attitudes are altogether reasonable in cultures that make support of one's own family a prime virtue. It may be considered a greater wrong to allow one's family to starve than to steal from a business owned by someone outside the group. Honesty in the abstract, without regard for who robs whom, commands little respect in many parts of the world even today.

Hence few families with savings in backward countries are likely to lend money to strange families or unknown institutions. It would seem the height of folly to entrust one's funds to some manager who has no family ties with the investor to protect him from dishonest manipulating or outright absconding. Until people in these countries cease to feel that their only real loyalty is to their immediate family or village group, private savings will not flow readily into indirect investment, and development will be restricted accordingly.

One explanation of why there are so few institutions to facilitate indirect investment is again this spirit of distrust. Illiterate and ignorant people are usually suspicious of what they cannot understand. But another reason is that the legal basis of many investing institutions is often of recent origin in underdeveloped countries. The most important channels for indirect investment in other nations have proven to be joint-stock companies, insurance companies, and savings banks.

Legally, establishment of a joint-stock and limited liability company is a privilege, and not a right. It was only toward the end of the last century that this privilege came to be granted almost automatically on application in Western countries. The essential grant is that investors are permitted to combine in order to establish and operate a business without being separately liable for its debts beyond the subscription price of their own shares. The corporation, as an institution, also permits a specialization of functions. People who are competent to manage a business, but have no wealth to invest in it, are not disqualified on this count. People with wealth, but no wish or ability to be managers, are not thereby precluded from investing. These extra degrees of functional freedom can be of great practical advantage. But they will only be so if government enacts and enforces measures that will protect shareholders from management and so increase their confidence in this kind of indirect investment.

Insurance companies usually collect more from premiums than they pay as benefits, and so they accumulate a financial surplus, which they must invest if they are to have a profit. Death insurance—more happily but less accurately known as life insurance—is the most important example. The current risks of death at any age are usually rather less than the "actuarial" risks, primarily because of advances in medicine, and to this extent net surplus is greater. The same is true of other forms of insurance, such as those against personal accidents, not to mention the insurance of property against fire and flood, for losses are generally on the decline per population at risk. Thus, in one way and another, almost all insurance companies augment national investment. But inflation, as explained below, deters people from taking life insurance policies.

Savings accounts are an important way of directing savings into investment in countries that have already attained sustained growth. But in some of the poorer and more backward countries they do not seem to have attracted more than a very small fraction of even the limited total savings. And this is despite government regulation that, by limiting the sorts of investments that the savings bank can make, also limits the risk of default to depositors. One explanation may be that the true rate of return on deposits is usually low, sometimes because of usury laws that do not bother individual moneylenders, but more often because of the ravages of perennial inflation.

There are few underdeveloped countries that do not experience at least a 5 per cent inflation of price levels each year. And annual inflation rates of 20 per cent are not uncommon. A nominal 8 or 10 per cent on a savings account can then represent a negative rate of interest. Life insurance premiums are paid in more valuable money than the eventual cash benefit. So once again the diversion of savings into jewels and gold, direct private investment, and speculation, and away from indirect investments, is partly due to government policy and a pervasive unwillingness to lend savings to strangers.

Government can encourage private saving for private indirect investment in a number of ways. An obvious and negative way is to remove the discouragement of persistent inflation. But there are also positive ways in which indirect investment can be made more popular.

A few countries still do not have any routine way in which a group of capitalists can obtain the privilege of forming a joint-stock and limited liability corporation. A special—and perhaps expensive—act of the legislature may now be needed to form a company. Businessmen may have instead to form a partnership and so incur the additional risks of unlimited liability.

Government can also, through regulation and inspection, do much to protect the stockholder from corporate managements. In these ways the confidence of the private indirect investor can slowly be gained. At present savers have too few investment alternatives open to them.

The attractiveness of corporate shares can be increased through the establishment of stock exchanges, perhaps operated or financed by government, so that the demand and supply for corporate securities can be focused upon one another. Certain items of information might be periodically required of management. A special stock control commission might even grade different issues according to their presumed security. In these ways new issues are more likely to find buyers, and shareholders have increased liquidity. Where the value of traded securities is not great, the government might on occasion enter the market to promote stability. Banking regulations can be amended so that certain categories of shares are always acceptable as collateral against loans. Shares can be excluded from the tax base when capital levies and death duties are being calculated. By law certain classes of securities might be rendered immune from attachment in the discharge of civil liabilities.

Most governments conduct small saving schemes, often through the post office, but deposits are usually meager when inflation exists or threatens. It is not inconceivable, though, that government might be prepared to protect these savings accounts, at least by increasing the minimum balance of each quarter by the same percentage as the rise in some cost of living index for the same period. Such savings might also be made immune from liens.

None of these measures to stimulate private indirect investment is without cost. Implementation might indicate that the cost is not worthwhile. However, it is hard to imagine how any country can develop economically without a rather large volume of indirect investment, and so almost any imaginative proposal to make bonds and stocks more popular with private savers deserves at least consideration.

HOW PROFITABLE IS REAL INVESTMENT?

It is usual to ascribe the low level of investment in backward countries to the inability of low income households to save. A frequent implication is that real capital investments would be extremely profitable if only they could be financed, because a strong demand and a weak supply of loanable funds should result in very high interest rates.

Interest rates not too dissimilar

A more careful examination of the evidence suggests that comparable interest rates are not very much higher in backward countries. It is seldom that they are more than twice as great on an average. Although there are variations from country to country, and from year to year, some recent Indian rates are perhaps representative. These include bank interest on time deposits at 4 per cent, mortgages taken by insurance companies at 7 per cent, and secured bank advances at about the same level. Scrutiny of shares listed on major markets—such as those of Calcutta, Buenos Aires, or Cairo—usually reveal prices and dividends that in a majority of cases yield returns of under 10 per cent a year.

It must be recognized that some of the "atrocity" usury rates often quoted are on loans to poor and desperate families who have no remaining security and can repay only slowly if at all. Hence the charged rate is much higher than the realized rate. Also, in some countries, the quoted interest rate is not per annum but on the loan: if repayment is over several years, the annual effective interest rate is reduced accordingly.

Many countries of Asia and Africa, during colonial days and before exchange control, had access to the world's capital markets. Moreover, the colonial governments of these territories often guaranteed, with their taxing power, bond issues which financed railways, tram lines, commercial wharves, and electric power. Capital was accordingly available at rates only slightly higher than the return paid by established public and private companies in Europe. It is unlikely that government officials in these administered areas, anxious to enlarge their activities, would have been backward in pressing for overseas capital for new projects. And yet the facts seem to be that, on a per capita calculation, rather modest amounts of social overhead capital were sought. Today, when the confidence of overseas private investors has been lost, it is alleged that very considerable and profitable investment opportunities of this kind exist now in these very countries.

Can these interest rate levels, usually not more than twice those of advanced countries and sometimes only slightly higher, be explained in terms of theory? One can try. It is evident that a useful investment can be employed either to increase output (other inputs unchanged) or to reduce some input such as labor (output remaining unchanged). But it is not so certain that such additional output can be sold, and it is not obvious that the saved labor has much opportunity value.

Inadequate effective demand

Investors cannot afford to assume that there will always be an adequate effective demand. It is all very well to invest in a new shirt factory, printing press, or paint plant, but will there be enough customers able and willing to buy the output at a profitable price? Many marginal investments are of a kind that can pay only if the general level of consumption increases per head. Every properly conceived investment contributes to this end. But each investment only very indirectly and most inadequately finances itself. The people who receive additional incomes from a new shirt factory will certainly not buy more than a fraction of its output. It is this problem that has given rise to various suggestions for a "big push" and certain kinds of "balanced" growth (see Chapter 16).

The art of profitable investment in an expanding economy with rising incomes per head is partly to invest after and not before there is a profitable effective demand. The other part of the art is to invest before and not after some rival concern has seized the same opportunity first. It is this difficult timing decision that, if repeated enough times to disprove luck, marks the truly gifted entrepreneur.

It is useful to distinguish between an economy that is growing but not advancing and one that is advancing but not growing. An economy may be said to grow when population, production, and consumption tend to increase in step with one another, but per capita welfare remains unaffected. In this case investment opportunities will mostly comprise additional facilities to make more of the same kind of goods as before. But economic progress is not merely having more equally miserable people per square mile of a country's area.

Real economic advancement means that individuals are consuming additional and more varied goods. Rising per capita consumption means that new kinds of goods are coming into use and that the whole sumptuary mix is altering. This means that many investments will be innovations and not merely duplications—with somewhat more modern equipment perhaps—of plants in existing industries. Improved consumption—in variety and amount—is the hallmark of economic progress.

It is a simple deduction that, if the availability of productive factors is not greatly altered per head of population, individual consumption can improve only because of innovations that increase productivity. It is the higher real income from increased productivity that creates an adequate effective demand for new sorts of consumer goods. Such a situation increases the investment demand for loanable funds and so tends to raise interest rates. A not unreasonable hypothesis is that the interest rates of backward countries are little higher than in advanced countries, despite the low rate of net saving, because of the slow and retarded rate of innovation.

Competition of labor

Investment, if it is not undertaken to produce something extra or novel, is usually made to eliminate labor. Real capital stocks are of course in competition with land also. But primarily, especially in industry, one thinks of capital and labor as substitutes within rather broad limits.

The productivity of capital, where additional output is unprofitable, depends on the number of workers it can displace and the cost of those workers. In industry, this cost is usually the wages, taxes, and rations that workers occasion. In subsistence agriculture the cost may be an implicit opportunity value. If displaced workers have nothing else to do, the rate of return is psychological, and depends on the utility of leisure.

In the market economy, and especially in industry, capital funds are rented partly to acquire real capital goods that will displace labor. However, this incentive is clearly less when wages are very low. Imagine an advanced country A in which a worker receives \$4500 a year, and \$1000 of capital funds costs \$50 a year to rent. A factory manager will then borrow capital if each \$1000 displaces $1/90$ (*i.e.*, $50/4500$) of a worker. Now imagine a backward country B where workers receive \$300 a year and \$1000 of funds costs \$100 a year. Then a producer will borrow only if each \$1000 displaces $1/3$ of a worker. Marginal capital, relative to marginal labor, must then be 30 times more productive in B than in A.

Generally, unless workers in A are vastly superior as individuals to those in B, one can expect that firms will want to invest much more capital per unit of output in A than B. It takes a lot of capital to force the marginal substitution between capital and labor to where it takes \$90,000 to equal one worker in output terms. It does not take much capital to reach a point where \$3000 of extra capital will occasion as much extra output as one extra worker. Why should there be a strong demand for loanable funds to invest productively when cheap substitutes for real capital exist?

Many poor and backward countries are in something that approaches a Schumpeterian circular flow. But it is a vicious sort of circle. No one producer has much incentive to invest in more capital, hence to borrow more funds, and hence to raise interest rates. So long as there are no innovations, there is a fairly widespread equilibrium, and most firms have all the capital and labor they want in the proportions they want. Innovations of a useful and profitable kind would probably result in more profits and higher rates of return. There would be a greater incentive to save if interest rates were higher. And, with higher real incomes as a result of successful innovations, there would be a greater ability and willingness to save at any given rate of interest. Innovation is one way—and perhaps the best way—to increase the capital to labor ratio and so assist workers to produce more.

The concept of capital absorption will be considered again. The essential idea though is that producers will wish to borrow only a limited amount of funds at any given interest rate. Moreover, in backward countries, their demand for capital funds may be such that it takes a much larger percentage drop in interest to induce them to borrow, say, an additional 10 per cent. Also, the time preferences of households are more urgent in these poorer countries. And their demand and supply of loanable funds may be such that interest rates cannot fall very far. There is always some competition for funds between certain households and firms. The demand of producers for capital must increase mainly through innovations in industry, agriculture, and commerce that increase productivity. Until then interest rates will not rise significantly to evoke more net domestic savings.

12

Government policies
to increase investment

There are many ways in which a wise and disciplined government can encourage investment and output. One is to encourage private saving for private investment in the domestic economy, as explained in Chapter 11. Another is for the government to borrow in order to finance productive capital projects. Creation of a budget surplus—through increasing taxes or reducing wasteful expenditures—may also result in worthwhile government investment. Governments that operate commercial enterprises can reinvest their profits. Bank credit, whether created for private or public use, is often but not always employed for productive purposes. But money creation, if not wisely controlled by government, can lead to inflation that in turn inhibits private saving. Fiscal and tax policies of the government can also be used to stimulate the use of land and labor and to encourage entrepreneurial risk taking. But many of these policies pull in opposite directions, more investment of budget surpluses resulting perhaps in less private investment, for instance, so that in the abstract there are no obvious "best" policies. A country's institutions, culture, and situation may dictate one set of measures in certain cases and other policies under other circumstances. Using government to encourage investment and output is an art possessed by only a few officials and politicians. Unfortunately it is an art that cannot be practiced by a government too subject to popular and ignorant pressures.

GOVERNMENT BORROWING FROM
PRIVATE SAVERS

If a government is financially sound and responsible, and does not permit continuous and obvious inflation, it can borrow considerable sums from private savers if it will only pay a high enough interest rate. Borrowing can be a substitute for or supplement to taxation. So long as borrowing by government is from households and firms, and not from a central bank that creates money with which to buy government obligations, it is not likely to be inflationary and can be deflationary. Although governments usually borrow in order to increase their own disbursements, there are no theoretical reasons why they might not under certain circumstances reloan some of their borrowings to private development projects, but at lower interest rates. Of course a government's ability to borrow is based on its apparent willingness to tax and the economy's ability to pay taxes.

Government borrowing for public investment

Most officials who favor government borrowing are eager that the proceeds be spent on government operations rather than be lent to private investors. The intellectual leaders of many backward countries incline to big government, and have little confidence in and some dislike for private enterprise, partly because most of them have little personal experience of it. Bureaucrats naturally desire an increase in the responsibilities of their own departments of government. Thus public health officials will inevitably recommend improved water and sewage systems in the course of their duties. Government engineers would be inhuman if they did not press for a new highway here and a new breakwater there. The agricultural department will assert the necessity of new irrigation canals. Hence ministers of finance can never satisfy all the demands of government agencies for funds as it is. The prospect of having to borrow and tax in addition, so that government funds can be used for private investment on a major scale, would horrify most treasury departments. So in the world as we know it, government borrowing is almost entirely for government operations.

It does not follow, though, that government borrowing is necessarily or even usually for productive public investment. Many governments borrow to maintain military establishments and police forces. Quite a number of countries have heads of government who are practically dictators. Some of them are anxious to extend their power into neighboring territories, and not all feel completely secure among their own subjects. But as armed forces are costly to maintain, the needs of development have often to be sacrificed in part to the ambitions and fears of present rulers.

Even in countries that are both backward and democratic—of which there are a fair number—a great deal of waste, nepotism, and corruption often prevails within the civil service. The ordinary activities of government are frequently far more costly than they should be. And when the functions of government are extended—as, for example, into comprehensive economic planning and regulation—the bureaucracy grows exponentially in size and cost.

If one examines government disbursements in backward countries during the past decade, the increase in expenditures for real development projects is likely to be a rather small fraction of the total increase in disbursements. Even if expenditures for extra education and health are included—and these are partly inflated by growing population—this fraction is unlikely to exceed one-half of increased spending. In a majority of cases—if extra education and health disbursements are excluded—it is probably under one-quarter. India, since receiving its independence, seems to have spent not much more than 15 per cent of all extra disbursements on recognizable development projects. This ratio is important, because it indicates the government's propensity to save, which may be less than the public's.

Another difficulty in assessing the relative desirability of government borrowing, even assuming that the resultant disbursements have been categorized into current and capital account expenditures, is that many government operations provide services that have undoubted value but for which no specific charge is made. This may be because the benefit is supposedly so general—examples are national defense and fire protection —or because it hardly seems worth the cost and trouble to charge users. It is possible to levy highway tolls but not always worthwhile. Most of the traditional functions of government, such as enforcement of law and order, are of this kind.

Now that capital expenditures by government are increasingly for industrial operations—e.g., transportation, steel manufacture, oil refining, and so on—comparisons of the productivity of public and private enterprises are more feasible. But many projects either do not capture all the benefits they provide or do not bear all the costs they incur. Financial profitability is not always synonymous with economic desirability.

This brings us to the present-day concept of "external" economies— and sometimes diseconomies too—that can be occasioned by any activity, whether it be privately or publicly owned and operated.

In economic theory, the concept of external economies was originated by Alfred Marshall, and he defined them as economies that accrue to a firm because the industry of which it is a member has increased its output. Thus these economies are external to the firm but internal to an industry. A distinction can also be made between pecuniary economies (e.g., some factor of production becomes available at a lower price) and technical economies (e.g., more efficient production methods are possible when an industry's expansion permits greater firm specialization). These strict meanings of external economies are seldom observed in current literature on economic development. Nowadays the term *external economy* is applied to what technically are buyers' and suppliers' surpluses in the Marshallian sense. But this is not the first time that officials have unknowingly misused economic terms.

Today's concept of external economies includes those lower input costs that other enterprises enjoy because some particular productive activity is in existence. Thus investments in improved fishing vessels and equipment presumably reduce the price of unloaded fish, and this is an economy to a fish cannery. Or the construction of an improved hard-surface highway reduces trucking charges and so is an economy to farmers who produce to supply a neighboring town. These economies are "external" because they are not enjoyed by the government or firm that makes them possible. The above examples are said to be "forward" external economies, because the activity that provides the economy has an output that is an input to the firm that benefits.

A still broader concept of external economies is one that includes "backward" economies as well. Investment in a fruit and vegetable cannery increases the demand for these products and so raises the prices obtainable by growers. In this case, the public or private user of the input provides the external economy, and the makers of the input good enjoy it as higher output prices.

Whether the "economy" is of a forward or backward kind, it is external when it is not or cannot be captured by the enterprise that creates it. The "lost" gain may be psychic or monetary. Promoters of a firework display, held within some stadium for which admission is charged, cannot prevent spectators outside the grounds having a free view of at least the rockets. Of course the private firms that provide external economies do not do so for love of mankind, and are quite frustrated by their "loss." The managers of government industrial corporations often feel the same way. They would very much like to "internalize," and so capture, all such economies if possible. To some extent they can succeed through discriminatory pricing and other devices to be considered later; but where forward or backward economies exist, some usually remain "external" or lost.[1]

The problems raised by alternative projects, giving rise to more or fewer external economies, will be considered in Chapter 15. They are important here because it is often claimed that government projects generate more net external economies per unit of investment than do private projects undertaken solely for profit. If so, and maximum net increases in productive investment are a policy goal, these extra external economies —if possible—are something to be considered.

The difficulty is that *pecuniary* external economies usually involve robbing Peter to pay Paul. The government ice plant that gives fishermen a better price for their catch—because it can be shipped further inland—lowers the price that interior meat suppliers can command. The fishermen get more suppliers' surplus and the cattle raisers get less. Adding suppliers' and buyers' surplus throughout an economy, and comparing changes in them, involves almost insurmountable conceptual and practical difficulties.

1 External *diseconomies* are discussed in Chapter 17.

Government borrowing for private investment

There is no theoretical reason why a government might not borrow from private savers in order to lend to private investors. It might establish a National Development Bank (NDB)—for want of a better name—that borrows money at interest rates somewhat higher than those it charges on its loans. The losses that it makes because of this difference in interest rates would be made good by government. In this way annual net productive investment is presumably increased. And private sector projects that are just submarginal in terms of financial profits, but which would be supramarginal for the economy because of substantial external economies, may thus be brought into existence. This is the major justification for subsidizing selected private projects.

Fig. 12-1 represents schematically the arguments presented so far. It illustrates a market for loanable funds. Without government intervention the interest rate is 7 per cent and the annual net lending is $100x$ in money units. If the NDB borrows at 8 per cent and loans at 5 per cent, it is assumed that total lending by private savers and borrowing by private investors will increase to $120x$. But at this higher rate of interest, private investors, unless somehow subsidized, will only borrow $90x$ worth of funds. If the private demand for loanable funds is given by the D schedule, the NDB must offer selected investors $30x$ worth of funds annually at 5 per cent. Its losses accordingly—without regard to administrative costs—will be 0.03 of $30x$ or $0.9x$. These would be covered by treasury grants to the NDB.

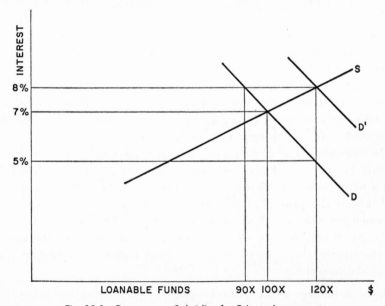

Fig. 12-1. Government Subsidies for Private Investment.

Why should taxpayers, through their government, subsidize private savers (some of whom get 8 instead of 7 per cent interest) and a few selected and preferred private savers (who get $30x$ worth of funds at 5 per cent interest)? There would be justification if the enterprises that were permitted to borrow at 5 per cent provided substantial external economies that were excluded from the demand schedule D. If another private schedule of demand for loanable funds could be constructed, *including* external economies, it might be D'. Investment of the marginal $120xth$ investment is then worth only a 5 per cent financial rate of return to the borrowing enterprise. But it may be worth 8 per cent to the economy. Annual net investment has been increased by $20x$ also.

Contrast the alternative of government borrowing for government operations. The treasury would have to offer 8 per cent to obtain $30x$ worth of funds for government use. If experience has any significance, it suggests that about one-third of this sum might be used to increase productive capacity. The balance would probably be used to finance current operations of government. Hence, unless government projects yield disproportionately more external economies than private ones, there will constitute less useful investments.

Another alternative would be for government, instead of spending $0.9x$ on subsidizing the NDB each year, to invest this sum directly in government projects. But it would take over 20 years, at $0.9x$ a year, to match the $20x$ of extra net investment achieved from the outset by the subsidized NDB. And this is assuming a rather inelastic *combined* demand and supply of loanable funds approximating 0.5.

The relative attractiveness of the three above alternatives depends of course on actual conditions rather than on the assumed relations of the diagram. Some scheme of government borrowing and relending, as described here for a mythical National Development Bank, will be more promising if (1) the external economies excluded from the demand schedule of private borrowers are substantial, (2) private lenders and borrowers respond strongly to any change in interest rates, and (3) transactions at the differential interest rates are almost all *extra* savings and investment. In certain countries and various times these circumstances will not prevail. Nevertheless, subsidization of private saving and investment is always a possibility to be considered, and there are more ways than one to achieve investment for economic development.

ABILITY OF GOVERNMENT TO BORROW
WITHOUT INFLATION

The ability of the State to borrow without incurring inflation is one that every government should preserve if possible. And if the national treasury is to borrow without inflation, it must normally obtain loans from private households and firms within the economy and not from its own central bank. These households and firms must be able and willing to lend to their government. But "ability" and "willingness" are highly subjective magnitudes. All that can be done here is to advance a few considerations.

Taxable capacity

The ability and willingness of persons and businesses to lend to government are intimately related to the level of national income. Higher incomes usually result in more saving. If incomes are higher, the tax revenues of government are also likely to be higher, and it is government's power and intention to tax that are the ultimate assurance that interest will be paid on its debt.

There need be no expectation that government will reduce the debt. It is only necessary that specific bond issues be redeemed upon their maturity. At that time they can be promptly replaced by new issues, perhaps sold to other savers, but mostly to the same people as before.

The ability of a central government to pay interest on its debt is obviously limited by its taxing powers. Constitutional provisions may permit it to levy certain taxes only. For instance, it is not every government that has always had authority to tax income and capital. A government that is legally restricted to a narrow tax base, and refuses to take credit from its central bank, may be able to carry only a limited debt despite a high national income. Hence, but only approximately, there may be some maximum fraction of national income that can be diverted by means of taxes through the treasury under existing limits.

Let us represent the maximum ratio of tax receipts (T) to national income (Y) by the ratio t. Then if government is compelled by political pressures to incur some constant expenditure for ordinary operation (O), the maximum sustainable national debt (D) can be represented by the equation

$$D = \frac{Yt - O}{i}$$

where i is the contractual interest rate on government obligations. If Y is $1000x$ money units, maximum t is 0.2, O is $150x$, and i is 0.05, then the maximum possible debt is $1000x$, which happens to equal the national income.

If the national debt is already at its supposed maximum limit in some year, it can presumably be increased each year only as national income increases; and in the absence of changes in population and labor force, increments in Y presumably depend upon increments in investment (ΔK) and annual improvements in the state of the arts (ϕ). The equation for maximum national debt increase is then

$$\Delta D = \frac{Y(\phi + sr)t}{i}.$$

where s is the average propensity to save and r is the normal rate of return on investment. If ϕ is 0.01, s is 0.1, and r is 0.1 also, the other values remaining unchanged, ΔD is $80x$ or 8 per cent of national income.

These formulae are of course only suggestive of the elements involved. There is really no obvious maximum limit to t. If people support their government enthusiastically, if economic progress can be seen on every hand, if increased consumption levels are expected after another few years of austerity and investment, then t will be higher. If government projects are useless, officials are corrupt, and there is general dissatisfaction with the regime, resistance to taxes will stiffen. And, in the long run, constitutional restrictions on taxing authority can usually be amended.

National debt burden

In the abstract, there is nothing good or bad about a large national debt, for it really depends upon how it was financed and used. In practice, most national debts are financed in part through new money created by the central bank, and so an increasing national debt is not surprisingly associated in the public mind with inflation. Also a large fraction of most national debts were incurred for the production of goods and services having almost no economic use—e.g., military armaments and service personnel—so that real national income and taxable capacity have not increased as a consequence. But here we are assuming for the moment that the national debt is financed from real savings. And most backward countries at least have the advantage of not being saddled with large debts from past wars.

If a government wishes to divert more of the economy's resources to its own uses, and refuses to increase taxes or expand credit, it can only do so by borrowing from the public and so increasing government debt. There is no other way it can increase its purchasing power as against that of private consumers and investors. Conversely, a reduction in the national debt, taxes and credit unchanged, means a greater private determination of national income composition.

There have been long controversies as to whether a national debt is somehow a burden on the home economy. A common and rather oversimplified argument is that, so long as the debt is owed exclusively to residents of the same country, any servicing of the debt merely involves indirect payments by resident taxpayers to resident holders of government obligations. If taxpayers and bondholders are resident in the same country, there is certainly no foreign exchange problem, and within a country all bondholders will be taxpayers. But all taxpayers will not be bondholders. And if taxpayers are required to service the national debt, it is not clear why they are relieved of their burden because bondholders live in the same country rather than in another country on the same planet.

Some developing countries—and especially the lands of current settlement—are long on resources but short on capital and labor. They need immigrants and funds from abroad. But if the underdeveloped country must tax away a considerable fraction of national income for debt service, potential immigrants and foreign investors may be deterred. Immigrants, as new residents of the debt-burdened country, will not be able to escape its heavy taxes. Foreign capitalists who venture their funds in the country will perhaps expose themselves to heavier taxes than elsewhere. And these inhibitions upon labor and capital inflows will be all the greater if the national debt was incurred for unproductive uses.

If a national burden has to be serviced from a narrow tax base, the objects that can be taxed must be taxed heavily, and this will inevitably distort the output and consumption mix of the economy. For example, if a central government could tax *only* industrial output, serious underinvestment in industry would probably result. National debt service would increase this distortion if the burden were heavy. It is therefore generally true that a large national debt can better be supported, given national income, if government has a broad tax base over which it can spread the burden to minimize distortion of the economy.

Reducing the burden through inflation

Short of outright repudiation of the national debt—which some revolutionary governments have done—rapid credit and price inflation can eliminate much of the burden of servicing it. The money paid as interest and principal has less and less purchasing power. The government is paying its obligations to private lenders by increasing its obligations to the central bank. The central bank in turn becomes more liable to the public. But its liabilities are legal tender currency.

The point hardly needs laboring that if a government permits a continued and considerable annual increase in price levels, it will not long be able to borrow any but insignificant sums from the public. A persistent inflation, despite a temporary illusion of money, is recognized sooner or later for what it is. People then attempt to transfer their assets from money claims into real property. And through such attempts prices are inflated sharply.

If private investors come to believe that the price level will rise about 10 per cent or more each year—and in some underdeveloped countries with ambitious governments the annual currency depreciation is considerably higher—they will only buy government obligations that annually yield considerably above 10 per cent in money terms. But governments are often under legal or political restrictions as to the rate of interest they can offer on their long term bonds. Their only recourse then, if they are to borrow from the public and not the banks, is to sell new bond issues at a fraction of their redemption value. In the end this only makes it harder for the treasury to withstand the temptation of demanding inflationary credits from the central bank.

CREDIT INFLATION TO DIVERT RESOURCES

Expanding bank credit to "force" saving is the method most commonly used by governments to divert resources into uses that they prefer. Politically, credit inflation is an easier way to reallocate resources than borrowing private savings and levying extra taxes. Economically, it may be the most costly means, however, and socially it is perhaps the most dangerous.

Diversion of resources

A government that is eager to force the pace of investment in the private sector can often arrange an expansion of credit. If the banking system is under government regulation, the minimum reserve requirements of individual banks may be increased by the amount of loans they have outstanding to specifically approved borrowers for approved projects. Or the government, through its central bank, may lower minimum reserve requirements and purchase securities on the open market while simultaneously restricting loans for consumption and other disapproved purposes. Thus more credit may be made available for extra investment in favored industries or localities.

However, this kind of credit inflation to force investment operates only indirectly. It presumes that private investors will apply for loans and that bank managers will grant them. Sometimes the investment climate may seem so unfavorable to private enterprise that neither businessmen nor bankers are interested at any price.

Government can inflate credit and divert resources more directly and certainly if it borrows for its own account and from the banking system when it needs more money than it has to make capital and current disbursements. The central bank merely credits the treasury's account, subsequently government writes checks on this account which are deposited in commercial banks by payees, and the banking system thereby increases both its holdings with the central bank and its demand deposit liabilities. These demand deposits, so far as the firms and households are concerned, are money. In this way, the stock of money in public hands is increased when government spends more than it is borrowing and taxing from private sources. The practical effect would be the same if the government were printing money instead.

When credit is expanded to finance development, whether the loans are to government agencies or private firms, the borrowers are able to compete more effectively against other potential users of scarce productive resources. Having obtained an increment of purchasing power, they can divert labor and equipment and land to employments of their own by paying slightly higher prices. If aggregate resources remain unchanged in quantity, but there is more money in the system, the general level of prices will almost inevitably rise unless the public for some reason wishes to hold a larger fraction of its income in bank balances and legal tender.

It is because credit inflation usually results in higher prices that it is often referred to as "forced" saving. The firms and households that have not received additional loans lose command of some goods and services to those who have. And banks mostly lend, not to consumers, but to enterprises that wish to expand their operations by investing in fixed and working capital. However, there cannot be extra investment without extra saving, because they are two aspects of the same phenomenon. And if resources and technology are unaltered, increased saving means decreased consumption. Households are forced to save because they cannot buy as many goods and services at higher prices.

Credit inflation, with higher prices, may not always result in more saving in the sense of fewer current goods and services. Government may borrow from the banking system to finance its ordinary operations, and not for development purposes. The public must then buy rather less of the things it prefers and "enjoy" the goods and services that government provides. These may be extra parks, airports, schools, telephones, bureaucrats, soldiers, or almost anything. Whether these things are more or less useful than the goods and services the public would otherwise have bought is not of importance here. The point is that credit inflation has diverted resources into making other goods and services.

Compounding of inflation

Credit inflation, when it results in higher prices, is rather like a drug: it has to be used in increasing doses in order to maintain the initial effect.

Suppose a country has a national income valued at $1000x$ in some base year. The stock of money is $250x$ and the annual velocity of money is 4.0. Gross national output and money stock are both increasing at 2 per cent annually while prices and money velocity remain unchanged from year to year. Ten per cent of the annual output is produced for or by the government to be distributed as public goods and services. Initially the budget is balanced.

Now imagine government decides to direct and allocate not 10 per cent but 15 per cent of the national output. Thus in the first three months (one turnover of money period) it must spend not $25x$ but $37.5x$ worth of funds. But it does not wish to increase tax rates, so it is given credits of $12.5x$ by the central bank instead. There has been a 5 per cent increase in the money stock in one quarter of a year. If output does not increase in response, there will be more money seeking approximately the same quantity of goods, and prices may rise by 5 per cent also.

In the next period the government still wishes to direct 15 and not 10 per cent of the country's resources. (Its share in national income derived from taxes is presumed constant at 10 per cent in spite of the rise in price levels.) The credit it must obtain from the central bank in the second period is 5 per cent greater in money units than before because of the price level increase. This will continue to be so period after period if the conditions assumed above remain unchanged. Thus after 5 years (*i.e.*, 20 periods) prices will have risen by 2.4 times, and after 10 years by 5.8 times.

A crude approximation of the multiplication of prices over N years, where d is the proportion of national income to be diverted by new government credits, and V is the annual velocity of money, is:

$$(1 + d)^{NV}$$

The anticipated percentage inflation after N years is sensitive to the annual turnover of money, here represented by V, which is the reciprocal of the fraction of annual income that businesses and people hold as cash balances on an average. So far it has been supposed that V remains unchanged. But sustained inflation is soon recognized for what it is by many firms and households. They consequently prefer to hold their assets in forms other than money. They will prefer stocks to bonds, building sites to life insurance, commodity speculations to bank balances, and so on. But everyone cannot transfer out of money simultaneously. The entire money stock must be owned by someone at any given moment. Hence, the harder people try not to hold money, the greater its turnover. And as V increases, prices will rise more rapidly. So the above equation understates compounding tendencies of credit inflation.

Consequences of inflation

What does it matter if a country experiences a continual price inflation? So long as all resources are employed, the economy is investing, and people are consuming, it seems like carping for economists to criticize policies that result in constantly rising prices. However, merely to mention three negative consequences, a steady price inflation inflicts personal injustices, inhibits the growth of a productive middle class, and atrophies the price and market system. A little inflation usually results in a lot more. Credit creation, like the use of a narcotic, has to be experienced in order to understand its dangers.

Unfair Incidence of Price Inflation.   Although not numerous, many of the residents in backward countries do have relatively fixed incomes, especially retired persons and their heirs. They may be beneficiaries of life insurance policies, holders of annuities and pensions, or owners of bonds and bank balances. Some of these people, either on account of their sex or age, may not be competent to risk their livelihood by speculating in land, stocks, and commodities. They need the comparative safety that fixed money incomes provide in the absence of inflation. Thus inflation robs these people of part of their wealth and income as surely as any thief might.

Inflation is not so hard on people who are productive and have something to sell, whether it be their own labor, output from agriculture, or natural resources. Those who are better informed, more energetic, and highly acquisitive may benefit from price inflation. It is the uninformed, infirm, or unworldly that suffer. But these last are in a minority. And it is seldom politically expedient to manifest a concern for those who have saved a fraction of their life's earnings.

No government should complacently adopt economic programs that violate accepted tenets of justice and decency. There is something extremely distasteful about policies that rob the weak and trusting for the advantage of the strong and predatory. And the ethics of those are suspect who, with a full understanding of its personal consequences, advocate price inflation as a means to economic development.

Inhibits Growth of a Middle Class.   An outstanding characteristic of most advanced nations is the existence of a substantial and educated middle class, comprising business and professional men, which is the main depository of the nation's specialized human talent and an important source of its savings. No nation can develop without an increasing proportion of engineers, chemists, agronomists, doctors, accountants, pharmacists, biologists, economists, and other professional people among its population. Their specialized knowledge and training are essential for progress. And because under ordinary circumstances they are able to earn more than they consume, this difference is available for investment.

Professional persons are nearly always salaried. Moreover they are frequently employed by institutions of a semipublic nature that have relatively inflexible wage structures. Hence a prolonged period of inflation will continually depress real earnings in these occupations. This must deter young men of ability who might otherwise embark on a long period of professional training. Persons already trained may be encouraged to transfer into business instead. Some may emigrate to another country.

Underdeveloped countries can barely afford as it is to provide a few years of elementary schooling to those children who live within or near towns and larger villages. Thus the tuition and living expenses of "higher" education must be borne for the most part by the middle classes. They understand the importance of investing in their children through education. The desire to put a son through school may be a major incentive to produce. But if inflation reduces the real earnings of the middle class, and partially destroys the value of its savings, there will be fewer educated and trained people in the next generation. And yet professional people are one of the scarcest requirements of economic development.

A middle class also provides entrepreneurs and managers for small enterprises. All save avowedly socialist nations need these risk-takers and resource-allocators. It is just such people, in their selfish and competitive search for private profit, who direct labor, land, and capital into making those goods and services that buyers seem to want most urgently. They hazard their wealth in the correctness of their judgment. These entrepreneurs, with their special knowledge of particular goods and localities, can probably perform this allocating function better than some comparatively disinterested and uninformed official. The cloak of authority does not ordinarily bring with it the cap of wisdom.

A majority of entrepreneurs do not wish to be speculators. Price speculation is a very particular form of risk-taking. Most owners and managers have enough to do ascertaining the wants of the market and satisfying them as economically as possible. Hence most businessmen and agriculturalists try to avoid gambling on prices if they can. Evidence of this are the numerous hedging devices that have been evolved, in advanced countries especially. Price inflation increases unwelcome risks and hence inhibits more worthwhile entrepreneurial activity.

Most backward nations are largely divided into only two classes. At top are a few wealthy families, owning land and industry, and sometimes operating large commercial enterprises. At the bottom are innumerable peasants, landless manual laborers, and a white-collared proletariat of office clerks. There is only a very small middle class of small capitalists and professionally trained men to provide a social ladder for outstanding families to mount over the generations. Such a sharp dichotomy between "haves" and "have-nots," and the absence of a middle class to permit vertical mobility, must inevitably result in political tension and instability.

Economic development creates a middle class (except in Communist systems) and a middle class furthers economic progress. A strong and vigorous middle class is also one of the greatest stumbling blocks to socialist advance. But a compounding inflation will undermine a middle class or prevent it from emerging by depressing its earnings, inhibiting ordinary enterprise, and reducing the savings with which it perpetuates itself through education. Hence it is no accident that socialists or Communists, eager to weaken this bulwark of private enterprise and independence, usually welcome rapid inflation as a device for social destruction.

Inflation Paralyzes the Price System.   Perhaps the most serious consequence of prolonged monetary inflation is that in order to mitigate some of the effects already mentioned, government is likely to impose price ceilings and quantity rations that may seriously distort the economy over any long period of time. The same political pressures that may induce government to inflate rather than tax may impel it to prevent any symptomatic increase in the cost of living. The final outcome, if the government has a large enough bureaucracy to administer all its market regulations, may be a sort of controlled disequilibrium that paralyzes economic self-regulation through the price system.

When credit inflation is more rapid than output expansion—sometimes described as more money chasing goods and services—prices will almost inevitably increase. In poor countries this impact will soon be felt in rising costs for food. And these are possibly more unpopular than higher taxes. Hence government may feel compelled to declare that old prices are legal maximum prices. At these ceiling prices, which now are sub-equilibrium market prices, supply naturally falls short of market demand. Food has not risen in price, but it is now often unavailable to would-be purchasers. The next stage of control is usually some form of quantity rationing that confuses equality with equity.

During short periods of time it might be possible to freeze the distribution and prices of consumer goods without misallocating economic resources. But over, say, a decade, during which all sorts of product, market, and technical innovations occur, old economic patterns become obsolete. The wrong goods will tend to be distributed to the wrong people in the wrong localities. Of course, to a limited extent, a large bureaucracy may be able to duplicate some of the adjustments that a free price system would make automatically. But this seems an unnecessarily cumbersome and costly substitute for natural law.

In all countries there is some evasion of price and rationing controls. Even during wartime, and with a majority of the public cooperating out of patriotism, profits from illegal transactions often proved too strong an incentive to illegality. In backward countries, where officials are poorly paid, such controls are certain to spread corruption throughout the civil service.

Steadily rising prices will put an end to most long term lending. The principal on maturity will have lost too much purchasing power. Not every potential saver feels capable of investing for himself in real property and common shares. Thus the economy will suffer a loss in aggregate saving and investment except to the extent that this is more or less offset by government investment financed through credit inflation. And backward countries are generally supposed to be particularly in need of increased investment. Inflation, so far as investment is concerned, is rather like pushing into a revolving door and finding oneself out on the street again.

Domestic credit inflation will cause increased external payments, disappearing foreign reserves, and eventual exchange control. Higher money incomes, reinforced by higher domestic prices, will increase imports. So a system of import licensing will be introduced to permit only "essentials" to be purchased from abroad. An actual or potential disequilibrium in the balance of payments may be counted upon to instigate an outflow of short term capital. Some exchange control measures are soon inevitable, but for a while nonresidents may not be subject to them.

Exchange control will not prevent two adverse reactions however. First, because of the domestic rise in prices and money incomes, producers who used to export will divert an increasing fraction of their output to the home market: this is because exchange control will pay only exporters who surrender foreign earnings at the official rate of exchange, which undervalues foreign currencies. Second, the imposition of exchange control, even if only on residents, is a storm warning that is likely to keep foreign investors safe in their own harbor. Both developments result in a reduced capacity to import producer goods from abroad. Many capital goods cannot be produced domestically, and yet certain industries cannot be established without them. Domestic output may partly depend on imported raw materials too. It is usually impracticable to prohibit all consumer goods imports so as to concentrate the use of foreign exchange on imported real capital. Hence it is often the foreign trade consequences of inflation that immediately do most to hamstring economic development in backward countries.

USING A BUDGET SURPLUS FOR INVESTMENT

If government wishes to invest for development, and is unable or unwilling to borrow from the public or the banks, its principal remaining alternative is to budget for a treasury surplus on so-called current account. Segregating receipts and disbursements into current and capital categories—as explained above—is not always a simple matter. To be done at all properly some sort of depreciation allowance must be estimated for each class of property. A new school building is a capital asset, but are expenditures to train extra teachers a current expense? In fact, such are the difficulties of categorization that most governments do not attempt to distinguish current and capital receipts and expenses. A less formal method of bookkeeping is to have some development loan account—or a National Development Bank as described above—to which the treasury makes transfers from its general revenue fund when it has a surplus in its "ordinary" budget.

More receipts or fewer expenditures?

Arithmetically, to obtain an "ordinary" budget surplus, a given reduction in expenditures is the equivalent of the same increase in receipts. However, the politics of public finance are such that the latter possibility may in fact be impracticable. There is also a tacit assumption that if government can have command over yet another increment of resources, it will be able to use them "better" than those who have been partially relieved of their purchasing power.

In a very real sense, government is not able to determine its receipts and disbursements, especially in the short run. The *rates* at which it taxes take time to change; meanwhile, fluctuations in economic activity and general prosperity will determine the tax base, and thus tax receipts. In advanced countries this is most obvious in the case of income tax yields. In backward countries, where half the national product may be derived directly or indirectly from agriculture, the receipts of government may vary from year to year by several per cent depending on the weather. On the whole, backward countries probably have less "elastic" tax receipts than advanced ones, their receipts varying proportionately less than a related change in national income.

Expenditures are also determined in part by external forces. In advanced countries, with social insurance schemes, unemployment means increased disbursements by government. In backward countries, a crop failure and threatened famine may occasion an unexpected expense. A few poor and backward countries are threatened by external aggression, more by internal subversion directed from abroad. Both of these threats may result in unexpected drains on the budget. (Thus the countries of Southeast Asia must worry about China's intentions, and not a few of them have diverted funds and resources from development to defense.)

Many governments are so vulnerable to pressures from special interests that they have very little discretion in raising tax rates, reducing various services, or ridding themselves of unnecessary employees. In some Latin American countries the landowners are so powerful a group that a government would have to possess very strong popular backing to increase taxes on land rents. In Southeast Asia, some governments subsidize the sale of food grains in the larger towns, and must probably continue to incur these costs if they are to avoid riots.

Also, costs of administration increase with economic planning for development, and at present salary scales, men of ability and energy are not likely to take government positions. The middle civil service grades in most backward countries include too many men who are on the public payroll only because they have been educated and possess connections. In not a few countries it is recognized that government officials, whose salaries are constantly being decimated by inflation, are strongly tempted to supplement their income by improper means.

The facts of corruption might as well be faced. In many poor and backward nations tax collectors accept "presents" in return for low property assessments. Purchasing agents accept low quality materials from their "friends." Postmasters have their little larcenies. The police do not prosecute if the payoff is prompt and adequate. Public school teachers neglect their classes to devote their time to special students whom they tutor for a fee. Customs officials look the other way. Projects are located so that a relative can sell his land at a good price. And receipt of foreign assistance is evidenced by the new cars that senior officials park outside their clubs. Where salaries are low, and are not increased in step with inflation, it is hardly surprising that people who have been reared to place family first should often be guilty of such malpractices. It is perhaps more surprising that a few governments—India's being outstanding—include so many fine and dedicated senior civil servants.

Eventually, if government is to play a more important part in economic life, it must be conducted by people of superior caliber. Many of them will have to be diverted from the professions and commerce by the prospect of really competitive salaries. These must be made proof against inflation. They might be automatically increased in accordance with some rising cost of living index, for example. But this means that the true and total costs of government administration must cease to be met in part from bribes and exactions and instead be charged to a public budget.

Increasing population means increased government expense. More must be spent on social welfare, such as primary schooling, public health clinics, and possibly urban housing (especially where internal migration is uncontrolled). In overpopulated countries, where population may be increasing 20 per cent each decade, the resultant increases in labor force may increase output by only half as much. Hence population increase probably occasions a larger relative increase in public expenses than in receipts.

For these and other reasons, and despite the existence of undoubted waste in all government operations, budget surpluses for development account will come from levying new kinds of taxes and raising the rates of old taxes. So far as possible these taxes should discourage consumption without discouraging production. Appropriate canons of taxation for underdeveloped countries—together with various examples—are described in some detail in the following chapter.

Government surpluses from industrial operations

Many backward countries are partly socialized and have public and private sectors of the economy. Government, in addition to operating the communication systems (*i.e.,* posts, telegraphs, and telephones), may also own and operate transport services (*i.e.,* railroads, some bus lines, and a shipping fleet). In not a few cases it will operate mining properties, steel plants, and oil refineries, and even engage in light industry. Government may monopolize the import and export of certain commodities. Some or all of these activities may yield a surplus that can be transferred to the treasury's development loan account.

Once government is operating enterprises that sell to the public, certain important pricing issues must be settled. For example, should government determine the price and output of steel so as to maximize its profits (*i.e.,* equate marginal cost to marginal revenue), to make the project self-financing (*i.e.,* equate average total cost to price), or to maximize economic efficiency (*i.e.,* equate marginal cost to price).[2] For want of better names, the first two alternatives might be called, respectively, the socialist's approach and the businessman's approach to government pricing.

Not a few socialists are eager for government projects to be operated so as to maximize profits. This ensures the largest possible surplus that government can use to acquire additional plants in more industries. In this way it is expected that the public sector will in part finance its own aggrandizement. It can then encroach upon the private sector, aided by the higher priorities that public concerns enjoy over private firms in such matters as obtaining import licenses and bank credits, until almost all of industry and a considerable fraction of commerce have been nationalized.

Almost the antithesis of this viewpoint is that of the businessman. He wants government projects, acquired in part with his taxes, to price their outputs as cheaply as possible and still cover all their costs. So long as these projects are financially sound, meeting depreciation allowances and paying comparable tax and interest charges, the businessman would like the external economies of new government projects to be distributed forward and backward in lower output prices and higher input prices. Exhortations of this kind are not disinterested of course, as in the case of building contractors who must buy their cement from a government monopoly, but in this case the interests of firms and households may be more in accord.

Accordingly, a major point at issue is whether the advantages of specific development projects should flow into the economy or into the treasury,

2 The theoretical rationale of the third policy is explained in Chapter 15.

and whether the public sector should assist the private sector or be used to contract it. If government enterprises set prices to maximize profits, there will be reduced output and sales, and as a result there will be fewer forward or backward external economies. The public is then denied some of the advantages of economic development so that a more socialist economy can be achieved at an earlier date.

Taxes, borrowing, and inflation

Government may be able to increase investment and hence output in the economy through a budget surplus (probably achieved through higher prices and tax rates), borrowing from the public (at higher than former market interest rates), or obtaining funds from the banking system (thereby raising prices and diverting resources). Each policy involves so many indirect counterreactions that there are no reasons for supposing that one policy rather than another will always occasion a larger increase in net public and private investment combined. Some of these repercussions are often overlooked.

First, the propensity of government to spend extra receipts on real investment projects, and not on ordinary current operations, may be quite low. It is a common delusion that governments of poor countries devote all increments in borrowings, taxes, or profits to development. Their propensity to invest may be less than those who pay the extra taxes. Thus an increment of $10x$ in taxes—because of higher rates, not higher incomes—may cause taxpayers to save $2x$ less. Ignoring possible interest rate changes as a result, and assuming the propensity of government to invest is only 0.15, the economy as a whole may then experience a decrease of $0.5x$ in net investment.[3]

Second, government borrowing must raise interest rates, and this in turn will reduce ordinary private borrowing. For example, reverting to Fig. 12-1, a rise in the interest rate from 7 to 8 per cent accompanied government borrowing of $30x$ worth of funds, but total borrowing in the market increased only $20x$. The difference was the decline of $10x$ in nongovernment borrowing. Thus 0.33 of the government borrowing was not a net addition to the economy's lending. If one can suppose that ordinary private borrowing is for real investment, and the propensity of the government to invest is less than 0.33, aggregate real investment in the country will decline as a result. The least unfavorable situation for an increase in net investing, given the government's propensity to save, is

---

[3] A more complete analysis would include the probability that a leftward shift in the supply of loanable funds in the market will result in a higher interest rate. To this extent, the reduction in total funds lent and borrowed will be smaller. In the extreme case of a zero interest elasticity of demand for loanable funds, there will be no decrease in lending, even though at former interest rates savers now would lend less.

when the supply schedule is much flatter than the demand schedule in the market for loanable funds.[4]

Third, the demand for loanable funds of private investors is naturally sensitive to the attitudes and actions of government, and a program of vigorous government competition over a wide range of industries may merely substitute government investment for private investment. Government fertilizer plants may mean fewer private ones. In this case the D schedule in the diagram is shifting to the left. And government will be able to borrow for public industrial projects at practically no increase in interest rates. But there will then be no extra investment in the economy either.

Fourth, although a government can divert resources to its own use by selling its obligations to the central bank for new credits, the resultant inflation will inhibit private savers from lending fixed sums at fixed interest at long term. Government may discover that most of its new credits are a substitute for the funds it might have borrowed from selling bonds and bills to the public. And to the extent that the public no longer will lend (*e.g.,* buy bonds), combined government and private net investment may hardly increase.

Fifth, the allocation of resources cannot be completely ignored in favor of increasing the employment of resources, for what is the gain from producing more of the wrong goods and services? Inflation, for reasons given, may result in a variety of government controls that perpetuate former production and distribution mixes long after they are obsolete. If government has only a narrow tax base, so that the rates of a few taxes have to be drastically raised to increase revenues, the taxed items will be discouraged and may fall considerably in volume. Borrowing from private savers does not threaten proper resource allocation in this way because the lender can contract all around his expenditure perimeter.

In conclusion, each method by which government can increase net investment in the economy has certain pros and cons. On strictly economic grounds, there is often little to choose between taxing and borrowing. However, for social reasons as well as economic, inflation should be avoided.

---

[4] One psychological argument against borrowing, and in favor of taxation, is that consumption may not be reduced as much when people buy government bonds instead of paying taxes of equal values. Bonds are wealth. Taxes are gone forever and paying them makes one feel poorer.

13

Tax policies for
undeveloped nations

Enlightened tax policies can contribute to the development of any free enterprise economy. In fact, the more emphasis a government and people place upon expansion of the private sector, the more important taxes become. But tax policies cannot of themselves perform an economic miracle and give an overpopulated country which lacks natural resources and a modern technology the higher output that it wants.

Many current tax systems are unable to finance the numerous services that aspiring peoples increasingly consider the responsibility of governments. A broadening and tightening of taxes in backward countries is hence essential if governments are to meet the many demands upon them, plus those of development, and yet avoid a compounding inflation of credit. But tax policies that may encourage and permit the most rapid expansion of output may also result in a distribution of income that seems inequitable to many.

Tax policies that are suitable for advanced countries may not be appropriate for backward ones. In poorer countries there can be less emphasis on anticyclical measures. Mass industrial unemployment is not so alarming a specter. The existence of a large subsistence economy in many underdeveloped countries also calls for unusual methods of tax assessment and collection. Backward countries have a great need for foreign private investment, and capital inflows can often be encouraged by reasonable tax concessions, although some countries seem willing to deny themselves in this respect.

Among economists there is some difference of opinion regarding the degree to which the tax and credit policies of government can actively contribute to more rapid economic development. A few writers feel that a "vigorous"—*i.e.*, inflationary—fiscal policy that includes a lot of government investment can somehow get the economy "off dead center," "prime the pump," and so on. But most economists eschew these simple physical analogies and accord a more passive role to government policy. Their feeling is that "good" tax systems are those which encourage individual firms and households to produce more and hence cause the economy to grow. But what tax policies are "good"?

TAXATION FOR GROWTH

The economic goals of society largely determine the more specific criteria that define a "good" or "bad" tax structure. It makes a difference whether the main objective is increasing output (which may be distributed "inequitably") or raising the incomes of the very poor (which may deter maximum output). Steeply progressive income and inheritance taxes are undesirable in the former case and desirable in the latter. A poll tax may force families in the subsistence sector to sell more of their food output to the towns ("good"), but it is highly regressive in its incidence ("bad").

A country that is in the earliest stages of economic growth, with very low per capita incomes, may well be advised to make increased output a major objective and more equal incomes a minor one. Goods and services must be produced before they can be distributed. Metaphorically, a larger pie usually results in a majority of people receiving more to eat, even though some may get a smaller fraction.

Historically, although the evidence is not conclusive, those countries that now exercise themselves so much about equitable distribution of income were among the earliest to acquire an outstanding capacity to produce it. A sound rule is probably that a people must win the struggle for production before wrangling over the division of output.

Even if we assume that this issue is settled, and that the equities of distribution are to be subordinated to the magnitudes of production, any list of criteria for the evaluation of alternative tax policies must be somewhat arbitrary and controversial. The so-called "canons of taxation," as promulgated by Adam Smith, were "equality" (taxes in proportion to ability to pay and benefits received from government), "certainty" (levies must not be arbitrary or retroactive), "convenience" (payment required when the tax-payer has funds), and "economy" (costs of collection small relative to yield). But the twentieth century is not the eighteenth, nor are the possibilities and needs of underdeveloped countries necessarily the same as those of more developed ones, so these formerly accepted criteria are not sacrosanct. Most modern economists would probably revise this list and define each criterion more specifically.

For a developing economy, in early stages of economic growth, a "good" tax system is probably one that meets the following tests. First, it should discourage production as little as possible. Second, it should reduce less "essential" forms of consumption, especially during the period when savings and investment are crucial to output expansion. Third, it should not distort the economy, for a misallocation of resources will result if taxes make the real and money costs of certain producers too disparate. Fourth, it should be income elastic in the sense that net government receipts increase proportionately more than national money income, as in some measure this will mitigate the effects of credit inflation and serve as a cyclical "stabilizer." Fifth, the tax system should be economical, particular taxes being inexpensive to collect in full relative to the revenues they realize.

There are certainly other "canons of taxation" that might be added. Some people would append the criterion that a good system retards (or accelerates) population growth in the case of countries that are overpopulated (or underpopulated). Those who feel that a stronger middle class is a cause as well as an effect of economic growth might favor tax policies that make it easier for families to provide their children with higher education. Probably most people—and after all a majority of any population have below average incomes—want to use the tax system to lessen inequalities. Some people hate or envy another particular class, and demand high taxes on its incomes as a practical way of confiscating its property. Many other supposed characteristics of a "good" tax system could be appended.

One genuine but subsidiary *desideratum* remains to be mentioned. In the case of underdeveloped countries having a federal system of government, the central and state governments should each have a taxable capacity appropriate to their responsibilities. At present the main cost of development falls upon the broader tax base of the central government, but specific projects are and must often be proposed and administered by the states. In India, for example, the states initiate and administer most projects concerning community development, agriculture and irrigation, and social welfare; but, as their taxing powers are inadequate, a considerable fraction of these schemes are financed by the central government.

In large countries, and where communication and transport are slow, labor recruiting and bill paying must be a local function. But, as local authorities frequently have only a land tax as a major source of revenue, the main cost of development must fall upon the income taxes and import duties that can be levied by the national government. Because so much development must be local in its inspiration and implementation, there is much to be said for reversing recent trends and transferring, so far as possible, some tax authority from central to state governments.

In backward countries where there are strong provincial and tribal loyalties, it is psychologically easier for a local government to collect taxes. There is more assurance that the money will be spent for local improvements, and there is greater emotional identification with completed public works. Projects need not wait for "coordination" by faraway officials without local knowledge.

It is evident that a particular tax that best satisfies one criterion may not satisfy other criteria. Treasury officials can no more find one tax that preëminently meets all requirements than an automobile engineer can design a car that is simultaneously fastest, safest, and cheapest. But it is possible sometimes to determine that some tax meets one requirement better, and other requirements no worse, so that alternative taxes can be rejected. To do this obviously requires judgment of a higher order than can always be exercised. But by disregarding political objectives—*e.g.*, "plucking the most feathers with the fewest squawks"—a greater contribution to growth is possible.

MINIMIZING PRODUCTION DETERRENTS

Nearly all taxes deter output more or less over prolonged periods. It is true that perhaps, because of accustomed notions of what constitutes a normal income, some families will work harder under heavier tax burdens in the short run. But a general working rule is that anything taxed—whether it be income, goods, or some activity—becomes less available as a result in the long run.

Tax on rents

A tax on pure land rent is the most notable exception to this rule. If all the landlords died overnight, the services of all natural resources would still be available on the morrow. The original growing powers of the soil, proved mineral and petroleum reserves, and existing water power would all be unaffected. It is therefore an old idea, popularized by the single-taxers, that government should so far as possible finance itself from taxes on pure economic rent.

Such a tax on rent cannot be shifted, for the supply of most arable and grazing land is perfectly inelastic. But where agricultural land has first to be cleared or drained, the owner's income includes a return on the capital and labor invested and so exceeds the pure economic rent. And in the case of depleting natural assets that have to be prospected and proven at some expense, a so-called tax on rent that was excessive might eventually discourage exploration for new ore deposits and new oil fields to replace exhausted ones.

There are undoubtedly instances of weak or corrupt governments granting mineral and oil concessions at unwarrantedly low royalties. In such cases of exploitation, higher royalties, or stiffer taxes on the rent element of profits, are often economically feasible and just. But there are dry holes for every producing one, and some useless mine shafts for every working one, so royalties should cover all costs of exploration whether or not such efforts are successful. Moreover, after more obvious and accessible resources have been found and depleted, costs of proving new reserves are likely to rise. Hence, although reducing the profits of extracting industries is always popular, government should proceed with restraint lest revenge for the past ruin the future.

In a society that does not permit private property rights in land, there can be no private income from its rent. But even socialist economies, if they are efficiently to allocate specific areas of land among different uses, must estimate what pure rent each area could earn in each of several competing employments. The real question is not whether useful land always earns an imputed land rent, because it does, but rather who shall receive explicit rent payments. A landlord receives income in capitalistic societies because financially land is like any other investment to a private owner. It would be a gross injustice to deprive him of pure rent income if he or his family purchased the land at something like its capital value within say the last twenty-five years. But when land has been owned by the same family for centuries, and was initially acquired perhaps by conquest or royal generosity, taxes on land rents are not so obviously inequitable.

There is less conflict between economics and ethics where *potential* land rent is markedly higher than actual incomes from rent and is taxed. Some unprogressive landlords who own much acreage may not use their land to best advantage. Some land may be in grazing that should be in cultivation. The crop that is grown may not be the most valuable. The landlord may live far away and his local manager may have no authority to make drastic changes in land use. Some very large landowners are "land poor"—unable or unwilling to raise the capital needed to improve their property and increase pure rents. Resident and cultivating owners may simply be ignorant of better land uses.

In all cases where land is not earning its potential economic rent— assuming this can be roughly estimated—there is something to be said for levying a tax equal to the difference between the possible and actual rent. It takes some time, however, to reorder operations in agriculture. And, as this is a tax on rents that are not being received, the tax might have to be suspended in hardship cases. Moreover, where the maximum possible land rent requires considerable associated capital, the State might have to make it available. This scheme also requires tax assessors who are expert in agricultural operations and can predict markets. Otherwise, in practice but not in theory, the levy will become like any other land tax.

A significant feature of levies on potential but unrealized rents is that they will yield no tax revenue when the landlord's rents becomes the maximum possible. Hence this kind of tax is financially productive only so long as owners of land refuse to use their land in the way the tax assessors think they should. In a sense it is a punitive tax, imposed for misusing land, and as such might set far-reaching precedents for levies on other productive factors. Thus self-employed persons who do not work many hours a day might be taxed with as much logic. The owners of factories that only work one shift a day could face similar penalties. Having tax officials give managers advice—with the threat of special taxes if their views are not adopted—could open a veritable Pandora's box.

Levy on capital

Annual levies on capital are often suggested as a way to raise tax revenues in backward countries. The incidence depends rather on what is included in the tax base as "capital." Under one definition the effect would tend to be that of a tax on "unearned" income, and under another the capital levy would not be unlike a general tax on property.

One possibility would be an annual uniform *ad valorem* tax on all a household's assets above a certain exempt value. This could include natural resources and agricultural land, produced means of production of all kinds, stocks, bonds, loans, insurance policies, bank balances, and cash. Assets owned by corporations might not be taxed in order to avoid double taxation. Of course it is always difficult to assess the value of certain assets, but so far as possible capital values would be estimated from potential net income. Thus under-utilized productive assets would be assessed according to their fully utilized values. The total labor of assessment would be reduced by having only the comparatively wealthy —say the richest 1 or 2 per cent of the population—file a return.

Government, by excluding certain kinds of property from the tax base, can shift assets. For example, corporate securities might be exempt to encourage indirect investment. Or bank balances might be exempt to stimulate public use of the banking system.

The rate of an annual capital levy must be very low or an abnormal confiscation of private investment would in effect result. If the normal rate of return in a country is 10 per cent, an annual 2 per cent tax on capital values would tend to reduce the capital value of all assets by 20 per cent. For instance, if an asset used to earn $100 a year, the capital value at 10 per cent is $1000 under simple assumptions. A 2 per cent capital levy would amount to $20 a year. So the net earnings of the asset after tax becomes $80 and its capital value $800. The confiscation of capital values approximates yt/r^2, where y is the asset's annual net income, t is the rate of tax on capital, and r is the "normal" rate of return in the economy.[1]

One reason advanced in favor of a capital levy is that it is often easier for government to determine privately owned wealth than privately

[1] A capital levy is equivalent to an income tax having a rate of roughly t/r so far as total tax receipts are concerned.

received income. This is especially so when most consumption is produced within the same family or village. A good deal of bookkeeping must be done by businesses and families in order to determine taxable income. Allowances for depreciation must be estimated, for instance, when families own a business or farm. The existence of most assets—land, buildings, livestock—is more readily ascertained. Owners can be identified because they have a selfish interest in asserting and even registering their property rights.

In order not to discourage private saving and investment unduly, the concept of capital might be expanded to include all consumer durables. If the base is broadened, a lower rate can yield the same revenues. Or durable consumer goods might even be taxed at a higher rate to encourage persons to hold their wealth in productive rather than sumptuary form. Idle assets—such as vacant land being held for speculation and currently out of use—might also be taxed at a higher rate. Taxpayers can be made to dance to all sorts of different government tunes.

Taxes on income

Corporate and personal income taxes, although the main source of government revenue in advanced countries, are comparatively unimportant in backward nations. This is because most incomes are so low that only a small fraction of all households have practically taxable incomes. Exemptions, even though small, may be several times greater than average family income.

There has always been a great deal of controversy regarding the effect of an income tax on the productive effort of those who may be liable. A superficial view is that so long as the rate of tax on income is under 100 per cent, people will always prefer to have more rather than less disposable income and so will seek to maximize gross income. But this assumes that the disutility of earning an extra dollar's worth of income—including the lost utility from sacrificed leisure—is always less than the utility of spending the few cents that may remain after tax from that dollar. This is extremely unlikely, especially in the case of those who must worry, risk, and work to obtain a large income, and it is more unlikely the higher the rate of progression in the tax on incremental income.

It is more or less possible to discourage the earning of specific kinds of income. Thus income from work may be taxed at a lower rate than income from land. Or if a progressive rate structure is used for unearned income, "earned" income may be treated as though it were received separately and be taxed at a relatively low uniform rate. Thus a person with a fairly large income from property is not discouraged from working for a salary.

Taxes on estates

A familiar variation of the capital levy is an estate tax or death duty. The difference is that such a tax is not levied annually but only upon the death of those who own property above some minimum value. To prevent wealthy people from evading the tax by making gifts to their relatives before death, it is usual to include in the tax base all property alienated during, say, the seven years immediately preceding death. Or taxes may be levied on gifts made at any time. The nature of the assets held by wealthier people can be influenced by taxing different kinds of property at different rates. Thus, if it is considered desirable to distribute land ownership more widely, inherited land might be taxed more heavily; conversely, if land ownership is too fragmented for efficient cultivation, land might be exempt from estate and gift taxes. Death duties discourage the accumulation of wealth to some extent, for parents produce and save partly for their children, but they probably encourage investment in the health and education of sons and daughters.

REDUCE NON-ESSENTIAL CONSUMPTION

If consumption can be decreased without affecting production, the difference must be public or private investment that should result in more output of consumer and producer goods in the years ahead. So long as reduction in consumption is greater than any reduction in output, there should be increased investment, but the immediate real cost is greater. And some taxes on consumption may even increase output in special circumstances.

Poll taxes

A uniform poll tax on adults is certainly regressive in that it must represent a larger fraction of the incomes of poor persons, but it may increase productive effort.

In a rough sort of way, and within limits, most men can vary the amount of real or money income that they acquire during a year. If self-employed, or engaged in subsistence agriculture, they have considerable discretion as to how much they work. And they can hire themselves out to do extra odd jobs if their need for money is very urgent.

One can perhaps imagine that most adult males achieve a rough hedonistic equilibrium, the "last" (*i.e.*, marginal) unit of income having about the same utility in spending as disutility in earning. Designate this marginal dollar in equilibrium before poll tax as $\$_m$ and its utility and disutility as U' and D', respectively. A poll tax of $10 means that the $(\$_m - \$10)th$ unit of *disposable* income will still have a disutility of D'

in acquisition. But the utility of spending the ($\$_m$ — $\$10$)$th$ unit of disposable income must be greater than U' if the $\$_m th$ unit occasions U' marginal utility. Hence the taxpayer will prefer to spend something more than $\$_m$ — $\$10$ and to earn more than $\$_m$. He will have to contribute more to production in some way.

In some backward countries a poll tax might be difficult to collect in remote back areas where government does not always know the identities, numbers, or whereabouts of all the population. So collection of the poll tax often comes to be associated with registration for voting or some other purpose. Avoiding the voting polls is then a way of evading the poll tax. The poor tend to be "disenfranchised" more than the rich. The counter argument is that if everyone has a right to vote because he is human, adult, and alive, then every citizen has a duty to contribute to the State for the same reasons.

Taxing "luxury" goods

It is commonly supposed that the "luxury" consumption of the middle and upper classes of society—because their sense of time preference is less urgent—can be reduced through taxation without their reducing their productive effort commensurately. This comforting assumption may or may not be justified. But the "better off" do have more capacity to pay taxes, and they do not have enough votes to protect themselves in universal suffrage countries, so in practice their consumption is likely to be taxed more heavily.

The simplest method is to levy an excise tax on certain durable consumer goods, such as motor cars, refrigerators, and factory-made furniture, that obviously are not owned by low-income families. In really poor countries most manufactured consumer goods are of this kind. The tax can then be collected from the manufacturer or the importer.

A more costly method of taxing is to have an assessor annually visit all homes of the rich and levy an *ad valorem* tax on all scheduled consumer durables that he finds. The schedule of taxable items might include silverware and jewelry if they can be discovered. The only argument for this more cumbersome procedure is that a government that has hitherto not levied an excise at the point of production or importation has "missed" all luxury consumer durables already in existence within the country.

The merit of a tax on luxuries is that although it is impossible to tax the marginal *unit* of some consumer good, it is feasible to tax an incremental *kind* of consumption. Government cannot selectively tax the "last" yard of cloth, say, that a family buys during the year. But it can tax radios, for instance. Of course as the general level of consumption in a country rises, goods that were "luxuries" a decade or so ago may come to be "necessities." Then if the items selected for taxation are not altered, what was once a tax on luxuries will tend to become a general consumption tax.

General sales tax

A really broad tax base can be obtained by levying a general *ad valorem* tax on all consumer goods at the point either of production and importation or final sale. Often certain "necessaries" such as food are exempted. Such a tax may be called a consumer sales tax or purchase tax.

Of considerable importance and some controversy is whether such a tax will increase or decrease the productive efforts of households. There are grounds for supposing that a general consumer sales tax, at a uniform *ad valorem* rate, will reduce contributions to production by households that have an elastic marginal utility of money income.

The argument runs something as follows. Suppose the *ad valorem* rate sales tax is one-third and represented by t. All earnings are spent on consumption. Suppose the last dollar formerly spent on consumption bought the $100th$ unit of consumption. The same last dollar will now be spent on the $100 (1 - t)$ or $67th$ unit of consumption. The $67th$ unit of consumption has more utility than the $100th$. But the $67th$ unit now probably costs $[\$1/(1 - t)]$ more of gross earnings than before because of the purchase tax. So the same "last" dollar of expenditure will now buy less satisfaction than before if the $67th$—or $100/(1 - t)th$—unit does not have a utility $1/(1 - t)$ times greater than the $100th$ unit.

This type of analysis is a little embarrassing to those who like to "soak" the rich. It is the poorer families that may experience more than a t change in marginal utility with a t change in units purchased. This suggests that a general sales tax may force the poor to work more.

It is obviously difficult to enforce a general consumption tax in a subsistence sector of the economy. A tax collector would have to be permanently posted in every village household to prevent families from eating their own food crops. This is one reason why it may be necessary to exempt many agricultural products from an otherwise general sales tax.

AVOID DISTORTING THE ECONOMY'S STRUCTURE

A good tax system should include taxes having a broad base; otherwise, the output and consumption mix of the economy may be altered undesirably. A tax is said to have a broad base if the item taxed has a large money value. The "broadest" taxes are hence indirect taxes on, say, private income or household spending. If a tax system includes many taxes, having a broad base, the receipts from each tax can be a rather small fraction of the tax base. The levy then bears down less heavily on the property, commodity, persons, activity, or money flow that is being taxed.

In contrast, a narrow tax system is one that includes only a few taxes, and these on items that have narrow bases. Thus a tax on salt, although very hard to shift, cannot yield much revenue. The total value of all salt production during a year is an infinitesimal part of total national income. And most commodities cannot bear taxes as can salt because they have far more elastic demands. If a commodity has substitutes, or if people are willing to do without it, any appreciable tax will result in the good practically disappearing from legal view and yielding no revenue. The cost of collecting such taxes may then amount to a significant fraction of the yield.

The ability of a heavy direct tax to drive certain goods out of existence—or at least out of legal trade channels—explains the *dictum* that "the power to tax is the power to destroy." In fact governments have sometimes tried to eliminate supposedly antisocial activities and dangerous products by taxing them heavily. Success depends on the elasticity of demand and supply. But all commodity taxes reduce output and use of the item to some extent, even when supply and demand are very inelastic, since there are no goods and services for which there are no substitutes—however imperfect.

Governments obviously prefer to tax inelastic demand and supply goods and services because these contract only a little in volume, thus yielding much revenue. However, if government is determined to increase aggregate tax receipts, it may be led increasingly into taxing items that yield very little because they contract so appreciably in volume. Hence all sorts of moderately useful goods and services may be largely lost to use. The composition of the national product is affected adversely.

Central and state governments are sometimes constitutionally limited in their ability to tax. Authority to impose indirect taxes such as income and purchase taxes may be lacking. Some backward countries have the same problem but for another reason. Income and sales taxes are hard to collect in countries where only a few of the largest firms maintain complete accounting systems and a considerable fraction of national output and consumption is neither bought nor sold. The easiest taxes to collect without widespread evasion may be narrow in base and few in number. The only practical alternatives for a government determined to increase its activities and expenditures may then be credit inflation or economic distortion.

INCOME ELASTIC TAXES

Although not as important in backward as in advanced countries, it is good that tax receipts should rise relative to money incomes when the latter are increasing. Then (especially if government has expenses for social welfare and unemployment relief) good times should cause a budget surplus and bad times a budget deficit. If a surplus is used to redeem government obligations held by banks, and a deficit is met by creating more money, the tax system may tend to reduce the amplitude of economic fluctuations.

The two ways to obtain an income elastic tax structure are to have indirect taxes on "superior" goods—*i.e.*, goods that people purchase more as their real incomes rise—and to have direct taxes at progressive rates. This is one rationale of a tax on "luxuries." It is simpler to have progressive tax rates on personal incomes because purchase taxes have to be at uniform rates.

There is a tendency to inflation in all backward countries that are trying to develop more rapidly than taxes and voluntary savings permit. But real incomes do not rise merely because money incomes do. Hence inflation will not lead to more tax receipts from superior goods becoming a greater fraction of national consumption.

ECONOMY OF ADMINISTRATION

The cost of collecting taxes—which includes assessing values, computing tax liabilities, and prosecuting for nonpayment—is in part an unavoidable cost of government. But as the labor and other resources so employed are presumably lost to alternative productive uses, tax administration costs are an outright loss to any economy. Hence there is every reason to keep them as low as possible. Logically, if no other considerations existed, government should try to devise its tax system so that the cost of obtaining the last dollar's worth of receipts from each kind of tax is the same. It makes no sense, *if* other things are equal, to spend 5 cents collecting the last dollar of land tax and 50 cents collecting the last dollar of dog tax.

The most economical direct taxes are those that fall upon commodities having only few supply points. Sometimes the supply point may be a single plant—such as a large oil refinery—and in general it is easier to collect so-called consumption taxes from a few producers than from thousands of retail stores. In the case of imported goods, the supply must pass through some one of several ports, or possibly along a single railroad line. Collection is then accordingly simple and economical.

In really primitive economies, almost all the most rudimentary industrial goods have to be imported, and so customs duties often provide over half the total government revenues of such countries. Moreover, as all consumer goods imports tend to be purchased by those with above average incomes, reliance on consumer import duties may actually impart some progressiveness to a country's tax structure.

Export taxes, especially in cases where a country ships a few agricultural or mineral commodities from a small number of supply points, can be very productive of revenue and economical to administer. But such taxes on production are less favorable to economic growth than taxes on consumption (see Chapter 25).

Another tax easily collected is a tax on land, for land cannot be hidden and most useful land is owned or used by some identifiable person, family, or village. If the tax does not exceed the economic rent, it cannot be shifted onto consumers of agricultural products. Moreover, in countries where land rents may account for a fifth or so of national output, the taxable capacity of land is substantial.

Most tax structures need an occasional overhauling. Taxes that once provided revenue may now be little more than nuisance taxes, for they may be levied on goods or property of a kind that has long been obsolete while the modern substitute may still be untaxed. (Of course some taxes are imposed not to raise revenue but expressly to prevent production and use of a particular good.)

One hidden but real cost of administration is corruption. The opportunities for corruption are greatest where tax liabilities are uncertain and the tax collector has considerable discretion in determining the amount of tax that is due. Any tax that is based on highly subjective estimates—e.g., the capital value of a mining property—suffers from this disadvantage. For this reason, specific rate taxes have some advantages over ad valorem taxes, but they are extremely vulnerable to inflation, and entail other difficulties besides.

Some governments may give undue weight to economy of administration in determining their tax systems. Historically countries have often taxed those things they found administratively—and also politically—easiest to tax. Other criteria should also be considered and economically may be more important. But there is no "scientific" way to decide among different taxes that satisfy one or more criteria while violating others. The economist has no more to contribute at this point. It is politicians who must then decide the matter.

SPECIAL PROBLEMS OF TAXATION IN PRIMITIVE ECONOMIES

The above discussion may not be too relevant to a few of the poorest and most retarded countries in which there may be large subsistence economies, little use of money except in the towns, and almost no foreign trade. Some rather unusual levies may then be imposed. Among them are turnover taxes, assessments in kind, and compulsory labor.

Taxes on turnover

One of the simplest taxes to levy, on any business that sells its output for money, is a constant rate turnover tax, because its determination requires only the most rudimentary kind of bookkeeping. Even small producers and shopkeepers who keep no capital or expense accounts may at least have a record of the money they take from buyers. Or except for itinerant traders and peasants, licensed retailers might be required to keep such information. Between the wars, the turnover tax in the Soviet Union was a major source of revenue, and it was originally imposed probably because of its ease of collection. The turnover tax has also been an important source of revenue to the state of São Paulo in Brazil. Where seaport cities and provinces have turnover taxes, shifted partly to find buyers, the people of the hinterland areas are bearing some of the burden.

An important advantage and disadvantage of the turnover tax is that unlike a manufacturers' sales tax, there is no need to determine at what stage in the making of a good is it "produced." Is a suit "produced" when the cloth is cut and sewn, or when the cloth is dyed, or when it is woven? These uncertainties are irrelevant if all firms pay a tax on their receipts.

However, where each stage of production is completed by a different firm, the turnover tax will be pyramided. There will accordingly be some tendency toward vertical integration to lessen the total tax burden. The tax will then bear most heavily on those final goods the making of which cannot be integrated, and this will result in some distortion of the economy. One solution is to tax not the receipts but the gross value added of each business. But such an assessment would also require that there be an accounting of material purchases.

Taxes in kind

Peasants in a subsistence sector of a national economy may consume most of their own output. There are then very few ways in which they can acquire money unless they seek paid work in the market economy. Sometimes government may impose taxes—e.g., a poll tax—partly to compel peasants to sell more output and to hire themselves out as paid laborers. However, if there is already undernourishment and unemployment in the towns, government may be more than willing to accept certain food grains in payment of taxes.

The tax may be a fixed quantity of grain, a specific assessment being made against the owner or cultivator of each hectare of land, in which case a bad harvest will cause more hardship than usual. Or government and taxpayer may share the risk by making the tax some predetermined fraction of output. Alternatively, government may assess a tax liability in money, but accept grains and certain other produce at local market prices. In such cases, a poor harvest, resulting probably in higher prices, means that a smaller quantity of produce will discharge the tax liability.

Government of course does not want to become a trader in chickens, goats, and other livestock. Nor will it accept perishable vegetables and fruits. In practice, therefore, it is only food grains, and perhaps certain fibers (such as cotton) that government will accept in lieu of money as taxes.

Compulsory labor on government projects

Compulsory or statutory labor was a commonplace in Europe several centuries ago and has existed in a number of European colonies during the recent past. Under this system every male adult may be required by law to work for the government so many days a year. Statutory labor is something akin to a poll tax that can be worked off.

Traditionally this labor has been on public works such as repairing roads, digging drains or irrigation ditches, and constructing government buildings. Often it is possible to schedule work on these projects at times when there is little agricultural activity and considerable under-employment. If the rural population can acquire very little money to pay taxes, and has little surplus produce of a kind acceptable to government, labor is about all that exists for government to extract. Why should government not accept payment in service if it will accept payment in goods?

Some flexibility can be introduced by allowing adult males to commute their statutory labor by making a stipulated cash payment. In this way men who have special skills are not diverted from possibly more valuable employment. In fact, because few government projects can be completed with only unskilled labor, men with special skills may be able to find seasonal jobs on these projects. For such men government must pay wages, and it will always have material costs too; hence compulsory labor can never provide more than a good fraction of local government's real and money incomes.

In countries that have a large rural population, clustered into innumerable small villages, the cost of community development projects may be predominantly labor costs. Or it may be possible to devise useful community projects that do not require much more than local unskilled labor under supervision of one trained government official. Ideally such projects should be of a kind that can be finished in one slack season, or else enthusiasm will flag. If it is not necessary for everyone to work on these projects simultaneously—that is, if individuals can work off their obligations at times that suit them—so much the better. Projects such as building aqueducts, digging water tanks, installing sewers, paving village streets, and constructing community ovens or a village grain mill may all meet most of these requirements.

Unfortunately, compulsory labor is often associated in the public mind with "slave" labor, brutal correction camps, and various atrocities. But statutory labor need not mean any of these things. For one thing, workers would not be transported away from home, but would live and work in their own community on projects that obviously benefit them. Really there is little difference between taxing away a sixth of a man's income—which means that the fruits of two months of his labor go to the government every year—and requiring him to work 45 days a year on a local government project. And if he has the right to pay so much a day instead of working, there is even less difference. The needs of community development are so great in most poor countries, and there is so much seasonal unemployment in many of them, that levies on labor seem desirable and inevitable (see Chapter 8).

14

Banking requirements
of backward countries

The economic consequences of tax and credit policies are so closely intertwined that it is not very useful to specify the sort of tax structure an underdeveloped country requires without also considering the kind of credit controls it should have. And credit controls cannot be discussed except in the context of a particular banking system. Tax structures and banking systems are twin institutions for implementing fiscal policy.

All nations have certain universal needs that could be met by any money and banking system. But backward countries also have a number of special requirements and problems that are often overlooked and cannot be satisfied by establishing slavish imitations of the banking systems of advanced countries. Unfortunately, as one authority has stated, circumstances have conspired

. . . to make some of the "new" countries rush into the establishment of central banks, and only gradually are they beginning to realize how essentially different are the financial climates in which these new institutions are functioning. The "new" countries alone cannot be held responsible for their misunderstandings; they often took British or American advice based more on familiarity with the City or Wall Street than on fundamental analysis of banking problems. Since then we have both lived and learned.[1]

This chapter is accordingly devoted to a description of the main requirements of any money and banking system, the special problems of underdeveloped countries, and the institutional arrangements that might satisfy these general and special needs.

GENERAL MONEY AND BANKING NEEDS

The general requirements of any banking and money system are reasonably familiar. There is of course scope for disagreement as to which

[1] R. S. Sayers, *Modern Banking*, 3rd ed. (Oxford, 1951), p. 297.

needs should be given priority. But the following list includes most of the more desirable characteristics.

First, money is one of the greatest of all social inventions, for it facilitates division of labor and so promotes efficiency in production. A major responsibility of government is to provide a legal tender in quantities that accommodate the changing needs of trade without alteration of its purchasing power. If money is the established means of payment, any prolonged expansion of trade will tend to depress money prices in a closed economy, and in this way the increase in activity may retard itself unless a larger money stock is made available. It is the task of government, using the symbols of the monetary equation $PT = MV$, to keep M and T in step when V is constant (P being prices; T, trade; M, money stock; and V, velocity of money), to keep M and T in step when V is constant.

Second, every economy constantly has opportunities to make investments that earn a positive rate of return. But the persons who recognize these productive opportunities may lack the money to exploit them, while the people who are most able or willing to save may lack entrepreneurial vision. It is hence important that institutions exist either to channel private savings indirectly to entrepreneurs or to extend credit to selected investors. Various relending institutions can do the former. And commercial banks perform both functions. Some fraction of new deposits can always be loaned to direct investors. Also, subject to certain drains, the commercial banking system can extend credit by creating demand deposits in favor of borrowing entrepreneurs. But the ability of a conventional banking system to finance efficient "roundabout" methods of production at low cost usually depends on the willingness of the public to own bank deposits rather than legal tender. In addition, in furtherance of this willingness, central bank operations and banking regulations must together ensure the solvency of each bank.

Third, economic decisions and events abroad will affect the balance of payments; this, in turn, will influence domestic activity and prices through changes in the local money stock—unless the central bank takes neutralizing action. Sometimes it may not wish to do so. But it should possess sufficient authority that, given the financial institutions and money markets of the country, it can influence domestic prices without administrative fuss and bother.

There are other subsidiary attributes of a "good" financial system. For example, it is desirable that credit facilities be managed by people able to select those loan applicants who have potentially the most productive investments. It is desirable that institutions other than banks—insurance companies, for instance—exist to channel private savings into longer term investments. It is also desirable that liquidity preferences be reduced, thereby increasing the willingness of people to hold their wealth in assets more productive than money, through making it easier to borrow funds on real assets in case of personal emergencies. And last but not least, in the case of countries that fear mass industrial unemployment, there is always the need for a banking and money system that can implement anticyclical fiscal policies.

Advanced countries have long possessed a variety of means to achieve these goals. In these countries the use of money as a medium of exchange is universally practiced: savers do not hide their hoards under loose floor boards but deposit them in a bank, buy life insurance, or purchase securities. There are commercial banks that hold deposits and make loans to promising entrepreneurs. Over-all credit creation and contraction are regulated by a central bank through open market operations, rediscount rates, legal reserve requirements, and so on. The workings of such a banking system are today highly developed and well understood. But backward countries have a number of special problems that can only be solved by rather different institutional arrangements.

SPECIAL PROBLEMS OF BACKWARD COUNTRIES

The peculiarity of most backward countries, at least in contrast to advanced nations, is that only rudiments of commercial banking exist because relatively few people own demand deposits. Also, in most instances, there is no short-term money market of any consequence. Hence the central bank—with no commercial banking system to regulate and no money market through which it can absorb and release funds—is primarily involved in stabilizing foreign exchange rates. Specialized institutions, such as savings associations, are so small or little known that long-term investment is handicapped. And in the back areas of more primitive countries, goods may often be bartered for want of an acceptable money.

Continuance of barter

Some of these countries lack a sound currency that people will accept in exchange for goods and use as a store of wealth. In the subsistence sectors of primitive countries, goods are bartered more often than bought and sold. Such a cumbersome method of exchange inhibits productive specialization, and its continuance is ordinarily attributable to a lack of circulating coinage with intrinsic value and to the public's distrust of circulating paper money with *no* value. No central bank has gold and foreign exchange holdings large enough to permit it to substitute valuable metal coins for most of its paper issue—and any such action would be rather ineffectual, for in conformity with Gresham's Law, the more valuable coinage would tend to be hoarded, while the paper money would circulate more rapidly. The real solution is for the monetary authorities to maintain the purchasing power of circulating bank notes so that eventually the public would have no good reason to distinguish between paper notes and metal coins.

Institutions for channeling savings into investment

People who save do not always know how to invest. And people who perceive good investment opportunities do not always have funds. In the more advanced countries, non-bank institutions function as financial middlemen. For instance, families may deposit savings with some building and loan association and receive interest on their accounts, while the association relends these funds at a slightly higher interest rate to persons acquiring shop premises, apartment buildings, homes, and the like. Life insurance companies, obtaining funds from policy premiums, lend to industry in addition. In all these cases the physical investment is made by the borrower. The financial saving is done by depositors and policy holders who never meet investors, and most of the loans are long-term.

Every country needs such non-bank institutions to channel the savings of one group into long-term investment by another group. But such institutions cannot exist unless they can attract savings. The problem in backward countries is that although private savings do exist, few savers want assets that are vulnerable to currency depreciation. Deposits in loan associations and claims on life insurance companies give the owner a fixed claim on money that may continually be losing a fraction of its purchasing power. Only very high interest rates can overcome this real loss of principal. And government, which is attempting to sell its bonds to private savers, may encourage such purchases by limiting the rate of interest payable on deposits.

Savers who own concerns in which they can make direct investments, as well as savers who have the courage or knowledge to invest indirectly by purchasing corporate stocks, are not ordinarily deterred by inflation. But savers are of various kinds. And many of them, especially among those not actively engaged in business, are too financially ignorant or otherwise occupied to select and supervise direct investments or share holdings. Most savers want safety first, and a widespread realization that money is continually depreciating in real value prevents a great deal of private saving. Unfortunately, few backward but aspiring countries have any other kind of money.

Few bank depositors

Few people and not many firms in underdeveloped countries have yet become accustomed to paying wages and bills with bank checks. The use of demand deposits as money is taken for granted in advanced nations—over 95 per cent of all dollar payments in the United States are made in this way. It comes as a shock to realize that "money" means circulating legal tender and not bank deposits even in Latin America. Well under 1 per cent of all families own checking accounts in the poorer countries. It follows that the total assets and liabilities of the commercial banking system—relative to national output each year—are much lower in these countries. The national central bank may practically constitute the country's entire banking system.

The main consequence of this public preference for cash rather than bank balances is that the ability of the commercial banks to expand credit is very limited. The currency drains on the private banks are too high. If the banking system's redeposit rate is, say, 0.1, this means that 0.9 of all payments made by check are not redeposited in some bank by the payees, and 0.9 of all newly created bank deposits will be drained away in demands for currency.

This would not matter if it were not for the fact that banks incur considerable costs in borrowing from one class of saver and lending to another class of investor. Investigating loan applications, negotiating loan contracts, supervising outstanding loans, collecting interest and principal, having recourse to endorsers, helping the borrower with his tax returns, and keeping the books, and so on, all take human effort and time. Over one-half of the gross income received on loans goes for unavoidable operating costs in many countries' banking systems. The effect of these costs is to enforce a spread between what interest banks can pay to those who deposit or invest funds and the interest they must demand of those who borrow from them.

This spread between interest paid and received has an economic significance that is too often neglected. The capitalists who form a bank, and those who leave time or savings deposits with it, possess limited opportunities for using these funds. For a variety of reasons they may be content with 4 per cent a year. But there may be many entrepreneurs with ideas that could earn a 10 per cent or better rate of return if only they had funds to command needed resources. It is in the interest of the economy that the first group not undertake direct investment, but "lend" through depositing their funds with a bank, and that the second group get funds. And the more the spread can be narrowed, with financial savers getting, say, 7 per cent and direct investors paying, say, 8 per cent, the better off the economy. The higher rate paid by banks may stimulate saving, and the lower rate charged by banks may increase investment.

If the administrative expenses of private bank lending are e times loans outstanding, and i is the rate of interest paid depositors, the minimum rate at which banks will lend (r^*) will depend on the proportion of customer loans, and so on, that drain away through withdrawals in currency (d). In fact,

$$r^* = id + e$$

when other than currency drains are ignored. Of course r cannot fall below e, because $d > o$.[2]

Substituting possible values, such as 0.9 for d, 0.04 for i, and 0.06 for e, the critical or "indifferent" zero net profit rate for r^* is 0.096. This is 0.056 above the rate paid to bank savings depositors. But if d were 0.1, r^* would be 0.064 or 0.024 above i. Clearly r^* is dependent on d. And d ranges from around 0.1 in advanced countries to 0.9 in backward ones.

This rather simple and incomplete analysis shows why it is that—other things equal of course—commercial banks will charge higher interest rates in countries where the public prefers coins and notes to demand deposits. The high cost of bank credit is, then, not entirely the result of a small supply of savings relative to the demand for them. Interest rates are higher than they might be because less credit will be extended by banks when currency drains are severe. The cost of borrowing credit could be rather lower if more businesses and people owned bank accounts and used them to settle debts. Anything government can do to extend the banking "habit" among the public should lower interest rates.

No money market

The Bank of England and the United States Federal Reserve System have traditionally affected the availability of credit through open operations in the money markets of the City and Wall Street, respectively. These two money markets are almost unique in financial experience. They exist because the British pound sterling and the United States dollar are two of the world's key currencies. Other central banks are therefore prepared to keep some of their foreign exchange reserves in London and New York. If they can employ these funds at short term, by discounting bills or purchasing short maturity bonds, so much the better. There is a good supply of these currencies—not only because so much

---

2 The derivation of this equation is as follows. If private banks borrow x units of money and pay i per unit for it annually, they must earn at least an equal net income from lending it after administrative expense. Assuming 100 per cent drains, x $(r - e)$ would have at least to equal $x \cdot i$. But if the bank's currency and other drains are less than 1.0 of loans, more than x can be lent, even though only x was borrowed. In fact x borrowed can become x/d loaned. So the indifference equation is

$$i \cdot x = (x/d)(r - e).$$

Multiply both sides by d/x, and then add e to both sides, and the equation in the text is obtained. This analysis ignores clearing house drains—presumably all private banks expand in step. Legal reserve drains are considered later.

international trade is conducted in sterling and dollars, but also because a majority of finance bills are also denominated in these two currencies. When foreign governments borrow, it is usually dollar or sterling obligations that they sell.

The only other money markets of any consequence are to be found in some of the European financial centers—such as Basel, Amsterdam, and Paris. But they are not significant in comparison with those of London and New York. No poor and backward country now has—or is likely to have in the foreseeable future—a money market of such importance as to permit credit control operations by the national central bank.

Central banks in the old financial capitals have traditionally sought, by altering their rediscount rates, to influence the discount rates charged by the commercial banks. However, to make the rediscount rate effective, the central bank must somehow force the commercial banks to borrow from it. The usual method is for the central bank to sell bills and other short maturities in the money market. Purchasers must draw orders upon the commercial banks in favor of the central bank. Unless the commercial banks have excess reserves in the form of surplus cash holdings or redundant central bank deposits, they must either rediscount with the central bank or borrow from it. And commercial banks will voluntarily lend only at interest rates above those they must pay the central bank. Thus the monetary authorities of Great Britain and the United States can usually compel an increase in the cost of commercial bank credit by selling debts on the money market.

This method of control cannot be used, however, if there is no domestic money market of consequence. If the Bank of Mexico were locally to sell securities that it owned, in an attempt to raise interest rates, its first difficulty would be that its negotiable debt holdings are mostly denominated in United States dollars and would ordinarily be sold in New York. (If it were to sell these assets for Mexican funds, it would be exchanging dollar assets for peso assets and in effect relinquishing foreign exchange to support Mexico's currency.) Normally the securities it sold in Mexico City would be peso-denominated. If the Bank of Mexico does not hold many different peso-denominated issues, it will have to sell a considerable number of bonds and bills of each issue. But the Mexican money market is rather thin, and would not be able to absorb any large offerings of a few issues without a sharp price break, which might prove unsettling to investor confidence.

In some of the newly independent countries that practice a limited socialism, the government's central bank *is* the country's banking system. It can accordingly limit credit expansion and raise interest rates directly. The remaining question is whether or not a government banking monopoly will satisfy the other requirements of a good banking system.

Fluctuations in balance of payments

Those underdeveloped countries that export a significant fraction of their gross national product—and many do—are subject to disconcerting changes in their balance of payments from year to year. This is because they export only a few products, usually raw or semiprocessed materials, that have fluctuating prices. As some of these are agricultural products, the quantity of exports may change quite drastically according to the harvest. In good years, these countries may find themselves accumulating short-term balances abroad with their export credits, and the converse of course in bad years. Moreover, if such a country has several good years, this may give confidence to foreign investors. The result may be long-term capital inflows. These will reinforce the tendency of the national currency to appreciate on foreign exchange.

Not a few governments are sorely in need of a little appreciation of their currency and hence are likely to welcome extra export credits. But some governments may fear that the inflow of funds will appreciate the national currency abroad and inflate prices and costs at home. Both outcomes reduce the country's ability to compete in export markets. So if the country's exports are large, the central bank may attempt to prevent an appreciation of the national currency abroad and seek to contract the local money stock. Unfortunately, if conventional measures are tried and no money market exists, success in holding the exchange rate may lead to failure in holding domestic prices.

The central bank, in order to prevent the national money appreciating on foreign exchange, must sell local currency and buy foreign bank balances. In fact, exchange control regulations probably require all exporters to sell their foreign exchange proceeds to the central bank through their commercial banks. Thus the central bank must make payments to the commercial banks in exchange for the foreign claims they have bought from exporters. This development is the opposite of what is needed to prevent an inflation of domestic incomes and prices. For if the commercial banks are becoming the creditors of the central bank (or no longer its debtors), raising the rediscount rate will be without effect. Of what relevance is the rediscount rate if the commercial banks have no need to rediscount?

If no adequate domestic money market exists, the central bank cannot sell securities to reabsorb the funds it must release in purchasing foreign exchange. Hence the central bank cannot simultaneously prevent an appreciation of its money abroad and prevent inflation at home through its rediscount rate policies. It has little power to insulate the national economy from the world economy in this case unless the national treasury coincidentally runs a large budget surplus. But the budget is determined by a variety of forces—many of them having great political strength—and so it is unrealistic to suppose that the treasury can be counted upon to absorb local money at the same rate at which the foreign exchanges compel the central bank to release it. Life is not renowned for such happy coincidences.

BANKING SYSTEMS FOR BACKWARD COUNTRIES

One might as well accept the fact that the more backward countries will possess neither a significant money market nor substantial bank deposits for a long time to come. Money in circulation will remain several times the total of demand deposits. The conventional methods by which a central bank regulates commercial banks and the money stock will not work properly under such circumstances. A different sort of banking and money system must be designed. It might include commercial banks or it might be a government banking monopoly. The privilege of note issue might be vested in the central bank alone or in the commercial banks alone. There is a wide range of possibilities. But the preferred system is one that can control the money stock in accordance with the needs of trade, allot resources through credit creation to the most productive investors, and permit insulation of the home economy from events abroad.

Mixed banking and money systems

Assume temporarily that the policy decision has been made to create a national banking system comprising a government central bank and a number of private commercial banks. It has been shown that the ability of the commercial banks to extend credit at nominal interest rates is severely limited by the propensity of the public to hoard rather than to deposit funds. What can be done to reduce the currency drain?

There are some things government can do to popularize the "banking habit." It might guarantee all private deposits in commercial banks up to some maximum value per depositor. The treasury might insist on making payments for its material purchases into a bank account owned by its trade creditors (and refuse to pay by cash or check), thereby compelling persons doing business with government to maintain bank accounts. Government might pay a small subsidy to commercial banks for each account they carry. In countries that have a capital levy it would be possible to exclude bank deposits from the tax base. Where bank checks are subject to a stamp duty—as is not unusual—this tax should be revoked. But all these measures together may not suffice to increase the ratio of demand deposits to circulating currency by very much.

A drastic alternative—and one that flies in the face of all accepted thinking regarding banking in advanced countries—is to give commercial banks the privilege of issuing notes and to declare these obligations to be legal tender for the discharge of interpersonal debts. Each private bank, upon withdrawal by a demand depositor, then substitutes its own note obligations in place of its reduced demand liability. It thereby avoids having to relinquish to the depositor any obligations of the central bank that it may have held.

Obviously this does not mean that government should permit each private bank to create money at will and without constraint. Far from it. Each private bank can be required to maintain a reserve deposit with the central bank equal to some stipulated fraction of the bank's total demand deposit and note obligations to the public. The fraction to be held in reserve would be subject to change from time to time by the national monetary authority.

How does a private bank make a deposit in this reserve? One way is to deposit the notes of other banks that it has received. However, as any clearing house drains of a bank will be met from its reserve account in the central bank, this will normally not be too important on balance. Another way is for the private bank to seek loans to its reserve account from the central bank. But the most important way is for the private bank to rediscount commercial paper with the central bank.

The only kind of "run" that can take place on Bank A under this system is if the public deposits abnormal quantities of A's notes in other private banks. The other banks will accordingly present A's bank notes at the clearing house operated by the central bank. Bank A, in order to maintain its minimum legal reserve, will have to rediscount more and more of the paper on which it has made loans. It would be a recognized policy of the central bank always to rediscount eligible paper on request by a private bank to settle at clearing house.

An important feature of this system is that although the notes of any bank are legal tender for the settlement of obligations among private firms and persons, no private bank can settle its debts to the central bank or to other commercial banks with its own obligations. It must instead present obligations of the central bank or other banks.

The only obligations of the central bank need be its deposit liabilities. Circulating central bank notes would be redundant and would entail various complications. The public might consider them more "safe" than private bank notes and so hoard them.

The public would have confidence in the private bank notes primarily because the total quantity of all private bank notes and demand deposits would be under a certain constraint, so any lack of public confidence would normally be due to lax regulation by the monetary authority. Second, there might be only a few large private banking chains rather than hundreds of unit banks, so that each private bank system would be comparatively well-known and substantial. Furthermore, there can be a "run" only through the clearing house drain, and the central bank stands ready to rediscount without limit to meet this drain. It might be advisable for psychological reasons to have the notes of the various banking chains absolutely uniform except for some minimum necessary identification of issuer. How many Americans know which Federal Reserve Bank's notes they are spending? (Minor denomination coins would be minted by the treasury, need not be legal tender, and could be bought by the central bank and sold to the private banks for issue to the public on demand.)

Credit control would be enforced by the central bank through its determination of fractional reserve requirements—to be held on deposit with it—and rediscount rates. Suppose the fractional reserve requirement is f and the rediscount rate is r_d a year. The commercial banks collectively cannot increase their deposit and note obligations by $1000 worth without obtaining $1000 \cdot f$) worth of credits to their reserve accounts with the central bank. These will cost them ($1000 \cdot f \cdot r_d$) in interest. It makes little difference whether they borrow from the central bank or rediscount paper with it. But assuming they rediscount when "loaned-up," about f times new discounting must be rediscounted. The central bank is prepared to rediscount eligible paper—at a price—and it determines the rate.

Hence the central bank indirectly determines the minimum discount rates at which the commercial banks lend. Their zero profit interest rate (r^*), where e is their administrative cost as a proportion of loans outstanding, is given by the equation

$$r^* = f \cdot r_d + e$$

where the currency drain has been eliminated by making private bank notes limited legal tender. So, if f is 0.2, r_d is 0.1, and e is 0.06, then r^* is 0.08. If f were 0.4—given the same r_d and e values—the zero profit interest rate would be not 8 per cent but 10 per cent.

The central bank, by increasing f and/or r_d, can raise the cost of lending to the public. At higher costs all private borrowers presumably seek fewer loans and there will be less credit expansion. And the central bank, having given advance notice, may refuse to rediscount except to enable a private bank to meet claims on it by other banks.

It is noteworthy that the commercial banks are continuously forced to come to the central bank to rediscount. As rediscounted paper matures, payment by debtors provides the central bank with private bank notes and deposits which it sells back to the obligated banks by debiting their reserve accounts. The private banks must then contract credit or rediscount other paper instead.

The treasury—assuming it to be distinct from the central bank—could maintain deposits with both the private banks and the central bank. A transfer of funds by the treasury from private banks to the central bank is deflationary because—other things being equal—the private banks must then contract other obligations by $(1 - f)$ times the transfer. Such transfers of treasury funds from one banking level to another might prove to be a useful instrument of fiscal policy, taking the place of market operations that are largely ineffectual in countries without a money market, except that in this case the initiative lies not with the central bank but with the treasury. It is to be hoped they cooperate to constitute a single monetary authority.

It is customary for a country's treasury to borrow from the national central bank. However, to the extent that the treasury borrows from the private banks, no over-all inflation of credit under this system would necessarily occur. Instead, other things equal, there would be a contraction of private bank credit to other borrowers. The private banks, in exchange for the privilege of issuing legal tender notes, might be required to grant credit to the treasury on demand. This credit might be exercised either at the going commercial bank rate or at the treasury rate for borrowing from the public.

International capital inflows can be readily "sterilized" in various ways under this system. Perhaps the simplest way is for the central bank, if it has an exchange stabilization fund, to keep the fund's local "money" assets on deposit with the private banks. Then if the fund sells domestic balances for foreign exchange, the total obligations of the private banks are not affected.

The central bank can also instigate a mild deflation, prompted perhaps by an adverse change in the international balance of payments, by withdrawing some of its deposits from the private banks. Such withdrawals, assuming no legal reserves are held against central bank deposits in private banks, really cancel the private banks' reserve deposits with the central bank by an equal amount. A multiple contraction of credit can thus be instigated in this way. By varying its deposits with the private banks, the central bank can exercise controls that are analogous to open market operations in countries that possess a real money market; in this respect the note-issuing private banks of backward countries take the place of the money markets of the most advanced nations.

The essentials of such a mixed banking system are as follows. First, the private banks are relieved of the currency drain by giving them the privilege of issuing limited legal tender notes, but each private banking chain must individually still be concerned with the clearing house drain. Second, a legal reserve requirement is established as a drain instead of the currency drain, the advantage being that this legal reserve drain can be determined and altered by the central bank, whereas the currency drain cannot be so controlled when private banks do not have the privilege of issuing legal tender notes. Third, the central bank earns an income from rediscounting paper, this income being $L \cdot f \cdot r_d$, where L is the value of private bank deposit plus note obligations and f and r_d have the same meaning as before.

Although there are private banking chains within such a system, they are in effect working for government. The gross profits of the private banks are $L \cdot r$. From this must be deducted costs amounting to $L \cdot f \cdot r_d$ (on account of legal reserves) plus $L \cdot e$ (for operating costs). It might be that e includes a small allowance for nominal profits. But the real receiver of interest under this scheme is the central bank. It is as though government were leasing its note-issuing privilege to the private banks and charging them a rent sufficiently high to eliminate all save nominal profits. The private banks are allowed only sufficient income from interest, after paying for the privilege of banking and note-issuing, to cover their costs of selecting and supervising loans to private persons and concerns. The justification for such a mixed government and commercial banking system is that the private banks, for reasons to be given, may be able to select and supervise loans better than could a government banking monopoly.

Government banking monopoly

The operations of a government banking monopoly—at least in a formal sense—are simplicity itself. Controls over credit can be direct. There is no cause to establish a complicated system of indirect controls if there are no private banks to regulate. Instead there are numerous branches of the government bank. And the head office of this bank chain discharges the responsibilities of a central bank in a mixed system.

The government banking chain would be the sole issuer—except perhaps for the treasury—of legal tender notes. It therefore need not fear any currency drain. There is no clearing house drain arising from domestic exchange of bank notes, and there need be no such drain on account of checks being drawn on deposits in specific banks. Capital inflows from abroad will result in the national bank's owning more foreign exchange and placing more domestic exchange in circulation. But this can be offset by contracting other loans so that the total volume of the banking system's obligations remain unchanged.

Obviously there will be an interaction, whether government monopolizes banking or banking is mixed, between the interest rate that the treasury offers to attract private savings and the rates that the banks—government or private—charge for commercial credit. As the treasury loan involves little risk of default—and both kinds of loans are equally vulnerable to inflation—the treasury rate is nearly always the lower of the two. But if the margin of difference is too great, there will be a tendency for private savings to be diverted from treasury bonds and bills into commercial loans. The banking system may then increasingly be called upon to meet budget deficits.

If there is a genuine capital funds market in the country, any reduction in interest rates will affect both the rates offered by the treasury for savings and the rates demanded by the banks of trade and commerce. The margin of difference between the two rates, allowing for differences in risk, should remain more or less constant. It is, then, of no consequence whether private savers lend to government, or the banks create credit for commerce, or vice versa. It is the combined demand and supply of loanable funds that determines interest rates. And it is the total extent of credit created by the banking system that influences the price level.

Government monopoly or mixed banking

The choice between a government banking monopoly or a mixed banking system is not based on economic considerations alone. Certain practical *pros* and *cons* do exist. But what is actually done in any country will usually depend upon the beliefs of the government and the public regarding the effectiveness of the private profit motive in recognizing good credit risks.

Practical considerations determine the establishment of one system or another. In a really primitive country, with no private banks of any consequence, the decision to have a national bank with branch offices is almost unavoidable. But the more usual situation is that a country already possesses two or three private banks, some with branches in the major towns, often founded a century or so ago by British, Dutch, or French capitalists. Underdeveloped countries, unlike the United States, do not typically have numerous small unit banks. The question then is how either to nationalize or regulate them.

Nationalization is always simple enough in theory. The State compels the private owners of the bank to sell—there is usually an element of confiscation in that the price is less than the capitalized values of the bank's expected future profits. The same banks then reopen under government operation and ownership. The head office, cooperating perhaps with the treasury, is then the national monetary authority.

Most countries in Latin America and Asia have adopted a mixed banking system. After World War II, a number of them established central banks for the first time. These banks were often modeled upon that of the United States or Great Britain, in the hope of having a regulated banking system and in order to keep up with the times. For a number of reasons—not the least of which is the inapplicability of American and British central banking techniques to backward countries with severe currency drains and inadequate money markets—these new central banks have not always been very effective.

The usual procedure in establishing formal central bank control is to designate the central bank as a sure lender of last resort, require the private banks to hold obligations of the central bank equal to some fraction of their demand deposits, and eliminate any note-issuing privileges of the private banks.

The first innovation—making the central bank a sure lender of last resort—has the merit of guaranteeing the solvency of the private banks. If they can always rediscount—admittedly at a slight loss—they can risk granting credit for longer term investments. They can select from among loan applications those that promise to be most productive rather than most liquid.

The main purpose of a minimum reserve requirement is to subject the private banks—through rediscounting or borrowing from the central bank—to the interest rates determined by the monetary authority. In many advanced countries, the private banks have become indebted to the central bank over the years, and so would be influenced by central bank rates in the absence of reserve requirements. But in more backward countries the newly created central banks probably do need authority to set and alter legal reserves if they are to control the national money stocks.

Eliminating the note-issuing privileges of the private banks is more debatable in countries where money is not demand deposits but circulating bank notes and minor coinage. A high currency drain, which banks must meet with government obligations that alone are legal tender, prevents the private banks from "diluting" their considerable administrative expenses. Hence the spread between the interest banks pay on time deposits and the interest they charge their customers continues to be considerable. Some capital funds, and hence the economy's resources, are probably misallocated as a result, and there is almost certain to be underinvestment.

Establishing a mixed banking system of the kind described in an earlier section—where all bank notes are issued by private banks—involves some special problems. For one thing, government note issues should probably be withdrawn. This can be done by having the public bring government notes to private banks—before some date at which they become invalid—and take the private bank's notes in exchange. The private banks then return the government notes to the central bank, which credits the private banks' reserve accounts, but only with the fractional reserve needed to back the private bank notes issued in exchange. Thus the private bank gets a "free" legal reserve credit equal to f times its redemption of government notes. Additional legal reserves, in support of its other obligations, are obtained by the private banks rediscounting paper with the central bank. It may take some time for the system to stabilize and for net clearing house drains to approach zero for each private banking chain.

The decision to establish a mixed banking system or a government banking monopoly may be based on the requirement that a good banking system is one that extends credit to those applicants who promise the most productive investments. Bank managers, like bettors at race courses, should be able to pick "winners." And for several rather intangible reasons, a mixed banking system may be able to do this better.

Private banks are in business to make a profit. Branch managers are likely to be promoted according to their showing in this regard. In deciding what loan applicants are to obtain scarce credit, each branch manager must balance the risk of loss against the promise of profit as best he can. The most productive investments, if they can be recognized as such, should also prove the most profitable. Private bank managers are not ordinarily concerned with the political affiliations of loan applicants or whether their projects have the blessing of government departments. And if the applicant cannot convince one private bank of the excellence of his application, he can always try another.

There are many people who fear that a government banking monopoly, combined with all the other authority that government already has over its subjects, would constitute a serious loss of economic liberty. Once refused a loan, an applicant would have no other bank to approach. Credit might be granted according to political considerations: businessmen who are not thought to be conforming enthusiastically enough with some plan for the private sector might find it hard to continue in business, their entrepreneurial abilities notwithstanding. Outspoken criticism of government policies regarding any subject may make a man *persona non grata* and so unable to obtain credit. In such ways a loss of economic liberty can also subtract from personal freedom.

15

Alternative

investment criteria

The preceding three chapters have considered ways in which a closed economy can accumulate capital. (*International capital* transfers are considered in Chapter 24.) But capital accumulation is the beginning rather than the end of the investment story. The acts of saving that provide capital do not resolve the uncertainties of how to use it. Only abstinence is needed to accumulate capital. Future vision, technical knowledge, and a wide awareness of possible alternatives, these are all necessary if capital is to be invested as economically as possible. Luck is probably important too. In any year, among all proposed investment projects, there may be more that will in the end waste resources than augment them.

It is an unfortunate but common fallacy that capital has merely to be invested in order to create extra output in the future. The truth is that saving merely provides a surplus of goods, supplied but not yet exhausted in use, including both producer and consumer goods. As Professor S. H. Frankel has stated:

All that capital provides . . . is what the past has created. It cannot buy time in any other sense than that it will aid men and women in exploring the future.[1]

Saving gives society a short breathing spell in the endless race to produce enough for population to consume. It gives time to experiment with roundabout methods of production and establish them if they seem productive enough. But there is no guarantee that, because some actual investment adds income, other displaced projects would not have added more to output. The poorer the country, and the more limited its savings, the more important it is that capital be employed not merely in

[1] S. H. Frankel, "The Kongwa Experiment: Lessons of the East African Ground Nuts Scheme," *The Economic Impact on Underdeveloped Societies*, Essay VIII (Cambridge, Mass.: Harvard University Press, 1955).

good but in best uses. Hence it is doubly tragic when an underdeveloped country wastes its capital on inferior or wasteful investments.

The considerations that formally determine private investments have long been developed and are implicitly understood by most business-men. However, for a variety of reasons to be explained later, there is a general belief among government officials that private investment, when a country is still underdeveloped, is more likely to be for the wrong things. Thus investment decisions in poor and backward countries are being made increasingly by public authority. But it is one thing to trans-fer responsibility for making decisions and another to ensure that they are made more wisely. To this end a number of economists have proposed investment criteria to guide officials when selecting among alternative objects of government investment. It remains to evaluate some of these government investment criteria and compare them with those of private capitalists.

GENERAL INVESTMENT CALCULATIONS

Every economy is always advancing resources against future output. One of the fundamental characteristics of production is the existence of a time lag between the first application of resources and the resultant final or useable output. This is as true of public as of private production.

It is important to realize that "capital," whether in the form of ad-vanced resources or invested funds, is the value of the stock of labor, materials, and plant that have been diverted from satisfying immediate wants to providing scarce goods a little later but in larger quantity. Hence the savings of a country are not all available for plant and equip-ment. Associated with these there will be increased stocks of materials and labor, also to be used in roundabout methods of production. All these are a charge against savings.

However, to a private entrepreneur planning his operation, "capital" means capital funds. These funds give him command over resources of equivalent value advanced by the economy against future production. He uses them to invest in fixed capital (*e.g.,* buildings and equipment), work-ing capital (inventories in process), and labor (wages prior to sale of out-put). Production, almost without exception, requires advances of funds for all three of these purposes. It is a rare entrepreneur who can arrange his affairs so that he pays for labor and materials *after* the goods they produced have been sold.

Management, if it is to maximize profits, must perform an almost impossible feat of balancing marginal costs and receipts in various di-mensions. It must distinguish between the flow of labor and materials that are needed to produce a unit of output and the capital funds it must invest in stocking capital goods and labor in advance of receipts from sales. It must also, in order to attain its theoretical goal of maximum profits, give different values to receipts and disbursements depending upon when they will occur. Because of the complexity of all these interactions and the inevitable uncertainty about future events, it is unlikely that either private or public entrepreneurs can really attain "maximum" profits. And to the extent that public managers are seeking to maximize a more intangible conception of "profit," their efforts are less likely to meet with complete success.

In maximizing profits it is necessary to distinguish sharply between a "static" situation—in which it is assumed that any decision will have the same effect on costs and receipts in this period, the next period, and forever after—and a "dynamic" situation—in which it is recognized that some decisions may occasion large costs now but receipts for many years thereafter.

Static case

Every student of elementary economics knows that the way to maximize profits is to adjust output so that marginal costs (MC) equal marginal receipts (MR). If there are two kinds of output, A and B, and one kind of input, X, it is necessary that $MR_a \cdot \phi_a$ equal $MR_b \cdot \phi_b$ where ϕ is the marginal physical product of the common factor in making A or B (as the case may be). Conversely, if there is one output and two inputs, X and Y, it is necessary that the factors be combined so that ϕ_x/MC_x equals ϕ_y/MC_y. The marginal cost of a factor will equal its price if the user has no monopsony power or if the supply of the factor appears to be infinitely elastic.

Of course even though only one kind of product is being made, there are independent variables other than output. Changes in product quality occasion incremental changes in receipts and costs just as much as do changes in product quantity. Promotional effort is yet another dimension to be considered in the making and selling of a differentiated product. Where m and n are independent variables—such as quantity and quality, respectively—the rule is that MR_m/MC_m should equal MR_n/MC_n. The rationale of this is that the last dollar spent for quantity or quality must occasion the same rate of financial return.

The concept of marginal cost includes more than meets the eye however. In spending a little more for quantity, say, two kinds of extra expenses are incurred, one for a flow and the other for a stock. Producing a little more output usually means not only that a little more material "disappears" into the product in each time period, but also, in all probability, that a little more material must be stocked on an average—and this necessity occasions more investment of capital funds. Also more wages will have to be advanced against future sales receipts. And an increase in space and equipment will also require more investment of capital funds.

Any investment of capital funds means an expense for interest. Hence the true marginal cost of output must include extra interest for advances for materials, extra interest for advances for labor, and extra interest for advances for fixed capital. The marginal cost of output will also include flow costs. And the ratio of interest expense to flow costs will usually differ considerably among working capital, labor, and fixed capital.

Suppose the receipts and costs occasioned by an incremental unit of output are both $1000, and that the breakdown of costs for the "last" output is:

	Extra Interest Expense	Extra Flow Cost	Total Extra Cost
Materials	$ 50	$200	$ 250
Labor	50	400	450
Plant & Equipment	200	100	300
Total	$300	$700	$1000

The extra interest expense, given the rate of interest, indicates the extra investment required to produce this incremental output—for instance, if interest is 10 per cent, the extra investment of capital funds is $3000. But one-third of this extra investment is not in fixed capital such as plant and equipment. It is needed to finance extra stocks of materials and labor.

It is important for profit maximizing that the extra $3000 of capital funds be allocated properly among these three uses. The extra plant and equipment should ideally contribute twice as much to output as the extra advances for materials and labor combined. This allocation of capital funds among these three objects—materials, labor, and plant— constitutes a sort of inner maximization. It is just as important that the extra $300 of interest be spent properly as it is that the other $700 of flow costs be incurred in producing this "last" unit.[2]

It is noteworthy that no capital funds are needed to finance the flow costs. They are supposedly covered in the same time period by receipts from sales. These receipts also meet the interest expense. Although an extra investment of $3000 is required to expand the scale of output by this one "last" unit, it is not treated as a cost. The only recognized expense is $300 for interest at 10 per cent for the period of one year.

This method of treating capital funds outlays, recognizing only their fractional interest expense, is valid only under rather special circumstances. One would be if the extra plant, materials and labor that are

[2] The flow cost of $100 for plant and equipment represents depreciation expense that occurs as a function of use and output.

stocked (and costing $3000) could always be sold at original cost less depreciation on the real capital. This is unlikely in the case of fixed plant and equipment capital. Costs of installation and dismantling alone would prevent sale without loss.

The other validating and more usual assumption of static analysis is that any management decision is timeless in the sense that it will endure indefinitely. If management decides to produce one more unit of output a year, it is supposed that the cost and receipt consequences are not limited to the current period but will be repeated in every subsequent period. Of course this is an unrealistic assumption, for management may next year decide to reduce output, improve quality, or even close down the operation. But without it capital outlays cannot be ignored. The device of only "costing" the interest occasioned by such capital outlays would otherwise have little warrant. It would be different if all expenses were flow costs and covered from sales receipts. But modern production involves "roundaboutness," and hence capital fund outlays—all of which make static analysis rather unrealistic.

Dynamic analysis

The essential characteristic of dynamic analysis is that every cost and receipt has a time date. Assuming that some positive rate of interest and time and liquidity preferences exist in every country, receipts of $1000 next year have less present value than $1000 to be received this year. Similarly, a disbursement of $1000 in 10 years' time represents a far lower present cost than $1000 that has to be paid this year; in fact, the present value of the future obligation is only 1000×0.9^{10} (*i.e.*, $349) when discounting compound at 10 per cent for 10 years.

Dynamic profit maximizing is concerned with actual money receipts and actual money expenditures. Unlike static analysis, it considers receipts but not revenues, expenditures but not expenses. A firm has a revenue when a buyer contracts to purchase, but it has a receipt only when the purchaser pays. A firm may have a depreciation expense (or cost) every year on a machine that is depreciating, but it has an expenditure (or disbursement) only when it first pays for it. And it will not have another expenditure until payment is made to buy a replacement. Standard accounting practices, but only to a limited and conventional extent, try to express various past expenditures as current expenses (*e.g.*, depreciation allowances). But to be "conservative," it is customary not to reflect future receipts as current revenues. Hence many accounting records tend to be understatements of a firm's net worth.

Any management decision will occasion extra receipts and extra disbursements at various dates in the future. Of course these cannot be known with certainty, but they can be estimated with varying degrees of reliability. Suppose some particular decision that management is contemplating would cause the year by year receipt and disbursement consequences shown in Table 15-1 (columns 2 and 3). Also, suppose that capital funds can be borrowed or loaned by the concern at 6 per cent discount. What should management's decision on this project be?

The answer depends on the present discounted values of the receipts stream (PVR) and disbursement stream (PVD). If PVR exceeds PVD, management should go ahead with the project, and *vice versa*. Column 4 in Table 15-1 gives net undiscounted receipts. Column 5 gives the present discounted values, for each year over a service life of 15 years, of future estimated receipts minus costs. It will be seen that, although there are heavy outlays in the early years (probably investment for plant, equipment, and materials) these are overbalanced by the long stream of future receipts (presumably from sale of output). Column 6 shows the present discounted value of the firm's accumulated net receipts. Until the 11th year of the operation, the firm is in the "red," and then climbs into the "black," finally emerging with an expected profit having a present value of $194. It is evident that PVR exceeds PVD—at least in anticipation— and that the project is "profitable."

What is the expected rate of return exactly? It is that rate of discount that would render the present values of the receipts and disburse-

Table 15-1

WHETHER TO INVEST OR NOT:

Determining the Present Value of Net Receipts in Future

(1)	(2)	(3)	(4)	(5)	(6)
			Receipts minus	Present value of	Accumulated net present
Years	Receipts	Costs	costs	difference	value
1	0	50	− 50	− 47.2	− 47.2
2	0	200	−200	−178.0	−225.2
3	0	200	−200	−167.9	−393.1
4	50	50	0	0	−393.1
5	100	50	50	37.4	−355.7
6	150	50	100	70.5	−285.2
7	150	50	100	66.5	−218.7
8	150	50	100	62.7	−156.0
9	150	50	100	59.2	− 96.8
10	150	50	100	55.8	− 41.0
11	150	50	100	52.7	11.7
12	150	50	100	49.7	61.4
13	150	50	100	46.9	108.3
14	150	50	100	44.2	152.5
15	150	50	100	41.7	194.2

ments streams equal to one another.[3] But not many people have the time or patience to recalculate the present values of these two streams at various discount rates until finally they converge upon the rate that makes them equally valuable now. It is quicker, and accurate enough, to assume some nominal discount rate (*e.g.*, 5 per cent) and compute the *PVR* and *PVD* of the two streams at that rate. If the *PVR* exceeds the *PVD*, calculated at a nominal rate (*i'*), the real rate of return is higher than *i'*. The true rate of return will approximate

$$i' \cdot \frac{PVR}{PVD}$$

Every project has many variants. A new factory building can be given a longer service life by constructing it with better materials: there is an extra initial cost but the implicit rental is received over more years. Additional mechanization means more cost for equipment now but less for labor later. It is always desirable of course to advance receipts and defer disbursements, thereby increasing *PVR* and decreasing *PVD,* whenever possible without loss. However, this usually cannot be done without some sacrifice, and so in considering project variants the rule is to adopt any contemplated modification only if (*PVR* −*PVD*) is increased when calculated at the rate at which the concern can lend or borrow funds.

Maximizing profits in dynamic analysis involves maximizing (*PVR* − *PVD*). For any possible schedule of output over time, there is conceptually some way of producing it that has the lowest *PVD* and some way of selling it that has the highest *PVR*. At higher discount rates, projects are more likely to be rejected if the costs all come at the start and the receipts come only after a number of years. There is then less incentive to mechanize or make structures durable. No private entrepreneur can plan profitably, especially if disbursements will greatly exceed receipts in the early years, in disregard of interest or discount rates.

PUBLIC INVESTMENT CALCULATIONS

Governments and other public authorities invest as well as private entrepreneurs. And every decade sees them owning and operating more and more enterprises. A crucial question is, in providing these useful goods and services, should they make investment calculations that are fundamentally different from those of profit-seeking capitalists?

Governments of underdeveloped countries invest quite substantially in what is termed "social overhead" capital. Transportation and communi-

---

[3] This statement ignores the difference between a rate of interest and a rate of discount. If $100 a year from now is discounted at 10 per cent, it has a present value of $90. But $90 now, at 10 per cent interest, will be worth $99 in a year's time.

cation are among the most important forms of this. Specific projects may
be marine docks, railroad lines and rolling stock, or an extended telephone and telegraph system. But multipurpose river dams and irrigation
canals are also high on the list. Not to be overlooked are more traditional
objects of investment such as local public utilities—water, sewage, and
electricity—and schools and hospitals.

A government, when investing in social overhead capital (SOC), is not
limited to maximizing profits in the sense that it seeks receipts having a
greater present value than that of the disbursements it must make. If
government is to economize in its use of the nation's resources, and this
is especially important in poor countries, it must do this and more. In
fact, government must make investment calculations more complex than
those of a private capitalist.

Distinction between real and money
costs and benefits

But what exactly should a government try to maximize when it is
investing the economy's resources on behalf of the nation? In some sense
it should consider "real" costs rather than money disbursements and
"real" benefits rather than money receipts. In any country there are
numerous reasons why money costs and receipts—both in the aggregate
and at the margin—may not be commensurate with real costs and benefits,
respectively.

Pigovian welfare economics provide numerous and familiar examples
of disparities that exist between the benefits and injuries that an entrepreneur can occasion for society and the revenues and expenses that
fall upon him as a consequence of these same acts. For instance, a factory
may pollute the surrounding air, so that a great deal of money and resources must be spent in the local community for extra washing and
cleaning. But this might be of little concern to a private owner of such a
factory unless he has to pay extra wages to induce workers to live in such
a locality. A government factory, it is to be hoped, would invest resources to reduce air pollution if this cost less than the extra expense the
public would otherwise have to bear for additional washing and cleaning.
It may very well be more economical to prevent the dirt from entering
the atmosphere than to remove it from people and clothing later. If so,
and the pollution is abated, more of the real costs of the enterprise are
included in the money cost curves of the public project. Alternatively, if
it is not more economical to prevent air pollution in this case, the public
enterprise must *imagine* that the indirect costs of washing and cleaning
are included in its cost curves.

Conversely, there are numerous instances of free enterprises that incidentally provide some useful goods and services free, so that their receipts curves understate the total benefits they supply the public. Suppose a private company which booms logs for towage by sea to a sawmill constructs a breakwater so that its log booms can be assembled in protected water. Such a breakwater will also benefit fishing boats and small coasting vessels. But the private lumber company, in constructing the breakwater, does not consider these incidental benefits unless it has authority to levy anchoring charges. A government sawmill would presumably *estimate* the fees that might be levied, and include them in a hypothetical receipts curve, even though never actually assessed.

In underdeveloped countries it is often maintained that almost any new enterprise is likely to provide all sorts of free advantages over and above the services that are sold. A private utility company may dam a river in order to produce and sell electric power, but there may be no ready means of collecting compensation from the people who live downstream and are no longer subject to flood damage. A government highway may be worth far more than the extra fuel tax it collects as a consequence. In both cases, a socially worthwhile product may not be undertaken because it does not seem to "pay" financially. This is because the full value of the services has not been transmuted into money receipts. Some of the most important examples, either from an unwillingness or an inability to collect for all services rendered, are provided by investments in social overhead capital.

Pricing policies for government enterprises

The receipts of a government project, the buyers' surplus that it occasions, and the value of the benefits it provides without charge, all depend on the price policies it adopts. The apparent "worth" of this or that project is determined by the price it charges. Hence a major problem when considering government projects that provide goods and services that can be sold is: What pricing policy should be followed? For instance, even if government can estimate real receipts and expense curves, should it attempt to maximize a sort of social profit by equating marginal real costs and marginal real receipts? Is the only proper difference between a private and public concern that the former considers only explicit money costs and receipts whereas the latter should make decisions on the basis of all real costs and receipts—including those that do not accrue to the concern itself?

There is certainly very little agreement regarding the answer to this question. There are people within the underdeveloped countries who demand that government projects be operated so as to maximize profits for reinvestment in the public sector, and this seems to be the pricing policy of government steel mills in India.[4] Others propose that government enterprises charge the lowest prices that will meet all variable and fixed cost; this is the policy adopted by many public power authorities, including those that operate the Kariba Dam in Rhodesia. Finally, but only among economists, there is a demand for "marginal cost pricing"—that is, output should be such that marginal cost equals the demand price.

These three contrasting policies can best be understood in terms of an example and a diagram. Suppose government is contemplating the construction of a harbor, with wharves and cranes for handling cargo, and has decided to make some uniform charge for every ton of cargo loaded or unloaded at the main wharf by crane. Light coastal cargoes are not charged if handled by ships' crews and without assistance from the port authority. Two interacting questions are (1) what charges to make per ton of liable cargo, and (2) whether the project should be approved at all.

In Fig. 15-1, the horizontal axis represents tons of cargo loaded or unloaded, and the vertical axis represents dollars. There is a uniform marginal cost (MC) of $1 per ton of cargo handled by crane. Curve D is the estimated commercial demand; at lower prices it is assumed that more cargo will pass through this port than through either of the two other harbors on the coast. From Curve D a marginal revenue curve (MR) can be derived. In this particular case the MC curve is also the

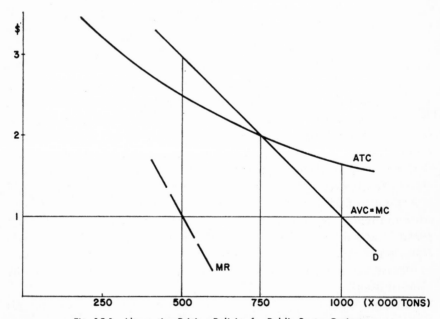

Fig. 15-1. Alternative Pricing Policies for Public Sector Projects.

[4] Possibly because there are other sources of steel, namely, imports and private concerns, and the government plants meet, rather than make, the market price.

average variable cost (*AVC*) curve. Fixed costs are $750,000 a year. The vertical distance between Curve *AVC* and the average total cost (*ATC*) curve is the average fixed cost, including annual debt service.

The first policy of maximizing profits would entail a charge of $3 per ton, as it is estimated that 500,000 tons a year would then be handled by the port authority, and marginal receipts would equal the marginal cost of $1 a ton. There are profits of $250,000 a year. The project pays, is financially sound, and is in all respects a banker's delight.

However there will be a demand—especially from importers and exporters—that the port authority set the lowest charges that will still cover all costs. After all, why should government extort the greatest possible profit from its own people, so long as it can meet all operating expenses and cover its fixed costs on schedule? In other words, assuming it estimates the same demand schedule, the commercial community may agitate for a $2 charge. If 750,000 tons a year materialized, the total revenue would cover all operating costs and the balance would exactly meet fixed costs of $750,000 a year. A few analysts might even note that although the government would no longer have a profit of $250,000, users would have extra free services worth from $500,000 to $750,000—at no cost to them.

Sophisticated economists, to the horror of the financially conservative, might suggest a third policy of setting a price that will result in an output equating marginal cost to marginal use value. Given current income distribution, the marginal use value is indicated by Curve *D*. Specifically, they would propose a charge of $1 a ton, as the resultant volume of freight (1,000,000 tons presumably) will produce a marginal use value equal to the marginal cost of $1. The extra freight handled at the lower price, which is 250,000 tons additional, has a use value of from $2 to $1 a ton. The value of the extra use of the port facilities by paying customers is hence about $375,000 and the value of the extra resources used is $250,000, so that the economy has gained $125,000 net. Aggregate fixed costs are unaffected. Of course there may be an annual loss, and in this case it is $750,000 a year. But economists may blandly propose that this be met in the case of a public project from the treasury's general revenue fund. It would be folly, in their view, to make the project self-financing, as this would require a charge of $2 a ton. And at such a "high" price, many persons would not use the port facilities, although the use value to them would be greater than extra resource costs.

The rationale of marginal cost pricing is most evident in short-run cases where the main investment has already occurred. If the wharves have been constructed, and the cranes installed, and so forth, the resources used are lost forever. They are a sunk cost. The problem now is to use these existing facilities as economically as possible. And this means lowering the charge and increasing use until the last ton handled adds use value equal to added resource expense. Public projects should have pricing policies different from those of private concerns—assuming that they can and do distinguish between marginal revenue and demand price —for the government is presumably trying to maximize not private, but social profit.[5]

The important economic consideration is that any enterprise, whether publicly or privately operated, finance itself in a way that makes the most economical use of its facilities. This means that it need not always cover all its fixed and variable costs from charges that vary proportionately with the extent it is used. A price sufficient to meet all costs may limit use to a volume at which the marginal use value exceeds marginal costs. The facility will then be underutilized. The balance of costs must be met from another source—in most instances the government. Taxpayers will meet those costs of a public concern that users do not. Private concerns can be bullied or persuaded into adopting marginal costs pricing by price ceilings or subsidies.[6]

What should be the long-run criterion for determining whether or not to invest in a project that has not yet been constructed? Various formulae are possible depending upon the assumed prevalence of monopoly and competition in the domestic economy. The most conservative test, and especially appropriate in competitive economies where highly differentiated products comprise only a small fraction of national income, is that the project could be rendered self-financing. Is there some price, however socially undesirable, that would result in enough volume so that total receipts covered total variable and fixed costs? If so, the project is economical *a priori,* even though this particular price is never charged and marginal cost pricing is adopted instead.

However, in interpreting this long-run criterion, public authorities must realize that total receipts obtained at each possible price may be less than the project's use value. Many people who benefit may escape paying, either because they use the good or service illegally, or because the process of collecting from them may be more expensive than it is worth. In the port facilities example, for instance, it was assumed that vessel owners did not pay for loading or unloading cargo alongside if they did not use the cranes. The harbor and dock were a free service for them under this circumstance. But this use value should be included as

[5] A consumers' cooperative should logically attempt to maximize the algebraic sum of its financial profits and the consumers' surplus it occasions. As marginal profits equal marginal revenue minus marginal cost, and marginal consumers' surplus equals price minus marginal receipts, this sum is equivalent to price minus marginal cost. Such a consumers' cooperative, were it to suffer losses, could assess its members some uniform amount each quarter or so. (See S. Enke, "Consumer Cooperatives and Economic Efficiency," *American Economic Review,* March, 1945.)

[6] See J. E. Meade and C. J. Hitch, *An Introduction to Economic Analysis and Policy* (New York: The Macmillan Company, 1946), Part II.

part of the project's worth even if this service is enjoyed *gratis* and so never collected.

Inclusion of this real but nonmonetized use value may make all the difference in deciding whether or not to go ahead with a project under consideration. Suppose, reverting to the last example, fixed costs had been not $750,000 but $1,250,000 a year. There would then be no price and quantity combination, given the commercial demand curve, that would yield enough revenue to cover all costs. Diagrammatically, this new average total cost curve (ATC') would lie entirely above the demand curve, and the project would never be undertaken by a private concern. However, the full use value is given not by the usual demand schedule but by a demand curve (D') that includes the use value enjoyed by those who do not use the cranes and so do not pay. Curve D' may lie above ATC' at some combination of quantity and price. The long-run decision for a public concern should be to go ahead and construct the facility. And this is so even though everyone knows that after completion the uniform charge will be one dollar, vessels not using the cranes will not pay, and there will be an annual loss of over a million dollars.

Assuming socially desirable income distribution

Some people would go further and say that a public authority, in estimating marginal use values, should try not to guess what people would be prepared to pay for some increment of good or service given existing income distribution but what they might be willing to pay given some alternative and presumably more socially desirable distribution of income.

Imagine a municipal bus service that carries half a million passengers a day at a ten-cent fare. But its passengers tend to be among those having the lowest incomes. If family incomes were less unequal, so that people who ride buses had more money, the use value of the 500,000th daily ride in money terms might be not 10 cents but, say, 13 cents. Unequal income distribution reduces any monetary measure of the use value of goods and services supplied poorer people.

All this is perfectly true. The theoretical difficulty is that differences in income are sometimes equitable and frequently useful. The practical difficulty is that there is no objective way of deciding what a socially desirable income distribution would be and what demand schedules would accordingly result. If public concerns sought to adopt pricing policies based on subjective estimates of demand under socially "good" distributions of income, there would never be agreement as to what prices should be charged. The final decision would have to be quite arbitrary.

PROPOSED INVESTMENT CRITERIA

Several economists have suggested a number of additional and more special ways in which disparities between social and private product may arise in backward countries. Some seem to feel that rural labor at least is a free good to the economy—because its marginal product in agriculture is supposedly zero—and that public investment criteria should therefore ignore all monetary costs of hiring labor. Others feel that projects which ease the strain on the national balance of payments—by increasing exports, for instance—should be favored over those which increase it. All of them expatiate on the importance of external economies and diseconomies and on the need to include them in the estimates of receipts and costs of public concerns that are being ranked. The balance of the chapter will describe some specific investment criteria—most of which are sensitive to pricing policies though—that have been proposed for selecting and rejecting rival government projects.

Maximizing output per unit investment

Governments of poor but developing countries have a limited amount of funds that they can invest in the public sector during any period; there is always a constraint on the amount of funds that can be borrowed, taxed, or created, and which the nation's leaders feel can be spared from financing current operations of government. To public planners the scarcest resource appears to be the limited capital funds placed at their disposal by government. From this it is a short step to supposing that capital is the only scarce resource in the economy as well.

Accordingly, it is not infrequently proposed that government should give priority to projects that promise to give the greatest output value increment per unit of investment. For instance, suppose Project *A* will have a gross value added of $1 million a year for an initial investment of $1 million, whereas Project *B* will have a gross value added of $2 million for an initial investment of $3 million. That is, Project *A* has an incremental capital to output ratio of 1.00, whereas Project *B* has an ICOR of 1.50. Many officials would unhesitatingly give priority to Project *A*. But it is most improbable that both projects will be operated over the same number of future years, for depreciation may put an end to one project far sooner than the other. It is therefore the present discounted values of the two future streams of gross values added that should really be compared in each case with the initial investment cost.

Enough has been written here already—especially in Chapter 7—to indicate that ranking alternative projects by their presumed ICOR's makes no sense whatsoever unless all inputs save capital are free goods. But labor cannot be assumed a free good for industry even though rural workers may be underemployed. It has been shown that such labor in industry will occasion associated urban costs, a larger aggregate food output requirement, and disutility costs that should be compensated for in any free society.

Anyway, even if labor were a free good in agriculture, it presumably is productive in industry. Hence any specific industrial project using labor must consider the opportunity cost of employing labor in other private or public *industrial* projects. Those contemplated public investments that have the lowest ICOR's will tend to be those that are most labor intensive. If these projects are undertaken, the drain of labor from other enterprises may be considerable and other industrial output will be lost.

A standing rule in economics, assuming there is more than one scarce factor involved, is never to maximize output divided by a single kind of input. The special input must then be combined with such large quantities of other and supposedly free inputs that their marginal productivities fall to zero. If these other factors are in reality scarce goods or services, there is certain to be some economic waste. Unfortunately, among government planners there is always a tendency to assume that what is a constraint for them is also *the* scarce element in the economy. Such misplaced egotism can cause wrong investment decisions.[7]

Investing to maximize profits and saving

Another not uncommon theme in economic development literature is that in really poor countries with rigid class divisions all saving—and hence most investment—must come from those who receive profits. Workers are too poor to save during the first stage of development. These assumptions are rather in accord with the thinking of the English classical school and of Professor W. A. Lewis.

Suppose it is agreed that the object of development is to attain the maximum possible national income (Y) in 1975. Increases in population, and accompanying proportionate increases in the labor force, are deemed exogenous. So maximizing Y is tantamount to maximizing per capita income. If the contributions of technology are also considered to be outside government influence, there is little left for it to do except maximize investment in each and every year so that the total stock of capital will be at a maximum in 1975. If national income equals profits plus wages, and only profits are a source of savings, it is necessary to maximize profits each year if investment and output are to be at their highest level in

---

[7] Professor N. S. Buchanan was one of the first to suggest that projects be ranked according to their value added to initial investment ratio. But many others have since recommended almost identical methods of ranking, and the current vogue for computing the ICOR of each rival project accepts this approach. Certain theoretical weaknesses have been exposed by Professor A. E. Kahn in "Investment Criteria in Development Programs," *Quarterly Journal of Economics* (February, 1951).

each and every future year. The Marxist prescription for rapid economic development is to do anything and everything to maximize surplus value, and maximizing this surplus for the State was a predominant theme during the 1920's and 1930's in the Soviet Union. Some would say the technique was successful. But the cost in human suffering was appalling.

This line of argument, for many people, means selecting capital intensive projects. See, for example, what follows from an assumption that output (or value added) per worker varies proportionately with capital per-worker. Holding the number of workers constant, this means that output varies proportionately with capital, so that with no capital there is no output, with x capital there is y output, with nx capital there is ny output, and so on. The marginal product of the last unit of capital is always y output. Thus the whole product is attributed to capital, and apparently labor makes no contribution to output. But workers have to be paid the going wage rate, every dollar of which is a dollar less profit. Although labor takes a wage it contributes nothing. Maximizing profits involves minimizing payroll. Priority should be given to projects that have high $K:L$ ratios.[8]

The principle of variable proportions negates the notion that the marginal product of capital, say, can be constant as the $K:L$ ratio is altered. If K and L are always combined in the most profitable proportions—i.e., if their marginal physical products are in the same ratio as their marginal costs to the employer—there is no particular reason to suppose that labor somehow "exploits" capital in the sense of taking more wages in than it contributes in output. The possibly valid initial assumption that profits are more important a source of investment than wages in a poor country does not seem logically to imply that priority should be given projects that are capital intensive. *A priori,* a more sensible conclusion would be that capital will have to be spread very thin relative to labor if it is to be allocated most productively. But this does not mean combining so much labor with each unit of capital that output per unit of capital is maximized, for this would entail a zero marginal product for labor.

Maximizing profit per investment unit

An improvement over selecting projects according to V/K—where V is value added—is to select them according to $(V - C)/K$. In this case C in-

[8] This argument is rather similar to ideas advanced by Professors W. Galenson and H. Leibenstein, "Investment Criteria, Productivity, and Economic Development," *Quarterly Journal of Economics* (August, 1955). However, they made the milder assumption that V/L is some function of K/L. Their conclusion that high K/L projects are preferable must imply that labor takes more in wages than it contributes to output. In the above paragraph the special instance of proportional variation between V/L and K/L is assumed because presentation is simpler. There is no obvious warrant for this supposition.

cludes labor payroll and other factor costs, and so rankings are likely to be less nonsensical than they would be if ICOR's were made the only rating device. Moreover, the $(V - C)/K$ criterion can be further refined by including various intangible external economies in V and diseconomies in C, as well as by distinguishing between receipts and payments that will be in foreign exchange and hence will normally be more valuable than those in the depreciated local currency.

Professor Chenery is one person who has followed this route. His proposed formula for determining the annual Social Marginal Product of a project is a good example of what can be attempted.[9] The main part of the $(V - C)/K$ formula—before foreign exchange and local currency are distinguished—is:

$$SMP = \frac{X + E - M - L - O}{K}$$

where X is market value of the output, E is external net economies, M is the cost of materials, L is the cost of labor, and O is overhead costs including depreciation. This can be more simply stated as $(R - C)/K$, where R equals $X + E$ and C equals $M + L + O$.[10] Logically, O should also include interest, although this will not affect SMP rankings. How one goes about determining net external economies is not disclosed and obviously this must be a very subjective assessment. Also, as explained in the preceding section, total receipts—and every other term in the numerator—depend very much on whether prices are set to maximize profits, or simply to cover costs, or to equate marginal costs. This criterion cannot be applied until price policies have been decided.

A majority of backward but developing countries have exchange control, and foreign exchange is really more valuable in terms of local currency than the official rate of the central bank alleges. This discrepancy between the real and official value of the local currency may be severalfold and is here represented (after Chenery) by r. Accordingly, an additional SMP credit must be given to projects that export some of their output, and a debit must be accorded those that must import materials. Hence a refined formulation, and one which recognizes that foreign exchange is worth more than local currency is:

$$SMP = \frac{R - C}{K} + \frac{r (aB_1 + B_2)}{K}$$

In this equation, r is the difference between the real and official value of foreign exchange, aB_1 is the annual amortized impact on the balance of

9 See H. B. Chenery, "The Application of Investment Criteria," *Quarterly Journal of Economics* (February, 1953).
10 Chenery uses V instead of R as equal to $X + E$, but V here means value added and so R has been substituted.

payments of servicing initial borrowings from abroad, and B_2 is the annual impact of the project's operations on the balance of payments. A positive B means an export; a negative B, an import. Hence a negative B_1 would indicate that some of the initial investment had been financed abroad, and a positive B_2 would indicate that exports of output exceed imports of materials to be processed. Of course if a government could maintain its fiscal house in order, there would be no need for this second modifying term in the equation.

Maximizing social profit

A fundamental question is whether or not the K denominator is part of a valid economic criterion. Suppose K refers only to fixed real capital. Then there is no special reason for having the annual cost of labor (L) in the numerator and the value of the capital stock (K) in the denominator. One might as well have the annual cost of capital in the numerator—as a deduction from value of output—and the number of employed workers in the denominator. It is true that government officials may have limited funds to invest in alternative projects and may therefore want to maximize value added per unit of funds invested, but the constraints for the economy as a whole include labor as well as savings.

However, it would be a mistake to go to the other extreme and suppose that no denominator should be included in an investment criterion. For example, a project should not be selected over others according to the absolute magnitude of its value added contribution, for this may be larger than others' simply because the project is immense in terms of total resources employed. One rather expects that between two projects— both involving the same investment perhaps—more gross value will be added by one that occasions $10 million of annual disbursements than one that gives rise to $100,000 of expenditure a year.

This suggests that, despite the natural desire of government officials to suboptimize by maximizing value added per dollar they invest in projects, they should really select that project having the highest social investment rating (SIR):

$$\frac{R - M}{L + Ka}$$

where R is market value of output plus ascertainable net external economies, M is cost of materials purchased from other firms, L is annual labor cost, and Ka is annual capital expense. (Depreciation of invested capital can be considered part of Ka.) This is certainly different from Chenery's SMP. And it differs from the ordinary capitalist manager's dynamic goal of maximizing profits per unit of capital funds invested.

These distinctions are not merely academic. Suppose two projects—
A and B—having the following attributes and hence rankings set forth in
Table 15-2. If labor were considered the constraint, Project B would be
preferred. If capital were the limitation, A would be selected, and Chenery's SMP is for A double that for B. But the SIR—or $(R - M)/(L + Ka)$
—is the same for each project.

Table 15-2

COMPARATIVE RESULTS OF ALTERNATIVE SYSTEMS FOR RATING PROJECTS

	Project A	Project B
	(millions)	
Assumed Values		
R, output value plus external economies	$2.5	$ 3.0
M, materials purchased	1.5	.5
L, annual labor cost	.5	.5
Ka, annual capital expense	.3	1.5
K, capital funds invested	3.0	15.0
Consequent Ratings		
V/K (Buchanan)	.33	.17
$(R - C)/K$ or Chenery's SMP	0.067	.033
$(R - C)/L$	.4	1.00
$(R - M)/(L + Ka)$ or S/R	1.25	1.25
$R - C$	.2	.5

N.B.: $V = R - M;$ $C = M + L + Ka.$

All this suggests that, before extensive estimates are made, a logical investment criterion needs to be determined. It should be based on the resource limitations of the economy, and not on that of some government
agency, although this point is often overlooked. There is usually no
obvious warrant for assuming that capital is scarce and labor is free.

Finally, the ways in which a social investment criterion should differ
from those of an ordinary investing capitalist need to be understood, for
significant differences do exist. As already indicated, the receipts and cost
curves of a public enterprise should include so far as possible those real
gains and injuries that each concern occasions, but which are not ordinarily monetized. Otherwise government investors should attempt what
private investors also theoretically essay under static conditions: to maximize the ratio of aggregate value added to aggregate factor costs.

Some "scientific" but political criteria

A number of governments—they might as well remain nameless—have
concocted some amazingly complex investment criteria. "Scientific" formulae can always be rigged to include a number of highly subjective

estimates, and the junior officials who make the various estimates usually
know the political requirements of their seniors.

In addition to estimates of tangible revenues and expenses—such as a
corporate accountant might make—government clerks may have to guess
at such things as (1) external economies and diseconomies, (2) the
amount of indirect employment that may be created, (3) the extent to
which this output may prove to be an import substitute, (4) the extent to
which the disbursements by the project are likely to be saved by their
recipients, and (5) the extent to which the output is a necessity or a
luxury.

For each seriously considered project, someone may have to complete
the following sort of worksheet, which is less of a caricature than one
would hope, and which is unlikely to be worth anything when finished
and submitted for action.

HYPOTHETICAL AND USELESS WORKSHEET FOR RATING A PROPOSED PROJECT

Name of Project: — — —
Initial investment over 3 years: $2,000,000

Estimated Annual Data	Basic	Weight	Value
Sales to public (weighted by necessity)	300,000	1.2	360,000
Free transfers to government units	50,000	1.0	50,000
External economies (weight by income level of recipients)	30,000	1.3	39,000
Indirect employment creation (weight by region)	20,000	1.8	36,000
Substitution for imports	120,000	1.5	180,000
Domestic disbursements likely to be saved by recipients	320,000	0.1	32,000
Total credits			697,000
Wages (otherwise unemployed excluded)	220,000	1.0	220,000
Domestic materials used	80,000	1.0	80,000
Imported materials minus output exports	30,000	1.5	45,000
Foreign interest payments	50,000	1.5	75,000
External diseconomies	20,000	1.0	20,000
Total debits			440,000

$$\text{Worth of Project} = \frac{\text{Credits} - \text{Debits}}{\text{Investment}} = \frac{697 - 440}{2,000}$$

In this particular case it is fairly evident that weighting for necessity,
external economies and diseconomies, indirect employment creation,
probable import substitution, and percentage of domestic disbursements
saved by recipients, must be very crude estimates at best. These items, in
the above example, total almost $400,000. A slight prejudice for or
against a particular project, placed in the estimator's mind by a few careful remarks from his superior, can enormously alter the "scientifically"
computed worth of the project and therefore its ranking with others.

These dangers of chicanery prompt the suggestion that any investment criteria employed by government should be as simple as possible. In estimating social "profit" the credits and debits should exclude all the extra modifications suggested for the first time in the hypothetical worksheet. In backward countries that seriously overvalue their local currency in terms of foreign exchange, an adjustment of the kind suggested by Chenery would seem appropriate.

This still leaves the difficulty of estimating external economies and diseconomies—the magnitude of which can make or break the apparent worth of many projects. The best rule is probably to include only as credits and debits those external economies and diseconomies, respectively, that can be cited and about which there is general agreement. And there are all the uncertainties regarding the proper definition of "total revenue plus external economies," as described in the preceding section. The most conservative approach, but not necessarily the most correct one, is to credit as an external economy the extra revenue that would be obtained if everyone who benefits could be charged at the prevailing price.

If all these strictures are accepted, the criteria for private and public investment may be rather similar except in special cases. Government should ordinarily give priority to those projects that give the most return under profit maximizing price policies. In the case of government monopolies, marginal cost pricing should be assumed when estimating the social investment rating (SIR) of a contemplated project.

16

A "big push" under
government direction

During the past decade or so, a number of views on how governments should directly force economic growth have become extremely popular with the public, and terms such as "balanced growth," "take-off," and the "need for a 'big push,' " are on many lips. Given the temper of the times, it is inevitable that some of the most popular of these should stress the desirability of very large "investments," financed and determined by government. The arguments for a large and costly "big push" program of investment stress the view that, because of inevitable "indivisibilities" in demand, supply, and saving, there is a certain *minimum* level of investment in most poor countries below which outlays for development will be largely wasted. These arguments for government direction and centralized planning often assert also that the market price system, as known in advanced nations, will not give proper "signals" to private entrepreneurs and capitalists in backward countries. Accordingly, they may not invest to produce goods that are warranted, and this "failure" of private enterprise can allegedly be avoided only if investment decisions are made by more omniscient government officials. The economic ideas that underlie these popular attitudes, and which are often cited by officials in justification of their activities, need to be understood much better than they generally are.

"BIG PUSH" ARGUMENTS

The "big push" approach toward economic development in backward countries has been summarized as follows:

"There is a minimum level of resources that must be devoted to . . . a development program if it is to have any chance of success. Launching a country into self-sustaining growth is like getting an airplane off the ground. There is a critical ground speed which must be passed before the craft can become airborne. . . ." Proceeding "bit by bit" will not add up in its effects to the sum total of the single bits. A minimum quantum of investment is a necessary (though not sufficient) condition of success. This is in a nutshell the contention of the theory of the big push.[1]

Thus economic growth is seen as a discontinuous affair, rather than a gradual one, with any effort below some minimum being comparatively ineffectual if not downright useless. The basis of the economic argument depends on three "indivisibilities" (*i.e.*, discontinuities) that are held to characterize the demand for consumer goods, most industrial production functions, and the supply of total private saving in poor countries.

Balanced growth (complementarity of demand)

Most people fully realize that, although in the long run aggregate production constitutes aggregate demand (Say's Law), a single firm cannot create a demand for its own product merely by making that product. A manufacturer of laxatives cannot count on his workers spending all their wages on his product; it would hardly be to their advantage. The proposed "solution" of this obvious inability of an individual firm to finance its own sales has been advocacy of widespread and simultaneous investment in a "big push." By immediately establishing many firms, producing a variety of products, it is thought that each new firm can count on selling a substantial fraction of its output to the workers of other new firms.

Nurkse explained the problem when he wrote:

Human wants being various, the people engaged in the new industry will not wish to spend all their income on their own products. Suppose it is a shoe industry. . . . People in the rest of the economy will not give up other things in order to buy, say, a pair of shoes every year, if they do not have enough food, clothing, and shelter. . . . As it is the new industry is likely to be a failure.

The difficulty is not present, however, in the case of a more or less synchronized application of capital to a wide range of different industries. . . . People working with more and better tools in a number of complementary projects become each other's customers. Most industries catering for mass consumption are complementary in the sense that they provide a market for, and thus support, each other. This basic complementarity stems, of course, from the diversity of human wants. The case for "balanced growth" rests ultimately on the need for a "balanced diet." [2]

[1] P. N. Rosenstein-Rodan, *Notes on the Theory of the "Big Push,"* Center for International Studies, Massachusetts Institute of Technology, March, 1957, p. 1. The author quotes from *The Objectives of U.S. Economic Assistance Programs,* prepared by the Center for the Special Senate Committee to Study the Foreign Aid Program, Washington, D.C., 1957, p. 70.

[2] R. Nurkse, "Some International Aspects of the Problem of Economic Development," *American Economic Review,* May, 1952, p. 572.

Unfortunately, despite the sense of the above quotation, other people have interpreted it in a nonsensical way. Clearly, if a country is expanding output anyway, it is important that it expand output of many different goods in a "balanced" way that accords with market demands. It is also evident that a new shoe industry, superimposed upon a poor economy of constant productivity and aggregate income, will normally fail for lack of demand. And it is also obvious that under these circumstances it is desirable that the new shoe industry should fail. The resources producing shoes should all or mostly be producing other more wanted goods. And this is so whether the resources employed in the shoe factories were previously employed or unemployed.

The nonsense inference from this very sensible diagnosis concerns public investment policy. For some have argued that the "leakage" problem of a single firm—i.e., that most of its disbursements for factors do not come back directly to it as sales receipts—can be significantly reduced by simultaneously establishing many new firms and expanding all kinds of output. The idea seems to be that each new firm, by spending on production, creates effective monetary demand for other firms making consumer goods. So the "solution" is to establish many new industries at once. They will survive and prosper by "taking in each other's washing."

Common sense suggests that all this must somehow be very irrelevant. Entrepreneurs, in contemplating an investment, ask themselves whether total receipts will more than cover total costs. They do not care who their customers are so long as they pay and buy enough. Firms do not customarily pin their hopes on selling most of their output to the factors of production they employ. Any realistic entrepreneur, unless "he" is a gigantic corporation or producing for a very local market, must expect 0.999 or so of his expenditures for production to "leak" away. They will not be respent on his own output. Practically, no development and investment program is ever going to do more than increase national output by more than, say, 0.1 in a year, so leakages of about 0.9 from the new subeconomy must be expected in the first year. And it is unlikely that the difference between a 0.999 leakage for a single firm and a 0.9 leakage for a tremendous new public sector will crucially affect private investment decisions. If the financial problem of new firms were really to recapture their own factor disbursements through their own sales—which it never has been—the "push" would have to be impossibly "big." In fact, an entirely new and closed economy—including agriculture, since people wish to eat—would have to be created to avoid any leakage. And within this new and closed economy any particular firm would still encounter difficulties if it did not produce a good that income recipients wanted enough to pay a price that covered its unit production costs.

Enough has now been written to suggest that the real problem is not whether the owners of productive factors employed by new firms buy the output of these new firms. Rather, it is whether the owners of productive factors employed by *old* firms will buy nearly all the output of the new firms at a price that covers their unit production costs. The real problem is the opposite of that presented by the shoe factory example.

Imagine that an economy had two firms, A and B, and that a new firm, C, now goes into operation. Homogeneous labor is the only productive factor. Assume first that C's workers were previously unemployed, but that total employment in the country is constant after C begins production. Hence the C output is truly incremental, as is the monetary income of C's workers. These C workers buy A, B, and C goods. But firms A and B cannot increase output—except at C's expense—for there are no more unemployed resources. For the output of A, B, and C to achieve the consumption mix desired by those who have earned money incomes from these firms it is necessary that the prices of A and B outputs not be increased by competitive consumer bidding.

The requirement in this case is that the workers of A and B want the C product enough that they are prepared to reduce their consumption of A and B goods by the same physical amount that C workers want to buy them. If A and B workers do not shift to consuming C by this amount, the prices of A and B goods will increase, and these firms can then afford to bid labor away from C and so reduce its output. Alternatively, if there is a very large demand for C output, the C firm will be able to expand output and so reduce the output of A and B by bidding away their factors.

The situation is not really very different when there is always full employment and C has had to use previously employed labor. In all cases the real requirement is that A and B employees buy the C output—priced to cover all costs—and not that the C workers do. In other words, the economy must want the new output, so that the real problem is to know what to produce.[3]

This is true whether an economy is merely growing or really developing. An economy can grow in the sense that its population and national income are increasing by the same proportion: at a constant per capita income, more of the same sorts of goods will be produced, but a particular firm must decide whether it is A or B that is relatively in short supply. More satisfactory is the case where increasing productivity raises per capita incomes so that a profitable demand for a new kind of good develops. Thus if improving technology results in more and more A and B

[3] The importance of knowing what to produce is an inherent part of any proper statement of Say's Law. Mill formulated it correctly when he wrote, "Every increase of production, if distributed without miscalculation among all kinds of produce in the proportion which private interest would dictate, creates, or rather, constitutes, its own demand." See J. S. Mill, *Essays on Some Unsettled Questions of Political Economy*.

goods being produced with a given employment, the time will come when consumers would rather have less extra A and B each and some C instead. So the advent of C output is not a cause but a consequence of higher per capita incomes. It is evidence of increased productivity in making more "necessary" goods.

On the whole, consumer goods fall into two classes, which might be termed "preferred" and "deferred." Preferred goods are those for which the demand, at constant prices, increases proportionately more than rising income. The demand for deferred goods increases less than proportionately. Very broadly speaking, in backward countries, industrial goods are preferred and agricultural products are deferred. And this is why industrialization depends in part upon increasing agricultural productivity.

So far the analysis has been in terms of a closed national economy; but even poor and backward countries indulge in international trade, so the open economy case should be mentioned in passing. It is, then, quite clear that the specious requirement—that workers buy their employers' outputs—can never be satisfied, however great the "big push"; there will always be a leakage from consumer goods imports. The real requirement in this case is that the consumers of the world want some contemplated increment of production enough to pay a price that covers unit cost, whether it be an old or new kind of good, and whether it be produced by old or new firms. (This is exactly the question that entrepreneurs are constantly trying to answer when they risk their funds.)

Finally, it should be indicated that "complementarity of demand" stressed by the "balanced" growth argument for a "big push" is not technical but monetary. Technical complementarity occurs when a consumer wants more of one good because he has more of another—for example, a man who buys a car will want gasoline to run it. The "complementarity" considered in the "big push" argument is really just interdependence. It arises because one firm, in making an output, disburses funds to factors and so creates a demand for the output of other firms. But this extra demand is monetary purchasing power and not necessarily real. It can be no more real than if government distributed new paper money to everyone in the country. If the output of the new factories is unwanted by everybody, and was made with resources taken from firms making wanted goods, real purchasing power will be less. If the new unwanted output was made with resources that were unemployed before, as is usually suggested would be the case, real purchasing power is unchanged. There can be a gain for humanity only when extra or new output is wanted, in the sense that it has a use value equal to or greater than the opportunity cost of producing it, and in the long run this comes only from using resources more effectively in general. A new and wanted industry, conventionally making some good that before few could afford, is ordinarily a consequence and not a cause of economic progress.

Capital "lumpiness" and increasing returns

The nature of production is another reason why some economists feel that "proceeding 'bit by bit' will not add up in its effects to the sum total of the single bits." Production is very frequently characterized by increasing returns. These are of various kinds that need to be distinguished.

Many firms—especially in industry—are subject to important internal technical economies. That is to say, at constant input prices, larger outputs involving different factor combinations can be produced at lower unit costs. This is particularly true in the short run, when some large investment occasioning a fixed cost can be used more or less intensively, but to a lesser degree this is often also true over longer periods. These internal technical economies are entirely independent of the influence on profits of those changes in factor prices that may be associated with different volumes of firm output.

Next there are true external economies—in the strict Marshallian sense —that are again technical rather than pecuniary and accrue to firms within an industry only because the output of their own industry is increasing. These economies are external to the firm that enjoys them in the sense that it cannot increase or decrease them through its own actions. But they are internal to the industry because it is the *industry's* output that occasions them. Most examples that come to mind are really diseconomies, as when vegetable growers in a dry region are collectively allowed so many acre feet of irrigation water, the result being that each acre of irrigated land gets less water the more acres are put into cultivation by growers.

Increasing financial returns—*i.e.,* pecuniary economies—often accrue to a "representative" firm because increasing production "outside"—whether in the industry, the economy, or the world—results in the price of its output increasing or the prices of its factors decreasing. This extremely broad concept, which, however, does at least exclude changes in taste, is really a grab-bag idea. It includes all the impacts on a firm's profits, through the prices that it pays and receives, of the interactions of joint demand and supply and rival demand and supply. Moreover, the causal direction is from some output increase external to the firm, whereas technical economies originate—and stay—within the group or industry. For example, a furniture manufacturer will experience a stronger demand for his output if government is building urban apartments. Unfortunately, these "general financial advantages" have come improperly to be termed "external economies," so all that remains is to distinguish them by the adjective "pecuniary."

From the above it is clear, then, that "lumpiness" of capital—*e.g.*, it takes a dam of a certain size and cost to block a river—may give rise to internal technical economies (in this case, in the production of hydro-electric power). This in turn will probably result in pecuniary external economies for the users of the output that is subject to these internal increasing returns. For example, the large power output from the dammed river may result in lower unit power charges, and this in turn will benefit heavy users of power. The supreme justification of large investments in transportation, power, and water is that this social overhead capital generates large pecuniary external economies for numerous other enterprises that use their outputs and services.

But what has all this to do with the need for a "big push"? For the sake of argument, let us suppose, not very realistically, that every kind of production—including agriculture—is subject to very substantial technical internal economies. Moreover, let us imagine that the most economical ways of producing different outputs involve some discontinuities (or "breaks") in firms' long-run cost-to-output curves.

Consider Fig. 16-1. The output is perhaps kwh of electric power. Only two alternative "plants" are supposed possible. One is a thermal plant

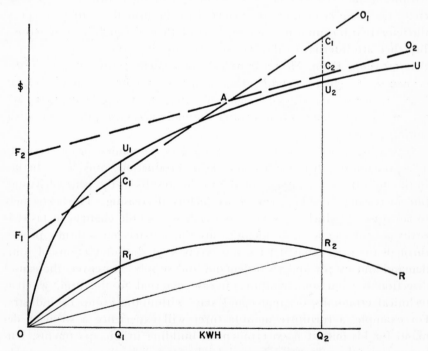

Fig. 16-1. Capital Lumpiness and Social Losses.

involving annual fixed total costs of OF_1 and a cost to output function F_1O_1. The other is a hydro-power project involving fixed annual costs of OF_2 and a cost to output function F_2O_2. The long-run cost-to-output function is OF_1AO_2 with a discontinuity at A. If inputs are assumed to have constant prices, regardless of electric energy output, internal technical returns are increasing in both the short and long run. Does this mean that the larger investment that occasions the hydro project with OF_2 annual fixed costs is somehow "better" because of capital "lumpiness"?

There can be no verdict unless something is known about use value and demand for electric energy. Suppose that the monetary measure of the total use value at different outputs is given by the curve OU. From this curve, assuming for simplicity's sake that all users are charged the same price per kwh at any time, the total revenue-to-output curve OR can be derived. For example, at a price indicated by the slope of line OR_1, the demand will be OQ_1 because the slope of the U curve at U_1 is then the same as that of OR_1. Similarly, a price of R_2Q_2 total revenue divided by OQ_2 total output (as represented by the slope of line OR_2) will result in exactly OQ_2 being sold because the slope of the monetary use value curve at U_2 is parallel to OR_2. Once the total revenue curve OR has been determined, it is possible to say something about the relative merits of the thermal and hydro projects for producing electric power, but not before.

The proper criterion, assuming competition is rather prevalent throughout most of the economy—i.e., there is no average monopoly gap and most firms have marginal costs equal to price—is what might be termed "social" profit rather than ordinary financial profits. In the present case, "social" profit is the difference between total use value in money terms (U) and total money costs (C) or, algebraically, the sum of ordinary profits and buyers' surplus. Financial profits are total receipts (R) minus total costs (C), and total buyers' surplus is total use value (U) minus total buyers' outlays (R). Given the facts represented in the diagram, will the thermal or hydro plant occasion the most social profit in this sense?

It depends on management's price policy. If a conscious effort is made to maximize social rather than financial profit, construction of the thermal plant should mean a price of OR_1, and selection of the hydro plant should result in the much lower price of OR_2, because the marginal costs of the thermal plant (shown by the slope of F_1O_1 at Q_1) are equal to marginal use value (shown by the slope of OU at U_1), just as the marginal costs of the hydro project are equal to marginal use value at Q_2 output. The rationale of such marginal cost pricing, even though it results in losses that must be met by taxpayers, was explained in the preceding chapter.

If a marginal cost pricing policy is adopted, the comparison is then:

		Thermal Plant	Hydro Plant
	Output	OQ_1	OQ_2
	Price	R_1Q_1/OQ_1	R_2Q_2/OQ_2
	Average cost	C_1Q_1/OQ_1	C_2Q_2/OQ_2
	Total revenue	R_1Q_1	R_2Q_2
less	Total cost	C_1Q_1	C_2Q_2
	Money profit	$-R_1C_1$	$-R_2C_2$
	Use value	U_1Q_1	U_2Q_2
less	Buyers' outlays	R_1Q_1	R_2Q_2
	Buyers' surplus	U_1R_1	U_2R_2
	Money profit	R_1C_1	R_2C_2
plus	Buyers' surplus	U_1R_1	U_2R_2
	Social profit	$+U_1C_1$	$-U_2C_2$

In this case the smaller investment makes the thermal plant preferable to the hydro project, even though the thermal plant involves higher unit costs, a higher price, and smaller buyers' surplus. The reason is that with each method of production considered at its most socially desirable price and output, the thermal plant yields a social profit of U_1C_1, whereas the hydro project occasions a social loss of C_2U_2. This is despite capital "lumpiness" in the form of large annual fixed investment costs (*e.g.,* OF_2) and production function "indivisibilities" (*e.g.,* the long-run cost curve has a "break" at A).

The moral is that one can pay too great a price for so-called external and internal economies. In this case the pecuniary external economies all go to the electric energy users—since factor prices to the power concerns have been declared constant—and in fact are identical with buyers' surplus. In other words, the external pecuniary economies are U_2R_2 for the hydro project, but only U_1R_1 for the thermal plant. Although there is some doubt as how best to measure internal technical economies, at the higher output the superiority of hydro power generation might in this respect be estimated at $C'C_2$. The whole trouble, in this particular instance at least, is that the increment in annual fixed investment cost of F_2F_1 was simply too large.

The above analysis is entirely static. In economies that are expanding—*i.e.,* more population and/or higher incomes per capita—consideration of future demands may properly cause public or private investors to construct facilities that will be financially or socially uneconomic for the next few years. A full dynamic analysis is then necessary. And this may indicate the long-run desirability of the plant that has lower unit costs when operating near its larger capacity.

A certain number of millions of dollars of foreign aid to a backward country will accomplish more if there are gradually increasing technical returns. But the fact that alternative methods of producing a good involve discontinuous investments to obtain different outputs merely means that one method and scale will be discretely better or worse than another. Neither increasing technical returns nor discontinuities in the production function justify the assertion that "a minimum quantum of investment is a necessary (though not sufficient) condition of success."[4]

Kinked supply of domestic savings

The third "indivisibility," often cited as justification of a large minimum foreign aid program by the United States, is that many poor and backward countries have a discontinuous relation between national income and domestic savings. Below a certain national income level there may be almost no domestic net saving. It is alleged that above this critical level the marginal propensity to save does—or could—involve a fairly substantial proportion of extra income. Perhaps investment provided from abroad might so raise income in poorer countries that they would begin to save.

According to Professor Rosenstein-Rodan:

A high minimum quantum of investment requires a high volume of savings, which is difficult to achieve in low income underdeveloped countries. The way out of the vicious circle is to have *first* an increase in income (due to an increase in investment which mobilizes additional latent resources) and to provide mechanisms which assure that at the *second* stage the marginal rate of savings be very much higher than the average rate of savings.[5]

If the interest elasticity of the domestic savings supply is very low or zero, and the income elasticity at some income level increases discontinuously from zero, the case for productive foreign aid is strengthened. But some people would go further and hold that minimum aid is that which so raises a poor country's income that it starts saving for itself. How, it is asked rhetorically, can a backward country ever attain higher net incomes if it cannot even save?

There are several possible models that would provide an increasing net income for a country without any domestic net saving by its residents. Only one will be presented here. It conforms with the historical development of a number of countries of recent settlement—*e.g.*, Australia and Argentina—that were really "underdeveloped" in the sense that their resources and culture gave promise of progress and so enabled them to borrow from the rest of the world to their own advantage.

Imagine a country that has accumulated within its boundaries a con-

[4] Rosenstein-Rodan, *op. cit.*
[5] *Ibid.*, p. 13.

siderable amount of productive capital goods—all of which have been financed with money from abroad but are operated by residents. The country's accumulated net savings are zero because its foreign indebtedness cancels its domestic capital stocks. Funds are obtainable from abroad in practically unlimited supply at 10 per cent interest a year. The actual domestic demand for foreign capital depends upon world interest rates and national domestic product. Given current domestic incomes, there is no domestic savings at any interest rate: *i.e.,* the production that accrues net to domestic residents is all consumed. Can such a country "grow" and increase the net incomes of its possibly stationary population?

Yes, if the average product attributable to capital is in excess of its 10 per cent assumed cost. The surplus will accrue to domestic residents if they are borrowing these funds and operating capitalistic enterprises for their own account. Moreover, as domestic net incomes rise, the demand for capital obtainable at 10 per cent interest will increase. As funds are borrowed, aggregate profits will be increased, because more borrowed dollars will be contributing a surplus to residents. There will be an accelerator effect at work, a given ΔY occasioning a given ΔK, and the ΔK will in the next period occasion a given ΔY. Given certain assumptions, this can go on for a very long time, for each ΔY will cause some firms to expand capacity to meet demand.

Of course some of this net domestic product is not net national income. Some of the product—amounting to, say, 10 per cent of total K— will have to be exported as interest.[6] Net national income is increasing in the aggregate, and per capita income also if there is no population increase, and yet domestic net saving is still zero.

The conclusion is that, although there may be some minimum national income below which no aggregate domestic net saving will occur, this income level does not have to be exceeded in order for there to be self-sustaining growth of advantage to domestic residents. Of course if there is some domestic saving, a smaller amount of foreign capital will be needed to obtain any given income increment. So no domestic saving means that a bigger push from outside is necessary. But if only the possibility of sustained growth is at issue, and not the magnitude of this annual increment of growth, there is no critical minimum capital inflow requirement. The only requirement is that some capital be obtainable from abroad at a cost that enables all but the marginal units to be invested for a net gain. There is no *minimum* amount of capital that is critical, and hence no minimum necessary foreign aid or investment "push," whether big or little.

---

[6] If K is increasing without domestic net saving, it must be that new gross borrowings exceed gross principal repayments. This is a fairly realistic case for some countries that have developed during the past hundred years.

INVESTMENT INCENTIVES AND THE PRICE SYSTEM

Closely related to arguments for a "big push" in investment is the belief that, in poor and backward countries, certain peculiarities of the market price system prevent a level of private investment that is economically justified. An advanced enterprise economy regulates itself—more than most people fully understand—through the interplay of demand and supply forces and the profit motive. But the price system allegedly does not work in still undeveloped countries. For a variety of reasons it is supposed to give variable, discouraging, and shortsighted "signals" to entrepreneurs. And so government must allegedly make its own large investment decisions on the basis of nonmarket data and other plans. (Practically, as any really large investment program must be financed with government funds, it is inevitable that it will make the investment decisions.)

Inelastic demands and price fluctuations

A common contention is that prices fluctuate more in poor and backward countries. Insofar as firms use prices as "signals," to tell them whether to expand or contract output, substitute one factor for another, or export or import, and so on, violent and unexpected price reversals may cause firms to make wrong decisions. They may "zig" when they should "zag."

A first question is whether prices do fluctuate "more" in undeveloped countries. There can be no statistical answer if only because it is almost impossible to define what constitutes a greater or smaller degree of price fluctuation: for example, does a price that varies 20 per cent in the same direction every year fluctuate "more" than one that varies 10 per cent in opposite directions every six months? There are a number of reasons for supposing that at least some prices may be rather stable in these countries. For one thing, there is often a large or "unlimited" supply of labor to be had from a subsistence sector at an almost constant real wage and—where labor is the most important cost of production—this must tend to stabilize many supply prices. Also, numerous domestic prices are linked closely to the price of some major export, and, while export prices certainly vary, they do not do so because of any peculiar characteristics of demand or supply within the underdeveloped and exporting nation.

Nevertheless, prices are commonly supposed to fluctuate more in poor countries, and the reason often advanced is that demands are inevitably inelastic to price where real income levels are low.[7] Hence a given proportionate change in the supply of some good will supposedly cause a more than proportionate change in the demand price for it. And the

[7] R. Nurkse, *op. cit.*

price elasticity of demand is supposed to be low because poor people are supposed to consume only "necessities" that they "must" have irrespective of price.

But there is no such thing as a demand for "food," "clothing," or "shelter." Instead, at least within the market economy, there are demands for rice, maize, wheat, fish, peanuts, palm oil, pawpaw, potatoes, meat, and other goods that provide "food." So it is with "clothing" and "shelter." And the very desperation that prevents poor families from saving makes them extremely sensitive to small price changes among substitute goods they can afford. The truth is that the price elasticities of a particular good, when it is one of several substitute ways of satisfying an essential need, are very high. Incidentally, relatively high income families can have inelastic demands for durable consumer goods that they are just about able to afford (*e.g.*, automobiles) and for goods for which their demand is practically satiated (*e.g.*, salt).

If only homogeneous and competitive staples are considered, the absolute price effect of an absolute shift in a demand (or supply) schedule will depend upon the slope of the opposing supply (or demand) schedule. And in countries where the good in question can readily be produced from now idle resources, the slope of supply schedules may be rather flat. To consider an extreme case, where supply schedules are horizontal, shifts in demand cannot alter price.

Monopolistic competition theory has taught us that most industrial producers do not equate their marginal costs to price but to a distinct and lower marginal revenue. Each individual firm itself determines price. It reacts not to its output's price but to its output's demand schedule. Where markets are "small"—perhaps because of costly transport—there may be many instances of such competitive monopoly within the economy. Then a shift in demand, or a change in input prices, has a diminished effect on the price charged for the output. (In fact, where marginal costs are independent of output, a shift in a demand schedule will have no effect on price unless the new demand schedule has a different price elasticity measured at the previous price.)

Discrete investments in limited markets

A related idea is that because the demand for products is allegedly very small in underdeveloped countries, and investment in factories is supposedly discrete, establishment of a new firm may drastically lower the price of the output. Professor Scitovsky has explained this possibility and some of its consequences:

The plant capacity most economical to build and operate is not very different in different countries; but, as a percentage of an industry's total capacity, it is very much greater in underdeveloped than in fully industrialized economies.

In underdeveloped countries, therefore, investment is likely to have a greater impact on prices, give rise to greater pecuniary external economies, and thus cause a greater divergence between private profit and social benefit.[8]

As a result, it is feared that investments that would benefit society may not be made because they would not prove profitable to private investors, and there will consequently be underinvestment.

This is a plausible notion, but it requires examination. First, although it can be accepted for argument's sake that an oil refinery, for example, that can process a barrel of crude oil at minimum cost will be of about the same capacity in most parts of the world, very few industrialists would ever invest in a plant of such size where there was a more limited demand. Relatively small-scale plants, having higher unit costs of output, are often established in areas where a comparatively small local market is sufficiently protected by transportation costs or import restrictions to permit a profitable price to be charged. It is possible that a majority of new plants are in fact designed to operate at an output less than the minimum long-run unit cost output. What may seem optimum to an engineer—*i.e.*, maximum output per dollar of inputs—is often neither a financial optimum for plant owners nor an economic optimum for society.

Second, backward countries often provide a larger market for some goods than do advanced countries, because specific product demands depend on per capita income and size of population. South Africa and Canada have about the same population, but the demand for bicycles is much greater—although per capita income is much lower—in South Africa than in Canada. India is poorer than New Zealand, but its population is much larger, so its demand for cotton textile cloth is much larger.

Third, if markets in backward countries were as small as is alleged, a new firm would presumably conduct itself as a monopolistic competitor. It might establish itself in the expectation of maintaining a high price, producing a small output, and perhaps maximizing profits at a volume where marginal costs are falling. The only question in the capitalists' minds would be whether demand and supply conditions permit a profit.

However, rather than argue about the facts, let us suppose that what Scitovsky says may happen upon investment does happen. The investment is made, the output increment is large compared to total demand at the old price, and so there is a considerable price decline. This of course is extremely beneficial to users of the product, who enjoy pecuniary external economies, and the using industry (if the good is a producer

[8] T. Scitovsky, "Two Concepts of External Economies," *Journal of Political Economy*, April, 1954.

good) may be stimulated to expand. This is all to the good. So what is the complaint?

The usual objection is not that this is harmful, but quite the reverse—that its very probability will deter the investment that would make it possible. A firm is less likely to establish itself if it knows that its own operations will seriously depress the price. It has no desire to create buyers' surpluses for other people. Total revenue is its concern. So unless it is able to convert some of the potential buyers' surplus into total revenue through price discrimination, an investment that would be worthwhile for the economy may not be worthwhile for private enterprise.

But this is essentially the old monopoly problem all over again, with its threat of underemployment of resources in occupations where entrepreneurs can distinguish between demand price and marginal revenue, and hence the usual remedies can be applied. In an economy where prices and marginal costs are almost equivalent for most firms, every monopolistic competitor should be induced to produce a little more. If the government is aware of the situation, and government is usually supposed to be rather omniscient in these matters, it can subsidize an incipient firm enough to make it invest in a plant and operate it. The only peculiarity about the Scitovsky example is that, because the adjustment is not one of expanding a present firm's output but rather of establishing a whole new firm, an element of discontinuity has been added.

Finally, three differences between this situation and that hypothesized by Nurkse should be noted. Nurkse presents inelastic demands and fluctuating prices as the chief dangers, but does not stress discontinuities of output; Scitovsky assumes nothing about the elasticity of demand, but emphasizes the difficulty arising from discontinuous output changes that are large relative to demand. Whereas Nurkse is concerned that prices will fluctuate more or less continuously and in both directions, Scitovsky is considering a single drastic and downward price change. Both feel that the price system coupled with free enterprise will cause underinvestment, but Nurkse tends to believe that investments (*e.g.*, a shoe factory) will be made but will fail, while Scitovsky implies that future losses will be anticipated and so deter the investment from ever being made in the first place.

Present prices and future conditions

Another complaint about prices as "signals" is that most prices indicate present relative scarcities of goods and services, not the economy's future needs. Although futures markets exist for certain staple commodities, some of which are important exports for underdeveloped countries, it is true that most of a nation's output is sold at more or less "spot" prices. As Scitovsky has written:

> In the market economy prices are the signalling device that informs each person of other people's decisions. . . . Market prices . . . reflect the economic situation as it is and not as it will be. For this reason they are more useful for coordinating current production decisions, which are immediately effective and guided by short run considerations, than they are for coordinating investment decisions, which have a delayed effect and—looking ahead to a long future period—should be governed not by what the present economic situation is but by what the future economic situation is expected to be. The proper coordination of investment decisions, therefore, would require a signalling device to transmit information about present plans and future conditions as they are determined by present plans; and the pricing system fails to provide this.[9]

Assuming for the moment that an entrepreneur has been "fooled" by the current prices of an earlier period into making an investment that he subsequently regrets, what does it matter?

It matters not at all if the unexpected price change is the unforeseen consequence of this particular firm's own establishment and operations. If the firm continues to produce at a loss, covering its short-run prime costs, its misfortune is the gain of others. If it must otherwise close down at the subsequent price, a government subsidy can probably keep it in operation, the justification being that it is providing exactly those pecuniary external economies that in the preceding subsection it was feared that more perspicacious firms would not willingly provide. And so the same outcome has been attained—inadvertently of course, but in economics it is not intentions but consequences that count.

On the other hand, if the unforeseen and adverse price changes are not due to the firm's own decisions, economic waste can certainly arise. A company might invest in establishing a rubber plantation, only to find that advances in synthetic rubber had halved the price of tree rubber, and the labor and materials used to clear jungle and plant trees could in retrospect have been better employed. But all this assumes that investments are made on the basis of current prices.

It is far more realistic to suppose that in industry and agriculture (except for small peasant cultivation) few potential investors are mesmerized by current prices. Capitalists who are considering investment in an oil refinery, a fertilizer plant, a box factory, or whatever it may be, are perfectly conscious that they will be stuck for decades with the consequences of their investment. They give far more thought to future market trends than to present prices. Not infrequently they expect to develop a demand that does not now exist, as when a luxurious hotel for tourists is built at a little known resort, or a soft drink bottling

9 *Ibid.*, p. 150.

plant is constructed in a new territory. Often they worry themselves ill
about future labor unions, zoning restrictions, local property taxes, government regulation, rival imports, domestic competition, and the like.
In any given trade there are many close personal contacts within and
among countries, and few major plans for expansion long remain secret
to other members of the trade. This is not to say that managers of larger
concerns are not unpleasantly surprised on occasion, but when this happens it is usually not for want of trying to foresee and almost certainly
not because they had expected present prices to continue.

SOME PRACTICAL AND THEORETICAL PROBLEMS

The notion that many of the obstacles to investment can be overcome
by planning a still larger investment program is intriguing, to say the
least. Certain weaknesses in the supporting economic theories have now
been explained. The time has come to mention other difficulties, some
of them theoretical, but most of them extremely practical.

First, two of the arguments for a minimum "big push" were the alleged
need for "balanced" investment to provide a growing but "balanced" effective demand, and the supposed prevalence of increasing returns, but
these two forces pull in different directions. If returns increase markedly,
a poor country will not want to invest in both a railroad and a super
truck highway between the same points, and it may have to choose between a steel mill and an oil refinery. Decreasing returns, not increasing
returns, favor balanced growth.

Second, the whole argument implies a closed economy and forgets
the outside world. One way a country can have balanced consumption
without balanced production, if it can make or grow or mine anything
the world wants, is to import goods it cannot afford to produce. Through
international trade, except in the provision of utilities and other services,
the obstacle of capital "lumpiness" can largely be circumvented. A nation can have large and advantageous accumulations of domestic real
capital without domestic net saving if the world will lend or grant it
international purchasing power. Many of the arguments for a "big push"
could have validity only in a closed economy.

Third, the essential rationale for organizing a brave new economic
sector from scratch is that in this way many pecuniary external economies
(stretching this concept as wide as we can to include the creation of
monetary purchasing power) can be internalized. A single firm would
ignore these effects. But a government expanding many outputs simultaneously can supposedly count on capturing these "economies." Unfortunately, there would also be pecuniary external diseconomies, and
these should not be ignored; when a number of industries are competing
for the same scarce labor skills, the same materials, and perhaps the same

energy sources, some factor prices will rise. If government could arrange to internalize all pecuniary external economies while avoiding all pecuniary diseconomies, the public sector might be able to finance handsomely its own rapid growth. But such an assumption is altogether too asymmetric to swallow.

Fourth, even if a "big push" public investment program were feasible, it would result not in economic development but in "dualism" of an extreme form. An important characteristic of real and lasting development is that people change their methods of production, adopt new attitudes to work and saving, and sell more of their output in exchange for consumption goods. The balanced growth doctrine would involve the superimposition of a modern public sector upon a private subsistence sector, with almost no exchange between them, and hence little penetration of the subsistence economy by the market economy. A considerable portion of the population and territory would remain untouched and stagnant. The new sector might have as little impact as some of the foreign direct-investment enclaves about which there is always so much complaint.

Fifth, although capital "lumpiness" of many public utilities and industrial projects is often given as a reason why large sums must be invested immediately, the experience of many recently developed areas suggests that many services can be provided less grandiosely at first. There are other ways of providing electric power than damming an enormous river; thermal plants may be built or private deisel-generating sets installed, and although these have higher operating costs per unit output, they incur comparatively low initial investment costs. If monetary capital is extremely scarce, a low investment-high cost technology may constitute an acceptance of high interest rates and be truly more economic, especially when effective demand is still small.

Sixth, who is going to organize the large public sector, with its multiplicity of products and numerous new industries? One of the laments of officials in poor and backward countries is that there are so few people who can understand modern business records, schedule materials in a factory, coordinate the outputs and inputs of different plants, and assess future demands. It is a quaint notion that very ordinary people, with only human intelligence and knowledge, become omniscient when placed on a government payroll. In essence, the "big push" doctrine is a form of escapism. It suggests that what cannot be done in a small way is somehow within the physical and intellectual resources of a poor and backward country if done in a big way. Even if wealthier countries were to provide many producer and consumer goods free, and also technicians, many necessary institutional and human prerequisites are simply not there. It is as though a builder, having trouble constructing the ground floor of an office building, were advised to forget it and build the next three floors instead and now. Or as Singer has stated:

The advantages of multiple development may make interesting reading for economists, but they are gloomy news indeed for the underdeveloped countries. The initial resources for simultaneous developments on many fronts are generally lacking.[10]

Seventh, in practice any implementation of the "big push" proposals would mean a large public sector, plus substantial socialism. Even if the government were to subsidize private firms, instead of operating public concerns, the extent of regulation would be enormous. One reason why "big push" proposals have been accepted so eagerly in some circles abroad is that they are seen as a first important step toward public ownership and operation of a country's land and capital.

It is on a psychological rather than an economic plane that perhaps something can be said for the idea of a "big push." People may be more ready to change their ways and views in a manner favorable to economic development if some widely publicized expansion program is underway. Perhaps families will save more, workers labor harder, and producers risk innovations sooner if they all feel that they are participating in a great patriotic endeavor. A "small push" might never jolt them from the rut of tradition. Perhaps the inevitable resource waste is not always too high a price to pay for cultural changes favorable to subsequent economic development.

[10] H. W. Singer, "Economic Progress in Underdeveloped Countries," *Social Research,* March, 1949, p. 7.

17

Unbalanced
industrial growth

A historical survey of economically developed non-Communist countries suggests that their growth was largely achieved by investments, made to supply a demand, which in turn created some other unsatisfied demand to be met by another investment. Sometimes the government took a hand in creating the imbalance, as when it invested in transport and utilities, hoping that low prices for their services would stimulate investment in industries using them. But most investment decisions were made by private entrepreneurs, the entire path of development although unplanned being perhaps predestined, and this may be the most effective way for some societies to achieve economic growth.

GROWTH THROUGH IMBALANCE

Many countries of the free world have increased per capita output, some of them very strikingly. And they have constantly altered the composition of their national outputs without any conscious planning. How were they able to do it?

Profits and entrepreneurs

A first subsidiary question is "What 'powered' development?." A desire to profit, or "make money," was probably the most important single incentive that led people to risk their capital and apply their energies in order to innovate some new enterprise in a particular market. But unusual egotism and an adventurous spirit should not be overlooked.

In early stages of economic development, when capital fund requirements are not very large, there are many persons who could afford to be entrepreneurs, but instead prefer a profession or leisure.

Only a certain sort of person wants to be an entrepreneur. However, in some cultures, free enterprise and making profits is a sort of game, where profits no longer have any sumptuary meaning but are simply a "score" that shows which players are winning prestige and power. Only a few persons really *want* to be entrepreneurs, however much successful entrepreneurs may be envied, and those people who are only happy as entrepreneurs are usually not the kind who would wish to make investment decisions as government civil servants.

It is one thing to want to be an entrepreneur and quite another to be a successful one. Many make the attempt, but few survive. Some of those who do profit may be successful not because of their superior acumen and effort but from sheer luck. But these are probably a minority. The probabilities are that a person who has started several different enterprises, and has made a profit on each before turning to the next, combines some set of qualities that most people do not possess. Some of these attributes may not be genteel—entrepreneurs on the make are ruthless and acquisitive—but what matters to society is that they are able to employ the economy's resources to such very good effect.

Of course entrepreneurs employ resources selfishly, to make money if possible for themselves and not for others. But if there is competition, the efforts of rival capitalists will eventually pass most of these once potential profits on to workers, savers, and landlords in the form of wages, interest, and rents. It is not even necessary that there be several rival entrepreneurs within the same "group"—whether it be grain millers in a rural town or coal mine owners in a country—for to some extent all producers are rivals for many factors or production and are in competition indirectly or directly for the consumers' and taxpayers' dollar. Hence an important responsibility of government is to prevent the grosser sorts of collusion and not itself to create unregulated monopoly situations, as through import restrictions for example.

The significance of profits is not only that negative profits eliminate the inept and the unfortunate from entrepreneurial circles and return them to the ranks of employees, but that positive profits are a source of producers' purchasing power. Some capital funds can be borrowed, often in very large sums, but an entrepreneur must always contribute some funds of his own, even though these may be a minor fraction of the total. Winning one round of the competitive game enables an entrepreneur to play another round. Hence, at any given time, a fair fraction of the players have proved themselves winners in the past. This increases the chances that the resources of a private enterprise economy will be used effectively.

Profit opportunities and "external economies"

To be successful an entrepreneur must perceive profitable "gaps" between demand and supply and fill them before someone else does. Sometimes these "gaps" may be fairly obvious and definite, and in that case the profits will be nominal, constituting not much more than "wages of management" after all factors have been paid. But other "gaps" are far more nebulous and uncertain, and perhaps can only be seen by capitalists who are placed at certain vantage points in the structure of the economy, these suspected "gaps" being very profitable if they do in fact exist. The more an investment constitutes an innovation, the more the initiator is an entrepreneur and not a manager, and the greater the profits or losses may be. This, but without his detail and subtlety, was an important feature of Schumpeter's theory of economic development (see Chapter 5).

The point to be stressed is that, during the course of development, investments that are "innovations" at an earlier stage become routine at a later period. And at any given stage in any country, there will be some marginal investments that are experimental and risky and so constitute innovations. The introduction of ballpoint pen manufacturing would be an innovation in the Congo today, but the introduction of one more ballpoint pen factory in the United States would not be very startling or daring, and other examples come readily to mind.

It has been pointed out many times already that certain investments give rise to pecuniary external economies that in turn give rise to other investments.

Favorable external effects arise when good A results in more joint supply of B or more joint demand for C. Thus the establishment of an oil refinery, to meet the domestic demand for gasoline and diesel fuel primarily, will also occasion a joint supply of asphalt that will make it cheaper to surface roads and make them "all-weather" highways. Or local manufacturing of oil lamps, if it lowers their domestic price considerably, may increase the demand for lamp oil as oil and lamps are in joint demand. In all these instances there is technical complementarity.

Unfavorable external effects arise when there is technical substitutability. This will occur if the output of D is increased and it is in rival supply with E (e.g., the availability of electric power at low cost may render the mining of certain coal deposits unprofitable). Or an increase in the output of F, which makes intensive use of product G, may inhibit the output of H because its production also requires a great amount of G. An example of such rival demand would be a very large concrete highway program that so increases the price of cement that various irrigation canal projects have to be deferred for a few years.

Investment, depending on what it is for, may also create buyers' and/or suppliers' surpluses, although no complementarity exists. These are the cases, already described above, where there is a productive sequence with one industry's output being an input to another industry. Establishment of a tannery not only increases the suppliers' surpluses of those who grow wattle trees for *quebrache,* but it also increases the buyers' surpluses of shoe manufacturers.

The point of all this is that one investment may lead to another.

An entrepreneur, in closing one "gap" may open up another because of the external economies thereby created. Either he or some other capitalist may close the second "gap," but in closing it, external economies may open yet another gap, and so on. Or if "imbalance" is substituted for the word "gap," balancing one imbalance may create another imbalance *ad infinitum*. In this way the economy may lurch from side to side as it moves along the growth path.

Imbalance a stimulant

The notion that "imbalance" may be "good" rather than "bad" for economic development in a backward country—besides being inevitable —has been popularized by Professor Albert O. Hirschman.[1] It is his idea that certain investments will create new investment opportunities and so provide a stimulus to further economic development. In fact, assuming they do not have too low a rate of return compared with other alternatives, the best investments may not be those that restore "balance" within the economy but rather lead it away from equilibrium. Or as Hirschman states it:

In general, development policy . . . must keep *alive* rather than eliminate the disequilibria of which profits and losses are symptoms in a competitive economy. If the economy is to be kept moving ahead, the task of development policy is to maintain tensions, disproportions, and disequilibria. That nightmare of equilibrium economics, the endlessly spinning cobweb, is the *kind* of mechanism we must assiduously look for as an invaluable help in the development process.[2]

However, new investments appropriate external economies as well as create them, and in certain unfortunate instances an investment may exploit economies while creating diseconomies. The building of a breakwater may lead to the establishment of a fish cannery that smells so bad that incipient office and residential construction in the area never occurs. The opposite possibility of this convergent series of investments, which finally comes to a dead stop, are divergent series in which each investment creates more economies than are appropriated and the stimulus to additional investment becomes ever stronger. In practice such divergent series may of course be hard to find. The contribution of theory is telling developers what to seek.

Hirschman calls those investments that are net beneficiaries of external economies—*i.e.*, that appropriate more economies than they create—*in-*

[1] A. O. Hirschman, *The Strategy of Economic Development* (New Haven, Conn.: Yale University Press, 1958), especially Chapters 3–5.
[2] *Ibid.*, p. 66.

duced investments.[3] By the same token, those investments that are links in a diverging chain of investments he might term *inducing* investments (but he does not), as they create more economies than they appropriate. From the viewpoint of the economy, induced investments may then be less valuable than they appear to be to private investors, whereas inducing investments may have a greater social than private net marginal product. At least this seems to be the opinion of Hirschman in a now familiar paragraph that summarizes his strategy of development:

An ideal situation obtains when . . . one disequilibrium calls forth a development move which in turn leads to a similar disequilibrium and so on *ad infinitum*. If such a chain of unbalanced growth sequences could be set up, the economic policy makers could just watch the proceedings from the sidelines.[4]

Of course this sort of analysis is very loose, partly because the concept of external economies has become so stretched and shapeless, as Hirschman would himself probably admit. And in practice, such are the numerous and twisted interdependencies of firms through their inputs and outputs that it will always be very difficult in a specific case to decide whether the beneficial complementarities outweigh the harmful substitutabilities. The crucial issue is whether these ideas can be translated into any development policies.

UNBALANCING THE ECONOMY WITH "INFRASTRUCTURE"

The jargon of this subsection's title means that one way to unbalance the economy—and so stimulate other investment perhaps—is to construct many forms of what has been called "infrastructure" and is now increasingly termed "social overhead capital" (*SOC*). Included in *SOC* are such things as transportation investments (*e.g.,* harbors, rolling stock, and airports), conventional public utilities (*e.g.,* water, power, and light), and communications (*e.g.,* telephone, radiotelegraphy, and postal services). This "infrastructure" has a number of characteristics that together tend to distinguish it from other investments.

First, *SOC* provides services rather than goods, and services have to be produced near where they are used: hence *SOC* services, unlike most kinds of production, usually cannot be imported. Second, the services of *SOC* greatly facilitate or are essential to the conduct of a wide variety of activities by potentially numerous firms and people, the effect often being very diffused. Third, *SOC* services are usually (but not always) provided by public authority, and they are supplied free or at regulated

3 *Ibid.,* p. 71.
4 *Ibid.,* pp. 71, 72.

prices. Fourth, there is a tendency for marginal costs to be rather constant up to capacity, and to comprise a small fraction of total costs per unit of output. Fifth, the large initial capital investment is often "lumpy" (or discontinuous), although perhaps less so in the long run than some enthusiasts for a "big push" investment would have people believe. Despite this enumeration of characteristics, it must be admitted that the concept of economic infrastructure is not as tidy as one would like, and many important public investments for economic development (*e.g.*, expenditures for health and education) are often excluded from the *SOC* concept. A pragmatic definition, offered half-humorously, is that *SOC* comprises those sorts of things that the International Bank for Reconstruction and Development (*IBRD*) tends to favor, as the behavioral sciences have been said to comprise all those endeavors which manage to obtain financial support from the Ford Foundation.[5]

A considerable majority of officials engaged in planning economic development currently subscribe to the view that a large investment now in *SOC* will encourage private investment later. Improved highways may stimulate truck farming; cheaper electric power may encourage light industry; a more frequent and reliable postal service at reduced rates may indirectly subsidize the publication of magazines and the distribution of knowledge. The basic idea is always that by perhaps temporarily overinvesting in *SOC* capacity, the costs of many directly productive activities (*DPA*) can be reduced and hence investment in these enterprises encourage. In effect, although it is seldom if ever described in such terms, the *SOC* approach to economic development is to "unbalance" the economy in the hope or belief that subsequently there will be important and private induced investments. This is one of the few instances in which full recognition has been given to "efficient sequences" of investment as described by Hirschman.

It is probably a fair comment that many *SOC* investments are made on the basis of faith and with no clear idea as to who the customers of the project will be and how much they will probably use its services. Even the Kariba Dam project in Central Africa, one of the largest development undertakings during the past ten years, was based on very cursory estimates of future power requirements. Hundreds of man-years went into the designing and planning of the dam and its equipment, but estimated future needs were based on little more than the probable demands of the "copper belt" (which had alternate but limited power sources anyway) and an observed tendency for power usage to increase by two different annual percentages in the principal towns and the rest of the country, respectively. This "failure" to make careful estimates of demand is not necessarily a fault. Perhaps such estimates are really not

[5] *Ibid.*, p. 83.

possible and it is better to guess frankly than to go through the hocus pocus of lengthy market "research." If this is the practical lesson that one of the largest international lending agencies has learned, one doubts the feasibility of nicely planned "balanced growth," with all capacities being matched by demands and all demands being supplied.

The justification of *SOC* investments is that they "subsidize" industry, agriculture, or commerce by cheapening certain inputs that they use or otherwise reducing their costs. An irrigation project may give farmers more and cheaper water. A telephone service—with intercity connections —may result in grain traders' keeping in closer touch with each other and thus with market conditions in different areas. But the *may* depends on the price charged for the service.

If the prices charged for irrigation water are no lower than previous costs of obtaining water, the farmers will not use any more water than they did before, and the potential value of the extra water will be lost because the water will never be used. If telephone charges are not reduced after additional intercity circuits are installed, the circuits will not be used more either. And it is tragic when the potential gains from damming a river for hydro-electric power are wasted because "sound" financing is supposed to require a price that covers all costs including debt service charges. In such cases the cost of power is hardly reduced, so there is little increase in consumption, and the river flows over the spillway rather than through the turbines. *SOC* investments will not stimulate private investments unless the former's services are provided cheaper, or unless they are vastly improved at no increase in cost to users. The proper yardstick for pricing the "last" units sold—as explained in Chapter 15— are marginal costs.

Because of the "lumpiness" of capital, and the optimistic belief that a growing population and rising income will soon increase all demands, public utility projects are often constructed with a capacity far in excess of present demands. This extra capacity is often reflected in higher unit costs of service at recent output levels. Any attempt to cover these extra unit costs in higher prices would be fatal of course to the whole purpose of the investment. Use might even fall off. Fortunately, because of political hostility to any increase in output prices, this is seldom done.

SOC investments that provide free services usually do not violate the marginal cost pricing rule, except where heavy use of the facility increases costs of maintenance or impairs the service itself. Thus the services of improved highways are usually provided free, and as a consequence the repair and fuel bills of trucking companies are reduced. The improved service, at no increase from a zero price, should stimulate extra trucking. And this is quite economical, unless it can be shown that each passing truck shortens the life of the roadway, in which case a special fuel tax on trucks might correct the matter.

Some of these problems of determining *SOC* investments were aptly summarized by Professor Hirschman, when from his experience he wrote:

The trouble with investment in *SOC*—or is it its strength?—is that it is impervious to the investment criteria that have been devised to introduce some rationality into investment plans. The computation of capital-output ratios often presents almost insuperable statistical difficulties (as in the case of highways) and is moreover considered to be misleading anyway because of the igniting effect *SOC* investment is expected to have on *DPA*. As a result, *SOC* investment is largely a matter of faith in the development potential of a region or country. . . .

The absence of an *ex ante* criteria is compounded by the weakness of sanctions when mistakes have actually been made. Underutilized ports installations, highways, and even power plants do not present nearly the same administrative and public relations problem as a factory that is idle or suffers losses because of insufficient demand.

Perhaps it is this absence of criteria and of sanctions that has endeared *SOC* so much to the developers. Development planning is a risky business and there is naturally an attraction in undertaking ventures that cannot be proven wrong before they are started and that are unlikely ever to become obvious failures.[6]

However, in defense of the policy of *SOC* investments in advance of demand, the point is often made that public investments in *SOC*-type projects are the only development investments that government can make politically in underdeveloped countries having predominantly free enterprise economies. Government investment in regular industry—with or without funds from abroad—would cause some very hostile reactions among the financial and business communities of many countries. The willingness of Western countries, all of which have private capitalist economies, to tax themselves in order to finance socialist experiments abroad is certainly limited. Investments for *SOC,* then, appear to many Western peoples in a favorable and contrasting light, for their rationale is that they stimulate private enterprise government being limited to providing the necessary infrastructure. Most other decisions to invest are still private and decentralized, hence the *SOC* approach is not much more than a modification of the government policies for favoring economic growth that were followed during the nineteenth century throughout North America and Western Europe.

LEADING WITH *DPA*

An opposite kind of imbalance can be created however. Conceptually at least, a government might directly or indirectly invest in *DPA* (directly productive activities) and allow *SOC* investments to lag. In other words,

6 *Ibid.,* pp. 84, 85.

instead of investing in *SOC* in order to induce *DPA* investments, government might lead with *DPA*. In time the shortage of *SOC* might lead to political demands for more public utilities of all kinds.

Some investment sequences are generated by profit expectations and others by political demands. Of course profit expectations only power the sequence from *SOC* to *DPA,* and political pressure can only force the sequence from *DPA* to *SOC*. However, to use Hirschman's phrase, the important requirement is that a "self-propelling" sequence be started: whether it runs by profit steam or political gasoline doesn't matter so long as there is a maximum increase in useful national product.

Because of the reluctance of some Western lending nations to finance government projects in competition with firms in traditionally private industries, coupled sometimes with a similar reluctance on the part of underdeveloped borrowing countries, government "investment" in *DPA* might have to be indirect. It could take the form of government loans to private firms for capital construction and equipment, or even outright subsidies of operating costs. Such aids might have to be combined with price ceilings to ensure that most of the benefits get "through" to users of the subsidized products and do not remain with the producers as profits.

A common reaction to such a proposed scheme is to attack it as wasteful. If a factory has to be subsidized in one way or another for it to become established and to operate, it is bound to be suspect. It may well be that the usefulness of its product is not in accord with the opportunity cost of making it. If this is really so, it would be perverse of government to promote such a malallocation of resources. But in this same sense all *SOC* investments are suspect. And many of them are probably wasteful by accident or design.

A contributing factor is that nearly all *SOC* projects are rather "lumpy" in their capital requirements. And this is particularly so of the *SOC* projects that most developers fancy, for among underdeveloped countries the prestige of government may suffer when public projects are not of the latest and largest kind. Because of this accentuated "lumpiness," the choice is often between having considerable excess capacity for at least a number of years or permitting public services to become grossly inadequate before anything is done to enlarge their scale, the former being an instance of *SOC* leading *DPA* and the latter exemplifying *DPA* leading *SOC*.

Which path of development will probably be most economical? Consider two ways government can promote transport of goods and persons by truck and bus. It has a choice of replacing present narrow and twisting interurban roads with modern four-lane highways (anything less being beneath its dignity) or subsidizing truck and bus companies directly.

It may be cheaper to "compensate" highway users for the bad state of the interurban road system than to improve it in some grossly discontinuous way. After all, if it costs $100,000 a mile to build a highway (which is under $20 a foot), the annual cost per mile (assuming a 25-year service life) is $4000. The saving to users may be $0.02 a mile. The road will "pay" if over 600 vehicles use every mile each day at least. If initial volume is likely to be less, it may be more economical now to subsidize road users by lowering taxes on gasoline and diesel oil used by vehicles. The scale of such assistance can be continuously and automatically adjusted in the aggregate. The more vehicles and driving, the more fuel purchased, and the more the subsidy. This is in contrast to the discontinuous expense of promoting road transportation by constructing super highways.

In a schematic way this same idea can be illustrated by modifying Hirschman's diagram.[7] In Fig. 17-1, the Q_1 curve represents an output of 150 units and Q_2 an output of 250 units. The horizontal axis shows the

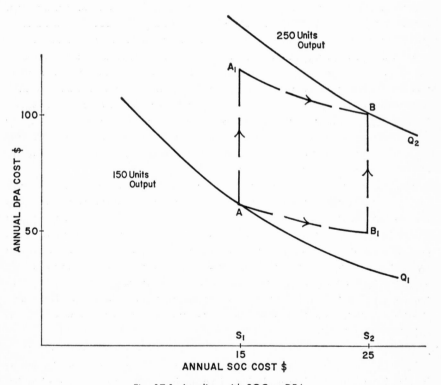

Fig. 17-1. Leading with SOC or DPA.

[7] Hirschman, *op. cit.*, p. 87. His diagram was evolved for the purpose of showing that a "self-propelling" sequence of growth might be realized through having either excess *SOC* capacity (and so inducing *DPA* through profit expectations) or a shortage of *SOC* (and so obtaining more through political pressures).

annual cost of available *SOC*. The vertical axis shows the total yearly *DPA* cost of producing each of these two outputs, including the annual cost of *DPA* investments. Note that the *DPA* cost of producing a given output increases if there is less *SOC* investment to help. It is assumed here that—insofar as adjustments can be made—there are constant returns to scale and that the economical combination is $4 of *DPA* annual expense to $1 of *SOC* annual expense. Although *DPA* expenses can be varied continuously, it is supposed that *SOC* comes in discrete "lumps" such as S_1 and S_2, so there is no direct and continuous route from *A* to *B*.

If an economy is at point *A*, and population and capital increments are expanding the national product, should it plan on moving discontinuously to B_1 (and then gradually to *B*) or gradually to A_1 (and then plan on a discrete move to *B*)? The first policy means excess *SOC* capacity most of the time. The second policy leads with *DPA*, belated adjustments of *SOC* being made only when the shortage becomes too agonizing.

Which expansion route is the most economical will depend upon the comparative inefficiencies at points A_1 and B_1, the length of time the economy might be at each point along one route or the other, and prevailing interest charges. But in general the choice is between incurring a sudden decrease in efficiency now (moving from *A* to B_1) which gradually ceases as output expands from B_1 to *B* or gradually becoming less efficient (while increasing output from *A* to A_1) with a sudden improvement much later (as extra *SOC* moves the economy from A_1 to *B*). If time preferences are high, as one usually assumes in countries with low per capita incomes and little capital accumulation, the present discounted value of the output via A_1 is probably higher than that via B_1.[8]

The ratio of population to land and other resources can be important in this connection. A sparse population makes the discrete *SOC* expenditures seem even more discontinuous. This can be seen most readily in the case of household utilities. With only 10 families distributed evenly per square mile, the cost "jump" between individual family septic tanks and a connected sewage system is too large. There is some critical population density at which rural electrification becomes cheaper than each family having its own lighting plant. The same principles apply in the case of *SOC* that supports industrial and agricultural output.

[8] These points can be understood more readily if total cost and total output values are assumed for each of the relevant points, such as:

	DPA Cost	SOC Cost	Total Cost	Output
A	60	15	75	150
B	100	25	125	250
A_1	110	15	125	220
B_1	50	25	75	180

N.B.: Costs are measured in terms of money units and output in terms of physical units.

Quite apart from which route from A to B might be more economical, there is the question of which route is more feasible, for there is little advantage in moving from A to A_1 only to find that sufficient pressure cannot be placed upon government to supply the SOC increment. There is no *a priori* answer to the question of whether those who own the DPA facilities have political influence. On the other hand, during recent years, there have been some very conspicuous cases of governments identifying themselves with monumental projects supposed to further economic development. Pyramid building—or at least its modern equivalent—did not end with the Pharaohs.

"LAST" INDUSTRIES FIRST

There is another kind of "imbalance" that can be exploited in the economic development of a country, one that is possibly more important than that between SOC and DPA, and which rests on the distinction between intermediate and final products.

In the making of industrial products, as distinct from agricultural goods, there are often several "stages" of production before the final good is ready for sale. A developing country mercifully does not have to undertake all these stages of production simultaneously—as many "big push" and "balanced growth" advocates propose—but can import various parts and finished materials for final assembly or production. There is no economic law that requires a nation to undertake all stages of production merely because it performs the final stage. International trade demonstrates that practice is the opposite. Many underdeveloped countries can best start to industrialize by first concentrating on "last stage industries."

In fact, this is exactly what many underdeveloped countries have done. Hirschman has described this evolution in the following terms:

In today's underdeveloped countries the textiles, food processing, and construction materials based on local materials are still of great importance, but, to a very significant extent, industrialization is penetrating these countries . . . through plants that perform the "final touches" on almost finished *industrial* products imported from abroad. Examples are the many converting, assembly, and mixing plants, the pharmaceutical laboratories, the metal fabricating industries, and many others.[9]

Such a process of industrialization, when once begun, can continue through lower and lower stages of production.

A majority of these "last stage industries" make consumer goods (*e.g.,* cloth, shoes, beer, pans, furniture), but a number of finally finished goods are producer goods of course (*e.g.,* wooden boxes, steel cans, barbed wire).

9 Hirschman, *op. cit.,* p. 111.

And in an expanding economy, where population and per capita income are increasing, the use of these goods must be increasing too. Thus goods that once could most economically be acquired as imports may in time reach a volume of use that justifies domestic "last stage production." In other words, in the making of those goods that are subject to increasing returns (*i.e.*, decreasing unit costs with increasing volume), there is a "threshold" quantity beyond which it pays to produce at home and before which it pays to import from abroad.

For some products (*e.g.*, beer) this "threshold" is attained by even a small country's market, but there are other products (*e.g.*, sewing machines) that require a large national market if home production is to be worthwhile. Sometimes the demand of an adjoining country should be included with estimates of the local market's volume of use. This is especially so when, in terms of transportation costs, the first country is located between the adjoining market and the principal alternate sources of supply in the outside world. For example, as regards transportation, Brazil lies between Argentina and Europe. In rather the same way, many coastal ports lie between a large hinterland and the major industrial centers of Western Europe and North America.

Once a country has established a variety of final product industries, one sort of imbalance has been largely eliminated, but another one has also been created. The last stage industries now in operation at home require many inputs. Whereas the final assembly (*e.g.*, bicycle or sewing machine) used to be imported, now it is parts that are coming in from abroad, and some of them are not too hard to make.

A good example is the battery-powered radio receiver—popular in the underdeveloped world. The vacuum tubes will be too difficult to produce domestically at reasonable cost. But many of the other parts, such as condensers, transformers, chassis, and cabinet are not. The job of assembly primarily requires manual deftness and, if the volume of output permits specialization among workers, can be done by illiterates—under supervision. A number of underdeveloped countries now produce radio receivers and many of the parts as well.

Although parts of manufactured goods are usually specialized and cannot be used in any other assembly, this is not always the case. And even when it is so, the same sort of equipment and skills that can make one part can make another, so that different orders can be filled with equal ease. Screws and bolts are used in many assemblies. And so are various electric components such as resistors and condensers. Moreover, the investment needed to make such parts is often not large. Hence at a fairly early period in its industrial growth, a country may acquire light metal-working and electric component industries.

Many finished products can be made from domestic materials without great investment or skill being required, if only some rather intricate and specialized equipment can be acquired from abroad. The cotton textile industry affords the best example for a country that grows cotton, as the spinning and weaving equipment can be imported and is not "lumpy." Shoes can be made from locally produced leather with the assistance of imported shoe machinery that can sometimes be rented. Glass jar manufacture, from local silicates, can be made with highly specialized equipment developed and produced abroad.

A great deal of industrial penetration downward from final demands, through lower and lower stages, may be undertaken by separate and independent firms. This has certainly been true of the textile industry in many countries, with some firms spinning, others weaving, and still others dyeing. But in other lines this downward penetration may take the form of vertical integration. A firm that begins by assembling sewing machines from imported parts may gradually produce more and more of the components. Building contractors may saw their own lumber, log their own timber, and make their own bricks. Usually integration occurs as final output volume attains levels that render financially feasible the making of subsidiary products. Successful companies usually "feel their way" in this regard. It is unusual for new concerns to come into existence as fully integrated companies. The largest corporations of advanced countries did not arrive on the scene all fully formed after the manner implicitly proposed by those who favor balanced growth according to an over-all plan.

A more practicable plan seems to be for government to stimulate industrial growth by exploiting the downward linkages that exist or can be created between final demands and intermediate products.[10] One way is by means of "development" tariffs (see Chapter 25) which are distinguished from conventional "infant" industry tariffs on three points. An alternative method is to subsidize certain key activities that may have linkages downward and upward. Examples are canneries, cold storage plants, dehydrating factories for the making of powdered foods, and in fact any and all methods of increasing and steadying the demand for perishable and seasonal products.

Government needs to scrutinize as many vertical industrial product sequences as it can. Many finished products can be imported, and some of the raw materials can be exported. Between the top and the bottom of this list of products are hundreds of thousands of intermediate goods, which interact in complicated ways, but some of the more important

---

10 Hirschman (op. cit., Chapter 6) refers to backward linkage—i.e., back from consumer demand—and so has a horizontal movement in mind. But the idea of a vertical movement, from higher to lower stages, is well established. Also, whereas Hirschman stresses the linkage from consumer goods, the linkages described here are from finished goods and may include some finished producer goods. Of course most finished goods, in the sense that they are not subjected to any more processing or refabrication or assembly, are probably consumer goods.

sequences can be traced. Certain industrial consumer goods bulk so large in family budgets that successively lower stages of product warrant study with a view to determining their imminent profitability. And exported primary products are not so numerous that the desirability of processing them more before shipment cannot be assessed.

To some extent input-output tables may indicate useful areas in which to conduct such a search for profitable product sequences. Such tables show, for each unit output of one industry, the units of input taken from every other industry. The "units" necessarily have to be in money value terms, so the resultant flow coefficients may show that a typical dollar's worth of output of industry A is made on an average with so many cents' worth of inputs from the industry B. These interindustry flows include goods of all kinds—fixed capital equipment as well as raw materials and finished goods—and the entire economy may be disaggregated into as many as a hundred "industries."

An input-output table lists in rows the industries that supply goods (including imports and labor) and in columns all the claimants or users (including exports and consumers).[11] It has been noted by at least one research team that industries tend to move their output "upward" rather than "downward." The "last" stage industries do not have outputs that are often used as inputs by "first" stage industries. In fact, the input-output tables of some countries can almost be "triangulated," with very little output being "lost" from the accounts because it has been used by a lower stage in industry.

Each intersection of a row (supplies) and columns (demands) constitutes a "cell" in the input-output matrix. And in that "cell" a coefficient indicates the importance to the column industry's output of the row industry's input. An interesting industry sequence would be one in which a final product industry buys heavily from a lower industry, which buys heavily from the next lower industry, and so on all the way down to the raw material supplying industry. Approximately, the larger the magnitude of a coefficient, the more important the downward linkage.

However, even the most disaggregated input-output tables are still highly aggregated, so that the flow coefficients reflect the movement of a wide variety of goods. Hence a lot of detailed examination of product sequences is still necessary after the input-output matrix has suggested where to look. And some profitable product sequences may not be revealed by the table.

The main idea and moral are obvious, however. A country can in time undertake lower and lower stages of production, and economically too, so long as it doesn't attempt to do everything at once. It must leave to more advanced countries—at least at first—the making of special equip-

[11] H. B. Chenery and T. Watanabe, "International Comparisons of the Structure of Production," *Econometrica*, 1960.

ment and especially difficult components. The main essential is that it does not attempt balanced growth in the sense of self-sufficiency.

SUMMARY

This and the preceding chapter have described two opposing views as to how economic development might be accelerated by government. The first was balanced growth under government direction, and the second is industrial growth through the skillful creation or exploitation of imbalances by entrepreneurs and government. The two approaches are in marked contrast on many scores. About the only point of similarity is that both favor some sort and degree of government participation to foster growth. *Laissez-faire* is not at issue.

Balanced growth, in the sense of deliberate sumultaneous investment in all lines of output according to some central government plan, has never been attempted outside the Communist states. Unbalanced growth by independent entrepreneurs is the way that advanced countries of the Western world have in fact realized economic development. So apart from Communist police states, the contrast is between theory and practice.

Balanced growth entails planning and central decision making. Unbalanced growth involves decentralized decision making and no over-all and conscious plan. But unbalanced development is not unplanned in a fundamental sense. Unbalanced growth, within the framework established by government, may well proceed according to an unconscious plan. Given the economic environment, as provided by nature and modified by government, independent profit seeking may guide development along an almost predestined route. The aggregate behavior of thousands of entrepreneurs is not as haphazard or as chaotic as many socialists would have people believe.

IV

Labor and
development

THE theme of this work is that output growth is a function of improved technology, additional capital, and extra labor. Part II stressed productivity advances through useful innovations; Part III emphasized the accumulation and use of capital. And so it remains to consider what determines the effective labor supply. Here it is important to distinguish between (1) increases in population alone, (2) extra hours of work per capita, and (3) more effective labor per hour of work. Extra population, without other changes, is likely to reduce per capita output because of diminishing returns (see Chapter 18). More hours per worker, and a larger fraction of people working, should increase output—but there is a real cost, if only because leisure is lost (see Chapter 19). Hence true economic development probably lies in increasing the effectiveness of an hour of work through increased health and training (see Chapters 21 and 22). Resources invested *in* people may earn a higher return for a nation than ordinary capital investments *for* them. The record of the advanced nations suggests that it is population "quality" that distinguishes them in most cases from backward countries. Of course there are spiral effects, with higher per capita incomes resulting in better health and more training and so higher per capita incomes again, the initial improvement being perhaps attributable to natural resources, geographic position, or superior political organizations.

This being understood, it is probably no exaggeration to say that the economic well-being of most countries today properly depends more than anything else upon the present character and culture of their inhabitants, and in many backward areas real economic development must wait upon fundamental changes in the people of these countries. As Adam Smith wrote, in the opening words of *The Wealth of Nations,* "The annual labor of every nation is the fund which originally supplies it with all the necessaries and conveniences of life. . . ." It is worth remembering that past and present human effort and ability are the ultimate source of all economic goods and services.

18

Dangers of overpopulation

A century and a half ago, economists in Britain were afraid that population would increase more rapidly than output and so depress individual consumption. However, in Europe at least, birth rates declined. And a series of technological inventions not only caused large increases in output per capita but also permitted food to be imported economically from overseas. For the advanced countries today, the dire predictions of Malthus seem obsolete. Yet in many backward countries, the threat of overpopulation looms large. Many of these countries are doubling their populations every 35–40 years. Lower birth rates, and a slower rate of population growth, would almost certainly permit a higher consumption per capita, and this in turn would presumably occasion more domestic saving and investment per capita. Hence population control is one aspect of economic development. India has government birth control clinics, for example: and some Indian states—such as Madras—offer small bonuses to husbands who have a vasectomy. But extra children, although lowering the consumption of others in these countries, can also be a great joy to their parents. Moreover, some of the world's major cultures stress fertility as a virtue, and one of its oldest religions prohibits specific contraception. Thus notions of what is an *economically* "optimum" population must always be reassessed within a broader context of human values.

THE POPULATION "EXPLOSION"

During recent years, a great deal of publicity has been given to the so-called population explosion that is occurring in many parts of the world. Population dynamics are extremely complicated. But the subject is so important that even an oversimplified description of this extremely rapid increase of the world's inhabitants is in order.

In comparatively primitive societies, including many large nations that are economically backward, the number of annual live births approaches the biological maximum that is possible under conditions of poverty: over 4 live births per hundred population. In other words, if almost all girls marry soon after adolescence, if they take no special measures to avoid pregnancy, and if they have an average number of abortions and stillbirths, the annual number of births divided by the total population will be somewhat over 0.04.

This crude birth rate depends of course upon the age distribution of the population and the life expectancies of females. In high birth rate countries a relatively large fraction of the population are children. And in poor countries females' life expectancies may be only 35 to 40 years at birth.

Many of these same countries, until a century or less ago, had crude death rates that were almost as high as the crude birth rates. With deaths almost as numerous as births, the growth of population was slow—certainly less than 1 per cent a year. Since then various causes of death have almost disappeared; among these are local famines (now prevented by improved transportation), tribal wars and religious massacres (ended during "colonialism"), and occasional epidemics of cholera, smallpox, and so on (almost eliminated by quarantines, inoculations, and other public health measures). Accordingly, for the time being at least, annual death rates in many of these countries have fallen to almost 2 per 100 inhabitants. The result is a 2 per cent annual increase in population. Such a rate, when compounded annually, means a doubling of population every 35 years.

In a few exceptional cases, including some of the Caribbean islands, more favorable living conditions have resulted in a longer period of childbearing for women and reduced infant mortality. As a consequence, crude birth rates are above 4 per cent, crude death rates are below 2 per cent, and the population is probably doubling about every 30 years. This would involve a tenfold increase in a century if such long-term extrapolations were ever fulfilled.

The situation in Central America—Costa Rica, El Salvador, Guatemala, Honduras, and Nicaragua—dramatically indicates the consequences of falling death rates. It is estimated by the United Nations that the population will have risen from 7.9 million in 1950 to 15.8 million in 1980, increasing by 2.4 per cent annually, under "medium" fertility assumptions. However, as one Latin American specialist has noted:

Assuming "high" fertility, or an annual increase in 1950–58 of 2.9 per cent, the estimate of Central America's population in 1980 climbs to 18,368,000. In the absence of any signs of a drop in birth rates and with further declines in death rates practically assured, it is far from clear how, or when, the natural increase in population will fall below three per cent annually. Migration will not greatly influence demographic trends. The population "explosion" is predominantly a phenomenon of longevity and unchecked fertility.[1]

The same author indicates that in 1950 the median age in Central America was 18 years and that 43 per cent of the people were under 15 years of age. And the ratio of "inactive" (i.e., under 15 or over 69 years) to "active" population ranged from 0.75 in El Salvador and Honduras to 0.82 in Nicaragua. The burden of dependency—with all the poverty that this implies—is thus accentuated by high fertility.

In the more advanced countries, where personal medical attention is available for almost everyone, most deaths are due to degenerative diseases and accidents that have nothing to do with poverty. Examples are heart attacks due to overweight and accidents involving motor cars. Old age ailments, such as cancer, are becoming increasingly common. Crude death rates range from about 15 to 20 per thousand a year. But with crude birth rates at or below 30 per thousand, it takes over 50 years for population to double.

The population "explosion" now occurring in many of the more backward countries is primarily the result of a relatively sudden cessation or reduction in certain kinds of deaths without any comparable reduction in births. It is hard to conceive of such a large disparity in crude death and birth rates being sustained for more than a few generations. The optimistic hope is that parents, as they come to realize that more of their children will survive to maturity, will deliberately reduce the number of babies that they conceive. A more tragic possibility—but one that may not be inevitable—is that the population growth will cause individual consumption levels to fall and deaths attributable to poverty to increase.

The European countries, during the past hundred years, have had a rather slow population increase, partly because of a large exodus of immigrants to overseas countries. This sort of relief is not so easily available to persons without white skins. North America and Australasia, for example, do not accept nonwhites as immigrants. The post-World War II influx of Indians and British West Indians into the United Kingdom may soon be limited. Chinese are not welcome in Indonesia. Another difference was that the birth rates in many European countries, notably France and Ireland, began to fall dramatically in the nineteenth century. Most important perhaps, public health measures had to wait upon knowledge and finance in the advanced countries, and hence they were extended slowly over many decades. The recently "colonial" countries sometimes established health programs within a generation. An amazing decline in mortality rates and the current population "explosion" are the aftermaths.

[1] Robert S. Smith, "Population and Economic Growth in Latin America," *Economic Development and Cultural Change,* January, 1962.

SOME POPULATION THEOREMS

The growth of population and its economic consequences were of major interest to the English classical school. The tendency for a growing population to depress the earnings of ordinary people close to a minimum of subsistence—as explained in Chapter 4—was an integral part of the doctrine of the English classical economists. But by the end of the nineteenth century these views were largely discredited. In Europe, at least, births had been reduced by contraception, output per capita had been enormously increased by many remarkable inventions, and improvements in refrigeration and transportation had made it possible to import food from overseas. For half a century or more, economists tended to ignore population issues. In fact, it is only since World War II, when the economic development of backward areas became of prime concern, that the threat of overpopulation has again come under attention. Accordingly, in this section, three different theorems are set forth regarding the possibility that population growth limits increasing per capita incomes. The first is a brief statement of Malthus' position. The second, contributed by Dr. R. R. Nelson, concerns the possibility of low level consumption "traps" being created by population growth. And the third, by the author, in various respects combines these two approaches.

Malthusian population determinants

Malthus (see Chapter 4) was primarily concerned not with what would be an optimum population but in stating the forces that would determine population size. An underlying assumption was that, particularly among brutish peoples in lawless societies, birth rates would approach the biological maximum. Population growth would outpace extra food output because of diminishing returns. Hence death rates would adjust in the long run to the birth rates. The positive check of deaths caused indirectly by poverty would limit the maximum possible population. The consumption of ordinary people would always be near the minimum needed for existence. The few wealthy families of landlords and capitalists might increase their numbers, and incidentally do the economy's saving, but they were too small a minority to affect Malthus' theory of population.

A logical consequence of this view is that, in the absence of saving or innovations, the natural resources of a country determine the equilibrium population. Any additional population, because of diminishing returns, lowers individual consumption and occasions higher death rates. However, as there is ample evidence that national populations have grown slowly and regularly, it is clear that the aggregate consumption of ordinary working people does increase at least proportionately with their numbers. Malthus' fear was that as landlords obtained an ever-increasing income from rents, profits and interest rates would have to fall and the incentive to save and invest would diminish. Few people were optimistic enough to believe that useful innovations would be sufficient to prevent economic stagnation and a stationary population.

Malthus' only recommendation was that working class couples delay marriage and thereby postpone having children. He did not believe that continence within marriage was possible. And he was opposed to positive methods of contraception. Were he to know that birth control advocacy would for a while be termed "neo-Malthusianism" he would probably turn in his grave. Instead, he relied upon the desire of young people to better themselves materially, hoping this would cause late marriages and hence fewer births.

In many respects the Malthusian model—if it can be so described—was a very simple one. Like his contemporaries, he gave little attention to the possibility that the work hours of a given labor force might vary. This may have been because working hours were then almost at a maximum. Women too had little leisure, many already hiring themselves out to work in factories, the others being engaged in cottage industry or domestic chores. Under these conditions it was perhaps not unreasonable to suppose that total hours worked vary more or less in proportion to the size of the labor force.

Malthus did not relate savings rates to per capita output. He assumed a rigidly structured society divided into those who worked and those who owned, the former being incapable of saving. He did not foresee a classless society, having lessened income inequalities, and with a majority of the population consuming more than necessary for subsistence while a large minority have net savings. In this respect his "system" does not fit the advanced countries as we know them. But it is still a fair description of some of the poorest and most socially backward countries of today.

Population traps with low consumption

A conceptual step forward is to relate not only the death rate to per capita output—as Malthus tended to do—but also the savings rate. Expressed more simply, and assuming a constant population for the moment, a larger output is likely to result in fewer deaths and more savings. Fewer deaths, assuming the birth rate is unchanged, will cause population to increase somewhat. The larger output will occasion more savings, and this extra investment will in turn contribute to production. If one ignores diminishing returns to labor and capital (because of limited natural resources), a rather simple little model can be evolved in which per capita income is the independent variable and annual rate of population increase and production increase are the dependent variables.[2]

At any given per capita output (Y/P), there will be some proportionate change in annual income (dY/Y). And at a slightly higher Y/P, there will be rather more aggregate and individual saving and hence a higher dY/Y. At any given Y/P there will be a certain dP/P, and at a slightly higher Y/P there will be a slightly lower death rate and hence a larger dP/P. At some Y/P values, dY/Y exceeds dP/P, in which case Y/P will be higher next year. At some other Y/P values, dY/Y will be less than dP/P, and so Y/P will be less next year. By making various assumptions regarding the way in which the death rate varies inversely with Y/P and the savings rate varies positively with Y/P, it is possible to create various "trap" situations in which per capita output is held down to some level because population would otherwise increase too rapidly.

Fig. 18-1 illustrates the argument. The horizontal axis represents Y/P; the vertical axis, positive and negative proportionate changes. The "income" curves, y, y', and y'', show dY/Y as alternative functions of Y/P. The population curve, p, shows dP/P as a function of Y/P.

Consider first the relation between Curves y and p. They happen to intersect at a Y/P that renders both dY/Y and dP/P zero. But they might just as well have intersected at a point which indicated a positive rate of increase.

If Y/P were higher than T (designating a "trap") but lower than W,

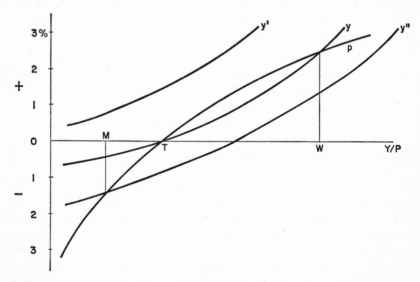

Fig. 18-1. Low Income Equilibrium Population Trap (neglecting diminishing returns).

[2] This has in fact been done by Dr. R. R. Nelson in "The Low-Level Equilibrium Population Trap," *American Economic Review*, December, 1956.

population would be increasing proportionately faster than income. Per capita income must then decline. Conversely, if Y/P were lower than TW, per capita income would rise. Hence TW is a sort of equilibrium trap. It can be escaped only if Y/P is for some reason greater than W, in which case dY/Y would exceed dP/P, and then Y/P could increase each year indefinitely.

The existence of this trap depends of course upon the position and slope of y and p, respectively. The income curve (y) rises more and more rapidly as it moves toward the right on the assumption that savings per head vary more than proportionately with income per head. The population curve (p) rises less and less rapidly as it moves toward the right on the assumption that deaths per head decrease less than proportionately with increases in income per head. All this assumes that returns on capital do not decline markedly as the capital stock increases and that birth rates do not decrease particularly with higher individual incomes.

However, accepting all these suppositions, it is possible of course that the income curve might be located after the manner of y'. Then the income curve never intersects the population curve and per capita incomes can apparently increase indefinitely. The low level equilibrium "trap" has not been escaped but avoided. Even though natural resources are limited, and no technical advances occur, such a relationship between the income and population functions asserts that there is no Malthusian problem.

Alternatively, the income function might be represented by y'', which intersects the p curve at a per capita income of M (designating misery perhaps). This is a stable Y/P. But rather amazingly it involves an equal rate of decline in population and output.

All three situations are theoretically possible. An upward shift in the income function might mean a higher savings rate at each and every per capita income or a higher incremental return on capital. A downward shift in the population function might be caused by an autonomous decline in birth rates at all per capita income levels.

This ingenious apparatus has one defect however. In some countries the ratio of *absolute* population and labor force to aggregate natural resources may be crucial. Changes in this relation may markedly affect incremental rates of returns on capital. It may not be true that a doubling of labor and a doubling of capital will double output. There may be diminishing returns to labor and capital because "land" is very scarce. Then the analysis cannot be conducted in terms of changes in Y/P alone: the absolute values of P and Y become important too.

Incidentally, this approach is not concerned with an excessive total population, but with a possibly excessive rate of population growth. In this sense the Nelson approach is always dynamic, whereas the Malthusian argument can become static. Fortunately, both approaches can be combined in such a way that the final outcome and its attainment can be perceived, the effect of income per capita on savings can be made explicit, and diminishing returns can be reintroduced into the argument.

Population and income and growth

Imagine a closed economy in which the state of the arts is unchanged for the time being. Birth rates are independent of per capita income. Death rates (d) vary inversely with Y/P. The rate at which income is saved (s) varies positively with changes in per capita income. There are limited natural resources that must be used more and more intensively as labor and capital increase. The labor force and total hours worked are deemed to bear a constant relation to population.

All the important interactions can be depicted in a single two-dimensional diagram such as Fig. 18-2. The horizontal axis represents population, P; or, it can alternatively represent labor (L), as labor is proportional to population. The vertical axis represents the capital stock per head of population, K/P, or, for the same reason, it can indicate K/L.

Consider a single curve such as $(Y/P)_1$. It is really an isoquant in that the value of Y/P is constant at every point on the curve. Because of diminishing returns to capital and labor, caused by limited natural re-

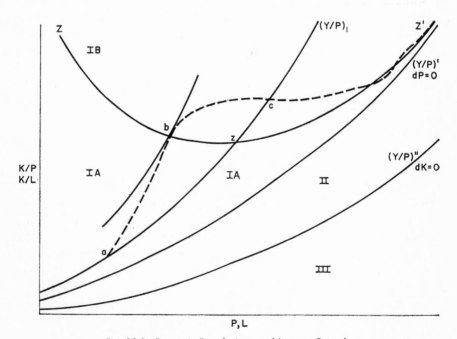

Fig. 18-2. Dynamic Populations and Income Growth.

sources, the $(Y/P)_1$ isoquant becomes positively inclined; that is, it takes a higher capital-to-population ratio in order to maintain a constant income per capita when population increases. Each isoquant has a specific Y/P label. Isoquants that are higher (in the sense that they involve a higher K/P for a given population) represent higher per capita incomes. Each isoquant also has a specific death rate (d) and savings rate (s) attached to it. Higher Y/P isoquants have smaller d values and larger s values.

Two isoquants have a rather special importance. One is $(Y/P)'$, for which the dependent death rate equals the independent birth rate so that population is neither increasing nor decreasing. The other crucial isoquant is $(Y/P)''$, for which the proportion of income that is saved is zero, so that the aggregate capital stock (K) is neither increasing nor decreasing.

$(Y/P)'$ involves a higher per capita income than $(Y/P)''$, and this is probably the most representative case for backward countries. In these areas the birth rates are very high. Death rates must be high if they are to equal the birth rates. Such high death rates must include many deaths from poverty. But there is considerable income inequality in poor countries also, and there can be positive saving by the rich, even though many poor people with no wealth to dissave are dying prematurely.

Suppose, in any specific period, a country is located somewhere in what is designated Zone II in the diagram. Zone II is characterized by a death rate that exceeds the birth rate (so that dP/P is negative) and a savings rate that exceeds zero (so that dK/K is positive). If population is decreasing and aggregate capital stock is increasing, the capital-to-population ratio must be increasing. Thus, in Zone II, any economy is "moving" to the left (smaller P) and upward (larger K/P). It must be achieving a higher Y/P. This will continue until the economy moves from Zone II into Zone I.[3]

Zone I, where P and K are both increasing, is the zone of real interest for economic development. This zone is divided into Zone IA (where Y/P is increasing) and Zone IB (where Y/P is decreasing). The two subzones are separated by a "zero improvement curve" designated ZZ'.

To understand why this is so, consider various points on a single isoquant $(Y/P)_1$, including Points a and z. At every point on this isoquant, saving per head is constant. In other words, the increment in capital

[3] Actually, the movement from Zone II into Zone I, across the $(Y/P)'$ boundary, must be straight upward as there is no population change when birth and death rates are equal. Movements in Zone III are not discussed here, as these situations are not very probable, and result in movements into Zone II and then Zone I anyway. These matters are discussed in S. Enke, "Population and Growth: A General Theorem," *Quarterly Journal of Economics,* 1963.

(dK) is proportional to P at every point on the curve. This follows from the fact that Y/P and s are constant for a given isoquant.[4]

However, if a given Y/P is to be maintained, a larger increment in K is needed for a given population increment when there is a large absolute population. Actual saving per head is constant throughout $(Y/P)_1$. But required savings per head—that is, the dK/P needed to maintain the same Y/P—is greater the further a point on $(Y/P)_1$ is from the origin. At Point z, where the zero improvement line ZZ' intersects the per capita income isoquant $(Y/P)_1$, the actual and required dK/P are equal. Nearer the origin—at a, for example—actual savings per capita exceed required savings per capita and income per capita increases. At c, on $(Y/P)_1$ but above ZZ', actual saving is less than required saving and Y/P is declining even though K and P are increasing absolutely.

Most—perhaps all—countries are in a Zone IA. Their population, absolute capital stock, stock per capita, and income per capita are all increasing. Thus if a country were located at a, it would move partly to the right (growing population) and partly upward (because higher Y/P isoquants can only be attained by moving upward if there is a rightward movement). Year by year, such an economy will move to higher income per capita isoquants (not shown in the diagram) until the zero improvement curve is encountered at, say b on ZZ'. From then on population will continue to grow, so a general rightward movement is maintained, but savings per head will be inadequate to sustain the b income per capita. There will be a movement to higher P values on lower Y/P isoquants.

In this way there will be an asymptotic movement toward that part of the ZZ' curve that is positively inclined and converging with the constant population isoquant $(Y/P)'$. A possible path of movement, from a through b and c, is shown by the broken line curve. Should some autonomous event occasion a discontinuous adjustment, so that an economy was "jolted" across ZZ'—but not $(Y/P)'$—income per capita would increase along with P and K/P until ZZ' was attained again at least.

The eventual destiny of an economy—assuming there are no "outside" changes in fertility, frugality, or technology of the kind discussed below —is a movement approaching ZZ' as the latter converges upon the zero population change isoquant $(Y/P)'$. In welfare terms, this means an ever slower decline in per capita income toward the level at which death rates equal birth rates. More and more people will be working with more and more capital per head. However, because of diminishing returns attributable to constant natural resources, the income per capita will be declining very slightly.

Is this the Malthusian prediction all over again? Yes and no. The

---

[4] Because $dK = s \cdot Y$, it also equals $s \cdot (Y/p) \cdot P$. But for any isoquant, Y/P is constant, and s has a unique value. So dK varies proportionately with P.

similarity is that, failing certain autonomous changes, an economy is destined for a declining per capita income, approaching, but never quite attaining that at which births equal deaths and population is stationary. The dissimilarities are two. The "destined" income per capita may be considerably in excess of the minimum necessary for subsistence, and population and capital continue to increase.

The analysis serves to underline the importance of less fertility. The definition of the zero population change isoquant $(Y/P)'$ is that the death rate equals the birth rate. If the birth rate is very low (because of contraceptive practices perhaps), the death rate must be low too. The only deaths may be attributable to causes *other* than poverty. So $(Y/P)'$ can be quite high if the autonomous birth rate is low. Malthus assumed a birth rate close to the biological maximum, so that death rates had to be high and include those attributable to poverty, but the high birth rate assumption is unnecessary under conditions today. A reduction in the birth rate, other things equal, means that a much higher per capita income isoquant becomes the $(Y/P)'$ isoquant. And $(Y/P)'$ is the income per head that is ultimately approached.

An increase in frugality, reflected by zero savings isoquant $(Y/P)''$ having a lower value, enlarges Zone II at the expense of Zone III. More important, if each isoquant has a higher s value than before, the zero improvement curve will shift upward and further away from the origin. This means an increase in the maximum per capita income attainable by a country now in Zone IA.

An advance in technology, if new innovations do not favor capital over labor or vice versa, will give each unchanged isoquant shape a higher income per capita value label than before. The zero improvement curve will also shift away from the origin. Interim and finally approached Y/P values will be higher and so provide more welfare.

In the real world, technological advances have usually prevented any declines in income per capita, despite large increases in population. And there are some who would argue—citing Japan perhaps as an example— that the very existence of a large population in a small geographic area may instigate useful innovations. However, for countries that still have very high birth rates, there is an obvious and alternative way to raise per capita incomes if their residents so desire.

OPTIMUM POPULATION NOTIONS

Quite distinct from the theorems which predict what populations and incomes will probably result are those that define what size of population is optimum. These notions regarding desirable population sizes also concern preferable birth rates. If population is supposedly supraoptimum, and death rates are determined without reference to development policy, then it follows that lower birth rates would be preferable.

There is not much agreement as to what constitutes an optimum population size. There are some who believe that, so long as at least some "decent" income is received by everyone, larger populations are desirable. This view may be based on the idea that national power and population are related—although in fact this is dubious. Or a large population may be the incidental outcome of the idea that children are a blessing, that the prevention of conception by unnatural means is a sin, or simply that more children make for happier homes. People who hold these latter views are likely to consider birth reduction practices selfish and materialistic where the objective is to increase income per head within an individual family. Nevertheless, among many economists, the notion that the best population is that which maximizes income per capita is an extremely prevalent one. It has been presented in varying degrees of simplicity and dogmatism. Three versions are described below.

Extreme static argument

The simplest theorem of all is that which identifies optimum population size with maximum income per head and treats the aggregate capital stock as an independent constant. Also, it is usually stated in static terms that ignore the effects upon income of transitions from one population size to another. This approach is presented first because it is probably the most familiar one.

In Fig. 18-3, the horizontal axis has number of persons as a unit of measurement, whereas that of the vertical axis is dollars. It is assumed that the effective labor supply is some constant fraction of population. There are two important "average" relations represented by the curves O'/L and Y/P. The O'/L curve indicates the value of output per worker produced by *labor* alone in the sense that the money value of this output is attributable to no other factor such as land or capital. The Y/P curve represents total national income—produced by land and capital as well as labor—divided by population and without any attempt to suggest how much income is attributable to one or another factor. If the effective labor supply is some constant fraction of population size— *e.g.*, one worker for every two people—these two average relations can be graphed according to different scales and compared. In this case, along the horizontal axis, one worker must be represented by the same linear distance as two persons, and along the vertical axis, one dollar of income per capita must be represented by the same distance as two dollars of output attributed to each worker.

Something must be assumed about the magnitude of capital's and land's contribution to total national output. The simplest supposition

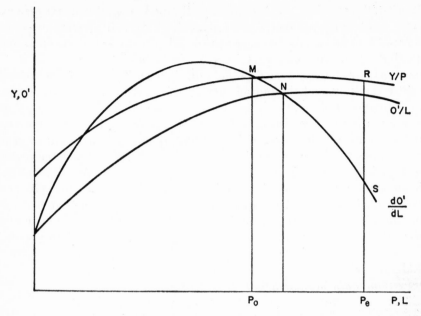

Fig. 18-3. "Optimum" Populations with Constant Capital.

is that this is constant and independent of population size and labor supply. (Of course this is not very realistic, for stock of capital depends upon the size of population, income per head, and the length of time an economy has been saving.) However, if this assumption is accepted for the moment, this means that output per capita attributable to capital and land is inversely proportional to population. Graphically, the Y/P and O'/L curves will slowly converge toward the right, but will never quite meet.

The third curve in the diagram—there marked dO'/dL—is the extra value output occasioned by an extra unit of labor. Mathematically, it is related to the average O'/L curve in such a way that the marginal value output curve (dO'/dL) must intersect the average value output curve at the latter's maximum value (N), and the two curves have a common value in the extreme case of one unit of labor being employed. But the population size associated with N is not optimum, although it does result in the maximum total output attributable to labor per head of population. For so long as capital and land are making a fixed contribution to output, this also means that total national output per capita will be larger with a slightly smaller population.

Maximum output per capita is P_o, associated with M, which marks the intersection of Y/P and dO'/dL (so long as the scales of the two axes have been adjusted for each curve as indicated above). In other words, at

P_o, dO'/dL equals Y/P. And, it is well worth remarking, dO'/dL exceeds O'/L. This means that it is better to have a little less output attributable to labor per worker in order to obtain rather more output attributable to capital and land per head of population. Maximum Y/P must occur at a smaller total population than maximum O'/L so long as L/P is constant and the output attributable to land and capital is also unchanging.

Why is it that the two average curves rise for a while with growing populations and then decline? A very small population, as all pioneer communities well know, can be most inefficient. Imagine a large region occupied by one family. It would hardly be able to afford roads into the homestead, the water supply would have to be from a nearby well, electricity might be out of the question. The school and medical facilities one family could support would be negligible. If more families live in the region they may find it worthwhile to organize public utilities and services. Social overhead capital can provide services only on a small scale at high unit costs. It is entirely possible for a region to have an uneconomically small population.

But against this is the fact that, especially in agriculture, more population may mean combining too much labor with natural resources in the sense that "direct" (or nonSOC) output per head is decreased. There is conceptually some happy balance between a population that is too large for maximum nonSOC output per capita and too small for maximum SOC output per capita. The optimum depends on the weighting of nonSOC and SOC consumption in the community. Poor countries depend heavily on food, hence upon agriculture, and generally on nonSOC activities. "Optimum" population depends on the consumption mix and hence on income per capita.

Reverting to Fig. 18-3, if the population were P_e and "excessive," SP_e would represent extra output occasioned by an extra person in the population, and RP_e would represent average production and hence average consumption in this closed economy. This means that a representative addition to population can be expected to consume his or her share of total available output (RP_e) but will cause an increase in production (SP_e) that is much smaller. So far as everyone else is concerned, this marginal person subtracts more in consumption than he adds through production. The rest of the population suffers a small loss in output per head. It is for this reason that some economists would consider any population excessive that results in a dO'/dL that is less than Y/P. And in some "overpopulated" countries of the world, although these magnitudes are hard to estimate in practice, the marginal product attributable to labor is probably less than half the average income per capita.

It may seem that this entire analysis is invalidated by the assumption that the quantity of land and capital combined with labor is constant But the determination of the optimum population may not be too vitiated by this unrealistic supposition. At optimum population, income per head is at a maximum, and so within any culture the accumulation of capital per capita is presumably at a maximum also. And the stock of natural resources is in fact constant anyway. This means that, at other than optimum population, Y/P may really be lower than illustrated and so even lower as compared with P_o. In a sense the "optimum" population is even better than the diagram indicates.

A more serious defect is that Fig. 18-3 illustrates a static case. It purports to show, for any given P value, an associated Y (the rectangle $P \times Y/P$) and an associated O' (the rectangle $O \times O'L$). This assumes that, for any P, the value of K (total capital stock) is constant; that is, the economy is in some sort of stationary state characterized by zero current saving.

Moreover, O' cannot be related uniquely to P, unless L/P is a constant. This means that the proportion of people too old or young to work and, in fact, the entire population age distribution, is a *datum*. This also means that crude birth and death rates are equal.

Accordingly, there are many difficulties of logic and definition involved in such a diagram, and it should be considered more of a schematic than anything else.

Subtraction of consumption vs. addition of output

The essential message of the above approach can be restated with less need for extreme and unrealistic assumptions. Several logical dangers can be circumvented if one considers a particular country with its existing population. This means that instead of trying to determine optimum absolute population at some timeless point along the horizontal axis, one determines the economic desirability or undesirability of extra population at this particular time.[5] Then the question becomes whether infants born during a given period are likely during their lives to produce more than they consume. Or will they have a negative value, so far as the existing population is concerned, by subtracting more as consumers than they add as producers?

Materialistically, ignoring parental pleasures and other psychic values, when are infants "worthwhile"? Some will die before they are old enough to work, so that they will have consumed during their lives and have been nothing but a loss to the population as a whole. Others may live a long time, and work many years, but their productivity may be low. This low productivity may not be the fault of these future workers, who

[5] Some of this increment might come from immigration, but here it is supposed that natural increase is alone responsible for population growth.

may apply themselves as industriously and capably as any others, but because there is too little land and capital to combine with them. The marginal product attributable to labor may be less than income per capita.

It is very difficult to estimate the net contribution of current infants to the output that will accrue in future to the now existing population. The stock of capital will be changing, for one thing, and the rate of accumulation will depend on income per head, so there is an interaction. The ratio of capital to labor will change over the next few decades because population is altering. This in turn will modify the marginal productivity of labor. The proportion of people who work may change slowly. There will be innovations. For all these reasons it is possible to estimate only very roughly the net economic contribution that current infants will make during their lives. However, there are some countries where the ratio of people to other factors is so obviously high, and the marginal product of labor compared with its average product so evidently low, that one can be sure that the net economic contribution of infants to the existing population will prove negative. Such countries can definitely be considered overpopulated.

Before continuing, one rather intangible element should be interjected, and that is the psychic value of children to their parents and older relatives. The analysis presented here is in terms of the incidence of infants upon the existing population. Part of that incidence is strictly economic— the additions to production and consumption that these "new" persons will make during their lifetimes—and this has now been explained in detail. A broader analysis might seek to give a monetary value to the psychic satisfaction that children may occasion their elders. Logically, this could be added to the value of their marginal production of ordinary goods and services. Alternatively (see Chapter 20), the psychic value of children to parents can be offset by their economic liability for the nation at large.

Resources for population or investment?

Any complete analysis of optimum birth rates must recognize that people represent a capital value that differs depending on their age and expectation of life. For the first fifteen years or so of life, a person is only a consumer and produces nothing of economic value. Then, unless death intervenes, most people produce more than they consume during the following thirty to forty years. Finally, if they survive their working years, there is a period until death when they are net consumers again. The capital value of a person too old to work—whatever his own financial assets may be—is negative. That of a person just old enough to enter the labor force may well be positive. What is the capital value in economic terms of a person at birth?

In order to estimate the present capital value of an infant at birth one might consider the future of typical boy and typical girl babies. For each of these, some estimate must be made of the value of their consumption for, say, each successive five-year period starting from infancy. Obviously, this will be low from 0–5 years of age, considerably higher from 30–35, and then low again from 70–75. The time shape of this future consumption stream might appear something like the *AC* (average consumption) curve in Fig. 18-4. In the same way, an estimate might be made for the expected contribution to output of typical boys in each successive period, beginning at 15–20 years of age. This contribution is the extra output that might be expected because of one person's addition to the population. The time shape of this future extra output stream could resemble the *MP* (marginal production) curve shown in the figure. (The output value of girl babies, when they mature, can be assessed in terms of the value of their services within the home.)

It may be wondered why the estimated consumption is average consumption while the estimated production is marginal production. A society does not discriminate among people working in any given occupation and pay each of them, according to the order in which they were hired, the marginal product he or she occasions. Within a subsistence agricultural family, each person of the same sex and age consumes about the same; but the product occasioned by any "marginal" family member to attain working age may be considerably less. Within any group of gainfully occupied persons, where no person is obviously more or less productive than another, there is no *identifiable* marginal worker. Ana-

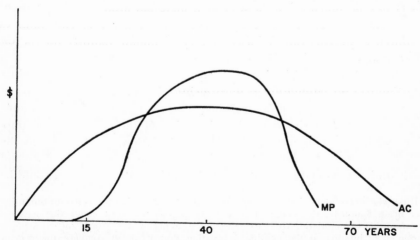

Fig. 18-4. Hypothetical Average Consumption and Marginal Product by Survivor's Age.

lytically, or in imagination, there is always a "last" or marginal person however.[6]

The *AC* and *MP* curves in Fig. 18-4 are supposedly for typical girl and boy babies. But the consumption and output of a male is rather different from that of a female, year by year, during their respective lives. So *AC* and *MP* must be representative of the sex distribution within successive age groups of the population.

Another complication is that humans are mortal at all ages. A typical infant will live fewer years than a substantial fraction of its contemporaries. And so estimates of *AC* and *MP* should be in terms of some representative group of infants born during a given period. If this "sample" is composed of 1000 infants, approximately half of whom are male and half female, the group becomes smaller year by year because of continual attrition. The *AC* and *MP* values for any age period thus represent the average consumption and marginal product of survivors only. (The curves in Fig. 18-4 have been smoothed so that discontinuous changes from one five-year period to another do not show.)

From what was written in the preceding subsection, it might seem that the "worth" of a new-born infant to the existing population is zero if the total areas under the *AC* and *MP* curves are the same. But this is so only if time preferences of economic societies are ignored. Then it does not matter that people consume for many years before they produce. Most poor countries have rather high time preferences—that is, consumption now is worth appreciably more psychically than the same consumption at a later date. Poor people usually have urgent wants with high marginal utilities. Poor countries are often comparatively short of capital, which accordingly has a rather high rate of return on cost when invested. For both these reasons it is unrealistic to ignore time preferences—as expressed in discount rates—in the case of underdeveloped countries. The "worth" of infants to the existing population in such countries is the present discounted value of their future marginal production minus the present value of their future average consumption.

In several poor and backward countries the sum of these two values may be negative at a discount rate such as 10 per cent per annum. In other words, at this rate of discount, the present value of the infants' future marginal production is less than that of their average consumption. If the discount rate used in such calculations corresponds to the rate of return upon extra real capital investment, which in any poor and truly underdeveloped country is probably at least 10 per cent, it could be

[6] For a closed economy that does not save, output per head must equal consumption per head. Similarly, the marginal product of population must equal the marginal consumption of population. It is when we are thinking of the "worth" of extra population (*i.e.*, infants) to the existing population that we must compare the average consumption with the marginal product of population.

said that infants having a negative present value are undesirable on economic grounds alone. The birth rate, whatever its level, is then too high
for the time being.[7]

For any given AC curve, combined with any given MP curve, there
will be some rate of discount that will give them present values that sum
algebraically to zero. This particular discount rate may in some instances
have a negative value. Such will be the case when, without any discounting, total average consumption exceeds total marginal production.

This special rate of discount—which equates the present values of
future AC and MP—might be termed the zero present value discount
rate. Logically, it should be compared with the discount rate that corresponds to the rate of return that can be earned on extra real capital investments. For example, if the zero present value discount rate is 0.04
and the discount rate obtainable on real investment is 0.10, then some or
all current infants are "undesirable." In extreme cases, where the zero
present value discount rate is negative, there can be no doubt about it.
The overpopulation of some countries may be that burdensome.

Very broadly speaking, an economy can invest in the production of
goods or population, the extra population occasioning extra production
later but extra consumption now. Rearing the future labor force constitutes an investment. Children must be fed and clothed, and educated if
possible, so that later they can produce in turn. In some high birth rate
countries, where roughly 40 per cent or more of the population is too
young to work, this annual unrecognized "investment" in future workers
exceeds the total net investment in factories and other forms of real
productive capital. It is certainly uneconomic to invest in population if
the rate of return on rearing extra people is much less than the rate of
return on extra physical plant, and if the psychic utility of children to
their own parents is ignored.

These ideas are restated graphically in Fig. 18-5. This diagram has
two parts. The left part shows alternative numbers of births for a particular country during, say, the next five years—reading from right to left
along the horizontal axis—and vertically it shows what the zero present
value discount rate will be for each alternative number of current births.
The right part of the diagram shows on the vertical scale the rate of return on capital that it is thought will prevail during the next decade or
so. Theoretically this will be determined by the intersection of loanable
fund demand and supply schedules—on the horizontal axis—during these
same decades.

[7] If the appropriate discount rate exceeds 10 per cent, it becomes relatively unimportant how approximately marginal product and average consumption have to be
estimated for periods 30 or more years in the future. For example, $1 worth of con-
sumption 30–35 years from now is today worth only about 2.5 cents, at 10 per cent
discount when compounded. And this is just as well for the analyst in view of the
uncertainties regarding technology and factor proportions so far ahead.

The optimum birth rate schematically is that which yields a zero present value discount rate equal to r_c in the diagram. And r_c is the discount rate corresponding to the rate of return on ordinary capital projects. This optimum birth rate is shown as B_o. But suppose the actual birth rate is B. This yields a zero present value discount rate of r_b on new births that is negative. And r_b is less than r_c. So the actual birth rate, in a narrow economic sense, is supraoptimum.

In the real world all these estimates are of course very hard to make. And so it is only cases of gross overpopulation and excessive birth rates that are likely to be distinguishable by statistical means. However, the essential principle is very clear, and it is that on economic grounds alone a country should invest in rearing population and accumulating physical capital so that the rate of return on each is similar. It makes no economic sense for a country to be simultaneously short of capital (*i.e.,* extra real investments earn a high return) and long on population (*i.e.,* extra infants earn a low or negative return). And yet that appears to be the situation of many poor and backward countries of today. These nations exemplify the need for cultural change if there is to be economic development.

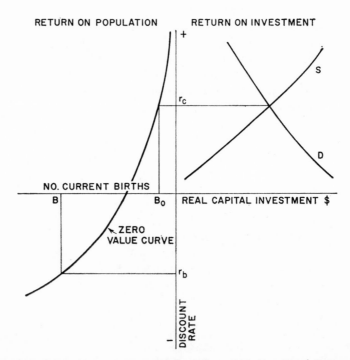

Fig. 18-5. Disequilibrium Between Resources Invested in New Populations and Rural Capital.

CONCLUSIONS

Enough has now been presented to indicate that, in many countries of the underdeveloped world, there are serious economic dangers arising from the natural tendency of population to grow too rapidly. As one noted economist has written:

In sum, population growth operates in four ways to retard the betterment of man's material condition. First, it increases the pressure of numbers upon a nation's land and resource equipment as of any given time. Second, it tends to accentuate this pressure through time by accelerating the rate at which the store of exhaustible and non-replaceable natural resources is used up and the costs of their use are increased. Third, it diminishes the rate at which capital can be accumulated, and this diminution is greatly accentuated when, as is the case in most overpopulated countries, much potential capital is utilized in maintaining for a few years children who eventually die before they reach a productive age. Fourth, given the rate of capital formation, the rate at which the equipment of the labor force can be increased is reduced.[8]

Because of recent advances in public health and attendant reductions in crude death rates, population is increasing most rapidly in the poorest countries. A doubling of population every 30-odd years, combined in many countries with diminishing returns on labor and capital, can only offset government programs to raise per capita incomes. And a great deal of foreign assistance, whether it takes the form of technical advice, capital advances, or food shipments, accomplishes little more than keep additional people alive at the same miserable consumption levels.

[8] J. J. Spengler, "The Population Obstacle to Economic Betterment," *American Economic Review, Papers and Proceedings,* May, 1951, 350, 351.

19

Population size
and labor hours

A great deal of theorizing by economists regarding population tends to assume that there is some more or less constant relation between population size and aggregate hours worked per time period. Over long periods of time, and population questions usually do concern changes over several decades, this may not be true. The fraction of population that is nominally in the labor force alters over time: falling birth rates lower the proportion of people too young to work, and female emancipation means more women working outside their homes. Moreover, the number of hours each individual works per week will vary depending upon his desire for money, his vitality, and wage rates available. However, for an economy, the extra output that is obtained by having a given population work more hours is not all net gain. One real cost that must be offset is the loss of leisure. Another real cost is that poorly nourished people cannot work more unless they have more and better food. Thus the real net gains from increasing the hours worked by a nation's people may be less than those occasioned by making them more effective workers, in the sense of accomplishing more per hour, through investments in education and health.

RATIO OF LABOR FORCE TO POPULATION

It is a tragedy of poor and overpopulated countries that a comparatively small fraction of their populations are of an age that places them in the labor force. General poverty results in higher death rates at almost all ages. Hence many children never survive to work, and many workers die while still otherwise productive. Society, partly as compensation, stresses fertility. And high birth rates result in over a third of the population being too young to work. Childbearing and rearing, in addition to other cultural inhibitions, prevent many adult women from taking useful employment outside the family. To be brief, too many consumers are being supported by too few producers, and low intake levels are the

result. The rather low ratios of labor force to total population, so typical of undeveloped countries, are both a cause and a consequence of
poverty.

Population dynamics are extremely complex. Here it is perhaps enough
to realize that the really fundamental factors, the ones that determine a
population's rate of growth and age distribution, are the birth and death
rates at each of several age groups. The so-called crude birth and death
rates—which are merely total annual births and deaths, respectively, per
thousand—provide rather superficial information.

Consider Fig. 19-1. It contrasts, for a hypothetical advanced country on
the left and a backward country on the right, two representative age distributions. The horizontal distances represent percentages of total population. The vertical distances represent age in years. The total enclosed
areas are the same for both countries.

It will be noted that the backward country has a broad base, with
many children of under five years of age relative to the number of people
from, say, 15 to 40 years of age, and this of course reflects the high fertility rates of those of childbearing age. On the other hand, the advanced
country's age distribution profile has a comparatively thick trunk with a
rather stubby top, indicative of low death rates until people are past their
prime of life. Wealthier countries benefit by having more of their infants
live to become productive members of the labor force and by having more

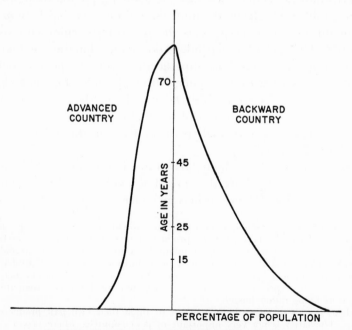

Fig. 19-1. Hypothetical Age Distribution (exaggerated).

adolescents survive the usual span of working years. However, as every-one must die eventually, death rates are considerable at older age brackets among advanced countries.[1]

There is sometimes a confusion as to whether the high percentage of people under 15 years of age in poor countries is primarily due to high death rates from birth to 15 years or to high fertility rates among women 15 to 40 years of age. Arithmetically, in a perfectly stable population (*i.e.*, a constant population over time at each age), the larger ratio of under 15's to over 15's in poorer countries might superficially be "ex-plained" by higher death rates among children. But it is mothers who bear children, and not children who produce mothers, and one must be careful about chronological sequences. The number of children born during a given period is determined by the number and fertility of adult potential mothers alive during that same period. Of course the number of fertile women alive now is partly attributable to past death rates among female children, but the ratio of very young children to parents of childbearing age reflects fertility rates.

The age distribution of a population is economically important be-cause it is a major determinant of the ratio of dependents to nonde-pendents.[2] Children under 15 years of age are normally dependents. So are most men and women over 55 or so in backward countries and over 65 or so in more advanced ones. The great problem of the more under-developed countries is that they have too many people too young to work. A minor problem of advanced countries, and one that has become more apparent during recent decades, is the number of senior citizens (and especially widows) who are dependent on savings, families, or taxpayers.

A partial offset, and one that superficially favors the poorer countries, is that children start working sooner. Although under 15, when children in wealthier countries would still be in school, they may be herding goats or frightening baboons out of the maize. But the opportunity cost of lost education is a very high price to pay for this relatively unim-portant kind of "work."

Another consequence of high birth rates is that married women are often unable to work. Either they are about to have a child or are rear-ing younger children. Hence, unless an older sister can be recruited for

[1] The "expected life" at birth is obtained by multiplying the probability of surviving successfully older age brackets until the product of these multiplications has fallen to 0.5. Of course this assumes that for an infant born today, death rates at older ages will not alter from what they have been. This is unrealistic in view of present public health measures in many backward countries. Thus an Egyptian infant may statis-tically have a life expectancy of, say, 35 years, but an insurance company could gamble on its living rather longer.

[2] Dependent, that is to say, either on others or upon their own past productive con-tributions. The latter is not very important in poor countries where people's savings are small. Hence older people there look to their children as old age providers.

supervision, youngsters are a serious drain on adult time and effort when there is no family planning. Nevertheless, when opportunity permits, "housewives" also labor in the fields according to the season, and sometimes participate in trading activities. One advantage of agriculture, and rural living in general, is that women can alternate more readily during the day between productive labor and homemaking chores.

One of the continuing revolutions of the twentieth century has been the taking of paid work by women. Previously there were almost no industrial jobs for women, except in textiles. Outside work was usually in other people's homes as cooks, maids, and governesses. There were probably more men than women employed as office clerks and secretaries, even in North America, prior to 1900. But two world wars have altered social attitudes in Western countries. For example, women banktellers are now commonplace, the electronics industry is "manned" largely with women, and female bartenders are not unknown. Women have come out of the home, except for a few deliberate confinements, to a degree that is extraordinary in comparison with less developed countries.

In Africa and Asia, domestic servants are more often men than women. There are more male than female school teachers in all countries save the most advanced ones. And except for a few "westernized" women of the more prosperous urban families, women escape domestic discipline and home chores only through marriage. Often this is the sole way that the virginity of young girls can be ensured. No African family, with prospects of receiving *lobola* for its daughters, is going to have them leave home "unmarried" and run the risk of being "damaged" prematurely. An Asian marriage broker is interested in representing girls who have been properly raised and guarded. And in Latin America, where most women have far more emancipation, traditional Spanish and Portuguese views still prevail among certain classes regarding proper chaperonage.

Moreover, once a married woman has borne her children, it is most unusual for her to go "out" to work. Homemaking is her only acknowledged profession. There is almost no divorce except in Arab countries and among Moslems elsewhere. Widowed women return to their families or seek the protection of a son or brother-in-law. Except in the Western world, remarriage of widows is not approved, but fortunately they do not outlive their men by so many years as in the United States.

These attitudes are all disappearing to some extent, but cultural changes of this sort do not occur suddenly, without revolution or war, and so for several decades at least it is unlikely that women will comprise more than a small fraction of the *hired* labor force. Urbanization is of course one slow but steady trend that occasions female emancipation. There are more available jobs for women in towns. Higher specific costs of children may encourage birth control practices that permit young wives to defer children and work longer. More urban women are also likely to have an education that trains them for paid employment. Of course outside paid work by women is not all a net economic gain, despite the conventions of national income accounting.

Nevertheless, one remaining feature of backward countries is that too few of the population are really effective members of the labor force, either because they are too young or because they are female. A reduction in birth rates would reduce the proportion of very young. And a change in social attitudes, combined with urbanization, is likely to place more women in outside employment. Both changes will revolutionize the traditional way of life of men and women, and the men especially will dislike these social adjustments of economic development, but "westernization" has its price and insists on payment.

HOURS OF WORK AND MOTIVATION

A man may be nominally in the labor force, but he may not work many hours a day or year, and he may not exert himself very much when he does. Could many gainfully employed persons in underdeveloped countries work longer and harder? Why don't they?

Inadequate employment opportunities

It is commonly held that much of the failure of men to labor harder and longer in poor and backward countries is because they cannot find gainful employment. These men presumably have no choice. They have no land or capital of their own with which they can combine their labor, so they must find work. But employers supposedly lack enough capital and natural resources to hire any more workers. These situations are most likely to occur in countries where the land is owned by a few families, where tenancy rights are by custom handed down from father to son, and the rich who save are banking abroad rather than investing in domestic industry.

The real situation is seldom quite so desperate, though. Most men at least have distant relatives who cultivate land as owners or tenants, and the obligations of consanguinity extend far in most uneconomic cultures, so that rural underemployment is more likely than unemployment. Some peasant families hire outsiders. It is very seldom that extra hours of work have no product at all times of year in agriculture.

So the real choice is often between various degrees of rural underemployment and urban unemployment. The distinction is often not very profound. In the city, a man may have to wait months for a few weeks' work, or a whole day for an odd job lasting an hour. In rural agriculture, he may have real work only during certain seasons, with a few hours a day at other times. Given seasonal peaks, there is likely to be some annual migration between country and city, and much of this internal movement has a real economic rationale.

Towns have certain well-understood financial advantages and disadvantages to rural people. One advantage is that work, if it can be obtained, usually pays more per hour than a man would get from an hour
of work on the family holding. Industrial jobs often pay relatively well.
Minimum rates may be established by law. Or wages may have been
raised through labor organizations. The possibility of getting such work
will often maintain a pool of underemployed in or near the towns. Another consideration is that a man who is away from his parents' extended
family may be able to keep most of his earnings for his own enjoyment;
after a few years, filial piety concerning home remittances may weaken.
Hence an hour of portering in the town may bring to the individual
as much as a day's hoeing on the land, and with far less disutility. A
serious disadvantage, on the other hand, is that living in town involves
many unavoidable and specific money expenses. It is more difficult to
have one's wife and children with one. So many young men, after the
novelty and excitement of the city have begun to pall, return permanently to their rural villages.

The real question about this customary pattern of employment, or perhaps underemployment, is whether and how it is uneconomic. If there is
involuntary urban unemployment, in the sense that at current wage rates
there are fewer jobs than qualified work seekers, then wages are too high.
If men prefer occasional and petty jobs in town to more productive work
in family agriculture because the real output of the latter must be shared
among many relatives, the extended family is an uneconomic institution.

On the other hand, if a man refuses to work more because the disutility of so doing is greater than his enjoyment of the extra he produces, his underemployment is economic. Undernourished and diseased
people may find it very hard to work for more than a few hours daily.
Given these circumstances, there can be no improvement in well-being
without an increase in capital, a decrease in population, or an improvement in the state of arts.

However, in not a few countries, there is evidence to suggest that some
rural underemployment and urban unemployment are man-made. Legal
wage minimums in industry are often to blame. Traditional sharing of output within peasant families reduces personal incentives to produce more.
In such situations there is economic waste because the rural areas are
clinging to a past culture and the urban regions are aping modern
occidental institutions. This combination of old and new can be especially unfortunate for an economy.

Backward sloping labor supply schedules

A frequent complaint, heard especially during colonial days, was that
the natives worked less if one paid them more. In politically independent
countries the same phenomenon is occasionally encountered. Subsistence

cultivators, for example, may supply less food grain to neighboring towns when prices for grain rise. If the wages of a father increase, perhaps some of his children will quit odd jobs, their earnings no longer being so necessary to the family. Why does this occasionally happen? Is such behavior undesirable or irrational in some sense?

At the outset, it is necessary to distinguish between the labor an individual will supply at different rates of remuneration and the labor a whole community will supply if hourly wage rates are raised. A single firm, hiring from a fairly large labor market, can nearly always persuade more people to apply to it for jobs by raising wages. Many workers will be diverted from other occupations. Hence the price system—i.e., relative wage rates—can usually be counted upon to allocate labor among different jobs and employers. But it does not follow that the working people of an area will offer more hours of effective work if *all* employers raise wages together. And an individual worker may offer less real labor if he receives more pay per hour or piece from his employer.

Most work, especially if repetitive and requiring exertion and discomfort, involves considerable disutility. No sensible person will work under such circumstances more than he "must." If the results of extra work have little value to a man, why should he work more, unless he has been reared in a Puritan culture that considers leisure somehow immoral?

Superficially, one would think that poor people would be especially eager to earn more, for lack of money income is commonly considered the essence of poverty. In towns this is more often so, for money wages can there be turned into better clothing and shelter, more entertainment and education, even into travel and financial security later. But this is not true of peasants, who are primarily subsistence cultivators. Extra output may be perishable and so cannot be stored. The peasant may know nothing about savings accounts, and paper money seems to lose its purchasing power all the time. The only general store in the area may carry a very limited line of goods. The way of life in the country renders many "city" goods relatively useless anyway. Once the peasant has enough to feed the family for the year, pay his taxes and his debts, and make a few improvements to his holding, extra money earnings mean less than Westerners subjected to advertising might suppose.

Many families in underdeveloped countries are partly in the subsistence economy and partly in the money-market economy. Their main support may come directly from their land cultivation. But other needs must be met with money and so are satisfied indirectly by taking paid employment. If wages for this "outside" work are increased sharply, and family wants do not change, an "outside" employer may find that his laborers report for work fewer days a week. This is especially true if his jobs are considered socially inferior—e.g., field labor cutting sugar cane— as workers will take other jobs first: they will only work for him enough to bring their total earnings to some necessary level. Thus it is that many an employer has found that he gets fewer hours of work when he raises hourly wage rates, particularly if there are no other paid jobs in the area.

The logic of why an individual worker may want to work fewer hours, when paid more per hour in money or in kind, can be explained in terms of ordinal utility. Each successive hour of work involves some disutility, and the fifth hour probably is more unpleasant than the fourth; every increment in purchasing power used for consumption provides some utility, but probably less and less. Hence the compensation that any worker requires just to induce him to work an extra hour—and leave him on the same welfare curve—involves a balancing of the extra disutility and the extra consumption utility occasioned by that hour's labor. But the extra consumption utility will depend upon the purchasing power already earned by intramarginal hours worked. If these "previous" hours were well paid, the less utility an incremental unit of purchasing power will provide, and the greater the necessary compensation to make the marginal hour a matter of indifference.

Suppose a man previously chose to work eight hours a day, at 25 cents an hour, and that his pay is now doubled to 50 cents an hour. As money still buys what it did before (assume prices unchanged) he will certainly want to earn more than \$2 a day at the higher wage rate. But he will want to work more or less than eight hours depending upon whether or not the fourth dollar a day has more or less than half the utility in consumption as the second dollar formerly had.

This is illustrated in Fig. 19-2, which represents hours along the horizontal axis, and money or real wage rates on the vertical. The W_2 line represents the 50 cents an hour rate and the W_1 line the 25 cents an hour rate. The D curves show the compensation needed at the margin to make one more hour of work indifferent. Thus at H_2 hours, the last hour must pay BH_2 if the worker has already earned $OH_2 \cdot H_2B$. And the H_1 hour, involving the more disutility, must pay AH_1 if the going wage has been at the lower rate of W_1 and accumulated earnings are so far $OH_1 \cdot H_1A$. In the diagram, H_2 at W_2 means less work than H_1 at W_1, but it is not necessary that higher wages evoke fewer hours.

When people earn more, initially they may buy more of the same sorts of things as before, but sooner or later they will try other goods and services. Eventually they will come to consider as "necessities" what once were thought to be "luxuries." The new and higher level of consumption becomes the "standard" of living. Poor people are often most conservative in their sumptuary habits during the short run. But over long periods people find their objects of desire are continually altering, and that their wants are almost insatiable.

Incidentally, so far as an entire community is concerned, economists should not worry if it has a backward sloping labor supply schedule over

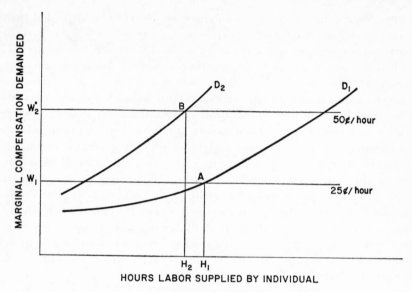

Fig. 19-2. Increased Labor Supply with Lower Wage Rates.

the long run. As real incomes per head of population increase, one would expect increased national productivity to be enjoyed partly as extra consumption, but also through extra leisure. It must never be forgotten that development is for man and not man for development.

Increasing work incentives

Governments can do much, negatively and positively, to increase the value of extra money earnings to ordinary people.

In rural areas, the establishment of stores can be an enormous incentive for people to farm for cash or work for pay. These general stores do not have to carry many lines, and the merchandise stocked must be inexpensive in price, for no other kind of retail operation could survive financially: but the quality of goods cannot be cheap, for backward and poor natives are shrewd buyers of merchandise. Thus public subsidies of store operators in remoter locations deserve serious consideration. One result might be the end of usury. But the main objective would be penetration of the subsistence economy by providing something useful that money can buy locally.

In urban areas a wider variety of consumer goods, at prices that most can afford, is an important way to stimulate work and productivity. Hence import restrictions on consumer goods that are within the means of a majority of households can be a serious handicap to development if comparable goods are not produced domestically. Many items that officials view as "luxuries" might in fact be purchased in volume if available. Their absence from the stores is a deterrent to work. Thus it is that inflation, because it leads to exchange control and limited sumptuary imports, is again to be avoided.

Many households would work to save if more of their savings could be safe. In time, economic security might increasingly come from owning liquid assets, rather than having many sons. But the most liquid assets— *e.g.*, savings accounts—are the most vulnerable to inflation. And peasants and coolies understand little of security markets and corporate stocks. Hence the provision of investment objects for small savers, safe from inflation, is another need (as previously explained).

Finally, mention should be made of advertising, the bane and boon of materialistic societies. Making people want things they cannot now quite afford is one of the most powerful ways known to make people work harder and more. People do not hanker for things they hardly know exist. And competitive consumption, of the "keeping up with the Joneses" variety, is partly a symptom of "successful" advertising. Of course there is no use in advertising motor cars to hungry people, but suits can be advertised to men already buying trousers, and there are always many goods and services that are marginal items for purchase. Hence it may not be entirely fanciful to suggest that government should subsidize certain advertising media. The resources so used may be more than offset through a larger supply of effective labor.

The majority of gainfully employed people in backward countries are working for themselves or their families. But the number of paid workers is steadily increasing. Most urban employment is of this kind. The question then arises as to whether these hired workers should be paid by the task, the hour, or the piece. If a task such as skinning so many slaughtered livestock is set, an employee more or less completes it at his own pace, and not much supervision is needed. If pay is by the hour, the employee works as little as he can without jeopardizing his job, and considerable supervision is needed. In neither case, except for the negative fear of dismissal, is there any real incentive to work harder and faster. The positive inducements are the other way.

Government might encourage, or even require, payment by the piece in certain industries. This would be particularly economical where each employee works with capital of considerable value. Employees, in working slowly, often waste some of the potential services of plant and equipment. This is true especially when real capital depreciates as a function of time rather than use. Capital-poor countries can least afford to combine lackadaisical workers with scarce factories and machinery. This is realized by many entrepreneurs, who for reasons of their own favor piece work, but most unions prefer time rates and governments have tended to also.

A last thought, but an important one, is that extra work is more likely to command substantial additional utilities if institutions exist that encourage trade and specialization. There is a limit to the extent that a family can enjoy more of the things it can make for itself. Division of labor is not only more efficient, it also makes a greater variety of consumer gooods available. Thus anything that inhibits internal or external trade of goods and services also tends to inhibit human economic effort.

HUMAN ENERGY AND HOURS WORKED

The classical economists were very conscious of the fact that extra output by working class people did not necessarily provide a net gain in available goods and services. Where employment calls for muscular exertion, extra output requires extra energy, and extra human effort requires a larger calorie intake. Some of the extra output is hence a cost of production and not a net gain in real income. This is particularly true of backward economies. The GNP of their national accounts includes essential food that perhaps should be deducted.

This relation between food intake and work output has tended to be forgotten in advanced countries, where a great deal of daily "work" is done sitting down, but human metabolism is the same as ever. So just as a Gaucho gives his horse some fodder before wrangling cattle, some employers still find it advantageous to give their workers extra food rations if they are performing heavy physical labor. The German government during World War II, at certain coal mines in the Ruhr Valley, discovered that output per worker per shift could be increased from 7 tons to 10 tons by providing 800 more calories on the daily ration. Today, in some mines in Africa and Latin America, workers are given free issues of bread and highly sweetened cocoa before going on shift.

There is a close physiological relation between calorie intake and energy output. A small-framed man, at complete rest in a warm climate, loses about 1400 heat calories a day. This is his basic metabolism requirement. He cannot perform much work over many weeks without more calories or without losing weight continuously. Any fewer calories will eventually result in his losing no heat at all!

Economically, a human worker is a complicated apparatus of unalterable design, having a calorie intake and an energy output. His performance function suffers from a grave discontinuity. A food intake just sufficient to meet basic metabolism needs would result in no prolonged and useful work. Hence the value of a worker's output, per unit of food or calorie intake, tends to increase as he eats and works more.

The following estimates of daily calorie requirements for a 70 kg adult man makes the point more definitely.

8 hours sleeping (at 65 cal/hr)	520 calories
10 hours sitting and talking (at 100 cal/hr)	1000 calories
2 hours walking (at 170 cal/hr)	340 calories
4 hours working (at 300 cal/hr)	1200 calories
Total	3060 calories

(Of course calories per hour of work depend on the job, carpentering requiring perhaps 240 calories an hour and felling trees perhaps 400 per hour.) The point is that if this man received just enough food for four hours of work as in the example, the calorie cost per work hour would be 3060/4 or 765. If he received enough food to work eight full hours—only sitting and talking for six instead of ten hours—the calorie cost per hour worked would be 3860/8 or 482.5. In other words, because of the considerable calorie cost of *existing*, the marginal calorie cost of an hour's work (*i.e.*, 200 calories) is much less than its average cost.

For most people in underdeveloped countries there is no need for Metrecal. Most of the work requires considerable physical effort. There is little electric power and few internal combustion engines to assist ordinary laborers with mechanical energy. The food supply tends to be spread among too many people, each needing a certain minimum to remain alive, and so the possible labor output in hours worked is less than it otherwise could be. It is conceivable, in countries where total food availability is comparatively fixed, that a smaller population might be able to work more hours in the aggregate.

Western writers are forever commenting upon the listless attitudes and widespread underemployment to be observed in most rural areas of the underdeveloped world. And yet *mañana*, when really analyzed, may be another name for undernourishment and debility. Given diminishing returns and existing technology, why should a man cultivate an extra hour if this results in less food output than the extra calories he thereby uses? Under these circumstances, maximizing personal well-being may mean maximizing leisure time rather than output. The man who has arrived is the man who has arranged his affairs so that he can spend the day talking with his friends and relatives under the shade of some tree. And until improved technology and extra capital make an hour of work more productive, there is little reason why he should alter his attitude to labor. Hence a major requirement of economic development, as it were, is to bring to life this vast potential labor supply.

20

Government measures
to reduce births

If the expected number of current births is deemed to be uneconomic and excessive—which is practically another way of saying a
country is overpopulated—there are broadly three ways in which the
situation can be improved. The crudest way is probably for government
to adopt one or more policies to reduce the birth rate. However, in many
countries this runs counter to the beliefs of the dominant religion, and in
most instances there are other alternatives. One way is to weaken various
cultural and institutional inhibitions on the amount and kind of work
that people perform: for example, in many countries women are not
supposed to work outside the family home or farm, and communal practices may encourage underemployment among men. Still another way,
and perhaps the most important of all, is not to limit the quantity of
population but to improve its quality: through public health and education, the younger generation of today can become much more productive than their parents. These two alternative ways of treating the
problem of overpopulation are discussed in the two chapters that follow.
In this chapter possible government measures to reduce births will be
considered.

THE VALUE OF PERMANENTLY PREVENTING
A BIRTH

A first essential for any government is some determination of the economic importance of reducing the birth rate. What is the "worth" of
reducing births—not just for a year but forever—to the people of a
country? If this can be assessed it is possible for government, acting as an
agent of the community at large, to decide how much it can spend in the
way of resources in order to reduce the birth rate.

The analysis in Chapter 18 indicated how such an assessment can be
undertaken. If the average consumption and marginal production curves
can be estimated for a typical sample of infants, and the rate of return on

capital is known, the present discounted value of an infant can be estimated. If this value proves to be negative, a reduction in current births is economically desirable, and this negative value suggests how much government can afford to prevent a birth permanently.

An example of the sort of calculations involved is provided by Table 20-1. It is believed to be representative of conditions in some undeveloped countries and is based on the future consumption and production of 1000 representative infants. Column 1 defines age groups. Column 2 gives the expected number of survivors at the middle of each age bracket. Column 3 suggests the average annual cost to the economy by age groups of each person for food, shelter, clothing, social services, and so on. Column 4 shows the assumed annual marginal product by age bracket per survivor. Column 5 gives the per capita aggregate excess of average consumption over marginal product—nearly always negative—by age intervals: it is Column 4 minus Column 3, all multiplied by Column 2 and divided by 1000. Column 6 is the compounded discount factor, at 10 per cent a year, taken at the middle of the age bracket. Column 7 is the product of Columns 5 and 6 times the number of years in the interval. Aggregating Column 7 indicates the estimated present discounted value of a representative infant. This total has a negative value. Under these assumptions it is worth approximately $127 to prevent a birth permanently.

However, this understates the importance of reducing births, because second-generation effects have been ignored. Female infants born today will be having their own children in 20 years' time. The consumption of these second-generation children has been excluded from the calculation;

Table 20-1

ESTIMATED FUTURE CONSUMPTION AND MARGINAL PRODUCT OF 1000
REPRESENTATIVE LIVE BIRTHS DISCOUNTED TO PRESENT VALUES

(Infant Mortality Rate 200/1000)

(1) Age bracket	(2) Survivors from 1000	(3) Annual consumption per head	(4) Annual individual marginal product per head	(5) Annual net contribution per head	(6) Discount weight for bracket mid-year	(7) Total present discounted value per head
0–1	900	$ 5	$ 0	− 4.5	.950	− 4.3
1–5	733	20	0	−14.7	.929	−54.5
5–10	652	30	0	−19.6	.353	−34.5
10–15	630	40	10	−18.9	.218	−20.6
15–20	610	50	25	−15.3	.122	− 9.3
20–25	583	60	45	− 8.7	.072	− 3.1
25–30	551	65	60	− 2.8	.043	− 0.6
30–35	515	70	70	0	.025	0
						−126.9

and their eventual production, because of compound discounting over 35 years and more, is of almost zero present consequence.

There are three main reasons why the present value of an infant is negative. First, it is average consumption and marginal product that are being compared. Second, consumption starts soon after birth (and so is discounted less), while production begins after about 15 years of age (and so is discounted more). Also, over a third of all infants die before they are old enough to work. These three forces, for reasons explained later, are apt to operate less strongly in advanced countries.

The estimated value of $127 for permanently preventing one birth may not seem very large by advanced country standards. It must be remembered, though, that the per capita annual income of many of the poorest countries is around $100. Thus the worth of preventing a birth may be equivalent to about 15 months' income per head. This probably approximates the situation in India, Egypt, and certain of the Caribbean islands. In some ways this ratio of the value of preventing a birth to income per capita may be the most significant way of assessing the degree of overpopulation.

The fact that a country has a high crude rate of population increase does not necessarily mean that it should seek to reduce births. Today the United States is experiencing population increases of over 1 per cent a year. Would it not be desirable that some of the more prosperous countries, with their rapidly growing populations, also adopt birth reduction policies? In some cases this may be so. But certain differences should be noted.

First, although crude birth rates *minus* crude death rates may not differ so markedly as between several advanced and backward countries, underdeveloped countries (as noted in Chapter 2), typically have higher birth rates and death rates than advanced countries do. Thus an advanced country might have birth and death rates of 28 and 13 per thousand a year, respectively, and a backward country 40 and 20, respectively. The proportion of any population that is too young to work—and so a drain upon resources for the time being—varies with the birth rate. The relative share of gross national product devoted to rearing children can be reduced by decreasing the birth rate. So the absolute value of the birth rate is important in itself.

Second, the ratio of labor to available capital and natural resources is not so high in the advanced countries, and hence there are less serious diminishing returns to labor as evidenced by a lower ratio of marginal product to average product attributable to labor.

Third, the life expectancies of people at the age that they can become usefully occupied tends to be greater in advanced countries despite the fact that useful employment may be postponed a few years for extra schooling.

Fourth, insofar as time preferences are less urgent where poverty is rare, discount rates may tend to be lower in advanced countries. This means that future output of current infants has a proportionately higher present value. This offsets some of the more immediate consumption of new-born children.

Fifth, even though infants in some advanced countries may have a negative present discounted value, it is perhaps not the absolute magnitude of this value that really matters. For any society, children are a source of pleasure, and the choice between children and consumer goods probably varies with family income. Suppose the present value of an infant is −$500 in an advanced country and −$125 in a backward one. However, income per head may be $2,500 a year in the advanced country and only $100 in the backward one. The more significant comparison may be that the value of permanently preventing a birth is 0.2 times the annual income per capita in the advanced nation and 1.25 times yearly income per head in the backward country.

Whether a government or people attempts to reduce the birth rate will depend on many factors. The relative economic burden of new-born children may well be one of them. Should a government decide to adopt birth reduction policies, it will need to know the value to the economy of permanently preventing a birth. In some undeveloped countries this may be on the order of $125. What government programs can then be afforded that will also be effective?

CUSTOMARY MOTIVES FOR MANY CHILDREN

Before this question can be answered, it is important to ascertain why most people in these poor and overpopulated countries do not now have fewer children than they do. Is it because they don't want to have smaller families? Or is it because they don't know how to have smaller families? In other words, is the problem primarily one of unwillingness or of inability to reduce births, is it one of motivation or method?

More definite information is needed on this point. There is little use in developing a contraceptive pill and distributing it free if rural women won't swallow it. It is also important to realize that whether families want more or fewer children is often determined by the culture in which they live. "Rational" economic motives may be overshadowed by religious beliefs or custom. To these people social conformity may be more important than material consumption.

There is considerable evidence to suggest that among rural peoples, who constitute more than one-half of the underdeveloped world, families are more unwilling than unable to have fewer children.

For one thing, among quite primitive tribes, there are many instances of successful birth control having been practiced in the past. Among some Central African tribes it was customary—before colonialism, when tribal wars were prevalent—for a woman not to have another baby until her youngest child was old enough to run: in this way she would not be encumbered with two children in the event of an enemy raid. Among the aborigines in northwest Australia, a very dry and desolate land offering little subsistence, a woman could not, upon pain of death, deliver a live child without permission of the local chief; such permission was usually granted only upon the death of someone in the tribe, and in this way the total size of the roving group was strictly controlled through contraception, abortion, and sometimes infanticide.

Where custom was definite and punishment severe there seems to have been a marked ability to prevent live births. The various methods are all hundreds if not thousands of years old. Among some African tribes men might not have intercourse with their wives while they were still nursing the latest baby. The Bible refers to the practice of interrupting coitus as a means of preventing conception. Among primitive people, and especially where women have a low status, various herbal and surgical means of abortion are familiar. And as a last recourse, especially in China until modern times, there was infanticide. The rather prevalent view that birth control is somehow an invention of the last century—a belief prompted by the innovation of new contraceptives—is quite fallacious.

As a general rule, and despite occasional special instances such as those mentioned above, incentives to have more rather than fewer babies seem to dominate poor and rural people. Some of these reasons are sound. They need to be understood.

Most families wish to perpetuate themselves. Parents want children who will later give them grandchildren. But if infant mortality is very high, and death rates among children are appreciable, a man and woman must have four or more infants to achieve this goal. For this reason, in many cultures it became customary to have large families. Nowadays, with death rates declining throughout the world, fewer children need to be born in order to perpetuate a family line. But it may take a generation or so before this is widely recognized. Birth rates may eventually follow death rates to lower levels. The crude rate of natural increase meanwhile is from 1 to 3 per cent a year depending upon the country.

Some form of extended family system prevails in most underdeveloped countries. The babies that men and women are now procreating will usually prove to be an economic asset to their parents when these parents have become too old and weak to support themselves. Peasants need sons who will tend the cattle and work the fields when they grow strong enough. In sub-Sahara Africa men pay a bride price to purchase a wife, hence girl babies have a future market value, and available statistics suggest that in this area girls have a lower death rate relative to boys than is usually true of primitive peoples. Moreover, within an extended family, newly married couples usually live with one or the other's parents; hence their babies and young children are not a direct economic burden upon them. In short, children are an immediate liability to the grandparents and are a future asset to the young parents, and so there is a real economic incentive for the latter to have as many children as possible. The parents gain in a narrow sense, but society loses in a broader sense, for someone must bear the cost of infants[1]

Special reasons for having large families prevail from country to country. Some religions require that a man's son perform certain services upon the father's death. For instance, in order to permit the spirit to depart, perhaps the dead man's skull must be smashed by the oldest available son; thus for a man without a son there is no spiritual peace after death.

Among most cultures, including until recently today's more advanced countries, fertility has always been stressed as a virtue. The position of unmarried women has usually been an unenviable one. The status of a young wife, often living under her mother-in-law's roof, is soonest improved by bearing a son. A barren wife can often be divorced and may be deemed accursed. Among agricultural people, who continually strive to increase the fertility of their fields and animals, human reproduction is considered no less desirable.

It is only among the increasing urban minority, and especially among the emerging middle class, that fertility is now viewed as a rather mixed blessing. Children occasion more direct costs in a city apartment house than in a peasant family. If the wife is emancipated, and especially if she is literate, outside employment opportunities exist if there are no children to care for. Neither "westernized" women nor their husbands evaluate themselves in terms of their breeding capabilities. And yet it is exactly these people of the emerging middle class—able to raise and educate children with various advantages—that are most needed in underdeveloped countries. From society's viewpoint, as is often the case in advanced nations too, the best parents are having the fewest children.

FIVE POLICIES TO REDUCE BIRTHS

A number of Asian governments are concerned that overpopulation should not offset their economic development programs. Examples include India and Japan, which already have large populations relative to capital and natural resources, and have experienced high rates of natural population increase. In some countries of Latin America the problem is

---

[1] In extreme cases—as in Table 20-1, where even during the best years the marginal production of population does not exceed its average consumption—infants are not even of potential value to parents.

no less serious, but government action—inhibited by religious attitudes—
is confined to measures of rather limited effectiveness.

If there are no political difficulties to be overcome, what can a national
government do to slow the rate of population increase? It can hardly
abandon public health programs so that the death rate will fall no
further, hence it must concentrate its efforts on reducing births. The
main possibilities are:

1. Advocating planned parenthood;
2. Raising the minimum age of marriage;
3. Legalizing abortion;
4. Establishing birth control clinics;
5. Taxing large families.

These are now considered in turn. No one measure may prove especially
effective in itself. But an integrated campaign that uses all these means
might substantially lessen the birth rate in some countries.

Advocating planned parenthood

Any successful government program to reduce births must counter the
various cultural and institutional motives for having large families that
were described above. In some countries there is not enough time for
government to wait in the hope that fewer births will result automatically
from gradual urbanization, female emancipation, and a growing recognition by young parents that fewer babies are now needed to perpetuate
a family. In the meantime, economic plans are being frustrated by growing populations, and the gap between economic aspirations and capabilities is widening.

Fortunately, in most poor countries seeking to develop, there is strong
emotional support of official development plans, and in many instances
it is considered unpatriotic to speak or act against The Plan. This is
especially true in countries that have gained their political independence
since World War II. These people are anxious to prove that independence brings economic progress and not retrogression.

Constant assertions by political leaders that high birth rates threaten
the development programs might bring some results. The propaganda
theme might be that large families under present circumstances are antisocial and constitute acts against the nation. Unfortunately, it takes considerable political courage for government leaders to campaign against
established cultural values, but a few have done so nevertheless.

Raising the minimum age of marriage

A majority of the world's poor and backward countries live in or near
the tropics. Adolescence is attained at an early age, and girls are not un-

commonly married at fifteen years of age or younger. If sexual intercourse could be deferred, through raising the age of marriage, a woman might bear fewer children during her life. (This was also of course the advice of Malthus to European countries around the start of the nineteenth century.) Hence it is often suggested that poor countries suffering from overpopulation should raise the minimum age of legal marriage. And India, long notorious for its child brides, has done so. But such prohibitions on very youthful marriages—even if enforced in rural areas—can have significance only in countries where cohabitation is normally legalized before it occurs. In numerous countries, most of Central Africa included, young men and women never go through a legal marriage ceremony. The truth is that any campaign to defer "marriage" must depend as much upon community support as upon legal prohibition.

Legalizing abortion

Many people believe that artificially to induce an abortion is a sin. Even those people who have no religious scruples are very conscious that abortion is sometimes psychically harmful and physically dangerous. As a positive act to prevent birth there is probably no one who would not consider contraception superior to abortion from all points of view. Accordingly, most countries, even though they permit instruction in contraception, have long made abortion illegal. Only a few countries have briefly legalized abortion.

One or two countries have recently ceased to prosecute abortionists. Moreover, they have publicized this change of attitude, so that abortion has become widespread. Of most importance, it has become much cheaper (no police pay-offs), safer (performed under proper antiseptic conditions), and easier to arrange (abortionists can advertise).

The outstanding example of such legalized abortion is Japan following World War II. In the course of one decade the birth rate was halved from 34 per thousand annually to 17. Experts have estimated that perhaps two-thirds of the attendant reduction in births was attributable to government toleration of abortion. But Japan is not a typical underdeveloped country. Its medical services are far more advanced than those of the poor and backward countries we are primarily considering. Thanks to a common language and a small territory, it is relatively simple for a Japanese government to explain the national need for birth control to the Japanese people, but this is not usual.

Establishing birth control clinics

As part of an expanding public health program, some governments have established birth control clinics, and these give information on methods of contraception. Sometimes they also distribute, free or at a price below cost, the usual variety of contraceptive devices and materials. India, as an example, allocated $8 million for birth control clinics as part of its Second Five-Year Plan: but this constituted less than 0.001 of the revised public sector budget over five years.

There is a limit to what birth control clinics, even when financed quite generously, can really accomplish. Usually they are located in the more urbanized areas and so are not very accessible to rural families. Many of devices and materials that they distribute are used more effectively if there are conveniences and privacy to a degree not usually found in a peasant's hut. Moreover, nearly all contraceptive methods require more discipline, intelligence, and knowledge than a majority of couples possess in underdeveloped lands. Young native women, poor and uneducated, are often unwilling to walk into a modern clinic to discuss such delicate and private matters with a strange doctor. They may not adequately understand what they are told or what they are given.

There is also the question of how to price contraceptive materials. If they are sold at cost they may seem too expensive to young couples for frequent use. And if they are distributed free there is a very human tendency for the recipients to value them accordingly. To ensure that at least an attempt is made to use contraceptive materials and devices properly, some low and subsidized price is probably necessary. Otherwise, they may remain unsold or be wasted carelessly.

It is partly to avoid the problems of knowledge and cost that the use of colored stringed beads to implement the "rhythm" method of birth control has often been stressed. The colors of the beads indicate "safe" days and "unsafe" days. If a wife moves one bead a day across the string, and starts with the right colored bead at a certain time of the month, she will presumably know when she can and cannot have intercourse without danger of pregnancy.

All these more or less conventional methods of birth control suffer from one marked disadvantage. A prerequisite of success is that couples, and especially younger married couples, *want* to have fewer children. Yet there is a great deal of evidence to suggest that it is unwillingness rather than inability to have small families that explains the high birth rate in most poor and backward countries.

Taxing large families

There remains the possibility of government establishing financial incentives to counter the various motives that now prompt most couples to want numerous progeny. A negative motivation, for example, would be to tax couples at a progressive rate for each additional child. Such a tax scheme would be income-regressive. Many economists would reject it on these grounds alone. Also, it is hard to collect taxes from the very poor, even though the tax might be commuted by labor on government projects at so much a day. The cost of collection might leave little net revenue. There is also the difficulty, in countries that lack vital records such as birth certificates and where large extended families are the rule, of how a tax collector from outside a village is to discover children born during the preceding year and identify their parents. In some cultures the only ascertainable parent may be the mother, and she may have no capacity to pay taxes, and she may have no legal and hence liable husband.

GOVERNMENT PAYMENTS FOR NONPREGNANCY

A democratically elected government may prefer to allow a subsidy to women who have no more than, say, two children. Such a subsidy would certainly be a fiscal novelty. And the practical difficulties of administering such a scheme would be many. Its success would depend also upon the amount of subsidy that government could afford to pay and still advance the general good. But the pressures of population are so great in some countries that every possibility of alleviation must be considered.

It has already been suggested that the value of preventing a birth permanently in some of the poorest and most backward countries is approximately $125. In these countries the fertility rates of young women are distinctly high: for example, in India it is about 0.270 a year per female of from 20–25 years old. This raises the possibility of having government pay a not insignificant subsidy to young women of from, say, 20–40 years of age who remain nonpregnant during this period.

Table 20-2 gives representative annual birth expectancies for women, by 5 year age brackets, in the second column. Assume the value of preventing a birth permanently is $125. Then Column 3 of this table, which is Column 2 times $125, gives the annual loss to the economy that a young woman of each age group will typically inflict upon it. This is in a sense a measure of her probable anti-economic behavior. This is also an indication of the maximum that government can afford to pay her annually, in its capacity as agent of the people, if she will refrain from such behavior.

How is government to be sure that a young woman, who volunteers to register for a subsidy, in fact has no children thereafter? The only certain method is to have each volunteer registrant report periodically for an examination at a local clinic. If the medical cost of the program is to be reasonable, the examination will have to be of a simple and quick kind that can be done by persons of very modest qualifications, and this in turn dictates a check every 17 weeks—*i.e.* 4 months. A finding that the woman is not pregnant would entitle her to a bonus. Failure of a registrant to report on schedule for an examination would be officially

Table 20-2

DETERMINATION OF NONPREGNANCY PAYMENTS TO REGISTERED WOMEN

(1) Age group (years)	(2) Assumed annual fertility per female	(3) Negative value of expected children born annually	(4) Proposed nonpregnancy payments each four months	(5) Years of negative examinations before cash payments
15–20	.193	$24.12	$ 8.04	4
20–25	.270	33.75	11.25	3
25–30	.252	31.50	10.50	3
30–35	.190	23.75	7.92	4
35–40	.140	17.50	5.83	6

considered an admission of pregnancy. The magnitude of the possible bonus each 17 weeks is given in Column 4.

Yet another complication remains. The $125 estimate is the supposed value of preventing a birth *permanently*. The worth to the economy of having a woman merely defer a baby from one year to the next is very much less. It would not do for a woman to register with a clinic, appear for several periodic examinations and collect her bonus, only to become pregnant next year. One way to overcome this difficulty would be to have the bonus paid into a blocked account until the accumulated credit amounted to the full value of a permanently prevented birth. Subsequently, and only afterward, would the bonus be paid in cash upon an examination confirming nonpregnancy. The blocked credit would be forfeited should a registrant be found pregnant or should she miss a scheduled examination. Otherwise the credit, with accrued interest, would be payable after menopause. If death intervened, the credit would be paid to her family. Table 20-2, in addition to giving possible bonuses each 4 months depending upon age, also indicates the number of negative examinations that must occur before cash payments begin if interest on the blocked credit is earned at 10 per cent a year compounded.

It is impossible to predict how effective such a scheme might or might not be. The maximum annual subsidy of around $30 is a considerable proportion of incomes per head in many poor countries. The prospect of forfeiting an accumulated but blocked account might provide a considerable incentive to both a woman and her mate to prevent conception. The actual method adopted could depend upon knowledge, availability, means, and, above all, conscience. The administrative cost of registration, examinations, and keeping the accounts, are all real resource costs and are hard to estimate in advance. Whether the actual bonus would be a resource cost or a transfer payment will be considered later.

The merit of the scheme, if indeed it has any, is that it mounts a counterincentive in opposition to the usual motives for having larger families. The blocked account, if eventually received, would constitute a possibly more effective insurance against old age than another child. The periodic cash payments, received after several years of accumulating the blocked credit, might finance the education of a previously born son. The main need is to establish some reason soon for many women and couples to want to have fewer children. How they achieve this end is a matter that can be left to them.[2]

THE BONUS-VASECTOMY SCHEME

There is one possible government program that might contribute to the willingness *and* ability of couples to have fewer children. This particular scheme has been adopted, but in a very modest way so far, by Madras, Mysore, and a number of other states in India. Under this plan, government offers a bonus to any married man who, having the consent of his spouse and two living children already, submits to a free vasectomy. The bonus paid has to date amounted to little more than a week's leave from work with pay.

A vasectomy (not to be confused with castration)—cutting and tying the vas ducts after an incision of the scrotum—is a very simple method of male sterilization. It can be performed under a local anesthetic, involves only a few minutes of actual surgery, and requires no subsequent hospitalization. The services of a fully qualified surgeon are not necessary and medicos could be trained without much expense to perform this particular operation. The resource cost to the economy of performing this operation is therefore very small. Under a large program, given the salaries of underdeveloped countries, the cost per operation might be as low as $2 or $3.

This means of sterilization does not affect enjoyment of sexual intercourse. It causes sterility without impairing virility. Psychologically, with the fear of pregnancy removed, female desire may actually be enhanced. There are no untoward consequences, such as change of voice or loss of hair, commonly associated with castration. There is no obvious change in physical appearance. Practically, the operation is irreversible, except perhaps at considerable expense shortly thereafter. In almost every possible respect, given the wish to have no more children, vasectomy is the most sure and simple means available.

However, and for many obvious reasons, only a few husbands per hundred are likely to volunteer for a vasectomy. Men may fear loss of virility, ridicule, or that some fatal accident may befall their present children. Terminating one's powers of reproduction runs counter to strong natural

2 This argument was developed by the author in "Government Bonus for Smaller Families," *Population Review,* Vol. 4, No. 2, July, 1960.

instincts. And in underdeveloped countries these normal inhibitions are reinforced by traditional social values.

The real question, if a large bonus were paid by government to husbands who volunteer for a vasectomy, is how large the response might be. In other words, what is the supply schedule of vasectomy volunteers, and how much larger a bonus is needed, say, to double the number of volunteers in a year? Moreover, over a decade or so, how much is this volunteer supply schedule likely to shift as more and more men have the operation and testify to its worth?

There can be no answer to these questions until some government implements the scheme—if only in a few areas as an experiment—and even then results in one country may not be representative of probable consequences in another.

However, if the monetary value to an economy of permanently preventing a birth is known, it should be possible to estimate approximately the maximum bonus government can afford to pay a vasectomy volunteer. This maximum reservation price on the part of government will be based on the number of subsequent children the man would otherwise be expected to sire. Such estimates require more understanding of family formation than now exists in most countries. It would be necessary, through sample surveys, to ascertain how many subsequent children husbands typically have at different ages, given their income, profession, religion, number of living sons and daughters, and of course the age of their wives. For example, these attributes having been established, a typical man may be expected to have three more children during the next fifteen years. The value of permanently preventing a birth may be $125 to the economy. Then, depending upon the probable spacing of future births and the appropriate discount rate, it might be determined that the maximum payable bonus is $260, for instance. Analogously, given the differences in U.S. and, say, Asiatic incomes per head, this would be the equivalent of about $6,500. Such payments should evoke curiosity about the government's offer.

The economic rationale of this bonus needs to be understood. In this case $260 is presumably the present discounted value of the future net consumption that the nation's existing population will lose if the volunteer does not have a vasectomy and instead sires the expected number of subsequent children. These extra children occasion a loss to the rest of society because they will add less to production than they subtract in consumption. Hence the economy, through government acting as its agent, is prepared to subsidize behavior on the part of parents that will be less harmful to it. And regarding other kinds of behavior, the use of subsidies to eliminate disparities between social and private welfare has long been an accepted practice.

Of course if government has to pay the full reservation price of $260 in this case, there is no "profit" remaining for the economy at large. The whole worth of the vasectomy has gone to those volunteering for the operation. Over several decades, if a bonus-vasectomy plan proved successful, government might be able to reduce the bonus appreciably and still have as many volunteers as it could treat at clinics. If this were a reasonable expectation, government might even pay more than the true maximum bonus for a few years in order to get the program underway. It is important that the bonus be lowered rather than raised over time if only to encourage volunteers now rather than later.

The program would have to include various safeguards. Consent of a volunteer's wife would probably be required. In order to perpetuate family lines, a man might have to have living children, including perhaps a son. A waiting period of several months between application and operation might be mandatory in order to prevent "impulse" vasectomies. Eventually, if a bonus-vasectomy plan were long in operation, a reduction in the bonus might be made for a man with an abnormally large family at his age: otherwise couples might deliberately have more children sooner, with the intent of then qualifying for the bonus.

The bonus might not be in the form of cash. There is a widespread and atavistic revulsion against the idea of selling one's reproductive powers. But strangely enough, if the payment is something tangible and productive, there may be more social acceptance. For instance, government might instead offer to finance the eldest son's education through secondary school, or extend peasants and artisans a free "credit" against which they could buy capital foods to increase their output. Any bonus-vasectomy plan would have to incorporate such alternative forms of reward for economic behavior.[3]

RELATIVE EFFECTIVENESS OF BONUS SCHEMES

How effective are bonus plans to reduce births likely to be—whether paid to husbands for vasectomies or to wives for remaining nonpregnant —in comparison with more conventional development projects? Are such programs a substitute or a supplement to traditional investments made to expand output? It depends upon the method of comparison.

One possible measure of successful economic development is the annual proportionate increase in the per capita income of a country. Income per capita is a ratio of course. It can be raised by increasing the output numerator or by decreasing the population denominator. Resources can be used for either purpose. For example, after a decade, $x worth of resources invested in real industrial capital might increase national output 0.0001 times more than it would otherwise increase. Different resources

[3] See also the author's "The Economics of Government Payments to Limit Population," *Economic Development and Cultural Change*, July, 1960.

but of equivalent value, employed in a vasectomy program, might after ten years result in a population 0.01 smaller than it would otherwise be. Then it could be said that, at least as a means of raising income per capita, traditional real investments are only $1/100$ as effective in terms of resources employed as are birth control schemes.

These ideas can be stated more precisely with symbols than in language. The relative effectiveness of traditional investments to bonus-vasectomy programs, per unit of resources involved, is $(\Delta Y/Y)/(\Delta P/P)$, where $(\Delta Y/Y)$ is the proportionate change in output and $(\Delta P/P)$ is the proportionate change in population that results from these alternative policies. The question is, at the end of some period, such as ten years, what will be the relative "change" in output compared to the relative "change" in population if different resources of similar value were used either to increase output or "decrease" population. By "change" is meant the difference between what output would be with and without resources worth $\$x$ invested in more output or spent for fewer births. Actually, population will normally be larger absolutely, whether or not there is a birth reduction program; but it will be not so much larger as a result, and this difference is ΔP.

How is the denominator in this effectiveness ratio—*i.e.*, $\Delta P/P$ to be approximated? Let V be the number of vasectomies a year and f the normal annual fertility of the volunteers' wives. Then for simplicity's sake ignoring gestation lags, the first year's vasectomies will reduce births after N years by $V \cdot f \cdot N$ births. The second year's operations will reduce births by $V \cdot f (N - 1)$ after N years from the start of the program. So, at the end of N years, the absolute "change" in births is for all practical purposes roughly approximated by $N^2/2$. So the proportionate "reduction" is $(V \cdot f \cdot N^2)/2 \cdot P$. This approximation is valid only for relatively short periods of time, such as 10–15 years, if only because the fertility of wives that is "lost" by vasectomies would in any case decrease. Also, this little formula assumes that vasectomies have an immediate effect on births at the start of the year they occur, which certainly is not realistic. But a time lag can readily be included.

How is the $\Delta Y/Y$ to be estimated? If the resource cost of a single vasectomy is c, then the resource cost of a constant scale vasectomy program is $V \cdot c$ each year. Different resources of equal value, if invested in factories and the like, would earn a rate of return of, say, i each year. So if we also assume no gestation period for ordinary investments, the proportionate change in national annual output at the end of N years is $(V \cdot c \cdot i \cdot N)/Y$.

It is evident that $\Delta Y/Y$ and $\Delta P/P$ have V and N in common. So these can be cancelled. Also, it is clear that P/Y is the reciprocal of income per capita. So the over-all relative effectiveness ratio can be written:

$$\frac{\Delta Y/Y}{\Delta P/P} = \frac{2 \cdot V \cdot c \cdot i \cdot N \cdot P}{V \cdot f \cdot N^2 \cdot Y} = \frac{2 \cdot c \cdot i}{f \cdot N \cdot (Y/P)}$$

In other words, the effectiveness ratio is twice the resource cost of a vasectomy times the annual rate of return on industrial investments, all divided by the fertility rate times the number of years in the comparison times the annual per capita income.

Let us substitute some imaginary but perhaps not too unreasonable values for these symbols. Suppose c is \$3, i is 0.1 per year, f is 0.2 per year, N is 10 years, and Y/P is \$75 a year. Then the over-all effectiveness ratio is \$0.6 over \$150 or 0.004. Verbally, at the end of the period, resources of given value will be 250 times more effective in raising per capita income if they are used to decrease the population denominator rather than increase the output numerator. Because income is an annual flow, and population a stock, the vasectomy program looks better the longer the period at the end of which the comparison is made.

What of the bonus payments? How is it that their expense is not included in the comparison? How is government to finance these bonuses in a way that will be a true transfer payment and not include a net resource cost?

For instance, suppose government diverts funds from other expenditures, including some investment for development. The superior effectiveness of the birth control program would then be reduced somewhat. However, if government reduced expenditures for all other purposes by the same proportion, the reduction in true capital outlays could be less than a fifth of the cost of the bonus payments. This is because all government capital outlays for development projects are seldom more than this fraction of all government outlays. And most governments, if it were thought urgent enough, might be able to finance the bonus payments by reducing bureaucratic wastes or military forces.

Alternately, government might finance the bonus payments through extra taxation, and some proportion of the extra tax proceeds would then come from taxpayers who might otherwise have invested more in ways that would enlarge the productive capacity of the country. However, most taxpayers consume more than they invest, so their consumption will be decreased more significantly. And if the bonus is not paid in cash, but in productive benefits such as technical education for present children, seed and fertilizers, hand tools, and light equipment, there is not merely a transfer of consumption from taxpayers to birth control volunteers. Instead, there is a transfer of resources from taxpayers' consumption to volunteers' investment. Also, no mean consideration, the social acceptance of the program will probably be greater if the bonus is paid in producer goods and services rather than cash that might go mostly for consumption.

Algebraically, the over-all effectiveness ratio can be rewritten to include this case, as follows:

$$\frac{P \, \Delta Y}{Y \, \Delta P} = \frac{2i[c + b \, (s_t - s_v)]}{f \cdot N \cdot (Y/P)}$$

Here s_t is the marginal propensity of the taxpayers to save, s_v is the marginal fraction of the bonus that remains as a net investment after receipt by the volunteer,[4] and b is the money value of the average bonus granted. It is important to note that, if the bonus is paid in capital goods and services, s_v may be greater than s_t, in which case (depending on the value of c), the whole numerator of the above equation could be negative. This would mean that the bonus scheme was an "infinitely" more effective way of raising per capita incomes. Or, expressed in economics, the vasectomy-bonus plan would then increase output *and* decrease births.[5]

As a practical matter, no bonus scheme to reduce births is likely to attract enough volunteers for the financing of payments to be a real problem, at least for the first decade or so. Also, if it ever were to become very popular, by then the bonus payment would probably be a fraction of the maximum price that the economy could afford to pay through government. Accordingly, in the years immediately ahead, any birth control programs that include a bonus should be viewed as a supplement to and not a substitute for traditional investments for economic development. Both are needed. Otherwise, many countries already suffering from overpopulation will continue to win output victories proportionately not much greater than their population defeats.

[4] Volunteers might sell some of their seed and fertilizer, and so on, even though this were illegal.
[5] See "Some Reactions to Bonuses for Family Limitation," *Population Review*, July, 1961.

21

Productivity
and education

Most discussions of labor supply by economists stress its quantity. However, so far as economic development is concerned, the quality of labor and population may be far more important. It is not only the number of hours of labor that the members of a given population work that matters. Of greater significance is what they do during those hours: are they human earth movers, carrying soil in baskets on their heads, or are they assembling bulldozers? An untrained labor force, however many hours it works a day, will have a very low income per head. It is mostly through increasing the productivity of workers, by investing in them and not merely in capital to be used with them, that individual consumption levels are increased in the long run. Ignorant people cannot construct, operate, and maintain elaborate equipment. Thus it is that government, through public education, may be able to increase the effective labor supply very considerably. Human capital may prove to be the most important investment of all for the public sector.

EDUCATION AND PRODUCTIVITY

It is probably no coincidence that one of the distinguishing characteristics of advanced and backward countries is the proportion of children at each age that attend school. In underdeveloped countries, only a fraction of youngsters attend even elementary schools, and the school-leaving age for most is in the very early teens if not earlier. Although education is partly a consumption service—and was particularly so in Europe a century ago—most people now value education mainly for the additional earning power that it usually bestows.

There is little doubt that education can increase a person's economic usefulness, as measured by the value of what he produces or what he can command as wages, if it is designed to do so. There is evidence to suggest that—in advanced countries at least—the average rate of return on college education is more than sufficient to justify a student's borrowing funds at nominal interest to finance his living and tuition expenses. In backward countries a man with almost any kind of technical training— except for clerical skills and sometimes law—is something of a rarity. The effective market demand for many technicians is occasionally small also, but it is often enough to enable a person to obtain double the ordinary wages which prevail for unskilled work, so that educational expenses can often be considered a true investment. The important thing is that the kinds of training made available be suited to the demonstrated needs of the country and not merely designed to satisfy the social aspirations of parents for their children.

The ability of schooling to "pay for itself" can be considered in the following simple way. If the student-teacher ratio is 50:1, and youngsters have 10 years of school, each graduated student has taken 0.2 years of an instructor's time. Perhaps all other costs, for buildings, books, and so on, increase the total labor cost per student over 10 years to 0.5 of a man-year at a teacher's salary. The student may work for 20 years. If all discounting is ignored, the educational investment will be worthwhile if each educated adolescent, during 20 years, increases his total output by more than the equivalent of what a teacher is worth for half a year. This means that the increase in the graduate's annual effectiveness must be worth 0.5/20 or 2.5 per cent of a teacher's salary. The actual difference in productivity between a person with 10 years' schooling and one with none must be many times this percentage.

Obviously, the economic importance of education cannot be assessed unless the kinds of subjects and training have been defined, for people with more schooling in the wrong subjects may command lower wages than others with fewer years of more appropriate education. When only the well-to-do could educate their sons, one traditional purpose of education was to increase enjoyment of life through enhancing the humanistic sensibilities and artistic appreciation of the leisure classes. Hence a knowledge of the Greek and Latin languages was indispensable for enjoyment of classical literature. This is not the sort of education that should be stressed for the majority of students in undeveloped countries today. However, such has been the strength of tradition in former dependencies and the need to pass examinations set in Britain, France, or Holland, for example, that far too much of the curriculum in poor and backward countries has until recently stressed what might harshly be described as irrelevant education. Now, among the newly independent countries, there are more alternatives regarding the selection of imported textbooks and external examination boards.

The sort of education that is needed in underdeveloped countries is not too hard to describe qualitatively—at least in general terms; the really difficult decisions are those of emphasis and resource allocation.

First, there must be an extension of literacy, although universal literacy may be too costly an objective for some decades. Most backward countries should soon be able to educate all urban children from about six to twelve years of age. An inability to read and write is an enormous handicap for anyone who will not be working in agriculture all his life. Too many ideas, instructions, and items of information come nowadays in written rather than oral form.

Compulsory and rather general education also permits government to stress some common "national" language. There is little social cohesion in a country that has no single language that at least all educated people use. And yet, outside of Latin America, the people of backward countries are divided linguistically to a politically dangerous extent. Government schools can at least require the learning of a common "second" language. Moreover, by stressing national political and economic history, an important measure of popular homogeneity (and sometimes "jingoism," too, unfortunately) can be created.

Included in "literacy" is arithmetic. No one today can look after his own interests, or those of his employer, without being able to add, subtract, multiply, and divide. The advent of compulsory public education in arithmetic also provides an extra opportunity to introduce a decimal system of measurement. In not a few underdeveloped countries in Asia there is now little standardization among regions in this regard. The former British colonies are still handicapped without a metric system. In this respect Latin America is again ahead.

Second, in addition to "the 3 R's," all children in underdeveloped countries need to acquire what might be described as a "sense of science." Agriculture is an important part of economic life, so some knowledge of general biology should be taught at least in the rural schools, the more so if a general education can be provided for eight rather than six years. And all children need to be given some knowledge of public health and personal hygiene. In urban schools particularly, elementary physics, including principles of heat, light, electricity, and perhaps mechanics, should be studied the last two years. By simple scientific explanations of commonly observed phenomenon—e.g., what causes thunder and lightning—a great deal of superstition can be overcome. Fear of the supernatural must be conquered through a knowledge of natural law if men and women are to take their destinies into their own hands.

Third, and most difficult of all, a public education system must strengthen the kinds of loyalties and values that are necessary for a specialized and impersonal economy to operate. The moral systems of many primitive cultures were well adapted—too well adapted one sometimes thinks—to their own preservation. Thus it may still be considered quite moral for a man appointed to be a local postmaster to steal from government if it is for the benefit of his family. Narrow group loyalties may excuse and encourage unethical behavior toward other sects or tribes. It is sometimes a novel idea that the weak do not exist to be exploited by the strong. Children everywhere have a hard time believing that in the end it is better to be right but poor than rich but wrong. None of this is to deny that non-Occidental religions teach important ethical truths. The point is that narrow loyalties, recourse to violence, and disregard for the rights of others are perhaps barely tolerable among politically disconnected and economically backward peoples. But for modern economies and politics they are quite disastrous.

In addition to these broad cultural preconditions, and the reading, writing, and arithmetic that all elementary school children should acquire, some fraction of elementary school graduates should go on to secondary school. Most of these should probably take vocational or technical courses of a kind that can be completed in from two to four years. These courses cannot and should not be duplicates of instruction given in the same subjects in, say, North America. The distribution of personal intelligence may be the same in all countries, but the quality of preschooling is not now and may never be similar. Nevertheless, curricula —adapted to local needs and capabilities—will be developed for the training of agronomists, veterinarians, civil engineers, accountants, radiologists, pharmacists, foresters, architects, and so on.

At a lower level there should be shorter courses for electricians, plumbers, bookkeepers, computers, mechanics, and various artisans. In some ways it is unfortunate that the old institution of apprenticeship—because to some it smacks too much of indentured service—is no longer available as a means of training. Hence, and particularly where private companies do not provide on-the-job training, government will have to undertake this responsibility.

Most of those who enter the secondary schools should probably take vocational and technical courses, examples of which have just been given. A minor fraction should seek a general education that will prepare them for higher education at college level. But experience in former colonies and elsewhere has proven that very few of those high school students who scorn to learn a vocation or trade do in fact go on to finish college and become professional men. Most lack the intelligence, means, and perseverance to become the fully qualified doctors, lawyers, chemists, geologists, engineers, economists, or secondary school teachers that these countries need. Far too many high school graduates seek white-collar clerical positions. But there are not enough such jobs available. Too often these idle and discontented young people drift into politics and subversion.

This is partly the result of a snobbery that sneers at people who work out of doors or with their hands. The unfortunate conclusion is that these countries get too few trained professionals, too few technicians and too many persons with a general liberal education but nothing useful to do.

Some underdeveloped countries misuse the educational facilities they already possess.

The sort of education that can really be considered an investment, apart from that which satisfies the three social needs listed above, is that which results in a person having an increased value in the labor market. A usefully trained and educated person is one who can command a higher wage or salary because he is more productive in supplying the goods and services that other people want. This, despite the pleas of traditional scholars, is the real and immediate test.

In nearly all the underdeveloped countries, so long as there are established and solvent governments, there will be a strong demand for most of the skills of the kind mentioned above. It will be surprising if young men, with four years of secondary work in a sensibly chosen field, cannot earn at least two or three times as much during their working lives as they can by going to work on leaving elementary school. This is partly because they will receive higher pay almost at once, but also because trained people can earn during more years than those who only have muscular strength to sell. Even in terms of personal finance, the monetary return on extra schooling is extraordinarily high, and parents who are fortunate enough to have intelligent children can always do much better investing *in* them through education than *for* them through property.

Obviously, in order to estimate the rate of return that is obtainable from education, one must define the extra cost and the extra income with some care. As every student knows, the cost of education to him is not only tuition and books, but also the earnings that he has to forego because he is studying rather than hiring himself out. And the rewards to him are not merely more money income—if he has equipped himself with the skills that are wanted—but also a rise in social status. A family may be able to raise itself to another class in society through education.

Actually, the "investment" is not very great for the individual, partly because government subsidizes most of the direct costs of secondary schooling when it is available. Moreover, a youngster of from 12 to 16 cannot earn very much, so the lost earnings cost is low too. By giving up the equivalent of rather more than four years' modest earnings, a youngster may be able to earn several times more annually for several decades. The life expectancy of a 16-year-old, educated and comparatively well-paid, is probably well over 30 years in even the poorest countries. Hence the personal and financial rate of return upon education must be considerably above that of any other kind of generally available opportunity to invest.

The rest of the economy, as distinct from the individual student, obtains a return of sorts from its investment in education. This is of course greater to the extent that the resource costs of the school system are covered by tuition. Even with subsidies, though, the nation at large shares in the benefits of spreading education, for there are technical external economies in a loose sense. A great deal of physical capital is a complement for trained personnel despite its frequent substitution for unskilled laborers. Hospital facilities are more useful if there are trained doctors and nurses to staff them. Imported equipment is of little value if it cannot be maintained for lack of trained mechanics. Industrial companies are not likely to remain solvent and operating for long with no accountants to establish financial record systems. A better trained labor force increases the rewards of property owners and others besides increasing the salaries of skilled personnel. Education is just as much a form of social overhead capital as a bridge or airport. It is no less real because it cannot be photographed.

SOME MAJOR ISSUES

In the abstract almost everyone favors more education for underdeveloped countries. But not everyone agrees on what the form of education is to be or who is to have it. If a government has budgeted a certain annual sum over ten years for "education," it still has many decisions to make, other than the choice between a liberal and vocational education already discussed. Should it stress a little education for all children or higher education for a few? Should it provide urban children with teachers and schools before rural children? Should it exclude girls above a certain age in order to educate more boys? Should it initially emphasize the training of teachers so that the educational system can be expanded more rapidly? Should it provide a college education within the country or subsidize study at foreign universities? Should private companies be paid for certain on-the-job training? To what extent should those who can afford it pay for tuition? With given funds and resources, more of one kind of education must mean less of some other kind, so these policy issues must be settled one way or another.

Who is to be educated?

There are some who feel that the first goal of education in poor and backward countries should be to eliminate illiteracy among children. Some would also favor adult classes in reading and writing. And while such a program would require many teachers, the qualifications of such instructors can be acquired within a few years. But the costs of salaries, books, and structures for educating all children, plus some adults, may be beyond the means of many poor countries.

Alternatively, the same budget might be used to give fewer students more years of education, assuming that sufficiently qualified instructors can be trained or imported. An extreme policy would be to select a very few children who seem most talented on the basis of intelligence and aptitude tests, and give them 16 years or so of instruction through college. Practically, this is not so simple, because many young children who seem excellent educational "material" may later prove to be deficient in effort or interest or health. The art of testing is not so advanced that one can predict whether a child of six will make a brilliant and industrious college graduate. So for every youth who should go to college when the time comes, many more children have to be started on their reading, writing, and arithmetic. For political reasons, no democratic society will deliberately create a small professional elite at public expense if the opportunity cost is most children remaining illiterate.

This issue relates to another, namely the extent to which an attempt should be made to educate rural children as well as urban ones, it sometimes being argued that funds should be used to give city children more years of schooling even though this entails less schooling for country children. The rationale of this argument is that it costs far more to educate rural children—because rural families live far apart and good teachers insist on high pay at remote posts—and why should society pay the cost of providing education to people who are scattered in the hinterland?

There is much to be said in support of this argument, especially where population *is* scattered, and costs per student *are* much higher. It is then sometimes impossible to give secondary schooling to rural children unless they attend city schools as term boarders. This means room and board costs that must be met mostly from public funds. Consequently, it may cost government less to give an urban boy a twelfth year at school than a rural boy his sixth year. And the need for technically trained people is such that the case for giving city children more schooling and country children less has many supporters.

In towns especially, where classroom space is a greater need and expense, there are many who would favor giving boys more years of training by giving girls fewer years of schooling. In many cultures, until women have gained more independence, education of girls appears less urgent. However, it is through education that women will become emancipated, and uneducated mothers inevitably perpetuate misinformation and superstition in their children. So the social cost of not educating girls is considerable too.

Westerners tend to think of education in terms of schooling children, because most adults in advanced countries have already attended school. In underdeveloped countries, because public education in many areas is so recent, there are many intelligent adults who are extremely eager to better themselves scholastically and financially. The considerable investments that are possible in adult education must not be overlooked. Moreover, these people are often willing and able to pay some tuition fees, and to the extent that they study outside working hours the usual opportunity costs are largely absent. However, if paid tuition covers only a small part of direct educational costs, government may want to think twice before it uses resources to increase the productivity of men who have fewer years of working life ahead of them.

On-the-job training is another very important way in which people can often be made more productive at a low public cost. Some skills can better be acquired on the employer's premises than in a government school. Company foremen may make better instructors for specific courses than regular school teachers. There is usually a definite increment in productivity when an employer is willing to provide the instructors and space—and sometimes the workers are students on company time as well. If governments were to subsidize certain kinds of on-the-job training, more employers would provide more workers with training in different skills, to the ultimate benefit of both.

All in all, it is not obvious that elementary schooling of *all* children should be the prime goal in backward countries because, with limited resources, more important educational advances may be gained if some children continue to receive no schooling for the time being. Experience seems to show that schooling children only two or three years accomplishes almost nothing but expense. It is the rural children, and perhaps girl children in the towns, who are likely to be deprived at first. Urban children, and especially boys, are likely to gain a secondary education as a result. These savings from discrimination can also be used to finance adult education and on-the-job training.

The main object of educational policy at the outset might well be to maximize the present value of present and imminent members of the labor force. Funds and resources used to educate girls in the hinterlands, or to establish a national university for a few native students, may be sadly misused according to this criterion. But the adoption of such a rule raises some very difficult issues of social justice.

Who should pay for education?

Compulsory schooling at public expense is now so taken for granted in most advanced countries that many people forget it was not always so. There was a time when schools and colleges were private institutions, often endowed by individuals, religious orders, or the State, and charging substantial tuition. One disadvantage of this system was that children without wealthy parents or considerable intelligence did not get an education. The government school systems of today ensure that they do. Attending school at public expense, along with the bright pupils, are now the dullards and lazybones. And these bored louts provide nothing but discipline problems.

Many underdeveloped countries will for some time lack the funds and resources to give all children a decade of schooling. Some groups of children, as explained above, will probably be excluded at first. And yet all families pay taxes that in the aggregate are more or less in proportion to income. If school attendance is not universal, but a privilege rather than a right, should not families whose children do get an education be charged a fee? Why should parents of children who have no school to attend pay taxes so that other people's children can be trained to earn higher wages later? This issue is very relevant in poor countries where only a few per cent of all children in their teens will ever see the inside of a high school.

An inevitable question, if secondary educational facilities are very limited, is whether to restrict admission through high tuition or hard exams. If education at this level is rationed by high fees, so that the effective demand is cut back to the available supply, the net cost to the public may be substantially reduced; but many brilliant youngsters may be excluded because their finances don't match their intelligence. Alternatively, if admission is by competitive examination, those already advantaged by brains will be further advantaged by an education at other's expense; and the extra productivity that results from training will accrue to them as individuals through higher earnings.

Can government arrange for the few to be educated for the benefit of the many? Can the brilliant who do receive secondary schooling be made a sort of indentured class of public servants? Could they be required to work for government for a certain number of years after school at rather low salaries? In a few countries the major employer of certain professional skills is the government, and as a labor monopolist it can recapture some expenses of education through poor salaries, but this may impair morale, private employers will be able to afford higher salaries that command the best people, and a few graduates may emigrate to other countries where their value is recognized. Another government recourse is of course a steeply progressive tax on earned income, but this has many disadvantages, not the least of which is the blunting of incentives.

Practically, a person who becomes more productive through training is unable to capture the entire increment as individual income, because so many other productive agents employed with him are complementary. So if high school facilities are limited, a reasonable compromise may be to create moderate academic and financial obstacles to admission. Tuition fees might be discriminatory, being lower for the very bright but poor, the average level being sufficient to pay about half the cost of educating all pupils.

These issues are less pronounced as regards the lower schools. The case for tuition fees is far weaker there. For one thing, proportionately more children will attend elementary schools. For another, the benefits derived from the first few years in school are more generally diffused throughout the body politic. It is in the common interest that everyone ultimately become literate in the same language, that there be a sense of science, and also a national consciousness.

Who should operate the schools?

Public financial support of education facilities does not mean that public operation of schools and colleges is the only possibility. In all countries there are some excellent private schools—and in backward countries mission schools have always been important—and these could be far more numerous and effective if they received government funds. But there is a basic if illogical distrust of proposals to have public money support private schools. Underdeveloped countries may have to overcome some of these prejudices if they want to get on with educating their children.

First, there are private schools and colleges already in existence in most backward countries, with established traditions, loyal graduates, and dedicated staffs. A government "takeover" will usually leave nothing but the same "plant" behind. Government should seriously consider providing either some annual grant per student to such schools, so long as they meet stipulated requirements, or numerous scholarships to superior pupils. These awards to students might only be usable at specific private institutions. Usually, however, such is the reputation of established private schools that students receiving "untied" awards will elect them anyway.

Second, where governments unfortunately favor national schools administered from the capital city, the public educational system cannot escape bureaucratic delays and inflexibility. It is one thing to have general standards established and enforced from the capital, but quite another to have all purchases and promotions determined centrally, with the resultant dangers of corruption and favoritism. A large degree of local autonomy is essential. And if there are educated and honest citizens who will serve, local school boards having at least an advisory role should be established. In some instances the local board may appoint the principal and determine part of the curriculum. Then in effect the central authority is using its taxing power to support schools that it does not administer. Once this is accepted as a sound principle, it is but a short step to a system of government subsidies to private schools that meet public requirements regarding staff, facilities, courses, and admission.

Third, the impracticality of government education is most obvious when it comes to higher education. Very small and underdeveloped countries cannot finance a national college of any kind, except perhaps for teacher training, and certainly cannot support graduate schools in the sciences. In one respect this is just as well, for in backward countries the college students who may be future leaders need more than anything else to go abroad for some years and "see the world." But the native student who goes overseas to college may not always come back. He may prefer to earn a livelihood in London, Paris, or wherever he has studied. Or he may choose to take an appointment in some other underdeveloped country. Thus it has been estimated that over a half of all Indian students who have obtained doctoral degrees abroad have not returned to India to stay. An alternative is to accept alien doctors and engineers as perhaps temporary immigrants, but this of course continues national feelings of inferiority and dependence.

EDUCATIONAL INVESTMENT AND NATIONAL ACCOUNTS

Enough has been written to indicate that education of the kind that is most needed by underdeveloped countries is primarily an investment. The element of consumption, which was the *raison d'être* of a humanistic education, should be a minor one for the next few generations. However, if education is to be considered an investment, most men and some women must be considered a special form of capital.

Unfortunately, for reasons stemming from antislavery movements of the past, most economists are reluctant to look upon gainfully employed persons as human capital. And yet if development is to be viewed in national terms, a government should be ready to invest in the productivity of its subject taxpayers. So long as it can extract considerable fractions of private earnings, it has at least a narrow fiscal interest in human investment, and its broader concern should be to allocate resources between physical and human capital so that the marginal contribution to gross national output is about the same in each case.

Actually, much of the output increases by advanced countries during the past century or so may be attributable to improvements in human quality, although they are often ascribed to innovations and technology. In Chapter 5, reference was made to a famous National Bureau study of the United States over an eighty-year period which indicated that less than a fifth of the per capita output increase over that period could be explained by increases in the stock of reproducible capital. But the gainfully occupied at the end of this period were not the same sort of people as those at its start. They had far more education and training and better health. In some respects they were no more the same sort of people as cars of today are the same as cars of 1900. Many persons are trained today in skills that were not imagined even fifty years ago. One cannot properly measure labor's contribution toward gross national product over time by comparing the number of gainfully employed persons in a country at very different dates.

A more realistic method of national accounting, but one that is certainly unorthodox and might be difficult to complete, would be to establish a capital account called "gross human investment." To this would be credited the consumption of all people of employable age who forego earnings in order to be trained, plus their direct expenditures for education and public health. The annual credits to such an account would be very considerable in advanced countries, and some very preliminary estimates have suggested that gross human investment may often exceed annual gross physical investment.

In considering the stock of education and training in the labor force, one should logically distinguish between gross and net human investment. Everyone dies eventually, even the most educated of persons, and this is in some ways analogous to the scrapping of equipment. Analytically, despite human ego, the service life of a trained person is not so different from the service life of a machine. Thus net human investment constitutes the increase in the number of gainfully employed persons who possess this or that special skill or training. One noted economist has tentatively estimated that the stock of education in the labor force rose about eight and a half times in the United States between 1900 and 1956, whereas the stock of reproducible capital rose about four and a half times.[1]

In striking contrast to what has happened in the advanced nations is what is usually prescribed for backward countries. Although all governments profess a great concern over increasing education, and individual parents are often frantically eager that their children get the education they missed, economic development plans of backward countries usually place much greater stress on physical investment than upon human investment. This is despite the fact that innovations are vital and that new techniques require new skills. The ability of a country to absorb capital funds, by using them productively enough to pay a return, is closely linked to advancing general education. One occasionally wonders whether some of the great international development agencies have not been waving the wrong end of the stick.

These doubts and dangers were ably expressed some time ago by the President of the American Economic Association:

My last policy comment is on assistance to underdeveloped countries. . . . Here . . . investment in human beings is likely to be underrated and neglected. It is inherent in the intellectual climate in which leaders and spokesmen of many of these countries find themselves. Our export of growth doctrines has

[1] T. W. Schultz, "Investment in Human Capital," *American Economic Review*, March, 1961, p. 11.

contributed. These typically assign the stellar role to the formation of non-human capital, and take as an obvious fact the superabundance of human resources. Steel mills are the real symbol of industrialization. . . . New funds and agencies are being authorized to transfer capital for physical goods to these countries. The World Bank and our Export-Import Bank have already had much experience. Then, too, measures have been taken to pave the way for the investment of more private (non-human) capital abroad. This one sided effort is underway in spite of the fact that the knowledge and skills required to take on and use efficiently the superior techniques of production, the most valuable resource that we could make available to them, is on very short supply in these underdeveloped countries. Some growth of course can be had from the increase in more conventional capital even though the labor that is available is lacking both in skill and knowledge. But the rate of growth will be seriously limited. It simply is not possible to have the fruits of a modern agriculture and the abundance of modern industry without making large investments in human beings.[2]

This important lesson has not yet been fully learned by the officials who either grant or request aid for economic development.

[2] Presidential Address by Professor T. W. Schultz at the Seventy-third Annual Meeting of the American Economic Association, St. Louis, Missouri, December 28, 1960.

22

Public health
and effective labor

Underdeveloped countries altogether spend even less upon health than upon education. In the United States, about one-twentieth of national income is devoted to education, and approximately another one-twentieth to health; about 80 cents of every dollar spent on education, and about 20 cents of every dollar used for health, are expended by government. In backward countries, private spending for health is almost negligible, and public expenditures for education exceed those for health. Some people seek to justify this emphasis on education rather than health on the grounds that improved health will aggravate population pressures. It is argued that whereas both education and health make adults more effective workers, better health increases the number of consumers by reducing the death rate. Moreover, improving public education might even lower the birth rate and so lessen diminishing returns to labor. Such common attitudes hardly contribute to the morale of public health officials serving the underdeveloped countries. And it may be that this widely held opinion is too simple a view. So in this chapter, expenditures for health are compared with investments for extra education as an effective contribution to economic development.

PUBLIC HEALTH IN BACKWARD COUNTRIES

Poor countries within the tropics and subtropics have many common public health problems. Some of the ailments from which they suffer, such as tuberculosis and venereal diseases, are common to temperate climates also. Certain diseases, now only found in the tropics, have been brought under control elsewhere. In addition, to a great degree, there are a number of purely "tropical" diseases that give rise to high morbidity or mortality rates. Many of them can be remedied or eradicated at resource costs that are cheap when assessed from even the narrowest economic viewpoint.

The more important of those widespread diseases that are debilitating, rather than crippling or killing, include the following:

Disease	Millions probably affected
Malaria	700
Hookworm	400
Trachoma	400
Yaws	50
Filariasis	250
Leprosy	2–12

Many natives suffer from more than one of these ailments at the same time. There are also other debilitating ailments—*e.g.*, gastro-enteritis and infant malnutrition—that are practically endemic. Extreme cases can cause serious disability and result indirectly in premature mortality. In addition, there are diseases that can prove fatal, such as smallpox, cholera, and yellow fever.

Any public health program must consider the surest and cheapest method of reducing the incidence of these diseases. The more important ones can be grouped approximately according to the most effective means of control. The real killers, such as smallpox, are today checked through inoculations: when an epidemic threatens, the affected area is placed under quarantine, and those not infected are immunized. Another group of diseases—including notably malaria—can be eradicated through eliminating disease-carrying insects. Still another group—which includes dysentery—can be controlled through better excreta disposal and improved water supplies. A fourth group requires personal medicine, including drugs and clinical treatment, and hence is many times more expensive per person benefited. Table 22-1 lists the best control measures for certain major diseases.

A selected number of diseases, and their control through public health programs, are described below. These diseases are malaria, yaws, bru-

CONTROL MEASURES AND DISEASE*

Immunization or vaccination	Control or eradication of disease-carrying insects	Control of human wastes	Prophylaxis or clinical treatment
Smallpox	Malaria	Hookworm	Yaws
Typhus	Typhus	Schistosomiasis	Malaria
Whooping cough	Plague	Roundworm	Leprosy
Poliomyelitis	Encephalitis	Cholera	Tuberculosis
Typhoid fever	Onchocerciasis	Amebiasis	Syphilis
Tuberculosis	Filariasis	Dysentery	Bejel
Influenza			Pinta
Cholera			Trachoma
Plague			
Yellow fever			

* *Source:* United States Senate Report of the Committee on Government Operations: The Status of World Health, 86th Congress, 1st Session, Senate Report 161, April 10, 1959, p. 58.

cellosis, infant malnutrition, and gastro-enteritis. These, together with hookworm and trachoma, still affect about two-thirds of the people in underdeveloped countries in the course of a year.

Malaria

Despite the high incidence of annual deaths, and though it is often a major cause of infant mortality, the importance of malaria lies in the chronic invalidism that it occasions. It is insidious rather than dramatic. Hence it has serious repercussions on agriculture, commerce, and industry. Many potentially fertile areas of the world are not cultivated because the local population has learned to avoid them for fear of malarial infection. Accordingly, and because of the large number of persons afflicted, a major campaign has been directed against malaria in various parts of the world since the end of World War II.

Malaria is usually transmitted from one afflicted person to others by a mosquito. Where population is dense, and there are not many areas of open and stagnant water, it is economical to prevent mosquitos from breeding by attacking the larval forms in the water. However, where population is sparse and there are many pools of water suitable for mosquito breeding, it is more economical to spray houses with a residual insecticide. Such spraying operations have a cost per house or family that is more or less constant irrespective of population density. The residual insecticide, sprayed on walls of houses, stays effective for several months. A gorged mosquito will usually rest immediately after it has taken blood, perhaps on a sprayed structure, in which case it will be killed. Thus the cycle of infection from person to person by mosquitos is broken.

Residual spraying has proved very effective. Malaria has been completely eliminated in Chile since 1945, and the most important mosquito vector has apparently disappeared. In Peru, DDT and residual spraying in four highly malarious regions have reduced parasite indices to less than 2 per cent of their prior level. Malaria has been drastically reduced in Mauritius, the Rhodesian copper belt, Ceylon, Fiji, Sardinia, and other areas. The cost in northern Ceylon has been a fraction of a dollar per person protected. In British Guiana the cost of hospital treatment of malaria patients was cut to less than one-fourth through an antimosquito campaign that cost about half this gross saving. But the real gain in these instances is of course the increased vitality of workers and others.

Yaws

The treponematoses are another major source of debility. In Europe and North America the emphasis has been on the treatment of venereal syphilis. But in the underdeveloped world, although the incidence of syphilis is often very high, yaws and bejel have recently been stressed. These treponemal infections are transmitted by other than genital contact. Thus they may be communicated by direct contact in juvenile play or through utensils for drinking and eating.

The disease is endemic in areas of the Pacific, Africa, and South America. Since the war, various treponema-immobilizing antibodies have been discovered, and it has been learned that all the organisms generally react favorably to penicillin. Hence, for the first time in man's history, control of yaws, bejel, and syphilis appears practical.

With assistance from the World Health Organization, there have been mass yaw-control campaigns in Haiti, Indonesia, and Nigeria. In Haiti alone, 50,000-odd people have been treated monthly; it has been estimated that this single program has returned 100,000 incapacitated people to work, and increased the Haitian national output by about five million dollars a year.[1] The Indonesian campaign against treponematoses during the 1950's was one of the largest national efforts of its kind ever undertaken: within six years, 23 million people were examined and over 3 million treated. With such mass campaigns the cost per person examined is around 40 cents, and the cost per person treated is a little under one dollar. The actual penicillin cost still accounts for half the expense of treatment.[2]

Brucellosis (Undulant Fever)

The evil of brucellosis lies in the reduced capacity for work and actual suffering of numerous agricultural workers plus considerable farm losses from the lessened ability of domesticated livestock to reproduce and give milk. In underdeveloped countries this is especially important in the case of goats, sheep, swine, and cattle. Human brucellosis almost inevitably results from contact with infected livestock or their products. Latin America is one of the areas principally affected. However, it is now believed that the disease may be significant in certain areas of Africa and Asia also. The Food and Agricultural Organization combined with the World Health Organization during the 1950's to establish uniform diagnostic procedures and to develop an internationally standardized anti-brucella drug to lessen livestock abortion rates. They also undertook vaccination programs in several underdeveloped countries where infection of sheep and goats is a serious problem. In these nations it is usually not practical to conduct test and slaughter operations.

[1] United States Department of State, Economic Cooperation Series 24, Publication 3719.
[2] The First Ten Years of the World Health Organization (Geneva: United Nations Health Organization, 1958), p. 206.

Infant malnutrition

Infants born in poor tropical countries are normally underweight—at least by Occidental standards—but many gain well during the first six months afterward. However, during the next six to nine months, they usually gain very slowly and may even lose weight. They often exhibit edema and suffer from rickets and anemia. These ailments are usually attributed to prolonged breast feeding, sometimes for 18 months or more, without adequate food supplements being given. This is partly the result of poverty, but also of custom and ignorance, and thus part of the remedy is education.

Human milk does not provide enough proteins, iron, vitamins, or even calories once a baby is over six to nine months. Iron deficiency is responsible for "suckling anemia," while rickets are attributable to lack of Vitamin D_3. Once a child is a year or older, the breast is more a comforter than a source of nourishment, but few families in poor and tropical countries prepare special foods for infants. Usually they will be given some of the pappier and starchier foods prepared for the family as a whole. Sometimes these will be heavily spiced with condiments. Available protein in the form of fish or meat or eggs is more likely to go to the adults or elder children. Animal milk is not always given even when available. Very young children are almost starched to death.

The rationale of prolonged weaning is that human milk direct from the breast is the safest of all nutriments. Animal milk may be carried in dirty and open containers, the milker's hands may have been used for other and unsanitary purposes. Meat and vegetables that have been covered with flies may also threaten the young child with dysentery if not worse. Or as one writer has said:

It can be emphatically stated that in overcrowded, unhygienic, tropical surroundings, any food or drink unnecessarily given to a small baby stands the greatest chance of producing an infective, debilitating, nutritionally hazardous, and often fatal gastro-enteritis.[3]

In fact there are few "safe" foods. One is the banana, for it can be peeled immediately before feeding, and it has a high sugar content when ripe. Eggs are also a potential source of safe protein, for they can be broken just before eating. However, in rural areas where chickens run wild, it is not always easy to discover newly-laid and still fresh eggs. Also certain groups have taboos against eating eggs. Another useful food source is peanuts—or groundnuts as they are usually called outside the United States—for they too come in their own shell.

[3] D. B. Jelliffe, "Infant Nutrition in the Subtropics and Tropics" (Geneva: United Nations World Health Organization, 1955).

Infant malnutrition or *kwashiorkor*—to use the West African term—does not only increase child mortality. Of more consequence perhaps is that it may render surviving children apathetic and listless. As young men and women they may always lack energy and initiative. Physically and mentally stunted adults too often result. Human quality suffers.

Gastro-enteritis

Gastro-enteritis, including amoebic dysentery, is the great infant killer through dehydration and general weakening. However, gastro-enteritis is also extremely debilitating for adults. The "tourist-stomach," which so many Americans fleetingly and mildly experience while on trips outside the temperate zones, is part of daily life for most people in many backward nations. Experienced in childhood, it can lessen a person's ability to absorb nourishment from digested food, thereby increasing total food requirements of a country.

Water plays a predominant role in the transmission of many enteric bacterial infections, such as typhoid and paratyphoid fevers, bacillary dysentery, and cholera. It is especially important that water supplies should not be contaminated with human excreta. In fact the principal way of preventing gastro-enteritis—not to mention other diseases—is to provide means for disposing of human wastes and supplying "safe" water.

Rural areas are often quite densely populated. And even where land is plentiful, the local culture may favor village settlements. With a few hundred people living in a small community, it is often not possible to separate the water supply from human excreta disposal sites, at least not without deliberate investment. Outhouses must be designed, built, and located so that people will use them: a central sewer system is even better and, in the end, more economical. Unpolluted water must be brought into the villages and distributed close enough to each dwelling so that families will not take water from some other handier but dangerous source. Experience has shown that, if there is some nearer stream or pond, women are unwilling to tote water from a safe water source that is further away. It has also been found that if water is carried from a distant source in an open container, and perhaps thus stored for later use, it is likely to become contaminated.

Lack of adequate water supplies often causes poor excreta disposal and inadequate personal hygiene. Nor is this surprising under some primitive conditions. As two experts have commented:

In countries . . . where surface water is scarce and underground water unobtainable, housewives spend most of their time in carrying a few litres of water in cans and jars from distant rivers and springs to their homes. Under such conditions the amount of water used is the absolute minimum required for survival. It is, by necessity, rationed for drinking purposes—little if any being left for the personal and household hygiene which loom so large in the epidemiology of diarrhoeal diseases.[4]

Without a lot of water, there won't be much washing, and there can be a great deal of "health" in a bar of soap!

On the other hand, if water is too readily available from open sources, it is too easily polluted. Villagers located on a small and sluggish river are likely to use this same water for washing clothes and bodies, disposing of human wastes, and slaking thirst. The typical village of Southeast Asia, with its water "tank" or pond in the middle, seems almost specifically designed to spread gastro-enteritis and increase infant mortality.

Nearly all economic development plans include investments in "social overhead capital." Some of these projects are lavish airports and other prestige items. Privies and boreholes are less dramatic and glamorous investments, but they are needed nonetheless.

INVESTING IN HEALTH

If it is economical for a society to invest in education, one would expect that it would also be worth its while to invest in health. In many important respects, as we shall see, investing in education and health are similar. But there are also some important differences.

Similarities between health and education

Health and education are often joint goods. If children have poor health, they will lose many days from school, so that better health may result in better education. If children die during their years in school, the cost of each addition to an educated labor force is obviously increased.

Health and education both provide sumptuary satisfactions and are not only investments. It is important to a man that he feel well and able to greet a new day with enthusiasm, although it may be his increased working ability that matters to others. Without good health, many ways of enjoying oneself are impossible, so good health also increases sumptuary pleasures. Similarly, as described in the preceding section, education of a humanistic kind enhances a person's ability to appreciate the finer things of life.

Health and education are alike in that their benefits accrue partly to the individual and partly to others. When a person is cured of tuberculosis there is also a gain for the people whom he might otherwise infect. When a person acquires vocational skills he benefits all those who own complementary factors of production.

Health and education can be increased only through some form of in-

4 E. G. Wagner and J. N. Lanoix, *Water Supply for Rural Areas and Small Communities* (Geneva: United Nations World Health Organization, 1959), p. 19.

vestment that entails a deferment of consumption. In the case of schooling, a child goes to work later, and there is the resource cost of the staff and plant needed directly for instruction. As regards health, an investment of resources is also necessary, not only for training doctors, nurses, and others, but because there may be a lag of several years before the morbidity or mortality rate declines. Meanwhile, the economy has advanced resources, and there must be an equivalent value in return—with interest—later.

Health and education both increase output. As regards education, there can be little doubt on this score, as the many students who have borrowed funds to finance their college years and have repaid their debts can testify. But the output effects of improved health are not so immediately obvious.

Increased output from improved health

Increased energy from improved health is one cause of extra output. A man suffering from dysentery, ridden with parasites, and experiencing occasional fevers is not going to work very hard for very long. It is beyond his powers. So far as possible he will defer a job rather than finish it now. He will tend to do the minimum acceptable amount of work and stop to rest more often.

Increased motivation is another contribution to output resulting from better health. As Dr. Selma Mushkin has written:

A people riddled with malaria, schistosomiasis, trachoma, intestinal worms, and a dozen other afflictions are not likely to care very much about community development.[5]

People in poor health will lack even the mental vigor to improve their lot.

People's expectations of life and death also influence motivation. A man well acquainted with death is likely to become fatalistic about his own future and that of his children. People are less inclined to work harder today for some improvement tomorrow if there is little assurance that there will be a tomorrow for them or their close relatives. A successful public health program may encourage people to better their situation in other respects also. Self-reliance is more likely to take the place of passive acceptances once a community knows, for example, that malaria can be overcome, infant mortality can be decreased, and yaws can be cured.[6]

[5] In a privately distributed monograph drafted for subsequent publication by the United States Department of Health, Education, and Welfare.
[6] Some indications of the effect of life expectancies on rational time preference in the United States and India have been developed by Professor Otto Eckstein, "A Survey of the Theory of Public Expenditure," *Public Finances: Needs, Sources, Utilization* (Princeton, N.J.: National Bureau of Economic Research, 1961).

Increased absorption of nutriment may result from a public health campaign that eliminates gastro-enteritis and internal parasites. Food that is swallowed provides less nourishment if it is passing through the alimentary tract too rapidly or is sustaining intestinal worms. Public health expenditures can—to a limited extent—decrease national food requirements.

Increased control of malaria and other diseases may augment usable land. In not a few countries some of the potentially best agricultural land is not cultivated because it has become notorious as a fever area. In Ethiopia the peasants often terrace far up the hillsides rather than work the better soil in the malarial valleys below. Parts of Africa are almost denuded of population, despite arable land being available, because of the prevalence of sleeping sickness. Many areas in Latin America—in the Amazon valley, for example—are not used because they have an evil health reputation.

Increased control of zoonoses not only benefits man but certain of his domesticated animals also. Various diseases are transmitted indirectly from man to his livestock and back to man. In underdeveloped countries, a family is closer to its animals, so that the total community for health purposes includes both animal and human life.

Increasing life expectancy

A major difference between health and education is that the latter does not affect the death rate—except very indirectly—whereas public health expenditures very definitely do. From a human viewpoint this is desirable. But the economic incidence is rather mixed.

Once a youngster has completed his schooling, or is otherwise about to commence gainful work, an increase in life expectancy is likely to be desirable from an economic viewpoint. But it all depends upon the kinds of work such a youngster will do and how long he may live. If he is destined for hard physical work, he may be past his prime at 45 years, but with many years of consumption still ahead. However, as a sorter of mail in a post office, for instance, he may be productive at 60 years of age. Suppose that before a public health campaign, a boy at 15 has a 0.75 chance of attaining 30 years, a 0.50 probability of attaining 40 years, and a 0.25 chance of reaching at least 45 years. Now suppose that after a public health effort, these three respective probabilities at 15 are for survival to 35, 50, and 60 years of age. Are matters improved?

More man-years of work will certainly be performed. But more man-years of consumption will also result. One must be balanced against the other. The answer will depend on how young a man becomes too old to work and how old a man becomes before ceasing to be a consumer. It is in advanced countries, where the productivity of people depends little on their physical strength, that one can certainly want youngsters of 15 to survive another 35 years or more.

The desirability of extending the life expectancy of infants is also a difficult question, for until about 15 years of age they only consume. Preventing a few-months-old child from dying is desirable on humanitarian grounds. But where is the advantage of saving a child from death in infancy if it thereafter has a life expectancy of only 20 years or so?

Considering people only as producers and consumers, which is certainly a most inhuman viewpoint, the "ideal" would be for everyone either to die at birth or to die at the end of a full working life. The worst and very imaginary situation would be for almost everyone to die at around 15 years, when he or she is just becoming old enough to be economically productive. The situation in the real world is somewhere between these two conceptual extremes. And the real issue is the extent to which the actual timing of deaths can be altered toward the later extreme. This means that the economy has an interest in reducing death rates at every age except roughly under 5 and over 55 years.

How to achieve such an outcome is a subject that economists are not qualified to discuss, and public health officials are sometimes reluctant to do so. Officially, despite population pressures in some countries, a reduction in death rates at any age is considered laudable. And it may be that medical knowledge regarding diseases and the interactions among them is still inadequate to reduce diseases that kill 10-year-olds without reducing those that kill infants. The problem must differ too from region to region, depending upon the incidence of various diseases, topography and climate, customary methods of cooking and sleeping, and many other matters. There are also many overlapping afflictions, so that expenditures to eliminate one specific disease may simply uncover another, there being less incentive to eradicate malaria in an area in which there is also widespread amoebic dysentery, for instance. Finally, medically trained people simply do not think in terms of minimizing the life expectancies of afflicted infants, and perhaps on grounds other than economic this is just as well.

The one economic distinction that does seem to be widely observed among health authorities is that between debilitating and fatal diseases. Of course this distinction is often very uncertain, for any ailment that weakens a person's constitution usually increases the risk of death from some other cause. But in general, so far as economic development is concerned, investment in health should ordinarily be to increase output rather than lives. Campaigns against diseases that occasion debility are probably more promising than efforts against diseases that either kill swiftly or permit survivors to recuperate fully.

Actually, for humanitarian reasons, early public health measures were against "killers" such as smallpox and cholera. It is only rather lately that major efforts have been taken against the "weakeners" such as malaria and hookworm. Partly this is a result of the historical sequence in which methods of disease control were discovered and perfected. Medical research gave priority to saving lives rather than strengthening life. Ironically, for the development of poor and overpopulated countries, it might have been better had this sequence been reversed.

ALLOCATING EXPENDITURES FOR IMPROVING HEALTH OR EDUCATION

During recent years there has been an increasing interest in allocating public health expenditures in some economically rational way. At least conceptually, there are some rather clear alternatives, although in practice the various lateral effects of any health activity are likely to be blurred. Some of these allocating yardsticks are now described.

Equalizing the cost per person

One can consider health expenditures as a way of purchasing the utilities of good health and well-being, much as though they were consumer services. Buying better health is, then, like buying any other useful service. And it might be argued that a "democratic" public health program should be designed so that everyone has an equal share of public funds spent on his behalf. One consequence would be that in very sparsely populated areas the level of public health services would necessarily be low because of the cost per head. Similarly, because some people choose to live in unhealthy regions, taxpayers would not be required to incur special and extra outlays to save them from the consequences of their decision. Another consequence might be to spend rather less on the "killing" diseases (a dead man doesn't feel ill anymore) and rather more on the "weakening" diseases (so that people feel better). In this latter event, because people who feel better usually work better, there would also be an incidental but useful productive contribution.

Minimizing expected deaths

Many people favor an allocation of public health outlays so that annual expected deaths are the lowest possible. Practically, this might tend to concentrate efforts upon reducing mortality among infants and the very young, although it does not follow of course that more lives can be saved per dollar among persons in age groups that experience high mortality rates. Logically, this criterion means that saving a 15-year-old who otherwise would have died in some year is no better or worse than saving a 75-year-old who otherwise would have died in the same year, although one has a productive period ahead of him and the other has not. This is of course incompatible with a more economic objective, such as maximizing the number of 15-year-olds who reach 55 years, or the unrealistic "ideal" of having everyone die either at infancy or at, say, 60 years of age.

Maximizing extra output

At the other extreme from those who look upon health expenditures as a means of buying consumer utilities are those who regard public health activities primarily as an investment in human capital, and thus as a means of gaining extra output from the economy during any year. Better health makes for a larger labor force and more energetic workers. Disease eradication may open agricultural regions that people now avoid as too dangerous to health. It is also conceivable that certain industrial activities, located in notoriously unhealthy areas, have to pay such high wages as a counterinducement that they have substituted expensive capital for labor: thus rendering the area healthy might "release" capital in the future. There seems little doubt but that a well-planned public health program could within a decade or so increase output very considerably in most backward countries where there are now short life expectancies. In this sense most public health activities "pay" for themselves, perhaps several times over in terms of extra output, and so appear eminently desirable. But economic criteria are seldom quite so simple.

The first difficulty is that improved popular health increases consumers of output as well as producers of output. If raising income per capita is considered an approximate goal of economic development, and the distribution of income is not unfavorably affected thereby, public health expenditures at least should be directed not toward maximizing extra output (dY) but to raising $(P \cdot dY)/(Y \cdot dP)$ as much as possible. This means that public health programs that make actual workers more effective without reducing deaths may be preferable to those that reduce deaths and thereby increase the absolute number of workers. The merits of one program over another will depend very much upon the population elasticity of national output. For example, if a 10 per cent increase in population and labor force over five years increases output by only 2 or 3 per cent (because land resources are relatively so scarce), it would be desirable to reduce population growth even if a potential worker had to be lost for each potential consumer less.

A more serious difficulty is that it is not the absolute effect of any program—including public health programs—that matters, but its comparative effect. If resources or funds are limited, more spent on health may mean less spent on education, or more spent on human capital may mean less spent on physical capital. Even within the area of public medical expenditures, funds can be used to reduce deaths or reduce births. And in Chapter 20 it was indicated that this last use of resources may be several hundred times more effective in raising per capita income than the use of equivalent value resources for traditional development projects. So it is essential to consider the opportunity costs of health investments.

Health vs. education

Public funds will assuredly be spent in all countries for both health and education. But marginal transfers of funds and resources are always possible. Conceptually, one could want to allocate investments in human capital so that the "last" dollar spent on health occasioned the same increase in income per head as the marginal dollar spent on education, hard though this may be to measure in practice. Education and health both increase the effective supply of labor. It is as though they added equivalent workers—who really don't exist—and this in turn added of course to output. But additional health measures also increase the real population by decreasing deaths. How is a comparison of expenditures for health and education to be made?

One possible approach—although it stretches the imagination—is to adopt the classical notion of a standard worker of standard productivity. Expenditures for education increase the "effective" but not the "real" number of workers in the population. It is as though, by educating people of all ages, more workers who do not consume are somehow added to the labor force. Thus one might say that educational expenditures E result in $E(dp'/de)$ more imaginary people, where dp'/de is the extra P' associated with a small extra E and the prime indicates that the "people" don't really exist but have been "created" by education. Thus, apart from the opportunity cost of using resources for health, there is a gain in output per head of real population.

Expenditures on health increase the real population, and hence the number of real workers and real consumers, but improved health also makes the actual population more energetic and hence more effective as workers. So two relations involving health expenditures (H) are involved. One is the extra effective population—including some more real people but also many extra equivalent ones—which might be written

$$\Delta P'' = H \frac{dp''}{dh}$$

where H is a small health expenditure, dp''/dh represents extra effective people occasioned by a small increase in health outlays, and $\Delta P''$ is the extra effective but not necessarily real population. The other relation, resulting from decreasing death rates, is

$$\Delta P = H \frac{dp}{dh}$$

where P is real population.

If we wish to compare the economic benefits resulting from equal expenditures of E or H, and the basis of comparison is to be income per capita (Y/P), we must recognize that E occasions dY but H occasions both a dY and a dP. We can also assume for convenience that a constant fraction of the real or imaginary population comprises effective workers in the labor force. Finally, it needs to be realized that a proportionate increase in the effective labor force does not cause an equal proportionate increase in national output because of diminishing returns.

Some sort of production function must be stipulated. We shall assume one of the Cobb Douglas type—see Chapter 9—such as

$$Y = aL^l K^k \cdot R^r$$

where a is a constant for converting units, K and R are real capital stocks and natural resources, respectively, some constant fraction of population is always the labor force (L), and k, l, and r sum to unity. With such a function an x per cent change in L occasions an $l \cdot x$ per cent change in output.

Such changes in the effective labor force can result from expenditures on health or education. For example, E dollars spent on education would result in a proportionate change in effective labor force equal to

$$\frac{P_1 + E \dfrac{dp'}{de}}{P_1}$$

Similarly, H dollars spent on health would result in a proportionate change in the effective labor force of

$$\frac{P_1 + H \dfrac{dp''}{dh}}{P_1}$$

But expenditures on health (H) will also increase real population, so that a comparison of populations as between periods 1 and 2 would give

$$\frac{P_1 + H \dfrac{dp}{dh}}{P_1}$$

for P_2/P_1. These equations look alike, except for the priming on the marginal ratios, p' indicating extra equivalent people caused by education, p'' extra effective labor supply resulting from more energetic workers and more people in the labor force, and p extra population of real people.

If the choice were between equal sums spent for education or health, and the dp'/de, dp''/dh, and dp/dh coefficients were all known, one might choose according to which raised per capita income most effectively. We would want to compare the $(Y_2P_1)/(Y_1P_2)$ ratio, where the subscripts 1 and 2 respectively indicate "before" and "after," for the case of expenditures for education (without extra expenditures for health) and of spending for health (without extra spending for education). If the dollar values of H and E are equal, but only one expenditure or the other can be made, both are equally desirable if

$$\left(\frac{P_1 + E\dfrac{dp'}{de}}{P_1}\right)^{l} \cdot \frac{P_1}{P_2} = \left(\frac{P_1 + H\dfrac{dp''}{dh}}{P_1}\right)^{l} \cdot \frac{P_1}{P_1 + H\dfrac{dp}{dh}}$$

In this equation the left side shows $(Y_2P_1)/(Y_1P_2)$ resulting from educational expenditures; because education does not affect real population, P_1/P_2 is unity, and this term can be dropped. The right hand side shows the $(Y_2P_1)/(Y_1P_2)$ resulting for health expenditures. In both cases, the proportionate increase in the effective labor supply is downgraded by the l exponent because of diminishing returns to labor.

From the fundamental equation above it is possible of course to obtain the "indifferent" value for any of the marginal coefficients that will make neither extra education nor extra health preferable to the other. Actually, whether health expenditures are superior, equal, or inferior to education, given expenditures of equal value, will depend upon whether:

$$\left[\frac{P_1 + H\dfrac{dp''}{dh}}{P_1 + E\dfrac{dp'}{de}}\right]^{l} - 1 \quad \begin{matrix} \geq \\ < \end{matrix} \quad \frac{H}{P_1} \cdot \frac{dp}{dh}$$

(The right side of the equation (Hdp/PdH) might be termed the health elasticity of population.)

The above statement may be more meaningful if numbers are substituted for symbols. Imagine a country in which P is 100 million people and expenditures on health *or* education are to be $100 million. Suppose that a dollar spent on health occasions 0.01 additional effective men (*i.e.*, $dp''/dh = 0.01$) and that a dollar spent on education (dp'/de) provides 0.005 effective extra person. The left side of the above equation will then be approximately .0025 if the labor elasticity of output (l) is 0.5. It is then a matter of indifference as to whether this human capital budget goes for health or education if $Hdp/Pdh = .0025$. If $1000 spent on health will save less than 2.5 lives, it would be better to invest in health, and vice versa.

The above formulation is of course most crude and approximate. Many intertemporal relations are ignored. Estimating the marginal coefficients can be no better than an informed guess. But the essential logic of any rational comparison is set forth above. And that is something anyway.

Education vs. industry

One opportunity cost of investing in human capital is an inability to invest in industrial capacity, social overhead capital, and other orthodox projects of development. If the alternative is $100 million on education (E) or factories (F), a rather simple comparison is possible because neither type of investment involves population effects. Extra factories will have an effect on output through K in the Cobb-Douglas function, as extra education will through L, and the test is which equal dollar investment will increase output more.

Thus industrial investment is superior, indifferent, or inferior, respectively, as:

$$\left(\frac{K+F}{K}\right)^{k} \gtrless \left(\frac{P + E\frac{dp'}{de}}{P}\right)^{l}$$

This can be reduced to

$$\left(1 + \frac{F}{K}\right)^{k/l} - 1 \gtrless \frac{Edp'}{Pde}$$

In this form it is analogous to the rule stated in the preceding subsection.

If k and l are each conveniently 0.5, and P is 100 million persons and E or F $100 million as before, the outcome depends on K and dp'/de. Suppose K is $5 billion, or $50 of capital per head, then the value on the left side of the last equation is 0.02. Education will then be preferable if each $100 spent on it can increase the "effective" population by more than 2 persons.

This particular indifferent value for Edp'/Pde of 0.02 should not be taken too seriously. It is very sensitive to the arbitrary magnitudes assigned to l and k. For instance, if k were 0.25 and l were 0.75, educational expenditures would be neither more nor less desirable than industrial investment if $1000 of expenditure increased the effective population by about two-thirds of a man. In many underdeveloped countries $1000 represents the combined annual salaries of two or more teachers!

Fewer deaths vs. fewer births

It seems probable that educational expenditures usually earn a higher economic return than do industrial investments. And we have seen that despite the tendency to increase population, public health programs may prove themselves as effective as education programs of equal resource cost in raising per capita income. A remaining question is whether public medical programs should be directed less toward improving health, which reduces deaths, or more toward reducing births.

A plausible criterion is again PdY/YdP. Under a vasectomy-bonus plan, the resource cost of the operation might be $3, the effect on fertility might be 0.2 infants annually, and altogether 2.0 infants over the postoperative life of the husband's spouse. Thus $100 would have a negative effect on a population of 66 persons after 10 years. The question is whether $100 spent once on improving public health could sufficiently increase effective labor as to raise per capita income equivalently. It seems unlikely.

Fortunately, the real choice is not so clearcut, and public medical programs often have indirect effects that are favorable. Thus a reduction in births may make for healthier youngsters in the family, having more food and energy, and enjoying a greater ability to acquire an education later. And lower death rates may within a few generations convince parents that only a few infants need be born to ensure adult sons and daughters. These supplementary interactions are hard to measure and can often be no more than sensed. But they are important nonetheless.

CONCLUSIONS

Labor contributes more than any other factor of production to national output. Labor has a double significance because the number of workers and inhabitants of a country are usually in some roughly constant relationship. Because natural resources are limited in all countries, there are diminishing returns to labor and capital, and in severe instances the ratio of labor's marginal to average product may be a fraction of unity. Hence it is that an increasing population—if other things were equal—would result in lower incomes per capita. Fortunately, capital per head is usually increasing, and there is a steady improvement in technology. Another variable is the ratio of aggregate hours worked per head of population in a year. However, and of great importance for welfare, human quality is far from unalterable. It is possible to invest in human capital and obtain very high rates of return. Education and health expenditures may enormously increase the productivity of those who are gainfully employed. Nor are public medical expenditures necessarily limited to improving health and therefore reducing the death rate. Given political support and establishment of necessary clinics, resources can also be used to reduce births and thereby prevent rapid population growth. If the object of development is to raise income per head without adversely affecting income distribution, supplementary programs for increasing education, improving health, and reducing births are all needed. It may yet be discovered that the economics of labor quality and population control have a much greater potential than ordinary capital investment for purposes of economic development. And as these investments in human capital and welfare will ordinarily be made by governments or not at all, the opportunity costs of public sector investments in industry may be too high to be met. Perhaps, as a very general rule, private investment should be in physical capital and public investment should be in human capital.

V

Development

through trade

I<small>T</small> is common practice to distinguish between "advanced" and "backward" countries, although many of the nations of today are really in an intermediate stage of development. Some of the advanced nations (*e.g.,* Australia) were once far less developed than certain of today's "backward" countries then were (*e.g.,* India). And two hundred and fifty years ago Scotland was in many economic respects not so much more developed than Egypt. It is important to understand why certain nations have moved ahead so spectacularly whereas others, except for population growth, have been comparatively stagnant. One explanation lies of course in basic cultural and institutional differences. But another striking feature of the advanced countries is their active participation in a world trading system. For economic purposes, with the exception of the Soviet bloc and China, the countries of the North Atlantic basin are the center of this system. From them there radiates to a vast global hinterland a flow of inventions, entrepreneurship, capital, and finished goods in exchange for raw materials and unfinished products. The end of colonialism has not altered this economic relationship. Although this highly organized trade in ideas and goods has not benefited all countries equally, it has almost certainly left them better off than they would otherwise be, one proof being the extreme backwardness of those countries that have hardly any exports. Because of the importance of international trade for economic development, and the need to expand this useful intercourse despite the tendency of many new governments to restrict it, the next five chapters are devoted to explaining the interaction between material advancement and foreign trade. A country that does not make use of the world economy will have a very much slower rate of economic growth.

23

World development
before the first war

During the past two hundred and fifty years, and associated with the spread of European culture and influence, ever larger areas of the globe have experienced a hastening economic development. And developments in ocean and rail transport after 1870 precipitated an enormous commercial upheaval. Thus:

These stupendous world movements emanating from England and France, transforming Germany and Russia, spreading to the United States, permeating South America, impinging upon Africa and reconstructing India and Japan, reacting on China, colonizing Australia and making its influence felt in remote Pacific islands, constitute the world revolution we have to examine.[1]

Although the seeds of this growth began with the great geographic discoveries by Europeans around 1500, it was not until about 1750 that a series of economic inventions which were to revolutionize agriculture, transport, and industry added impetus to European penetration and settlement of the world. Where there were sparsely populated lands in the temperate latitudes (*e.g.,* North America, Argentina, and Australia), the culture and institutions of the European homeland were soon planted. But where the Europeans came upon established native populations, sometimes of very ancient culture, the usual difficulties of development were complicated by racial tensions. Nevertheless, where Europeans penetrated, they usually went as traders, missionaries, and later as governors. In time these colonies and economic satellites became an important source of primary materials and tropical produce. After the technological revolution, and the resultant emphasis on industry, the leading countries in Europe increasingly imported food as well. This chapter describes the spread of European culture and influence through a vast overseas hinterland prior to World War II.

[1] L. C. A. Knowles, *Economic Development in the Nineteenth Century* (London: Routledge and Kegan Paul, 1932), p. 5.

SPREAD OF EUROPEAN INFLUENCE AND CULTURE

Modern economic development began with the great geographical discoveries made by Europeans from around 1500. Within a century the
Spanish were established in much of Central America and the Philippines,
and the Portuguese had a foothold in Brazil, around Africa, and in
Macao. By 1700 the Dutch were in the Indies and at the tip of South
Africa, while the British and French were on the east coast of North
America and had "factories" at ports on the African West Coast, in India,
as well as in the Far East. The British began to settle Australia (originally
with convicts) somewhat before 1800. But it was not until the end of the
nineteenth century that there was European control throughout equatorial Africa.

Wherever Europeans went exploring, they of course discovered natives,
but sometimes they found almost empty territories while at other times
they encountered ancient cultures. In the temperate zones especially—for
example in North America, Argentina, and Australia—the land was
sparsely populated and the natives followed a nomadic life. Neither the
North American Indians nor the Australian aborigines could assimilate
or successfully oppose the onrushing Europeans. Instead, they were
brushed aside, relocated in reservations, or killed by European diseases
and bullets. Accordingly, within a century or so, the inhabitants of these
temperate and "empty" lands were mostly of European stock. The social
values and economic institutions of Western Europe were simply transplanted thousands of miles across the oceans to places like New England
and New South Wales. The new immigrants and their descendants understood the uses of capital, the advantages of specialization, and the operations of a price system. They worked the land as individual farmers.
Political and religious freedom were highly esteemed. Indeed, for many
nonconformists and socially underprivileged, the new lands gave promise
of a better life.

But in Asia the Europeans encountered established communities governed by local and sometimes powerful rulers, so that the early trading
expeditions had to negotiate for commercial privileges. Initially they required permission to establish a resident factor or agent, with a factory
or warehouse in the port, and sometimes a particular company would
obtain monopoly rights over the import and export of certain goods. As
volume of trade increased, and the number of company employees in
these ports grew, the Europeans were often ceded areas where they could
govern themselves in their own way. As the expanding trade often originated with inland communities and tribes, it was inevitable that the
coastal settlements should extend their influence further inland. And
except in China, this process was often expedited by participation in

local dynastic wars. However, so firmly established were the local cultures and so numerous the natives in countries such as India that the intruders were eventually either eugenically assimilated or politically evicted. The strong official attitudes of the British and Dutch regarding miscegenation—although it did not prevent the emergence of an important class of Eurasians—did ensure that the early colonists' pure-bred descendants would in the end have no choice but to go.

The history of Europeans in Latin America was somewhat different. The Spaniards had first to conquer the established indigenous empires of the Central American plateaus. But social attitudes toward intermarriage with native women—except among a few noble houses—were far more tolerant. In Argentina and Chile, the European stock gained ascendancy; but in the rest of Latin America, the opposite was the case, the racial problems of Brazil being further complicated by the importation of African slaves for plantation and mine work. Despite this confused racial situation in many South and Central American countries, the culture of these countries follows many traditions of the Iberian peninsula even to this day. Although political independence was gained throughout Latin America as a consequence of the Napoleonic Wars, almost three centuries of Spanish and Portuguese administration had rooted European influence throughout these territories. The missionary efforts of the Catholic Church in Latin America, so much more successful than in Asia, have been another powerful factor in maintaining an essentially European culture among influential circles. Accordingly, although the populations of Central America are predominantly not of European stock, these countries have economic institutions largely similar to those of their original mother countries.

Sub-Sahara Africa has peculiarities of its own. Except for South Africa and Southern Rhodesia, where there are considerable European settlements, the population is almost entirely black African. The local culture was extremely primitive, and the native tribes (apart from those around the ports) have had only limited contact with Europeans for barely the past hundred years or so. It is for these reasons that economic development in Equatorial Africa may prove to be so difficult. Political principles of self-determination, applied hastily without regard to levels of political and social development, have resulted in casting adrift people whose own cultures are not only inferior (at least economically) but who have not yet had time to acquire Western values and institutions.

This brief and superficial survey is included because economic development, at least in the sense that it has occurred in North America, is an aspiration of hundreds of millions of people with inherited social cultures that are incompatible with substantial material advance. History suggests that European institutions and attitudes, such as characterize North America and also European Russia, are a necessary but insufficient condition of economic development. If so, this means Asians and Africans may have to choose between traditional cultures and material well-being. This is far less so of Latin Americans, and does not apply at all to white South Africans and Australasians.

THE ECONOMIC REVOLUTION IN WESTERN EUROPE AFTER 1750

Why is a European way of life apparently so conducive to material prosperity and economic development? It is not really that Europeans—and their North American "cousins"—have so much capital to combine with their labor and natural resources. Great Britain, and other European countries too, had initially to save their own real capital investments. The efficiency of European-type economies seems to stem rather from a combination of political liberty, private organization, and decentralized decision-making in production; extremely personalized incentives to work, save, and risk; continuous exploration of natural and biological phenomena for useful applications; maintenance of law and order; and honest government. Historically, the Protestant Reformation was both a cause and effect of the intellectual skepticism and curiosity that were to result not only in Newtonian physics and Darwinian biology, but also in modern agriculture and industry. This broad social and intellectual movement also gave rise to the various economic revolutions that originated in Great Britain after 1750.

It is customary to identify these changes with a series of mechanical inventions that occurred in British industry around 1800. But the Industrial Revolution in its broadest sense included equally significant and quite essential revolutions in agriculture and transportation. Moreover, although the new textile machines and subsequent steam engines attract attention, they were preceded by important organizational changes. As mentioned before, Adam Smith wrote his book prior to 1776, and before the rise of modern industry with all its power-driven machinery. And yet this author had witnessed sufficient economic changes already in his life to warrant an inquiry into the causes of the wealth of nations (see Chapter 4).

Agriculture

Many of the changes that revolutionized agriculture in Great Britain between 1750 and 1850 are relevant to agricultural reform elsewhere. These changes increased the domestic output of food, and thereby enabled the industrial population of the country to increase rapidly. Before the last quarter of the nineteenth century, when steamships and railroads began bringing North American grains, Argentine beef, and

Australasian farm products to British dining tables, British industrial development depended upon domestic agricultural productivity.

A major innovation, introduced by Jethro Tull (1674–1741) was the substitution of a mechanical seed drill for hand sowing and the use of an animal-drawn multiple hoe for cultivating the soil. The possibilities of increasing the output of meat, wool, and milk through deliberate and selective breeding of livestock, was dramatically shown by Robert Bakewell (1725–1795). By 1750, partly under the impetus of Viscount Townsend, the four-course rotation of wheat, turnips, barley, and clover had begun to replace the manorial practice of leaving each field fallow one year in three.

Most important perhaps was the completion of the Enclosure Movement between 1760 and 1815. The effect was to consolidate the numerous strips in the various large open fields which villagers had traditionally worked so that each tenant or freehold owner had a single parcel of land to farm. This meant that each villager, who previously had some good and some bad, some fallow and some cultivated land now had the complete use of particular holdings. These were enclosed by hedges to prevent other farmers' livestock from entering. And the quality of such land, plus the extent of the improvements and structures upon it, determined its rental or sale price. These drastic changes made it possible for individual farmers to experiment with novel ideas; change their crops and livestock in accord with market demands, and invest capital in drainage, equipment, superior breeding stock, hedges, and better barns. Another and frequently less happy result of the enclosure system was that many villagers, with modest and insecure land use rights under the old system, were expelled without compensation and left with no alternatives but to become agricultural laborers, industrial workers, or emigrants.

One new agricultural practice was the use of fertilizers other than ordinary manures. By the middle of the nineteenth century, the scientific understanding and use of fertilizers had become widespread. For a time Peruvian *guano* was imported in large amounts. But by 1843 the production of artificial superphosphates had begun. During the following years the principles of nitrogen fixation, methods of crossing plants to obtain desirable hybrids, and numerous other features of modern scientific agriculture were discovered.

In many ways this agricultural revolution was as considerable as the Industrial Revolution with which it was associated. Few people in 1750 would have thought it possible that within two hundred years there would be great nations such as the United States, almost self-sufficient as regards food, and with barely an eighth of their gainfully employed population occupied in agriculture. Only through fantastic increases in rural output per man has it been possible for so many people, engaged in industry and commerce, to be fed by so few.

Transport

As late as 1750, the travel of persons and the transport of goods in Western Europe was primarily by water or on the backs of animals. The state of the undrained dirt roads, especially in winter, was such that wheeled vehicles were of little use beyond the cobbled streets of the towns. Hence countries with indented coast lines, good harbors, and long navigable rivers enjoyed considerable advantages.

In Great Britain, there was a great road-building period from about 1760 to 1830. Many of the first turnpikes were constructed for profit by private syndicates that charged tolls. The peculiarity of the new roads was that they were "metalled," with a hard cambered surface of fine angular stone fragments, and were raised or drained to prevent flooding. Good roads made it possible to travel by stagecoach rather than horseback, for merchandise to be moved by cart rather than by packhorse, and for inland towns to gain in importance.

The same period was one of extensive canal building, often privately financed by mine owners eager to move coal to urban and industrial centers. Because of the cheapness with which heavy materials can be moved by water, river improvement and canal interconnections were also pressed in the Low Countries, France, and Germany, but primarily after the European wars that followed the French Revolution. Road-building and canal construction, by making transportation easier and cheaper, together served to extend the market and encourage productive specialization.

Although steam engines were originally used for mine-pumping and hoisting, their use as railroad locomotives proceeded apace after 1830, and in many ways the steam railroad had an importance in the nineteenth century similar to that of the gasoline-driven motor car in the twentieth. It was inevitable that in time the steam engine would be installed in ships, but it was not until development of the propeller (in place of paddle wheels) that ocean-going steamships became practical and profitable. By the last quarter of the nineteenth century the new steamers were driving sailing ships from the seas. Because steamers did not have to follow longer routes to obtain favorable trade winds, and could navigate under the fitful breezes of the Red Sea or Gulf of Panama, for example, the Suez and Panama Canals became projects to be seriously considered.

Regular (and often refrigerated) ocean transportation made it profitable to produce wheat on the Canadian prairies, butter and lamb in New Zealand, wool in Australia, and beef in Argentina. New steam railroads, as a means of bringing raw produce to and from ports, also played a part. The farms of the New World became almost as much part of the economy of Western Europe as its own agricultural lands. By exporting these foods, fibers, and raw materials, the "empty" lands of recent settlement were able to service the capital debts incurred in London and Paris for development. Division of labor came increasingly to be practiced on a truly international scale.

Industry

There were many changes occurring within the "industry" of Great Britain and France before new mechanical discoveries—such as Hargreave's spinning jenny in 1767—introduced what is often described as the Industrial Revolution. These tendencies were drastically accelerated by the advent of water- and steam-powered equipment in industry. Other important developments included the undermining of the guilds, the weakening of the apprentice system, and the establishment of factories. Because these changes in organization are less spectacular than the new machines in textiles, steel, and mining, they are often overlooked. But these and other cultural and institutional changes of almost two centuries ago in England may have in large measure to be duplicated in some of today's more backward countries.

"Manufactures"—as the word itself indicates—were originally products made by hand. The "manufacturer"—the merchant artisan—was usually a member of a trade association, called a "guild." Silk-makers, silversmiths, coopers, and others each had a separate organization. The guilds regulated markets, enjoyed certain privileges from the Crown, but sometimes were not permitted to sell directly to consumers. They employed experienced journeymen who ordinarily were paid by the day, and also trained apprentices indentured to their master for seven years or so. The journeymen were skilled workmen, often fine craftsmen, and in theory the apprentice gave several years' labor in return for board and lodging and instruction in the skills of his chosen trade. These merchants and craftsmen were town dwellers, beyond or exempt from any serious feudal obligations, and some guild members accumulated considerable capital over the generations. They constituted the backbone of the growing bourgeois class.

There was also "manufacturing" in the poorer agricultural regions, performed at home by the women folk of peasant cultivators, as a means of supplementing their income. During most of the year, women are not needed to work in the fields, and in areas where crops are meager there is always an urgent need to earn additional income. Accordingly a special kind of entrepreneur would purchase raw materials (such as cotton), distribute them among cottagers in villages around the towns, and pay them for working-up the goods (such as spinning and weaving). This "putting-out" system lasted for many decades and involved considerable costs for capital (to buy materials) and transport (by packhorse). Other family responsibilities and emergencies sometimes resulted in the work not being completed in time for the next visit of the itinerant employer. And so, even before power-driven machinery was introduced, there was a tendency to assemble women and children into "factories." There were definite hours for work could be established, materials could be processed for resale more rapidly, and standards of quality could be better enforced.

The new textile innovations—such as Arkwright's water frame and Crompton's "mule" for spinning and winding—could not be turned by hand but required water power. This involved dams, flumes, and shafting with belts to produce and transmit power from water to machines. Not only were capital requirements greatly increased, but it became necessary for "manufactures" to be produced under one roof near the source of power. The "putting-out" system was doomed. More violent, though, was the impact of machinery upon certain guild members and their journeymen employees. The latter were skilled and grown men, but the new machines made their skills almost useless. Moreover, the new textile machinery could be tended by women and children, who were available at very low wages. And even unskilled farm laborers, forced off the land perhaps by enclosures, could immediately compete on even terms with skilled artisans who had served many years of apprenticeship.

"Industrialization" also threatened and finally eliminated many other artisans, such as the smith, the potter, and the shoemaker. The same conflicts of interest that occurred in Great Britain around 1800 have been duplicated in most underdeveloped countries during the past half-century. And in more remote and backward regions, and especially in rural subsistence areas, the village artisans still have an economic role to play.

These transitions involve the same interaction of forces today. Improved transportation permits a greater scale of production and more intense specialization by extending the market. The use of machinery increases capital requirements and forces employees to work under factory discipline rather than as self-employed artisans at their own pace. These innovations inevitably arouse fierce resistance. But cultural change and economic development go hand in hand.

Emergence of entrepreneurs

One feature of European economic development between 1750 and 1900 was the increasing importance of entrepreneurship. Many of the innovations in machinery and equipment in transport, textiles, and iron and steel were actually introduced by others than the inventors. Moreover, these energetic and imaginative innovators had often to find someone else with capital to finance their ventures. To be successful, they had to bring together capital, labor, and equipment in novel and gainful ways.

No one can be certain how or why some nations in some periods seem to develop an entrepreneurial class that can innovate, make investment decisions, and command capital of its own and others. The immediate cause may be a political upheaval, such as the French Revolution, which removes the heavy hand of inherited privilege. Sometimes a religious schism may stimulate intellectual inquiry and practical experimentation.

The circumstances most conducive to entrepreneurship seem to include spiritual liberty, an atmosphere of pragmatism, a sense of change and progress, government by law, legal protection of individual rights and property, and a minimum of government interference in economic affairs save when the general welfare demands it. These favorable conditions were enjoyed by most of Western Europe and North America throughout the nineteenth century. They do not exist to any marked degree in the less developed countries of today.

A major question for social scientists is whether these conditions were peculiar to these particular countries or to the nineteenth century itself. In other words, can they be duplicated in backward countries during the latter half of the twentieth century, or is it that times have irrevocably changed? There are some who feel that only government officials can perceive economic opportunities nowadays, and that only taxpayers and government bond buyers can provide capital in adequate quantities, so that development must await public entrepreneurship.

This was very much the attitude of European statesmen during the sixteenth century and for some time later, and the mercantilists especially believed that national power and wealth could be enhanced most readily by government economic regulation. As these attitudes were slowly eroded there was an unspectacular but steady material improvement in Western Europe during most of the seventeenth and eighteenth centuries, but its principles remained unheralded until Adam Smith. The *laissez-faire* economists who followed him essentially supplied a theoretical rationale for an economic development that had already started.

Sources of capital

European development was financed by domestic savings. This is significant today in view of the widespread clamor for capital assistance among the more backward countries. Europe didn't borrow during the early stages of the Industrial Revolution—there were no other countries able to lend. How, then, were they able to save?

The Spanish obtained silver and gold from their overseas possessions, especially during the sixteenth and seventeenth centuries, and often by force. Much of this bullion and specie was distributed throughout Europe through Spain's trade with Holland, Britain, and other countries. Thus Spain was able to accumulate capital in part because of a favorable trade balance financed by colonial gold. But the other European countries that desired an export balance with Spain, partly because they needed specie and bullion as money, were also able to accumulate producers' goods.

It is evident that these countries, although their per capita incomes were not high in real terms, produced more than they consumed. Despite wars and epidemics, some people were apparently willing and able to save over the generations. The lower classes presumably saved very little, but on the other hand they lacked the assets to dissave, so that landlords, merchant-capitalists, and a few exceptional freehold farmers must be considered as the original sources of investment during this period.

Among the merchants—many of whom were puritanical in their spending habits at least—their property's relative safety from seizure must have been a consideration. But also important were the opportunities for gains from trade—especially overseas trade—from which large fortunes could sometimes be made despite great risks. Thus individual merchants would buy a small fraction of interest in some syndicate outfitting ships for trade in the Far East, slave-buying along the West African Coast, or occasionally raiding enemy ships. There was also considerable social mobility, and commercial successes often led to the acquisition of some lesser title of nobility. But these more spectacular exploits of merchant adventurers were probably less important altogether than the year to year denial of consumption by individuals for their own future advantage. There was litle productive investment by government during this period.

After the Napoleonic Wars, most countries permitted their colonies to trade with other countries (subject to some duty penalties), and prohibition of the slave trade was enforced when possible by the British navy. Profits and savings of European powers during the nineteenth century therefore tended to come from conventional trade with more backward countries as well as from commerce at home. These savings were presumed—at least by contemporary English classical economists—to come from the surplus value accruing to landlords and capitalists.

In this way many landlords became capitalists as well, selling farms to invest in coal mines, ship canals, and—later—railroads. The new industrial towns, often constructed on previously vacant land, provided additional incomes to landlords from which they could save. However, while landowners were often the immediate investors, the ultimate source of savings was improved technology in agriculture (which permitted individual tenants to purchase farms) and in industry (which permitted adequate wages to pay for food).

The poor and backward countries of today cannot become technological leaders, save in a few special lines, for many decades or even centuries. However, to facilitate saving, improvements in technology over time within a country probably matter more than the country's state of arts at any one time relative to that of other nations. A people becomes accustomed soon enough to a new level of consumption; former luxuries come to be deemed necessities. Many of today's underdeveloped nations with very low rates of saving from annual income probably have higher per capita incomes in a real sense than did some Western European countries in 1800. An advancing technology, with continual and useful innovations, makes people feel better off year after year so that they save appreciable fractions of their income. This is yet another reason why saving depends on entrepreneurship. A stationary economy, where consumers have long ago become accustomed to their incomes, is likely to have lower savings rates from equivalent incomes per head.

Growth of population

The populations of European countries, despite substantial emigration, doubled and tripled during the nineteenth century. Compared with the natural increase of former centuries, this multiplication was rapid indeed, but it falls short of present population growth rates in many undeveloped countries. This may prove to be a significant difference.

There is some evidence to suggest that the birth rate began to fall in France soon after the Napoleonic Wars. It began to fall in most of Protestant Europe and America during the last half of the nineteenth century. Throughout the present century, among the white races in countries of predominantly European culture, the birth rate has been far below the biological maximum. It appears that the birth rate in Europe was *already* falling at the time that death rates began to fall in response to such new medical techniques as inoculation and sterilization. Public health activities began to be effective by the latter half of the past century, and this explains the rapid population growth in Europe during the Victorian period. But even so the rate of increase fell considerably short of the 2 per cent a year so typical of many Asiatic countries today.

Moreover, unlike contemporary Asians, Europeans have during the past hundred years been able to emigrate to the new lands of recent settlement. Thus the Irish potato famine helped to populate Boston. The annual exodus from certain other European countries exceeded 1 per cent for several years. These emigrants did not only voyage to North America—which has received as many as a million immigrants in a single year—but also to South America, South Africa, and Australia and New Zealand. While migration on this scale is now impossible, largely due to United States immigration restrictions established shortly after World War I, it was an important relief from population pressure for several generations. Thus an annual population loss of 1 per cent through emigration, if it reduced the growth of resident population from 2 per cent to 1 per cent yearly, would mean a doubling rather than a quadrupling of population every 75 years or so.

The important point is that economic development in the Western countries was well underway before modern medicine caused death rates to decline markedly. And by the time public health measures began to take effect, a falling birth rate and substantial emigration were combining to check population growth. The contemporary situation in many poor and backward countries is almost the opposite. Public health innovations have reduced the fatal incidence of many diseases before sustained economic development has got underway. Thus there is a rise in population rather than in per capita incomes. Moreover, to make prospects more bleak, there is in most Asiatic countries neither evidence of a decline in fertility nor the opportunity of emigration to "new" lands.

EXTENDING THE OLD WORLD INTO THE NEW

Today the term *underdeveloped country* refers usually to one that possesses ancient cultures or at least a long record of settled population and land cultivation. However, as late as 1840, the term could better have been applied to the "empty" lands that were still largely "new" to Europeans. These included not only the Great Plains and Far West of North America, but almost all of Australia and New Zealand, besides much of South America and southern Africa. And during a relatively short period—roughly from the American Civil War to World War I—these lands were explored, pioneered, subdued, occupied, and otherwise developed. There has been nothing like it before or since in the history of the world. In fact it constitutes so extraordinary a phenomenon, and from an economic viewpoint was so amazingly successful, that its peculiar characteristics need to be understood.

First, there were more than enough usable resources, so that labor was always at a premium. Population pressure, whether in the *pampas,* the prairies, or the *out-back,* was unknown. The land was of course too abundant to have much value, and in fact the wide open spaces involved special transport costs initially, but the lure of land to be had for the taking was a powerful attraction to emigrants from the Old World. Another consequence was the availability of food, including wild game and fish, so that a comparatively small fraction of the population's efforts had to be directed to feeding itself. Its released energies could be and were devoted to making capital improvements of all kinds. In a very real sense, once the early discomforts and dangers had been overcome, these were "lands of opportunity" for healthy, alert, and industrious men and their families. But the indirect cause of all these advantages was the paucity of population relative to resources.

In several instances the first impetus to permanent settlement was the discovery of gold or other minerals. Central California was moving toward a pastoral pattern of agriculture when the discovery of gold, on the lower western slopes of the Sierra Nevada (1849) opened a hectic interlude of rush and riches. The discovery of gold in the Australian State of Victoria (1851) provided a similar stimulus to immigration, transport, construction, trade, and local food production. And gold finds in the Transvaal territory of South Africa (1886) precipitated an influx of "uitlanders" that was to transform the high veld within a few decades. But it is interesting to note that these various discoveries were the result of economic development already in progress—the first California gold nugget was found in the mill race of what was to be Sutter's new flour mill—and that within a few decades after these finds many other economic activities had become established. Even without major mineral discoveries, there would have been economic development in the new and empty lands of recent settlement, but this growth would of course have been slower and along different lines.

As mentioned before, these lands were only "new" and "empty" to Europeans, not to the indigenous populations. The latter were usually driven back by the early white settlers, and pioneer families on remote farms were liable to attack as recently as less than a century ago. But the Europeans had firearms, diseases to which they were largely immune, and missionaries on their side. So in the end the North American Indian, the Australian aborigine, and the Cape Hottentot met rather similar fates. In all cases the encroaching settlers were determined to occupy the new lands, and were quite ruthless toward any native tribes that attempted resistance, so that in time these hard characteristics became typical of social life on the frontier.

Second, immigrants and capital went out to the new lands together, and one would have been little use without the other. The capital additions increased the marginal product of labor. And the extra labor in turn increased the marginal product of capital. In fact, although comparable capital-to-labor ratios were higher in North America than in Western Europe, the former borrowed from the latter. For the times, the flows of capital and migrants were enormous, and relatively quite beyond anything seen since World War II. Thus in the nineteenth century, something like 60 million Europeans migrated overseas. And during the fifty years preceding World War I, Britain alone exported capital at an annual rate of from 4 to 7 per cent of its national income.

The *kind* of immigrant was important too. Many were poor, and some—in the case of Botany Bay "colonists" in Australia—were convicts. But they came from a materialistic and experimental culture, they knew how to exploit natural resources to best advantage, and they were familiar with the construction, use, and maintenance of all sorts of structures and equipment. In short, they came from an innovating and capitalistic society, and economic development could proceed without cultural change.

The willingness of institutional and private investors in Europe to lend to North America, South America, and Australia, among other countries, was partly based on their belief that the governments of these countries would respect investors' property interests and enforce their rights. In Latin American countries there was always some danger of adverse legislation, even before World War II, but the rights of European investors were normally considered secure in those countries settled predominantly by other Europeans. And in some cases, such as that of Britain and New Zealand, creditors and debtors were sometimes distantly related. Economic development of the British dominions, prior to World War I, was almost a family affair.

About two-thirds of the capital outflow went into what today would be called social overhead capital, and altogether about half went into railroads. These projects were normally undertaken as an act of faith and before there was anything like enough traffic to justify them. In fact, the new railroads—such as the Canadian Pacific—actively recruited immigrants from Europe to settle the areas through which their lines ran. Because of the heavy losses suffered during the early years, these railroads had to be subsidized, frequently through land grants along the right of way. Most major projects were either undertaken by government (*e.g.*, water systems and street-paving) or with its support and assistance (*e.g.*, railroads, grain elevators, and ferries). So far as indirect investments through bonds were concerned, there were few spontaneous *laissez-faire* undertakings in which government had no hand. The magnitude of private venture capital is harder to assess, but it seems to have been minor in comparison.

The great contrast between nineteenth century investment in the empty and temperate lands and today's hopes for investment in tropical and sometimes crowded countries is that capital then moved with labor that could use it properly, whereas today the capital has normally to be placed in the hands of people possessing notable but uneconomic cultures. Nor is it possible, because of restrictions on immigration, for labor to migrate from Asia and Africa to be combined with capital in the so-called "white" nations. One way out of this impasse is direct foreign investment by Western concerns, such as mining and petroleum companies, but this sort of "development" has its own problems (see p. 489).

Third, the new lands would never have attracted capital and immigrants had they possessed no export prospects, for expanding exports are normally a requirement of international borrowing. It is quite satisfactory to have imports exceed exports—the balance representing capital inflows—but gross exports should promise increases if foreign investors are to have confidence enough to buy state and local bonds, corporate stocks, and so on. Thus it was that the advent of steamships and steam railroads, by bringing Canadian wheat and Australian wool much closer in time and cost to Europe, contributed greatly to the growth of these truly underdeveloped countries. The subsequent introduction of refrigeration provided yet another stimulus, for Argentine beef as well as hides could then be exported, and New Zealand butter and bacon could compete in Europe with those of Denmark. These exports earned foreign exchange to pay interest and dividends on the new countries' international debt.

Now a major and probably unique chapter of social history is over. The lands of recent settlement are mature communities. Some of them enjoy the highest per capita incomes in the world. These vast territories, which once provided barely enough to keep a few nomadic tribesmen alive, are today inhabited by many millions of people. North America has become an industrial giant which serves as an "arsenal of democracy" and invests in the new enterprises of the European Common Market. In the world of the 1960's, few development frontiers remain in which the old pioneer life still continues, except in out-of-the-way places such as Northern Queensland or Southern Rhodesia. The once underdeveloped countries of the middle latitudes have become developed nations.

The great question in the twentieth century is whether this nineteenth century experience has any relevance for the long-settled and economically backward countries of the tropics. The basic theme, in the case of Australia, Argentina, Canada, and similar countries, was economic development without cultural change. Indigenous tribal groups did not have to be converted to capitalism, induced to work for a wage, or taught a new kind of agriculture (except in South Africa). There was always plenty of land, improved transportation after 1870 made regular exports profitable, and considerable domestic saving was possible almost from the start. Also, Europeans were willing to lend capital to members of their own race and culture who observed familiar commercial principles and were governed by the same institutions. European societies and activities were simply transferred across the oceans, the same play being acted on a new stage, with nothing much altered. It has been said that:

These countries—the "regions of recent settlement"—were offshoots of European civilization. For Britain, or at any rate for Europe as a whole, investment in these areas was essentially a process of capital widening rather than deepening. Indeed, when Britain sent capital out to work with Swedes, Poles, Germans, and Italians emigrating overseas, she may have done so at the expense of the deepening which her own economy is said to have needed in the period just before the First World War.[2]

These are very different circumstances from those that exist today in, say, Indonesia, the Congo, or Honduras. The economic growth of North America in the last century is not an augury for material progress in Southeast Asia in the twentieth century. Economic development with cultural change and without abundant natural resources relative to population pressures is much more difficult and far less certain.

DEVELOPMENT THROUGH COLONIALISM

As already mentioned, Europeans were extending their influence throughout the world from the time of the great geographic discoveries around 1500, and especially from 1750 until World War I. In Southeast Asia, and indeed in all the tropical regions, native populations and civilizations were encountered (although less so in sub-Sahara Africa). This was the period in which the British, French, and Dutch Empires were founded and consolidated, and it is their former colonies that today include most of the poorest countries of the world. Accordingly, if we are to understand some of the present problems of these countries, we must know something at least of their more recent history. The economic advantages and social disadvantages of colonialism from, say, the Napoleonic Wars to World War II need to be clearly recognized. Unfortunately, since the Communist propagandists have succeeded in making "colonialism" a nasty word in international discussions, any brief and impartial description of this emotional subject is difficult.

As Adlai Stevenson has said:

. . . the horse of colonialism, whose dead body is so maltreated, was not a wholly monstrous creature. It had wicked traits, to be sure, but it was in some respects a highly useful animal. It bore many burdens whose grievous weight we are only beginning to realize as, in the aftermath of empire, we are forced to assume our share of them.[3]

How most recent colonies were established

It is important to recognize the mixed motives and varied circumstances that led to the establishment of recently acquired colonies (such as the Dutch East Indies, Ceylon, and the Congo) as distinct from those that led to the establishment of the self-governing dominions (such as Canada, New Zealand, and South Africa).

[2] R. Nurkse, "International Investment Today in the Light of Nineteenth-Century Experience," *Economic Journal,* December, 1954, pp. 747, 748.
[3] Adlai Stevenson, "The Sequel to Colonialism," *Optima* (December, 1957).

These former dependencies, usually in the tropics, were ordinarily considered not to have a "white man's climate" and hence not suitable for mass immigration. Resident Europeans tended to be posted government officials, mine and plantation managers waiting to retire "home," trading company agents, and some missionaries. The primary purpose of Europeans in these countries, apart from officials and missionaries, was originally to buy agricultural and mineral products. (Subsequently they came to supervise the mining or growing of exportable commodities also.)

The first European traders exchanged manufactured goods (*e.g.*, cloth and knives) for raw materials (*e.g.*, spices and tea) with the natives found along the coasts and in the ports. As the volume of trade increased, the coastal tribes became "middle-men," and European goods were traded much further inland for precious metals. Where the coast natives were prepared to enslave people from other tribes in order to sell them—as was the case in Africa—humans became a major export until this trade was suppressed by the British government in the early nineteenth century.

Increasing population and prosperity in Europe after 1840 greatly increased the effective demand for tropical products such as sugar, coffee, tea, cocoa, and palm oils; hardwoods such as teak; spices such as cloves and vanilla; and fibers such as sisal and jute. After 1900 there was also a growing demand for latex. Other important exports included such minerals as tin from Malaya and mica from India since the last century and copper from Northern Rhodesia and bauxite from Ghana in the present century.

European colonizers soon discovered that in order to obtain a greater export volume of these products at a lower supply price, it was necessary to organize their production. Thus "estate" agriculture came into being (tea estates in Ceylon and rubber plantations in Malaya); only Europeans had the necessary vision, capital, and perseverance to establish and operate these plantations. The extraction of minerals, except surface deposits, had always to be organized and financed by non-natives: mining at depth was an exclusive specialty of foreigners.

The early trading companies—such as the East India Company—discovered that their operations were seriously jeopardized by the general lack of law and order in many of the areas they served. Goods might be stolen along the highways, agents kidnapped, and warehouses robbed. It was not long before they were exercising police powers on a considerable scale. But their home governments eventually became disturbed over the practically sovereign powers of these private companies. Inevitably there were financial scandals. A frequent recourse was formally to annex these territories, making them Crown colonies, and maintaining order there according to more definite legal principles. Really, despite the saying that "trade follows the flag," it was more often the other way around.

One exception is Central Africa, explored mostly by missionaries within the past hundred years. The "scramble for Africa" was an extension of Anglo-German power struggles and had little commercial motivation. This is in contrast with colonization of the Far East—considered a source of trading profit since before Columbus—and cannot be considered typical.

Colonial government was usually indirect and operated through the tribal system. Chieftains were sustained in their customary jurisdiction over natives and appointed as petty magistrates. Natives were initially employed in all the lower civil service posts and eventually in all save the highest ones. Neither whites nor natives could elect representatives except to local bodies. But governors, appointed by "home" governments, might appoint advisory councils.

These colonial administrations usually invested in such "infrastructure" as harbors, railroads, telephones and telegraphs, streets and roads, and urban public utilities. These were financed by bond issues sold in European financial capitals and secured by colonial taxes. In this way India was able to borrow in London for its excellent railroad system at interest rates sometimes lower than those obtained by private railroad companies in North America.

Colonialism also entailed a limited investment in human capital. Education had to be subsidized and encouraged if only to provide literate office clerks for commerce and government. As disease is no respecter of race, public health measures of limited scope were undertaken for all—if only for the protection of the privileged. It is sometimes useful to remember that universal education and widespread inoculations against a few specific diseases such as smallpox, were not yet established practice in all European countries prior to World War I. All in all, considering the very limited tax base for financing colonial social services, what was accomplished was often both laudable and remarkable. Some of the credit must also go to missionaries, to private corporations that subsidized medical care and evening classes for their employees, and last but not least to the taxpayers of the metropolitan powers.

Colonialism served also to introduce and promote—partly through education and partly through administration—a common European language among the emerging tribes in each territory, thereby increasing personal mobility and intellectual exchange. In Africa, during the last hundred years, the imperial powers suppressed tribal wars, abolished slavery, almost eliminated cannibalism, and did much to reduce the evil influence of witch doctors. In India the British sought to prevent child marriage and long ago prohibited the voluntary immolation of widows (suttee). In nearly all colonies attempts were made to conserve wild life from extinction, and extreme instances of cruelty to animals were prevented where possible.

Of great importance was the creation in most colonies of an efficient and honest native civil service, buttressed by impartial and trained courts of law, bringing good government to millions of people for whom such values had been practically unknown hitherto. This same point has been expressed elsewhere:

. . . it was through the imperial link that thousands of Asians and Africans made their first contact with Western education and administrtaion. The numbers affected were small, constituting an elite among the subject peoples. . . . As a result, for over a hundred years a community of training, learning, and scholarship helped to create in India, for example, a small but decisive class of men and women who came to feel at home with Western techniques and concepts.[4]

Today, with almost every former colony now politically independent, these aspects of civilization are in some territories being overrun by a returning barbarism.

These recent colonies came into existence because Europeans arrived in Asia and Africa to trade. Their commerce eventually resulted in the founding of empires, not so much for the glory and panoply of imperialism, but because profitable trade required political stability. Having assumed the responsibilities of government and confronted with a growing awareness of humanity among their electorates at home, these European governments were increasingly compelled to extend social service to natives who a century before had often been considered little better than animals. Accordingly, colonialism established the preconditions of economic development in most backward countries—although this was not its original intent.

Alleged colonial exploitation

Many people think of colonialism, and even the liberal colonialism of the interwar period (1918–1939), as a form of exploitation. This misrepresentation has been sedulously maintained by native politicians seeking power, Western intellectuals who have never seen these countries, and Soviet propagandists. There are three common complaints. One is that the colonies were forced to trade with the imperial power under disadvantageous terms. Another is that they were prevented from industrializing. And still another is that native wages were deliberately held at low levels. Each of these allegations is probably true of some colony at some date. But the general situation, during the present century at least, has been very different. Certain facts and principles deserve to be known.

4 Ibid.

"Exploitation" through trade.   Until the end of the Napoleonic Wars, the colonial territories of all the European powers—particularly the Spanish possessions in the New World—were required to trade with the mother country in accordance with the mercantilist views of those days. But the loss by Britain of its American Colonies in 1776, together with the spread of *laissez-faire* attitudes among policy-makers, resulted in more liberal regulations during the nineteenth century. Preference tariffs were increasingly substituted for exclusive trade. From 1860 to 1919, Great Britain maintained an "open door" in India and in most Crown colonies, exacting only low revenue duties. Colonies like Hong Kong were virtually free ports. By World War II such nominal preferences as still existed were often mitigated by trade agreements incorporating "most favored nation" treatment. The Congo, prior to independence, daily exercised its right to export to whatever buyer would pay the most and to import from any seller that charged the least.

Although many colonial markets gave preferences to imports from the mother country prior to independence, almost all colonies sold on the world market except to the extent that they received a preference in the mother country. For instance, the British West Indies long had a preference on cane sugar exports to the United Kingdom market. Today, years after independence, a wide range of tropical products of considerable value enter the European Common Market under specially favorable terms. Natives from the colonies have also traditionally been able to migrate to the mother countries, either as permanent residents or as temporary workers, and this has been a great boon since the last war to natives from the British West Indies.

A popular view is that the kind of trade conducted by the backward colonial countries with more advanced nations (including the United States) provided very little gain for the tropical exporters of raw materials and foodstuffs. The prices of primary goods have not risen as rapidly as those of industrial goods—but then the quality of the latter has often improved enormously. It is also held that in the long run the demand for these primary materials cannot grow as rapidly as the demand for finished goods: by way of proof it is usually stated that the income elasticity of demand for food is less than unity. Forgotten, however, is the fact that food exports from the tropics are often not the simple and staple nutriments of advanced countries (such as potatoes) but more exotic goods (such as cocoa) with high income elasticities. As for materials, the advanced countries are rapidly either depleting their own ore reserves or losing their comparative advantage in supplying minerals. Europe and North America have increasing import demands for newsprint, tin, copper, bauxite, asbestos, and other materials. Except for reusing scrap metals, the industrial nations are dependent on other countries for many materials, and increasing prosperity in Europe is making this evident.

The greatest threat to some of the backward countries is really that of synthetics—substitutes for silk and rubber, for example—but as though in exchange the petro-chemical industries are innovating new products (*e.g.*, fertilizers) of potential significance for underdeveloped countries.[5]

It is also necessary to distinguish between those tropical exports that are ordinarily grown by small holders (*e.g.*, cocoa in Ghana) and those that are produced on great "estates" with foreign capital and under foreign supervision (*e.g.*, sugar in the Caribbean area). The latter are really outposts of the advanced economies, geographically situated in a backward country perhaps, but to a considerable extent isolated from its economy. These direct investments by North American and West European companies result in the payment of taxes, export duties (sometimes), royalties (in the case of mineral concessions), and wages. However, profits are banked in London, New York, or some other financial capital, and sales are usually for pounds sterling, dollars, or some other hard currency. Thus a change in an export's price may affect a company's profits rather than its disbursements in the producing country.[6]

Analytically and statistically, it is impossible to assess the relative gains for backward and advanced countries from trade between them. If the underdeveloped countries have gained less, in some hard-to-define and impossible-to-estimate sense, it has not been because of price-rigging in the world markets in which these primary products are normally sold. And the real question, also without any possible answer, is: How would this native labor have otherwise been employed? Would the Sinhalese and Tamils who grew and picked tea in Ceylon have developed vigorous industries equally capable of exporting against competition from more developed countries? Would the Bolivian tin miners have otherwise formed a cooperative to produce radio sets? Wasn't it better to learn and earn something rather than earn nothing? And colonial exports, although the product of foreign capital and management, did place foreign exchange earnings—and hence goods—in the hands of native workers and local governments.

Preclusion of industry. The failure of many poor and backward colonies to industrialize has been laid at the door of imperial policy. It is alleged that colonial governments, out of concern for manufacturing interests at home, prevented the establishment of competitive manufactures. This is something that is very hard to prove or disprove for the present century.

However, the imperial powers were also producers of capital equipment, and the companies concerned were just as eager to sell their

---

[5] This subject of secular terms of trade changes is discussed in some detail in Chapter 25.

[6] The pros and cons of direct investment, as against loaning capital to native entrepreneurs in the backward countries, are discussed in Chapter 26.

machinery abroad as they were to sell it domestically. Thus the British manufacturers of cotton textile machinery were more than willing to equip Indian textile factories, despite the loss in trade this meant ultimately for Lancashire. In fact, especially since World War I, the leading imperial countries have had a considerable stake in the industrialization of less advanced nations for this same reason. Industrialization means all sorts of sales by producers of machinery. Backward countries don't happen to make large electrical generators, heavy earth-moving equipment, electronic control devices, wharf cranes, diesel locomotives, and so on.

Colonial officials, although sometimes subservient perhaps to industrial interests in the mother country, were usually also eager to develop new sources of local tax revenue and foreign exchange. Often a strong emotional identification would attach a governor to his colony, or a native commissioner to his district, and it was usually official policy to start new economic activities so long as they showed some promise of paying their way. Many experiments to see whether some alien crop could be grown locally are little known because they proved unsuccessful. Major achievements, such as tree rubber production in Malaya, are naturally fewer.

Although impossible to prove conclusively, it is more likely that industrialization in the colonies has been slow because their comparative advantages lie in other directions, and notably in the supply of minerals and tropical vegetable products. It is hard to believe that the management and resources that went into exporting Manilan hemp, Caribbean sugar, or Malayan tin, for example, could have been better invested in, say, local plants for making motorcycles, refrigerators, or turret lathes for export. Finished goods exported from colonies tend to lack style (if consumer goods) or be obsolete (if producer goods). In practice, industrial goods exported from former colonies tend to go to still less developed countries, and especially toward markets that lie "away" from competitive advanced countries in terms of transport costs. The more modest sort of industrialization that usually pays is putting more value added into material exports (i.e., limited processing of raw materials) and almost finished imports (by assembling tractors locally, for instance).

The limited state of industrialization in former colonies is probably best explained by Engel's law—assuming finished exports offer no real opportunities—which states that industrialization must wait upon increased food supplies and increasing incomes per head. It is only through improved agricultural techniques that rural labor can be released to urban industry and manufacturers can find domestic markets for their products. If colonialism is to blame for a lagging industrialization, it is really to blame because per capita income did not rise more rapidly under foreign rule, and to assess this "guilt" one could examine whether family consumption levels and food intake have risen faster or more slowly since independence.

Wages too low. The wages of natives in the colonies, as in other backward but independent countries, appear to be inhumanly low to most North Americans. These men *must* be "worth" more! They are surely being "exploited"!

It is often overlooked that native labor in the colonies, lacking many personal traits and skills that are taken for granted in more prosperous countries, is often of value for its muscular strength and little more. And native workers may be physically weak from disease, parasites, and poor nutrition. They were and are frequently illiterate. They may be unreliable and clumsy, and so may damage expensive equipment or fail to maintain it. Except under close supervision they may work as little as possible. When needed they cannot be found. Special safeguards may be necessary to prevent theft of tools and materials. In Africa especially, "cheap" labor has often proved very expensive, although the truth of this statement may be hard for anyone to believe who has not worked with it. Labor productivity depends largely on basic cultural attributes.

The need for fundamental changes in attitude among ordinary workers and peoples in Central Africa has been well stated by a man who has given most of his life to helping them. Some years ago Dr. Albert Schweitzer wrote:

The task of the whites is to make good and worthy people out of the natives. . . . This work of education is only in its initial stages. It will take time. In order to meet new demands the native must develop and strengthen certain qualities. Seriousness, faithfulness, sense of responsibility, honesty, trustworthiness, love of work, devotion to the calling in which he is placed, enterprise, prudence in the management of his material welfare, independence—these qualities are what constitute character. . . . We, the whites, have won this character in a long development. With the native it will also take generations.[7]

So long as there is competition among employers in a region, wages that are too low will be evidenced by vacant jobs that cannot be filled, but in the colonies the situation was and is more often the reverse. Thus in the copper mines of Northern Rhodesia, there are far more applicants than jobs, and the African labor turnover is lower than that of any major industry in Europe. Whether out of human altruism or political perspicacity, subsidiaries of Anglo-American corporations sometimes pay more than the market really requires.

The basic reason why wages are low in most former colonies is that job applicants have such unrewarding alternatives in native subsistence agri-

[7] Albert Schweitzer, "Our Task in Central Africa," reprinted in *The Africa of Albert Schweitzer* (New York: Harper & Row, Publishers, Inc., 1948). Of course Dr. Schweitzer was referring to natives of the interior, who have only had comparatively recent contact with the outside world.

culture. This is mostly due to low rural productivity, attributable in turn to wasteful practices, or excessive population in relation to usable land. And within the subsistence family, the fruits of extra work are shared by many mouths.

Low wages in native industry were and are attributable to ineffectual employers. Where owners lack managerial skills, technical knowledge, or adequate capital, productivity and wages will be low. Bad entrepreneurs are a misfortune to themselves and to their employees, but they can hardly be said to exploit the latter.

Initially, low wages are a stimulus to economic development, harsh though this may seem. Sometimes low wages serve to attract foreign capital, especially if useful natural resources are available. If a company's other costs of production are high—*e.g.*, transportation to market, fuel and power, and installation of equipment—it will only start an enterprise in a region if real labor costs are offsettingly low. If enough outside capital is attracted into an area, wages or employment will usually increase soon enough, for the truth is that unskilled native labor and skilled foreign management are complementary factors of production.

Wage comparisons between advanced nations and colonial economies are usually meaningless, for the cost and way of living, the incidental real income that does not go through any market, and the appropriate rate of exchange for translating local earnings are all so difficult to assess. Of more significance is whether real wages and earnings have increased over time in these present and former colonies. In many cases they have, and very markedly indeed as statistics and observation indicate, but in other cases there has been relative stagnation. The latter tend to be those colonies that are hopelessly overpopulated and practically devoid of natural resources, have developed no important exports, and possess a native population lacking the physical and spiritual vigor needed to help itself.

CONCLUSION

Human life involves more than economics though. And it is fashionable to explain that colonialism, while it may have helped to fill men's stomachs, has embittered their hearts and poisoned their minds. Racial antagonisms have been exacerbated. Today, in the United Nations and in the conduct of United States foreign policy, these consequences are a curse. Colonialism, with its usual color bars, was not entirely responsible for these racial tensions however. It is inevitable that there will be antagonisms when people who are wealthy, educated, and employers have skin of one color and those who are poor, illiterate, and employees have another. Even among whites, the poor do not like the rich, nor workers their bosses.

Now that colonialism is passing into history, a fair appraisal should be possible, and the economic gains set against the social costs. Government by Europeans, depending on the territory concerned, put an end to wasteful local wars, exactions by local princelings, slavery, and cannibalism. The position of women was improved. Colonialism also brought the advantages of honest civil service, administration of justice by impartial courts, and modest advances in public education and health. Transportation and communication projects, water and sewage utilities were other benefits. Sound monetary and reliable tax systems were not the least of colonialism's contributions. Some backward countries today are in danger of losing such preconditions of real economic development.

For these and other reasons, it can be stated that colonialism *was* economic development, given earlier conditions of progress. It is hard to imagine how these political and economic foundations of growth could otherwise have been established in the nineteenth century. Colonialism was apparently an inevitable but passing stage, and it is important to realize that the world's social conscience has begun to waken only quite recently, so that many conditions that seem inhuman today were entirely acceptable before. It is perfectly natural and proper that economic development in the twentieth century should operate in other political forms and with other social values than hitherto. We can only agree with Tennyson that

> The old order changeth, yielding place to new:
> And God fulfils himself in many ways,
> Lest one good custom should corrupt the world.

24

Making use of
the world economy

No country that is small and backward can hope to advance materially if it attempts to exist in isolation outside the world economy. For all, save countries which are as large as continents and contain a wide variety of natural and human resources, autarky and stagnation go together. Even the Soviet Union, despite forced saving and labor consumption, has found it advisable to trade rather extensively with its satellites. The countries considered here—some of them quite small in population and limited in resources—cannot hope to progress without investing foreign savings, employing foreign skills, and using foreign goods. Somehow, the exigencies of the Cold War notwithstanding, payment must usually be made for hiring other people's money and using other people's services and goods. And the only method of payment is to export goods and services in return. Hence a government that deprecates exports, and adopts policies that must sooner or later end capital inflows, is making its subjects pay a high price for something. The something may be a desire to escape "colonial" trade patterns or to prevent certain symptoms of domestic monetary inflation from becoming too apparent. Often the difficulty is that domestic political considerations result in national economic policies that the world commodity and financial markets find unsound and impracticable. The results of such a verdict—for example, capital outflows and export declines—are often more than a proud and opinionated government will accept. It may then be tempted to impose exchange controls and import restrictions.

NATIONAL ACCOUNTS AND INTERNATIONAL
TRANSACTIONS

The manner in which a nation "pays its way" in the world can best be understood through a description of various accounting records that today are standard analytic tools among economists. One is the nation's balance of payments with the outside world. Also important are the accounts that reconcile a nation's production, investment, and consumption with its imports and exports. For example, it is conceptually possible for a country to experience an increase in domestic product but an unchanged national income. Also, borrowing from abroad may take the form of consumer rather than producer goods imports. A certain amount of familiarity with international economics is essential for an understanding of economic development, especially when backward countries are small and produce only a limited range of goods—as is usually the case.

Balance of payments

It is possible to estimate for a given period (such as a year) all the credits and debits that accrue to the residents of a particular country from their transactions with nonresidents. Credit transactions are those that give residents claims to payment on others, such as exports or the sale of securities. Debit transactions are those that give nonresidents claims upon residents for payment.

Examples of credits and debits. A typical underdeveloped country such as Pobakland will have various primary exports—mostly mineral and agricultural products—that occasion credits. Its major debit transactions are likely to be imports of finished producer and consumer goods. If it is borrowing from abroad, it is selling bonds and stocks whose foreign purchasers (the lenders) must pay for their securities (subscribe the capital); hence the borrowing contract gives rise to credits in the debtor country's balance of payments for the year. Underdeveloped countries usually owe interest and dividends on balance, and these occasion some debits.

It is worth noting that an act of payment is a credit for the paying country and a debit for the payee country. This is because the payor has canceled an obligation to pay by actually paying. Hence an increase in foreigners' ownership of local bank balances is a credit in the balance of payments of the local country for—other things being equal—there has been a reduction in the claims of foreigners to payment.

The major accounts. A nation's balance of payments is usually divided into various categories. The most important of these are the current account, the long-term investment account, and the short-term account. Each of these is subdivided in turn. A common scheme of classification with hypothetical values is given below.

It is usual to list the total credits and total debits for each subclass, together with the net balance for each, a credit balance being termed a "positive" or "active" balance. The grand total of all debits should equal the grand total of all credits. This simply means that the net values of the major accounts must algebraically sum to zero.

	Credits	Debits	Balance	
Current Account				
Merchandise trade balance	40	55	−15	
Services	5	10	− 5	−35
Interest, dividends, and profits	2	17	−15	
Long-Term Investment Account				
Direct investment	28	3	+25	+20
Indirect investment	1	6	− 5	
Short-Term Account				
Bills of exchange	2	1	+ 1	
Bank balances	11	2	+ 9	+15
Gold	5	0	+ 5	

The representative account balances given in the above example illustrate several things. First, Pobakland has an "unfavorable" balance of trade, export credits being less than import debits. Second, the residents have made considerable use of foreign transportation and other services. Third, the country is apparently a debtor nation, for it owes more on interest, dividends, and paid-out profits than it is owed. Fourth, the current account as a whole is negative, which means that the nation must be borrowing on balance to settle this current deficit. Fifth, long-term capital is moving in both directions in the same year, foreigners tending to make direct equity investments in this country and residents tending to make indirect investments abroad. Sixth, the gold holdings of the country (probably held by the central bank) have declined. Seventh, the short-term account as a whole is positive, which means that the nation's liquid assets have been partly depleted in order to meet that portion of the current account deficit that was not offset by long-term capital inflows.

Analysis of liquidity and disequilibrium. The international solvency or liquidity of a country deteriorates when it has a positive balance in its short-term account. A time will come when it has no more liquid assets with which to meet the net imbalance in the rest of the accounts. Hence a positive short-term account over several years is likely to encourage withdrawals by frightened capitalists. There will be an international "run" on the central bank, people will sell local currency at a discount, and devaluation is likely in the absence of exchange controls.

Almost all underdeveloped countries do have some degree of exchange control however. Usually residents are required to sell foreign exchange earnings to the national central bank at a price defined in local currency. Residents must also buy foreign exchange from the central bank if they wish to import merchandise or buy foreign securities. The central bank, in order to husband its reserves of gold and overseas bank balances, will probably sell no more foreign exchange to domestic importers and lenders than it is buying from exporters and borrowers.

A nation's balance of payments is said to evidence disequilibrium if the short-term account either has been positive for some time or would be positive in the absence of exchange control. This is not an equilibrium situation because it cannot be sustained when the more liquid assets are exhausted. Conversely, a prolonged negative balance in the short-term account would be a sign of increasing liquidity, and the national currency would tend to appreciate on free markets.

Long-term analysis. Assuming the short-term account is more or less in balance, and over a period as long as a decade it must be approximately so, long-run analysis of a country's balance of payments is concentrated upon the relation between its current and long-term accounts. If the current account is negative, the country is either becoming more of a debtor or less of a creditor. The actual situation is usually indicated by the interest and dividend subaccount, for if this is negative the country is likely to be an absolute debtor, and if it is positive the country is probably a creditor.

Many of today's advanced countries were or are very considerable debtors, examples being the United States prior to 1917, Canada, Australia, Argentina, and South Africa. An old distinction is that between an immature debtor country (one that has a negative balance of trade) and a mature debtor nation (one that has an export merchandise balance). Some of today's most prosperous countries have graduated from being immature debtors to being mature debtors (*e.g.*, Australia), and some have graduated further to become immature creditors (*e.g.*, the United States) with an export balance but a creditor status. It is advisable for a country to go into debt if productive assets of greater value than its indebtedness can thereby be acquired or developed within the country.

Accounting for aid. Many underdeveloped countries today receive grants-in-aid that are not loans but gifts. The result is that the receiving country can import more without exporting more or borrowing more. For the recipient, the aid grant is an accounting credit, and its immediate effect is usually to reduce its need to sell its remaining liquid assets. Accordingly foreign aid might logically be included by the receiver in its short-term account. There is special merit in such accounting, if the aid is not certain from year to year, for by tradition the short-term credits in the balance of payments are those that are not obviously sustainable. However, perhaps for reasons of tact, grants-in-aid are more often listed in the current account as though they were analogous to earned export credits.

The balance of payments is neither an income account nor a balance sheet, but rather a list of claims and counterclaims to payment arising from the transactions of residents with nonresidents over some period of time. It remains to link the balance of payments with national income and investment accounts. Such a reconciliation is more exact if the physical aspects of these financial settlements are also considered.

The physical flows

It is helpful to consider the physical flows that result from economic activity within a country. In doing so one must distinguish between producer goods (including services) and consumer goods (including services). Also one must distinguish between goods that are exported and imported and those that do not enter trade. Accordingly, we shall symbolize producer goods by k and consumer goods by c, the subscripts d, e, and i indicating, respectively, that the goods are domestically produced and used, domestically produced and exported, or domestically used and imported. (Goods that are imported for export are not considered.)

It is obviously possible to describe a number of familiar national accounts in terms of these symbols. For example:

Gross Domestic Product (GDP)	$= k_d + k_e + c_d + c_e$
Exports (E)	$= k_e + c_e$
Imports (I)	$= k_i + c_i$
Gross Capital Accumulation (GCA)	$= k_d + k_i$
Consumption by residents (C)	$= c_d + c_i$

If exports and imports include all goods and services other than charges for the use of other people's savings, their algebraic sum is equal to the sum of the first two balance of payments subaccounts listed on p. 446. That is, exports *minus* imports *equal* current account *minus* net earnings of residents from the use of their real property and capital funds by foreign nonresidents. (This last is positive for a creditor nation.) The net earnings that residents obtain from tangible and intangible property abroad will simply be called Net Profits. If these net profits are zero, any surplus of exports over imports means that the country is lending to foreigners, assuming the short-term account is always balanced. Hence an important international equation is:

$$\text{Exports} - \text{Imports} = \text{Net Lending} - \text{Net Profits}$$

Of course many backward countries have an import balance for goods and services, so that the left side of this equation is negative. This indicates that the country is a net borrower if net profits are zero. But backward nations are usually debtor countries so that net profits—including interest and dividend payments—have a negative *magnitude*. This makes the net profit *term* positive, so that a given excess of imports over exports is consistent with even greater net borrowing.

If a country is receiving aid, it doesn't need so many exports to sustain the other magnitudes in the equation. Hence aid can be deducted from the right side of the equation if received or added if it is given. This gives us the following equation for an assisted country:

$$\text{Exports} - \text{Imports} = \text{Net Lending} - \text{Net Profits} - \text{Aid Received}$$

International trade and national accounts

All this should now be reconciled with more familiar national account relations. For example, it is generally held to be axiomatic that

$$\text{Production} = \text{Consumption} + \text{Investment}$$

But some of the production that occurs within a country does not belong to residents but to foreigners who own tangible and intangible property in it. Some of the investment by residents may not take the form of domestic capital accumulation but of lending to foreigners instead. Domestic capital accumulation usually exceeds domestic saving in underdeveloped countries.

Domestic capital accumulation is one magnitude that economic developers are usually concerned about. Physically, as we have seen, this is $k_d + k_i$. But how is it financed?

Part of it is financed by residents and the balance by nonresidents. To understand the exact details one must first realize that gross domestic product, which for all practical purposes here is gross value added, divides into V_r to residents and V_f to foreigners so that $V_r + V_f = k_d + k_e + c_d + c_e$. In addition, residents have some gross returns ("profits") from assets abroad designated V'_r, and when V_f is subtracted from V'_r the difference is net profits as described above. $V_r + V'_r$ *equals* gross national income of residents.

Gross capital accumulation by *residents* is hence Gross National Income − Consumption − Gross Lending Abroad. And gross domestic capital accumulation by nonresidents is simply the gross "borrowings" of residents. If these two contributions to domestic capital accumulation are summed, one has GDP − Consumption − Net Lending Abroad + Net Profits. Foreign aid should also be added. It happens that (see above) Net Profits − Net Lending + Aid Received = Imports − Exports. In other words,

$$\text{Gross Capital Accumulation} = \text{GDP} - \text{Consumption} + \text{Imports} - \text{Exports}$$

The proof is that:

$$k_d + k_i = (k_d + k_e + c_d + c_e) - (c_d + c_i) + (k_i + c_i) - (k_e + c_e)$$

and all terms on the right side of the equation cancel save k_d and k_i.

The residents of a country should not necessarily seek to maximize domestic capital accumulation. There is no advantage to them in having a great turmoil of economic activity within the country if a disproportionate share of the resultant domestic product goes to nonresidents. It all depends upon whether the country really has undeveloped potential resources and the extent to which their exploitation is for the benefit of residents rather than aliens. Nonresident capital is inclined to generate fewer benefits for the residents of a country if it is direct investment. The most favorable situation is usually where the people of a truly promising but underdeveloped country can borrow capital funds that they themselves manage. The investment of aliens is indirect in this case. Whether residents benefit depends on the productivity of capital under their management and the cost to them of hiring overseas capital.

If a people wish to maximize their real income in the future they should save now. But the allocation of these savings between domestic accumulation and foreign investment should depend upon marginal rates of return at home and abroad. In other words they should emphasize domestic accumulation *plus* net lending abroad. This is equivalent to stressing the gross savings of residents. Thus a more fundamental objective is to maximize:

Residents' Gross Savings = GDP — Consumption + Exports — Imports

the last two terms comprising the balance of trade.

Hence one prescription for development is to maximize collectively domestic output minus consumption plus the balance of trade. This is in contrast to maximizing the equation for gross capital accumulation as given above. Both formulae include output minus consumption. But maximizing domestic accumulation stresses an import balance, and maximizing residents' savings emphasizes an export balance. Other things being equal, which they so seldom are, increasing domestic economic activity requires more imports, but increasing resident national income requires more exports. It makes a difference whether a geographic area is being developed economically for the benefit of nonresidents or for that of local residents.

USING THE SAVINGS OF OTHERS

Nations vary enormously in annual savings per capita. The yearly savings of an advanced country may be around $250 per person. Among the poorest countries they may be as low as $10 a head. Eventually the marginal rate of return on domestic investment is likely to fall in advanced nations, at least relative to that in backward countries, so that were it not for political risks one would expect an increasing flow of private savings from advanced to backward nations. As we have seen, this is what happened in the nineteenth century, with the countries that acquired a modern industrial technology first lending capital funds to those developing later. Today, because fewer governments of underdeveloped countries respect the private investments of foreigners, such capital is available only to a limited number of nations. For example, the Canadian economy can borrow readily but that of Ghana or Ceylon or Brazil cannot. One of the tragedies of modern times is the increasing cost of private overseas capital that many poor countries have brought upon themselves. Backward countries that do not have a "Western" regard for private rights in property have significant access to overseas capital only through intergovernmental loans and gifts.

Advantages of borrowing

Nevertheless, the economics of borrowing from abroad are much the same as ever: it is advantageous for an economy to borrow if its residents can hire funds at a lower cost per unit than the resultant net product is worth. If value added per worker is $100 per year greater when combined with $800 extra capital obtained from abroad at an annual cost of $60, it is to the employer's advantage to borrow this capital. This means that some of the extra domestic product "belongs" to foreign lenders but that there is also a surplus for the resident entrepreneur who borrowed these funds. Moreover, there is usually some capital-widening as well as capital-deepening, so these borrowed funds may result in more workers being employed in the modern capitalist sector instead of engaging in traditional subsistence cultivation. It is therefore very much in the interest of all truly underdeveloped countries that international capital be available to them at a low rate and that individual producers use enough so that its marginal value product equals its unit cost.

Capital inflows increase gross imports

However, loans that foreign governments and international agencies are prepared to make have to be transferred. And for various reasons the transfer must take the form of goods and services that appear as debits in the borrowing country's balance of trade. If the government of Pobakland borrows dollars made available in New York, it can spend them in the United States or it can sell them to someone who wants to buy United States exports. Perhaps it sells them for Dutch guilders because it wants to import goods from the Netherlands. It might even sell the dollars to its own residents who want to import goods from the United States. In any event Pobakland—unless its central bank wants to increase its foreign exchange reserves—will import more as a consequence.

In most cases the link between capital inflow and commodity inflow is more obvious and certain. Most international development loans are "tied," the lending country advancing its own currency as a means of financing its exports. This is one reason why there is usually in advanced countries a domestic export lobby that favors foreign aid.

Governments ordinarily borrow foreign exchange to cover as much as possible of the so-called "foreign exchange component" of their economic development projects. Insofar as local materials and labor can be used, there is no direct need for foreign exchange. Some simple components may also be domestically produced. But much equipment will have to be imported, along with structural steel and electronic controls, so that many projects cannot even be constructed without using overseas funds. For public sector investments, the average foreign exchange component—depending of course on the country and projects—may approach one half the initial total cost. (For instance, for India's Second Five-Year Plan, the foreign exchange component for public sector projects was about one quarter on an average; it is estimated to be much less for the Third Plan, but realistically it will probably be around one-fifth.)

Even if the direct foreign exchange component of public sector projects were zero, the government of an underdeveloped country would often have to borrow overseas to finance planned investments. This is because direct construction labor must be paid. Even if labor's marginal product in subsistence agriculture is zero, laborers will not work for love of country or government, and hence unless conscripted they must be given wages that will enable them to establish a command over goods and services. This will occasion rising prices for food and other wage goods that, unless offset by imports of appropriate consumer goods, are unpopular and sometimes politically dangerous. Alternatively, if domestic resources employed in an expanded public sector were previously employed, the same outcome can be expected because the same workers' payroll is now seeking fewer consumer goods.

If a country suddenly accumulates domestic capital on a much larger scale than before, either wage goods prices must rise while aggregate consumption remains about the same (*i.e.*, all publicly employed labor previously had a zero product), or consumption must fall in the aggregate as wage goods rise in price (*i.e.*, these same resources were previously employed usefully), unless more consumer goods can be imported. The smaller the foreign exchange component, the greater the tendency for consumer goods prices to rise and real consumption to fall. Thus a foreign exchange increment is always needed to offset the consequences of rapid domestic accumulation of capital.

In other words, domestic capital accumulation involves some combination of k_d and k_i. If k_d is expanded and there is something like constant underemployment, c_d, k_e, and c_e will fall. If exports fall, imports must decline, unless the country can borrow or receive aid. If imports fall, and k_i

must be maintained, c_i must fall. If c_d has also declined, total domestic consumption must then fall—unless of course there is a capital inflow as loans or grants.

Accordingly, foreign exchange is needed whether or not new domestic projects need imported equipment and components. In one case the need is obvious: a country cannot have a power plant without a generator, and perhaps no generators are produced within the country. In the other instance the need for exchange is more subtle, and is based on the political necessity of keeping food prices and consumption stable, but in the end this foreign exchange requirement may be no less real. This second situation explains why food grain loans—extended by the United States under P. L. 480, for example—are so useful for countries with large planned investments (see Chapter 27).

Expanding exports necessary

During a capital inflow period, gross imports are normally much larger, but the availability of extra foreign capital is often dependent upon expanding gross exports by the borrowing country. This is because lenders, whether governments, private banking syndicates, or individual capitalists, must consider not only the solvency of the borrower but also the international liquidity of its local economy. The borrowing economy must be able to service its debts abroad, and this means increased exports, even though the trade balance may remain negative.

Specific loans (*e.g.*, bonds) have maturity dates, and the particular borrower must not only pay interest but also repay the principal, these contractual remittances usually being denominated in dollars, pounds sterling, or the currency of the lender's country. It is only recently that so-called soft loans have been made repayable in the borrower's currency. Foreign buyers of Pobakland's securities purchase them on the supposition that they can repatriate their capital at their own discretion without considerable exchange losses. The probability of satisfaction in this regard is much greater if the borrowing economy is constantly expanding its exports.

Here it is important to distinguish between principal repayment by the actual borrower and by the borrower's economy. The specific borrower presumably expects to repay. But the central bank of the borrower's country probably expects that new loans to some resident borrower will more or less replace those that mature in any given year. National economies may incur increasing international indebtedness for decades or even centuries before the tide of capital reverses itself, but individual loans will mature much sooner. Meanwhile, although the economy need not make net principal repayments, it does have to pay an ever larger amount of interest, dividends, and profits to overseas owners of local assets. These increased current expenses must normally be financed through increased exports. A national economy cannot long borrow to meet its current costs on externally supplied capital. Hence an increase in gross exports is an encouraging sign to major lenders abroad. They are always concerned over the ability of the borrowing economy—as distinct from the contractual debtor—to pay current interest and dividend liabilities.

However, in expanding exports, a country usually imports more. Increased exports induce increased imports of producer goods. If mineral extraction is increased, more parts must be imported to keep mine equipment in repair, and pit props and other imports will be needed for the mine itself. If agricultural exports are being expanded, there may have to be more imports of equipment and materials. Industrial expansion usually means increased imports of fuel and raw materials.

If the underdeveloped and borrowing economy is export-oriented, as many of them are, some given percentage increase in exports will tend to increase residents' incomes by a percentage that may not be much smaller. Part of any increased spending by these residents will be for durable consumer goods and other items that are only available as imports. Thus extra exports may induce increased imports of consumer goods also.

There are some small and developing countries where the export propensity to import is about two-thirds. That is to say, $100 of extra exports induces about $67 more imports of producer and consumer goods together. There must be many other countries for which this propensity is at least one-third.

These ideas can be expressed symbolically. Suppose that extra induced imports of producer goods is m_p times extra exports. Also suppose that induced imports of consumer goods is m_c times extra resident income. Moreover, extra resident income is y_e times extra exports. Then a given increment in exports (ΔE) occasions extra induced imports (ΔI_i) such that:

$$\Delta I_i = \Delta E \, (m_p + y_e m_c)$$

For example, if m_p is 0.35, y_e is 0.7, and m_c is 0.5, the marginal propensity for exports to occasion imports (m) is 0.7.

This tendency for exports to induce imports of both producer and consumer goods makes the economic burden of external debt service greater for the borrowing economy than is always apparent. The local economy, in order to provide say $10 million a year of extra debt service, must increase gross exports by $1/(1 - m)$ times as much. In the above example, where m is 0.7, this would mean extra gross exports of $33.3 million a year because there would be extra induced imports of $23.3 million.

The significance of this is that an individual project—such as the Kariba dam and power project in the Central African Federation—may be able to earn its contractual debt service readily enough in terms of local currency. But the economy will have to increase its gross exports by three or more times as much to transfer this debt service into dollars, pounds sterling, and other creditors' currencies. Thus with debt service on Kariba around $10 million a year, the question is whether this project will directly and/or indirectly increase exports (including import substitutes) by $30 million or more a year.

The specific borrower must consider the contractual debt service, but the government of the borrowing economy must worry about the ability of the project to increase gross net exports by several times as much. The greater the increase in imports induced by extra exports, the greater this multiple will be, and for small economies the export propensity to import can be anything from about one-third to two-thirds. The cost of induced imports is one aspect of capital transfers for economic development that has not always been sufficiently appreciated by debtors or creditors.

Apart from grants-in-aid, well-conceived international capital transfers should benefit both creditor and debtor. The borrower can presumably use these savings to better purpose than the lender. Accordingly, even though the debtors pay somewhat more for the money than the creditors could earn in their own country, they too earn a surplus. Of course this does not always happen, because particular projects may not live up to their promise. Moreover, the governments of many poor and backward countries are under political pressure to confiscate foreign-owned assets, and through exchange control they may block the repatriation of capital. These various inhibitions on capital movements from poor to rich countries have retarded economic development in backward countries. It can be a great handicap for a poor country to be forced to rely on its own savings when accumulating capital.

Finally, it would be impossible for people in one country to use the savings of people in other countries were it not for international commodity trade. It is through imports that borrowers receive loans, and it is through expanding gross exports that debtors service borrowings. There can be capital movements only if there are commodity movements. Loans cannot be transferred without net merchandise trade balances. But this is only one of the important contributions of trade to development.

GAINS FROM TRADE

International commodity trade, even if imports were always to equal exports, would occasion other considerable gains in welfare. The general arguments in favor of trade among nations are so strong that the burden of proof is always upon those who would restrict it. These gains from trade have three sources. First, a given national output can provide more consumer satisfaction if some of it is exported in exchange for imports, these being the so-called short-run gains from trade. Second, and more important, by longer-run changes in the composition of its output a nation can increase its international purchasing power. Third, and perhaps most important of all, trade in producer goods may enormously increase a nation's ability to make consumer goods. These general arguments are given immediately below: specific counterarguments in favor of restricting international trade are given in Chapter 25.

Welfare gains from trading a fixed output

Imagine a national economy which produces two goods—"cloth" and "food"—its alternative and efficient output possibilities being represented by the transformation curve TT' in Fig. 24-1. Initially it is an entirely closed economy without international trade. The closed equilibrium is shown at Q_1. The exchange rate between food and cloth is given by the line Q_1a_1. This line, passing through Q_1, is tangent to both the transformation curve TT' and the community indifference curve I_1, which is based on the income distribution at Q_1. At Q_1, the amount of cloth that cannot be made if an extra unit of food is produced is equal to the amount of cloth that consumers would forego to obtain an extra unit of food, which means that the marginal rate of substitution between cloth and food is the same for production and consumption.

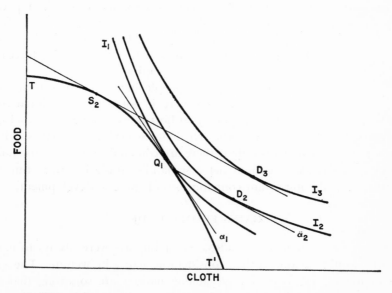

Fig. 24-1. Gains from Trading Consumer Goods Short and Long-run Cases.

Each and every point along the community indifference curve repre-sents the minimum mix of cloth and food that could be distributed so that each and every household would be as well off sumptuarily as it was with no international trade. Hence any point above or to the right of I_1 represents a mix of commodities that *could* be distributed to give each and every household extra satisfactions. The question is: Given the transformation curve, how can these people command a mix of goods superior in welfare to that actually produced? The answer of course is that unless by some accident world prices are the same as closed equilibrium prices, represented by a_1, Q_1 output can be exchanged for a consumption mix that provides more satisfaction than any mix on the community indifference curve I_1. The diagram shows an international commodity exchange represented by the line Q_1a_2. Hence, if food is exported and cloth imported, the economy can command mixes of goods that can be distributed to provide more welfare. Perhaps the new open equilibrium, with national output still unchanged, involves a superior aggregate consumption of D_2 instead of Q_1. This requires that D_2 lie above and to the right of I_1. Some trade will always be better than no trade.

Of course if Q_1 is to be produced and D_2 consumed, the government will have to intervene so that the price of cloth measured in food is higher to producers than to consumers. So this short-run optimization is not a complete optimization. This source of gain is merely included to show that redistributing an unchanged national output through world trade can increase the welfare of residents.[1]

Increasing purchasing power by adjusting national output

A more complete optimization, if a country engages in international trade, is to adjust its output so that the opportunity cost of producing one good in terms of another is equal to the world commodity exchange rate. For example, if the international price of cloth in terms of food is represented by the slope of the line Q_1a_2, at the Q_1 output far too much food is lost in producing the last unit of cloth. The best domestic output mix is indicated by S_2, for at this point a line representing world prices is tangent to the transformation curve, and the cost in food of gaining one more cloth unit is the same whether it is acquired through a very small change in output or by exporting food for cloth imports.

An open economy should always adjust domestic output so that it has a maximum value at world prices. In this way external purchasing power

[1] For various footnotes, as it were, to this argument, see S. Enke, "Trade Gains in Short Run: Reply to Mr. Kemp," *Canadian Journal of Economics & Political Science,* November, 1961.

is also maximized of course. Then the people of this country can command any mix of goods indicated by the line—parallel with $Q_{1}a_{2}$—that passes through S_2 and D_3.

Such an adjustment of national output to external prices has the potentiality of increasing welfare unambiguously, because, for any point from Q_1 through D_2, there are combinations somewhere on S_2D_3 that represent more food *and* cloth. And more specifically, considering D_2 itself, there will be many mixes along S_2D_3 that lie above and to the right of the community indifference curve (I_2) that passes through D_2. If D_2 is a free trade equilibrium, given constant output, I_2 will be tangent to $Q_{1}a_{2}$ at this point.

International trade in these two goods—combining gains both from short-run redistribution and long-run output adjustment—alters this country's production from Q_1 to, say, S_2 and its consumption from Q_1 to, say, D_3. As a minimum, one can assert increased welfare if D_3 lies above and to the right of Q_1, for this means that more cloth and food can be given each and every household. But it is possible that D_3 might involve absolutely more food but less cloth as compared with Q_1. However, so long as D_3 lies above the community indifference curve (I_1) that is based on the income distribution associated with Q_1 output, a change from no trade to this degree of trade would be advantageous viewed from the no trade income distribution.

Each possible output along the transformation curve involves some distribution of income among households. This income distribution is presumably unique if the transformation curve indicates the quantities of food and cloth that each and every household will collectively produce at each different commodity exchange rate. Then, if S_2 and D_3 are the free trade production and consumption mixes, respectively, the I_3 community indifference curve based on D_3 will be tangent to the international exchange line through S_2D_3. Accordingly, all points on I_3 can be distributed to give the same satisfaction as D_3, some parts of I_3 must lie above and to the right of Q_1 and no part can lie below and to the left of Q_1. Thus free trade, given the income distribution among households associated with it, provides potentially more welfare than does no trade.

In conclusion, then, the goods an economy produces cannot be redistributed *without* foreign trade so that each household will be as well off as it would be under free trade. There are a number of consumption mixes that an economy can command by *some* international trade that could be redistributed so that each and every household is better off than it would be at the closed economy equilibrium. These gains from trade are especially obvious where an economy reallocates its resources to maximize the value of its altered output mix at open prices.[2]

[2] The logic of this subsection is contained in S. Enke, "Welfare and Trade," *Kyklos*, No. 3, 1962.

Trading producer goods

Well over half the total value of world trade comprises imports and exports, not of finished consumer goods, but of producer goods. Most of these are partly processed materials, but some are finished capital items. It is obvious that a country does not benefit itself through trade solely by exchanging one consumer good for another. Nations find that they are able to increase their output of consumer goods by trading in producer goods. Through such trade effective transformation curves can be moved further out from their origins. The whole production block, which is the area under the transformation curve, can be expanded through producer goods exchanges.

Suppose again that a country consumes and produces food and clothing. But in addition it produces animal feeds and fodder (f) for the raising of food (F), and it likewise produces various textile fibers such as cotton (c) to make clothing (C). If this country were entirely self-sufficient, its production block for F and C would be given in Fig. 24-2 as $TT'O$. However, through trading, say, c for f, its production block for F and C might really be $BB'O$.

Perhaps the closed economy is producing Q. It can produce more F at a cost of less C output, probably making more f and less c too, or vice versa. However, this country may have a marked comparative advantage in c, so much so in fact that it is worthwhile producing c for export and importing f of equal value at external prices. As a result more F and less C will be produced at home. These possibilities are shown by the tt'

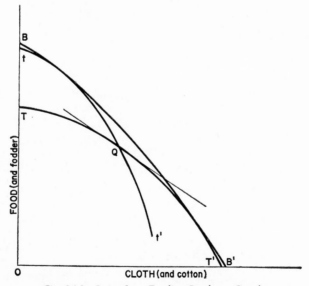

Fig. 24-2. Gains from Trading Producer Goods.

curve passing through Q. The substitution of F for C results not from trading *them* but from exchanging c for f.

It is noteworthy that tt' intersects TT' at Q. The more f that c can command in world markets, as compared with the c opportunity cost of producing f at home, the steeper tt' will be compared with TT'. The greater the fractional value of F provided by f, as for example if labor and capital contributed little of the value added, the greater the difference in the slopes of TT' and tt' near Q.

There will be a specific transformation curve, analogous to tt', passing through each point along TT'. (These other possible curves are not shown however.) To these specific transformation curves the open production block $BB'O$ will be fitted as an envelope. And for every point along BB' there is a curve analogous to tt'. It is possible that at one point TT' and BB' will coincide, which would be at the food and clothing mix that makes trade in fodder and cotton an indifferent possibility. Except for this one case, there will be trade in producer goods, if the value of producer goods imports and exports always balance. An enlarged and open production block for food and clothing results.[3]

Thus international commodity trade is a source of three gains to the residents of the country. A given output of consumer goods can be traded for a more satisfactory mix. An adjustment of output can provide a production mix that provides more command over a more valuable mix that occasions more consumer satisfaction. And the production block itself, which together with external prices determines international purchasing power, can be enlarged through trade in producer goods. All these arguments are entirely general and apply equally to backward and advanced countries.

BALANCED CONSUMPTION AND UNBALANCED PRODUCTION

The most important national use of the world economy is perhaps the simplest of all to state. Through international trade a country is relieved of the necessity of producing exactly what it wants to use. Any producer or consumer goods can be used, so long as something—of equal value if the country is not borrowing—is exported in return.

The abilities of peoples to provide different goods, given the different resources, climates, and locations of their countries, are more varied than their wants as producers and consumers. Naturally the inhabitants of every country somewhat adjust their lives to what is available—for in-

[3] The constraint that producer goods imports and exports balance in value is necessary, given the limitations of two dimensional geometry, to construct the specific transformation curves. Hence a somewhat more satisfactory maximization is really possible. See S. Enke, "Some Gains from Trade in Producers' Goods," *Quarterly Journal of Economics,* November, 1961.

stance, by eating produce of local origin whenever possible. But it would be a dismal and hopeless world if only nationally produced goods were ever available.

One index of rising income levels is the distance that consumer goods travel from their material origins to their final use. Were it possible, it would be interesting to estimate the miles moved per dollar value of each final good a household uses. A poor family in a primitive country mostly consumes local produce, often from its own holding, but this is certainly not true of, say, a prosperous American family. And the farther goods travel, the more likely they are to cross a boundary and enter international trade.

These ideas are as old as economics itself. Adam Smith described the advantages of national specialization as an example of the general economies of division of labor, and Ricardo explained how it was that differences in factor supplies and natural endowments resulted in every country having comparatively low costs in some lines of production. For generations no one has seriously argued that a people wanting a balanced diet should struggle to produce a matching output. It would usually be most uneconomic for a people to attempt production of all the goods that they wish to use. The implied goal of many development planners today— that the domestic economy should produce a complete line of consumer and producer goods—would have seemed nonsensical to economists of the past.

It also follows that no laments are necessary if, say, a cigarette lighter factory is not established in a backward country for lack of effective demand. The marginal import cost of buying a lighter from abroad may be far less than average costs of domestic production. Making cigarette lighters might directly and indirectly withdraw resources from export activities that earn enough foreign exchange to import several times as many lighters as could be made domestically.

Moreover, the availability of varied consumer products, offering good value for money, is one of the requirements of development in a backward country. After a family has satisfied its more urgent needs for food, clothing, and shelter, the utility of extra money income depends upon the availability of attractive consumer goods at practical prices. Most of these consumer goods, at least during the early stages of a country's development, are available only as imports. Excluding such imports reduces the importance of extra money earnings. And this in turn dulls the incentives that play upon a family to produce and earn more.

Many governments of new countries have an affinity toward economic planning. Each industry is supposed to fit into some program matrix, so much of industry A's output becoming an input of industry B, and so on. But planning of this kind is extremely difficult because everything cannot be foreseen. This is why exports and imports are important. For example, if industry B doesn't want industry A's output after all, the output can be sold abroad. Alternatively, if industry B has to curtail operations because it cannot obtain enough of industry A's output, the deficiency can usually be corrected by imports. The existence of an external market, where unplanned surpluses can be disposed of and unplanned shortages covered, has been an unrecognized and unappreciated blessing to many a bureaucrat in more than one planned economy.

DISCIPLINARY ROLE OF WORLD MARKETS

Another important function of international commodity and capital markets, unless a government completely isolates its subjects from the world economy, is that they reveal and penalize mistakes.

Not all products are really worth producing. They may prove to be too high in price or too low in quality. Hence they cannot be sold as exports and they cannot compete against imports. If a private firm were the producer of such a good, it would lose money and soon close down, and the resources that it was misusing would be released. However, if the inefficient producer is the government itself, responsible officials are often tempted to protect it by establishing import controls. This does not necessarily mean that private enterprises are more efficient than public undertakings, or that private companies will never seek protection, but it does mean that inefficient public activities are more likely to receive enough protection to continue their misallocation of resources.

Some countries enjoy good government, but some do not. People's lives or possessions may not be safe. Impartial justice may not be obtainable. Revolution and violence may always seem imminent. Arbitrary officials may determine what goods and funds can be moved internationally. Money may be useless as a store of wealth. Success in business may invite a shakedown. Then the main incentives of all but the poorest may be not to produce and earn more but to get themselves or their capital out of the country. Thus capital outflows, in the absence of exchange control, are often a symptom not only of fiscal irresponsibility but also of bad government.

The authority of every government, however, is ultimately limited by world markets. Government may prevent imports of goods and exports of capital by residents of a country. But it cannot force nonresidents to purchase the country's commodity exports or to lend the country capital. Every country must import some kinds of goods—not a few of which are for government—and usually it would like to import many more. However, its importing will be seriously curtailed if foreigners will not buy its goods or lend it capital. This can hurt severely. Thus, in the final analysis, most governments of small countries are subject to the economic sanctions of world markets.

In contrast, stable governments of sound economies have little to fear. If the home market can produce goods of quality at low cost, imports will not pose a serious threat, and foreign exchange can be earned through exports. Exchange controls are not required to restrain capital that would otherwise flee the country.

These favorable conditions exist in varying degree among the more advanced countries. But they exist in very few of the backward ones. Here is yet another of the many vicious spirals to be found in any study of economic development. The more prosperous countries are able to submit themselves to international competition, and the disciplinary effect has proved salutary, if painful. Governments of the poorer nations, and especially those experimenting with unsound policies, are normally unwilling to have their mistakes demonstrated for all to see: and yet they are the ones that can least afford continued economic mistakes and inefficiency.

25

The new autarky

It is the more backward and poor countries—apart from the Communist states—that have the most controls over trade imports and capital exports. Those countries that have become politically independent since World War II happen to be among the most restrictive. This new autarky is justified in various ways. Some of the economic arguments are questionable, to say the least, but there are often political and emotional explanations also.

WORSENING TERMS OF TRADE FOR PRIMARY EXPORTS

A common complaint by all countries that export primary goods— and the more undeveloped countries export little else—is that the terms of trade are continually shifting against them and that accordingly they should transfer resources into industrial employment. This is a complicated subject (already discussed in Chapter 7 as regards agricultural and industrial sectors within a single nation) so that no policy conclusion should be reached hastily. One complication is that there are three different concepts of the terms of trade.

Barter or commodity terms of trade

The simplest concept of the terms of trade is that which measures the quantity of exports that exchange for some quantity of imports. If prices of exports are declining as compared with those of imports, it will take more coffee exports to buy car tires, more lumber exports to import refrigerators, and more tin exports to import typewriters, and so on. Thus the barter terms of trade supposedly worsen if some export price index rises by a smaller percentage than some import price index does. Such an event is sure to evoke all sorts of outcries about exploitation of poor countries by wealthy ones. But there are analytic difficulties.

The trouble is that price index comparisons of this kind are largely meaningless. Primary exports by their very nature do not change much from decade to decade: copra is still copra, tin is still tin, coffee is still

coffee. But the industrial goods imports of undeveloped countries are almost constantly improving in quality. The automobile tire of today has
more miles in it than the tire of several decades ago. Tractors, trucks,
radios, and all the durable producer and consumer goods that are imported into these countries now provide better and longer service than in
the past. Basically, if it were possible to construct price indices that reflected quality changes in goods, it might well be that many primary export countries are receiving more in exchange for a barrel of oil, a ton
of copper, or a bag of cocoa today than, say, thirty years ago.[1]

Nevertheless, a commonly expressed argument is that the barter terms
of trade must worsen over time for primary goods exporters, because of a
secular and relative increase in effective demand for finished goods. As
incomes per capita rise throughout the world, households spend proportionately less on food and more on intricate consumer goods, and the
prices of the latter reflect not so much material costs as industrial value
added. Is it not madness, then, to go on stressing the export of goods for
which demand is relatively declining throughout the world?

The answer depends upon the extent to which gainfully occupied
persons throughout the world shift from primary to finished goods production, the relative increases in productivity achieved in making
primary and finished goods, and the tendency of households everywhere
to spend proportionately more on finished consumer goods rather than on
primary materials (including food stuffs) as their real incomes rise.

Consider the following very simple case, which assumes a large international economy trading freely and two categories of goods called, respectively, "secondary" (or "finished") and "primary" (including materials
and foods). Output in this international trading community was 100
units per head a decade ago. Of this, 40 units were value added in primary
production and 60 were value added in secondary production. Income per
head was the same in the two sectors.

Total output has increased to 120 units a head. Consumer preferences
are now such that households spend not 40 but 35 per cent of their
budgets on value added in primary activities; hence they now spend not
60 but 65 per cent on value added in secondary industry. Let us also suppose that output per head has increased 5 per cent in primary activities
and 30 per cent in secondary industry. (Hence the primary industry produces 42 units of value added, and the secondary industry produces 78
units.) In this case, without any shift of labor from one sector to the

1 Some barter terms of trade indices have been biased by comparing the prices of
industrial exports f.o.b. the producers' countries (*e.g.*, United States, the United Kingdom, Holland) with the prices of primary imports c.i.f. these same countries. But ocean
freights, although increasing absolutely over the past decades, have fallen relative to
the prices of most other goods and services. The barter terms of trade would have
looked better for the undeveloped countries had net prices of imports and exports
at *their* ports been compared.

other, the increase in output of each sector has matched the increase in demand for that sector's supply. The barter terms of trade, based on relative primary and secondary prices, have not altered.

This outcome is unaffected by whether all primary goods workers are in one set of countries and all secondary goods workers in another set, or whether workers of both sectors are to be found in the same proportions in each and every country. The moral is that the barter terms of trade do not have to worsen because effective global demand for secondary goods is increasing relative to that for primary goods. The decreasing relative efficiency of primary goods producers in many less developed areas of the world, as in the example above, may prevent this.

The barter terms of trade would have worsened for primary output producers if there had been a rather larger productivity improvement in primary activities and a rather smaller one in secondary industry. It would also have worsened if households had a still higher marginal propensity to buy secondary rather than primary values added as their incomes rise. In either case, there would be incentives for some primary goods labor to move into secondary goods lines in all countries, this depending in part upon national comparative advantage.

Transportation costs, quite apart from government obstacles to trade, tend to compartmentalize any international economy, so that there is a tendency for the allocation of labor between primary and secondary activities within a country to reflect its per capita income. This is one reason why one expects to find proportionately more people in primary activities in backward countries than in advanced ones. Most backward countries—quite apart from the requirements of international trade— would comparatively stress primary outputs of some kind because they have low incomes per head.

Factoral terms of trade

One suspects that the barter terms of trade concept—although popular with many special pleaders—is not useful for measuring changes in welfare. It is surely of little solace for a country to know that its barter terms of trade are not worsening because it is becoming relatively less efficient as a producer! Thus a more fundamental consideration is

$$\frac{\phi'}{\phi} \cdot \frac{P_e'}{P_e} \cdot \frac{P_i}{P_i'}$$

where ϕ is a measure of productivity per worker, P_e is an export price index, P_i an import price index, and the primes indicate the present as contrasted with some base period.

If the barter terms of trade worsen slightly (neglecting quality changes), but productivity increases considerably, people engaged in making primary products are better off than before. For example, farmers in the United States are always arguing that they should obtain "parity" prices for their output, so that the prices they receive will have the same relation to the prices they pay as they did many decades ago: but it just happens that for many crops, the output per farm worker is now several times what it was in the base period. How important is this point when it comes to countries exporting primary products?

It is necessary at the outset to distinguish between agriculture and mining (including petroleum extraction). The extractive industries are usually conducted in backward countries by large international corporations having considerable direct investments and employing the latest methods. Output per worker is usually high. The problem for the underdeveloped country is, then, to ensure that more of the output per worker stays in the country and less is distributed or banked as profit in the United States or some other rich country.

Another important distinction in agriculture is between large capitalistic plantation or estate agriculture (*e.g.*, bananas in Guatemala) and small holdings of sometimes primitive cultivation under native management (*e.g.*, coffee in Brazil). Productivity in large agricultural estates has often increased considerably. For instance, new strains of rubber trees developed since World War II give latex yields several times as great as before, and the introduction of pesticides and irrigation have sometimes raised estate output severalfold.

There is nothing about primary products, whether minerals or fibers or foods, that prevents the innovation of improved methods. There are many instances of management applying science and capital so that the net value of output per worker has risen markedly. But of course there are many cases where traditional methods are still employed so that productivity has not increased. In such cases the apparent purchasing power of rural families has declined because of adverse changes in the prices they receive and pay. Then the fault probably lies not with the product but with the producer.

Double factoral terms

A rather esoteric comparison over time involves the changing ability of a typical worker in a backward country to "command" the services of a typical worker in, say, an advanced country. If a primary product worker labors for one hundred days, will his output exchange for output that takes a secondary product worker more or fewer days of work than before? This approach to the terms of trade does not consider whether the typical primary worker is absolutely better or worse off, but only whether he is better or worse off relative to secondary product workers, and such is human nature that this comparison may have political importance.[2]

There are certainly a number of backward countries where productivity is now little or no higher absolutely than it was before, so that relatively it is now below that of those countries that have innovated. The governments and peoples of the former sense that real incomes per capita from producing primary products are falling as compared with increasing real incomes per capita obtained in foreign countries from producing secondary goods. Illogically, but very humanly, they blame their plight on the nature of the goods they produce and export. Everything would supposedly be better if only they were producing industrial goods instead. There seems to be a widespread belief that, if a people cannot acquire capital and skills to improve agriculture, they are qualified to establish and operate industries with efficiency instead.

It is fairly obvious that, just as in the past half-century, in the future one the output of a worker in an advanced country is likely to "command" the labor of many workers in what are now considered undeveloped countries. This inequality may also become greater before it lessens. As the world grows ever smaller, in the sense that people in poor countries realize more clearly how people in the rich countries live, this difference is likely to be a constant source of political tension.

PRICE INSTABILITY OF PRIMARY EXPORTS

Another complaint regarding primary goods exports is that their prices supposedly fluctuate more than industrial product prices. Certainly, because primary products are sold on commodity markets, their prices do fluctuate from day to day while many industrial goods are sold at what are sometimes called "administered" prices. Moreover, because agricultural output is always subject to crop failures and animal disease, the export earnings from rice, sugar, coffee, and the like are vulnerable to sudden and often drastic reductions. Many underdeveloped countries earn almost all their foreign exchange from one or two exports, examples being Brazil (coffee), Bolivia (tin), Northern Rhodesia (copper), Ceylon (tea), and Iran (petroleum). A 5 per cent reduction in the world price of an export may, depending upon the commodity and country of course, reduce its foreign exchange supplies more than would a complete cessation of all foreign grants and loans.

Given this problem, does it follow that these countries should curtail their export lines in favor of diversification, which usually means the domestic manufacture of some import substitute? There is no simple categorical answer. If the countries have a proven comparative advantage

[2] The equation is the same as above (see p. 466) except that it is multiplied by ϕ_f/ϕ'_f where ϕ_f is the productivity of some foreign workers.

in their export lines, and these must be curtailed for other kinds of production to be started, the opportunity costs of new enterprises may be too high. But if idle resources can be employed, so that old exports can be continued and others added, there is much to be said for this development. The trouble is that new industries are more likely to be import substitutes than export supplements. Undeveloped countries have a hard time competing with the advanced countries when it comes to finished producer and consumer goods.

The hard truth is that diversification, when it requires the contraction of activities that can earn foreign exchange, is likely to lose average real national income over the years but gain a reduction in income dispersion from year to year. The economic cost of diversification is then a sort of premium paid as insurance against income fluctuations. So long as a government and people know what they are paying and buying through self-sufficiency policies, it is for them to make the decision.

However, there may be a less expensive way to stabilize the incomes of export producers, and that is for the government to create buffer stocks of major commodities and monopolize their foreign sales. The resultant operation involves state trading by a marketing board. And this marketing board will have to work rather closely with the national central bank.

During a period of "high" international prices for the export, the marketing board buys from producers at a lower but "normal" price, paying in local currency. It sells the current supply, plus some inventory accumulations, at the world price for foreign exchange. The board sells this foreign exchange to the central bank for local currency. Thus the board has increased its cash balances and decreased its commodity inventories, and the central bank has increased its foreign exchange holdings.

If a period of "low" prices follows, the marketing board continues to buy current production at the "normal" price. It sells rather less on foreign markets than it buys domestically and so accumulates inventories. The local currency it receives from selling foreign exchange earnings to the central bank are inadequate to meet the current cost of buying local output, so it has to exchange cash for inventories.

As the country needs to import goods every year, and must pay in foreign exchange, the central bank sells foreign exchange to importers for local currency. When export prices are high, the central bank accumulates foreign exchange. When prices are low, it will lose foreign exchange and gain local currency.

Such a scheme may seem more attractive in theory than in practice. First, it is very hard for any commodity expert or statistician to estimate what a "normal" world price for some primary good should be in the near future, and long-run price trends are very treacherous. Second, the scheme has to be started during a "high" price year, which means that domestic producers are initially being denied the full external price: politically, "stabilization" schemes are acceptable to producers only when prices are abnormally "low." Third, if prices are "low" some year, this may be an early indication that world supply will exceed demand within a few years at what were once considered to be normal prices: by maintaining local prices, the marketing board is not encouraging producers to decrease output.

The generic defect of all stabilization schemes is of course that by definition they eliminate the regulatory effects of price changes. They also require a government wise enough to estimate future commodity markets and strong enough to withstand producers' influence on the marketing board to post unduly high buying prices. Although some governments use marketing boards deliberately as a source of revenue—notably in West Africa—few governments are both wise and strong.

CONTROL OF EXPORTS FOR REVENUE

The tax systems of many underdeveloped countries are necessarily primitive, rather narrowly based, and not very productive of revenue. And yet these governments need current budget surpluses with which to finance real capital investments. If there are one or two valuable export commodities that have to be shipped out of the country from one or more ports, it is administratively feasible and financially profitable for the government either to tax these exports or to establish a State trading monopoly. The economic incidence, but not the legal forms of course, can be almost identical whether the revenue is taken as taxes or profits. Thus Bolivia has an export tax on tin, and Ghana has a cocoa marketing board with a profitable export monopoly. The principles governing a statutory export monopoly can best be explained by Fig. 25-1.

Suppose there are a number of producers of some export commodity and that their collective supply schedule—as seen by the marketing board, say—is positively inclined and resembles the S curve in the diagram. If the country in question contributes only a very small part of the world supply, the apparent demand curve (D) will be horizontal, but some undeveloped nations are sufficiently important suppliers of certain commodities that the estimated demand for its exports has some recognizable negative inclination. At what price should the marketing board buy domestically and sell foreign?

Usually it will not buy and sell at the equilibrium price (indicated by the intersection of the supply and demand curves) because this will not alter competitive outcomes and will not occasion profits for government. Presumably it will buy at a price lower than that at which it sells, adjusting these two prices so that the quantity bought is sold. The differ-

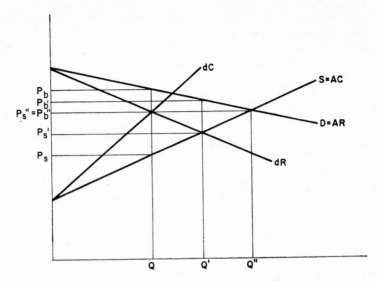

Fig. 25-1. Alternative Policies for Pricing Exports.

ence between these two prices is its gross profit per unit. But it cannot
have a reasoned price policy, even with perfect knowledge, unless it
knows what it wants to maximize.

There are at least three distinct possibilities. First, it can try to maximize profits for government. Second, it can try to maximize both government revenues and domestic producers' surplus. Third, it can try to
maximize the domestic producers' surplus.

So far as the marketing board is concerned, the supply curve (S) is an
average cost curve, and so a marginal cost schedule (dC) can be derived
from it in the usual way. The demand curve (D) appears as an average
revenue schedule, so a marginal revenue curve (dR) can be calculated.
The board's profits will be maximized at an output (Q) which results in
a P_s seller's price and a P_b buyer's price, because this equates marginal
cost and marginal revenue.

But perhaps the board wishes to maximize collectively its own profits
and the suppliers' surpluses of domestic producers. Total suppliers' surplus is shown by the area, up to the quantity purchased, that lies between
Curve S and Curve dC. And the marketing board's profits plus fixed costs,
up to the quantity bought and sold, is indicated by the area between
Curve dC and Curve dR. Hence suppliers' surplus plus government
profits are represented, up to any given quantity, by the area above the
supply curve and below the marginal revenue curve. This area is maximized at the quantity (Q') corresponding to an intersection of the S and
dR curves. The result is a buyer's price of P_b' and a seller's price of P_s'.
Government profits will be smaller than before, but this loss is more than

offset by increased surpluses for local producers. In effect the government is exploiting foreign buyers through its monopoly power, the existence of which is indicated by the negative inclination of the demand curve for the country's exports. The benefits of the exploitation go partly to domestic producers and partly to the national government.

If the government's marketing board were only concerned with maximizing domestic producers' surplus, it would set a buyer's price of P_b'' and purchase Q''. But it could only dispose of this quantity at an identical seller's price of P_s''. There would then be no profit for the board, and no reason for its existence, for P_s'' (or P_b'') is the equilibrium price without State intervention.

What the marketing board attempts to maximize is likely to depend upon government's attitude to local suppliers. If these constitute numerous small producers, and happen to have considerable political influence, something like the second price policy (giving Q' volume) may be adopted. But if the producers are financed and controlled by foreigners, and government is eager to convert some of their surpluses into revenues for itself, maximizing government profits (the Q volume) may well be the marketing board's goal.

It is noteworthy that the same outcomes could have been realized by levying export duties rather than by operating a State export monopoly. Government could maximize tax revenues by establishing a duty per unit equal to $P_b P_s$. Or it could maximize duty revenues plus suppliers' surpluses together through a unit tax represented by $P_b' P_s'$. Which method is followed is largely a matter of administrative convenience.

Whenever government tries to share in earnings from exports, it is of course making itself vulnerable to adverse fluctuations in other countries' demand and supply schedules for the commodity. This can be extremely serious if the government of a small country—with no significant monopoly power in the sale of its product on world markets—depends heavily upon its tax duties or trading profits. For example, suppose the government's profit margin were 0.3 of the world price, and that these profits comprised 0.4 of government's ordinary revenues: then a 0.15 fall in the world price could reduce the board's profits by 0.5 and government receipts by 0.2. Government, when it tries to share in earnings from exports, inevitably becomes a risk-taker.

PREVENTING THE TRADE CONSEQUENCES
OF INFLATION

One of the most common and compelling reasons why so few undeveloped nations can make full use of the world economy is their inability or unwillingness to exercise monetary restraint. Their governments want to spend more than they receive as taxes and loans, and so they create money for their own use, which means that domestic inflation becomes almost inevitable. The international consequence of such national currency depreciation would normally be external insolvency were it not that some form of exchange control is nearly always introduced. The immediate effect of these exchange restrictions is to interpose the government between the domestic and foreign economies. And the ultimate result is likely to be that the nation either does without various imports or produces them at opportunity costs that exceed external prices.

The immediate effect of domestic financial inflation is always increased effective monetary demand at home. Money in circulation increases rapidly. Commercial bank loans to private businesses are unlikely to contract and are quantitatively unimportant in backward countries. For a time this money expansion may occasion the employment of previously unemployable labor and capacity. But sooner or later domestic prices will rise in terms of local currency.

This means that, at the official exchange rate between domestic and foreign currencies, external prices come to appear relatively low because they have not risen as domestic prices have already done. Imports are increasingly substituted for domestic output. Moreover producers who used to export will now find local prices more profitable and will shift sales from foreign markets to domestic markets. This tendency for the home market to absorb former exports will be especially marked if these commodities are consumer goods favored by low- and moderate-income households. The combined effect of reduced exports and growing imports is of course to worsen the balance of trade and instigate a drain upon the foreign exchange reserves of the national central bank.

A serious worsening of the trade balance, in the absence of government intervention, would cause many residents and nonresidents to export their capital. And any free foreign exchange valuation of the domestic currency would fall to a small fraction of the former rate. But few governments will tolerate either of these developments. A fall in the external valuation of its own currency is interpreted as a criticism of the government's financial policies. Also, such a depreciation will render the local money cost of servicing foreign loans—which are usually denominated in dollars, pounds sterling, or the currency of the lender—much greater than had been expected. However, should the government support its own currency on foreign exchange markets by purchasing it with gold and exchange, its central bank's reserves will soon be exhausted and the country will be insolvent. Hence the inevitable outcomes are exchange controls and officially determined exchange rates.

There are various degrees of exchange control that may be imposed. All restrictions on money transfers may initially apply to residents only, especially if nonresidents now have few investments in the country and there is still some hope of inducing them to risk additional funds in its development. Or the restrictions may at first relate only to so-called capital transfers by nonresidents and residents, importers supposedly being free to acquire foreign exchange for this purpose, but actually finding it often unavailable at official rates.

Most exchange regulations require exporters to sell all foreign exchange earnings to the central bank at the official rate. The government then uses some of this foreign exchange for its own purposes. It sells the balance to importers. If it sells at an official rate that is the preinflation rate, the demand for foreign exchange will be much greater than the government can meet, and hence it will soon commence selling exchange only to those importers and for those imports that it favors. Importers of "luxuries" for public sale may not be able to buy foreign exchange, but importers of various capital goods "required" for development probably will, and in this way government can determine what is imported. Similarly, by selling exchange to persons wishing to import from one nation but not from another, it can play favorites among alternative countries of origin. Some exchange controls have become very complicated, with different prices being charged importers for exchange, depending on what they buy from where.

However, although exchange control permits government officials to determine what is imported from where, they cannot determine how much is to be imported altogether. They can sell no more foreign exchange than is available. This means that the exchange control is limited to selling the amount of exchange that exporters can earn, minus what government takes for its own supposed needs.

At the official rate of exchange, producers may find export demand and prices less attractive than those of the domestic market. Of course government can plunge deeper and deeper into regulation of enterprise, setting fractional output quotas that particular industries and firms must export if they are to receive permits to import equipment and materials. But the experience even of nations with fairly effective bureaucracies has been that complicated schemes of this kind are so ponderous and slow that initiative is handicapped and incentives are destroyed. Most undeveloped countries do not have enough honest, intelligent, and expeditious officials to waste in this sort of employment. There is also a serious danger that exchange control will result in importers' corrupting ordinary bureaucrats and thereby undermining the civil service's reputation.

When the domestic market cannot import all the goods that it can afford in local money because not enough foreign exchange is available at official rates, there is a tendency for domestic firms to commence making some of these scarce goods. In some cases, the quality of these substitutes may not be too inferior, and sometimes underemployed resources may be employed as a result. These consequences, plus the incidental industrialization of the domestic economy, are often cited as arguments in favor of monetary inflation with exchange control.

The counterargument is that although many import substitutes can be made domestically after a fashion, their opportunity costs may be unreasonable. For instance, it may be physically possible to make kitchenware and farm implements internally, but resources of equal value to those so employed might be able to produce exports that would exchange for many more kitchen pots and pans—and field plows and harrows, too. Moreover, there will always be many goods that are wanted and that cannot be made domestically at sensible prices, so that the choice of available producer and consumer goods is always reduced by the controlled disequilibrium that follows inflation.

The basic rule is that whether goods are imported or produced at home should depend not on what is physically feasible but on what is economically advantageous. Unfortunately, by establishing artificial exchange rates for its currency, government reduces exports and hence the imports that can be financed. Certain kinds of goods are then obtained directly but inefficiently from home production. Other goods simply become unavailable, and the nation must learn to stumble along without them.

Given domestic inflation, the best solution may be to impose exchange control on capital transfers by residents (and perhaps by nonresidents), but allow an unrestricted market and free exchange rate on all current transactions. The control on capital transfers means that the country does not have to use resources to produce exports in order to finance capital outflows. A free exchange rate on current transactions means that domestic producers will find that export sales are now more attractive. More foreign exchange will be earned by the nation's exporters. Also, as the domestic money cost of imports will be higher, the effective demand for imports will be reduced. The price system will have brought current demand and supply for foreign exchange into balance on *current* account at least.

Under this scheme the government will not be determining what is imported from where—except insofar as it imports on its own account— and those who believe that government knows best may consider this a disadvantage. But it matters less what is imported if more can be imported in value because exporters are earning extra foreign exchange. There are also some who doubt that government officials are equal to such responsibilities.

Nevertheless, a somewhat different mix of goods will be imported when the price system performs an impersonal regulation. For instance, more "luxuries" may be imported, but it is exactly those consumer goods which cannot be purchased by poor people that are so often an incentive to the ambitious and successful to become even more productive. Durable items such as automobiles and air conditioners may become more available to businessmen and less available to government officials after current exchange transactions have been freed. Firms can then make plans that need not be contingent on the uncertain approval of several different bureaus. The private sector of the economy can accomplish more.

Freeing current transactions and allowing a flexible exchange rate to regulate exports and imports is of course only a suboptimization. The task of distinguishing current from capital transactions cannot be accomplished without a certain degree of official interference and regimentation. Moreover, the imposition of exchange control on capital transfers will hardly encourage private investment in the country from abroad. A capital inflow, in the form of more imports, would enable the domestic economy to acquire more equipment and materials from other countries for its own development. Thus one cost of inflation is that the nation is deprived of imports that are financed through ordinary borrowing. Government must instead seek "soft" loans and grants. And applicants for charity, even when governments, usually must sacrifice some measure of independence.

PROTECTION FOR INDUSTRIALIZATION

As mentioned before, the governments and people of most undeveloped countries tend to equate industrialization with economic development, although the former is more likely to be a consequence than a cause of the latter. It is therefore not surprising that a number of arguments have been concocted in favor of protecting new domestic industries that otherwise seem to have no financial viability. A *minority* of these arguments do have some merit, depending on circumstances, and are described below.

When industrial money costs exceed real costs

Arguments for free trade subsume that money costs and receipts as experienced by private firms do approximate the real costs and benefits accruing to the economy. If this assumption is patently wrong, there is a case for government intervention of some kind. Whether or not this intervention should take the form of protection against imports is another matter though.

Nevertheless, it is often argued that certain industries in undeveloped countries should receive tariff and quota protections, a common assertion being that money labor costs to industrial employers are higher than real labor costs to the economy. It may be alleged that trade unions have managed to raise industrial wage rates too high, in terms of their members' productivity, or that minimum wage regulations are to blame. Or it may simply be asserted that nonindustrial labor has a zero marginal product and hence is really a free good to the industrial sector, although for some unexplained reason it has to be paid for work in urban industry. Also the associated urban costs that industrialization includes—as described in Chapter 7—are often ignored.

Imagine a country that produces apples (agriculture) and suits (industry), in which labor is the only important productive factor. In the course of a year a rural worker can produce 500 apples for his own subsistence; the same man in industry can produce 1 suit. Urban wage rates are such, though, that a manufacturer would have to pay him a wage that would enable him to buy 1000 apples. The reason for this discrepancy may really be that for each man directly employed in urban industry, there is another "shadow" man constructing and maintaining urban facilities of a kind not needed for rural living. In this case the net rewards and productivity of the marginal worker have really the same value whether he is making apples or suits. And many alleged cases of divergent real and money costs of labor are revealed as spurious upon a closer examination that includes associated activities. But in order not to terminate the argument so promptly, we shall pretend that suit-making labor does cost twice as much as apple-growing labor in terms of its marginal value product.

We then have the rather astounding situation depicted in Fig. 25-2. The vertical axis represents apples; the horizontal axis, suits; and AM, the real transformation curve. However, as we are assuming constant returns and considering only labor, this "curve" is a straight line. For some unexplained reason the money transformation curve, based on what suit-making employers must pay in wages, is twice as steep as AM and is represented by AP_i. Moreover, we will assume that world prices for suits and apples are such that the external commodity exchange line (AP_e) has a slope that is more negatively inclined than AM and less inclined than AP.

Under these remarkable conditions, private firms and subsistence producers would concentrate exclusively on apple-growing, the output mix being represented by A and the consumption mix perhaps by C, some community indifference curve (I_1)—tangent to AP_e—passing through C. But this outcome can hardly be the best possible for the economy, if one can believe the diagram, for a substantial segment of AM is above and to the right of C. It has therefore been argued that a complete embargo on suit imports, together with price fixing, bonuses, or taxes, might locate the economy's consumption mix at some point such as D that makes more suits and more apples available.[3] Each household could then be rendered

---

[3] This has been suggested for example by Professor E. Hagen, "An Economic Justification of Protection," *Quarterly Journal of Economics* (November, 1958), and incidentally commented upon by S. Enke in "Food Constraints on Industrial Development," *Southern Economic Journal* (April, 1961).

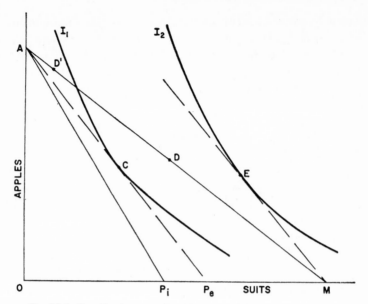

Fig. 25-2. Free Trade versus Protection to Induce Industrialization.

better or no worse off than before through various lump sum transfers enforced by government. And with no imports or exports, autarky would be complete.

Accomplishing all this might be extremely difficult administratively. Full employment must be maintained, for otherwise the economy's output may fall below the AM line, and prices of apples and suits to households must be adjusted through domestic taxes and subsidies so that the final consumption mix does not prove to be at some point such as D' "below" the I_1 community indifference curve. But let us suppose all these difficulties are overcome.

The real objection to this argument for protecting domestic industry against imports is that this *better* outcome is not the best solution for the country. If it can be arranged for the economy to produce some output such as D, why not subsidize industrial firms in paying wages, for example, and so make the internal commodity exchange rate correspond with the "real" transformation curve? Then the producers in the country will specialize in suit-making. Located at M, and given world prices, the economy's consumption mix can then be anything along the line from M through E. Some point on this line (parallel to AP_e), such as E (through which I_2 *passes*), is certain to provide more welfare than D.

All this suggests that a disparity between real and money costs of producing industrial and agricultural goods does not logically mean more protection and greater self-sufficiency. On the contrary, the conclusion may be that national specialization and extensive trade are desirable, but that divergent real and money costs may result in exports and imports of an incorrect kind. Desirable government intervention is, then, not to limit or prevent imports, but to tax and subsidize in such a way that real and money costs of production are reconciled within the country, so that the best and not merely a better outcome is achieved through free external trade.

Protecting infant industries—a new version

Ever since the late eighteenth century, when Alexander Hamilton sought to establish new American industries in the face of competition from British imports, pleas have been advanced in favor of protecting infant industries during their early stages of development. It has usually been argued that these new industries cannot become established without tariff duties to raise the price of imports, but that within some reasonable period they will become viable without this indirect subsidy, so that protection is temporary. This argument has always been a sort of Trojan horse within the free trade citadel. Once the principle has been admitted, the practical consequences have included permanent protection for submarginal concerns. Another outcome has been continual protection for sturdy adolescent industries now strong enough politically to prevent removal of their hidden subsidy. So specific applications for infant industry protection must always be scrutinized very carefully.

A rather new version of this old argument deserves to be considered though. It involves a negotiated agreement between government and whatever concert of capitalists is prepared to establish domestic production under stipulated conditions. One novelty of the arrangement is a requirement that local prices charged by new and protected firms be no higher than the price of imports outside the customs area.

Suppose an undeveloped country normally imports a rather large number of rubber tires of certain standard sizes for trucks, cars, and bicycles. Some of these tires will be Brand X, others Brand Y, and still others Brand Z, and so on. For practical purposes, these different tires of similar size are of the same quality. However, brand preferences being what they are among buyers, it would be very difficult for a new domestic company to make Brand A tires and sell enough at competitive prices to cover its unit production costs. In fact the entire local market for tires would barely be sufficient to support a single domestic producer.

As the domestic market grows and uses and imports more and more tires, the volume may reach a level at which government might consider "handing over" the local buyers to some single domestic tire producer on condition that he produce tires of similar qualities and sell at prices similar to those now imported. This possibility is reached where total local demand is represented by DD' in Fig. 25-3. The present import price of some standard tire size is represented by P, and the unit cost curve of a domestic plant of appropriate capacity is represented by AC. Apparently a domestic tire producer, if he had the entire local market to himself, could just cover all unit costs at the present import price.

The government can "deliver" the market to such a firm by imposing an import embargo or a very high duty rate. But if it did this, and no more, the new tire firm would probably charge a price such as P', and make large profits at the expense of buyers. Thus the government must make protection depend upon the domestic producer selling at prices that are equal to what the price of imports would be if they could enter free. There would also have to be some minimum quality stipulation to prevent the new domestic manufacturer from pricing competitively but adulterating the product. This sort of government protection on "good behavior" would best be administered by a government agency, not the legislature.

Another peculiarity of this new version of infant industry protection is that negotiations between government and business must precede any real action. The government can promise to prevent imports only when the new plant is ready to produce. And the firm in question can promise to establish such a plant and sell at external prices only if the government does provide the indicated protection. It would make no sense for government to place an embargo on tire imports and then wait to see whether any firms were interested in establishing a plant. Nor can

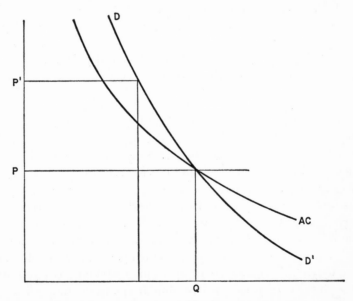

Fig. 25-3. Infant Industry Protection—a New Variant.

firms be expected to invest in plants on the chance that they can later persuade the government to grant protection.

Firms that are prepared to negotiate such arrangements with government are often corporations that already import their products into the developing economy. Any plant they establish under some agreement will be a species of branch factory. If the local market for the good is small, and exports of it do not seem likely, protection against imports may apply only to finished or highly processed versions of the product. Certain component parts and materials may even be placed on a free list as part of the agreement. Where there are several competing brand imports, each producing firm may be eager to have its rivals excluded so that government may be able to pick and choose among them. Alternatively, the company that "signs" may induce the government not to approve any other tire manufacturers in the country for some period of years, so that a continued increase in demand can give it some profits at constant prices.

Deals of this kind are not uncommon in developing countries. But a certain amount of government participation in the supposedly private affairs of corporations results. There may have to be some supervision of prices and quality, and also of profits to be allowed prior to another firm's entry. Hence there is a danger that the protected company, established by arrangement with government, will become a sort of public utility, without much incentive to improve its product, duplicate innovations abroad, or reduce costs and prices.

Industrializing by performing more processes

The complaint of backward countries against advanced ones has always included the charge that they are "compelled"—by foreign capitalists no doubt—to export primary products and import finished goods. Sometimes, to make the allegation more poignant, finished imports are made from the same materials that are exported. Thus a country may export crude petroleum and have to import gasoline, export hardwoods and import furniture, export copra and import soap, and so on. To the uninitiated, such trade flows seem unnatural and wasteful, so much so that many persons soon suspect that there is something sinister and selfish about it. Usually it is not altogether simple to explain why, when overhead and freight costs are considered, this "colonial" trade pattern is rational.

However, as the domestic market for finished goods increases, it becomes feasible to undertake more processes domestically; thus bicycle parts may be imported and assembled, unstained furniture may be imported and finished by indigenous labor, photo offset plates may be imported but final printing and binding may be domestic, and so on. Also, when it comes to exports, materials can be sold abroad in a less or more processed form; thus copper ore can be transformed into electrolytic copper, sisal can be made into rope, tobacco can be made into cigars, and so on. A country that exports its goods in rather more processed form and imports goods that are not so nearly finished may discover that these are economic uses of its resources. Unfortunately, some primary exports do not lend themselves to this sort of thing, and not much can be done to process exported bananas, sugar, coffee, or tea, for example, beyond cleaning, grading, and packaging. Thus developing countries may be more successful in their efforts to subtract value added from imports than to add such values to exports.

The eventual outcome, as the local economy does more processing of exports and imports, may be that the lower and higher stages "meet" in the sense that all stages of producing some goods are undertaken domestically. This kind of self-sufficiency may be economic. It all depends upon volume, fixed costs, efficiency, local factor prices, and the protection that transportation expenses may provide. The important thing is that government planners not be doctrinaire—i.e., in favor of industrialization as a goal in itself—but ready to ascertain the financial facts and prospects as well as they can. Any enterprising community of entrepreneurs will probably be doing the same thing. Sometimes government and business can then agree on a common program of industrial expansion that is financially viable and economically justified.

CONCLUSIONS

It is natural enough that many governments, and especially those that have recently acquired political independence, should be opposed to anything that smacks of colonialism. Unfortunately, trade patterns that involve raw material exports and finished goods imports are often so stigmatized. It is also regrettable that lack of domestic monetary restraint, resulting in inflation of prices, causes serious declines in exports, so that governments feel compelled to regulate and limit imports more closely. Identification of industrialization with development is also common. Hence it is not surprising that many arguments favoring protection of local industries against imports should have been devised over the years. Some of them are too ingenious by far. But this does not mean that valid justifications for protection do not exist in special circumstances.

26

International capital movements

The most publicized aspect of international economic development today is the making of grants and loans by advanced countries to backward ones. Financial assistance completely overshadows technical assistance both as regards cost and attention. These international "capital" movements take many forms. Some are channeled bilaterally and others multilaterally, some originate with governments and others with private investors, some are direct investments and some are indirect portfolio purchases. The varied motivation and incidence of these different kinds of capital movements are explained below.

ALTERNATIVE MEANS OF TRANSFERRING CAPITAL

An international capital movement is essentially a transfer of purchasing power from the residents of one country to those of another. It may be the cause or consequence of trade. The actual mechanics of the transfer, which has the effect of giving the receiver command over goods and services previously possessed by the creditor or donor, depend upon the kind of transfer. Today, international agencies, governments, and individuals have evolved many different ways to transfer purchasing power from advanced countries to backward ones.

Most bilateral grants and loans by governments are "tied," in the sense that the proceeds must be spent in the local economy of the donor or creditor, so that the "assistance" is also an export subsidy. This aspect of "foreign aid" has not escaped the attention of those domestic industries that benefit—ranging all the way from producers of bulldozers to publishers of textbooks. This facet of "assistance" has also been noted abroad by recipients and helps to explain in part their common lack of gratitude. Few national governments—except West Germany—regularly extend "untied" credits in local currency that can be used to buy exports from third countries.

Governments sometimes make "loans" by "selling" surplus commodities that they have on hand. The debt is then often denominated in the "soft" currency of the debtor country. Frequently there is a tacit agreement that debt service will not be repatriated without notice and consent so as not to burden the balance of payments of the importing country.

Private loans may be indirect, in the sense that some individual saver in an advanced economy subscribes to bonds or other evidences of indebtedness issued by a corporation or government in a backward country. Traditionally such securities are denominated in the comparatively hard currency of the capital market where they are sold. This is why so many bonds, especially in Latin America, are still denominated in dollars and pounds.

When an undeveloped nation sells securities in foreign money markets, it normally acquires hard currency balances which permit it to import from the country where the bonds or notes were sold. Or this currency may be used to buy other nations' currencies with which to purchase their goods and services. Only in rare cases are the proceeds of borrowing effectively used to supplement the foreign exchange reserves of the recipient's central bank. The more customary reason for borrowing foreign exchange is of course to permit a worsening of the current account without having to liquidate short term assets that are negotiable abroad. Then the debtor's balance of payments for the current period has a positive long-term entry and a negative current account entry as a result of borrowing.

The long-term private capital that a backward country "receives" is often direct foreign investment. The similar accounting entries that ensue should not conceal the different nature of such capital movements. Direct investment occurs, for example, when a foreign corporation—through a local subsidiary company perhaps—constructs buildings and installs equipment for its own use. The structural steel and equipment that are imported into the receiving country are recorded as an import. A long-term capital inflow is also entered as an offset. The local labor that the foreign corporation hires and pays—employed perhaps in constructing company housing or clearing land for cultivation—may be financed by selling hard bank balances for local currency. The backward country's balance of payments then has negative short-term capital entry and a positive long-term capital entry in principle.

Today, more than ever, governments of prosperous nations make outright grants to governments of poorer countries. A flow of goods into recipient countries ordinarily results. And in those nations' balances of payments, an import debit is offset by a "grant" credit.

The main point of this discussion is that except in short-run periods when central banks are gaining or losing liquidity, international capital movements are simply another aspect of merchandise trade movements. Sometimes a loan or grant is made so that goods can subsequently be exported. But the instigating transaction is often a merchandise sale that is subsequently financed by the seller extending funds to the buyer. This is true of public and private capital movements, whether direct or indirect investment, as well as of loans and grants.

Another point is that "capital" is a rather euphemistic term to apply to all financial transfers from advanced countries to backward ones. There is no assurance that there will be a corresponding real capital accumulation in the borrowing or receiving country. Of course this cannot be ascertained from observing changes in the merchandise trade of the capital inflow country. It may import food, for instance. However, if this is to release domestic labor from agriculture to construct new factories, the financial capital inflow should occasion real capital accumulation. Alternatively, structural steel imports might result from international borrowings, but this could conceivably be more than offset by domestic labor transfers from building wooden structures to producing food for the domestic market. A nation obviously should not go into debt internationally unless it can acquire assets of equal or greater worth domestically. Moreover, transfers of purchasing power can be for consumption as well as for accumulation, and so all grants and loans are not necessarily a measure of net investment.

Finally, despite the tendency to identify capital inflow with economic development, a nation must already possess certain rudiments of a political economy if external capital is to benefit its labor and culture. Enough social justice must prevail so that ordinary people are motivated to innovate and work in the confident knowledge that they and not some privileged class will benefit. Or as a noted economist who has also served as United States Ambassador to India once noted:

Capital becomes the touchstone of development, the limiting factor, only in countries that are well along. . . . Indeed, there is a distinct possibility that capital provided to countries in the earliest stages of development will be wasted. Only in a relatively sophisticated stage of development can it be well and wisely used in any considerable quantity.[1]

RELATIVE IMPORTANCE OF DIFFERENT KINDS OF CAPITAL TRANSFERS

Before we consider the relative magnitudes of recent capital movements in the more developed nations and those in the underdeveloped world, it would be well to classify explicitly the main kinds of transfers. These are:

Private Capital Movements
   Direct investment (e.g., United States company expands tire factory in Indonesia through a subsidiary company);
   Indirect bilateral investment (e.g., purchase of securities of a Brazilian public utility company);

[1] J. K. Galbraith, *Economic Development in Perspective* (Cambridge, Mass.: Harvard University Press, 1962), p. 14.

Multilateral indirect (*e.g.*, purchase of International Bank bonds needed to finance a dam in Liberia);

Public Capital Movements
Bilateral hard loans (*e.g.*, British loans in pounds sterling to Kenya government);
Bilateral soft loans (*e.g.*, United States "sales" of foodgrains to India for blocked rupee balances);
Multilateral grants (*e.g.*, Canadian contributions to the Colombo plan);
Reparations (*e.g.*, West German Republic payments to Israel).

During recent years the total net contribution of the comparatively advanced OECD nations (plus Japan) to those more backward countries, including all the above forms of capital movement, have amounted to approximately $8 billion annually.

Table 26-1 indicates the relative importance of each kind of investment when the United States is excluded and included. It is noteworthy that while public capital transfers amount to about three-fifths of the total, private financial movements on long term aggregate over $3 billion net yearly. Also outstanding is the vast predominance of bilateral to multilateral capital movements: the ratio when the United States is excluded is about 6:1, and for the United States it is 10:1. Still another feature is the United States contribution of roughly $3.8 billion—almost half the total—in 1960.

DIRECT PRIVATE INVESTMENT

An important distinction in the case of private bilateral investment is that between direct and indirect investment. At the turn of the century most of the private capital flowing from Europe to the undeveloped countries constituted indirect investment: individual savers purchased bonds and other securities issued by foreign governments and public and private corporations. But since World War II probably over half of all private investment has been direct. Exact estimates are not available. However, of the $2.37 billion of private bilateral lending in 1960 by the OECD nations (plus Japan) to undeveloped countries, at least $1.12 billion was direct and another $0.44 billion consisted of reinvested earnings. Much of the latter were foreign earnings that could not be repatriated because of exchange controls and so were directly reinvested. Hence well over half of all private bilateral lending probably takes the form of direct investment. And this is as true of lending by the other advanced countries as it is of the United States.

Because of the magnitude of private direct investment and the controversies that it has aroused, something needs to be said regarding its rather special economic and social incidence.

Table 26-1

TOTAL PRIVATE AND OFFICIAL CONTRIBUTIONS TO UNDERDEVELOPED COUNTRIES
AND MULTILATERAL AGENCIES BY OECD NATIONS (PLUS JAPAN) IN 1960
(*in millions of dollars*)

	Net private lending and investment			Net public loans and grants					
	Bilateral	Multi-lateral	Total	Bilateral	Multi-lateral	Total	Total Bilateral	Total Multi-lateral	Totals
Austria	5	—	5	—	—	—	5	—	5
Belgium	64	14	78	82	19	101	146	33	179
Canada	33	27	60	48	27	75	81	54	135
Denmark	24	—	24	1	6	7	25	6	31
Finland	—	—	—	—	1	1	—	1	1
France	435	9	444	783	60	843	1218	69	1287
Germany	270	4	274	242	101	343	511	105	616
Italy	169	—	169	39	89	128	208	89	297
Japan	100	—	100	114	42	156	214	42	256
Luxemburg	—	—	—	—	—	—	—	—	1
Netherlands	199	—1	198	25	22	47	224	21	246
Norway	—	—	—	1	20	21	1	20	21
Portugal	49	—	49	34	—	34	83	—	83
Sweden	38	—	38	1	6	7	39	6	45
Switzerland	115	30	145	2	2	4	117	32	149
United Kingdom	470	—3	467	298	92	390	768	89	857
Subtotal (excluding United States)	1971	81	2052	1670	487	2157	3640	568	4208
United States	893	124	1017	2529	235	2764	3422	359	3781
Total	2864	205	3069	4199	722	4921	7062	927	7989
Percentages	36	2	38	53	9	62	89	11	100

Source: OECD, *The Flow of Financial Resources to Countries in Course of Economic Development in 1960*, Paris, 1962.

The bulk of direct investment is undertaken by large international concerns with head offices in New York, London, Amsterdam, or some other major financial center. Although a subsidiary company may be legally established in each country of operation, these subsidiaries are wholly owned or at least entirely controlled by a holding or parent company, owned in turn by shareholders in North America and Western Europe. From the viewpoint of people in, say, Latin America, who know that the largest companies in their country are controlled from, say, New York, Communist claims of Yankee economic imperialism are not hard to believe. (Even Canadians are not universally happy about having over half their country's mineral resources controlled by United States corporations.) For these reasons, direct private investment has many political connotations, in contrast to indirect private investment.

Direct private investment is most strikingly apparent in the extraction of crude petroleum and nonferrous minerals; examples are oil in Venezuela and Libya, tin in Bolivia and Malaya, and copper in Chile and Katanga. But plantation agriculture, whether of palm oil, rubber latex, cane sugar, or merely bananas, should not be overlooked. In nearly every case the object of large-scale direct investment by corporations of advanced nations in subsidiaries in backward countries is the acquisition of raw materials and primary food stuffs. And the original motivation for these investments was to supply market demands in North America and Western Europe.

The managers of these international concerns cannot politically afford to ignore the local inhabitants—some of whom are needed as workers anyway—but otherwise the native peoples are rather incidental to these major direct investments. In fact management would have fewer worries, so long as workers were available, if there were no other people living in the countries where oil fields, mines, and plantations are located. At least this is a fair caricature of managerial attitudes until recently. Although top positions in subsidiary companies had necessarily to be filled by Americans, Britons, Hollanders, and so on—especially where scientific and technical skills were required—few serious efforts were made to open careers for educated young men of the exporting country. Nor were unskilled laborers accorded many opportunities to acquire more than very rudimentary training. Investment in local human capital was usually at a minimum. Moreover, in situations of international tension or hostilities, it has always been felt that imported local managers are more concerned to act in the interests of, say, the United States or Great Britain than in the true national interests of, say, Bolivia, Chile, or Malaya. Finally, because company managers and officials ordinarily live with their families in specially constructed areas or compounds, apart from the native population, acute social antagonisms have often arisen.

An economic complaint, touched upon before, is that these direct investment companies don't bring as much money into the country as they could or should. When a Venezuelan petroleum subsidiary sells its crude oil output on the world market, very possibly for dollars, it is likely to bank the proceeds in New York if it has a United States parent company. These funds will be spent in the United States for equipment and supplies, and distributed profits will go to shareholders, most of whom reside in the advanced nations. In fact funds will be remitted to Venezuela only to the extent that wages, royalties, and taxes must be paid there. If oil prices are high, perhaps less than half of all sales receipts will flow into the country where it was extracted, although this percentage will be higher of course during periods of depressed prices. An offset, however, is that fluctuating prices for primary products have less violent local repercussions when a subsidiary company's financial reserves are held abroad.

National governments have naturally attempted to regulate foreign subsidiaries located within their boundaries. Foreign-owned companies are sometimes required to provide vocational training and minimum health services for all indigenous employees. Such concerns may be required to hire a certain fraction of citizens for higher-echelon positions. Subsidiary companies may have to be registered in the country of operation. And the government may reserve the right to appoint one or more directors to their boards. Subsidiaries will probably be under notice that some fraction of their foreign earnings banked abroad must be made available to the national exchange control on demand.

Many of these requirements are not unreasonable. Unfortunately, patriotic xenophobia and human venality have been known to result in excessive and crippling demands. Both alien companies and native peoples need one another. Certainly, given the relative disappearance of private indirect investment, the direct variety should not be unnecessarily discouraged. In 1960, private investors in the United States, Great Britain, France, and the Netherlands together made net and novel direct investments in undeveloped nations—excluding reinvestment of earnings —of roughly $1 billion. This is admittedly not a large sum by modern standards. But it represents one-eighth of all capital movements—including grants and loans—from advanced nations to backward ones. Thus the art of economic statesmanship is to divide the gains of direct investment between each alien company and its local economy in ways that promote efficiency and cooperation.

NATIONAL GRANTS AND CAPITAL LOANS

In the sphere of public rather than private investment, Table 26-1 indicated that over five-sixths of grants and loans extended by national governments of advanced countries to less developed areas are bilateral. The bulk of these transfers are grants rather than loans. The largest single government contributor is the United States, whose foreign assistance programs are described in Chapter 28. Here the contributions of other governments will be considered.

Table 26-2 gives some additional data regarding the transfer forms and national origins of disbursements for economic development. Grants are distinguished from loans. Bilateral and multilateral objectives are again separated.[2]

2 Tables 26–1 and 26–2 do not always appear to agree because the former is based on commitments and the latter on disbursements.

Table 26-2

GOVERNMENT GRANTS AND LOANS FOR DEVELOPMENT
BY SELECTED COUNTRIES IN 1960
(*in millions of dollars*)

	Bilateral Grants	*Bilateral* New loans	*Multi-lateral*	*Total disbursements*
Belgium	86	—	13	99
Canada	48	—	17	65
Denmark	1	—	3	4
France	708	114	52	874
Germany	8	151	50	209
Italy	9	19	12	40
Japan	2	80	9	91
Netherlands	26	5	16	47
Norway	1	—	3	4
Portugal	2	32	—	34
Sweden	1	—	6	7
Switzerland	2	—	2	4
United Kingdom	165	184	45	394
United States	1481	854	235	2570
Total	2539	1440	461	4441

Source: OECD, *The Flow of Financial Resources to Countries in Course of Economic Development in 1960*, Paris, 1962.

A feature of the table is the considerable disbursement of France in grants and loans. French foreign economic assistance on public account has been indispensable to the franc zone. The average annual contribution during 1956–1960 was $820 million gross. This contribution amounted to about 1.8 per cent annually of French GNP. In percentage terms, this represents a greater capital outflow than that of any other country, including the United States.

The United Kingdom has always granted public assistance to its colonies, although new commitments have normally not been made after independence. These grants and loans were normally made through institutions established under the Colonial Development and Welfare Act. In 1960, total public bilateral grants amounted to $357 million gross, for commitments of $298 million net.

The West German Republic has only recently begun to make substantial public transfers of capital. Under recent legislation a policy of favoring long-term loans rather than grants-in-aid has been enunciated. New credit disbursements amounted to $151 million gross in 1960, considerably more than in the years immediately preceding, and these annual transfers are expected to rise.

Although supposedly neither loans nor grants, guaranteed private export credits have lately become a major additional commitment of governments, and totaled almost $0.5 billion in 1960. In many instances the exports in question comprise equipment and other producer goods. An exporter's government, by protecting him against noncommercial risks, in effect encourages his bank to finance sales abroad. The domestic political motivation for extending such credits is clear enough. But the underdeveloped importing country is also a beneficiary.

Another recent occurrence has been a lengthening of government bilateral loan commitments to underdeveloped countries. In 1960, 6 per cent of such commitments were from 1–5 years, 16 per cent were from 5–10 years, and 78 per cent were for over 10 years in value terms. In this respect the example of the International Bank may have been useful.

Certain nations have at times formed more or less formal organizations to promote special projects of mutual interest. The Alliance for Progress, including the United States and the Latin American countries, is a loosely-knit and still ill-defined example. The Organization of American States in 1960 established the Inter-American Development Bank to which the United States pledged $150 million. In 1958 the European Economic Community established the European Development Fund, to which about $100 million a year is now being subscribed. Under the Colombo Plan, which includes most members of the British Commonwealth, the more prosperous nations (such as Canada) undertake projects to benefit the poorer ones (such as India). In 1961, Canada, France, Germany, the United Kingdom, and the United States, together with Japan and the International Bank, agreed to raise $2,225 million in support of India's Third Five-Year Plan.

The Indus Basin Development Fund is another example of a modern tendency to form international consortia for specific purposes. The governments of Canada, Germany, Great Britain, and the United States, together with Australia, New Zealand, Pakistan, and the International Bank for Reconstruction and Development (IBRD), agreed in 1960 to finance irrigation and other water works in the Indus Valley. The total sum involved amounted to $786 million, with over half being contributed by the United States. Completion of the project depends, however, upon settlement between India and Pakistan of various outstanding issues.

The immediate prospect, although mitigated by intergovernment partnerships such as described above, is for nations to contribute grants and loans bilaterally rather than multilaterally. There are many reasons for this preference. For one thing, many governments "tie" their contributions, so that they have to be used to purchase exports from the granting or lending country. But equally important, bilateral financing often permits the contributing country to exact some sort of *quid pro quo,* whether it be a modification by the receiving country of its exchange control practices or its vote on some issue before the United Nations General Assembly. For exactly these reasons the underdeveloped nations, who must beg and borrow capital, would prefer that aid be channeled through special multilateral agencies of the United Nations. However, although the future trend may be from bilateral to multilateral assistance, the former will dominate for many years to come. In international affairs, as in humbler activities, the piper likes to call the tune.

THE INTERNATIONAL BANK AND ITS AFFILIATES

An important complex of multilateral lending agencies, each of them nominally a specialized agency of the United Nations and technically reporting to its Economic and Social Council (UNESCO), has been assembled in stages since the end of World War II. This group includes the IBRD, established in 1944; the International Finance Corporation (IFC), established in 1956; and the International Development Association (IDA), established in 1960. Each has a separate charter, and each is a separate financial institution legally and for accounting purposes, but the staffs of the IBRD and IDA are identical.

The International Bank for Reconstruction and Development

The first established, best known, and most important of all multilateral lending agencies is the IBRD.[3] It was established together with the International Monetary Fund as a result of the Bretton Woods conference. Membership in the Fund is prerequisite for membership in the Bank and the organizations are located in adjacent buildings in Washington, D. C.

Although over fifty countries are now members of the Bank and its affiliated organizations (see below), share holdings and associated voting rights of member nations vary considerably. United States participation amounts to one-third of the total. The other major subscribers, in descending order, are Great Britain, France, Germany, India, Canada, the Netherlands, and Japan.

Initially the authorized capital of the International Bank was $10 billion, but this was increased in 1959 to $21 billion, almost all of which has been nominally subscribed by members. However, each member pays in gold or United States dollars only 2 per cent of the par value of its subscription, and another 18 per cent in its own currency. The remaining 80 per cent of the subscription price remains on call in *local* currency as a guarantee. Such a general call has never been made to date.

The Bank was originally envisaged as having two main functions. One was to lend subscribed capital to governments for development projects. The other was to guarantee the bonds of member governments when

3 The IBRD is often inaccurately cited as the "World Bank"; but none of the Communist powers is a member, and several Western powers, such as Switzerland, have also abstained.

issued for projects that the Bank approved. Actually, no such guarantee has ever been made to date, so that this function remains a dead letter. Instead, the Bank has made unexpected use of its right to sell bonds of its own, lending the proceeds to members for specific development projects. Such transactions became particularly important once national governments and individual states in the United States amended their laws to permit financial institutions to purchase IBRD bonds for trust accounts. Thus the Bank's two principal activities in practice have been (1) lending subscribed capital and (2) borrowing to relend.

The magnitude of the Bank's operations has been nothing like the scale that the $20-odd billion of subscribed capital might suggest. Even the approximate $4 billion of paid-in capital exaggerates the practical ability of the Bank to lend its own capital and relend its borrowings. This is because almost half the subscription quotas comprise very "soft" national currencies that are barely negotiable internationally. New York investment houses are not going to buy IBRD bonds with dollars when half of their ultimate backing is afghani, colons, quetzal, hwan, baht, piastre, and so on. Prudent purchasers of such bonds are only interested in their "hard" currency backing, and hence in the Bank's potential command of United States dollars, pounds sterling, and German Deutschmarks.

This is the explanation of why the Bank, prior to 1959, began suggesting an increase in its authorized capital from $10 billion to $21 billion, at a time when its outstanding funded debt was still between $1–2 billion. By the middle of 1958 nearly all the outstanding debt of the Bank was payable in United States dollars (although about 40 per cent was held outside the United States), and this amounted to almost four-fifths of the United States' contingent guarantee. In effect, private purchasers of IBRD dollar bonds had been buying against the United States government's dollar subscription to the Bank, and this "line of security" was approaching exhaustion.

These difficulties of the 1950's underline an important need of the 1960's: namely, an increase in the number of "hard" national currencies, and especially a hardening of the currencies of those nations that are principal subscribers. Thus the Bank, in seeking to develop the more backward areas of the world, has a more than passing interest in the economic advance of all OECD members who provide most of the share capital.

The Bank's operations have also been limited in other ways, partly by its charter and partly by its own adopted policies, and especially as regards the purpose of loans and the identity of borrowers. First, the Bank can lend only to or with the approval of a member government, in the case of a project under its jurisdiction. Second, its loans are for particular projects, and not for the general financial support of a member. Third, its loans are normally limited to the so-called foreign exchange component of a project. Ordinarily, it has tended to favor transportation, communication, and public utility projects—that is, social overhead capital that provides services that are sold to users rather than provided free. It has generally eschewed investments in "human capital," through financing, say, hospital and school buildings, although there are signs that this policy may be relaxed.

All of these restrictions can be argued pro or con. For the most part, they tend to limit the Bank's risks, and so promote the negotiability of its own bond issues. For example, by financing only the foreign exchange component of a project, the local government is usually committed to about half the total project expense. By stressing utilities that charge for their services, there is some measure at least of the value of a project. Anyway, these specific restrictions are not a practical limitation, for the real constraint of the Bank is the value of its hard currency subscriptions.

The Bank's loans are not "tied." Unlike the IMF its loans do not have always to be repaid in convertible currencies. Also it makes comparatively long-term loans: some have been for 25 years, the average is for about 14 years, and none since 1951 has been for less than 5 years.

The over-all impact of the Bank as a means of channeling capital has been significant. By mid-1961 it had made 298 loans aggregating nearly $6 billion. Although United States dollars were used for most of the earlier disbursements, other currencies have been increasingly employed. At present over half the current disbursements are in nondollar currencies. Thus the Bank is truly becoming an international development institution.

The Bank's charges—ranging from 4–6 per cent annually—are not considered unreasonable. When relending, it levies 1 per cent over the cost to itself of borrowing, plus a service charge of one-fourth of 1 per cent annually. The former charge is to accumulate reserves against bad loans. The service levy is to cover the cost of general administration and of assessing and supervising projects.

In fact the advisory or consulting function of the International Bank provides an important *raison d'être*. It has been aptly observed by a distinguished British economist that the Bank

. . . has acquired authority in the exercise of other functions. It has built up a special *expertise* in the peculiar blend of engineering, economics and administrative skill necessary for the appraisal and supervision of large projects of construction. It has also a unique experience in the formulation of comprehensive programmes of economic development. This experience leads member countries to turn to the Bank not only for finance, but also for advice and guidance; while the Bank, in devising techniques by which it could put its experience at the service of member countries, has come to think of itself as a consultant quite as much as a financial institution.[4]

The truth of the matter is that many of the smaller and poorer countries still lack the engineers and economists necessary to conceive and specify development projects. Unofficially, in the course of evaluating an ill-prepared proposal, the Bank's staff in effect may "shape it up" so that it is acceptable. And while such a paternalistic attitude is sometimes resented by less backward national applicants, many countries appreciate this staff assistance.

International Finance Corporation

Another organization affiliated with the IBRD is the IFC, with a capital of $100 million, subscribed almost entirely in dollars by the United States. It was established in 1956 to finance undertakings outside the scope of the IBRD. Thus the IFC can make loans to private enterprises without the approval of the government of the country in which the concern resides and operates. Since 1961 the IFC has been able to purchase the equity shares as well as the bond obligations of private corporations. It is permitted under its charter to finance local currency costs as well as the foreign exchange component of approved undertakings. By the end of 1961, the IFC had made 45 commitments for projects in 18 countries, involving a total investment equivalent to almost $60 million. Although the IFC is a relatively small-scale institution, its special function is an important one, namely the financing of private enterprise in underdeveloped countries.

International Development Association

In 1960 the IDA was established. The employees of the IBRD and IDA are one and the same people. Membership in IDA depends on membership in the IBRD. Its initial authorized capital was $1 billion, nearly all of which was immediately subscribed, and three-quarters of which will be in freely convertible currencies by the end of 1964.

A feature of the IDA organization is that there are distinct Part I members and Part II members. Part I members include fifteen "advanced" nations, whose subscription installments shall all be convertible. Part II members include 40-odd countries that are relatively backward: most of them have small quotas, and only one-tenth of these paid subscriptions must be convertible. In practice, the Part I members will advance funds to the Part II members for development purposes. India,

---

[4] A. Cairncross, *The International Bank for Reconstruction and Development, Essays in International Finance*, No. 33 (Princeton, N.J.: Princeton University Press, March, 1959), p. 6.

Pakistan, Mexico, and Spain are among the more important Part II countries.

The IDA was established so that it could benefit from the experience of the IBRD—hence the common officers and staffs—and yet provide capital on more liberal terms. The first IDA loans have been for 50-year terms, without interest, repayment commencing after 10 years of grace. Principal repayment is to be at 1 per cent a year for the second 10 years and at 3 per cent annually for the last 30 years. A service charge of three-quarters of 1 per cent is charged annually on outstanding indebtedness.

It may be significant that the first IDA loans were for highway construction. This is a type of project normally eschewed by the IBRD. It is expected moreover that water and sewage systems that contribute to health, as well as structures and equipment that contribute to education, will also be financed by the new organization.

DEVELOPMENT AGENCIES OF THE
UNITED NATIONS

For the sake of completeness, brief mention should be made of the Special United Nations Fund for Economic Development (SUNFED) and of the United Nations Expanded Program of Technical Assistance (UNEPTA), both administered directly by the United Nations from New York through such specialized agencies as the Food and Agricultural Organization, the World Health Organization, and the International Labor Organization. Both activities are financed from voluntary contributions by United Nations members. SUNFED, established in 1959, has been operating on an annual budget of approximately $50 million. UNEPTA is an older institution and disburses about $30 million annually.

Neither SUNFED nor UNEPTA involves loans (although SUNFED can make reimbursable grants), but instead provide assistance through surveys. Projects supported by SUNFED include mineral and soil surveys, land and water surveys, and surveys of locust migrations. Both SUNFED and UNEPTA have financed training courses in such specialized courses as watershed and fish hatchery management. For political reasons these United Nations agencies must have projects in as many member nations as possible. Hence, given the small size of their total annual budgets, individual projects are very small in terms of expenditure.

The long-run significance of these two United Nations agencies may prove considerable however. Surveys made under the auspices of SUNFED may result in major project applications to the IBRD at a later date. For example, a mineral survey may reveal an important deposit, which would repay extraction and justify a narrow gauge railroad to transport the output. Moreover, the Afro-Asian members of the United Nations tend to look upon SUNFED as "theirs," whereas, for various reasons, they do not have the same emotional identification with the IBRD and its affiliates. Accordingly, depending upon the shifting balance of power between the "haves" and the "have-nots" in the General Assembly, the importance of SUNFED may rise or fall.

TRADE OR AID?

Having considered various specific ways in which purchasing power is being transferred from advanced to backward nations, and before turning to a consideration of United States aid programs, it is advisable to place aggregate capital movements in context. How important is aid—in the sense of grants and loans—relative to trade? Unfortunately, the data needed to answer these questions are sparse and frequently unreliable, but rough orders of magnitude can be indicated.

As the world entered the 1960's, the exports of what might be termed advanced countries[5] to backward countries[6] amounted to $24 billion annually in round figures.[7] The reverse exports of these same backward countries to advanced ones were approximately $16 billion. These combined merchandise trade flows constitute a small fraction of total world trade—only about one-third of about $120 billions in fact—as the main volume of trade in value terms is among the more developed and wealthy nations.

Impressionistically, these estimates of trade, between advanced countries on the one hand and backward countries on the other, need to be compared with the net flow of annual capital from the former to the latter. In an earlier section this was put at $8 billion in 1960. Very roughly, then, about one dollar in three of exports from advanced countries to backward ones was financed by the net donor-lenders, and the backward countries "earned" only two of every three dollars' worth of imports.

Another view of the matter is that the backward countries would have to increase their export earnings by one-half in order to import the same value of goods and services without financial assistance in the form of loans and gifts.

Some countries might be able to achieve such an increase in export earnings if certain of the wealthy and developed countries were to eliminate import quotas and other protectionist barriers. For example, Argentine exports of frozen and canned beef to the United States might expand very considerably if the United States Department of Agriculture

---

5 Including the United States, Canada, continental Western Europe (excluding Finland, Yugoslavia, and Spain), the United Kingdom, "white" British dominions (including South Africa), and Japan.
6 Including Latin American republics, former overseas territories of European continental countries, the Middle East, India, Pakistan, and the Far East.
7 Developed from the United Nations *Monthly Bulletin of Statistics*.

did not assume that most Argentine beef imports would also introduce foot and mouth disease. Imports of Venezuela crude oil into the United States have also been limited in the past out of regard for the political strength of small oil producers in eastern Texas and elsewhere. Nor are Indian textile imports welcome in certain New England and Southern States. Also, because of the low wages involved in their production, manufactured imports from backward countries into advanced ones are always vulnerable to emergency protection under peril point and antidumping enactments.

There can be little debate over the need of underdeveloped nations to import many kinds of equipment, a wide range of producer goods, and many finished consumer goods from the wealthy and advanced nations. The real question is whether they could expand their exports and so increase their current account credits significantly if this were made a first major objective of planning and development. This would entail both the production of suitable exports in increased volume within backward countries and a willingness of governments in advanced countries to accept these goods as imports.

The underdeveloped world produces various distinct kinds of goods for export. Tropical vegetable products are an important category; primary mineral and petroleum products are another. A less important class at present is simple consumer goods such as textiles, shoes, and furniture. Each kind of export is confronted by different problems.

Tropical vegetable exports encounter the least political resistance in advanced nation markets. Cocoa, tea, coffee, bananas, spices, and sisal, for example, are not produced in North America and Western Europe. However, although such items are noncompetitive, the demand for them tends to be limited. Price elasticities of demand are probably low. The state of demand probably depends more on population growth and increasing income per capita. Not many new-type products are now envisaged. A possible exception, based on rapid tropical growth, is wood pulp for newsprint.

Primary mineral products are a different matter, but only for those countries that have proven and workable deposits of course. Demand in the industrial countries is rapidly increasing. Known domestic deposits of such depleting assets in the United States are not being "replaced" by new discoveries. Unfortunately, although market prospects are not unpromising, it is exactly these kinds of exports that tend to be the result of direct investment by large foreign corporations. And as explained above, the incidence of such direct investments from abroad often leaves something to be desired.

A real test of conscience for many of the more developed countries may prove to be their willingness to accept simple and comparatively low-quality consumer goods as imports. The standards of many European consumers—especially on the Continent itself—are not so high that all imports from undeveloped countries of finished goods should prove to be unsaleable. As a noted British economist has observed:

. . . greater freedom of entry into the markets of Western countries should be extended to the products of the underdeveloped countries of Asia, Africa, and South America without any comparable *quid pro quo*. In this case a vast market would exist in the Western countries for the cheap labor-intensive manufactures which it was relatively simple for many densely populated underdeveloped countries to learn to produce.[8]

The day may not be far distant, if it has not already arrived, when countries such as Brazil, India, and Egypt will be able to export quantities of light manufactured consumer goods to some of the European nations in the absence of protective restrictions.

Perhaps one of the most startling developments during the coming decade may be not trade between advanced and backward countries, but trade among now underdeveloped nations. Traditional trade patterns are like the spokes of a wheel that radiate from the countries of the North Atlantic basin to the comparatively backward areas of the outside world. The historical rationale of this arrangement was described in Chapter 23. However, as the backward nations begin to develop, increased productivity will create more effective demand. For example, it may become economical to ship beef from Argentina to Ghana, cocoa from Ghana to Egypt, and cotton textiles from Egypt to Argentina. Ocean "tramping" may acquire a new lease on life. And as effective demand and transport volume increase, greater national specialization can further increase productivity.

Whether or not significant increases in trade among the undeveloped countries are a serious possibility remains to be seen. Unfortunately, because advanced nations are financing and hence "managing" so much of the economic development planned for more backward countries, conventional trade patterns between advanced and backward countries remain overstressed. New and supplementary trade patterns may be needed. Especially if private enterprise were given more of a chance to trade wherever it perceived a potential profit, there would be more experimentation. Bureaucratic planning and exchange control operations always tend to freeze the status quo. One way for newly independent nations to escape the traditional "colonial" trade pattern that they so dislike, without turning their backs on the advantages of national specialization through foreign commerce, is to approach new customers with new trading items within the underdeveloped world.

[8] J. E. Meade, "The Future of International Trade and Payments," *Three Banks Review,* June, 1961, p. 17.

But even so, such new trade patterns would be no more than supplementary to those now in existence, for certain kinds and qualities of finished producer and consumer manufactures are not likely to be obtainable at a reasonable price save from advanced countries for some time to come. "Hard" foreign exchange must always be earned, borrowed, or received as grants if these particular imports are to be financed. The point is rather that there are some less specialized and durable consumer goods that may in time be available to undeveloped countries from undeveloped countries. Payments could be made by clearing through the International Monetary Fund. Finally, to the extent that such new trade patterns do evolve, there will be a diminished need for capital contributions to the more backward nations from those already developed.

CAPITAL TRANSFERS AND DOMESTIC ACCUMULATION

A remaining consideration is the actual and potential importance of international transfers—whether as loans or gifts—relative to accumulations of domestic capital within the less developed nations.

Most backward countries have understandably meager and unreliable national accounts. However, it is possible to form some impression of the extent of gross domestic capital formation as a percentage of gross domestic product. This relation varies markedly from country to country, as might be expected. Thus it is very approximately 40 per cent in the Rhodesias, 20 per cent in Venezuela, 12 per cent in Malaya, 10 per cent in India, and 6 per cent in Guatemala. (Gross domestic capital formation and gross domestic product refer of course to accumulations and output, respectively, within the geographic confines of a country, without regard to ownership, some of the accumulations and output ordinarily belonging to nonresidents.)

From somewhat more reliable balance of payments statistics, it is possible to estimate the receipt of loans and gifts, as given in Table 26-3. Most backward countries have small annual fluctuations in their payments accounts, and so capital inflows approximate negative current account balances, positive current accounts indicating capital outflows. However, in making such estimates, it is important to exclude grants-in-aid from the current account: the latter should comprise only goods and services (including financial services).

Of considerable interest, especially to those who must request and recommend foreign assistance programs, is the relative importance of these international capital inflows as a source of domestic capital formation in underdeveloped countries. Both absolute values and ratios are significant in this connection. However, for comparison's sake, the following examples of the importance of net capital inflows from abroad are given in Table 26-4 as relatives of gross domestic capital formation.

Table 26-3

BILATERAL AND MULTILATERAL GRANTS AND LOANS RECEIVED
BY SELECTED COUNTRIES 1958–1959*
(in millions of dollars)

	Bilateral		Multilateral			Grants as per- centage	Loans as per- centage	Total grants	Total loans
	Grants	Loans	Grants	Loans	Total				
Latin America									
Argentina	0.3	103.5	1.8	0	105.6	2	98	2.1	103.5
Brazil	15.7	105.2	2.6	4.7	128.2	14	86	18.3	109.9
Ecuador	5.5	0.9	1.5	9.0	16.9	41	59	7.0	9.9
Guatemala	29.2	−0.9	1.2	7.9	37.4	81	19	30.4	7.0
Mexico	2.7	99.2	5.5	21.0	128.4	6	94	8.2	120.2
Peru	13.7	108.0	1.9	9.4	133.0	12	88	15.6	117.4
Venezuela	0.2	2.2	0.7	0	3.1	29	71	0.9	2.2
Asia									
Burma	2.2	4.5	7.9	7.6	22.2	45	55	10.1	12.1
Ceylon	31.7	4.1	148.3	24.1	208.2	87	13	180.0	28.2
Fed. of Malaya	25.2	−1.3	0.6	0	24.5	106	−4	25.8	−1.3
India	160.3	171.3	13.0	280.4	625.0	28	72	173.3	451.7
Pakistan	194.6	95.9	2.8	29.6	322.9	61	39	197.4	125.5
Thailand	49.1	2.7	2.3	11.2	65.3	79	21	51.4	13.9
Africa and Near East									
Egypt	18.5	27.0	2.0	0	47.5	43	57	20.5	27.0
Ghana	3.8	0	0.8	0	4.6	100	0	4.6	0
Guinea	0.2	0	0	0	0.2	100	0	0.2	0
Iran	36.5	61.3	4.6	49.0	151.4	26	74	41.1	110.3
Iraq	6.3	0	1.3	0	7.6	100	0	7.6	0
Lybia	57.5	0.9	1.8	0	60.2	98	2	59.3	0.9
Nigeria	19.3	0	0.7	0	20.0	100	0	20.0	0

* *Source:* United Nations, *Statistical Yearbook*, 1960, Table 155.

It would seem from this table, although such estimates are notoriously unreliable, that certain countries (*e.g.*, Argentina) have reasonably high rates of capital formation relative to GDP and are able to finance this from local savings. Other countries, such as India, are relatively far more dependent on external capital for domestic accumulation: and in this case the "capital" inflow represents grants rather than hard loans. Explanations of these differences are not hard to find. Argentina has a per capita income three times higher than that of India. And Guatemala has been something of a client state.

Nevertheless, although a few countries can attract capital, the only realistic prospect is that a majority of poor and backward countries must themselves finance all save a small fraction of their domestic capital accumulation. As a vice-president of the International Bank has stated:

Table 26-4

(Average of 1958 through 1960)

Country	Net capital inflows as per cent of GDP	Gross capital accumulation as per cent of GDP	Ratio of net capital inflows to gross capital accumulation
Argentina	.5	18	.03
Brazil	1.3	15	.09
Burma	.9	19	.05
Ecuador	1.3	13	.10
Guatemala	2.7	6	.45
India	1.7	10	.17
Mexico	1.9	17	.11

* *Source:* United Nations, *Statistical Yearbook*, 1962.

By any statistical measurements and any numerology that you can invent, in the long run the great bulk of the capital requirements for development must be generated in the countries themselves. Outside assistance can only be marginal, at best.[9]

Substantially the same views have been expressed by a deputy manager of the United Nations Special Fund.[10] It seems harsh that poor and backward countries, many of which truly have something to develop, should be constrained in domestic investment to their own savings at a time when other nations have such a large surplus of output over consumption.

The advanced and developed nations could "afford" far more than the $8 billion that they now give and lend annually to more backward countries tactfully described as "being in the course of economic development." These advanced countries—plus the Soviet Union and Red China —spend far in excess of $100 billion yearly on combat equipment and forces. The resources used to support these military establishments, given time for factor redeployment, could better be used to export capital goods for purposes of economic development. The populations of the developed countries would be no worse off in real terms—and would possibly be safer from nuclear devastation besides—if such a change were made. And if backward countries with uneconomic cultures could absorb most of the resultant capital, there can be little doubt that their people would benefit. Soviet and Chinese threats of aggression and subversion,

[9] Mr. J. Burke Knapp, at a seminar held under the auspices of The RAND Corporation in the summer of 1957.
[10] Professor W. Arthur Lewis, at a graduate seminar held by the author at Yale during 1959–1960.

coupled with refusal to accept disarmament with "cheat-proof" inspection guarantees, is accordingly a major reason why international capital is comparatively scarce.

However, even in view of the military necessities of the Cold War, international capital is relatively in shorter supply today than it was half a century ago. During the fifty years prior to World War I, Great Britain exported as capital about 4 per cent of its gross output. For a few years immediately prior to that war the capital export rate approached 7 per cent. The United States alone, were it to duplicate this feat today, might contribute from $22–$38 billion annually. Or if the entire OECD membership plus Japan were to provide capital at such a rate, approximately $100 billion would be available each year.

The tragedy of today's world is that, whereas the wealthier countries could afford to make such enormous commercial loans, there is no incentive to make grants larger than Cold War exigencies dictate. Lending money—which is the way that capital was transferred during the pre-1914 period—is one thing. Giving it away, except for the export industries that taxpayers thereby subsidize, is quite another. Private lending—direct and indirect, bilateral and multilateral—has shrunk annually to under $4 billion, as we have seen. Government grants have increased from zero to over $4 billion. Any explanation of why international capital is so hard to attract—when absolute savings within advanced countries are so great—must explain the decline of private foreign investment in undeveloped countries that has been such a feature of the mid-twentieth century.

The explanation is not hard to find for those who want to find it. There was a time when the world was safe for private international investment. Most of today's aspiring countries in Asia and Africa were European colonial territories until the last decade. And in Latin America, especially in the Caribbean area, there was until 1933 always the threat of a United States Marine landing should any government seek to confiscate United States property or abrogate its lawful rights. It was during this period, however great the damage to local pride and autonomy may have been, that so much of the less developed world was able to progress with the assistance of outside capital. Moreover, especially before 1914, most of this external capital constituted indirect investment in transportation, utilities, and other kinds of social overhead capital. It was only during the 1918–1939 period that direct investment began to bulk so large.

Against all this, much of the increase in gross domestic product that resulted did not comprise gross national income for the residents of these countries. Part of the gain in economic activity was naturally for the foreign investor. And the colonial peoples had the constant annoyance and humiliation of being ruled by people of an alien culture with loyalties to foreign lands.

To date political independence has unfortunately been associated with property confiscation, exchange control, and public corruption. Under these circumstances bilateral private investment is simply too hazardous for any ordinary householder to consider. Today indirect private multilateral investment in newly-independent Africa appears too risky to most people. Direct private investment by Americans, Britons, Germans, and so on, is often inhibited by a realization that Western governments will not support their citizens' property rights abroad except with words. Such a refusal, given the hostile attitude of many officials in certain undeveloped countries, goes far to explain why private foreign investment in these countries is limited to a few direct operations of major international corporations.

Political maturity, and not merely political independence, is necessary if economic development is to be achieved sooner with the aid of foreign capital. There is a limit to the charity of the great powers—whether based on generous impulses or Cold War fears. If the independent people of the less developed nations could provide the environment that free capitalism requires—which need not entail alienating their natural resources to foreigners at ridiculously low prices—private indirect and bilateral capital would probably be available again to finance many of the industrial projects that the undeveloped nations so urgently desire. For some societies it may be that political independence and economic development are alternatives. The balance of this century will provide the answer.

27

The United States'
aid programs

For many years, the United States has been by far the most important contributor to the economic development of poorer and backward countries, with past aid being more in the form of grants than loans. Today assistance includes development loans, grants-in-aid, mutual assistance (*i.e.,* military) subsidies, export guarantees, and an agricultural surplus disposal program that amounts to gifts of certain foods. All these activities, together with some new ones such as the Peace Corps, were incorporated in the Foreign Assistance Act of 1961. Since then the Kennedy Administration has worked hard to bring more conscious purpose, longer-term planning, and greater practical realism into the conception and implementation of the nation's foreign aid program. All these reforms were certainly needed. It remains to be seen whether they can be accomplished.

BRIEF HISTORICAL REVIEW

The United States government—and the American taxpayer—had its initial taste of foreign assistance during World War II when the first $7 billion Lend-Lease Act was passed. After the war, the European Recovery Program assisted the countries of Western Europe in reconstructing depreciated and destroyed capital and rehabilitating normal economic institutions. Assistance to Greece and Turkey, threatened by Communist subversion, also originated during this period.

This postwar European program began to taper off sharply in the mid-1950's. From VE day to the end of the 1956 fiscal year, out of a global $57 billion for economic and military support, roughly $26 billion represented nonmilitary disbursements for Europe. Most of this accrued to the more advanced and industrialized nations, such as Great Britain, France, Germany, Italy, and the Netherlands. During this same period the Latin American republics received $1.2 billion, while the Near East, Southeast Asia, India, and all of Africa together accounted for $1.9 billion of nonmilitary assistance. A cynic might remember that, in the late 1940's, the Cold War had not yet spread to the underdeveloped world; nor had half the present members of the General Assembly yet achieved political independence.

The Marshall Plan for Europe has always been rated a great success. In the 1960's it is more than evident that continental Europe at least has recovered beyond the most sanguine expectations. Germany's industry has been rebuilt and France's agriculture is being modernized. Under the impetus of the European Common Market, efficiency and productivity are rising, and in third area markets United States exporters are learning to respect the commercial competition of reborn Europe. In many respects this renaissance of spirit and invention on the continent that cradled Western civilization is one of the most gratifying developments of the century. But how much of this extraordinary outburst of energy and creativity can be attributed to the Marshall Plan?

Although this question has no clear answer it is worth considering briefly. There are some who would argue that the reconstruction of Europe demonstrated our ability to develop backward territories through commensurate infusions of money. In opposition are those who believe that Europe recovered because it is where Europeans live. Europeans are not only accustomed to most kinds of equipment, they also invented much of modern technology. They did not have to learn how to operate public power grids: they only needed help in rebuilding them faster. The European nations did not have to be taught about central banking and limited liability corporations, for the truth is that these lessons were mostly taught the New World by the Old. Today, the skeptical view, that Europe *recovered* because it already possessed an advanced economic culture, is gaining acceptance, but this was not so in the 1950's when the United States began reprogramming its foreign assistance resources for the development of backward countries.

From 1956 through 1960, the emphasis of United States aid programs turned toward the development of the poorer and more backward countries, especially those in Asia and Africa. During this period the yearly average assistance was $2.6 billion gross. About three-fifths of this aid was in grants: but these grants included a substantial fraction of military assistance, providing little or no economic benefit (see pp. 516–518). Rather more than one-fifth went for loans. Somewhat less than one-fifth financed net sales of surplus agricultural commodities, for local currencies, at prices and terms that some allied governments considered to be nothing short of international dumping.

Until 1961, foreign aid was channeled through different bureaus, some of which were notorious for their apparent inability to make decisions or act with dispatch. The most important agency was the International Co-operation Administration, operating under authority of the Mutual Security Act of 1954, superceded in 1961. The agricultural surplus disposal program had been operated under P.L. 480. The Development Loan Fund, although operating with funds provided under the Mutual Security Act, had been a distinct corporate entity before 1961. And the Export-Import Bank (Eximbank) had been the designated recipient of loan currency repayments for agricultural surpluses. These fragmented responsibilities were consolidated by the Foreign Assistance Act of 1961 into a new Agency for International Development (AID) within the Department of State.

Barring unforeseen changes, foreign assistance during the 1960's is likely to differ from that in the 1950's in at least the following respects: (1) greater emphasis on loans rather than grants, and especially on longer-term loans at low interest rates, with an attempt to provide various nations with something like a "line of credit" (Congress permitting); (2) a renewed attempt to provide technical assistance, with more emphasis on the areas of health and education and less on industrial know-how; (3) more encouragement of private participation, through export loss guarantees and private investment survey subsidies.

One hope of the Kennedy Administration is to place more stress on economic development and less on military support, to take a long view rather than a short one, and to consider the apparent needs of the recipient country more than the immediate and often transitory desires of the United States. The Senate Committee on Foreign Relations, which partially drafted the Foreign Assistance Act of 1961, echoed these sentiments when it commented:

. . . programs must be clearly related to the long run goals of a recipient country, as defined within a general economic and social development plan. Heretofore, our programs have been too heavily influenced by military considerations, by "impact" projects, by temporary and sometimes illusory political urgencies.[1]

However, with subversion and insurgency threatening in Asia, Africa, and Latin America, the exercise of such laudable restraint will prove difficult.

THE CURRENT UNITED STATES DEVELOPMENT PROGRAM

The current United States foreign aid program includes a number of features, some of them novel, as described below. In order of importance and interest these are

[1] Report of the United States Senate Committee on Foreign Relations on S1983, 87th Congress, 1st Session.

1. Long-term "development" loans (repayable in dollars);
2. "Food for Peace" (disposal of agricultural surpluses abroad on easy terms);
3. The Export-Import Bank (assists exports with loans and political risk coverage);
4. Private investment opportunity surveys (to encourage the flow of private funds into backward countries);
5. Development grants for technical assistance (mostly to improve human quality, make resource surveys, and establish necessary institutions);
6. The Peace Corps (an attempt to apply American youth and idealism usefully in service abroad);
7. Development research (learning how to spend money profitably and avoid past mistakes).

Since 1961, except for Eximbank and the Peace Corps, all these activities have been administered by AID.

1. Long-term loans

Since 1961 the United States has placed increased stress on long-term loans up to 50 years, repayable in dollars. Thus for the fiscal year ending in 1962, $1,112.5 million—or roughly 60 per cent of the $1,835.5 million appropriated by Congress—were for development loans. The first of these loans (one to Brazil) was for 40 years, with a grace period of 10 years, and carried no interest provision; however, a "service" charge of three-quarters of 1 per cent is levied on the unpaid balance. Loans under this program are not necessarily limited to financing the so-called foreign exchange component.

Criteria for lending are determined generally by statute and specifically by an interagency Development Loan Committee. Certain of the stipulated tests—such as creditworthiness of the economy and technical soundness of the project—are unexceptional enough as regards intention although sometimes hard to apply in practice. More novel criteria are (1) availability of assistance from other free world sources, (2) the recipient country's capacity for self-help, and (3) possible effects on unemployment in the United States.

The first requirement partly reflects a strengthening belief that many of the more prosperous OECD countries are not assisting development as generously as they should. The United States would like to encourage the governments of underdeveloped countries actively to solicit loans and grants from European countries, whether multilaterally through OECD or government-to-government. For example, it is felt that Germany should do more, and its somewhat ostentatious preference for "untied" assistance makes United States officials wince. More important really, the emphasis on other free world sources is a warning to those governments who work both the West and East sides of Assistance Alley.

The second requirement is partly prompted by an increasing exasperation with those countries that relax internal efforts to help themselves and rely on external assistance instead. For instance, why should a government collect existing tax levies seriously if Uncle Sam is ready with funds, and what is the advantage in increasing agricultural output if the United States will accept and hold local currency in exchange for foodgrains? As a retired President of the International Finance Corporation has stated:

. . . I am troubled by the extent to which there is growing up the insidious consequences of too great reliance on foreign aid. Everyone repeats the platitudes that each country must be primarily responsible for its future and that others can only supplement its own efforts. Nevertheless, there are too many instances where the obvious attitude is that the chief responsibility of a government is to secure the maximum help from abroad, with lesser responsibility to mobilize its own resources, and to take action so that all resources are most effectively applied, and that internal conditions which hinder development are improved.[2]

The trouble is that, in international affairs as among families, charity can pauperize. Moreover, although often without conscious intent, the foreign assistance bureaucracies of donor and lending countries favor increased spending whatever the consequences.

The third requirement, that loans be considered in regard to unemployment in the United States, is obvious enough. Certain loans will result in certain exports for that country. This protectionist attitude is consistent with the increasing tendency by the United States to grant "tied" loans in defense of its international payments situation.

The issue of "tied" versus "untied" loans has always been a vexed one. In the 1950's, when the dollar was a "scarce" currency, the United States could afford to be magnanimous. However, what with military expenditures abroad and an increasingly competitive Europe and Japan, this is no longer the case. Section 604(a) of the 1961 Act permits off-shore procurement provided that the President determines that such procurement will not adversely affect the domestic economy or the net balance of payments position of the United States. Thus Congress has turned the political heat on the White House. President Kennedy has subsequently stated that no funds for nonmilitary programs are to be expended for procurement in other OECD countries, South Africa, or Australasia, among other places. The Administration policy is that dollar exchange can be made available to uncommitted backward nations, but not to military allies having developed economies. It is the latter that tend to have competitive exports and favorable payment balances. Although understandable as a short-run measure, this policy sets an undesirable

[2] R. L. Garner in an address to the 1961 meeting of the Board of Governors, International Finance Corporation, Vienna, September 21, 1961.

example and is unsound in principle. Countries best able to extend credit are only coincidentally those best able to provide the equipment and other products required by the borrower for development. For various reasons, among them the intricate labor-saving design of modern United States equipment, it would often be better if backward countries with cheap labor and little maintenance capability were permitted to purchase elsewhere.

The Administration has sought long-term financing from Congress for the development loan program. To date this has been denied. However, although still appropriating from year to year, Congress has authorized AID to enter into loan commitments of up to $1.5 billion a year for each of the four fiscal years succeeding 1961–1962. With this implicit promise from Congress, AID can evolve a more rational program for each country over time. This innovation somewhat alleviates the traditional and enforced practice, as described by one AID official, of "tackling twenty-year problems with five-year plans, staffed with two-year personnel working with one-year appropriations."

2. Agricultural surplus disposal

The United States has an ever-growing surplus of food grains and other agricultural products stored—and in effect owned—by the government, and there are many hungry people in the poorer countries. Moreover, in backward nations that attempt deficit financing, soaring food prices are the most immediate and politically dangerous symptom of inflation. Domestic investment programs also tend to draw some labor away from agriculture, and hence from food production. The United States, for humanitarian and strategic reasons, is also committed to assist many of these countries. Given these circumstances, what happier solution could be devised than to have the United States ship surplus foodgrains and other products to poor and backward countries?

The procedure evolved under the Agricultural Trade Development and Assistance Act (P.L. 480) was that the United States "sell" foodgrains or other products to governments of undeveloped countries. The purchasing government, except under defined famine conditions, in turn sells these products in its domestic market. The local government normally credits the United States government with an unofficially "blocked" account in local currency. The effectual blocking results from an undertaking by the United States government to use these funds for limited purposes only—*e.g.*, covering local Embassy expenses—that in value terms constitute only a small fraction of the sums involved. The fiscal effect in the domestic economy is of course to withdraw circulating money from public hands. The United States in effect is granting a loan, for it does not use the purchasing power placed at its command.

The principles are essentially continued under the original Act as amended in 1961.[3] In 1961 Congress authorized purchases from the Commodity Credit Corporation (CCC) during 1962 through 1964, not to exceed $4,500 million, the "purchases" to be made available to users and for uses as determined by the Department of State and AID. Expenditures of up to $300 million a year during this same period were also authorized for famine relief. But as exported surpluses are purchased from the CCC at *its* cost, which is about one-half more again than world prices, these authorizations exaggerate the scheme's benefits. Local currency accruals are now used to pay additional United States obligations abroad, to purchase strategic materials, to make loans to United States firms operating abroad, and to sell against dollars to United States tourists. In general, as the strain on the United States' international payments balance increases, more ingenuity goes into devising ways of using local currency to offset gold and dollar drains.

Although the Administration is under admonition from Congress not to disrupt world markets of commodities disposed under the program, everyone knows that some measure of dislocation is inevitable, and none are more sure on this score than some of the nations that normally earn their way by exporting these same products. The Canadians and Australians regard the United States disposal program—despite its Madison Avenue title of *Food for Peace*—as nothing short of international dumping. Burma, which also receives assistance from the United States and has traditionally acquired export credits by selling rice to India, now finds this market far less profitable. There is much substance to these complaints. Hence during the next few years, the United States may discover that taking humanitarian credit for exporting commodities below domestic prices is a game that others can play also. The final outcome, after the usual bickering and dealing, is likely to be some combined scheme including Canada, Australia, and the United States.

3. The Export-Import Bank (Eximbank)

In connection with exports, mention should be made of the Export-Import Bank, one of the oldest lending agencies of the United States. It was established in 1934, engages in international lending according to conventional banking principles, and has capital of $1 billion; however its major resources are borrowings from the United States Treasury,

---

[3] From 1955–1956 to 1960–1961, about 30 per cent on an average of all United States agricultural exports were financed under P.L. 480, and an additional 7 per cent roughly under Sections 402 and 55 of the Mutual Security Act as unamended. In 1956–1957, government-assisted exports of surplus agricultural products amounted to almost two billion dollars. Wheat, cotton, and soybean oil are among the most important assisted items in value terms.

which it relends, and this authorized lending now totals $7 billion. During recent years, annual new lending has averaged around $750 million.

The purpose of Eximbank is to promote United States exports, and its most important method is to grant export credits and guarantees. Principal categories of loans include: (1) one-year financing of specified raw materials and foodstuffs, (2) medium-term "exporter credits" up to 7 years for exports of durable capital goods and consumer goods, especially where foreign suppliers are offering too competitive credit terms, and (3) guaranteed loans of 5–10 years to finance specific investment projects abroad. Loans are ordinarily payable only in dollars, financing usually covers only the cost of materials and equipment produced in the United States, and interest rates are normally 6 per cent annually or a little lower. From its inception to January 1, 1962, Eximbank had authorized credits of $11.8 billion and had had $3.8 billion fully repaid. Of the remaining $8 billion of active dollar credits authorized, $3.4 billion were to Latin America and $1.8 billion to Asia and Africa. This geographic distribution partly reflects conservative banking views of national creditworthiness around the world.

An important function of Eximbank is to guarantee United States exporters against losses from "political" risks in friendly countries. "Political" risks include such dangers as unanticipated inconvertibility or nontransferability of local currency, cancellation of import permits, new import restrictions, and losses arising from expropriation, civil disturbances, and actual war. Eximbank will also on occasion insure against commercial risks—*e.g.,* bad debts—although most of these are undertaken by a voluntary and unincorporated group of major United States insurance companies known as the Foreign Credit Insurance Association (FCIA).

Although exact details of insurance vary with the duration of loans, and the scheme was amended again in 1962, the United States exporter must normally place all his export business through Eximbank if he wants "political" coverage. Commercial insurance is usually compulsory on short-term business and optional on longer-term transactions. Export deals, to be eligible, must normally include a 10 per cent down payment by the foreign buyer: the United States seller must assume 15 per cent of the risk himself. Fees charged for comprehensive political and commercial assurance averaged 1.5 per cent per annum on outstanding balances prior to 1962. Since then they have been on a sliding scale ranging from $0.20 to $1.72 per $100, depending upon payment terms and country of purchase.

The whole program of export guarantees against political risks, in addition to conventional export loans, started in 1953 at about the time that European and Japanese exports became competitive again with those of the United States. More recent pressures upon the United States balance of payments have quickened Administration interest in such schemes. (Many foreign governments give similar subsidies to their exporters.)

4. Private investment opportunity surveys

A novel provision of the Foreign Assistance Act of 1961—but involving a maximum of $5 million only—was the establishment of a fund to finance surveys in less developed areas of opportunities for private United States investment. Such feasibility studies can be contracted directly with private industry on its initiative. Should a company not complete a contracted study within a specified time, its findings to date become public property. Extractive industries such as petroleum and mining are excluded from benefits under this legislation. In many ways this Title of the Act may prove to be little more than a gesture to those Congressmen who feel that the foreign assistance bureaucracy is not sufficiently enthusiastic in promoting small domestic business interests abroad.

5. Development grants and technical assistance

In accord with the new policy of stressing loans rather than grants, Congress has tended to appropriate rather less than formerly for technical assistance. Thus less than one-fifth of all appropriations for AID in 1961–1962 were for these purposes (in contrast to three-fifths for loans). It is recognized that some grants may be used for structures such as hospitals and schools in those countries that do not qualify for loans. Emphasis is increasingly on technical assistance to develop human resources. Grants are also to be used to conduct resource surveys, improve housing, promote agricultural credit institutions, advance community development, and stimulate land reform. These provisions constitute something of a policy shift away from engineering technical assistance. They result in part from a belated recognition that factories without people to operate and maintain them may prove costly failures.

6. The Peace Corps

A highly publicized innovation of the new Administration in 1961 was the Peace Corps. Starting with roughly a $30 million budget, increased to $63 million for the fiscal year 1962–1963, the operation is planned to attain a $100 million annual level. The purpose of the Peace Corps is to send young American men and women abroad for two-year periods to provide various kinds of technical assistance. It is hoped to tap the idealism and vigor of youth for the benefit of underdeveloped countries, to demonstrate through personal contact the interest of the United States in the economic plight of such nations, and incidentally to give more Americans a better awareness of conditions in these countries.

Corpsmen (and women) do not have to have college degrees, although a majority do, the emphasis being on technical experience as much as academic accomplishment. Although there is no upper age limit, the modal age of "volunteers" is around twenty-four, and—since many posts will be in rural areas—an above average degree of physical fitness is required. All volunteers save supervisors must be unmarried. Corpsmen ordinarily undergo training at an American college for several months—during which they acquire a smattering of a native language they will need. This may be followed by some months of training in the "host" country. Thus volunteers are on the job from about 18 to 21 months of the 24-month "hitch." They receive $125 a month while on duty, plus $75 a month termination pay (blocked until separation), various leave allowances, medical care, and other benefits.

In terms of vocational skills, over half have gone abroad as teachers, mostly in secondary schools. The next most important skill categories are in agriculture and forestry. There is a relatively small number of surveyors, medical technicians, engineers, geologists, arts and crafts instructors, and so on. An increasing number of volunteers—currently over half —are women. Apparently because of superior financial alternatives at home, men and women who have acquired real competence and standing in recognized professions are not electing to work with natives in back areas under difficult conditions for $200 a month. Most current volunteers—except for a few unmarried school teachers anxious for a change— seem to be young men and women prepared for a little adventure before they settle down at home with family responsibilities. Volunteer work in Africa or South America seems rather more exciting than taking a poorly paid social service job with a municipality in the United States.

However, this is not to gainsay the importance of the work being done, as indicated by a frank letter submitted in evidence by the Peace Corps to Congress as part of its appropriation request. As a young Corpsman wrote from Chile:

. . . the most important thing we can teach the *campesinos* is what they can do for themselves. Through hints, discussions, sometimes outright suggestions, we will try to organize the efforts of individuals into community projects. The possibilities are limitless. In one area, the farmers are running out of firewood and in a few years will be using their floors or fences for winter heat. We want to encourage a community plan to buy seedlings of Monterey pine trees which grow so rapidly they can be cut in ten years. On one *fundo* we are arranging a competition in rabbit care. I'll organize the youngsters, teach them about proper sanitation and feeding for the rabbits and arrange for them to buy a buck and doe very cheaply. Janet will teach the mothers some tasty ways to serve rabbits and we might succeed in getting them more protein during the winter.[4]

Evidently, in small but numerous ways, the Peace Corps can contribute to the lives of the world's underprivileged billions.

Accordingly, although costs per volunteer may seem high, this does not necessarily mean they are inordinate. At the end of its second fiscal year the Peace Corps will have expended something like $93 million and will have had a cumulative volunteer strength of 6700.[5] Long division puts the cost per volunteer "on board" at roughly $14,000. The annual cost per volunteer—including travel, overhead, and the like—is likely to remain rather above $9000. Some people may consider that this is an expensive way to arrange for Mary Doakes of Grand Rapids to teach English to secondary students in Nigeria, and proficient teachers of English could certainly be recruited more economically in Great Britain, but who can judge what is best when the national image and presence are involved? Moreover, through the Peace Corps, thousands of young Americans will gain an understanding of rural conditions in many backward lands.

7. Research for development

The Foreign Assistance Act of 1961 provided $20 million for a program of research, development, and scientific evaluation of the effectiveness of the United States aid effort.

The appropriation of these research funds is a belated recognition that United States foreign assistance for economic development has had a very low rate of return to date. Boondoggles in some areas have been fabulous. Partly this has been caused by naive enthusiasm in the field coupled with bureaucratic inefficiency in Washington. But more than anything else it has been the result of rushing in with resources before enough officials had an understanding of the problem. After the success of the Marshall Plan, when the United States turned its attentions to the poorer regions of the world, a common viewpoint was that "capital" was the answer. Repeated failures are now causing many people to have second thoughts. It is beginning to be understood that agriculture is a necessary base for industrialization and that the science of tropical agriculture is still in its infancy. Human capital as well as physical capital is beginning to receive its share of attention. It is now realized that good intentions are not a substitute for local knowledge.

Unlike other world powers, the United States was confronted with problems of the underdeveloped world before it had acquired any sub-

[4] *The Peace Corps,* Congressional Presentation, 1963, pp. 3–4.
[5] *Ibid.*

stantial colonial experience, and so mistakes can be excused. Apart from a few missionaries, and some oil and mineral geologists, Americans tend to have seen the world as tourists rather than as responsible district commissioners. Any efforts that cause our understanding to match our new and increasing responsibilities would be invaluable.

MILITARY ASSISTANCE PROGRAMS

Many of the countries that receive economic development assistance from the United States are also its military allies in SEATO and CENTO. These nations are strung discontinuously along the southern perimeter of Asia, from Greece and Turkey to Taiwan and Korea, with "neutral" countries such as India and Burma as gaps along the way. And other countries, not military allies, receive annual economic assistance while supporting military and security forces that are often a considerable drain upon their resources. Activities for "defense" sometimes supplement development programs, but more often they are in competition for labor, imports, and taxes. In any event, military preparedness and economic development interact in most countries, occasionally in complex ways.

Support assistance vs. military assistance

The United States has always distinguished between what, under various names at different times, might be termed "support" assistance and military assistance. The latter was costing about $1.8 billion a year in 1962 and 1963. The program is administered by the International Security Administration in the Department of Defense.

Military assistance includes "hardware" for the most part; that is, aircraft, artillery, small arms, landing craft, weapon carriers, jeeps, trucks, communications equipment, ammunition, and spare parts for maintenance. The kind and quantity of equipment depend upon anticipated enemy capabilities and intentions and the character of the supposed military threat. Taiwan's defense is against a water-borne invasion embarking from particular ports. Pakistan's defense—so far as the United States is concerned—is against a Soviet push through Afghanistan and over the Khyber Pass. The threat in Laos is a Chinese guerilla infiltration through mountainous jungle terrain.

Allied governments may have rather different ideas regarding the source and character of hostile threats than do the military advisory groups attached to the United States embassies in these countries. For example, Pakistan may be concerned over India's military expenditures, and some rulers may be more afraid of internal revolt than of external aggression. The United States is then in a difficult position. If it supplies armored cars and antiriot arms, it is placed in the position of supporting a regime that may be overthrown, and the next government may resent former United States assistance to political enemies. And if the United States insists on supplying military hardware suitable primarily against external threats, the present government may threaten to "go to Moscow" for what it needs. This would result in the local government becoming dependent upon the Soviet Union for ammunition, spare parts, maintenance, and training, which is something to be avoided if possible.

Another difficulty is that neighboring countries are often traditional rivals. A $1 million of military equipment to A may lead to demands for $2 million from B on the pretext that it is now vulnerable to attack. Thus grants of military equipment have a way of accelerating into a regional arms race. Suspicion and tension increase and local resources tend to be transferred from economic development to military preparation. A nation that supplies arms to others needs a tough conscience.

The main financial cost of these military programs to the United States is not so much the cost of the hardware provided. More times than not the aircraft, artillery, and arms supplies are practically obsolete equipment that is about to be phased-out anyway. Naturally, governments of poorer nations don't appreciate these military hand-me-downs, and for reasons of prestige demand the latest series and models.

The real financial costs to the United States—despite the large dollar tags on hardware gifts—are usually in the support assistance category. For example, in 1962, support assistance was $425 million as against $1409 million for development loans and grants, or rather more than one-quarter of the total. The stated purpose of this appropriation is to help friendly countries to support their own military effort, to maintain United States base rights abroad, to prevent economic instability which would threaten United States political interests, and to save countries from exclusive economic dependence on Sino-Soviet aid.

How is nonproject support assistance used? Military forces, even when equipped at zero cost, have many current operating expenses in peacetime. These include pay and allowances for personnel; shelter, food, and clothing of officers and men; POL, warehouses, communication links, airports, and certain highways. One way and another, there is a great deal of logistical infrastructure, and all imported components have to be paid in foreign exchange.

If the local national government attempted to meet these costs through deficit financing and exchange control, inflation would soon set in and many imports needed for economic development would be unobtainable for lack of foreign exchange. Under support assistance, the United States has attempted to counter these two dangers in different ways. "Eligible" goods have been consigned *gratis* to the local government, which has sold them to importers and, through distributors, for use as local currency. By absorbing legal tender in this way, the government does not have to create so much additional credit to meet current military expenses. In principle, the foreign exchange problem can be solved in much the same way, where the eligible goods supplied by the United States are commodities with international markets. Otherwise, where the country in question can demonstrate a loss of exports because of resources transferred to military activities, support assistance has on occasion included advances of foreign exchange.

Support assistance vs. economic development

It remains to be considered whether support assistance must be a substitute for economic development or whether it can be a supplement to it. Superficially, funds needed to enable a country to maintain security forces would hardly seem to contribute to economic output, and in an advanced country this would normally be true. However, depending on the use that is made of support assistance, it can serve a limited economic purpose.

Conscripting young men from rural and urban areas, and employing them in army and police forces, would occasion a loss of output in most countries. And so it probably does in backward ones, although rather less so, because marginal labor productivity is low in both agriculture and industry. But there may be offsets. Men under discipline can be given the rudiments of an education, they can be physically strengthened through better diet and enforced prophylaxis, and with imaginative indoctrinations they can be given a reason for protecting their country. They may learn how to maintain equipment. Moreover, in army engineering corps, they can be employed in constructing public works of all kinds. A healthy, youthful, and disciplined labor force, even if it does wear a uniform and exercise at times with weapons, is a real development asset if intelligently employed.

A great deal of military infrastructure has incidental civilian uses that are often substantial. Military roads are seldom located so as to maximize commercial use; however, in countries where there are very few roads anywhere, peasants who live near roads will eventually use them. Certain small enterprises may relocate along roads to gain easy transportation. Actually, although military highways may end at uninhabited frontiers, their sources are usually at the same ports that connect the local economy with the outside world. (Historically, while the railroad system constructed in India by the British was partly for military purposes, it has been of inestimable benefit to the economy also.)

Water and sanitation systems, although constructed initially perhaps for military camps, usually extend their benefits to others also. Military telephone systems should not be monopolized by the security forces when no other rapid means of communication exists. It is in the military tradition to take exclusive control of utilities and assets, but often this is not a necessity, and in poor countries it may be too expensive a luxury to permit.

In practical affairs, one must always consider alternative costs, and assess what would happen if some policy were abandoned. Along the perimeter of Asia, if native troops can be made into effective combat units, the cost of support assistance to the United States is something of a bargain. If ground forces are needed in a particular area—and guerilla infiltration cannot normally be countered by modern jet aircraft travelling too high and too fast—the choice is between a native soldier or, say, a United States Marine. The loss in production is far less if a native soldier is recruited from his economy. And the costs of billeting and provisioning him are lower because standards differ. Transportation halfway across the world is avoided. One man employed in the United States economy can produce the military support requirements of many native soldiers in, say, Thailand or Pakistan. Nations have comparative advantages and disadvantages in providing military elements no less than in producing civilian goods and services.

Maintaining economic stability

In a few countries, the immediate object of the United States is not to increase per capita incomes dramatically but to stave off political collapse and economic disintegration. This is especially so where the United States has base rights that it wishes to retain. Because of geography, these bases may be needed to detect Soviet nuclear tests, give warning of Soviet attacks or deploy United States forces in a crisis, and "host" governments are not slow to stress the dangers of retaliation to which they thereby allegedly expose their countries. In order to maintain these base rights, and particularly where the local economy and administration are close to collapse, pressures for assistance are hard to resist. Or as the State Department diplomatically expresses it:

Supporting Assistance programs . . . are proposed for five countries to help maintain their economic life with some semblance of order. Four of them would be faced with the distinct possibility of economic disintegration if such aid were not available. Their difficulties stem from recent ruptures of external political and financial relations, internal instability coupled in some instances with administrative incompetence and maladministration, and adverse trends in world markets. For each of these states, the only likely alternative to continued U. S. support is increased unrest and political chaos, affecting not only the inhabitants of the state concerned, but the peace and stability of the states surrounding them.[6]

However, if clay cannot make bricks without straw, one sometimes wonders whether money can make an economy without effective government.

SOME CONCLUDING COMMENTS

The United States has expended many billions of dollars on foreign assistance—even excluding military hardware transfers—since the mid-1950's when it began to assume responsibility for raising per capita incomes in most of the poorest countries of the world. Bilateral economic assistance has averaged about $2 billion a year since then. Absolutely, these are large sums, and, compared to Sino-Soviet credits assistance of around $1165 million to many of the same countries in 1960, they still appear considerable. But when viewed as $12 per United States resident a year, or as 0.4 per cent of GNP, they do not seem impossibly large.

The real question is not whether the United States can afford to use equivalent value resources for the benefit of such countries—for obviously it easily can—but whether or not there is a reasonable return of some kind that can be increased. The answer is difficult because not many people agree on national objectives. "Winning the struggle against Communism" expresses an attitude but cannot be translated into anything operational.

It is often stated that people in poor and backward countries will "turn to Communism" unless their per capita incomes rise. This may be quite true. However, with the exception of China, the countries where the Soviets have made the greatest inroads are not among the poorest and most backward of the underdeveloped countries. Cuba, for example, was one of the most prosperous of the Latin American nations; and one of the largest Communist parties outside the Communist bloc is in Italy. A certain amount of economic and cultural advancement—evidenced by some industry and increasing literacy—may actually "ripen" a country for a Communist takeover. It is just conceivable that the struggle to gain control of this country and that one may involve very specific measures, such as influencing particular generals, politicians, intellectuals, and trade union leaders, and this in turn may require programs with more focus than anything so vague as "giving the poor more to eat." The very poor and hungry, mostly rotting in rural areas, are seldom the people who start revolutions.

Nevertheless, supposing one discards *realpolitik* and supports economic development for humanitarian reasons alone, how can resources best be

[6] United States Department of State, *An Act for International Development: A Summary Presentation* (Washington, D.C.: USGPO, June, 1961), p. 86.

used? The moral of the last decade is surely that nonhuman resources are of very little significance without their human partner in production. Nor can the economist by himself give much guidance as to measures that will best promote a higher standard of living. He must work with agricultural and industrial experts and—above all—with political scientists and social anthropologists. The most useful people in the area of economic development are moral philosophers with youthful idealism.

These two attributes of understanding and idealism, although sometimes in apparent conflict, were nicely counterpoised in a recent Congressional statement and a Presidential declaration. The Senate Foreign Relations Committee has rightly warned:

[A] . . . critical need in most of the newly independent countries is competent public administration. A society is unlikely to progress very far in the absence of effective and orderly government. An efficient tax structure, sound banking system, and sensible fiscal and monetary policies are the hard but necessary attributes of a government determined to move its people across centuries of time in a few short years.[7]

And as President Kennedy has bravely proclaimed:

. . . we are launching a decade of development on which will depend, substantially, the kind of world in which we and our children shall live.[8]

A nation is fortunate in having a government that can keep both feet on the ground and yet raise its face to the heavens.

[7] Report of the United States Senate Committee on Foreign Relations on the Foreign Assistance Act, 1961, p. 13.
[8] Special Message to Congress on Foreign Aid, March 22, 1961.

VI

Prospects for
development

28

Development prospects
and government policies

In varying degrees, the people of each country can decide the political structure and economic policies that govern their lives. Everyone favors economic development in principle. But not everyone agrees on the "best" means. Hence it is important to distinguish some of the major alternative routes by which economic development can be attained. Among those underdeveloped countries that are still uncommitted in the Cold War, these issues form the struggle by which they are now being torn, so our preceding economic theory must be supplemented by broader political considerations.

MATERIAL PROSPECTS OF DEVELOPING COUNTRIES

Considering first the material prospects of economic development, it is important to realize what probably can and cannot be done, for eventual frustration of impossible hopes may instigate political upheavals and destructive revolutions.

There is not much question but that today's poor and backward countries will *grow*. Births will continue to exceed deaths so that populations will increase. Savings per head, although certainly small, will normally be positive. And this accumulation, together with slow improvement in technology, will result in a larger aggregate gross output. But such growth is not necessarily development, in the sense of higher output per head, unless there are rather drastic and favorable changes in fertility, technology, and frugality.

The question is how much more economic gain than this will be politically good enough. And voters are not discontented only when they fail to obtain what is possible. It may be that the people of the underdeveloped world are being led to believe that, without basic changes in culture and customs, they can have larger material gains than in fact are feasible.

Obviously, even among those who bother to formulate such ideas at all specifically, there are likely to be different economic expectations. The following are some possibilities:

1. Increasing annual income per head;
2. Achieving proportionately a more rapid rate of increase in income per head among the backward than among the advanced nations;
3. Reducing the absolute difference in income per head between rich and poor countries.

Modest success on the first score is very probable, although annual increases of over $15 per head a year are unlikely, for the drag of rapid population growth is serious. The second objective appears unlikely to be achieved by any country with a really high crude rate of increase in population. The third conceivable goal is impossible of attainment under almost any circumstances. These three prospects can be seen in a rough sort of way, depending upon what parameters are assumed, if one supposes that output growth can be characterized by a modified Cobb-Douglas equation (see Chapter 9).

First, consider what is required if per capita income is to increase, which means that $(P\Delta Y)/(Y\Delta P)$ must exceed unity. The aggregate production function may be such that

$$\frac{P\Delta Y}{Y\Delta P} = \frac{\left[\left\{(1 + \phi)(1 + \frac{s}{C_r})^k (1 + b - d)^l\right\} - 1\right]}{(b - d)}$$

where Y is base year national output, ϕ is the annual productivity increment, s is the proportion of annual income saved and invested, C_r is the observed ratio of capital stock to annual income, b and d are the annual crude birth and death rates, respectively, and the k and l exponents indicate the relative shares of capital and labor in aggregate output. It is assumed that the employed labor force is a constant fraction of population. Perhaps "typical" parameters for a poor and backward nation are those given in the first column below:

	Backward country	Advanced country
Y/P	$100.0	$2500.0
ϕ	.015	.025
s	.08	.15
C_r	1.0	2.5
b	.04	.025
d	.02	.015
k	.2	.3
l	.6	.6

The value of $(Y\Delta P)/(P\Delta Y)$ for a "typical" backward country is then roughly 4.4 per cent annually or an increase in Y/P of about $4.40 a year. Without a 0.015 annual improvement in the state of the arts this value would have been under $3. Had the initial income per capita been $300 a year (more typical of Latin America) instead of $100 (representative of some of the poorest Asian countries), these two Y/P magnitudes (with and without innovations, respectively) would have been approximately $13.20 and $8.70. However, estimates of this kind should be treated very circumspectly, for they give only rough impressions of the magnitudes involved.

The second possible objective mentioned above was to achieve a yearly rate of per capita income advance in the backward countries that is more rapid than in advanced countries. Symbolically, where the subscripts b and a refer in turn to backward and advanced nations, this would mean that

$$\frac{P_b \Delta Y_b}{Y_b \Delta P_b} > \frac{P_a \Delta Y_a}{Y_a \Delta P_a}$$

The equation for $(P\Delta Y)/(Y\Delta P)$ has been given above. This means that, if we use the parameter values listed above, in the backward country income is increasing about 2.1 times as fast as population. But if we use the values suggested above for the advanced country, the annual percentage increase in total output is around 4.9 and that of population is 1: hence income is increasing 4.9 times as fast as population. Even if both countries were assumed to have a population increase rate of 1.5 per cent annually, the poorer country would be falling behind relatively, and this would be so if alternatively one were to assume that they both experienced technological improvements worth 0.02 a year.[1] Even if the rate of annual saving from income were to increase in the poorer country from 0.08 to 15, everything else remaining as listed above, the rate of per capita income increase would be faster in the more advanced country.

The third objective mentioned above was to narrow the absolute gap in incomes per head that now exists between developed and undeveloped countries. This involves making

$$\left[\frac{Y_b'}{P_b'} - \frac{Y_b}{P_b}\right] > \left[\frac{Y_a'}{P_a'} - \frac{Y_a}{P_a}\right]$$

where the primes indicate the subsequent year and the nonprimes the base year. It has already been suggested that the absolute increase in annual per capita income is about $4.40 for the backward country. An advanced nation, using the parameters listed above, for instance, would have a comparable annual increase in income per head over a year of

[1] In these examples it should be noted that a doubling of labor and capital increases output by 1.8 times in the advanced country and 1.6 times in the backward country because diminishing returns attributable to overpopulation are supposed to be more severe for the latter.

$100. The gap is rapidly widening rather than narrowing, and in fact is increasing each year by an amount greater than the entire annual income per head of some poor countries.[2]

Although these comparisons are sensitive to the assumed parameters, there seems to be a political lesson, and it is worth noting. World tensions are not likely to decrease in poor and backward countries if large segments of their people are victims of an international demonstration effect. The relative differences in consumption levels will remain about the same when measured in money terms and the absolute differences will increase. Of course doubling money income probably does not double psychic income in some vaguely understood sense, and so it may be that subjectively the relative differences between rich and poor nations may become less marked than they are. But this is probably not what people in the undeveloped countries have in mind when they ask for foreign assistance.

Aid through technical advice and capital advances will lessen political tensions in the more poor and backward countries only if some obvious improvement in ordinary consumption levels soon results. It is to be hoped that people are more interested in comparing how well or badly off they are this year as compared with, say, five years ago than they are concerned with international comparisons with the wealthiest nations. Keeping the economy "moving" is a popular goal even in the United States.

GOVERNMENT INTERVENTION FOR ECONOMIC DEVELOPMENT

Every national government, whether a dictatorship, a "people's democracy," or a body genuinely elected over political opposition, must pay some heed to popular demands for higher consumption levels. But the degree of economic intervention that results and the kinds of development policies adopted naturally depend upon the degree of political freedom that exists within the country. Most people agree that economic and political freedom tend to be gained and lost together.

The issue is not one of government intervention as against *laissez-faire*. For over a century no serious economist has suggested that government has no responsibilities for promoting economic growth. Even Adam Smith assigned to government the duties of maintaining a sound and sufficient currency, preserving law and order while enforcing contracts, and providing improved transportation whether by land or water. Patent and apprenticeship laws were long ago enacted to encourage inventions and increase the number of skilled workers. Development of the lands of recent settlement was hastened by government guarantee of private utility

[2] The advanced country has a $\Delta Y/Y$ of about 4 per cent annually.

companies' bond issues, contributions to the fares of immigrants from overseas, and all sorts of other subsidies. Many prosperous but "new" countries of the British Commonwealth have not been above luring industrial capital with promises of infant industry protection.

The policy decision that is being made over and over again, and in most parts of the world, is whether government intervention for economic development should be primarily direct or indirect. In the case of Communist and socialist countries the die has been cast—and probably irrevocably—in favor of widespread and detailed controls over economic life. But in the "uncommitted" and underdeveloped world, although a general drift toward socialism is obvious enough, there are a number of countries which may yet find it possible to turn the tide by providing material well-being and economic freedom.

It is also important to realize that many policy matters that appear to be capable of independent settlement are really part of a whole, and that "mixed" economies are therefore seldom stable. Controls generate controls. Liberalizing of some regulations usually makes it easier to loosen other restrictions later. It is usually no more possible to have serious deficit financing without exchange controls than it is to have forced industrialization without food rationing in the cities. Government investment in industry is hardly compatible with private initiative in the same industry. Increased taxation usually reduces private saving and direct investment. Thus the larger choice behind almost every narrow decision is the issue of direct versus indirect intervention for development. Does government contribute more for development when it provides an environment that encourages innovation and work or when its officials try to order the economy as though it were one giant enterprise?

Accordingly, in this chapter, there seems little point in comparing the pros and cons of, say, exchange control or commodity rationing in isolation. They are part of a whole and reflect a basic attitude toward government roles and private initiative. Instead, a brief description of a typical underdeveloped and independent country will be offered; this is then followed by a comparison of the ways in which it can tend either to drift toward socialism or to attain a degree of economic democracy.

Typical economic policies of undeveloped nations

No actual country is ever really typical of course. But travel and inquiry in undeveloped nations, including only those that are politically independent, reveal many similar policies in most if not all of them. Existing conditions probably serve to deter rather than promote rapid economic growth.

Fiscally, most governments of these countries spend more than they can borrow or will tax, so that central banks finance budget deficits with newly-created balances. As new money stocks come into the public's hands, they are used to buy wage goods and other simple articles of consumption. But as the supply of these goods has not increased commensurately, food and other prices are bid to ever higher levels. In fact price inflations of from 5 to 20 per cent, compounded every year, are more common than rare.

The effect on the balance of payments is predictable enough. With rising domestic prices and money incomes, exports decline and imports increase, so that foreign exchange reserves soon decline. This results in exchange controls, first upon residents' current and capital transactions, next upon nonresident capital transfers, and finally on nonresident current earnings. The associated licensing procedures are usually employed to restrict "luxury" consumer goods for private use, the more so if capital equipment must be imported for new government industries, but the unfortunate consequence is that professional and skilled employees have fewer incentives to earn salaries if they cannot spend them on what they really want. Controls over nonresident transfers naturally cause foreign investors to place their funds elsewhere. In the end, although governments can divert the employment of domestic resources to their own uses through deficit financing, they are undone by their continued reliance upon independent foreign importers (who fail to buy a country's overpriced exports) and upon independent foreign capitalists (who refuse to invest in an irresponsibly governed country). These are ultimate sanctions that any government of a minor power must recognize and respect sooner or later.

Soaring domestic prices make money a useless store for wealth. Indirect investment by means of any contract denominated in money terms—such as mortgages and bonds—all but ceases because redeemed loans will not be renewed voluntarily. This tendency will be exacerbated if laws against high interest rates exist and are enforced. People of wealth will come to invest only where they see some prospect of a good and quick capital gain. Many of them will succeed in transferring their funds out of the country in some illegal way, thus placing an additional drain upon the economy.

Higher prices, especially of food and housing, are resented by all who live in towns. As urbanites are politically vocal, price and rent ceilings are likely to be imposed, with the result that market demand far exceeds market supply. If these price controls are applied strictly, waiting and unsatisfied consumers will become a commonplace unless specific commodity rationing is imposed. Rent controls will normally prevent new construction of dwelling units, deter the adaptation of older structures into multiple apartments, and encourage those who already have accommodation to waste it. Inability to find a place to live in a new town hardly encourages the labor mobility that is needed when the importance of different industries and areas is altered through economic development.

Because development is considered more a cause than a consequence of industrialization, such additional capital as can be mobilized is directed not into agriculture, but into manufactured goods. Frequently these new manufactures must be sold domestically because they cannot compete in world markets, sometimes being a little out of date in specification or style. Thus industrial goods tend to sell domestically at worsening terms of trade with agricultural commodities. This not only requires rationing of higher priced food in the cities but also tends to hold peasants in the rural areas.

Agriculture, except in a few model villages, tends to continue as it always has. Although sadly lacking in capital and innovations, it gets little of either from government, and the rural underemployed are left where politically they are least dangerous. Food output per head in the nation as a whole remains about the same from one development plan to the next: and the extension of food grants and loans under United States P.L. 480 inevitably reduces further any serious government attention to agriculture.

Government investment in heavy industry and transportation is limited of course by inability to obtain funds—except through bank credit creation—although efforts will certainly be made to exploit the Cold War struggle and thereby gain development assistance from both West and East. The local government may favor some spectacular project which will take many years to complete, so that for some time it will remain a promise of better things to come. Less dramatic projects, but possibly of more benefit to ordinary people, may be eschewed. Here there is sometimes a contrast between Soviet and American aid. The former often gives what is wanted, however uneconomic it may be, while the latter may insist on giving what the country seems to need.

Expenditure requirements may result in a search for extra tax receipts. A first step may be to enforce the collection of existing levies, if the plugging of tax loopholes is not made an excuse for serious riots, as has sometimes been the case. Another possibility is to impose altogether new taxes. Higher taxes on landowners may be imposed if they are more unpopular with the masses than powerful within the government. Taxes on capital or income, if made progressive enough, are another possibility. The fact that such taxes reduce savings and private investment more perhaps than any other taxes of equivalent yield may not be considered serious. Poll taxes, although a powerful means of making peasants work harder, may be discarded as smacking too much of former colonialism.

Unfortunately, although taxes may be increased considerably, this does not necessarily mean that government has much more ability to finance new development projects. Corruption among tax collectors may lose some fraction of potential government receipts. Often more important is the inability of government to control current expenditures for ordinary operations. There are too many relatives needing some sort of position on the public payroll. Popular pressures for subsidized food, political uncertainties that make a larger police force seem necessary, the need to buy local goods produced for export but unsaleable abroad at "fair" prices, all such demands constitute drains upon the national treasury. Moreover, domestic development projects usually require imported equipment, which means foreign exchange that no tax gatherer can provide. All in all, the government's ability to invest is more limited than its growing tax collections might suggest.

The selection of development projects for government investment must usually be made on the basis of economic judgment and political exigencies. Despite the various "scientific" criteria of investment that have been evolved, complete with terms supposed to be metrics of such intangibles as external economies and indirect job creation, final decisions will turn on other considerations in the case of social overhead capital. It is too easy to make work sheets give results desired by the cabinet minister involved.

Where the output of projects is to be sold and capital is considered the only scarce good, those projects may be favored that give high ratios of value added to capital investment. This is tantamount to treating labor as a free good, although it has to be paid of course. Newly hired labor gains purchasing power with which it can bid consumer goods away from others, so its marginal product must equal its wage, unless others are to suffer a loss.

Many governments favor investment in almost vertically integrated industries that will make import substitutes. However, it is sometimes preferable to accept imports—but at an early stage of processing—so that later processing can be done domestically. Conversely, as a means of increasing the value added of exports, it is often possible to process them through an extra stage than has been done in the past. Unfortunately, for prestige purposes, there is a tendency on the part of some governments to scorn this modest incremental approach to increasing export credits and decreasing import debits. Instead, partly for ease of planning, there is a psychological prejudice in favor of large integrated industries with little relation to external trade.

All governments are naturally anxious to expand public education and health. In order to avoid the creation of an intellectual elite, educated for many years at public expense, there is a tendency to favor mass education for a few years. Public health controls are usually more simple and effective against certain killing diseases than against the weakening ones. As a consequence the death rate has in all probability decreased more dramatically than the working strength of existing people has increased. The dominating consequence has been a rapid increase in population. Where natural resources are limited, diminishing returns have become worse, and this has not obviously been offset by workers becoming more vigorous.

With population increasing proportionately at a rate half as rapid (or more) as national output, there is increasing concern over methods of reducing births—except in Latin American countries where religious dogma precludes official programs for this purpose. Elsewhere clinics have sometimes been established to provide contraceptive information. However, although income per head is a ratio of output to population, so far a hundred times more thought and funds have gone to increasing output than to slowing population growth.

This brief recital of typical conditions in many undeveloped countries is certainly gloomy and cynical. In a majority of the least developed countries economic conditions are probably too confused and inefficient to long endure, and political instability is to be expected. This is partly a consequence of weak government and immature electorates. Most governments, even when they rule through the police rather than through the courts, are not strong enough to levy necessary taxes, refuse political expenditures, maintain a sound currency and hence international trade, permit high food prices in the towns, protect people with capital in their investments, and so on. Hence direct economic intervention by government is begun in a few instances to placate some vocal or influential group. This leads to maladjustments that in turn require rectification. Incentives are reduced, initiative is trammeled, and productivity declines. In the end, public exasperation may bring a "strong man" into power, but it may also establish a new political party that has been organized by alien elements. The sort of chaos that results from "mixed" economies in immature countries is surely conducive to the introduction of some form of Communist control later.

"People's democracies" in tropic lands

The first Communist "people's democracies" are now becoming established in the undeveloped lands of the tropics. This is a major "first" for the Soviet and Chinese Communists. And the policies of the Western powers, including those of the United States and Great Britain, have often unwittingly assisted this slide toward collectivism. Here we can only indicate very briefly the sorts of circumstances that finally cause such a sharp political break and transfer of power. The other concern in this section is to describe the economic policies of development that will probably follow.

Political discontent may have many sources, especially if there is a local organization to magnify sedulously every real or alleged grievance and to organize protest marches whenever possible. The corruption and arbitrary exercise of power by government leaders may be one constantly fanned source of unrest. Police brutality and denial of civil liberties is rightfully an inflammatory issue. Supposed racial or religious discrimination or the rumored intention of one language group to have other languages excluded from the schools may be exploited into a useful riot. If some people are shot by government forces, so much the better, for a new and better issue is thereby created. Martyrs are worth far more dead than alive. Idle city mobs, with no pay to lose and much to gain from looting, can often be organized quite cheaply. An old technique is to move systematically from one part of town to another, adding people to the march, initially by force if necessary. After some factories and shops have been smashed and entered—including a few wine shops to encourage added violence—the riot will become worth a newspaper headline in Washington and London.

Many sources of discontent are economic. But it is by no means inevitable that generalized poverty is the fundamental issue. Although poverty makes people feel that they have less to lose and perhaps something to gain from a drastic political change, the situations that precipitate revolutions are usually far more specific. Extreme inequalities in land ownership, even though the present tenant might be little better off as an owner paying taxes, are such an issue. A revised system of taxes, incorporating new levies or perhaps improving collection methods, can wreck a town. The closing of American-owned mines or plantations, however valid the reasons for so doing, results in unemployment and an emotional issue. Youths who have passed through secondary school, or even attended a college, often cannot find jobs worthy of their self-esteem: it is not long before some are joining conspiratorial groups, mimeographing clandestine pamphlets, and making inflammatory speeches.

However, frustration can cause as much unrest as low consumption levels. Any excessive direct intervention by government in an economy, because it creates maladjustments that the price system is no longer permitted to remedy, can be a powerful cause of annoyance and discontent. Workers can't get the goods they want with their money. Producers can't get the imports they need to keep operating. A general feeling of "What's the use?" develops.

Perennial inflation not only decimates some of the more stable classes in an emerging society, but it also leaves each person with the sense that his industry or union or group is falling behind others in having its demand for higher wages and salaries met. When members of each group are suspicious of every other, and able to compete effectively for income adjustments only through the exercise of political rather than market pressures, social disintegration is not far away.

Economic frustrations and human injustices, whether real or only skillfully alleged, may eventually make it possible for a supposedly "popular front" movement to come into power. Some of the more powerful personalities, still out of sight but close behind the new and popular leader, may have clearer and longer-held ideas than he has regarding the economic and political reorganization of the government and country. The legislative assembly, after delegating broad emergency powers to the new government, adjourns—perhaps forever. Any future elections will be referendums for the government as a whole, where the observed voter marks "Yes" or tries to spoil his ballot. Individual representatives from individual constituencies become a nostalgic memory. The trade unions continue, but as organs of government, with union leaders chosen by the Minister of Labor. Political commissars will be appointed for each city block, each industrial plant, and most large villages. Many religious orders will be proscribed, places of worship will be closed, and some religious leaders imprisoned. Once control has been firmly established, the new economic policies can be put into effect.

Most industries are brought into the public sector. Former private owners may be paid in blocked bonds, later to be repudiated, or simply have their property confiscated. Foreign-held companies will be used as hostages until it becomes evident that foreign assistance is no longer forthcoming. The new factory managers, appointed by government, have physical quotas to meet. Their own remuneration and continued health may depend upon their ability to show a profit at the prices attributed by government to inputs and outputs of the concern.

The outputs of each plant are supposedly determined by a master economic plan. But there are bound to be unplanned material deficits and surpluses. Unless government is willing to adjust prices domestically, these planning failures will have to be rectified by imports or exports from world markets, which not infrequently prove to be a great convenience.

The new government may not establish industries to produce the consumer goods that people want and might otherwise soon have been able to afford. The master economic plans are probably designed to increase the production of fixed capital goods, develop sources of power, improve transportation, and increase the armed forces. Real investment is accelerated by preventing increases in private consumption. These major capital investments can be financed, not only from a few remaining taxes, but mostly from government industries and monopolies.

Land reform is one promise that will be kept, not so much for the good of the former tenants, but because landowners as a class must be eliminated. Large estates may be divided among the peasants initially. However, if the landowners formerly provided technical advice, advances for seed, or marketing facilities, output may decline in the short run. Moreover, if tenant families no longer have to pay a rent, they will be inclined to work less than before. But all this is unacceptable to the government, which has to feed a growing industrial labor force in the towns. Sooner or later, government will assess heavy taxes, payable in money or grain, as onerous perhaps as any rents paid before to taxpaying landlords. Government may also decide that fragmented land holdings are too small for efficient working. Collective farms may be organized, the output from which belongs to the State. Thus in the end the former tenant may be worse off when government has become the master landlord of all.

Communist governments' resource problems are more real than financial. With government establishing workers' and farmers' wages and setting the prices at which food is to be sold to consumers, the State has little need to tax or borrow in conventional ways. Government can have a balanced budget and a stable currency within a closed economy.

Foreign trade will be a State monopoly. Agreements that are essentially barter deals will be made with countries in the Communist bloc whereby tropical raw materials are exchanged for various manufactured goods, including heavy equipment imports for development. Thus long-established comparative advantages of the local economy are exploited to the full. All private exchange dealings will be illegal without special permission.

Public health for the sake of physical fitness is likely to be stressed, especially among certain favored groups such as the security police, skilled industrial workers, and Party members. Although mass education for the sake of literacy, the learning of a single official language, and other kinds of indoctrination will all be emphasized, special attention will tend thereafter to be focused on a comparatively small group having superior intelligence and loyalty and an aptitude for technical and scientific subjects. The State is happy to educate these men and women, for later it will be employing them at its own wage in the jobs it prescribes.

All these enforced innovations may not make for spiritual contentment. And there may be very few material benefits. But there will be more activity and employment. Peasants may find they are working longer hours to grow the rice and other quotas demanded of them. Some factories may be working double shifts. There is no problem about distributing certain consumer goods, for they can always be put "on the ration," and at a very low price that makes them appear almost free. The omnipotent State, by controlling almost everything, can survive most major mistakes.

On the positive side, certain social discriminations may have been removed: so long as a man is intelligent, industrious, and loyal, he may be able to rise as far as his achievements will take him, regardless of the color of his skin. Workers may feel that their real wages are not very high, but they are at least not working for a rich employer who "exploits" them. True, the factory manager has a good car and a better villa by the shore, but he rose from the ranks and did not inherit the job from his family.

And in the final analysis, whether or not most people like their tropical people's paradise matters very little any more, for their preferences will not be consulted again. With the best intentions and highest hopes they originally aid a political revolution that is really under the control of others. What happens afterward is no longer revocable.

Economic development with personal freedom

A challenge for the Western world is to evolve a more efficient economic system that preserves all important personal freedoms and convinces officials and peoples in undeveloped lands of its fundamental excellence. Within large measure, the private capitalist economies of the past hundred years constituted just such a system, and the fact that North Americans are the richest and freest people in the world today should be a rather convincing proof. Unfortunately, many intellectual leaders in the poorer countries are long on human culture but short on economic understanding, and they do not realize that the same institutions and principles with minor modifications might also bring comparative prosperity to their own countries. Too many of them imagine that the "mixed" economies in which they live, handicapped as they are by all sorts of direct controls and weak policies, exemplify "capitalism."

The potential advantages of private capitalism are numerous and important. One of them involves incentives. Another is the opportunity to have decentralized decision-making.

Extra output comes from people working harder, saving more, and innovating more aggressively. Because people want something they cannot readily produce, they help to make something else for money. The more they help—whether as worker, investor, or entrepreneur—the more they produce. In the end this increases everyone's purchasing power and hence everyone's real income.

Most incentives to be effective must be highly personal and rather drastic. The trouble with many backward economies, as explained in Chapter 2, is that monetary incentives are dulled by all sorts of traditional attitudes and institutions. Thus a great deal of this book has been devoted to suggesting ways in which material incentives could be made more effective. The truth is that in this respect the undeveloped countries—if only because of the prevalence of the extended family system—have never really experienced modern capitalism. If they do not attain such an economy soon, and continue to demand more than they can produce, a Communist regime may give them material gains in exchange for freedoms.

Private capitalism, to be an outstanding success, must have entrepreneurs to keep it moving ahead. These men need not be wealthy themselves, but they must have access to capital, either from lending institutions or rich men. They must be able to see new needs and ways of satisfying human needs, to organize resources in these novel patterns, and to provide the personal drive needed for any undertaking to succeed.

Entrepreneurs cannot be produced at the call of government. They seem to result from certain political and social situations. They are in greatest supply when direct government intervention in the economy is at a minimum. They certainly do not perform well when government is preventing certain innovations on the demand of more powerful interests that would suffer from their introduction. Governments that cannot stand against such pressures and fail to provide a favorable environment for less scheming entrepreneurs perform a disservice to free economic development.

When production is organized by thousands of units, each under more or less independent management, these units are still guided by current and future prices and costs. The situation is far less chaotic than those ignorant of economics often suppose. The market place provides an impersonal discipline that is sharp and prompt and from which there is no appeal.

So long as there is some independence, there can be a measure of experimentation and specialization of a kind that is quite impossible under State socialism. These variations prove or disprove the worth of unusual ventures. The survival and growth of certain firms and the death of other competing enterprises permit a sort of natural selection. A monolithic government industry, with far-off officials making decisions regarding proper use of equipment, materials, and labor for a whole country, can avoid serious mistakes only by making very cautious changes.

There is little object in repeating the more specific economic policies that a government should adopt if there is to be development with freedom. Generally, gains in output should be shared so far as possible, and serious efforts should be made to alleviate the gravest poverty. The worst inequalities of wealth based on inheritance should be mitigated.

Taxes should be of a kind that cannot easily be shifted, such as land rent taxes and poll taxes. Taxes should be on consumption rather than on production. And above all, they should not discourage entrepreneurship and saving, as progressive income taxes often do. A tax on net value added on each turnover commends itself in primitive countries where accounting records are rudimentary (see Chapter 13).

Serious efforts should be made to increase taxes and control wasteful and corrupt expenditures, so that deficit financing can be avoided. With reasonable credit, it should be possible to mobilize domestic savings, and even borrow from abroad to some extent. If exchange control can be avoided, perhaps by allowing the exchange rate to fluctuate within limits set by stabilization operations, so much the better. If the country has only a few major exports, possibly raw materials, government may wish to institute buffer stock operations (see Chapter 25). Infant industry protection, under the safeguards enumerated earlier (Chapter 25), may provide economic import substitutes.

If a government were seriously interested in creating a class of entrepreneurs and small capitalists, it could do many things to encourage indirect private investment: grant concessions, permit limited liability share issues, exempt certain securities from death or income taxes, guarantee limited loans on the face value of certain bonds, and so on. Government might be prepared to join with private capitalists in syndicates.

Agriculture will be a serious and basic problem for any national administration. Productivity on the land must be increased. Land tenure rearrangements, so long as fragmentation is avoided, are one possibility. The substitution of fixed rent for rent shares may sometime raise output. But depending upon the crop and climate, the solution may sometimes be to force many small tenant cultivators into a farm laborer class. If adjoining tenant cultivations could be enclosed into larger single units, each under the management of a man who would follow expert advice in exchange for small subsidies and the possibility of eventual ownership, farm output might increase. Other possibilities have been explained before (see Chapter 8).

In severely overpopulated countries—especially in which further declines in the death rate are probable—radical government efforts to reduce births are essential. Obviously, any such plan must be voluntary, but this does not mean that public authority should not offer modest inducements. For this reason, the vasectomy-bonus plan (see Chapter 20) deserves careful consideration and an early but limited trial.

Everything possible must be done to promote human liberty and multiply personal choice. The advantages of individualism, both materially and spiritually, are often not realized. Accordingly, it may be useful to quote Lord Keynes on this subject:

Let us stop for a moment to remind ourselves what these advantages [of individualism] are. They are partly advantages of efficiency—the advantages of decentralization and of the play of self-interest. The advantage to efficiency of the decentralization of decisions and of individual responsibility is even greater, perhaps, than the nineteenth century supposed; and the reaction against the appeal to self-interest may have gone too far. But, above all, individualism, if it can be purged of its defects and abuses, is the best safeguard of personal liberty in the sense that, compared with any other system, it greatly widens the field for the exercise of personal choice. It is also the best safeguard of the variety of life, which emerges precisely from this extended field of personal choice, and the loss of which is the greatest of all the losses of the homogeneous or totalitarian state. For this variety preserves the traditions which embody the most secure and successful choices of former generations;

it colours the present with the diversification of its fancy; and, being the handmaid of experiment as well as of tradition and of fancy, it is the most powerful instrument to better the future.[3]

One trouble is that most of the underdeveloped world has never really experienced Western-style private capitalism, in a middle-class sense, as part of its own daily life. Tremendous direct investments by Anglo-American corporations, located often in a remote part of a backward country, are not representative of the best that free enterprise has to offer. Today the idea is far too prevalent in poor countries that "capitalism" means something large, foreign, and predatory, and that "individualism" means personal freedom to abuse others who have less financial bargaining power. But a socially regulated and locally rooted system of enterprise capitalism is not limited to international corporations on the one hand and rapacious village moneylenders on the other. The advanced nations have evolved an economically efficient and socially acceptable compromise —although it has taken them many years to do so—and it is this experience that needs to be understood and perhaps emulated by people in less developed nations.

The eventual alternative to economic development with personal freedom is State socialism under the tutelage of alien Communists. It is unlikely that the present confused, inefficient, weak, and overregulated "mixed" regimes now tottering in many of the undeveloped countries will long endure. What is needed is not simply "capital" (*alias* foreign exchange grants from richer countries abroad), but a real understanding in Washington, London, and elsewhere, of the policies and forces that support and undermine progress with freedom in these lands.

DOES ECONOMIC DEVELOPMENT PREVENT COMMUNISM?

The advanced nations of the Western world intend to prevent a further extension of Soviet and Chinese Communist "influence" into areas of Asia, Africa, and Latin America that are now economically or politically oriented toward the nations of the North Atlantic basin. Containment has been planned in military terms around the lower perimeter of Asia, although there and in other continents the dangers include insurgency and revolution. Hence foreign assistance programs for economic development of neutral and backward countries are ordinarily "sold" Congress and the public as affording the best means to counter "belly-Communism." This is because of a common belief that poverty results in Communism and that a rising consumption level is a necessary, if not sufficient, means of keeping undeveloped countries neutral or even

[3] J. M. Keynes, *The General Theory of Employment, Interest and Money* (New York: Harcourt, Brace, & World, Inc., 1936), p. 380.

friendly. This comforting if expensive notion is not always supported by the evidence. As one experienced observer has noted:

It is not true that poverty breeds Communism. Before the war Communism was very weak in the relatively poor countries of Eastern Europe; the only influential Communist party was in relatively prosperous Czechoslovakia. To-day, the strongest Communist parties in Western Europe are in France and Italy, and they draw their support mainly from the industrial areas, rather than from the poorer rural areas. India made some economic progress from 1952 to 1957, and the Communist vote grew from 4 million to 12 million. If any generalization on this subject is valid, it is that in a poor country the growth of education and industrialization is likely to lead to discontent and a search for ways of speeding up economic growth; a soil in which the seeds of Communist propaganda may thrive.[4]

The truth of these observations is suggested by the following cursory review, continent by continent, of the varied nature and organization of the Communist threat.

The Communist threat

It is important to realize from the outset that the nature of the Communist threat varies from continent to continent and from country to country. Moreover, when Communism makes a serious bid for power, it is never entirely spontaneous and indigenous but is organized in part from outside. Hence it is necessary to distinguish between Soviet and Chinese Communist infiltration, because they involve different methods.

Latin America. Events in Cuba during the first years of the 1960's offer a good example of what the United States wishes to avoid in Latin America during the balance of the decade.

In nearby Cuba, a personal dictatorship of the old style was overthrown by a revolutionary combination of urban workers, land-hungry peasants, liberal intellectuals, political adventurers, disaffected military officers, and hard-core Communists. As is usual, the Communist elements remained in the background at the outset, but were well enough organized to take over crucial government posts later. Within a few years many people who once thought they were among the leaders of a popular reform movement found that they had opened the door for Soviet Communism. The professional classes were either cowed into silence or scared into emigration, external trade was diverted to Communist countries, and the island became a springboard for Soviet infiltration into Central America.

It is hard to relate these events to lack of economic development in

4 F. Benham, *Economic Aid to Underdeveloped Countries* (Oxford: Oxford University Press, 1961), pp. 89, 90.

Cuba. As it happens, among all the countries usually classed as under-developed, Cuba was among those with the highest per capita income. The emotions that gave power to the revolution were rooted only in-directly—if at all—in poverty. Hatred of the corrupt and brutal Batista regime was what inspired the professional classes that originally sup-ported Castro. Historical resentment of Yankee "imperialism," aggra-vated by plantation agriculture controlled by absentee United States corporations, would probably not have disappeared had consumption levels been higher than they were. And a well-fed peasant is not obviously less hungry for foreign-owned land if he thinks some new government will give it to him.

One might even argue, regarding countries that have a more or less European culture, that a certain degree of economic development "rip-ens" a backward nation for an eventual Communist takeover. Such de-velopment, after all, increases urbanization, creates worker organizations, and destroys village loyalties. It may be relevant that Communism as a form of government first became established in European Russia with initial leadership and support from industrial workers and bourgeois in-tellectuals. Soviet-style Communism, although barely intelligible to tribal natives in African jungles, can always captivate a militant minority once an industrialized and hence urbanized nation begins to emerge from backwardness.

The truth seems to be that economic development provides an oppor-tunity to both the Western and Soviet blocs. As a country emerges, espe-cially if its influential classes have a basically European culture, it may become increasingly attracted to either bloc's form of political and eco-nomic organization. Which way it will incline may depend upon the quality and Cold War allegiance of its government. If a corrupt and undemocratic government is in power, and if this government is a "client" of the United States, any eventual revolution will probably be surrepti-tiously organized and led by pro-Communists.

This places the United States in something of a "heads I win, tails you lose" dilemma. In the long run it may be worse than useless to support certain existing governments. And in the short run—even if it had much experience or ability in such clandestine matters—it would be dangerous for the United States to cooperate with "moderates" in the instigation of revolutions. Partly because they have had little rivalry from covert agents of the United States, the Communists have been able in the past to monopolize subversive movements in Latin America, and realistically this is the way the situation is likely to continue. Thus the United States is left with little option but to exert all possible pressure on certain govern-ments to eliminate flagrant abuses. If it cannot engage in revolutions, it must press for reforms. Some of these reforms will also give an impetus to economic development and so be additionally welcome for humanitarian reasons.

Southeast Asia.   Because of geography and culture, the main threat in Southeast Asia (and possibly India) comes from Chinese rather than Soviet Communism, through the special appeals and techniques that the present government of mainland China has perfected during its slow progress to undisputed power.

Chinese Communism has its roots among peasants and not among labor unionists and drawing-room intellectuals. Its strength grows in the rural hinterland, progressing slowly and sometimes unnoticed from village to village, until the industrial centers are surrounded and finally taken. The revolution does not go from the capital city to the countryside but from the villages to the seat of government. Hence Chinese Communism, with its emphasis on infiltrating village after village, is well-suited to backward and predominantly rural countries. This path to power is also a very difficult one for the United States to block effectively through its embassies abroad.

It is also important to realize that the Chinese Communists do not primarily spread their control from one village to another merely because living standards are low. First, a considerable minority of the population of Southeast Asia are of Chinese extraction, so there are ethnic links. Second, most rural communities are traditionally "agin" the distant central government, and all the more so if the government appears to be the puppet of a non-Asian nation such as the United States. Third, rural Chinese Communism is politics at its most practical and personal; its material appeal during the first stage is not that everyone will be better off but that early adherents will gain power and hence goods by being on the side that will win.

Chinese-style Communism does not progress from village to village by promising economic development. The agent that goes ahead has a more limited objective. Somehow he must recruit a small minority of the villagers, perhaps not more than a tenth, and organize them to intimidate and coerce the others. Stubborn individuals who overtly stand against this disciplined minority can usually be handled in one way or another. Once the village has been cowed, more tightly organized political and military elements of the revolutionary movement can be moved into the area, to be supported with food and news from the villagers.

The point again is that this carefully organized technique, evolved over several decades in China, is largely independent of the sort of economic development programs drafted in Washington and elsewhere. Villagers take sides, not according to whether national per capita income has risen four or five percentile points during the year, but according to whether the legal government is going to protect them in their resistance to nearby "bandits" in the jungle. Otherwise, their huts may be burned down, they may lose their bullocks—or their lives. An unorganized majority cannot withstand a militant minority in areas where the government is unable to enforce law and order.

The importance of economic development in these areas—as is explained later—is not so much that incomes per capita are increased as that one of its preconditions is effective government.

Central Africa. Both the Soviet and Chinese Communists have shown some interest in Central Africa. Although their long-run plans may conflict, they probably have the same immediate objectives, and these seem to be limited to subtracting Central Africa from the North Atlantic economy rather than adding it to any Communist bloc. It is worth remembering that Europe is as dependent on Central Africa for certain minerals, such as copper, as it is upon the Near East for petroleum. Moreover, although not a vital matter perhaps, the Soviets and Chinese would rather see Central Africa politically independent and in economic chaos than an organized region within the hegemony of the West. Other things being equal, it is always better to contract the sphere of influence of a rival power, especially if this can be done at almost no risk or cost.

The cost is almost zero because of the colonial issue. The European powers did not have to be driven out of Central Africa: political opinion at home resulted in a voluntary withdrawal of imperial authority by Britain, France, and Belgium. It was recognized by many officials that these regions were not yet ready for political independence, and that their economies might disintegrate for lack of trained supervisors and private capital, but vocal opinion throughout the world was unusually unanimous that "colonialism must go."

The immediate danger in this area, so far as international Communism is concerned, is that the Soviets may be invited to provide technicians and capital to fill the impending vacuum. African language institutes in Moscow have had large enrollments during recent years, but Soviet specialists do not understand Central African conditions as well as former Europeans who lived there, and they are also handicapped by their white skins. Hence unless the whole region is to revert to tribalism and the bush, Central Africa must receive technical assistance and capital funds from some international organization that is not tainted by "colonialism." The immediate task would be to re-establish effective government, public services, and sound currencies.

Why economic development?

An obvious question, if the preceding analysis has some validity, is whether foreign assistance by the United States to these three regions of the world can counter the progress of international Communism. Would a higher per capita income make certain military dictatorships more acceptable to those who now conspire and organize against them? Would a full stomach cause Asian villagers to resist intimidation more forcefully?

Would a doubling of consumption levels preserve effective government in Africa? It seems doubtful.

The importance of economic development, so far as international Communism is concerned, has a different but related basis. It is that some of the same preconditions that are needed for dramatic income increases later are also necessary to resist Communist infiltration now. One of these preconditions has here been loosely termed "effective government." This means enforcement of law and order, provision of social services and public utilities, and so on. Most of the things that a government must do to enable the economy to advance are also things that can strengthen its internal position.

For example, law enforcement makes intimidation by insurgents difficult or impossible, and it also encourages investment. Reliable and rapid means of transport and communication extend the physical and propaganda presence of the legal government throughout the country, besides constituting important kinds of economic infrastructure. Eliminating government corruption and introducing an equitable tax system removes resented abuses and supports the government's finances. The extension of vocational training and apprenticeship schemes can give young men a sense of status and contribution—so they no longer need to seek these through political adventures—and increase national output besides. Other examples have been given in earlier chapters of actions and policies that strengthen the economy but also strengthen the present government.

In the case of most undeveloped countries, although there are some obvious exceptions in Latin America and Asia, the struggle is still to establish the preconditions for development rather than to provide capital fuel for an income takeoff. These preconditions are important both for economic and political reasons. Thus successful efforts to attain substantial economic advance eventually also have an immediate political justification.

Obviously, these remarks require many caveats, and one of these is that rising incomes per head may be a necessary although insufficient counterforce to spreading Communism. As explained before, people the world over have come to believe that government can and must provide higher consumption levels every year. GNP percentage increases are part of politics everywhere, and "growthmanship" has become an element of the Cold War. Accordingly, any government that cannot demonstrate such annual increases is politically vulnerable, even though satisfactory economic performance does not alone render it secure. This means that, so far as United States foreign economic assistance is concerned, a secure and popular government can be continued in office longer if it can be helped to show economic gains. But even dramatic economic progress will not suffice to keep bad governments in power.

What organization for economic development?

A remaining question is whether it really matters to the United States how an undeveloped nation receiving assistance organizes its economy for purposes of development. Is it to the advantage of the United States that the assisted country imitate the free enterprise system of its supporter? Or can United States officials view with equanimity the rapid progress of certain assisted countries toward a socialism that it is hoped can somehow be democratic also? Bluntly, should the United States finance socialism abroad, in order perhaps to secure diplomatic neutrality in the United Nations and elsewhere? This is a far from academic problem at the present time.

The answer must depend upon whether or not one believes economic and political freedom are divisible in the long run. Can a person be free in any meaningful sense if he lives in an economy where the State is the only employer, the only teacher, the only provider of goods and accommodation, and the only source of medical care? There are some who think he can.

There are others—including not a few who escape from East Germany—who believe that economic development through State socialism must eventually lessen freedom. And it is hard to understand how traditional Western institutions can operate as satisfactorily if most countries have predominant public sectors and permit private enterprise only on sufferance in limited areas. In the end, regulation breeds regulation, and not only intranationally.

Both Communism and socialism—however inferior they may later prove to be in practice—are positive and concrete ideas. They can be overcome only with ideas that have at least as strong an emotional appeal. Hence it is a modern tragedy that at a time when the world is locked in an ideological struggle, so few people in the West appreciate fully the institutions they have inherited but not earned.

If political and economic freedom are indivisible in the end—and nineteenth century Europe demonstrated that economic advances and political advances ordinarily go hand in hand—the basic justification of economic development is that it increases freedom by multiplying the choices that people have available to them in their daily lives. Freedom is exercised when a selection is made among occupations or jobs, among places to live or work, between working or loafing, between investing or consuming, between vacationing at home or abroad, and so on. Higher incomes are of less value when they cannot be acquired or spent in the manner that people prefer. State socialism in practice meets only the crudest material demands of mankind while failing to satisfy spiritual needs that are as fundamental. This is Communism's basic inadequacy.

Appendix A

Industrialization through greater productivity in agriculture[*]

There has long been disagreement as to whether industrialization is a cause or effect of economic development. Specifically, does a comparatively rapid increase in agricultural productivity cause a labor migration from or to non-agricultural sectors of a backward economy? Until lately, the classical and majority view was that industrialization had to wait upon an increased agricultural surplus that would create a demand for the output of industry and feed its workers. It will be demonstrated here that, given various innocuous assumptions specified below, two reasonable conditions are together sufficient to validate the traditional opinion that a comparative increase in agricultural productivity expands industry in a closed economy. One is that rural families do not increase consumption of their own output, at unchanged prices, proportionately *more* than any increase in such output per family.[1] The other condition is that for rural households, in inter-sector equilibrium, the income effects outweigh the substitution effects of a change in the price that a fixed agricultural output can command.[2]

STATEMENT AND PROOF OF THEOREM

The usual theorem seems to be that an increase in output per agricultural worker, there being no change in industrial productivity, must de-

[*] Based on a Note in the *Review of Economics and Statistics,* February, 1962.
[1] For example, a family that was producing 100 units of farm output and consuming 60 units of it, would not consume over 72 units if output increased to 120 units and prices did not alter. This is no more than a paraphrase of the ordinary assumption that food is a "deferred" good in the sense that it comprises an ever smaller fraction of increasing consumption levels. And there are no convincing reasons to suppose that this accepted rule of economic behavior is affected by the degree to which a peasant family is part of a subsistence or market economy.
[2] Thus, e.g., at higher prices for a fixed output, a peasant family consumes more food. This is commonly observed. Incidentally, when certain regions have suffered crop losses, a frequent complaint in backward Asiatic countries is that cultivators in undamaged areas take advantage of higher prices to sell less grain to the towns.

crease the real earnings of rural workers *relative* to urban workers.[3] The reasoning is that rural families, wishing to increase their consumption of industrial goods, will so depress the price of agricultural output in attempting to dispose of it that their real incomes will fall compared with those of urban families. The supposed significance of this is that there will be a migration of labor from country to town, and a larger contribution by industrial production to national output, the whole process producing higher incomes per head.

The various innocuous but necessary conditions are as follows. First, there is no foreign trade, for otherwise an increase in agricultural productivity may simply expand exports.[4] Second, the sectors exchange some of their output, for otherwise there is no problem to analyze. Third, the two sectors are normally in stable equilibrium, so that any exogenous change in sector productivity will "move" the economy from one determinate position to another.

The meaning of "stable equilibrium" needs to be specified however. Here we shall suppose that, before an increase in agricultural output per rural family, the consumption of agricultural and industrial output on an average was the same for both rural and urban families. Hence the relative sizes of the urban and rural populations are a function of the labor cost of producing industrial and agricultural output, the income level per family, and the comparative preferences of the public at such an income level for the two sectors' outputs.

These equilibrium requirements, together with some more crucial ones, are illustrated in Chart 1A. The relevant box diagram, before a 20 per cent increase in agricultural productivity, is $ARBU$. The origin for rural families is R and that for urban ones is U. The equilibrium price is AP, and this is marked by the intersection of the rural families' offer curve (O_r) and that of urban families (O_u). Social indifference curves, for the families of each sector, are shown as I_r and I_u, respectively, for the equilibrium situation. C_r (starting from R) and C_u (starting from U) indicate preferred consumption mixes for the families of each sector at the equilibrium cloth price of grain. These iso-price consumption curves indicate that agricultural and industrial goods are, respectively, "deferred" and "preferred" in the sense that their consumption changes, respectively, less and more than proportionately with income.[5] The AP price means

[3] Hereafter the analysis will be of a closed economy, with an agricultural and industrial sector producing grains and cloth, respectively, rural and urban workers being in turn synonymous with agricultural and industrial labor.

[4] This might greatly advantage the country, but it would not constitute economic development, at least in the eyes of those people who identify development with industrialization.

[5] The consumption curves are, given the other assumptions, necessarily tangent at P. There is also a contract curve (not shown) passing through P. On such a contract curve, P is the only point at which consumers will exactly clear the market for each good. In other words, the Scitovsky community indifference curves of rural and urban families are not only tangent to each other at P, but also to the price. That AP is a stable equilibrium price is indicated by the fact that a higher grain price for cloth

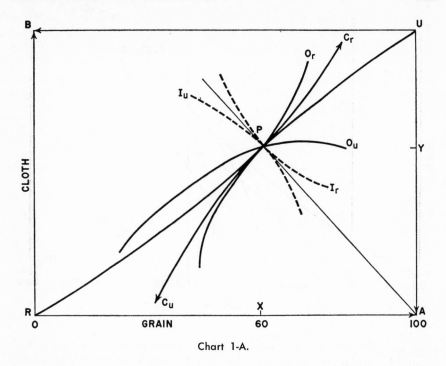

Chart 1-A.

that rural households exchange XA grain for YA cloth. Families in both sectors in general are equally well off and consume in the same proportions.[6]

Now consider Chart 1B and assume that innovations increase the individual and collective output of rural households by .2 so that the new grain output is initially $R'A$. The same balance of well-being between rural and urban households will only be maintained if the grain price of cloth increases by .2 also. Then both sets of households will have either a .2 higher income measured in grain or the same income as before measured in cloth. Hence the "indifferent" price change is from AP to AP'', for AP'' is constructed to lie .2 further away from UA than does AP. However, given the two conditions already stated, it can be shown that the new equilibrium cloth price for grain must be lower than AP''.

R', and not R, is the origin for rural households. A new offer curve

will occasion a market surplus of cloth and a deficit of grain. The two offer curves depend for their derivation on an assumption that temporarily the output of every rural and urban family is constant, although perhaps unequal. Then, at each possible price, the quantities that each family will wish to consume of each good is determinate, and a point on each offer curve can be obtained through summation. For any given price, such as AP, the Scitovsky indifference curves show for each sector the minimum alternative quantities of the two goods that would provide each family with an equivalent real income. See P. A. Samuelson, "Social Indifference Curves," *Quarterly Journal of Economics*, LXIX (February, 1955).

[6] P is on an imaginary line drawn from R to U.

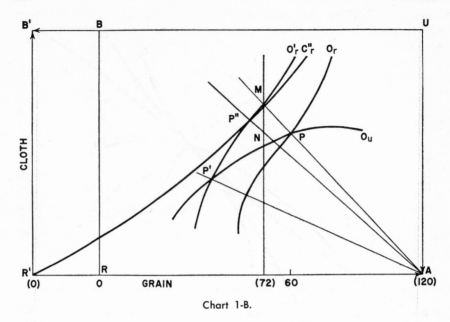

Chart 1-B.

must be derived from their unchanged consumer indifference maps. And something about the location of this new O'_r can be surmised, given the assumptions.

Suppose that the output elasticity of consumption by rural households, of their own output, is unity at unchanged prices. Then rural households will consume .2 more grain than before. For example, if P previously represented a rural household grain consumption of 60 units (measured from the vertical line RB), M represents a consumption of (72) units of grain (measured from $R'B'$). And, if N on AP'' is on the same horizontal plane as P (as it is by construction), N must be on the same vertical plane as M (by assumption). Hence O'_r must pass through M. And, if O'_r is positively inclined, it must intersect O_u somewhere below and to the left of N. The new equilibrium price of grain, expressed in cloth, must then be lower than the critical AP'' price.[7]

The "final" cloth price for grain, prior to migration of some families from agriculture to industry, is likely to be lower than AP' as given by the intersection of O'_r and O_u. This is because O'_r is constructed on the

[7] This is because, in addition to O'_r passing through M, O'_r is positively inclined. It is a geometric paraphrase of the assumption that, in the region of equilibrium, rural households have a stronger income than substitution reaction to a change in the price of their output. Approximately, the larger their relative consumption of their own product, the greater the income effect of a price change on direct subsistence use. C''_r is the iso-price rural consumption curve drawn for a price AP''. Any divergence between it and the O'_r curve is attributable to substitution effects. Price elasticities of demand are likely to be lower than income elasticities for commodities described so broadly as "agricultural" and "industrial" goods.

limiting assumption that rural households consume a 0.6 constant portion of their own output at a given price. If their output elasticity of demand for their own output is less than unity—and the iso-price consumption curves of rural households are drawn on this assumption—O'_r should really lie further to the left than shown. The terms of trade will then initially move more against the rural sector. In any event, the final price of grain in cloth will be lower than the "indifferent" price AP'', and resources should be released to industry.

CONCLUSIONS

In a closed economy, given realistic income and price elasticities of demand among rural peasant families, a comparative increase in agricultural productivity will expand the industrial sector.[8] It is also true that, say, a .2 per cent increase in productivity for agriculture *and* industry would normally cause some migration from rural to urban areas because industrial goods are "preferred" consumption items.[9] But the governments of many backward countries want to "industrialize"—in the sense of having more people working and living in a capitalistic and urban sector—as rapidly as possible. So when there is a choice between a given percentage increase in worker productivity in one sector or the other, such governments should stress agricultural productivity. Industrialization tends to be a consequence and not a cause of economic development.

The situation is markedly different in an open economy.[10] The prices of agricultural and industrial commodities are then determined by international markets. These prices are hence data for the backward country. An increase in agricultural productivity could then reduce the relative importance of industry and cities. People might gain, but domestic industrialization as a political objective would suffer. This may be one reason why so many economically backward but politically independent countries incline toward less trade and more autarky.

Finally, to close on a real difficulty, it is often simpler to raise productivity in industry than in agriculture because fewer producers and workers are involved and they are less set in customary ways. Innovation means persuading people to do things differently. And the most limited resource in some backward economies may be the number of effective and available "persuaders," not only in towns, but especially in the countryside. The choice may sometimes be between an increase in industrial worker productivity or no productivity gain anywhere. Then it

---

[8] It is not so certain that a comparative increase in industrial productivity will expand the agricultural sector, the reason being that an x per cent increase in industrial output (prices not changed) might well result in urban families increasing their consumption of industrial goods by more than x per cent.

[9] *I.e.*, an increase in income results in a more than proportionate increase in the consumption of such goods.

[10] Assuming transportation costs do not obstruct commodity trade.

may be justifiable to subsidize certain new industrial concerns, even though they experience losses because of shifts in the terms of trade against industry, but the burden of proof in these alleged situations must be placed upon those who identify industrialization and development in countries where people are hungry and poor.

Appendix B

Some aspects of India's Third Five Year Plan : A case study in planning for development*

INTRODUCTION

The preliminary design of India's Third Five Year Plan (1961–66) became available in 1959. The draft Plan Frame was prepared by the Perspective Planning Commission. These provisions included a total planned investment of Rs 10,000 crores, with Rs 6,700 crores in the Public Sector, external assistance supposedly limited to Rs 1,000 crores, and no deficit financing.[1] A cursory evaluation of this draft Plan Frame, later amended slightly, indicates something regarding the availability of resources for the Five Year Plan and the impending problems of the economy of India. It also suggests the sorts of questions and assumptions that are part of almost any development plan.

A Five Year Plan in India is a political document, and its preparation is a political activity. In India, where the economy is barely keeping ahead of population, no government can announce goals so low that they can be met from mobilized domestic resources alone. Practically, the planned goals may attract more attention and be more significant than actual performance at a much later date, by which time attention may be on proposals for the next plan.[2]

* This essay was written while the author was in India during 1959, and it was later published in the *South African Journal of Economics,* June, 1960. At that time the author acknowledged with appreciation, the time spared him by, among others: Dr. J. J. Anjaria (Chief, Economics Division, Finance and Planning Commission); Tarlock Singh, I.C.S. (Additional Secretary, F&PC); Professor P. C. Mahalanobis (Director, Indian Statistical Institute); Mr. Pitambar Pant (Head, Perspective Planning Division, F&PC); Dr. P. C. Lokanathan (Director General, National Council for Applied Economic Research); Dr. V. K. V. R. Rao (Vice-Chancellor, Delhi University); Dr. Douglas Ensminger (Director, Ford Foundation Mission); Mr. E. P. W. da Costa (Editor, *Eastern Economist,* Delhi); Mr. J. Robert Fluker (Economics Officer, U.S. Embassy); and Pandit Jawarhalal Nehru (Chairman of the Planning Commission, and Prime Minister of India). However, the conclusions of this essay are of course the author's.
[1] A crore is 10,000,000. A rupee is worth about 20 cents at par. Roughly a crore of rupees is worth $2 million in U.S. currency.
[2] The Second Five Year Plan started off very badly in 1956–58.

A "bold" plan,[3] besides being politically desirable at home, may be a requirement of extensive aid from abroad. Such aid is especially important as only about 5 per cent of India's output is exported, food has to be imported, her own sterling reserves are largely depleted, and she makes few industrial producer goods. A Third Five Year Plan that prospectively required no foreign aid might get none promised. The best strategy for the Indian Government may have to be devious. It should perhaps design the Plan to incorporate, on paper, all the foreign aid that seems available; but it should estimate expenses and receipts "boldly," and the resultant emergency may evoke extra assistance.[4]

In an essentially political matter such as economic planning there is usually a jumble of economic goals. One hardly expects to find a single criterion, such as maximizing per capita consumption, for selecting and rejecting specific projects. Within limits, however, decisions are made with an eye to economic consequences, and officially the most important of these is probably preventing further *urban* unemployment.[5]

Although everyone recognizes that India will long be a predominantly rural country, the village peasants are in a world apart from top policy makers and government officials. The emotional aspirations of the latter usually include steel plants, oil refineries, and industry. Patriotic pride requires that India have at least the same sorts of plants—even to an atomic reactor—as do the most advanced economies. A minimum of industrialization, partly for display purposes, has for many become a goal in itself.

As industrial output rises, population is also increasing, thanks to improving public health. The death rate, set at 31 per thousand in 1951, has been estimated at 25.5 in 1957, and projected to 21 in 1965 and 15 by 1975.[6] Fertility rates do not appear to be declining. As a result, the All-India population will probably increase from 384 to 424 million during 1956–61 (the period of the Second Plan) and from 424 to 473 million during 1961–66 (the period of the Third Plan). To maintain per capita consumption, the Second Plan had to raise consumer goods production by 10 per cent, and this was just accomplished. But it seems doubtful that much more than a third of the increase in national output attain-

---

3 "Bold" is a favorable adjective in India when applied to the Plan.

4 This is not an allegation that the Second Plan "emergency" was by design. It was drafted during a period of heady optimism while the modest First Plan was attaining its goals and benefiting from good harvests. Only a few academic economists, such as Professor Shenoy, protested that the Second Plan was too ambitious. Moreover, in 1955, India still had considerable sterling reserves. Today the situation is very different, and it would be surprising if leading officials, in drafting the Third Plan, did not consider the external assistance "feedback."

5 Politically, urban unemployment is of great importance, as the more desperate unemployed come to the towns on the off chance of finding work. The more apathetic and resigned usually stay in the villages. The Indian peasant tends to be the forgotten man of the economy.

6 Ansley J. Coale and Edgar M. Hoover, *Population Growth and Economic Development in Low Income Countries: A Case Study of India's Prospects.* Princeton, N.J.: Princeton University Press, 1958.

able under the Third Plan will be a per capita increase in consumption.[7]
Economic progress in India is a matter of three steps forward and two
back.

GENERAL FRAMEWORK OF THE DRAFT
PLAN FRAME[8]

The basic objective of the draft Plan Frame was stated to be absorption
in gainful occupations of at least all the additional labor force that will
seek work or self-employment during the period of the Third Plan. The
increase in the rural labor force during the Plan is estimated at 2.4
million a year, or 12.0 million altogether; that of the urban areas at 1.1
million a year for a total of 5.5 million. These estimates assume annual
increases in rural and urban populations, respectively, of 5.6 and 3.5 million annually, that is percentage increases of roughly 2 and 4 per cent
in turn, the difference being mostly caused by internal migration. By its
own statement this draft Plan Frame does not expect to *reduce* unemployment, but rather seeks to prevent further increases, at least in the
towns. As regards rural unemployment, the draft Plan Frame states without explanation that agricultural output will increase 5 per cent (*sic*)
annually, thereby generating more work in the country.

It is hoped that the Third Plan, in 1959 prices, will increase national
income from Rs 12,500 crores in 1960–61 to Rs 17,000 crores in 1965–66.
This would be a simple average annual increase of 7 per cent. Matched
against an annual compounded population increase of 2 per cent this
would presumably raise per capita money incomes by 4 to 5 per cent
each year.

Table I gives the capital outlays originally suggested, by major industrial heads, for both Public and Private Sectors. The Public Sector includes investments by both the Central and State Governments. The
Private Sector projects are financed by private funds and obligations.

The anticipated foreign exchange position during the five-year period
is given in Table II. Total foreign exchange requirements were set at
Rs 5,390 crores, credits from exports were estimated at Rs 4,375 crores.
It was hoped that the resultant deficit of about Rs 1,000 crores would be
met with external assistance.

The authors of this draft Plan Frame asserted that it could be financed
after the manner outlined in Table III. There was no provision for
deficit financing since the Second Plan has a very bad reputation in India.
Almost half the expected surplus from government enterprises was supposedly to be earned by the expanding steel industry, while the profit

[7] The draft Plan Frame accepts a crude All-India population increase of 2.0 per cent
annually, instead of the conventional 1.3 per cent. This recognition of the population
problem is an important advance. The consequences are of course a one-half increase
in the resource requirements of increasing per capita consumption.

[8] All rupee magnitudes mentioned in this and following sections in connection with
the Third Plan are at 1958–59 values.

Table I

(in Rs crores)

Investment head	Public Sector		Private Sector		Total	
	Expenditure	%	Expenditure	%	Expenditure	%
Basic industries	800 Rs	12	200 Rs	6	1,000 Rs	10
Organized large-scale in- dustries	500	7	500	15	1,000	10
Power	650	10	50	1	700	7
Mining and oil	200	3	100	3	300	3
Sub-total	2,150	32	850	26	3,000	30
Transportation and com- munications (incl. roads)	1,650	25	50	1	1,700	17
Small-scale industries	200	3	100	3	300	3
Agriculture	600	9	200	6	800	8
Irrigation	500	7	200	6	700	7
Sub-total	1,100	16	400	12	1,500	15
Housing	600	9	1,200	37	1,800	18
Schools and hospitals, etc.	500	7	100	3	600	6
Other construction	100	2	300	9	400	4
Addition to stocks	400	6	300	9	700	7
Total	6,700	100	3,300	100	10,000	100

Table II

(in Rs crores)

Debits		Credits	
Imports	Draft Plan Frame*		Draft Plan Frame*
Machinery and equipment:		Exports	Rs 4,375
Third Plan investment	Rs 1,200	External assistance	1,000
Replacement	} 690	Sterling reserves	15
Components and assembly			
Industrial and raw materials	3,000		
Consumer Goods	500		
Total	Rs 5,390	Total	Rs 5,390

* Assuming Rs 10,000 crores investment during Third Plan.

from trade in food grains envisaged a government operation that did not then exist.

Some comparisons with the Second Five Year Plan (1956–61) are provided by Table IV. The Public Sector in the Second Plan was originally set at Rs 4,800 crores. But in effect, when difficulties were encountered in

Table III

ASSUMED FINANCING OF PUBLIC SECTOR BY THE DRAFT THIRD PLAN
(in Rs crores)

TAXES		8,250
SURPLUSES:		
Railways	350	
Steel industry	450	
Fertilizers	50	
Coal, oil, machinery, drugs, etc.	150	
Total Surpluses		1,000
Profit from trade in food grains		850
Net savings and borrowings		1,800
Total receipts		11,900
Government (Central and State) expenditures on administration and current development outlays		−6,200
Available for Third Plan		5,700
External assistance		1,000
Total public sector investment		6,700

early 1958, this was reduced to Rs 4,500 crores, and may prove to be only Rs 4,200 crores. Thus the Public Sector envisaged for the Third Plan is about half as large again in current rupees. An obvious question is whether it can be financed without the deficit financing of the Second Plan and with less external assistance.[9]

AN EVALUATION OF THE DRAFT PLAN FRAME

The following evaluation of the draft Plan Frame is preliminary to a statement of the maximum economic progress the author considers feasible during 1961–66.

Size

The probable over-all "size" of the Third Plan is a compromise between what potentially available resources permit and what is demanded by the National Congress Party and others. Thus economics and politics are in collision. The actual goal of Rs 10,000 crores has the merit of not

[9] This is not the place to dwell on the things that went wrong with the Second Plan. Important factors were (1) higher prices due to deficit financing; (2) a melting away of the sterling reserves, partly due to the Suez incident, but mainly because of serious underestimates of the cost of imported investment components and working capital; (3) a bulge in military expenditures, which may not prove temporary since the Chinese invasion of Kashmir; (4) the increasing cost of the growing bureaucracy; (5) the disappointing response of the public to the small savings and loan schemes; (6) the inability or unwillingness of some States to mobilize resources promptly enough through extra taxes; and (7) the perverse performance of the monsoon, which resulted in poor harvest years. (See "Appraisal and Prospects of the Second Five Year Plan," Planning Commission, Government of India, May, 1958.)

Table IV

COMPARATIVE INVESTMENT ALLOCATIONS OF PUBLIC SECTORS OF SECOND
AND THIRD PLANS
(in Rs crores)

Item	Third Plan Public Sector	Second Plan Public Sector*		
		Total	Central	States
Large and medium industries	1,300	790	769	21
Mineral	200	90	88	2
Power	650	400	—	400
Sub-total	2,150	1,280	857	423
Transportation and communications (incl. roads)	1,650	1,345	1,181	164
Villages and small industries	200	200	60	140
Agriculture and community development	600	568	65	503
Irrigation	500	460	72	388
Sub-total	1,100	1,028	137	891
Housing	600	100	27	73
Schools, hospitals, welfare	500	763	294	469
Sub-total	1,100	863	321	542
Miscellaneous	500	84	37	47
Total	6,700	4,800	2,593	2,207

* Revised allocations, as of May, 1958. At this date it was officially admitted that total outlays for 1956–61 would probably not exceed Rs 4,500 crores. Since then, despite further inflation, this has unofficially been revised to Rs 4,200 crores.

only being a bold round figure, and with an impact on the public mind, but it is also extremely close to the magnitude suggested for the Third Plan at the time the Second Plan was being approved.[10]

The main concern of the government's planners is naturally with the Public Sector. The suggested magnitude of Rs 6,700 crores is one half as large again as the estimated final size of the Public Sector investment of the Second Plan (Rs 4,500 crores). It is also twice the size proposed for the Private Sector under the Third Plan. This proposed ratio of 2 to 1 represents a change in the approved direction—for India is an avowedly Socialist nation—and is again a round number.

Actually the real significance of this ratio is not as great as one might suppose, for the Private Sector is not as precisely determined as paper plans often imply. As a practical matter, investments "planned" for the Private Sector may, in fact, be exceeded (unless prevented later by regulatory officials), or may fall short (leaving officialdom helpless except to substitute public projects). More important is the magnitude and nature of the Public Sector, and the extent to which it competes with certain private enterprises, sometimes inhibiting ordinary investment.

[10] In the next section it is suggested that the total plan, including about Rs 2,100 crores of external assistance, can hardly exceed about Rs 7,000 crores in 1959 prices.

National income projections

The projected rise in national income from Rs 12,500 crores in 1960–61 to Rs 17,000 crores in 1965–66 is important to the planners, not merely as one possible index of general economic well-being, but as an increasing source of taxes and for savings. If national income does not rise as planned, deficit financing will have to be continued, assuming the new investment goals remain unmodified. What grounds exist for supposing this Rs 4,500 crores increase—a yearly simple growth of 7 per cent in national income—will occur?

Such an estimated increase—allowing for delays before new plants can produce—implies a capital-to-output ratio of two, unless some part of it is attributed to extra labor forces and unspecified "secular" forces. However, as Table I indicates, over half the planned investment may be in industry, transportation, irrigation, etc., all of which tend to be capital-intensive. In fact, only about 10 per cent is scheduled for such "uncapitalistic" enterprises as small-scale industry and agriculture. It is practically inconceivable, even assuming directly employed labor and taxes are not considered a cost, that the cumulative net value of output produced by this Rs 10,000 crores of investment can equal its capital cost within two years of completion.

What does the record of the past suggest for the future? Table V, in constant 1948–49 prices, gives estimated increases in national income, by industrial groups, for the entire period of the First Five Year Plan plus

Table V

SOURCES AND INCREASES IN NATIONAL INCOME, AT CONSTANT (1948–49) PRICES

(Rs in billions)

(1)*	(2)	(3)	(4)	(5)	(6)	(7)
						Average
			Increases			Annual
	Sources of Income		During	Increases	Increases	Percentage
			First Five	During	During	Increase
	FY 1948–49	FY 1950–51	Year Plan	1956–57	1957–58†	1949–58
A.	Rs 42.5	Rs 43.4	Rs 6.8	Rs 2.4	Rs −5.1	Rs 1.3
B.	14.8	14.8	2.8	0.8	NA‡	NA
C.	16.0	16.6	3.1	1.1	NA	NA
D.	13.4	13.9	3.4	0.9	NA	NA
E.	44.2	45.3	9.3	2.8	3.0	4.1
F.	86.7	88.7	16.1	5.2	−2.1	2.8
G.	−0.2	−0.2	+0.2	+0.1	+0.1	NA
H.	86.5	88.5	16.3	5.3	−2.0	2.8

* A. Agriculture, animal husbandry, forestry, and fishing.   B. Mining, manufacturing, and small industry.   C. Commerce, transport, and communication.   D. Services, including government.   E. Non-agriculture.   F. Net domestic product at factor cost.   G. Net earned income from abroad.   H. National income.
† Preliminary estimates only. Source: "Estimates of National Income," Central Statistical Organization, Cabinet Secretariat, Government of India, March, 1958.
‡ "Not available."

the first two years of the Second Plan. India is still a country approaching a million villages, and almost half of all national production is agricultural output. The first Plan benefited from a number of extremely favorable monsoons, while 1957–58 was an unfavorable year; the agricultural index, with 1948–49 as a base, has been 116, 124, and 113 during 1955 to 1958. It seems that agricultural output, since 1948–49, was increasing at an annual rate of under 2 per cent.[11] This was below the rate of population growth. Non-agricultural output rose on an average about 4 per cent a year. National income appears to have been rising by about 3 per cent, was lower in 1957–58 than in 1956–57, and altogether has been far below the simple average increase of 7 per cent estimated for 1961–66 in the draft Plan Frame.[12]

Foreign exchange and external assistance

In the draft Plan Frame, external assistance was originally set at Rs 1,000 crores for the period of the Third Plan (see Table II). Moreover, it was asserted in a supporting document that "while in 1960–61 net foreign assistance would account for Rs 350 crores out of Rs 1,400 crores of new investment (25 per cent), in 1965–66 it should be Rs 100 crores out of Rs 2,400 crores (4 per cent)." It was also stated that by the end of the Third Plan, assuming some curb on domestic consumption, merchandise exports might be increased by Rs 100–120 crores.

It does not seem very likely that the foreign exchange component of investment can be cut from 25 per cent to 4 per cent in five years, even though new domestic production (e.g., steel and cement) may displace some imports. For one thing, the investment proposed for 1965–66 is about 70 per cent greater than that proposed for 1960–61. For another, as industrialization increases, investment in more complex equipment outweighs investment in construction, continuing dependence on imports.

In the past, estimates of foreign exchange requirements have been too low; thus in 1958, for all industrial projects in the Public Sector, estimates had to be revised upward by one third. In basic industries over half the investment has been spent on imports, and for the entire Second Plan to date, this rate of investment to related imports has been 4 to 1.[13] Some of the balance-of-payments deficit has been caused by recently completed plants requiring unanticipated imported materials and components if they are to produce at planned rates.

What may imports be during the Third Plan? Table II gives the breakdown of the draft Plan Frame's total estimate for imports of about Rs

[11] This average annual increase is 1.3 per cent if the final year is the "bad" one of 1957–58, or 1.6 if it is taken to be the "good" one of 1956–57.
[12] In a following section a simple model of the author's estimates 1966 national income at Rs 15.6 thousand crores, the average national income for the period being Rs 14.0 thousand crores, in contrast to draft Plan Frame estimates of Rs 17.0 and 15.0 thousand crores respectively.
[13] *Appraisal and Prospects of the Second Five Year Plan*, Planning Commission, Government of India, May, 1958, p. 15.

5,400 crores. The implicit estimate of Rs 1,200 crores for foreign exchange, if incidental to a Rs 10,000 crores investment program, seems distinctly low; for a slow decline in the foreign exchange component of new projects of, say, 2 percentage points a year from 23 through 15 per cent during 1962 through 1966, this exchange drain would amount to roughly Rs 1,900 crores rather than Rs 1,200 crores. It is very difficult to assess the Rs 3,700 crores of imports to be used by industry as materials and components and for replacement, but experience shows how easy it is to underestimate this item; also the severity of recent import controls can hardly be continued without slowing capital projects and reducing output in the Private Sector. Finally, with the rising population and poor agricultural record, Rs 500 crores for all consumer imports (including purchased food) appears inadequate.

On exports, the post-Independence record of the Indian economy has not been impressive. In current prices exports were slightly higher in 1950–51 than in any subsequent year through 1956–57. India does not have many products that the world wants. Substitutes for jute are increasing. There is some evidence that textile exports decline with good domestic harvests and reduced impoverishment at home, while the increasing population provides an increasing and competitive domestic demand. For merchandise exports, Rs 650 crores a year in 1959 prices is not an unreasonable estimate, in the absence of domestic consumption curbs. Including annual credits of Rs 50 crores for income on foreign investments (net) and services (net) this would yield total "export" credits of Rs 3,500 crores during the Third Plan.

Reviewing Table II, the draft Plan Frame estimate of Rs 5,400 crores of import debits appears to be at least Rs 700 crores too low, the presumed demands of domestic industry for imports to process being taken on faith. The export credits of about Rs 4,400 crores may be Rs 900 crores too high. In round numbers, if the proposed scale of investment does occur, external assistance could be not 1,000 but 2,600 crores of rupees.[14]

(Incidentally, in the summer of 1962, a consortium of ten countries and the International Bank pledged approximately Rs 500 crores to cover the *second* year's external "gap." Help during the *first* year of the Third Plan was about of the same order. Over five years external assistance will almost certainly exceed Rs 2,000 crores.)

Financial resources of public authorities

This is a very difficult matter to probe. However, the experience of the Second Plan indicates three distinct tendencies on the part of the plan-

[14] However, the "size" of the over-all plan is more likely to be limited to Rs 7,000 crores, in which case the imbalance which needs to be covered by external assistance could be about Rs 2,100 crores; this assumes that the foreign exchange component can be reduced to an average of 20 per cent of investment, consumer imports can be limited to Rs 500 crores, and *all* other material imports have not been badly underestimated.

ners. First, to overstate surpluses available from the current accounts of the Center and the States, partly because ordinary expenses of government (including national defense) have risen unexpectedly. Second, to assume too rapid schedules for physical completion of projects. Third, to underestimate the cost in rupees and foreign exchange of specific projects. To date, the second tendency has at least offset the third, so that scheduled outlays on Plan projects are sometimes larger than actual outlays. This record prompts one to suspect estimates for the Third Plan.[15]

The Second Plan was framed in rather an optimistic and "painless" mood, it being thought that domestic loans and savings, the normal surpluses of railways, external assistance, and deficit financing would together meet about 80 per cent of the Plan outlays.[16] Much was soon learned, and new taxes had to be levied by both the Center and the States, which in a full year yield about Rs 167 crores and Rs 47 crores extra, respectively, thus increasing the total tax burden by one fifth.[17]

The draft Plan Frame for the Third Plan, as shown in Table III, assumes that the Central and State governments will have receipts from all sources during this period of Rs 11,900 crores. This is supposed to leave Rs 5,700 crores for "investment" during the Third Plan, after allowing Rs 6,200 crores for expenditure on "current development" and all usual activities of governments. Although it is impossible to know what the available funds will be, the estimate of Rs 5,700 seems distinctly high, and some magnitude below Rs 3,500 crores would be more reasonable.[18]

Taxes

Receipts from all existing and proposed taxes are set, in Table III, at Rs 8,250 crores for the full period of the Third Plan. This would be 11 per cent of average annual national income, assumed to be Rs 15,000 crores. Actually, because of the additional taxes and higher rates levied recently by the Center and the States, the total take will already, by the end of the Second Plan, be about 10.8 per cent. (This is in contrast to 9.0 per cent in 1956–57.) However, the average national income is more likely to be Rs 14,000 crores (see next section), and at 10.8 per cent this would yield Rs 7,560 approximately over five years.

Various new taxes and rates have been proposed in different quarters, including (over 5 years) Rs 450 crores from extra taxes on textiles and

15 For example, for 1957–58 the Plan outlay for Center and States was Rs 966 crores (likely actual 861); Plan domestic resources available Rs 430 crores (likely actual 297); Plan external assistance Rs 150 crores (likely actual 100); Plan deficit financing Rs 386 crores (likely actual 464).

16 Thus for 1957–58 it had originally been assumed that surpluses from governments' current accounts would contribute only Rs 107 crores toward the Plan outlay of Rs 966 crores.

17 The imposition of further taxes, apart from ordinary political obstacles, is complicated by the constitutional allocation of taxing power between the Center and the States.

18 Explanation immediately below.

manufactures, Rs 400 crores from extra taxes on wealth and income, and Rs 1,400 crores on agricultural land and output.[19]

Nobody can predict what a Parliament will vote in taxes and what an economy can bear without adverse output effects. Past tax increases raised very considerable controversy, and the increase in the cloth tax had mostly to be repealed. Conceivably, to finance the Third Plan, tax receipts of all governments could be increased by 1.5 percentage points to 12.3 per cent of national income. This would yield about Rs 8,600 crores over the five-year period. However, such a rate of taxation would be almost 40 per cent as high again as it was at the start of the Second Plan.

Surpluses

The Central Government has long relied upon annual surpluses earned by the railways, and the possibility now arises of also earning substantial profits from some of the newer industries such as steel. In Table III, during the Third Plan, these are estimated at Rs 1,000 crores.

Railways. The railway surplus has been rising in recent years, partly as a result of higher rates, new investments in capacity, and increased movements, although earnings are somewhat dependent on agricultural output. Table III assumes they will average Rs 70 crores a year during the Third Plan.[20]

Steel. By the end of the Second Plan mill steel capacity is expected to be two million tons a year, and during the Third Plan annual output on an average should be about double. Imported steel products are landed now at an average cost of about Rs 750 a ton, and it is asserted that production cost at capacity operations will be Rs 250 a ton.[21] If this differential were to continue, and the government exploited this potential profit to the full, the Rs 90 crores a year surplus assumed in Table III should be available.[22]

Other Government Enterprises. As the government becomes an increasingly important producer of fertilizers, cement, coal, oil, machinery, drugs, and other things, there may be important potential profits, especially in those cases in which India remains partially dependent on imports that incur heavy transportation costs; however, when private enter-

[19] These agricultural taxes would have to be levied by the States rather than the Center. During the recent upward tax revisions, the States were only prepared to increase the returns from land and agricultural output by Rs 4 crores a year, not Rs 280 crores a year. In fact such an increase would be over five times all the additional taxes levied by the States in three years.

[20] Against this it should be noted that the railways' contribution was Rs 34 crores in 1956–57 and approximately Rs 45 crores in 1957–58. In 1952–53 it was Rs 22 crores, so it has doubled in the past five years and might increase further as estimated.

[21] Shri Pitambar Pant. However, much of this steel will be sold to the public sector, in which case some "profits" are offset.

[22] Considerable controversy has already arisen over the price policies of goods produced by the new government enterprises as there are many potential users who had hoped to obtain these products at lower prices than must now be paid for imports.

prises are producing alongside government plants, what price policies should be permitted the private concerns?[23]

Altogether, something like Rs 1,000 crores from surpluses of government enterprises seems available during the Third Plan, the real question being the politics of their realization.

Profits from trade in food grains

The government has often considered trading domestically-produced food grains, but the item of Rs 850 crores in Table III was wholly conjectural. It is based on the assumption that there is a marketable surplus in food grains of 34 million tons annually, which the government acquires at collection points and subsequently sells in the cities and towns. The assumed profit would be about Rs 2 per maund, or Rs 54 a long ton.[24]

It does not follow that the entry of the government into this trade will yield it a surplus. In poor crop years, rather than force the price to farmers down and that to consumers up, the government may have to subsidize instead. Moreover, this is the sort of enterprise in which the operating costs of a bureaucracy are likely to exceed those of private traders. There is also the likelihood of smuggling from country to town should the price spread become too great. In view of the probable delays in implementing such a scheme, and the obvious possibility that it will prove a fiscal drain, it seems unlikely that this particular Rs 850 crores of revenue will ever materialize.

New savings and borrowings

To what extent can the Public Sector (the Central and State Governments) induce those with savings to "invest"?[25] In considering this question several factors are important. First, as schemes such as the small savings drive have yet to reach down to the semi-urban and rural areas, the savers who provide significant investments are the relatively few

[23] Should the government be the price leader, with private profits either taxed away or prevented by suitable excise taxes on private output, in which case what of incentives to enterprise to invest and produce? Or if the government sets low price ceilings on private output, the enforcement of allocations will be difficult and someone will inevitably gain windfall profits. Alternatively, if public and private concerns price according to the market, private investment will be encouraged even though some of the profits are removed by general income, corporate, and wealth taxes.

[24] Naturally the prices of food grains vary from place to place and fluctuate over time depending on the state of the crop, the amount peasants hold back for their own consumption, and the validity of U.S. grains distributed at lower prices in rationed amounts. An average price of around 16 to 18 Rs a maund is what the public likes to consider as "normal"; prices in the high twenties signal an emergency and provoke political agitation. In view of the increasing population, and the probable poor performance of agriculture in the future, it would be a very brave government that decided to undertake the bringing of food grains to the larger urban areas.

[25] As the government has a monopoly on all life insurance, and operates a small savings scheme, these premiums and savings are automatically mobilized as investments.

urban families of the upper and middle classes. These people have been the object of recently imposed taxes, and there is the prospect of additional levies in the near future. To some extent they will substitute tax payments for invested savings. Second, although India experienced no secular rise in prices from the war until the Second Plan, the fear of persistent future inflation now exists because of deficit financing, and will inevitably inhibit both small savings deposits and investments in gilt-edged securities. Third, although relatively high returns in the money market do help to finance Private Sector investments and increase over-all saving, they also divert capital funds from government.

Table III assumes that the governments can, on an average, tap savings of Rs 360 crores a year, partly from the sale of obligations and partly from increased savings deposits. However, these and other sources contributed (net) only Rs 144 crores annually during the first two years of the Second Plan, or about 1.3 per cent of national income. This was when the total tax take was already averaging about 9.8 per cent of national income.

If taxes are increased to 12.3 per cent of national income during the Third Plan, the percentage of "loans" to governments is likely to decrease to, say, 1.0 per cent providing net savings over five years of Rs 680 crores. Or even if taxes are not increased beyond current yields of 10.8 per cent, so that the annual saving rate is 1.2 per cent, loans may not exceed Rs 840 crores for the full Plan period unless the government is extraordinarily successful in popularizing the small savings scheme, or in realizing some new flow.[26] The Rs 1,800 crores assumed in Table III is not independent of the assumed tax yields, and appears to be about Rs 1,000 crores too high, barring some exceptional circumstance.

Current government expenditures

Clearly, it is an impossible task to estimate ordinary expenditures and current development outlays of the Central and State governments in detail during a period two to seven years ahead, even supposing no change in the value of the rupee. While the government once proposed a 10 per cent reduction in the defense budget for 1959–60, tensions resulting from the Chinese invasion and India's encroachments in Kashmir preclude it. The bureaucracies of government are becoming considerably more costly and unwieldy; this is difficult to combat in a country where family ties are strong and underemployment is rife, and it may become accentuated as the government undertakes more numerous and intricate activities. Other and possibly more serious costs in coming years are "*current* development outlays": in the end these may drastically limit the new development *investments* that can be financed.

The draft Plan Frame, as shown in Table III puts Central and State Governments' current administrative expenditures and development out-

---

[26] It has been proposed that life insurance, monopolized by the government, be made compulsory; declining death rates could earn handsome profits if such a scheme were administratively possible.

lays at Rs 6,200 crores for the full period. In the opinion of one senior official and his staff, however, this estimate is thought to be from Rs 1,000 to 800 crores too low. The main reason advanced for the discrepancy is that the Perspective Planning Division failed to allow adequately for current development outlays.

The Central and State Governments have separate capital and current budgets and accounts: naturally this distinction is sometimes blurred and difficult to determine in practice. Thus the construction of new schools is a capital outlay, but the training of additional teachers to staff them is a current development outlay. Plant construction is capital, but raw material inventories may be current expenses. It is easy to overlook many of these sorts of costs.

Some officials in designing the Third Plan seemed to believe that nearly all additional tax receipts will normally be available as a current surplus for investment. Yet experience shows that current expenditures increase almost as rapidly as current receipts. In fact, considering the six years, 1952–53 through 1957–58, receipts increased yearly at 8.4 per cent and current expenditures at 8.2 per cent. Of the total increase of Rs 428 crores in annual receipts during this period, Rs 370 crores went to increased current expenditures, and only Rs 58 for increased current surpluses. Without wishing to imply any "law" of budget development over time, past pressures do often persist; and, if *current* receipts and expenditures continue to increase at the percentage rates of the past, they would be, respectively, Rs 8,100 crores and Rs 7,050 crores for the full period of the Third Plan.[27]

Summary.   Table VI summarizes this subsection.

Table VI

ESTIMATED FINANCING AVAILABLE FOR THE PUBLIC SECTOR FROM DOMESTIC RESOURCES*
(in thousands of Rs crores)

Existing taxes	7.3
Special taxes for Third Plan	1.3
Total taxes	8.6
Total government current expenses	−7.1
Current government surplus	1.5
Government enterprise profits	1.0
Savings available to government	.8
Available for investment in Public Sector without external assistance	3.3

* Based on discussion in text, and compared with Table III, for the Third Plan.

The main differences from Table III are that no profit of Rs 850 crores from trading in food grains is included, the revised estimate of net sav-

[27] The former approximates the current tax receipts appearing in Table III, and falls below that suggested here as possible; the latter conforms closely with the views (already mentioned) of senior and experienced officials.

ings and borrowings available for investment is Rs 1,000 crores less, and future current government expenses are expected to be Rs 900 crores higher. However, new taxes of about Rs 350 crores higher yield are assumed. The final result, ignoring external assistance, is an estimate that the Indian governments can almost finance Public Sector investments valued at about Rs 3,300 crores during the Third Five Year Plan.[28] Even this apparently "low" estimate in terms of *domestic and mobilized* resources available for the Public Sector exceeds this same realized item in the Second Plan.

Resources available to the Private Sector

It is far more difficult to estimate resources available to the Private Sector because necessary data on private saving and investment are so incomplete. However, studies made by and for the Planning Commission suggest that the combined rate of public and private saving is about 8 per cent of national income. Obviously this percentage may vary over five years, but probably not more than one or two points.

Private saving may be inversely related to public savings when these are financed from extra taxes. Nor are there clear grounds for supposing that the rate of private saving will increase substantially, for there is no likelihood of any considerable increase in income per capita. A favorable prospect, though, is that government enterprise profits will increase public saving by Rs 750 crores during the Third Plan.

As a rough estimate for the Third Plan, public and private investment for the five years may be 40 per cent of national annual income, plus the Rs 750 crores additional government enterprise profits.[29] This totals to about Rs 6.35 thousand crores. If Rs 3.3 thousand crores is subtracted for the Public Sector, this leaves private savings of Rs 3.0 thousand crores in private hands. However, some of these savings will be used by the savers to improve their farms and stores, purchase simple equipment, and so on.[30] If we assume that about Rs 750 of these private savings is self-invested, this leaves Rs 2.25 thousand crores as an approximation of Private Sector investments, or Rs 5.6 thousand crores for total "plan" investment of domestic resources.

28 In case this seems a very low figure, in contrast with the suggested Rs 5,700 crores investment in the Public Sector, final estimates for the *Second* Plan, in thousands of crores of rupees, are: Current Government Surplus, 0.76; Government Enterprise Profits, 0.250; Savings Available to Government, 1.01; for a total of 2.02. (See "Appraisals and Prospects of the Second Five Year Plan, *op. cit.,* Table V.) The Second Plan in the end will probably use Rs 1,200 crores of deficit financing and over Rs 1,000 crores of external assistance, investing Rs 4,200 crores in the Public Sector.

29 This implies an aggregate saving rate for the economy which may be high for productive investment.

30 While these ordinary investments of small proprietors are beneficial to the economy, they are not the kind that normally are considered part of the Private Sector of the Plan: fortunately they are also the sort of thing that may escape the notice of studies on savings and investment, so there may be more resources than realized.

Additional jobs created

A basic objective is to create enough additional jobs through the Third Plan to prevent more *urban* unemployment. The draft Plan Frame assumes a yearly migration of 800,000 persons from rural to urban areas, that 33 per cent of the rural population will seek work, and 40 per cent of the urban. This means, combining Coale and Hoover's estimate of a Third Plan population increase of 49 million,[31] 12.0 million more rural and 6.3 million more urban job seekers.

In planning circles an attempt is made to calculate and apply capital-to-job ratios for different industries and heads of investment. For instance, in Iron and Steel it is supposed to take Rs 35,000 to 60,000 to create a job directly, and Rs 9,000 to do so in the large-scale manufacture of consumer goods.[32] If one accepts this approach—to which there are serious theoretical objections as well as practical difficulties—it would appear that a total of even Rs 7,000 crores, allocated along the lines of Table I, will create the extra *urban* jobs needed. However, there will probably be no reduction in urban unemployment, primarily because of the emphasis on heavy industry with high capital-to-job ratios.

Rural employment is another matter. For one thing, most investments in rural areas either improve local welfare (e.g., uncontaminated water supplies for each village), or lessen onerous chores (e.g., grinding grain), but do not create jobs. Many of the large investments that increase agricultural output (e.g., in fertilizer and simple farm equipment plants) directly create employment in *non-rural* areas. In the long run, the solution of rural underemployment must come from institutional changes and new practices that increase agricultural output, combined with migration to new urban jobs.[33] During 1961–66 existing underemployment will worsen, despite an estimated migration of almost one-and-a-half million job seekers from country to town, the increase in rural underemployed possibly being nine million.

A THEORETICAL REAPPRAISAL

In evaluating further the draft Frame Plan, use can be made of a modified Cobb-Douglas formulation (see Chapter 9), expressing the growth of an economy. It can be supposed that relative increases in annual income are some function of (1) technology (ϕ) improvements; (2) labor force (L) additions; and (3) capital (K) increments. It can be stipulated that (approximately):

[31] *Op. cit.*
[32] Professor P. C. Mahalanobis, "The Approach of Operational Research to Planning in India," SANKHYA, Vol. 16, December, 1955, Appendix to Chapter 4.
[33] In the short run, judging from Table V, increased output from agriculture is likely to be small; certainly there are no grounds for supposing, as does the draft Plan Frame, that it will suddenly increase each year by 5 per cent instead of 2 per cent a year.

$$\frac{Y'}{Y} = (1 + \phi)\left(\frac{L'}{L}\right)^{l}\left(\frac{K'}{K}\right)^{k}$$

where primes indicate subsequent year values. We shall further suppose that annual ϕ is .01, l is .5, and k is .3, there being diminishing returns to labor and capital amounting to .2 because of natural resource limitations. If the base national output in fiscal year 1960–61 (Y) was Rs 12.5 thousand crores, at 1959 prices, what is the national output likely to be in 1965–66 for (Y')?

Any estimate of ϕ must be very subjective, but agriculture accounts directly and indirectly for almost half the domestic product, so rather arbitrarily and hopefully ϕ is set at .05 over five years. If labor force grows with population at .02 a year, extra labor will have increased national annual output by 5 times .02 times .5 at the end of 5 years, or by .05. Should the K/Y ratio be unity, which is a crude guess, the 8 per cent or so of saving from annual income, with $k = .3$, will provide another 5 times .08 times .3 or an increase in output of .12 by the end of the Third Plan. These various proportionate increases sum to .22. And .22 of Rs 12.5 thousand crores is Rs 2.75 thousand crores.

Thus national domestic product, ignoring output contributions from new external assistance that is invested, may at the end of the Third Plan be around Rs 15.25 thousand crores in 1959 prices. Should one fifth of all investment be externally financed—which would be around Rs 1,400 crores for the total five years—there would be roughly another Rs 350 crores of output if a rate of return of 25 per cent can be obtained and gestation periods are ignored. The final outcome is an estimate of Rs 15.6 thousand crores for the last or fifth year. The mean annual domestic product is then about Rs 14 thousand crores during the Third Plan.

PROSPECTS FOR ECONOMIC GROWTH DURING
1961–66

In summary, the following are some major prospects for economic development in India during the period of the Third Plan, at 1959 prices.[34]

First, the domestic savings likely to be available to the Public and Private Sectors during this period amount to about Rs 5,600 crores, assuming no deficit financing, and an 8 per cent annual saving from income.

Second, although a reselection of investments could alter it somewhat, the foreign exchange component of investments under the Third Plan may amount to around 20 per cent. As India's own foreign exchange reserves are near the operating minimum, lack of external assistance may impose a more severe constraint on the size of the Third Plan than do domestic resources. Export credits are likely to be Rs 3,500 crores, about

[34] The following estimates, although stated categorically for brevity, are obviously very rough; but their margin of error is unlikely to be so great as to include estimates of the draft Plan Frame in cases where they differ.

enough to cover minimum consumer imports plus industrial and raw materials needed for processing. Hence all exchange needed for the investment program must be obtained from some kind of foreign assistance, in addition to Rs 700 crores for components and material needed for processing and replacing. For the entire Rs 5,600 crores of domestic resources to be invested during 1961 to 1966, foreign exchange amounting to about Rs 1,400 crores may be needed to finance the associated imports. The total exchange "gap" is then Rs 2,100 crores.

Third, assuming Rs 1,400 crores investment aid from abroad is forthcoming and domestic resources can be mobilized to the degree described, total Third Plan investments can scarcely exceed Rs 7,000 crores. This ignores all other constraints, such as lack of trained personnel, and all unanticipated administrative delays and errors. Although less than the

Table VII

EVALUATION OF THE DRAFT PLAN FRAME
(in thousands of crores rupees and at 1959 prices)

Item	Estimated here	Draft Plan Frame
National output in 1966	15.6	17.0
Average yearly output, 1961–66	14.0	15.0
Total domestic resources invested	5.6	9.0
Foreign exchange "gap"	2.1	1.0
Public Sector investment	4.7	6.7
Private Sector investment	2.3	3.3
Third Plan investment, including assistance	7.0	10.0

original investment goals of the Second Plan, establishing targets does not attain them, and total investment under the Second Plan was considerably less than anticipated.

Fourth, the Public Sector under the Third Plan might be Rs 4,700 crores, including external assistance. Part of the foreign exchange from this aid will be sold by the Center in support of approved investment in the Private Sector, but this does not effect the total value of its resources, and the foreign exchange component of the Private Sector's investments is relatively less. The estimate of investment in the Private Sector is thus about Rs 2,300 crores.

Fifth, national income will be less during the Third Plan than anticipated if total investment is not Rs 10,000 crores, but Rs 7,000 crores. National income at the end of the Third Plan may have risen from Rs 12,500 crores to about Rs 15,600 crores. It is estimated here that the economy's average annual income during the Plan will be Rs 14,000 crores.

Sixth, new jobs created under a Rs 7,000 crores Plan may be almost ten million if something like the relative allocations of Table I are maintained. Of these, new urban jobs would be slightly under seven million. If so, allowing for a migration of almost one-and-a-half million workers from the country to the towns, urban unemployment may be held at present levels. But apart from possible increases in agricultural output, which in turn create rural jobs, the underemployed in the rural areas may increase by nine million persons.

Seventh, agricultural output has increased very slowly in the past, by about 1.5 per cent a year. Despite additions to irrigated acreage there seems little prospect of annual increases of even 2 per cent annually, unless there are radical changes in agricultural practice and village life. It is most unlikely that these can occur to any significant extent within five years.

Eighth, population will increase by almost 50 million (i.e., 11 per cent) during the Third Plan. In every age group there will be more people than before, many of them adults seeking jobs, and all wanting food and other consumer goods. As we have seen, there is likely to be increased unemployment, and agricultural output may increase less rapidly than population. The prospect of over 18 million extra people in urban areas, allowing for migration, is a particularly alarming one. The ratio of estimated available consumer goods to population—1.22 to 1.11—indicates an increase in per capita consumption of only 11 per cent over five years. Consequently, unless India is willing and able to curb the rate of population growth, the economic status of her people can only improve by about 2 per cent a year per capita under favorable circumstances.[35]

[35] An interesting and promising alternative open to the Central Government is to pay bonuses, under certain conditions, to married couples of child-bearing age who reduce the expected size of their families. These bonuses, which are transfer payments, and not a reflection of resource cost, could be quite high, in some cases exceeding by several times the per capita annual consumption. This is partly so because the marginal product of population in India must be very low relative to its average product. Under certain conditions, if the object is to maximize per capita consumption, the economic return on resources invested in reducing the rate of population increase may be 500 times greater than in the case of traditional development investments. However this is another story, and it is told elsewhere. (See my paper, "The Gains to India from Population Control: Some Money Measures and Incentive Schemes," *Review of Economics and Statistics*, May, 1960.)

Bibliography

PART I—*ENVIRONMENT FOR DEVELOPMENT*

Adler, J. H. "World Economic Development—Retrospects and Prospects." *Review of Economics and Statistics* (August, 1956).

Bauer, P. T., and J. B. Wood. "Foreign Aid—The Soft Opinion." *Banca Nazionale del Lavoro Quarterly Review* (December, 1961), 403–18.

Baxter, J. *A Gift for Gomala.* Philadelphia: J. B. Lippincott Co., 1961.

Benham, F. *Economic Aid to Underdeveloped Countries.* New York: Oxford University Press, 1961.

Black, E. R. *The Diplomacy of Economic Development.* Cambridge, Mass.: Harvard University Press, 1960.

Bonne, A. *Studies in Economic Development.* London: Routledge and Kegan Paul, 1957.

Boulding, K. E. "Religious Foundations of Economic Progress." *Harvard Business Review,* (May, 1952).

Brandt, K. "Economic Strategy of Agricultural Development." *Proceedings of Mont Pelerin Conference.* Venice (September, 1954).

Brown, Harrison. *The Challenge of Man's Future.* New York: The Viking Press, Inc., 1954.

Dupries, L. H., ed. *Economic Progress.* Louvain: International Economic Association, 1955.

Enke, S. "Government Bonuses for Smaller Families." *Population Review* (July, 1960) .

Haberler, G. "Critical Observations on Some Current Notions in the Theory of Economic Growth." *L'Industria,* Milan (April–June, 1957).

Kuznets, Simon. "Quantitative Aspects of the Economic Growth of Nations." *Economic Development and Cultural Change* (July, 1960).

Lee, Douglas. *Climate and Economic Development in the Tropics.* New York: Harper & Row, Publishers, 1957.

Lenin, N. *Imperialism—The State and Revolution.* New York: Vanguard Press, 1929.

Mason, E. S. *Promoting Economic Development.* Pasadena, Calif.: Claremont College, 1955.

Malenbaum, W. "India and China: Contrasts in Development." *American Economic Review* (June, 1959).

Maynard, G. "Inflation and Growth: Some Lessons to Be Drawn from Latin American Experience." *Oxford Economic Papers* (June, 1961).

Millikan, M. F., and D. L. M. Blackmer. *The Emerging Nations: Their Growth and U.S. Policy.* Boston: Little, Brown & Co., 1961.

Myrdal, G. *Economic Theory and Underdeveloped Regions.* London: Duckworth and Company, 1957.

Nurkse, R. *Problems of Capital Formation in Underdeveloped Countries.* New York: Oxford University Press, 1953.

Shonfield, A. *The Attack on World Poverty.* New York: Random House, 1960.

Spengler, J. J. "Economic Factors in Economic Development." *American Economic Review, Papers and Proceedings* (May, 1957).

Chapter 1—The politics of development

Bronfenhenner, M. "The Appeal of Confiscation in Economic Development." *Economic Development and Cultural Change* (April, 1955), 201–18.

Clark, C. *Growthmanship.* London: Institute of Economic Affairs, 1960. Paper No. 10.

"Economic Motivations and Stimulations in Underdeveloped Countries," *ISS Bulletin,* Vol. VI, No. 3. Paris: UNESCO, 1954.

Frankel, S. H. "United Nations Primer for Economic Development," *The Economic Impact on Underdeveloped Societies.* New York: Oxford University Press, 1953.

Hoffman, Paul G. *One Hundred Countries–One and One-Quarter Billion People.* Washington, D.C.: Lasker Foundation, 1960.

Knorr, K., and W. J. Baumol. *What Price Economic Growth?* Englewood Cliffs, N.J.: Prentice-Hall, Inc., 1961.

Kuznets, S. "Economic Growth and Income Inequality." *American Economic Review* (March, 1955).

Mead, Margaret. *Cultural Patterns and Technical Change.* Paris: UNESCO, 1953.

Smithies, A. "Rising Expectations and Economic Development." *Economic Journal* (June, 1961).

Viner, Jacob. "Stability and Progress: The Poorer Countries' Problem," in *Stability and Progress in the World Economy,* edited by D. C. Hague. London: The Macmillan Company, 1958.

Chapter 2—Common characteristics of poor countries

Barber, W. J. "Disguised Unemployment in Underdeveloped Economies." *Oxford Economic Papers* (February, 1961).

———. "Economic Rationality and Behavior Patterns in an Underdeveloped Area: A Case Study of African Economic Behavior in the Rhodesias." *Economic Development and Cultural Change* (April, 1960).

Bauer, P. T., and B. S. Yamey. "Economic Progress and Occupational Distribution." *Economic Journal* (December, 1951).

Belshaw, H. *Population Growth and Levels of Consumption.* New York: Institute of Pacific Relations, 1956.

Berg, Elliot J. "Backward-Sloping Labor Supply Functions in Dual Economies –The Africa Case." *Quarterly Journal of Economics* (August, 1961).

Boeke, J. H. *Economics and Economic Policy of Dual Societies*. New York: Institute of Pacific Relations, 1953.

Edey, H. C., and A. T. Peacock. *National Income and Social Accounting*. London: Hutchinson's University Library, 1954.

Enke, S. "Labor Supply, Total Land Rents, and Agricultural Output in Backward Countries." *Southern Economic Journal* (October, 1962).

Higgins, B. "The Dualistic Theory of Underdeveloped Areas." *Economic Development and Cultural Change* (January, 1956).

Hoselitz, B. F. "Non-Economic Factors in Economic Development." *American Economic Review* (May, 1957).

Huntington, E. *Civilization and Climate*. New Haven: Yale University Press, 1915.

Jones, W. O. *Food and Agricultural Economics of Tropical Africa*. Food Research Institute, Stanford University, February, 1961.

Lerner, Daniel, and L. W. Pevsher. *The Passing of Traditional Society: Modernizing the Middle East*. New York: The Free Press of Glencoe, Inc., 1958.

Meenan, James. "The Political Economy of Development." *Journal of the Statistical and Social Inquiry Society of Ireland*, XX, I, 1951–52.

Myint, Hla. "An Interpretation of Economic Backwardness," *Oxford Economic Papers* (June, 1954).

United Nations' Yearbook of National Accounts Statistics. UN Department of Social and Economic Affairs, 1961.

Chapter 3—Economic differences among poor countries

Bauer, P. T. "International Economic Development." *Economic Journal* (March, 1959), 105–23.

Clark, C. *The Conditions of Economic Progress*. London: The Macmillan Company, 1951.

Fischoff, E. "The Protestant Ethic and the Spirit of Capitalism." *Social Research* (February, 1944).

Lekachman, R., ed. *National Policy for Economic Welfare at Home and Abroad*. New York: Doubleday & Company, Inc., 1955.

Mason, E. S. *Economic Planning in Underdeveloped Areas: Government and Business*. New York: Fordham University Press, 1958.

Nutter, G. W. "On Measuring Economic Growth." *Journal of Political Economy* (February, 1957).

Zimmerman, E. W. *World Resources and Industries* (rev. ed.). New York: Harper & Row, Publishers, 1951.

PART II—*INNOVATIONS AND DEVELOPMENT*

Adelman, Irma. *Theories of Economic Growth and Development*. Stanford Calif.: Stanford University Press, 1961.

Agarwala, A. N., and S. P. Singh, eds. *The Economics of Underdevelopment*. New York: Oxford University Press, 1958.

Allen, H. B. *Rural Reconstruction in Action: Experience in the Near and Middle East*. Ithaca, N.Y.: Cornell University Press, 1953.

Brozen, Y. *The Role of Entrepreneurship in Generating Technological Advance.* New York: 1951.

Bruton, H. J. "Contemporary Theorizing on Economic Growth," in *Theories of Economic Growth,* edited by B. F. Hoselity. New York: The Free Press of Glencoe, Inc., 1960, pp. 239–98.

Buchanan, N. S., and H. S. Ellis. *Approaches to Economic Development.* New York: Twentieth Century Fund, 1955.

Co-operatives and Land Use. Rome: Food and Agricultural Organization, 1957.

Enke, S. "Development with Limited and Unlimited Supplies of Labor." *Oxford Economic Papers* (June, 1962).

Goodwin, R. M. "The Optimal Growth Path for an Underdeveloped Economy." *Economic Journal* (December, 1961).

Grossfield, K. "Inventions as Business." *Economic Journal* (March, 1962).

Hagen, E. E. "The Process of Economic Development." *Economic Development and Cultural Change* (April, 1957).

Holton, R. H. "Marketing Structure and Economic Development." *Quarterly Journal of Economics* (August, 1953).

Jacoby, E. H. *Interrelationship Between Agrarian Reform and Agricultural Development.* Rome: Food and Agricultural Organization, 1953. Study No. 26.

Johnston, B. F., and J. W. Mellor. *The Nature of Agriculture's Contributions to Economic Development.* Food Research Institute Studies. November, 1960.

Jones, W. O. *Economic Man in Africa.* Food Research Institute Studies. May, 1960.

Leibenstein, H. *Economic Backwardness and Economic Growth: Studies in the Theory of Economic Development.* New York: John Wiley & Sons, Inc., 1957.

Lewis, W. A. *Theory of Economic Growth.* Homewood, Ill.: Richard D. Irwin, Inc., 1955.

Myers, H. E. "Dry Land Farming Practices." *Proceedings of the Conference on Middle East Agricultural Development,* Middle East Supply Center, Cairo, 1944.

Schultz, T. W. *The Economic Origin of Agriculture,* New York: McGraw-Hill, 1953.

Singer, H. W. "The Mechanics of Economic Development." *Indian Economic Review* (August, 1952).

Slotkin, James S. *From Fields to Factory.* New York: The Free Press of Glencoe, Inc., 1959.

Stigler, George. "The Division of Labor Is Limited by the Extent of the Market." *Journal of Political Economy* (June, 1951).

Tinbergen, J. *Design for Development.* Baltimore: The Johns Hopkins Press, 1958.

Chapter 4—Development ideas of early economists

Bloug, M. *Ricardian Economics—A Historical Sketch.* New Haven: Yale University Press, 1958.

Fay, C. R. *Great Britain from Adam Smith to the Present Day.* London: Longmans, Green and Company, 1928.

Letiche, J. M. "Adam Smith and David Ricardo on Economic Growth," *Theories of Economic Growth*. New York: The Free Press of Glencoe, Inc., 1960, pp. 65–88.

Malthus, T. R. *Essay on Population* (1798). London: The Macmillan Company, 1926.

McKinley, Erskine, "The Problems of Underdevelopment in the English Classical School." *Quarterly Journal of Economics*, Vol. 69 (May, 1955).

———. "The Theory of Economic Growth in the English Classical School," in *Theories of Economic Growth*, edited by B. F. Hoselity. New York: The Free Press of Glencoe, Inc., 1960.

Ricardo, D. *Principles of Political Economy and Taxation* (1817). Cambridge: Cambridge University Press, 1951.

Smith, A. *The Wealth of Nations* (1776).

———. "John Stuart Mill on Economic Development," *Theories of Economic Growth*. New York: The Free Press of Glencoe, Inc., 1960.

Spengler, J. J. "Adam Smith's Theory of Economic Growth." *Southern Economic Journal* (July, 1959).

Chapter 5—Development through science and technology

Abromovitz, M., ed. *Capital Formation and Economic Growth*. National Bureau of Economic Research. Princeton, N.J.: Princeton University Press, 1956.

———. *Resource and Output Trends in the United States Since 1870*. National Bureau of Economic Research, 1957. Occasional Paper 53.

Ames, E. "Research, Invention, Development, and Innovation." *American Economic Review* (June, 1961).

Belshaw, C. S. "The Cultural Milieu of the Entrepreneur: A Critical Essay." *Explorations in Entrepreneurial History* (February, 1955).

Brimmer, A. F. "The Setting of Entrepreneurship in India." *Quarterly Journal of Economics* (November, 1955), 553–57.

Brozen, Yale. "Entrepreneurship and Technological Change," in *Economic Development—Principles and Patterns*, Englewood Cliffs, N.J.: Prentice-Hall, Inc., 1954.

Fforde, J. S. *An International Trade in Managerial Skills*. Oxford: Blackwell, 1957.

Gerschenkson, A. "Social Attitudes, Entrepreneurship, and Economic Development." *Explorations in Entrepreneurial History* (October, 1953).

Jewkes, J., D. Sawers, and R. Stillerman. *The Sources of Invention*. London: The Macmillan Company, 1958.

Jones, W. O. *Manioc in Africa*. Stanford, Calif.: Stanford University Press, 1959.

McLaurin, W. R. "The Sequence from Invention to Innovation and Its Relation to Economic Growth." *Quarterly Journal of Economics* (February, 1953).

Rimmer, Douglas. "Schumpeter and the Underdeveloped Countries." *Quarterly Journal of Economics* (August, 1961).

Schumpeter, J. A. *The Theory of Economic Development*. Cambridge, Mass.: Harvard University Press, 1934.

Chapter 6—Economics of innovation

Brozen, Y. "Technological Change in Underdeveloped Areas." *Explorations in Entrepreneurial History* (February, 1951).

Eckaus, Richard S. *The Choice of Technology in Economic Development.* MIT Center for International Studies, October, 1959.

Enke, S. "Capital Intensity as a Mitigation of Inferior Labor: A General Theorem." *South African Economic Journal* (November, 1961).

Fabricant, S. *Basic Facts on Productivity Change.* New York: National Bureau of Economic Research, 1959. Occasional Paper 63.

Hicks, J. R. *Value and Capital.* New York: Oxford University Press, 1939.

Hirschman, A. O. "Investment Policies and 'Dualism' in Underdeveloped Countries." *American Economic Review* (September, 1957), 550–70.

Sen, A. K. "Choice of Capital Intensity Further Considered." *Quarterly Journal of Economics* (August, 1959), 466–84.

Spengler, J. J. "Product-Adding Versus Product-Replacing Innovations." *Kyklos* (1957).

Terborg, G. *Dynamic Equipment Policy.* New York: McGraw-Hill Book Co., 1949.

Tinbergen, J. "Choice of Technology in Industrial Planning." *U.N. Industrialization and Productivity,* Bulletin No. 1. New York: UN Department of Social and Economic Affairs, 1958.

Chapter 7—Expansion of agriculture or industry?

Balogh, T. "Agricultural and Economic Development." *Oxford Economic Papers* (February, 1961).

Enke, S. "Food Constraints on Industrial Development in Poor Countries." *Southern Economic Journal* (April, 1961).

———. "Industrial Expansion Through Agricultural Productivity." *Review of Economics & Statistics* (February, 1962).

Georgescu-Roegen, N. "Economic Theory and Agrarian Economics." *Oxford Economic Papers* (February, 1960).

Johnston, B. F., and J. W. Mellor. "Agriculture in Economic Development." *American Economic Review* (September, 1961).

Mellor, J. W., and R. D. Stevens. "The Average and Marginal Product of Farm Labor in Underdeveloped Countries." *Journal of Farm Economy* (August, 1956).

Moore, W. E. *Industrialization and Labor.* Ithaca, N.Y.: Cornell University Press, 1951.

Nicholls, W. H. "Industrialization, Factor Markets, and Agricultural Development." *Journal of Political Economy* (August, 1961).

Policies to Support and Stabilize Agricultural Prices and Incomes in Asia and the Far East. Report of the FAO/ECAFE Center. Rome: Food and Agricultural Organization, 1958.

Processes and Problems of Industrialization in Underdeveloped Countries. New York: UN Department of Social and Economic Affairs, 1955.

Rosenstein-Rodan, P. N. *How to Industrialize an Underdeveloped Area.* MIT Center for International Studies, 1959.

Schultz, T. W. "The Supply of Food in Relation to Economic Development." *Economic Development and Cultural Change* (December, 1952).

Chapter 8—Agricultural innovations and community development

Ames, D. W. "Manioc in Africa." *Economic Development and Cultural Change* (October, 1960).

Barlowe, H. "Land Reform and Economic Development." *Journal of Farm Economy* (May, 1953).

Binns, B. O. *The Consolidation of Fragmented Agricultural Holdings.* Rome: Food and Agricultural Organization, .

Cameron, R. J. *Investment in Agriculture.* Washington, D.C.: International Bank for Reconstruction and Development, 1955.

Community Development and Economic Development. Bangkok: U.N. Economic Commission for Asia and the Far East, 1960.

Grilickes, Z. "Research Costs and Social Returns: Hybrid Corn and Related Innovations." *Journal of Political Economy* (October, 1958).

Hill, Polly. *The Gold Coast Cocoa Farmer.* New York: Oxford University Press, 1957.

Honigmann, J. J. "A Case Study of Community Development in Pakistan." *Economic Development and Cultural Change* (April, 1960).

Jones, W. O. "Manioc: An Example of Innovation in African Economics." *Economic Development and Cultural Change* (January, 1957).

Keen, B. A. *The Agricultural Development of the Middle East.* London: H. M. Stationery Office, 1946.

Klein, Sidney. *The Pattern of Land Tenure Reform in East Asia After World War II.* New York: Bookman Associates, Bookman Monograph Series, 1948.

Land Reform, Defects in Agrarian Structure and Obstacles to Economic Development. New York: UN Department of Social and Economic Affairs, 1951.

Leach, E. R. *Pril Eliva—A Village in Ceylon.* Cambridge: Cambridge University Press, 1961.

Lewis, W. A. "Issues in Land Settlement." *Caribbean Economic Review* (October, 1951).

Lindholm, R. W. "Analysis of the Land Use and Land Taxation Policies of Non-Communist Underdeveloped Areas." *Economic Development and Cultural Change* (April, 1960).

———. "The Farm, the Misused Income Expansion Base of Emerging Nations." *Journal of Farm Economy* (May, 1961).

Malaviya, H. D. *Land Reform in India.* New Delhi: All-India Congress Committee, Economic and Political Research Department, 1954.

Millions Still Go Hungry. Rome: Food and Agricultural Organization, 1957.

Nicholls, W. H. "Investment in Agriculture in Underdeveloped Countries." *American Economic Review* (May, 1955).

Progress in Land Reform. New York: UN Department of Social and Economic Affairs, 1954.

Special Supplement on Land Tenure, *Journal of African Administration* (October, 1952).

Tannous, A. I. "Land Reform—Key to the Development and Stability of the Arab World." *Middle East Journal* (Winter, 1951).

Warriner, D. *Land Reform and Economic Development.* Cairo: National Bank of Egypt, 1955.

Chapter 9—Some growth and development models

Bauer, P. T. "Lewis' Theory of Economic Growth." *American Economic Review* (September, 1956), 632–41.

Bronfenbrenner, M. "A Simplified Mahalanobis Development Model." *Economic Development and Cultural Change* (October, 1960).

Bruton, H. J. "Growth Models and Underdeveloped Countries." *Journal of Political Economy* (August, 1955), 322–36.

Buttrick, J. "Toward a Theory of Economic Growth: The Neo-Classical Contribution." *Theories of Economic Growth,* New York: The Free Press of Glencoe, Inc., 1960, pp. 155–92.

Domar, E. D. "Expansions and Employment." *American Economic Review* (March, 1947).

Enke, S. "South African Growth: A Macro-Economic Model." *South African Economic Journal* (March, 1962).

Fellner, W. "The Capital-Output Ratio in Dynamic Economics." *Money, Trade, and Economic Growth; Essays in Honor of John Henry Williams.* New York: 1951.

Harrod, R. F. *Toward Dynamic Economics.* New York: The Macmillan Company, 1949.

Kahn, R. F. "Exercises in the Analysis of Growth." *Oxford Economic Papers* (June, 1959).

Kaldor, N. "A Model of Economic Growth." *Economic Journal* (December, 1957).

Lewis, W. A. "Economic Development with Unlimited Supplies of Labor." *The Manchester School* (May, 1954), 139–91.

———. "Unlimited Labor: Further Notes." *The Manchester School* (January, 1958), 32.

Meade, J. E. *A Neo-Classical Theory of Economic Growth.* New York: Oxford University Press, 1961.

Ranis, G., and J. C. H. Fei. "A Theory of Economic Development." *American Economic Review* (September, 1961).

Reddaway, W. B. "Some Observations on the Capital-Output Ratio (With Special Reference to India's Third Five-Year Plan)." *Indian Economic Review* (February, 1960).

Chapter 10—Historical stages of economic growth

Cairncross, A. K., "Essays in Bibliography and Criticisms, XLV: The Stages of Economic Growth." *Economic History Review* (April, 1961).

Gras, N. S. B. *Business and Capitalism.* New York: F. S. Crofts & Co., 1939.

Hobson, J. A. *Evolution of Modern Capitalism*. London: Allen and Unwin, 1949.

Hoselitz, B. F. "Theories of Stages of Economic Growth," in *Theories of Economic Growth,* edited by B. F. Hoselitz. New York: The Free Press of Glencoe, Inc., 1960.

Kurihara, K. K. "Dynamic Growth Programming for the 'Take Off Path.' " *Indian Journal of Economics,* XLI July, 1960.

North, D. C. "A Note of Professor Rostow's 'Take-Off' Into Self-Sustained Economic Growth." *Manchester School of Economics and Social Studies* (January, 1958), 68–75.

Ohlin, G. "Reflections on the Rostow Doctrine." *Economic Development and Cultural Change* (July, 1961).

Rostow, W. W. *The Process of Economic Growth.* New York: W. W. Norton & Company, Inc., 1952.

———. "The Stages of Economic Growth." *Economic History Review* (August, 1959).

———. "The Take-Off into Self-Sustained Growth." *Economic Journal* (March, 1956).

Spengler, J. J. "Mercantilist and Physiocratic Growth Theory," in *Theories of Economic Growth,* edited by B. F. Hoselitz. New York: The Free Press of Glencoe, Inc., 1960.

PART III—*CAPITAL AND DEVELOPMENT*

Chenery, H. B., and P. Clark. *Interindustry Economics.* New York: John Wiley & Sons, Inc., 1959.

Ellis, H. S. "Accelerated Investment as a Force in Economic Development." *Quarterly Journal of Economics* (November, 1958), 485–95.

Ghosh, Alak. *New Horizons in Planning—A Study of Planning Techniques with Special Reference to India's First and Second Five-Year Plans.* Calcutta: World Press Private, Ltd., 1956.

Gurley, J. G., and E. S. Shaw. "Financial Aspects of Economic Development." *American Economic Review* (September, 1955).

Hicks, Ursula K. *Development from Below.* New York: Oxford University Press, 1961.

———. *et al. Federalism and Economic Growth in Underdeveloped Countries.* New York: Oxford University Press, 1962.

Higgins, B. *Indonesia's Economic Stabilization and Development.* New York: Institute of Pacific Relations, 1957.

Hirschman, A. O. "Economic and Investment Planning—Reflections Based on Experience in Colombia." *Investment Criteria and Economic Growth.* Cambridge, Mass.: MIT Center for International Studies, 1955.

Lewis, W. A. *Aspects of Industrialization.* Cairo: The National Bank of Egypt, 1953.

Mahalanobis, P. C. "The Approach of Operational Research to Planning in India." *Sankhya* (December, 1955).

Mason, E. S. *Economic Planning in Underdeveloped Areas: Government and Business.* New York: Fordham University Press, 1958.

Meyer, A. J. *Middle Eastern Capitalism: Nine Essays.* Cambridge, Mass.: Harvard University Press, 1959.

Nurkse, R. "Reflections upon India's Development Plan." *Quarterly Journal of Economics* (May, 1957).

Programming Techniques for Economic Development. Bangkok: U.N. Economic Commission for Asia and the Far East, 1960.

Robinson, Joan. *Accumulation of Capital.* Homewood, Ill.: Richard D. Irwin, Inc., 1956.

Shenoy, B. R. "Some Fallacies of Plan Finance," in *Problems of Indian Economic Development.* Madras: University of Madras, 1958.

Singer, H. *Problems of Industrialization of Underdeveloped Countries.* Institut Recherches Economique et Sociales, Lovain, 1955.

Swan, T. W. "Economic Growth and Capital Accumulation." *Economic Record,* XXXII (Nov., 1956).

Chapter 11—Private saving and domestic investment

Belshaw, H. *Agricultural Credits in Economically Underdeveloped Countries.* Rome: Food and Agricultural Association, 1960. Study 46.

Chandavarkar, A. G. "The Nature and Effects of Gold Hoarding in Underdeveloped Economies." *Oxford Economic Papers* (June, 1961).

Felix, D. "Structural Imbalances, Social Conflict, and Inflation: An Appraisal of Chile's Recent Anti-Inflationary Effort," *Economic Development and Cultural Change* (January, 1960).

Fisher, I. *The Theory of Interest,* New York: Kelley and Millman, Inc., 1954.

Higgins, B., and W. Malenbaum. *Financing Economic Development.* MIT Center for International Studies, 1955.

Kaldor, N. "Economic Growth and the Problem of Inflation." *Economica,* 1 (August, 1959).

Methods of Financing Economic Development in Underdeveloped Countries. New York: U.N. Department of Economic Affairs, 1949.

Rangnekar, D. K. *Poverty and Capital Development in India.* New York: Oxford University Press, 1958.

Wolf, C., and S. C. Sufrim. *Capital Formation and Foreign Investment in Underdeveloped Areas.* Syracuse, N.Y.: Syracuse University Press, 1955.

Chapter 12—Government policies to increase investment

Bernstein, E. M., and I. G. Patel. "Inflation in Relation to Economic Development." International Monetary Fund Staff Papers. Washington, D.C., November, 1952.

Bhagwati, J. "Deficit Financing and Economic Development." *Indian Economic Review* (August, 1956).

Federal Reserve Bank of New York. "Inflation and Economic Development." *Monthly Review* (August, 1959).

Ghosh, S. *Inflation in an Underdeveloped Economy: A Study of Inflation in India.* Calcutta: World Press Private, Ltd., 1959.

Goodrich, C. *Government Promotion of American Canals and Railroads.* New York: Columbia University Press, 1960.

Hicks, U. K. "Budgeting for Development." *Bulletins of the Central Bank of Ceylon* (June–July–August, 1957).

McKean, R. N. *Efficiency in Government Through Systems Analysis.* New York: John Wiley & Sons, Inc., 1958.

Mobilization of Domestic Capital: Report and Documents of the First Working Party of Experts. Bangkok: UN(ECAFE), 1951.

Prakash, O. "Industrial Development Corporations in India and Pakistan." *Economic Journal* (March, 1957), 40–48.

Sunkel, Osvaldo. "Inflation in Chile: An Unorthodox Approach." *El Trimestre Economico* (1958).

Chapter 13—Tax policies for undeveloped nations

The Effects of Taxation on Foreign Trade and Investment. New York: UN Department of Social and Economic Affairs, 1950.

Heller, W. "Fiscal Policies for Underdeveloped Economies," in *U.N. Taxes and Fiscal Policy in Underdeveloped Countries,* New York: UN Technical Assistance Administration, 1954.

Hicks, U. K. "Direct Taxation and Economic Growth." *Oxford Economic Papers* (October, 1956).

———. "The Search for Revenue in Underdeveloped Countries." *Revue de science et de legislation financière* (January–March, 1952).

Kaldor, N. *Indian Tax Reforms.* New York: The Free Press of Glencoe, Inc., 1960.

Taxes and Fiscal Policy in Underdeveloped Countries. New York: UN Technical Assistance Administration, 1955.

Wald, H. P. *Taxation of Agricultural Land in Underdeveloped Economies.* Cambridge, Mass.: Harvard University Press, 1959.

Chapter 14—Banking requirements of backward countries

Bloomfield, A. I. "Some Problems of Central Banking in Underdeveloped Countries." *Journal of Finance* (May, 1957).

Davies, S. G., ed. *Central Banking in South and East Asia.* New York: Oxford University Press, 1961.

Economic Development with Stability. International Monetary Fund Staff Papers. February, 1954.

Hammond, B. *Banks and Politics in America.* Princeton, N.J.: Princeton University Press, 1957.

Sayers, R. S. *Central Banking After Bagehot.* New York: Oxford University Press, 1957.

———. *Modern Banking.* New York: Oxford University Press, 1951.

Sen, S. N. *Central Banking in Underdeveloped Money Markets.* Calcutta: Bookland, 1952.

Chapter 15—Alternative investment criteria

Aubrey, H. G. "Investment Decisions in Underdeveloped Countries," in *Capital Formation and Economic Growth*. Princeton, N.J.: Princeton University Press, 1955, pp. 397–440.

Balogh, T. "Equity and Efficiency—The Problem of Optimal Investment in a Framework of Underdevelopment." *Oxford Economic Papers* (February, 1962).

Baton, F. M. "On Capital Productivity, Input Allocation, and Growth." *Quarterly Journal of Economics* (February, 1957).

Bell, David E. "Allocating Development Resources: Some Observations Based on Pakistan Experience," *Public Policy*. Cambridge, Mass.: Harvard University Press, 1959.

Bohr, K. A. "Investment Criteria for Manufacturing Industries in Underdeveloped Countries." *Review of Economics and Statistics* (May, 1954).

Eckstein, Otto. "Investment Criteria for Economic Development and the Theory of Intertemporal Welfare Economics." *Quarterly Journal of Economics* (February, 1957), 56–85.

Galenson, W., and H. Leibenstein. "Investment Criteria, Productivity, and Economic Development." *Quarterly Journal of Economics* (August, 1955), 343–70.

Hotelling, H. "The Relation of Prices to Marginal Costs in an Optimum System." *Econometrica* (April, 1939).

Kahn, A. E. "Investment Criteria in Development Programs." *Quarterly Journal of Economics* (February, 1951).

Millikan, Max F., ed. *Investment Criteria and Economic Growth*. New York and Cambridge: Social Science Research Council and Center for International Studies, 1955.

Solow, R. "A Contribution to the Theory of Economic Growth." *Quarterly Journal of Economics* (February, 1956).

Vakil, C. N., and P. R. Brakmanand. *Planning for an Expanding Economy: Accumulation, Employment and Technical Progress in Underdeveloped Countries*. New York: Institute of Pacific Relations, 1956.

Chapter 16—A "big push" under government direction

Arndt, H. W. "External Economies in Economic Growth." *Economic Record* (November, 1955).

Fleming, Marcus. "External Economics and the Doctrine of Balanced Growth." *Economic Journal* (June, 1955).

Furuya, H., and K. Ivada. "Balanced Growth and Intertemporal Efficiency in Capital Accumulation." *International Economic Review* (January, 1962).

Ohlin, P. G. "Balanced Economic Growth in History." *American Economic Review* (May, 1949), 338–53.

Peacock, A. T., and D. G. M. Dosser. "Input-Output Analysis in an Underdeveloped Country." *Review of Economic Studies* (October, 1957).

Rosenstein-Rodan, P. N. "Notes on the Theory of the 'Big Push.'" MIT Center for International Studies (March, 1957).

Chapter 17—Unbalanced industrial growth

Hirschman, A. O. *The Strategy of Economic Development.* New Haven: Yale University Press, 1959.

Montias, J. M. "Balanced Growth and International Specialization: A Diagrammatic Analysis," *Oxford Economic Papers* (June, 1961).

Shehan, J. "International Specialization and the Concept of Balanced Growth." *Quarterly Journal of Economics* (May, 1958).

Streeten, Paul. "Unbalanced Growth." *Oxford Economic Papers* (June, 1958).

PART IV—*LABOR AND DEVELOPMENT*

Blaisdell, T. C., Jr. "Problems of Evaluating the Effectiveness of Development Measures." *Economic Development and Cultural Change* (January, 1954).

Coale, A. J., and E. M. Hoover. *Population Growth and Economic Development in Low-Income Countries.* Princeton, N.J.: Princeton University Press, 1958.

Dublin, L. I., A. J. Lotka, and M. Spiegelman. *The Money Value of a Man.* New York: The Ronald Press Co., 1947.

Enke, S. "The Gains to India from Population Control." *Review of Economics and Statistics* (May, 1960).

Hagen, E. E. "Population and Economic Growth." *American Economic Review* (June, 1959), 310–27.

Hauser, P. M., ed. *Population and World Politics.* New York: The Free Press of Glencoe, Inc., 1958.

Hoselitz, B. F. *Sociological Aspects of Economic Growth.* New York: The Free Press of Glencoe, Inc., 1960.

Leibenstein, H. "A Theory of Economic-Demographic Development." Princeton, N.J.: Princeton University Press, 1954.

McCleary, G. F. *The Malthusian Population Theory.* London: Faber & Faber, 1953.

Minan, R. "An Analysis of Malthus' Population Theory." *Journal of Economic Behavior* (April, 1961).

Mincer, J. "Investment in Human Capital and Personal Income Distribution." *Journal of Political Economy* (August, 1958).

Schultz, T. W. "Investment in Human Capital." *American Economic Review* (March, 1961).

———. "Investment in Human Capital: Reply." *American Economic Review* (December, 1961).

Shaffer, Harry. "Investment in Human Capital: Comment." *American Economic Review* (December, 1961).

Spengler, J. J. "The Population Problem: Yesterday, Today, Tomorrow." *Southern Economic Journal* (January, 1961).

Taeuber, Irene B. *The Population of Japan.* Princeton, N.J.: Princeton University Press, 1958.

Taft, D. R., and R. Robbins. *International Migrations.* New York: The Ronald Press Company, 1955.

U.N. Demographic Yearbook, 1960. New York: UN Department of Social and Economic Affairs, 1961.

Wagner, E. G., and J. N. Lanoix. *Water Supply for Rural Areas and Small Communities.* US Federal Power Commission. n.d.

Woytinsky, W. S., and E. S. Woytinsky. *World Population and Production: Trends and Outlook.* New York: Twentieth Century Fund, 1953.

Chapter 18—Dangers of overpopulation

The Determinants and Consequences of Population Trends, New York: UN Statistical Office, 1953.

Enke, S. "Population and Growth: A General Theory," *Quarterly Journal of Economics* (1963).

Frank, A. G. "Human Capital and Economic Growth." *Economic Development and Cultural Change* (January, 1960).

Johnson, S. C. *A History of Emigration: From the United Kingdom to North America, 1763–1912.* London: Routledge and Sons, 1913.

Meade, J. E. "Mauritius: A Case Study in Malthusian Economics." *Economic Journal* (September, 1961).

Minani, R. "An Analysis of Malthus' Population Theory." *Journal of Economic Behavior* (April, 1961).

Nelson, R. R. "A Theory of the Low-Level Equilibrium Trap in Underdeveloped Countries." *American Economic Review* (December, 1956), 894–908.

Penrose, E. F. "Malthus and the Underdeveloped Area." *Economic Journal* (June, 1957).

Spengler, J. J. "Aspects of the Economics of Population Growth," Parts I and II. *Southern Economic Journal* (January, 1948).

————. "Economics and Demography." *The Study of Population.* Chicago: University of Chicago Press, 1959.

Thompson, W. S. *Population Problems,* 4th ed. New York: McGraw-Hill Book Co., Inc., 1953.

Villard, H. H. "Some Notes on Population and Living Levels." *Review of Economics and Statistics* (May, 1955), 189.

Warriner, D. *Land and Poverty in the Middle East.* London: Royal Institute of International Affairs, 1948.

Chapter 19—Population size and labor hours

Hoselitz, B. F. "The Role of Cities in the Economic Growth of Underdeveloped Countries." *Journal of Political Economy* (June, 1953), 195–208.

Joosten, J. H. L. "Perverse Supply Curves in Less Developed Economies." *Netherlands Journal of Agricultural Science* (May, 1960).

Peacock, A. T. *Theory of Population and Modern Economic Analysis.* New York: The Free Press of Glencoe, Inc., 1956.

Rottenberg, S. "Income and Leisure in an Underdeveloped Economy." *Journal of Political Economy* (April, 1952).

Spengler, J. J. "Population Change: Cause, Effect, Indicator." *Economic Development and Cultural Change* (April, 1961).

Wolfbein, S. L., and A. J. Jaffe. "Demographic Factors in Labor Force Growth." *American Sociological Review* (August, 1956).

Chapter 20—Government measures to reduce births

Demeny, P. "The Economics of Government Payments to Limit Population: A Comment." *Economic Development and Cultural Change* (July, 1961).

Enke, S. "A Rejoinder to Comments on the Superior Effectiveness of Vasectomy-Bonus Schemes." *Economic Development and Cultural Change* (July, 1961).

————. "The Economics of Government Payments to Limit Population." *Economic Development and Cultural Change* (June, 1960).

————. "Some Reactions to Bonuses for Family Limitation." *Population Review* (July, 1961).

Villard, H. H. "A Note on the Economics of Birth Control." *Review of Economics and Statistics* (February, 1958), 78–79.

Chapter 21—Productivity and education

Becker, G. S. "Underinvestment in College Education." *American Economic Review* (May, 1960), 346–514.

Miller, H. P. "Annual and Lifetime Income in Relation to Education, 1939–59." *American Economic Review* (December, 1960).

Nicholson, J. S. "The Living Capital of the United Kingdom." *Economic Journal* (March, 1891).

Schultz, T. W. "Capital Formation by Education." *Journal of Political Economy* (December, 1960).

Weisbrod, Burton A. "The Valuation of Human Capital." *Journal of Political Economy* (October, 1961).

Chapter 22—Public health and effective labor

Brock, J. F., and M. Autret. *"Kwashiorkor in Africa.* Geneva: World Health Organization, 1952. Monograph Series #8.

Davis, K. "The Amazing Decline of Mortality in Underdeveloped Areas." *American Economic Review* (May, 1956).

The First Ten Years of the World Health Organization. Geneva: World Health Organization, 1958.

Jelliffe, D. B. *Infant Nutrition in the Subtropics and Tropics.* Geneva: World Health Organization, 1955.

Mudaliar, Sir A. "World Health Problems." *International Conciliation* (May, 1953).

Mushkin, S. J. *Toward a Definition of Health Economics.* Public Health Reports, U.S. Government Printing Office, September, 1958.

Spengler, J. J. "Some Economic Aspects of the Subsidization by the State of the Formation of 'Human Capital.' " *Kyklos* (1950).

Wagner, E. G., and J. N. Lanoix. *Excreta Disposal for Rural Areas and Small Communities.* Geneva: World Health Organization, 1958.

Winslow, C. E. A. *The Cost of Sickness and the Price of Health.* Geneva: World Health Organization, 1951. Monograph Series #7.

Yearbook of Food and Agricultural Statistics. Rome: Food and Agricultural Organization, 1962.

PART V—*DEVELOPMENT THROUGH TRADE*

Chenery, H. B. "Comparative Advantages and Development Policy." *American Economic Review* (March, 1961).

Diamond, W. "Economic Problems of Foreign Trade and Investment in Underdeveloped Countries." *Ohio State Law Journal, 3* (1956).

Dubey, V. "International Trade and Economic Growth." *Indian Journal of Economics,* Allahabad, India, XLI, July, 1960.

Ellis, H. S., and H. C. Wallich. *Economic Development of Latin America: Proceedings of International Economic Association.* New York: St. Martin's Press, Inc., 1961.

Enke, S. "Why Apologize for Recent Colonialism?" *Optima* (February, 1962).

Friedman, M. "The Reduction of Fluctuations in the Incomes of Primary Producers." *Economic Journal* (December, 1954).

Haberler, G. *International Trade and Economic Development.* Cairo: National Bank of Egypt, 1959.

Jones, G. P., and A. G. Pool. *A Hundred Years of Economic Development in Great Britain.* New York: The Macmillan Company, 1940.

Kuznets, S. "International Differences in Capital Formation and Financing." *Capital Formation and Economic Growth.* Princeton, N.J.: Princeton University Press, 1955.

———, W. E. Moore, and J. J. Spengler. *Economic Growth: Brazil, India Japan.* Durham, N.C.: Duke University Press, 1955.

Meade, J. E. "The Future of International Trade and Payments." *The Three Banks Review* (June, 1961).

Myrdal, G. *An International Economy.* New York: Harper & Row, Publishers, 1956.

Ropke, W. *International Order and Economic Integration.* Dordrecht, The Netherlands: D. Reidal Co., 1959.

Singer, H. W. "Distribution of Gains Between Investing and Borrowing Countries." *American Economic Review* (May, 1950), 472–92.

Supple, Barry E. "Economic History and Economic Underdevelopment." *Canadian Journal of Economics and Political Science* (November, 1961).

Thomas, B., ed. *Economics of International Migration.* London: International Economic Association, 1958.

Viner, J. *International Trade and Economic Development.* New York: The Free Press of Glencoe, Inc., 1952.

Wallich, H. C. "Underdeveloped Countries and the International Monetary Mechanism," in *Money, Trade and Economic Growth.* London: Macmillan & Company, Ltd., 1951.

Chapter 23—World development before the first war

Allen, G. C., and A. G. Donnithorne. *Western Enterprise in Indonesia and Malaya.* London: Allen and Unwin, 1957.

Baldwin, R. E. "Patterns of Development in Newly Settled Regions." *Manchester School* (May, 1956), 161–79.

Fay, C. R. *Life and Labor in the 19th Century.* Cambridge: Cambridge University Press, 1920.

Feis, H. *Europe, the World's Banker 1870–1914.* New Haven: Yale University Press, 1930.

Hobson, G. K. *The Export of Capital.* London: Constable, 1914.

Hoffman, W. G. *British Industry 1700–1950.* Oxford: Basil Blackwell, 1955.

Knowles, L. C. A. *Economic Development in the 19th Century.* London: Routledge and Kegan Paul, 1932.

Nurkse, R. "International Investment Today in the Light of 19th Century Experience." *Economic Journal* (December, 1954).

———. "Some International Aspects of the Problem of Economic Development." *American Economic Review* (May, 1952).

Chapter 24—Making use of the world economy

Chenery, H. B., and M. Bruno. "Development Alternatives in an Open Economy: The Case of Israel." *Economic Journal* (March, 1962).

Commodity Trade and Economic Development. New York: UN Department of Social and Economic Affairs, 1952.

Copland, D. B., and R. H. Barback. *The Conflict of Expansion and Stability: Documents Relating to Australian Economic Policy 1945–52.* London: Angus and Roberson, 1957.

Enke, S. "Some Gains from Trade in Producer Goods." *Quarterly Journal of Economics* (November, 1961).

———. "Trade and Welfare." *Kyklos*, 3 (1962).

———. "Trade Gains in the Short Run: A Reply to Mr. Kemp." *Canadian Journal of Economics and Political Science* (November, 1961).

Leubuscher, C. *The Processing of Raw Materials: A Study in Location.* London: Colonial Office, 1951.

Mason, E. S. "Raw Material and Economic Development." *Quarterly Journal of Economics* (August, 1952).

Nurkse, R. *Patterns of Trade and Development.* New York: Oxford University Press, 1962.

Robinson, Romney. "Factor Endowment and Comparative Advantage." *Quarterly Journal of Economics* (May, 1956), 169–92.

Chapter 25—The new autarky

Atallah, M. K. *The Long-Term Movement of the Terms of Trade Between Agricultural and Industrial Products.* Delft: Netherlands Economic Institute, 1958.

Baldwin, R. E. "Exchange Rate Policy and Economic Development." *Economic Development and Cultural Change* (July, 1961).

Ellsworth, P. T. "The Terms of Trade Between Primary Producing and Industrial Countries." *Inter-American Economic Affairs* (Summer, 1956).

Instability in Export Markets of Underdeveloped Countries. New York: UN Department of Social and Economic Affairs, 1952.

Myint, Hla. "The Gains from International Trade and the Backward Countries." *Review of Economic Studies* (1954–55), 129–42.

Prebisch, Raul. "The Role of Commercial Policies in Underdeveloped Countries." *American Economic Review* (May, 1959).

Raj, K. N., and A. K. Sen. "Alternative Patterns of Growth Under Conditions of Stagnant Export Earnings." *Oxford Economic Papers* (February, 1961).

Wallich, H. C. *Monetary Problems of an Export Economy*. Cambridge, Mass.: Harvard University Press, 1950.

Chapter 26—International capital movements

Avramovic, Dragoslaw. *Dept Servicing Capacity and Postwar Growth in International Public Indebtedness*. Washington, D.C.: International Bank for Reconstruction and Development, 1957.

Barlow, E. R., and I. T. Wender. *Foreign Investment and Taxation*. Englewood Cliffs, N.J.: Prentice-Hall, Inc., 1955.

Cairncross, Alec. *The International Bank for Reconstruction and Development*. Princeton University Essays in International Finance. Princeton, N.J.: Princeton University Press, 1959.

Colonial Development Corporation, *Reports*. London: HM Stationery Office, 1962.

External Public Assistance for Development Available from National and Regional Sources. Washington, D.C.: International Bank for Reconstruction and Development and International Development Association, 1962.

Financing of Economic Development—The International Flow of Private Capital, 1946–52. New York: UN Department of Social and Economic Affairs, 1954.

The Flow of Financial Resources to Countries in the Course of Economic Development in 1960. Paris: Organization for Economic Cooperation and Development, 1962.

Garner, R. L. *Address to the 1961 Meeting of the Board of Governors of the International Finance Association*. Vienna: September, 1961.

Heilbroner, R. L. *This Growing World: Economic Development and the World Bank*. New York: Public Affairs Committee, 1956.

Knapp, J. "Capital Exports and Growth." *Economic Journal* (September, 1957), 432–44.

Koo, Anthony Y. C. "A Short-Run Measure of Relative Economic Contribution of Direct Foreign Investment." *Review of Economics and Statistics* (August, 1961).

Rosenstein-Rodan, P. N. "International Aid for Underdeveloped Countries." *Review of Economics and Statistics* (May, 1961).

Spengler, J. J. "IBRD Mission Economic Growth Theory." *American Economic Review* (May, 1954).

Theil, H. "International Inequalities and General Criteria for Development Aid." *The Economist* (1953).

The World Bank—Policies and Operations. Washington, D.C.: International Bank for Reconstruction and Development, 1960.

Chapter 27—U. S. aid programs

An Act for International Development: Summary Presentation to Congress. Washington, D.C.: USGPO, 1961.

Castle, E. W. *Billions, Blunders and Baloney*. New York: Devin-Adair Company, 1955.

Colorado State University Research Foundation, *The Peace Corps—Final Report*. Boulder: Colorado State University, 1961.

Dobyns, H. F. "Blunders with Bolsas," in *Underdeveloped Areas*, edited by L. W. Shannon. New York: Harper & Row, Publishers, 1957.

Foreign Policy Clearing House. *Strategy for the 60's*, Washington, D.C.: 1960.

Galbraith, J. K. "A Positive Approach to Economic Aid." *Foreign Affairs* (April, 1961).

Hawthorne, A. *History of the Operations and Policies of the Export-Import Bank*. Washington, D.C.: USGPO, 1954.

Hunt, Chester L. "Cultural Barriers to Point Four." *The Antioch Review* (Summer, 1954).

Marriott, M. "Technical Changes in Overdeveloped Rural Areas." *Economic Development and Cultural Change* (January, 1957).

Report of the Committee on Foreign Relations on S1983. U.S. 87th Congress, Senate Report No. 612. Washington, D.C.: USGPO, 1961.

Reuss, H. S., *et al.* "Peace Corps Trilogy." *International Development Review* (June, 1961).

Richter, J. H. "Agricultural Surpluses for Economic Development." *Journal of Political Economy* (February, 1956).

Wolf, C., Jr. *Foreign Aid: Theory and Practice in Southeast Asia*. Princeton, N.J.: Princeton University Press, 1960.

PART VI—PROSPECTS FOR DEVELOPMENT

Berliner, J. H. *Soviet Economic Aid: The New Aid and Trade Policy in Underdeveloped Countries*. Council for Foreign Research. New York: Frederick A. Praeger, Inc., 1959.

Enke, S. "Preliminary Thoughts About India's Third Five-Year Plan." *South African Economic Journal* (May, 1960).

Hazlitt, H. *Will Dollars Save the World?* Irvington-on-Hudson, N.Y.: Foundation of Economic Education, 1947.

Hirschman, A. O. "Economic Policy in Underdeveloped Countries." *Economic Development and Cultural Change* (July, 1957).

Millikan, M. F., and W. W. Rostow. *A Proposal: Key to an Effective Foreign Policy*. New York: Harper & Row, Publishers, 1957.

Spengler, J. J. "Public Bureaucracy, Resource Structure, and Economic Development: A Note." *Kyklos* (1958).

Staley, E. *The Future of Underdeveloped Countries.* New York: Harper & Row, Publishers, 1954.

Youngson, A. J. *Possibilities of Economic Progress.* New York: Cambridge University Press, 1959.

GENERAL

Allen, G. C. *Japan's Economic Recovery.* New York: Oxford University Press, 1958.

Balassa, B. "Towards a Theory of Economic Integration." *Kyklos* (1961).

Barber, William J. *The Economy of British Central Africa.* Stanford, Calif.: Stanford University Press, 1961.

Bauer, P. T. *West African Trade.* New York: Cambridge University Press, 1955.

————, and B. S. Yamey. *Economics of Undeveloped Countries.* Chicago: University of Chicago Press, 1957.

Benham, F. *The Colombo Plan and Other Essays.* London: Royal Institute of International Affairs, 1956.

————, and H. A. Holley. *A Short Introduction to the Economy of Latin America.* Oxford: Oxford University Press for Royal Institute of International Affairs, 1960.

Black, J. "The Formulation of Development Plans in the British Colonies." *Economic Journal* (June, 1959), 255–74.

Bruton, H. J. *A Survey of Recent Contributions to the Theory of Economic Growth.* Cambridge: MIT Center for International Studies, 1956.

Clough, S. B. *The Rise and Fall of Civilization: An Inquiry into the Relationship Between Economic Development and Civilization.* New York: Columbia University Press, 1957.

Cohen, J. B. *Japan's Postwar Economy,* Bloomington, Ind.: Indiana U. Press, 1958.

Cole, A. H. "The Relations of Missionary Activity to Economic Development," *Economic Development and Cultural Change* (January, 1961).

de Vries, Egbert. *Finance for Agricultural Development.* (Speech delivered at the Conference of Agricultural Economists, Mysore, India, in August, 1958.)

Enke, S. "Western Development of a Sparsely Populated Economy: The Rhodesias as a Case Study." *American Economic Review* (June, 1960).

Farmer, B. H. *Pioneer Peasant Colonization in Ceylon.* New York: Oxford University Press, 1957.

Firestone, O. J. *Canada's Economic Development, 1867–1953.* London: Bowes & Bowes, 1958.

Frutschi, Alexander, and Marian Crites. *An Annotated Bibliography of Small Industry Development.* New York: The Free Press of Glencoe, Inc., 1958.

Government of India Planning Commission, *The Third Five-Year Plan.* New Delhi: Manager of Publications, 1960.

Harrod, R. F. "An Essay in Dynamic Theory." *Economic Journal* (March, 1939).

Hence, W. A. *African Economic Development.* Council on Foreign Relations, 1958.

International Labor Office. *Studies and Reports, New Series.* Geneva: 1956.

Isard, W., *et al. Methods of Regional Analysis: An Introduction to Regional Science.* New York: John Wiley & Sons, Inc., 1960.

Kalmanoff, G. *Joint International Business Ventures in Colombia.* New York: Columbia University Press, Country Studies No. 1, 1957, Country Studies No. 1, 1959.

Kindleberger, C. P. *Economic Development.* New York: McGraw-Hill Book Co., Inc., New York, 1958.

Kuznets, S. *Six Lectures on Economic Growth.* New York: The Free Press of Glencoe, Inc., 1960.

Lockwood, W. W. *Economic Development of Japan.* Princeton, N.J.: Princeton University Press, 1954.

Myers, C. A. *Labor Problems in the Industrialization of India.* Cambridge, Mass.: Harvard University Press, 1958.

Neuberger, E. "The Yugoslav Investment Auctions." *Quarterly Journal of Economics* (February, 1959), 88–117.

Niculescu, B. M. "Underdeveloped, Backward, or Low Income." *Economic Journal* (September, 1955).

Oliver, H. M. *Economic Opinion and Policy in Ceylon.* Durham, N.C.: Duke University Press, 1957.

Oshima, H. "Underemployment in Backward Economies—An Empirical Comment." *Journal of Political Economy* (June, 1958).

Pim, A. *Colonial Agricultural Production.* London: Royal Institute of International Affairs, 1946.

Report of Royal Commission on East Africa, 1953–55. London: HM Stationery Office, 1955.

Robinson, E. A. G., ed. *Economic Consequences of the Size of Nations.* The 1957 International Economic Association Papers. New York: St. Martin's Press, 1960.

Robinson, Joan. "Equilibrium Growth Models." *American Economic Review* (June, 1961).

Shiomi, S. *Japan's Finance and Taxation 1940–56.* New York: Columbia University Press, 1957.

Singer, M. *Traditional India: Structure and Change.* Philadelphia: The American Folklore Society, 1959.

Spengler, J. J. "Economic Factors in the Development of Densely Populated Areas." New York: American Philosophical Society, 1951.

———, and O. D. Duncan. *Demographic Analysis and Population Theory and Policy.* Homewood, Ill.: Richard D. Irwin, Inc., 1957.

Stillman, C. W., ed. *Africa in the Modern World.* Chicago: University of Chicago Press, 1955.

Swaswamy, K. G. "Indian Agriculture—Problems and Programs." *Pacific Affairs* (December, 1950).

Tew, B. "The International Monetary Fund: Its Present Role and Future Prospects." *Essays in International Finance.* Princeton, N.J.: Princeton University Press, 1961.

Thomas, Brindley. *Migration and Economic Growth.* New York: The Macmillan Company, 1958.

U.N. Economic Commission for Asia and the Far East, "Deficit Financing for Economic Development with Special Reference to ECAFE Countries." *Economic Bulletin—Asia and the Far East*. ECAFE Research and Statistics Division, (November, 1954).

Warriner, Doreen. *Land Reform and Development in the Middle East.* London: Royal Institute of International Affairs and Oxford University Press, 1957.

White, C. M. N. *A Preliminary Survey of Luvale Rural Economy*. Manchester: Manchester University Press, 1959.

Wolf, C. "Institutions and Economic Development." *American Economic Review* (December, 1955).

Yang, C. K. *A Chinese Village in Early Communist Transition*. Cambridge, Mass.: Harvard University Press, 1959.

Zinkin, M. *Development for Free Asia*. London: Chatto & Windus, 1956.

Index

Index